Exercise Your College Reading Skills

Developing More Powerful Comprehension

Second Edition

JANET ELDER

Richland College, Professor Emerita
Dallas County Community College District

McGraw-Hill Higher Education

Boston   Burr Ridge, IL   Dubuque, IA   New York   San Francisco   St. Louis
Bangkok   Bogotá   Caracas   Kuala Lumpur   Lisbon   London   Madrid   Mexico City
Milan   Montreal   New Delhi   Santiago   Seoul   Singapore   Sydney   Taipei   Toronto

The McGraw·Hill Companies

McGraw-Hill
Higher Education

EXERCISE YOUR COLLEGE READING SKILLS: DEVELOPING MORE POWERFUL
COMPREHENSION
Published by McGraw-Hill, a business unit of The McGraw-Hill Companies, Inc., 1221 Avenue of
the Americas, New York, NY 10020. Copyright © 2008, 2004 by the McGraw-Hill Companies, Inc.
All rights reserved. No part of this publication may be reproduced or distributed in any form or by
any means, or stored in a database or retrieval system, without the prior written consent of The
McGraw-Hill Companies, Inc., including, but not limited to, in any network or other electronic
storage or transmission, or broadcast for distance learning.

This book is printed on acid-free paper.

Printed in the United States of America.

6 7 8 9 0 QDB/QDB 15 14 13 12

ISBN: 978-0-07-351347-8
MHID: 0-07-351347-4

Editor in Chief and Publisher: *Emily Barrosse*
Sponsoring Editor: *John Kindler*
Development Editor: *Jesse Hassenger*
Executive Marketing Manager: *Tamara Wederbrand*
Project Manager: *John Shannon*, Pinetree Composition, Inc.
Production Editor: *Melissa Williams*
Design Manager: *Kimberly Menning*
Cover Design: *Lisa Langhoff*
Interior Design: *Susan Breitbard*
Senior Production Supervisor: *Tandra Jorgensen*

This book was set in 10.5/12 Times Roman, PMS # 2597, by Laserwords Private Limited, and
printed on 45# Scholarly Matte by Quad/Graphics

Library of Congress Cataloging-in-Publication Data

Elder, Janet.
  Exercise your college reading skills : developing more powerful comprehension / Janet Elder.
    p. cm.
  Includes bibliographical references and index.
  ISBN-13: 978-0-07-351347-8; ISBN-10: 0-07-351347-4
  1. Reading (Higher education) 2. College readers. 3. Reading Comprehension. I. Title

LB2395.3E43 2008
428.4'071'1—dc21   200707842

www.mhhe.com

"Come to the edge," he said.
They said, "We are afraid."
"Come to the edge," he said.
They came.
He pushed them.
And they flew.
—Guillaume Apollinaire, French poet

This edition is dedicated to the courageous students who take the leap—and discover they can soar—and to the caring teachers who give them that gentle nudge.

About the Author

Janet Elder is a reading specialist whose teaching experience includes secondary and undergraduate levels, as well as clinical remediation. For three decades, she taught college reading improvement and study skills courses at Richland College (Dallas County Community College District) and served as a reading program coordinator for many of those years. She also implemented the college's Honors Program and directed it for six years before returning to teaching full time. In addition to teaching reading courses, Dr. Elder periodically served on honors English and humanities teaching teams. Dr. Elder was three-time nominee for excellence in teaching awards. Disability Services students also selected her three times as the recipient of a special award for "exceptional innovation, imagination, and consideration in working with students with disabilities." She is a recipient of the National Institute for Staff and Organizational Development's Excellence Award. In fall 2004, she left teaching to write full time, but continues her affiliation with Richland as a professor emerita.

Dr. Elder was graduated summa cum laude from the University of Texas in Austin with a B.A. in English and Latin, and is a member of Phi Beta Kappa. She received a government fellowship for Southern Methodist University's Reading Research Program, which resulted in a master's degree. Her Ph.D. in curriculum and instruction in reading is from Texas Woman's University, where the College of Education presented her the Outstanding Dissertation Award.

Dr. Elder is also the co-author of *New Worlds: An Introduction to College Reading* and *Opening Doors: Understanding College Reading* and is the author of the introductory-level text, *Entryways into College Reading and Learning.* A frequent presenter at professional conferences, she has a deep interest and expertise in "brain-friendly" instruction.

Brief Contents

Contents

PART SIX

COOLDOWN
Welcome to the Cooldown 320

PART SEVEN

GRAND SLAM: PLAYING IN THE BIG LEAGUES
Welcome to the Grand Slam 392

To the Instructor

WHAT DISTINGUISHES THIS TEXT FROM OTHER TEXTS?

First, and most important, is the abundant opportunity for students to practice applying skills. Moreover, the practice moves from a set of structured multiple-choice items to two sets of increasingly sophisticated, real-life, open-ended items. All developmental students need extensive practice to strengthen their reading skills. Mid- to upper-level students often do not need additional instruction so much as they need extensive, targeted practice. Practice—rehearsal—is crucial for learning any skill and essential for transferring material into long-term memory. Repeatedly practicing something actually causes the brain to assign extra neurons to the task. In general, the more practice in a variety of ways, contexts, and formats, the better. Providing multiple contexts for learning the same thing creates the most neural pathways. This is why this text asks students to apply reading skills to passages from a range of college textbooks and other appropriate sources, and why there is recursive practice throughout the text.

Second, and obviously, the book has a sports framework. However, it neither assumes nor requires that you or your students have any prior knowledge about sports. The principles, practices, and attitudes that lead to success are the true focus because they apply to academic learning—and reading improvement—as much as to sports. Even students who are not involved in sports readily grasp the parallels and can relate to them. Moreover, metaphors make learning easier for the brain.

Third, *Exercise Your College Reading Skills* contains several brain-friendly features that capitalize on ways the brain learns naturally. (See A User's Guide to the Brain in the text, as well as the array of resource material in the Instructor Online Learning Center.) The instructional approach is based on certain assumptions derived from research on how the brain learns:

- Learning is an inborn ability in human beings.
- Human beings *want* to learn, because learning is inherently pleasurable.
- Learners must start from wherever they are because to learn new information, they must connect it with existing knowledge.
- The brain is a better pattern seeker than data gatherer.
- Appropriately challenging problem solving combined with collaborative learning opportunities is the best way to grow students' brains.
- Given appropriate instruction, all students can learn.
- The combination of appropriate challenge and low threat is optimal for learning.

The book's brain-friendly approach is also reflected in its constructivist approach: The foundation is laid before a subsequent concept or skill is introduced. For example, because the topic is always part of the main idea sentences, students learn to determine the topic before they are asked to locate or formulate implied main ideas. Approaching learning in a constructivist manner is not simply a nice idea; it's a necessity. Other brain-friendly features include The Replay, which allows students to record key chapter concepts themselves rather than simply read a list of them. There is recursive practice and integration of skills. The Learning Styles Tips in Appendix 5 will help each student discover ways to make learning easier. In addition, auditory learners in particular benefit from the "drill instructor chants" that summarize key skills.

Fourth, the tone of *Exercise Your College Reading Skills* is less formal, more personal, and more supportive than other reading improvement texts. This is brain-friendly because it reduces stress and makes learning more engaging and enjoyable. For example, there are reminders to students to stand up and stretch or to take a few deep breaths before starting each exercise set.

Fifth, the process of inferring is a common thread that links many of the vocabulary, reading, and study skills. For this reason, it is presented as a unifying skill, which students find reassuring. It is integral to deducing word meanings from context and word-structure clues, determining the topic, formulating implied main ideas, and recognizing an author's writing pattern. It is also involved in drawing conclusions, interpreting an author's intended meaning, determining an author's tone and intended audience, and interpreting figurative language (which is presented in Appendix 6 and more fully in a module on the Online Learning Center). Many fundamental comprehension skills that are based on making inferences are themselves the basis for other skills, including most study skills. For example, students must first understand the skill of determining the main idea before they can produce a summary or outline or take notes from a textbook.

Sixth, students have the opportunity to evaluate their progress at crucial points throughout the text and decide whether they need more help or need to change anything in their approach, effort, or attitude. It is crucial that students learn to metacognitively monitor their own understanding, pinpoint sources of confusion, and assume the responsibility for solving the problem.

Seventh, the skill chapters include these unusual, innovative, brain-friendly instructional features:

■ *The Trainer: Observe the Skill,* which allows underprepared students to peek inside the head of an effective reader to see that person's thoughts while processing a passage and applying a skill. This unique metacognitive feature provides a model that helps students learn to monitor their own comprehension. It also disabuses them of the notions that good readers never make comprehension miscues and that on their first try they effortlessly and accurately understand everything they read.

■ *The Replay: Remember the Essential Information from the Chapter,* which allows students to record the essential information in the chapter. Reviewing the material, then rehearsing it in certain ways, and finally writing it has several benefits. Writing forces students to be precise, it's an on-the-spot check of their comprehension, and it helps transfer the information into long-term memory.

■ *The Edge: Pointers [about a skill],* which goes beyond the "basics" of skill instruction. It alerts students to pitfalls to avoid when applying a skill; it reinforces crucial points and presents subtler considerations for advanced students.

Eighth, great care went into selecting the excerpts. They reflect the broad range of material students are likely to encounter in college courses. More importantly, the selections, which come primarily from *current, widely used* textbooks, were chosen because they are interesting and contain information that should be part of college students' general fund of knowledge. In addition to the formidable range of textbook excerpts, there are excerpts from other publications and online articles. (The Online Learning Center module on reading literature includes essays, fables, parables, poems, and excerpts from speeches, novels, short stories, and an autobiography. The cross section encompasses ethnic and historical diversity and includes a host of well-known writers.) To enrich your teaching options, there are text selections that play off each other. These are cross-referenced in the Teaching Tips in the Annotated Instructor's Edition.

Ninth, most of the study skills appear toward the end of the book. It makes sense for students to learn at the start of the semester how to preview their textbooks and approach their textbook assignments, of course. For that reason, Handle Your Textbooks and Your Textbook Assignments Like a Pro is placed near the beginning of the book, but the other study skills appear in Chapter 14, near the end of the book. The reason for this is that to be able to mark textbooks intelligently, take good notes, create an accurate outline, or write a correct summary, students must first be able to determine the main ideas and identify the details in a selection. To take notes and make outlines or maps, they must first understand how primary details relate to the main ideas, and how secondary details relate to other details. In short, trying to teach students study skills before they have mastered the basic comprehension skills that underlie those skills is putting the proverbial cart before the horse. (Students are welcome to look ahead to Chapter 14, but it will make much more sense after they have completed the preceding chapters. Also, Appendix 2 contains extensive material about preparing for tests, terms used on essay tests, handling various types of test questions, and reducing text anxiety. Of course, you should alert students to it and encourage them to read it early on.)

And last, the instructor resources are unparalleled. The Annotated Instructor's Edition is unique in its thoroughness and extensiveness. It contains a wealth of supplemental information, instructional strategies, and suggestions for energizing the classroom. In addition to explaining the correct answers, there are explanations of why *incorrect* answer choices are incorrect. (If students miss items without understanding the reason, the opportunity to learn is lost.) The Instructor Online Learning Center contains up-to-the-minute information on brain-friendly teaching and learning, informal assessment techniques, end-of-class activities, classroom management strategies, collaborative learning, and a comprehensive webliography of instructor resources.

WHICH KEY FEATURES WERE RETAINED FROM THE PREVIOUS EDITION?

- A strong emphasis on comprehension, the heart of the reading process
- Clear, focused, to-the-point explanations
- Scaffolded approach that moves students toward independence in applying skills
- Terminology consistent with *Entryways, New Worlds,* and *Opening Doors*
- Uniquely motivating, supportive approach and tone
- Comprehension-monitoring questions to help students apply each skill
- Exclusive use of excerpts and reading selections of the sort students are likely to encounter in their college course work: in other words, the "real thing"
- Continuous emphasis on the interrelatedness and integration of reading skills
- Emphasis on writing out answers (Set 2 and 3 exercise sets), because this is what students must do when they use college textbooks and because it reinforces the interrelatedness of reading and writing
- Three comprehensive review chapters: the "stretching" chapters (7 and 12) and The Grand Slam (15) that provide extensive, recursive, integrated practice of *all* skills introduced to that point in the text
- Study skills presented as they pertain to learning from college texts and preparing for college tests
- Flexibility in adapting your use of *Exercise Your College Reading Skills* to the particular needs of your students, your reading courses, and overall program
- Coverage of skills that typically appear on state-mandated reading competency tests (basic skills tests) and exit tests

- User-friendly format that includes perforated pages and labeled page edges
- Lower cost than comparable texts

WHAT ARE THE NEW FEATURES OF THE SECOND EDITION?

- More than 200 new and updated excerpts, selections, and photos
- More than a dozen new and updated graphs, diagrams, and charts in Chapter 13, Interpreting Graphic Aids
- Addition of longer and full-length selections in the final chapter, The Grand Slam, increasing the total to 12 selections
- Selections from a broad range of textbooks with timely, engaging topics such as terrorism, the stem cell controversy, threats to computer security, myths about video games, baby boomers and generation Xers, and strategies for managing cash
- A section on previewing textbooks and handling textbook assignments
- A User's Guide to the Brain, which tells about the brain's inborn ability to learn; emotions, stress, and the brain; and the care and feeding of the brain
- A new vocabulary chapter on word-structure analysis (Chapter 2)
- Expanded coverage of authors' writing patterns, as well as the relationship among ideas within and between sentences (Chapter 6)
- Additional Bonus Set in Chapter 9, Make Inferences and Draw Conclusions
- Expanded list of tone words and definitions in Chapter 10, Determine an Author's Purpose, Tone, Point of View, and Intended Audience
- Explanation of inductive versus deductive reasoning added to Chapter 11, Evaluate an Author's Argument
- Description of review cards added to Chapter 14, Organize Information for Study
- Extensive learning style tips (throughout and Appendix 5)
- New appendixes on propaganda and fallacies, conducting research using the Internet and evaluating websites, and learning style tips; an expanded section on preparing for and taking tests, and reducing test anxiety
- Rich, updated Online Learning Center (OLC) that includes new material and activities on propaganda and fallacies, commonly confused and misused words, as well as a comprehensive list of spelling demons
- Full-length modules on comprehending literature, interpreting figurative language (formerly chapters in the First edition), and the Bonus Items (formerly in the Advanced Stretching chapter) now available on the OLC
- Instructor OLC that is unmatched in terms of up-to-the-minute information and strategies for brain-friendly teaching, collaborative learning, informal assessment, and many other helpful topics.

I hope that *Exercise Your College Reading Skills* proves to be energizing, engaging, and effective for you and your students. My best wishes for a successful semester.

Warmest regards,
Janet Elder

ACKNOWLEDGMENTS

The following people contributed greatly to this edition, and I am grateful to each of them. John Kindler, Sponsoring Editor, Jesse Hassenger, Developmental Editor, and Melissa Williams, Production Manager, each lent their time and talent to the undertaking. Special thanks to John Shannon, Senior Production Manager at Pine Tree Composition, for proficiently transforming the manuscript into book form, and to eContent Specialist Paul Banks for making sure the Internet-related information in Appendix 4 was up-to-the-minute accurate. I am also grateful to Manuscript Editor Karen Slaght, Text Permissions Editor Marty Moga, and Marketing Manager Tamara Wederbrand for their contributions. In addition, I thank Media Specialist Alex Rohrs and Media Project Manager Marc Mattson for updating the Online Reading Lab.

I deeply appreciate the continued support and friendship of my former dean at Richland College, Mary Darin, and of reading professors Kathleen Riley of Polk Community College and Susan Pongratz of Thomas Nelson Community College. In addition, I thank Joe Cortina, my co-author of two other texts and former colleague at Richland College, for his friendship and support.

These thoughtful reviewers provided constructive criticism, helpful feedback, and supportive comments from which I benefited greatly:

Mary Dubbe
Thomas Nelson Community College

Valerie Hicks
Community College of Baltimore County

Elizabeth Jarok
Middlesex Community College

Marisol Regidor
Miami Dade College

Kathy Riley
Polk Community College

Edelin Rubino
Collin County Community College

Linda Stonebreaker
Riverside Community College

Elizabeth Tatko
Ohio University

And last, but never least, my heartfelt gratitude to my husband, Jim, for his boundless love and support.

Janet Elder

Introduction

Reading is to the mind what exercise is to the body.
—Joseph Addison, 17th-century English essayist

WHY "EXERCISE" YOUR COLLEGE READING SKILLS?

Welcome to *Exercise Your College Reading Skills*. Why "exercise" your reading skills? For the same reason you do physical exercise: *to become stronger*. In this case, though, you will be strengthening your college-level vocabulary and reading comprehension skills. The subtitle of this book is *Developing More Powerful Comprehension*. The goal is for you to *empower* yourself as a student by increasing your reading skills. You'll be doing this by using carefully chosen and sequenced practice exercises.

Here's what one knowledgeable person, Dr. Ben Carson, has to say about education, reading, and practice in his book, *The Big Picture*. It might be helpful for you to know a little about him first. Ben Carson is an internationally known, highly respected doctor who was appointed the head of the pediatric neurosurgery department at Johns Hopkins Hospital in Baltimore, Maryland, in 1984 when he was only 33 years old. It is a position he still holds today. It wasn't easy for him to achieve this, however. He endured extreme childhood poverty after his parents' divorce. He had a high temper that got him in trouble. His grades in elementary school were so terrible that the other students nicknamed him "Dummy."

When he was in the fifth grade, Ben's mother was desperate to help her failing sons. Part of the answer she came up with was to limit the amount of time Ben and his brother could watch TV each week (two programs a week, and she chose the programs). The more important part of his mother's solution, however, was that instead of watching TV, the boys were required to read two books a week and to write reports on them. That's more than 100 books a year! You can imagine the difference that much practice made in their reading, and becoming a good reader was what saved Ben Carson. (His brother became a very successful engineer.)

In *The Big Picture*, Carson says, "Ultimately, the quality of your education is up to you. It is a choice only you can make. You decide for yourself how much you are going to empower yourself through learning and knowledge. How far you go is determined, largely, by how far you are willing to go." He continues, "Any student who so desires can achieve a high quality education, whoever or wherever he or she may be—as long as the student can read, because once you can read, you can achieve the world's greatest education" (p. 202).

When Ben Carson found it difficult to concentrate on his reading assignments in medical school, he devised an effective solution: he would stand up—and even

Dr. Ben Carson, Director of Pediatric Neurosurgery at Johns Hopkins Hospital, is internationally known for his success in separating twins who are joined at the head and for his pioneering work in hemispherectomies (removal of half of the brain). Carson is also a professor of neurosurgery, plastic surgery, oncology, and pediatrics. He is the author of nearly 100 neurological publications and three best-selling books, and he has been awarded 24 honorary degrees.

walk around his room—while he read. He would do this for 45 minutes, then reward himself with a 15-minute break. I'm not suggesting this is a technique you should use, but I am suggesting that, like Ben Carson, you do whatever it takes to develop the skills and techniques that help you learn effectively.

Here's what Ben Carson has to say about practice and reading: "What is true of so many things in life is definitely true of reading: *The more you do it, the easier it gets,* the more efficiently you can extract relevant data from the printed page—not just breadth of information but also depth" (p. 203). He concludes: "Reading is mental exercise for the mind and imagination. As with physical exercise, the more you repeat it, the more agile and flexible you become. So whether you read or do brain surgery, the same principle applies: practice makes perfect" (p. 204).

Whether it's hitting a tennis ball or playing the piano, the way you become more skillful at something is through practice. The old adage "Practice makes perfect" contains a great deal of wisdom. Realistically, of course, practice may never make you absolutely "perfect" at something. Unquestionably, though, practice increases your competence. The fact is, unless you practice, you will never improve your skills, whether those skills pertain to sports, music, a career, interpersonal relationships, or academics.

Instead of "Practice makes perfect," it is more accurate to say, "Practice makes *permanent*" and that "*Perfect* practice makes perfect." Whatever you do over and over again becomes a habit: Through repetition, the brain learns to do it faster and faster until it becomes a habit. If you are sloppy and careless when you practice, you will be teaching yourself to perform in a sloppy, careless manner. If you want to learn to do something perfectly, then you should practice it as perfectly as possible. As you can see, if practice consists of sloppy, mindless repetition or merely "going through the motions," it is a waste of time. There is another old saying that goes, "If you do what you have always done, you will get what you have always gotten." Over the years, have you been sloppy and careless when you read? If so, you need to change your approach, or you will continue to be a less-than-effective reader. In *Exercise Your College Reading Skills,* your practice will consist of the exercises you will do. Do each exercise carefully and thoughtfully so that you can obtain the greatest benefit.

Effective practice means practicing with *concentration,* not just doing something over and over again. It's not just the amount of time you spend at practice that counts; it's *what* you put into the practice. Effective practice involves *thinking* about what you are doing and monitoring your performance. This means that, like an athlete, you are *constantly using feedback to improve your skills.*

Regardless of what you are trying to achieve, preparation, hard work, and learning from failure are important. Does your tennis serve always seem to go wide of the line? Do you make the same mistake every time you play a particular part of a song on your guitar? Perhaps you get confused every time you try to insert a picture into a document you are typing on the computer. Once you identify a trouble spot and the cause of the problem, you can determine what you need to know or change to fix the problem. As former UCLA All-American and pro-basketball superstar Bill Walton put it, "You celebrate the victory, but you analyze the defeat." In reading, this means you monitor (continuously assess) your comprehension, and if you haven't comprehended (understood) what you read, you immediately take steps to remedy the situation.

Exercise Your College Reading Skills is built on the principles of thoughtful practice and using feedback consistently to improve your performance. For example, if you can't figure out what unfamiliar words mean when you are reading, you must become aware that this is a problem. Next, you must pinpoint the *cause* of the problem ("I don't know any strategies to help me figure out the meaning of unfamiliar words"). Then you can take steps to fix the problem ("My instructor suggested I learn how to use context clues to help me figure out what words mean"). At that point you can learn and practice the skill until you become proficient at it.

Like an athlete, you can usually identify the cause of a problem: Perhaps you jumped in without really warming up (you leaped off into the exercises without really understanding the skill first). Perhaps you didn't put in enough practice time (you need to do more exercises or go over the ones you missed on those you've already done). Perhaps you need to adjust your attitude (maybe you let negative thoughts get in the way). At the end of almost every exercise set, you'll have a chance to reflect on your performance and think about any changes you need to make. Your instructor can also help you identify problems as well as the steps you need to take to correct them.

As you are using this book, you'll have me as a coach. I'll be talking to you throughout the book, giving you tips and pointers, making suggestions, and giving you encouragement. Your instructor will also be your coach, of course, so you have two experts to help you. When you work collaboratively with classmates, you'll have their help, as well.

So here's what it all boils down to: To improve your reading skills, you must practice them, just as you need to practice any skill you want to improve. You need to practice (do the assignments) mindfully; otherwise, you will not benefit from doing them, and your skills will not improve. You must monitor your comprehension by using feedback on your assignments to figure out what you are doing wrong and what you need to change. A special feature of this book is that you'll have at least two "coaches": your instructor and me, the author of the book. Follow our suggestions: We care, and we're here to help.

THE GAME PLAN: HOW *EXERCISE YOUR COLLEGE READING SKILLS* IS STRUCTURED

The Preliminaries

Before the skills chapters begin, there are three important sections that can contribute greatly to your success. They are

■ The "Secrets" of Success. Learn how to overcome barriers to success, along with keys to success borrowed from athletics, which pertain every bit as much to academic success.

■ A User's Guide to the Brain. Empower yourself by learning about your incredible brain: how it is "born to learn," how emotions and stress affect it, and its care and feeding.

■ Handle Textbooks and Textbook Assignments Like a Pro.

How the Chapters Are Sequenced

The instructional material in *Exercise Your College Reading Skills* is structured much like any other "strengthening" program: from simpler skill levels to more advanced ones. Here's the plan of the book:

Part 1: The Warm-Up (Chapters 1–2)

The first two chapters focus on vocabulary. Chapter 1 deals with using *context clues* to figure out the meaning of an unfamiliar word. This skill will be an important skill every time you read a college textbook. Chapter 2 targets *word structure analysis,* using prefixes, roots, and suffixes to help you unlock or confirm a word's meaning.

Part 2: The Basic Workout (Chapters 3–6)

The Basic Workout concentrates on *basic comprehension skills*, the minimum skills that you need in order to comprehend your college textbooks. You must be able to

■ Determine the *topic,* what a paragraph is about. (Chapter 3)

■ Identify the stated *main idea* sentence, the author's most important point about the topic, and identify the *supporting details,* additional information to help readers understand the main idea completely. (Chapter 4)

■ Formulate the *implied main idea,* a main idea sentence created by reader if the author does not included a stated main idea. (Chapter 5)

■ Recognize the *author's writing pattern,* how the author organized the information that is being presented, and learn about transition words and metacomprehension. (Chapter 6)

Think of the elements of the Basic Workout as comparable to the basic elements of any physical workout. In a physical workout, you need aerobic conditioning for the heart and lungs, as well as strength training to make individual muscles stronger. Until you develop both to a certain level, you're not physically fit: You need more practice. It's the same with basic vocabulary and comprehension skills: Until you develop both sufficiently, you need to keep practicing. Once you have mastered these skills, your day-to-day use of them will *keep* them at a high level.

Part 3: Basic Stretching (Chapter 7)

In these exercises you practice applying *all* the basic skills you have worked on up to this point. In other words, you will read a paragraph and determine its topic and main idea, locate the supporting details, and identify the author's writing pattern, as well as determine the meaning of unfamiliar words by using the context and analyzing word structure. Integrating all these skills rather than focusing on them individually (as you did in the Warm-Up and the Basic Workout) may be a bit of a "stretch" for you (hence the chapter title). However, you will already be "warmed up" and conditioned by your basic workout—making this the perfect time to stretch and extend your "mental muscles." And, as you know, total fitness requires not only aerobic conditioning and strength training, but also a third component: flexibility. And you can only gain flexibility by stretching after your muscles have warmed up.

Part 4: The Advanced Workout (Chapters 8–11)

The Advanced Workout consists of critical reading skills that go *beyond* the basic ones. These critical reading skills are

- Distinguishing between *facts and opinions:* determining whether information can be proved or whether it represents a judgment. (Chapter 8)
- Making *inferences* and drawing *conclusions:* understanding the implications of what you have read and arriving at logical conclusions. (Chapter 9)
- Determining the *author's purpose,* the reason the author wrote something; *tone,* the author's attitude toward the topic; *point of view,* the author's position on the issue; and *intended audience,* who the author had in mind as readers. (Chapter 10)
- *Evaluating an author's argument:* critically evaluating written material. (Chapter 11)

Think of the Advanced Workout as comparable to the extra training people would do if they wanted to be not just in good shape, but in excellent physical condition. They accomplish this by using heavier weights and more sophisticated training techniques. You can do this in your reading by applying increasingly sophisticated skills to increasingly complex material.

Advanced Stretching (Chapter 12)

Now that you've developed your advanced reading skills, you'll once again have a chance to "stretch" your abilities by applying *all* of them to practice passages. You'll be using longer selections because your skills are better and stronger.

Cooldown (Chapters 13–14)

In this section, you learn to apply two other important skills: interpreting graphs and organizing information to learn it. After these study skills are explained and modeled, you have an opportunity to apply them to longer textbook selections.

- Interpreting *graphic (visual) aids:* bar graphs, line graphs, pie charts, flowcharts, and tables. (Chapter 13)
- Organizing information you need to learn: marking a textbook by *underlining, highlighting,* and *annotating; taking notes* from a textbook; *outlining* textbook material; making a *concept map* of textbook material; and *summarizing* textbook material. (Chapter 14)

You may wonder why the study skills for organizing material, unlike the section on reading textbook assignments, aren't placed at the beginning of this book. After all, don't you want to use those skills from the very beginning of the semester? Of course you do, but here's the problem: To be able to understand and apply those study skills effectively, you must first practice and master the comprehension skills in the Basic Workout. Otherwise, it's like trying to play baseball without being able to throw or hit the ball accurately: It's frustrating, and you strike out. Think of these study skills as similar to a cooldown after a physical workout. You've already done the "heavy lifting," the hard work of thinking about and comprehending what you read. These study skills are ways to consolidate and record (literally!) your gains. You're welcome to look ahead at Chapter 14, but keep in mind that it will make even more sense after you've studied the chapters that precede it.

The Grand Slam (Chapter 15)

In this final chapter of the book, you have a chance to apply all the reading and study skills to several textbook excerpts and to other nonfiction selections. Moreover, the selections are longer. You'll have the opportunity to "test-drive" your skills on a variety of materials that span several subjects and types of reading.

In summary: Some skills may seem easy and feel like a review; others will be new or seem more challenging. Don't be frustrated or discouraged if you can't apply a skill perfectly at first. Make a commitment to yourself to practice and strengthen your reading skills. *Exercise Your College Reading Skills* assumes that you already have some familiarity with most of the reading skills, but just need more practice applying them. The parts of the complete "strengthening program" (the entire book) are the Warm-Up, the Basic Workout, Basic Stretching, the Advanced Workout, Advanced Stretching, the Cooldown, and the Grand Slam.

How Each Chapter Is Organized

Because the focus of this book is *practicing* vocabulary and reading skills, you receive a concise explanation of each skill, followed by abundant opportunities to apply it. The practice passages represent a broad cross section of topics and college textbooks, and they range from single paragraphs to lengthy selections.

Your brain likes to know in advance how things are organized. The sample minipages on the following pages illustrate the chapter parts in the order in which they occur.

The Skill

A brief description of a vocabulary skill or comprehension skill. You'll discover why it is important to know the skill and how it fits with the other skills.

The Technique

Pertinent information about applying the skill. The explanation is accompanied by one or more examples that illustrate the application of the skill to college-appropriate material.

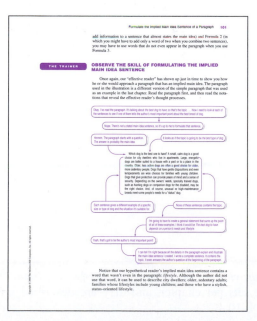

The Trainer

A peek inside the head of a skilled reader to see that person's thoughts while applying the skill to a sample passage. This unique feature lets you observe the reasoning process that effective readers use as they work through a passage.

The Edge

Additional tips to help you apply the skill even more effectively. These pointers alert you to pitfalls and give you an extra edge applying the skill correctly.

The Replay

A do-it-yourself review of the important chapter information. It helps you evaluate how well you understood the chapter. In addition, it allows you to consolidate the essential information and transfer it into your long-term memory.

The Practice

Exercise sets that provide an opportunity to apply the chapter skill(s). There are three sets per chapter, and they are described in detail on pages I–9 and I–10.

How the Chapter Practice Exercise Sets Are Structured

In strength training, one of the proven principles is called *muscle isolation:* working a muscle separately (in isolation) from all the other muscles to strengthen it. This gives superior and much faster results than skipping around from one muscle group to another. People who do that may think they're getting some benefit, but they will not make any real progress.

The same is true of developing your reading skills. Separate skills are presented in the Warm-Up, the Basic Workout, and the Advanced Workout because this gives you a chance to focus hard and concentrate on each individual reading skill. The Basic Stretching and the Advanced Stretching will give you an opportunity to put the skills together when applying them to paragraphs. The final chapter of the book, The Grand Slam, gives you a chance to apply *all* of the reading and study skills to longer textbook selections and other selections.

There are three sets of exercises for each skill in the Warm-Up, Basic Workout, and Advanced Workout. The Basic Stretching and Advanced Stretching chapters are review chapters that have three sets of exercises to which you apply *all* the skills.

If you have ever lifted weights as part of a strength training program, you know that one highly effective, widely used approach is to do three "sets" of an exercise. Each *set* consists of a certain number of *repetitions*. Each item in an exercise is one repetition or "rep." In strength training, the three sets are often completed using a technique called "pyramiding." *Pyramiding* means that you use slightly heavier weights for each set, but you do fewer repetitions in each set. That's the trade-off: You add a little weight, but you do fewer reps. So why pyramid? Because it lets you

SUMMARY CHART OF CHAPTER EXERCISES			
	Set 1	**Set 2**	**Set 3**
Warm-Up (Ch. 1—Context Clues)	12 multiple-choice questions	10 open-ended questions	8 open-ended questions
(Ch. 2—Word Structure)	20 multiple-choice items	20 open-ended items	25 open-ended items
Basic Workout (Chs. 3–6)	12 multiple-choice questions	10 open-ended questions	8 open-ended questions
Basic Stretching (Ch. 7)	12 paragraphs; 50 multiple-choice questions	10 paragraphs; 50 open-ended questions	8 paragraphs; 50 open-ended questions
Advanced Workout (Chs. 8–10)	2 passages; 10 multiple-choice questions	3 passages; 8 open-ended questions	2 passages; 6 open-ended questions
(Ch. 11—Author's Argument)	1 passage per set; 7 questions per passage; sets increase in challenge		
Advanced Stretching (Ch. 12)	11 multiple-choice questions	18 open-ended questions	11 open-ended questions
Cooldown (Chs. 13–14)			
(Ch. 13—Graphic Aids)	3 sets of 5 types of visual aids that increase in complexity		
(Ch. 14—Study Skills)	3 excerpts of increasing length and challenge, to which the 5 study skills are applied		
Grand Slam (Ch. 16)	12 selections: 6 with open-ended reading skills questions; 6 selections with 10 multiple-choice comprehension questions, 10 vocabulary items, writing prompts, and Web resources		

get the most out of your workout without burning yourself out. By starting with easier exercises, you warm up naturally. Because you will be doing fewer reps in each subsequent set, you stay motivated. When you get to the more challenging sets, you think, "Just a few left to go. I can manage this!" The way the exercises are structured in difficulty and length is one of the features that make this book unique. The chart on page I–9 that summarizes the quantity and type of exercises.

In summary: All passages in the exercises come from college textbooks or other college-appropriate material. The reading skills in the Warm-Up, the Basic Workout, and the Advanced Workout are first practiced "in isolation" rather than trying to learn and apply several skills simultaneously. You "pyramid" by doing three sets of exercises that increase in difficulty, but decrease in length.

When you do the Basic Stretching and the Advanced Stretching, you put the skills together by applying all of them to paragraphs or reading selections. Again, you will pyramid, using three sets of exercises that increase in difficulty, but decrease in length.

In the Cooldown section, you study sample graphs and passages used to illustrate the application of certain study skills. Then you apply those same skills to three increasingly complex multiparagraph passages. In The Grand Slam, you apply all skills in *Exercise Your College Reading Skills* to several longer textbook selections and other relevant selections.

To Make Even Faster Progress . . .

Exercise Your College Reading Skills is designed to help you develop the skills you need to comprehend and retain college textbook information. It's fairly safe to say that most students don't read their textbooks for pleasure, and yet reading in general can be one of life's great delights. The more you read, the better you become at it, and the greater your enjoyment becomes. Toward that end, consider setting aside just 15 minutes each day for leisure (pleasure) reading. It doesn't matter initially what you read: the front page of the newspaper, a magazine, a mystery, or a novel. The point is to establish the habit. Keep a paperback book handy for those free minutes when you are waiting for the bus or for a friend to meet you. Read for a few minutes to relax before you go to sleep. Anyone who gets hooked on the joy of reading never loses it. It's a gift only you can give yourself.

Human beings enjoy learning. We are by our very nature meaning-seeking creatures who learn continually. As A User's Guide to the Brain explains, one reason we learn continually is because learning feels good. When you read an excerpt or a selection in the exercise sets, go the extra mile: Look up names, places, and events you don't know. Look up words if you're not able to deduce their meaning from the context. Expanding your knowledge base is satisfying, but there's an even more important reason: When it comes to reading comprehension, the more you know, the more you *can* know. The reason is that the brain learns by connecting new information to information you already know. The more *prior knowledge* (background knowledge), you have, the more you have available to anchor new information.

Now that you know *why* you need to "exercise" your reading skills, how the chapters are sequenced, how each chapter in *Exercise Your College Reading Skills* is organized, how the exercise sets are structured, and what some of the unique features of this book are, you're ready to get started—almost. There's one other very important thing to discuss first, though: the "secrets" of success.

The "Secrets" of Success

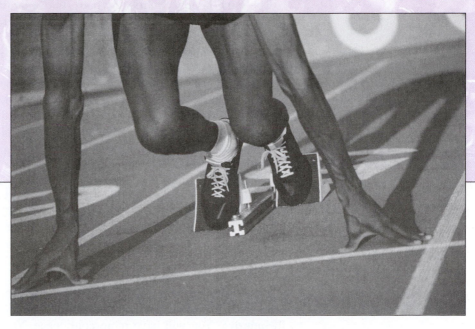

Welcome to a very important part of this book. Please read it carefully and completely. Take the time to do the activities in it. When you're asked to stop and write something or to read it aloud, stop and do exactly that. *Getting started on the right foot will make all the difference.*

This section focuses on preparing yourself mentally to succeed. It lays the foundation for everything that follows. It presents proven techniques, many of which are adapted from sports: They are the same techniques that make athletes successful. Body builders and other athletes know the crucial role their minds and attitudes play in their success—or failure. When they compete, they know they need to "have their head in the game."

No exercise program, whether it is designed to strengthen your body and athletic skills or your academic skills, is of any value if you don't follow it. But how do you get the motivation and discipline to do that? This section explains how. (The Online Learning Center has information about self-created barriers to success. It will help you to read it first and complete the short self-assessment activities.)

KEYS TO SUCCESS: IMPORTANT LESSONS YOU CAN BORROW FROM ATHLETICS

In this section, you will learn strategies and techniques that will move you farther along the road to success. Which ones of these do you already do? Which ones do you need to add?

1. Recognize the Importance, Cost, and Benefits of Making a Commitment.

The ancient Greeks understood the powerful connection between the mind and the body. To them, the perfect person was one who had "a sound mind in a sound body." The body and mind have a profound effect on each other. Neuroscience, medical, and cognitive psychology research confirm this. You know from your own experience, for example, how hard it is to concentrate when you are exhausted, and that sadness can drain all of your energy.

The mind largely controls the body, but sometimes your mind and your body don't always agree. Your mind says, "You know you need to study," but your body says, "I want to stretch out on the couch and watch TV." You have to *decide* what you want. The mind generally makes the ultimate choice. The exception would be physical illness or injury, in which case, the body will probably "win." For example, if you have the flu, you may in fact be too ill to study or go to class. For the most part, though, people do what they *decide* to do. You have to decide what is important to you. You have to *commit*. (Of course, there may be times when there are circumstances that are truly beyond your control: a family emergency or your apartment catches on fire.)

Just how important is it to make a commitment? In *The Mental Game of Baseball: A Guide to Peak Performance,* the authors report a study conducted by Charles Garfield, a clinical psychologist at the University of California School of Medicine. Garfield interviewed approximately 1,500 high achievers at the Peak Performance Center, which he directs. He found that "the single most powerful predictor of success in the long run is commitment," the willingness and desire to work hard toward achieving clearly defined goals (p. 45). The high achievers were more than just *willing* to work hard: They *wanted* to work hard.

There are many benefits of making a commitment to strengthen your reading skills. You will feel better about yourself as a person and as a student. Your grades will improve. You will have more confidence. You will become more and more motivated as one success builds on another. You will have better career opportunities as a result of having strong reading skills. You will probably improve your personal life, too, because you will be happier, more sure of yourself, and more successful. And if you're single, keep in mind that people tend to attract people who are similar to themselves. As you become a more skilled, successful student and person, you're increasingly likely to attract an equally capable, high-achieving person. In the realm of friendship as well, quality attracts quality.

What is the cost of achieving these wonderful benefits? A few hours a week. It may take three hours or it may take six hours. It depends on what "shape" you are in when you start: Do you just need to polish up and tone your reading skills, or do you need more intensive training? It also depends on whether you are working on your own or whether a coach or "personal trainer" (an instructor or tutor) is directing your "workout." It will probably take at least a semester. Regardless of the number of hours per week or whether it takes 10 weeks or 15 weeks or more, it is a small price to pay for very important gains. Everyone wants a "quick fix," but that's as unrealistic for improving your reading skills as it is for achieving physical fitness.

2. "Work Out" (Study) at the Right Time and in the Right Place.

When should you "work out," or in this case, study? Obviously, your class times and certain other items in your schedule are fixed, but you may have some flexibility with regard to when you study. Just as you wouldn't try to do a physical workout when you were exhausted, hungry, or had just finished a big meal, you shouldn't try to study under those conditions either. Identify the time of day when you are most alert and rested: morning, afternoon, or evening. Find the time that lets you get the most out of your "workout" (study session). Then *study at that same time every day.* If you give it three weeks, it will become a habit. (For a blank study schedule, go to www.tulsa.oklahoma.net/~jnichols/StudySchedule.html.)

Find a place where you can concentrate. Silence your telephone or cell phone; let the answering machine or voicemail take your calls. Because the brain finds it stressful to multitask, most students do better if they turn off the TV, iPod, and CD player. (See Appendix 5 for specific suggestions geared to each learning style.) Hang a "Do not disturb" sign on your door. After all, if you don't respect your study time, why should anyone else? Respect and protect your study time.

3. Avoid Negative Self-Talk and Negative Verbalizations.

Do you have the habit of negative self-talk? Almost without realizing it, you start saying to yourself, "This is too hard," "I'm not smart enough," "I'll never get this," or "This is hopeless." Whenever you have a thought like this, STOP IT. Immediately replace it with a positive thought: "Yes, this seems hard, but I can do it," or "I'm smart enough to know that if I stick with it, I'll eventually get it," or "The only thing that can stop me is myself, and I'm not going to do that!"

Just as negative thoughts have a damaging effect, so do negative comments that are made by you or by others. *Don't accept negative comments about yourself and don't make them.* If you find yourself knocking your ability in front of a classmate, for example, correct it right then and there: "No, I *used* to think I couldn't do this, but I *know* I can if I just work at it." If someone else makes a negative comment such as, "Why do you bother with that? It's a waste of time," don't let them hook you. In fact, you don't even need to respond. Don't agree or disagree. Just give them a polite smile, and then change the subject. Even if the comment isn't about you, don't buy into it. If a classmate says, "This homework is going to be impossible!" you can think to yourself or even respond aloud, "Yes, it's challenging, but not impossible." If your mother comments, "No one in our family was ever any good at math," you can think to yourself, "Well, *I'm* planning to be the first."

Complaining is certainly a form of negative verbalization. It adds to your stress and depletes your energy. Complaining causes you to become unfocused and to lose sight of what really matters. When you realize that you are complaining, you should stop, look, and listen: *stop* complaining, *look* at what is good in the situation rather than what is wrong; and *listen* to what you are saying because complaining becomes a habit. If need be, ask trusted friends to help you change. (They'll help you. They don't like to listen to your complaining either!) Because you can't change a habit unless you are first aware of it, arrange for your friends to give you a certain signal whenever you are complaining. Then replace the habit of complaining with a new, better habit, such as laughing or smiling instead. (A bonus is that laughter has mental, physical, psychological, and social benefits!)

4. Decide What Kind of Person You Want to Be.

It's been said that sports don't build character, but that they reveal it. The same can be said about being a student. What you do as a student doesn't build character. Rather, it reveals your character. The kind of student you are reveals the kind of person you are. *If you want to change the kind of student you are, change the kind of person you are.* If you think you're a responsible, mature, hardworking person, yet you skip classes, make excuses, or don't do your assignments, you're fooling yourself.

5. Train the Way You Want to Play.

For athletes and those who aspire to improved strength and performance, using good technique when they practice is everything. If they use sloppy technique when they work out or if they don't give a 100 percent effort, the results reflect it. Training sloppily and half-heartedly prepares you to perform sloppily and half-heartedly. In short, you play the way you practice. To put it another way, "Train the way you want to play."

In practicing your reading skills, you need to *do the same things in the same way as you will when you use them in actual situations.* This means practicing with the real thing, college-level material. It means thinking, focusing, and giving your best effort on every set of practice exercises. Keep in mind that you are preparing yourself ultimately to use these same skills to help you master your subsequent college textbooks. You get out of it what you put into it. Train carefully. Train regularly. Train hard.

6. Expect to Hit Plateaus and Be Prepared to Deal with Them.

When you are learning to apply a reading skill, your progress will be uneven. Athletes know that improvement isn't a graceful, smooth process. They know that sometimes they are "in the zone." Everything seems to go exactly right. On other days at other workouts, they are "flat"—yet they know they need to persevere regardless. They know they'll hit plateaus that make them feel stalled out, and that they'll be tempted to get discouraged. But they also know that when they least expect it, their performance suddenly improves: their tennis serve is faster and more accurate, their golf swing improves dramatically, they can lift more weight or run faster or farther than at any time in the past.

In a similar fashion, you may also hit an occasional plateau. A *plateau* is a period of time in which you don't seem to be making progress. It may last a few days or a week or two. When using this book, it may take the form of a certain comprehension skill that seems hard to grasp. You may stumble through the first set of practice exercises in a chapter, or maybe the first two, or perhaps all three. The important thing to keep sight of is that plateaus are *normal*, and they are *temporary:* If you hang in there, pay attention, and keep striving to understand, you will eventually be successful. Also, remember that trying hard to solve a problem or learn a new skill causes brain growth—regardless of whether you solve the problem or gain complete mastery of the skill.

There will be times when you think, "I'll never get this!" There will be days when you just don't feel like "working out." What you are feeling is normal, but *do the assignments anyway.* Persevere: you *will* make progress. (Someone once observed, "If you can find a road with no obstacles, it probably doesn't lead anywhere.")

Baseball great Hank Aaron said, "My motto was always to keep swinging. Whether I was in a slump or feeling badly or having trouble off the field, the only thing to do was to keep hitting." Take Hank Aaron's words to heart: Keep swinging. Unless you keep swinging, you will never have any "hits." Billy Jean King, a pioneer in women's tennis, said, "Champions keep playing until they get it right." So should you.

7. Breathe.

Deep breathing is another technique you can borrow from athletics to make you more successful as a reader and a student. Yes, *breathing.* Sounds too easy, doesn't it? Everyone who is alive breathes, of course. In fact, we breathe about 26,000 times each day. But when we get tense, we often begin to take shallow breaths without realizing it. (You also know that when some people experience intense fear or panic, they begin breathing so shallowly that they start hyperventilating and gasping for breath.) No one—athlete or student—can concentrate, be focused, learn, or perform if he or she is feeling too much stress. The body needs oxygen to function efficiently and calmly. The brain needs oxygen for you to function well mentally, to feel relaxed, and to stay alert—that's the reason people yawn when they are drowsy, fatigued, or bored. Your breath is the bridge between your mind and your body.

Take several slow, deep breaths when you sit down to study. (Sit up straight in a good chair: You can't inhale fully if you are slouched.) Put your feet flat on the floor. Rest your hands in your lap and close your eyes. Exhale completely through your nose. Now inhale through your nose until you have filled your lungs from the bottom up. If you are doing this correctly, you will feel your abdomen extend, then your ribcage will expand, and your collarbone will rise. Finally, you will feel your throat fill with air. (You may find it helpful to place one hand on your abdomen and the other on your chest so that you can tell if you are doing this right.) Unless you breathe this way, you will only be filling the top part of your lungs. Hold the breath for several seconds, and then exhale the stale air slowly and completely through your mouth. It's important to empty the stale air out of your lungs. As you exhale, reverse the process: empty the air out from the top down. You will feel the air leave your throat and your collarbone lower, then your ribcage will contract, and finally your stomach. Exhaling is the most relaxing phase of breathing, so take about twice as long to exhale as to inhale. (This may require a little practice. If it makes you feel lightheaded or dizzy at first, just go back to breathing normally for a few minutes, and then try again. You'll eventually get the hang of it.) Complete your breathing exercise by taking several more slow, deep breaths. Then open your eyes. Shrug your shoulders; interlace your fingers behind your head and press your elbows back as you press your shoulder blades together; rotate your head in a circle in either direction. Open and close your fists. Relax the muscles in your face.

This simple breathing procedure will calm and refresh you. It will clear your head and leave you ready to focus. If you find yourself feeling stress while you are doing an assignment (or when getting ready to make a presentation or take a test), stop and breathe. You can always take a few deep breaths anywhere, any time. Slow, deep breathing becomes even more effective with—what else?—practice. You can't always control your circumstances, but you can control your breathing.

A word about smoking: It interferes with your studying and your concentration. It's disastrous for your lungs, body systems, skin and other organs, immune system, and brain. (You already know the specific health risks, and you are probably aware of chewing tobacco's carcinogenic effects on the mouth, throat, and rest of the body.) If you don't smoke, that's terrific. Keep on *not* smoking. If you do smoke, make the decision to quit. It's a tough habit to break. Cigarette smoking is considered more addictive than cocaine, but if you want to quit, you can. It's one of those life decisions you have to make—not an easy one, but one that will have a profound impact on the length and quality your life, on the lives of those you love, and the lives of those who love you. (Although the recommendation not to smoke is solidly based in decades of medical research, it represents my bias. I cannot speak for all college professors.)

8. Use Visualization.

Another strategy you can borrow from athletes is *visualization*, imagining yourself doing something successfully before you actually begin it. It's like a movie you run in your head. Gymnasts, track stars, golfers, swimmers, divers, figure skaters—nearly all champion athletes use this powerful, confidence-building form of mental rehearsal. According to Terry Orlick, "In sports, mental imagery is used primarily to help you get the best out of yourself in training and competition. The developing athletes who make the fastest progress and those who ultimately become the best make extensive use of mental imagery. They use it daily as a means of directing what will happen in training, and as a way of pre-experiencing their best competition performances." For example, at the 2000 Olympics in Sydney, Australia, American platform diver Laura Wilkinson took the gold medal. What was amazing about her performance was that she had broken some bones in her foot six months prior to the Olympics, and until just a few weeks prior to the competition, most of her "training" consisted of visualizing the dives. Visualization worked: She executed the winning dive almost perfectly. Like these athletes, you can use mental imagery to help you achieve at your best as a student.

While you are sitting quietly doing the breathing exercise with your eyes closed, visualize yourself understanding the material you are about to study. See yourself being excited about your success and feeling good about your study session and what you have learned. "Your thoughts are your destiny," someone once said. The more you begin to view yourself as a hardworking, successful, motivated student, the more you are likely to perform that way. Civil rights leader Jesse Jackson made famous a slogan that has helped many disadvantaged children become successful: "If I can conceive it, I can believe it. If I can believe it, I can achieve it." It works for anyone. Try repeating it to yourself every day, several times a day, for at least three weeks. It will make a difference because it becomes reality to your brain.

Here's one more strategy related to visualization. Champion skier Jean-Claude Killy noted that, "The best and fastest way to learn a sport is to watch and imitate a champion." You too can pattern yourself after someone who is outstanding, such as someone who is a top student and reader. This is the reason every skills chapter of this book includes a section called "The Trainer," in which you can see the "thoughts" of a skilled reader. Analyze what this hypothetical student/reader does to be successful. Visualize yourself understanding and applying the skill correctly. Then do it.

Watching what a pro does can be very instructive. Well before the 2000 Olympics, 29-year-old Rulon Gardner of Wyoming set his goal: to win the gold medal by defeating the reigning Greco-Roman wrestling champion, a Russian named Alexsandr Karelin. Karelin had been unbeaten since 1987; he held nine World Championships and three Olympic gold medals. Gardner, on the other hand, had never competed in an international match prior to the Olympics. Gardner traveled to Russia, where he spent several months learning wrestling techniques and studying videotapes of all of Karelin's earlier matches. He watched them over and over again, analyzing his opponent's style. Then he went out and took the gold medal away from him. It was a stunning upset. Gardner's approach illustrates the importance of learning from those who are more skilled than you are as a way to help you evaluate and improve your own performance.

9. Focus on Your Own Game.

Athletes know that if they are focusing on what someone else is doing, they are not paying attention to their own game. If they are constantly seeing how the "competition" is doing, they lose concentration on what they should be doing.

A misplaced focus on others and their progress can hurt students' performance too. If you are constantly seeing how others are doing, or trying to evaluate how easy or hard it is for them, you are not thinking about your own performance. Also, it can cause you to make hasty, incorrect judgments. For example, you might conclude, "It's easy for them" or "Everyone else is getting this except me." Perhaps you feel that if someone else makes a higher grade than you do, that you are somehow diminished. You feel that you are "less than." You might even feel sorry for yourself and begin to view yourself as a victim. ("Poor me! It's just not fair! Everyone else has it so easy and is doing so well!") Or perhaps you find yourself thinking, "If they're successful, then I can't be." Now that's an illogical conclusion! There's plenty of success to go around. When you find yourself thinking any of these irrational thoughts, recognize that they are excuses you give yourself to quit trying.

Track star Carl Lewis said that his thoughts before a big race are usually pretty simple. "I tell myself: 'Get out of the blocks, run your race, stay relaxed. If you run your race, you'll win. . . . Channel your energy. *Focus.*'"

Remember, too, that all famous athletes had a first day, a first month, a first year of training and practice. They fell down, missed the ball, or failed a hundred times to execute a basic maneuver correctly. Don't make the mistake of thinking that something has always been easy for people who are good at it. Although "natural athletes" may progress much faster than others, even they must work to develop and perfect their skills. And like all the rest of us, they either "use it or lose it." They had to work to get in shape, and they have to work to stay in shape. (A colleague of mine who has run in dozens of marathons told me that each day when he goes out to run, the first three miles are always still hard.) You would think someone was crazy if they said that pro athletes never have to train or practice. Anyone who tells you that highly successful students don't have to study and work hard is making an equally silly statement.

It's tempting to look at someone who is achieving at a high level without focusing on what the person went through to get there. Take Lance Armstrong, seven-time winner of the Tour de France, a grueling three-week 2,200-mile bicycle race around France. Some people look at Armstrong and think, "Hey, the guy's a natural, someone blessed with tremendous athletic ability." The reality is, Armstrong has always trained harder than his competitors.

Yes, Lance Armstrong is a gifted athlete, but what you might not know is that he finished last in his first pro race. That's right: last. He was so devastated that he considered giving up cycling. His mother talked him out of it. Two weeks later he came in second in a World Cup race, and the next year he won the world championship, the U.S. pro championship, and a stage—one segment of the race—in his first Tour de France. He picked up a $1 million bonus for winning all three races in cycling's "Triple Crown" event that same year. Did you know that Armstrong failed even to *finish* three of his first four Tours de France, and that he finished 36th in the fourth one? He was then diagnosed with advanced testicular cancer that had spread to his lungs, abdomen, and lymph nodes. When doctors realized it had also spread to his brain, he was given only a 40 percent chance of surviving. After winning what he describes as the toughest battle of his life, defeating cancer, he came back to win seven consecutive Tours de France (1999–2005). No American cyclist had ever won more than two consecutive ones. When you look at anyone who has succeeded, don't assume that it was easy for them.

10. Develop Mental Toughness and Maintain Focus.

Stress and setbacks are part of everyone's life. Not everyone perceives them the same way, however. Do you perceive stress and setbacks as challenges, or do you allow them to make you feel overwhelmed? Each time you cope effectively with stress and setbacks, you build greater endurance and confidence in coping with them in the future. That's why it's important for you to think about how you're going to handle them *before* they occur. That's why it's important for you to recognize the strengths you already possess that can help you cope successfully when difficulty arises.

Every professional athlete will tell you that his or her success is grounded in the mental part of the game. Olympic decathlon winner Bruce Jenner was the epitome of physical strength, coordination, and speed. Despite his formidable physical ability, he viewed it this way: "I always felt that my greatest asset was not my physical ability, it was my *mental* ability." Olympic swimmer Cathy Ferguson goes so far as to say, "Ninety-eight percent of success is in the head and the heart." Even for a professional athlete, it only takes a minor lapse in concentration to lose a point, a race, a game. The mental edge is usually what separates those who almost won from those who actually did.

For students, the counterpart is what you would expect: You, too, must maintain your mental toughness and your focus. You must stay mentally alert and be committed to achieving your goals. If you spend your time worrying about the future or regretting the past, you will lose the opportunities you have at present. Maintaining focus means concentrating on the present so that you can make the most of every moment.

11. Learn to Distinguish between Problems and Facts.

It can also help you if you learn to distinguish between a problem and a fact. A problem is something that can be fixed. If you are dealing with a circumstance that cannot be changed or fixed, then it's no longer a "problem," it's a fact. For example, you're frustrated because you really want to attend a private four-year university in another city. Your financial situation makes it impossible, however, so you must live at home and attend a small, local college. If that's the reality of the situation, then not being able to go away to school is not a problem, it's a *fact*. Because it's a fact, there's no reason to waste emotional energy feeling frustrated over it. Don't subject yourself to unnecessary stress. Save your precious time and energy for problems that you can actually *do* something about.

12. Have High Expectations for Yourself.

Michael Jordan once said, "You have to expect things of yourself before you can do them." He's right. You generally get what you expect. If you expect to barely get by in school, that's usually what happens. If you have high expectations of yourself, however, you will perform at a higher level. It's been said, "The minute you start talking about what you're going to do if you lose, you have lost." Keep in mind that it is *your* expectations of yourself that matter, not what others' expectations are (regardless of whether they are positive or negative).

In addition to Lance Armstrong (mentioned earlier), countless other champion athletes have had to overcome severe physical challenges and handicaps. At one time or another, all successful athletes have gone on to victory despite illness or pain. For example, at the 1996 Olympics, the world watched transfixed as 18-year-old gymnast Kerri Strug gritted her teeth and sprinted down the long runway for her final vault. On her previous vault moments earlier, she had landed wrong and ripped the ligaments in her right ankle. She was the USA's last hope for victory over the Russian team. She performed a spectacular vault, nailed the landing, and held it for the required number of seconds. She then collapsed from pain and had to be carried off by her coach. She had done it.

Why mention this example? It is because it shows the power of the human spirit and the effect it can have on a person's life and success. Although he wasn't speaking of athletics, American writer Ralph Waldo Emerson made an observation that applies to any field of endeavor: "A hero is no braver than anyone else; he's just braver five minutes longer." When you get discouraged, try hanging in there for another five minutes. Then hang in for another five. Then another . . .

Take a minute now to write out a statement of your personal expectations regarding yourself as a student and a reader. Writing these down is essential. If you don't even care enough to write them down, you probably are not ever going to accomplish them. Unless you write them down, they're just wishes, not goals. Basketball superstar Julius Erving stated it plainly: "Goals determine what you're going to be." Bill Copeland says that unless you have a goal, you can spend your life running up and down the field and never scoring. Goals give you purpose and direction. They provide a way for you to measure your progress. In life as in football, it helps to know where the "goalposts" are.

Your goals statement can be long or short, but make it specific. Avoid vague statements such as "I want to do better" or "I want to do well." Word your statement positively. (Your brain understands and responds better to positive statements. It comprehends "Stand up!" more quickly and easily than "Don't continue sitting down!") Start your statement with "I will . . ." (for example, "I will obtain a degree in computer science"). Avoid wording your statement negatively ("I won't drop out of college before I get my degree"). Be sure you're firmly committed to a goal before you write it down. Write your statement of goals on the next page, or use notebook paper if you need more space.

■ **My Academic Goals**

_____

_____

_____

_____

_____

_____

_____

_____

Rewrite or photocopy your goals statement, and then put it where you can see it—perhaps above the desk where you study or on your bathroom mirror. Carry a copy in your billfold. Reread your statement often, preferably aloud. You can update or modify your statement from time to time.

We all need a payoff or reward for our efforts, even if it is simply the satisfaction of having given our best. It helps keep us motivated and focused. What would be the payoff for you if you achieved the goals you just wrote? Would it lead to enhanced success in school? Greater confidence and pride? A better, more satisfying career? Fame? Fortune? List the possible payoffs for meeting your expectations and achieving your academic goals:

■ **Payoffs for Achieving My Academic Goals**

_____

_____

_____

_____

_____

_____

What are you willing to do to achieve your goals? Are you willing to make a commitment to them? Former Oakland Athletics owner Charlie Finley observed that "Sweat plus sacrifice equals success." What sacrifices are you willing to make? What will you do to be sure that you stay with your plan? Write your responses as I-statements (for example, "I will sit away from friends in class so that I'm not tempted to goof off" and "I will attend a library orientation session so that I can learn how to use the college's library").

■   **What I Am Willing to Do to Achieve My Academic Goals**

_____

_____

_____

_____

_____

_____

_____

_____

_____

What effort or sacrifices did you list? Perhaps you listed that you were willing to commit whatever amount of time it takes to complete all of your assignments. Or that you are willing to cut back on your social life if it interferes with your academic work. Perhaps you wrote that you will get tutoring or extra help whenever you need it . . . repeat a course . . . take summer courses . . . cut back on hours at work (and perhaps do without a few things because you will have less income) in order to have enough time and energy to study . . . give up playing on an athletic team . . . avoid people who are not serious about school, who are negative, who drag you down . . . change roommates . . .

Someone once said that none of us can ever go back and make a fresh _start,_ but we can begin today to create a new _ending_. What kind of ending do you want for this course? For the semester? For your entire college experience?

13. Show Up for Practice—Even When You Don't Feel Like It.

As mentioned earlier, students who are struggling academically often have the mistaken idea that "good students" don't have to work hard, that they effortlessly understand and remember everything they hear in class or read in their textbooks. Wrong, wrong, wrong! That's like saying that top athletes never have to train or work hard to be successful, which is obviously ridiculous. Most top students work _very_ hard. They attend class diligently, they take good notes, and they do every assignment to the best of their ability. They seek help if they are having trouble in a class. They use written and verbal feedback from teachers to help them improve their performance in a course. They strive constantly to acquire reading and study skills and to refine them. Make no mistake about it: other than the phenomenally rare genius, everyone else—the other 99 percent of all students—must work at their academics to be successful. Top students sound a lot like successful athletes, don't they? Both skillful athletes and skillful students work hard. They show up for practice and class. They work out and do their assignments. They seek feedback from their coaches and teachers. They strive constantly to improve their techniques and skills.

Whether it's becoming a top athlete or a top student, there are no shortcuts, and nothing is a matter of luck. In reality, students don't make high grades because they're lucky or make low grades because they're unlucky. Lots of students, however, want to believe that success is due to luck and that failure is due to lack of ability or other factors "beyond their control." It gives them an excuse not to try. Dennis Waitley says, "The winners in life think constantly in terms of I can, I will, and I am. Losers, on the other hand, concentrate their waking thoughts on what they should have or would have done, or what they can't do." Failure is not falling *down;* failing is not getting *up.*

Winners show up for practice whether they feel like it or not. Former L. A. Lakers power forward A. C. Green is a perfect example. By the end of the 2000 season, when the Lakers won the NBA championship, Green had played in almost 1,100 consecutive games. (He missed three games during his second season, but it was his coach's decision.) That's 14 seasons without taking a day off or calling in sick, 14 years of showing up for practice despite muscle pulls, joint sprains, and knocked-out teeth. He was fond of saying, "If I can walk and I can breathe, I can play." He could just as accurately have said, "If I can walk and I can breathe, I can show up for practice."

The 2002 Olympics had a wonderful Team USA ad. Referring to the athletes, it said, "They're not out there every four years. They're out there every day." It's easy for the rest of us to forget the years of dedicated practice that lead up to the relatively few minutes that athletes spend in actual Olympic competition. Show up for practice.

Lou Gehrig, from the day he was substituted for an ailing Yankee first baseman, *never* missed a game for the next 14 years. He played in an astounding 2,130 consecutive games. In 1995 Baltimore Orioles' shortstop Cal Ripken finally broke Gehrig's record. Ripken played in 2,632 games. You know that neither of these athletes always felt like playing, but they played anyway. It's why they are two of the greatest players ever. Like Gehrig and Ripken, you can control your *effort.* You can show up. You can stay in the game, even when you don't feel like it. That's where discipline comes in.

Discipline is a word that is often associated with athletic training. But discipline doesn't mean forcing yourself to do unpleasant activities. The word actually comes from the Latin word that means "to learn." (The word *disciple* comes from the same root.) Discipline has to do with learning to regulate your own behavior and make good choices. It has to do with making choices that help you accomplish what you want to accomplish. "Discipline is remembering what you want," David Campbell says. When you are torn between doing your homework or momentarily more appealing activities such as watching TV, playing a video game, or going out with friends, ask yourself what it is you want. Think about what you *really* want, not just what you want at the moment. If what you *really* want is to do well in school, succeed in college, and feel good about yourself, you will choose to study. Discipline is remembering what is *really* important to you. When he was coach of the Houston Oilers, Bum Phillips said, "The only discipline that lasts is self-discipline."

Be disciplined. Work hard. No one ever drowned in sweat.

14. Monitor Your Workouts and Evaluate Your Progress.

You probably know that pro football teams review game films to analyze their performance. It enables them to see what they're doing right and what they need to improve. All professional athletes constantly monitor and evaluate their performance: that's one reason they made it to the professional ranks. Similarly, you should monitor your "workouts" in this book. It's crucial that you assess your own performance as well as use instructor feedback to help you identify any points of confusion. If you don't find out why you missed items, then you've lost the opportunity to learn—and you've wasted the time you spent doing the activity.

If you do not understand a reading skill or even a particular paragraph, it's important that you identify as precisely as possible what the problem is and what you think the cause might be. It also enables your instructor to be of greater help. If you make a vague comment, such as "I just don't get implied main ideas," it doesn't help you or your instructor know where to begin in solving the difficulty. Do you mean that you do not understand the difference between stated and implied main ideas? Or perhaps it's more basic than any of those things: You're not sure how to tell when you've written a complete sentence. The point is, the more precisely you define the problem, the quicker and the more efficiently you can address it.

15. Always Give Your Best Effort.

Tommy Lasorda once quipped, "There are three types of baseball players—those who make it happen, those who watch it happen, and those who wonder what happened." You have to decide if you're going to be one of those who make it happen or one of those who wonder what happened.

Whether it's a practice or the real thing—actual competition—true athletes give their best effort. Yankee slugger Mickey Mantle said that he never swung at the ball that he "didn't try to hit it out of the park." There's nothing more to say. Giving your best effort enables you to feel satisfied regardless of the outcome because you will have no regrets. Make it a habit to "go for the gold." Make it a habit to try to hit the ball out of the park.

16. Follow Instructions.

For athletes to be successful, they need to understand and follow their coach's directions. They can't carry out the game plan if they don't know what they're supposed to do. In the classroom, your instructor is your coach who gives the instructions; in your textbooks, it's the author.

Throughout this book, you will be reading sets of directions—directions about how to apply skills and directions in sets of practice exercises. *Read, mark, and follow every set of directions carefully.* Not only will you learn more and make higher grades, you'll get in the habit of paying attention to directions.

Following directions is a relatively simple skill. The problem is that students don't always read them: They just assume they know what to do and plunge in. If you're like most students, you've lost points on tests and assignments because you didn't follow the directions. (By the way, employers say that one of their big—and most costly—problems is employees who don't follow directions. Employers value employees who are skilled at following written directions.)

Here's a quick rundown on what you need to know about the skill of following written directions:

1. Read the *entire* set of directions *carefully,* even if you think you know what you're supposed to do.

2. *Circle* or *box* any clues that *signal steps* in the directions, such as numbers or the words *first, second, then, next,* and *finally.* Remember that not every step will be announced by a signal, however. When that's the case, number the steps. (This will prevent you from accidentally overlooking or leaving out a step.)

3. In each step *underline key words* that tell what you're supposed to do. On a test, for example, these might include *explain, compare, justify,* and *list in order.* (Pay attention to the general instructions as well, such as "use ink," "write answers on the answer *sheet* provided for you," etc.)

4. Carry out the steps *in order.* You can see how crucial this is when you're working with a set of instructions for computer software or a science experiment, but it's important with any set of directions.

17. Get Help from a Coach.

A final concept you can borrow from athletics has to do with coaching. Athletes view their coaches as their teachers. As a student, it will help you to view your teachers as "coaches." Ideally, your college professors are there to help coach you (and to cheer you on!) to success. Listen to them. Do what they advise. Seek their counsel when you need help, support, or advice. Ask for their guidance in class, and outside class, too, if you need it. Some students complain that they can never get any help from their instructors, yet they never *ask* for individual help or make an appointment to talk with their instructors outside class. It's *your* responsibility to let the instructor know when you need additional help.

If you have ever participated in athletics, you know that part of any coach's job is to push and inspire athletes to higher levels. Good teachers, like good coaches, won't let you get by with sloppy work, missed "workouts" (missed class sessions or missing assignments), or a bad attitude. They'll push, prod, and nag. They won't accept excuses. They'll see ability in you that you may not yet be able to see yourself. So when a teacher "gets on your case" or refuses to accept less than your best effort, or for that matter, when your teacher praises your effort and acknowledges your success, say "thank you." It means that teacher *cares* about you.

You may be wondering why the word secrets in the title of this section of *Exercise Your College Reading Skills* is in quotation marks. Real secrets consist of information that only a few people are permitted to know. Sometimes less successful students are convinced that highly successful students must know some secrets for success, but that's not true. The word is in quotation marks because the secrets in this book really aren't secrets at all: They are simply behaviors and attitudes that lead to success. They are available to anyone who chooses to use them. Now you know them—and you know the most important "secret" of all: There is no substitute for hard work and mindful practice.

In summary: It is important that you make a commitment to improve your reading skills, that you realize that it entails making some sacrifices, but that it will pay you great rewards. Make it a habit to study at a time and in a place that helps you rather than works against you. With regard to your academic abilities and endeavors, avoid the traps of thinking negative thoughts, of making negative comments, and of listening to or accepting the negative comments of others. If you want to change the type of student you are, change the type of person you are. In practicing your reading skills, you should do the same things in the same ways as you want to do them when you use them in actual situations. When you hit a plateau (a period of time when you seem not to be making any progress), keep going. When it's time to study, do some slow, deep breathing to center yourself and move into a state of relaxed alertness. Use visualization to help you achieve success. Focus on your own performance, not others'. Develop mental toughness and maintain your focus on what you are trying to achieve. Set high expectations for yourself and commit your goals to writing. Motivate yourself by determining what the payoffs would be for attaining your goals. Decide specifically what it is that you are willing to do to achieve your goals. Show up for practice, even when you don't feel like it. In other words, develop the self-discipline that allows you to do what you need to do at those times when you don't feel motivated. Always give your best effort so that you will not ever be plagued with doubts of whether you could have done better if you'd just tried a little harder. Seek help and support from someone who is knowledgeable.

TIME TO GET MOVING!

Now is the time to get moving—literally and figuratively. It's time for you to start exercising your reading skills. I'd be remiss, however, if I overlooked this opportunity to mention a couple of things. One is that I'm not a huge sports fan. What interests me about sports is that they offer so many valuable lessons in so many areas of our lives. They illustrate the astonishing capacity of the human brain, heart, spirit, and will. They teach us that the only person who limits us is ourselves. That's what *I* love about sports. And that's why I chose to create a book that draws on those lessons. (Those of you who excel in other areas know that the same is true for them—for example, art, music, dance, theater, computers, chess, or even video games.)

It's time for you to decide how committed you are to strengthening your reading skills. Read carefully through the contract below and think about it for a few minutes. Don't sign it unless you are absolutely committed to honoring it. It's really a contract with yourself, so if you scribble your name in the blank and sign it without truly intending to honor it, you've already broken faith with yourself, and that's not a good way to start. If you find that you honestly can't bring yourself to make the commitment, then don't sign it. Instead, give serious consideration to waiting and taking a reading improvement course when you're more ready to learn.

I, _____ , commit to give my best effort as I
   (fill in your first name)
work through this book.

I will complete every assignment to the best of my ability.

I will do my own work.

I will strive hard to understand the material.

I will ask for help when I need clarification or further explanations.

I will be patient with myself when I struggle with new material or hit plateaus.

I will use my strengths and my positive personal qualities to help me succeed.

I will take the best care possible of my health because it affects my ability to learn.

I will recognize and celebrate my successes along the way.

_____   _____
            Signature   Date

If you read this and signed it in good faith, congratulations! Place it (or a copy of it) where you can read it often. As you know, making a commitment in writing can be a powerful stimulus for success.

Now roll up your sleeves. Take a few good, deep, slow breaths as you close your eyes and visualize yourself a semester from now, successfully reading and learning from your college textbooks. Ready to begin? See you in the end zone!

Sources

Carson, Ben, and Gregg Lewis. *The Big Picture*. Grand Rapids, MI: Zondervan Publishing, 1999.

Dorfman, H. A., and Karl Kuehl. *The Mental Game of Baseball: A Guide to Peak Performance*, 2d ed. South Bend, IN: Diamond Communications, Inc., 1995.

Jones, Charlie. *What Makes Winners Win*. New York: Broadway Books, 1999.

A User's Guide to the Brain

It is not the answer that enlightens, but the question.
—Eugene Ionesco, playwright

Inside your head is the most complex thing in the universe: your brain. This soft, three-pound mass is your single most important tool for survival. It is the hardest-working organ in your body. It is responsible for more functions than any other organ in your body.

Most people don't know too much about how their incredible brain works, especially what happens when they learn. Knowing more about your brain and how it learns, though, can help you succeed in school and other areas of your life.

It is primarily through learning that human beings stay alive. Imagine how long a child would live if he or she couldn't learn. Even as a newborn baby, you started learning what is safe and what is dangerous, what feels good and what feels painful, and what other people's facial expressions, words, and tone of voice mean. Those are just a few of the millions of things you almost seemed to absorb. No one gave you classes in these things, so how is it that you learned them and the millions of new things you learn every year?

BORN TO LEARN

The fact is, you are born to learn. Think about something you are really good at. If nothing comes to mind immediately, think about how you like to spend your free time. Is there a hobby or particular interest that you have? It might be a sport, singing or playing an instrument, playing computer games, repairing cars, cooking, or doing a craft of some sort. Perhaps you have an artistic hobby, such as drawing or painting, or a people skill, such as being an excellent listener or leader. Perhaps you're an excellent driver. How did you get good at the activity? Whatever you're good at, you have undoubtedly spent a lot of time doing it. It might not have seemed like "practicing," but that's exactly what you were doing. In addition to practicing, you may have had someone who was already good at it coach you, encourage you, or give you lessons. Perhaps you spent time around them, observing or watching. You sought feedback from them. You asked questions. You probably learned, too, by trial and error. You learned from your mistakes.

Now that you know you're born to learn and how you learn, here are other points to keep in mind.

■ *Mistakes are absolutely necessary.* They are the bridge between inexperience and mastery. Each mistake gives you a chance to learn. View mistakes as "friends" who are there to help you, if you just pay attention to them. When you make a mistake, think about it. Ask yourself what you can do differently (and better) next time. At school, listen to feedback from teachers, knowledgeable peers, and tutors. In fact, seek it from them. Learn to see the important value in making mistakes. If you are making the same mistake over and over, that's a different matter. It means you are not taking advantage of the opportunity to learn from the mistake. Making mistakes is normal and useful. Just try to make better, "smarter" mistakes each time!

■ *Smart people aren't always the ones who come up with the answer most quickly, and they don't always get the right answer on the first try.* They use trial and error to help them eliminate wrong answers and "bad choices." This is what makes them smarter—their ability to eliminate wrong answers and avoid bad choices in the future. They know that learning doesn't come about by having someone give them the right answer and simply repeating (or copying!) it.

■ *Learning is natural and normal and, under most circumstances, enjoyable.* It is satisfying to learn. It gives people a feeling of pleasure when they make progress. They have a sense of pleasure when they can control what they are doing. (Remember the first time you successfully tied a shoelace? Learned to shoot free throws in basketball? Learned how to send e-mails?) You know from experience how good it feels when you make a discovery or have an insight. It's that wonderful "Aha!" feeling. It's the good feeling you get when you learn something new, understand something for the first time, or understand something in a new or different way.

■ *Your brain wants you to continue learning throughout your life.* It has a very clever way of accomplishing this: It rewards you for learning! It rewards you by making you feel good physically. If you exercise regularly or play a sport, you've undoubtedly experienced the sense of well-being after a successful workout that's referred to as a "runner's high." It occurs because the brain rewards you for exercising your body. Your brain sends the same "feel good" chemicals to the rest of your body when you work hard trying to learn. When you are working on something you enjoy, though, it doesn't seem like "work." In fact, a great deal of time can go by very quickly when you are absorbed in something you enjoy. The point is, your brain is brilliantly designed to provide built-in, natural motivation.

■ *Making the effort to learn something challenging causes your brain to grow and you to get smarter.* Challenging yourself to think of a solution to a problem or to learn something new is the key to getting smarter. Notice that it's the mental *effort* that makes your brain grow, and not whether you come up with the right answer or solve the problem. It's certainly nice when that happens, too, of course! But as the quote at the beginning of this section indicates, simply asking good questions and thinking hard about possible answers is what "enlightens" our brain. It doesn't depend on getting the right answer. Being in college offers you constant opportunities to learn new things and to "grow your brain."

■ *You learn by connecting new information with information that you already know.* Let's say, for example, that you pick up a book about computers. If you already know a lot about computers, you can probably understand it without too much trouble. But what happens when there's nothing in your brain for the new information to hook up with? In other words, what if you don't know anything about computers? What do you do then? The answer is that you have to go back and pick up the missing information. (You can do this by talking with or observing someone, reading about it or reading an easier explanation of it, or watching a video.) Often, when people have trouble understanding something new, they assume it's because they're just not very smart. That usually isn't the problem at all. The "problem" is often that they simply do not have enough prior knowledge about the subject. They don't have anything to build on, nothing to link the new information to. The new information is like a boat rope that has been tossed to the shore with no one there to catch it.

Suppose that you are reading, and you do not understand (comprehend) what you are reading. This can happen frequently in college. Certainly you should strengthen your overall reading strategies and skills. That's why you've enrolled in a reading improvement course and are using this book. The number one cause of reading comprehension problems, however, is the reader's lack of background knowledge. So if you find yourself struggling with a subject, it may be because it's new to you and you don't know very much about it. You can fix this by getting the background information that you need. (Sorry! There are no shortcuts!) You can do this by reading easier books on the topic, talking with the instructor and other students, or going to your college's tutoring center. By the way, each time you read and learn new information, you get a bonus: You expand your knowledge base. You then have more knowledge to link new learning to. In short, the more you already know, the more you can learn.

ADDITIONAL POINTS ABOUT HOW THE BRAIN LEARNS

Here are a handful of other useful things to know about your marvelous brain.

- *Your brain is a natural pattern seeker.* It looks for patterns because they help you make sense of the world. There are patterns everywhere: writing patterns, speech patterns, behavior patterns, mathematical patterns, musical patterns, and patterns in every aspect of nature (such as the seasons, life cycles, and weather patterns), to name only a few. If you are a chess player or a football fan, you've learned to recognize the pattern of "moves" in each game. (Seeing patterns is also a skill you will use in this book.)

- *Your brain gathers information many ways and from many sources.* Although all brains learn by the same physiological process, each person has a preferred learning style (usually visual or auditory). The person can learn in other ways, but his or her primary or main one is the one that makes learning most comfortable. Once you know your learning style, you can take steps to make learning easier and more efficient. This book has special features that take advantage of the natural way the brain learns and what works best for each learning style. (Appendix 5 has tips for various learning styles.)

- *Your brain can do something else that's remarkable: It can think about its own thinking.* There is a fancy word for this—metacognition—but what you need to know is that it is important for you to monitor or evaluate your learning. When you read, you need to ask yourself, for example, "Am I understanding this?" If the answer is no, then you need to ask yourself, "Why not?" Once you have pinpointed the problem, ask yourself, "What do I need to do to fix the situation?" Asking and answering these questions will enable you to make useful changes.

- *For learning to be most effective, you need to see the relevance or importance of it to you personally.* How does it relate to your own experience and your own life? Can you see a connection or make one? For example, suppose you want to add the word *agile* to your vocabulary. You look it up in the dictionary and find that it means "able to move quickly and with ease, skill, and control." You could create your own sentence using the word and, better yet, include information that is personally meaningful to you: "My brother has won several gymnastic competitions because he is so agile." You can even visualize your brother skillfully and agilely completing a gymnastic routine.

- *Your brain learns well when it experiences information in what are called "multiple contexts."* That sounds complicated, but all it means is that your understanding is deeper if you have opportunities to experience or apply information in different ways and in different situations (contexts). For example, when you are learning a new vocabulary word, your understanding (and recall) will be stronger if you use the word in sentences that you write or speak. (It's also helpful, of course, if you hear the word being used and come across it when you are reading.)

■ *When it comes to brain power, it's "use it or lose it."* If you do not use your muscles, you lose strength and flexibility. If you stop playing a sport, your performance level decreases. Your brain, like the rest of your body, operates on the same "use it or lose it" principle. If you do not use information, it fades away. This is terrific when you want to change a bad habit, do away with negative beliefs about yourself, or "erase" incorrect information. Most of the time, though, you want to understand and remember information. The way to do that is to keep your brain active and challenged. You must keep "practicing" by thinking and by using the concepts and knowledge you already possess. Staying mentally active may also prevent or delay brain disorders and diseases that can occur as you grow old.

BRAIN CELLS AND BRAIN FUNCTION

Your brain has approximately 100 billion brain cells, called neurons. Each neuron forms as many as 10,000 connections with other neurons. Neurons link together to form neural networks. As you learn more and more about a topic, the networks themselves can link together. (When that happens, you get that wonderful Aha! feeling.) Each neuron sends complex chemical and electrochemical "messages" to thousands of other cells at the rate of about 200 miles per hour. Your amazing brain can process two million bits of information per second.

Different parts of your brain are specialized to do distinct tasks. Reason and logic, emotion, and aspects of memory, for example, occur in different regions of your brain. This is why you can instantly see a good solution to a problem (the lightning fast reasoning part of your brain handles this), and yet still feel upset (the emotional system in your brain operates at a different speed). These specialized areas of the brain are also why it's usually helpful to people to get the same information through several "channels," such as seeing and hearing it, and reading and talking about it. The brain processes and stores the information in different places and in different ways. That makes the learning and recall stronger.

EMOTIONS, STRESS, AND THE BRAIN

A few words about how emotions and stress affect the brain:

■ *Emotions affect thinking, learning, and remembering.* Fear, sadness, or anger, for example, interferes with these processes. These emotions create stress. The brain reacts by ordering the release of certain "stress chemicals." Although this can be a good thing, and even a lifesaver in an emergency, being under long-term stress is not good. Over time, the constant release of these stress chemicals damages all the organs of the body, and it increases the likelihood that you will become ill.

■ *It's important that you develop healthy ways to deal with stress.* Exercise is a great way to reduce stress, and it has the added benefit of getting lots of oxygen to the brain. Taking a few slow, deep breaths and exhaling completely is another great stress reducer. Maintaining a positive outlook can also make a world of difference. So can letting go of "small stuff," not holding grudges, and not being too hard on yourself or others.

■ *All learning is state-dependent.* That means that the brain and the body have ongoing effects on each other. At any given moment, you are in a particular state: for example, joyful, excited, calm, scared, ill, frustrated, or tired. Although you might not ever have thought of it in these terms, you do things constantly to change the state you are in. You close your eyes for a few minutes. You take a deep breath. You eat a cookie or drink a cup of coffee. You make a phone call. You stretch and yawn. You take a nap. You take an aspirin. In short, you move continuously from one state to another. Learning to manage your states in appropriate ways can make you more effective as a student, as well as in every other area of your life.

You have already learned millions of things in your lifetime. Your magnificent brain already knows how to learn. Different people learn at different rates, of course, and different people have different amounts of background knowledge. Clearly, some people have special aptitudes for certain things.

In college, you will learn some concepts and subjects faster and more easily than other students do. There will be other students who learn things faster and more easily than you. But fast or slow, by practicing over time, you will become "smarter" and you will learn.

THE CARE AND FEEDING OF YOUR BRAIN

It's important that you take care of your brain. Your brain runs your body, and your body affects your brain. If you owned a unique, priceless, one of a kind automobile, you would make every effort to take great care of it and to protect it. You'd be careful to use the right kind of fuel, change the oil, and keep it polished and tuned. Your brain is infinitely more important, and so it deserves the best care you can give it.

■ *One key to caring for your brain is to eat a well-balanced diet.* Even though a human brain is small enough to hold in the palm of your hand, it uses 20 percent of the body's energy. Without the right "fuel," it cannot function at its full potential. You become forgetful, overly emotional, light-headed, or confused. Your brain's "diet" consists of only two things: glucose, which is a blood sugar, and oxygen. The body produces glucose from foods rich in the necessary nutrients.

■ *After you've been asleep all night, your brain is low on glucose, so it's important to eat breakfast.* The brain prefers numerous small "meals" or snacks throughout the day, rather than three big meals. It's hard to think clearly after a large meal, especially if it is high in saturated fat, because it makes you sleepy. The "good fat" is the kind found in fish (omega-3 oil) and in unsaturated oils, such as cottonseed oil, olive oil, and the oil in avocados.

■ *A brain-healthy diet includes quality protein and complex carbohydrates.* Quality protein is found in foods such as eggs, tuna, chicken, turkey, soybeans, and yogurt. Complex carbs are "good carbs" and are found in whole grains, beans, brown rice, whole grain cereal and breads, nuts, and sunflower seeds, to name a few. They give the body sustained energy. You also need to eat a variety of fresh green, yellow, and red vegetables (such as spinach, broccoli, green beans, asparagus, carrots, squash, yams, peppers, and salad greens) and fresh fruit. Blueberries seem to be particularly good for the brain. So are bananas, avocados, oranges, strawberries, and tomatoes. (That's not a mistake; avocados and tomatoes are actually fruits.) You can also take a multivitamin; just don't rely on it to make up for unhealthy eating habits. Keep in mind that severe dieting and "lose-weight-quick" fad diets can be just as disastrous for the brain and body as a junk food habit.

■ *View certain items as once-in-a-while "treats."* These include items that are filled with sugar (cookies, cake, candy, ice cream, and the like) and refined carbohydrates (packaged cereals, potato chips, pasta, crackers, white rice, and white bread, for example). Sugar, refined carbs, and far too much fat abound in most "fast foods," such as shakes, tacos, fried chicken, and French fries. They are filled with empty calories that offer little nutrition, but cause you to pack on the pounds.

- *Avoid or limit caffeine and alcohol.* Caffeine-laden coffee and cola drinks can leave you jittery. Alcohol not only impairs your judgment and memory (which are functions of the brain) and makes you sleepy, but it also kills brain cells.

- *The brain can go without oxygen for only about three minutes before permanent damage or death results.* So where does the oxygen come from? Of course, it comes mostly from breathing. Taking several slow, deep breaths not only supplies your brain with oxygen, but it also has a calming effect. Yawning is your brain's ingenious way of getting more oxygen for itself when you feel sleepy.

- *You need to breathe clean air.* Smoking cigarettes or inhaling someone else's secondhand smoke reduces the oxygen to your brain and harms it along with the rest of the body. In fact, the nicotine and chemicals in any form of tobacco are damaging.

- *Regular exercise, even in the form of brisk twenty-minute walks, benefits the brain.* It increases your circulation, so brain cells receive more oxygen and nutrients. Vigorous exercise also triggers the release of certain "feel-good" chemicals that enhance your mood. Physical exercise is one of the simplest, most effective ways to stimulate the brain and boost learning.

- *Sufficient water is also necessary for proper brain function.* Eighty percent of the brain consists of water, so it is no surprise that dehydration and poor learning are connected. Without enough water, blood pressure and levels of certain stress hormones increase. In addition to other beverages you drink each day, you need at least eight glasses of fresh, pure water.

- *Give your brain the rest it needs.* Inadequate sleep affects your mental sharpness and ability to concentrate. It impairs new learning and long-term memory. It results in a confused, groggy mental state and causes errors in judgment. Besides, being sleep-deprived makes you grumpy and irritable!

- *Protect your brain from impact injuries.* Remember when you were a child how your mother insisted you wear your seat belt in the car and a helmet when you did certain other activities? She was right. Even though your brain is encased inside your skull, that isn't enough to protect your brain from injury from a dangerous fall or from a serious car, motorcycle, or bicycle accident. Helmets make sense for skateboarders, motorcyclists, and bicyclists of any age. Football players would suffer a great many more head injuries if it were not for the helmets they wear. Boxers, in contrast, are much more likely to suffer brain damage because they wear no protective headgear. Crying babies are sometimes shaken violently by exhausted, frustrated parents who lose control of themselves. Tragically, the babies suffer permanent brain damage.

- *Your brain needs exercise in the form of mental stimulation.* Try to learn something new every day. Stay mentally active: read, keep a journal, solve puzzles, get involved in challenging projects and hobbies.

Your brain is one of the most awesome creations in the universe. It has been said that everything you are, everything you have ever been, everything you will be depends on your brain. Treat this precious gift with the care and respect it deserves.

Handle Textbooks and Textbook Assignments Like a Pro

It has been estimated that in college approximately 80 percent of the material you are asked on tests comes directly from your textbooks. That means it's more important than ever that you have a plan for handling textbook reading assignments. It goes without saying that you should read your assignments before going to class. You'll be better prepared to contribute in class, you'll understand what's going on, you'll be more engaged, and you'll be able to take better notes.

FIRST THINGS FIRST: PREVIEW YOUR TEXTS

Before we talk about how to approach specific assignments, let's talk about a simple thing you can do at the beginning of each semester that will help you in every course: preview the textbook. You only need to preview a textbook once, and the few minutes you spend doing it will pay big dividends. Here's all you need to do:

- Read the book's *title*.
- Skim through the *table of contents*. How many major sections are there? What are they? Read the chapter titles to see what is covered in the book and how the information is sequenced.
- Read the *introduction* to the book. It may be called "Introduction," "To the Student," or some other such name. In this section, the author tells you about the book, how it is organized, its special features, what certain symbols mean, and so forth.
- Look at the *information at the back of the book*. What features are included in the appendixes? Is there a *glossary* that defines key terms used in the book? Depending on the type of textbook, there may be a list of formulas, maps, or other special information. Is there an *index* that tells you the pages that specific information appears on? If so, is there anything special you need to know about it, such as page numbers in bold to indicate that the term is defined on that page? Is there a separate index of names of people mentioned in the book?
- Pick out a *chapter* and examine it more closely. What is the chapter format or organization? Is there a mini table of contents or outline of chapter topics? A list of learning objectives? An introduction? A list of key terms? Are key terms defined in the margin or somewhere else, such as the end of the chapter? Do key terms appear in special print? Are there icons (symbols) in the margins that provide tips or direct you to related online resources or lab activities? Are there special boxes that present case studies, ethical issues, or other related material? Is there a chapter summary or list of key points? Are there chapter quizzes or discussion questions?

A GAME PLAN FOR READING TEXTBOOK ASSIGNMENTS

Just as every successful coach and athlete goes into a game or competition with a game plan, you should approach your reading assignments in an organized way. Perhaps you're used to sitting down and flipping to the first page of the assignment. After a few minutes—or even a few paragraphs—your mind begins to wander. After a few more minutes, you feel frustrated and overwhelmed. You give up and close the book. Or perhaps you actually keep going. You finish reading the assignment, but then discover in class the next day that you don't remember any of it. When it's time for a test, you try to review by rereading as much of the material as you can. If any of these describes you, you'll be happy to know that there's a better way to handle textbook assignments. There are many different methods, but this is what they have in common: All of them consist of certain strategies you apply *before* you read, *as* you read, and *after* you read. (Of course, you should incorporate strategies that work well with your learning style.) The sections below describe the strategies in each part of the game plan.

Prereading Strategies

Preview

Many college students complain that everything in a chapter seems important. What they're really saying is that they don't know how to determine what is important. Because everything seems important and because no one can remember everything, they feel hopelessly overwhelmed. One solution is previewing, which is also called surveying or overviewing. ***Previewing*** means *looking at an assignment prior to reading it to see what it is about, how the information is organized, and what is important.* Previewing a textbook assignment is like looking at a map ahead of time to see your destination, how you are going to get there, and what you might encounter along the way. Your brain likes seeing the "big picture" in advance.

To preview an assignment, start by turning through the pages to determine (1) what the assignment is about and (2) how the information is organized. (If you are a global learner who likes to see how all the parts fit together, look at the titles of the chapters that come before and after so that you can see how that particular chapter fits into the even bigger picture.) Once you've turned through the chapter, examine these chapter features. (Of course, not every text will have every feature.)

- Read the *chapter title*. What, if anything, do you already know about the subject? Bringing this to mind helps you focus your attention and gets you ready to read.

- Read the chapter *objectives*. They tell you what you should know or be able to do after studying the chapter. They also help you focus your attention.

- Read the *chapter table of contents*. This "mini-outline" tells you the structure of the chapter. Your brain likes to see how the topics fit together.

- Read the chapter *introduction*. It describes the overall purpose and major topics. Read it carefully because it presents important concepts and may also provide background information you need in order to understand the chapter.

- Read the *headings and subheadings*. They indicate the major topics and show how they are organized. In other words, they provide an outline of the chapter.

- Read *words in special print* (**bold**, *italics*, or color). If there is a *list of key terms* at the end of the chapter, skim through it. Words in special print, lists of key terms, and definitions in the margin all alert you to information that's important. (Expect to be asked the meaning of those terms on tests!)

- Look at *pictures, diagrams,* or *other graphic aids* in the chapter.

- Read the *chapter summary*. Read it carefully because it presents the main points of the chapter. It may be called "Summary," "Chapter Highlights," "Key Points," or "Chapter Recap." (On tests you will typically be asked questions about key concepts that appear in chapter introductions and summaries. Don't skip over these important chapter features!)

- Read any *study questions* in the chapter. (These might also appear in an accompanying study guide or on a handout your instructor gives you.) Study questions are designed to guide your reading so that you can read purposefully. Chapter questions or quizzes let you assess your understanding of the chapter. Read them first, though. They tell you in advance what you need to understand by the time you finish the chapter.

Plan Your Reading Session or Sessions

Now you're ready to develop your plan of attack. In this prereading step, you assess your **prior knowledge,** *information you already know about the topic.* More than any other factor, prior knowledge determines how much you are likely to understand. The more you already know, the easier it will be to understand the material you are reading. If you have limited background knowledge, you may have to read even more carefully or take some additional steps to fill in gaps in your knowledge.

Based on how much prior knowledge you have and the length of the assignment, plan your reading session or sessions. In other words, estimate how long it will take you to read the assignment, and decide whether you need to divide the assignment into smaller chunks. If it seems too long to read all at one time, divide it into smaller parts and place sticky notes or paper clips at logical stopping points. You can then read a section at a time, spreading it over several study sessions. For example, you might have 24 pages to read before the class meets again in two days. You could divide the assignment into three eight-page segments that you read at three study sessions spread throughout one day. Or, you might read eight pages on the day you get the assignment, eight the next day, and the last eight the following day before the class meets. You can determine what works best for you.

These prereading strategies take only five to ten minutes, yet they can dramatically increase your comprehension and reduce the time it takes you to read the assignment. You wouldn't want to get in a car and start driving with only a hazy idea of your destination, with no clear idea of the route you're going to take, the important landmarks to look for along the way, and logical points at which to take a break if it's a long drive. Wouldn't you willingly spend ten minutes looking at a map and planning your trip to avoid the frustration and wasted time of wandering around, lost? Doesn't it make just as much sense to spend a few minutes planning your approach to a college reading assignment?

"During Reading" Strategies

Once you have previewed the chapter or assignment, you know where you're going, have assessed your prior knowledge, and have planned your study session or sessions, you're ready to read the chapter. But what can you do *as you are reading* to help you understand the material? The answer is: Pose a question. When you ask yourself a question, your brain swings into action. Questions grab your attention and focus your concentration. When you read with the purpose of finding answers to specific questions, your comprehension increases dramatically. That's why the "during reading" strategies include asking and answering questions.

Ask Questions as You Read

When you read, the most effective way to focus your concentration is to turn each chapter heading into one or more questions by asking *when, where, who, what, why,* or *how.* For example, if the heading says, "The Three Branches of Government," you should ask yourself, "*What* are the three branches of government?" Then read the section to find the answer to your question. Asking questions as you read is like going to the grocery store with a shopping list. Because you know what you're "shopping" for, you're more focused and purposeful. You can complete your shopping (reading) more quickly and efficiently, especially if you know the layout of the store (chapter). It's a lot less frustrating than wandering around the store (chapter) hoping that when you get home (go to class or take a test), you guessed correctly about what you needed.

Turning headings into questions is the simplest way to come up with questions, but there are other sources of questions as well. First, the textbook chapter may include them. Second, there may be a study guide that accompanies your text that includes questions. Third, your instructor may supply study questions. These questions help you identify important points from the start and to begin preparing for tests from the moment you read an assignment.

Answer Questions When You Reach the End of Each Section

Here's the next "during reading" strategy: When you come to the *end* of a section, stop. To find out if you understood the section, try to answer the questions you posed about it. For example, suppose you read a section in a health or nutrition textbook called "Complex Carbohydrates," and you turned the heading into the logical question, "What are complex carbohydrates?" If you can answer the question, you comprehended what you needed in the section. The *process of evaluating your understanding of what you read and correcting the problem whenever you realize that you are not comprehending* is called **comprehension monitoring.** Effective readers monitor their comprehension.

When you answer the questions, answer them out loud if you are an auditory learner. If you are a visual learner, jot the information down without looking at the book. If you are a visual-spatial or a tactile-kinesthetic learner, make a sketch that explains a concept or term. All of these are more effective than just "thinking" the answer in your head. If you do that, it's easy to be vague ("Complex carbohydrates are carbohydrates that are complex . . .") and to fool yourself into believing you understand more than you actually do. If you write information down, you can use notebook paper, the margin of the textbook if there is enough space, note cards, or sticky notes. (Chapter 14 describes techniques for marking and annotating textbooks, as well as recording textbook information so that you can learn it. You are welcome to look at it now, of course. You will be able to apply the techniques even more effectively once you have studied the comprehension chapters that precede it, which is the reason it appears near the end of the book.)

Wait until you reach the end of a section to answer questions about it. If you try to answer them or write down information paragraph-by-paragraph as you go, you'll be constantly switching back and forth between reading and writing. This fractures your comprehension and slows you down tremendously. You will find it difficult to follow the author's train of thought, and you will soon feel tired, frustrated, and discouraged.

What if you read a section and find that you cannot answer the questions you posed about it? One or more of these strategies will help:

- Reread the section or certain paragraphs in it.
- Keep reading (read the next paragraph or section) to see if things become clearer.

- If you do not understand a key term, look it up in the glossary or a dictionary.

- Do some extra reading. As noted, it is difficult to understand material if you have limited background knowledge in the subject (and in college, many subjects will be new to you). If you read a simpler explanation of a topic online or in an easier book, and then go back to your college textbook, it will seem much easier.

- Ask a classmate, members of your study group, or your instructor. Consult a tutor if your college offers tutoring.

- Don't get discouraged if you do not understand all the material. Read it again the next day. Give your brain time to process the material—even to "sleep on it."

- If you are still confused or unable to answer some questions, write a question mark in the margin beside the heading or paragraph, or jot your unanswered questions on notebook paper. That way, you can get answers well before you are tested on the material.

"After Reading" Strategies

You're on the home stretch! The "after reading" strategies consist of *reviewing* and *rehearsing* the material you have just read. The shocking fact is that if you do nothing but read an assignment, you will have forgotten half of the material by the time you close your textbook! Within a couple of weeks, you will have forgotten nearly all of it. You might remember one or two main points per chapter, which isn't enough to do well on a test. How can you change this natural forgetting process? The answer is to take steps to transfer the information into long-term (permanent) memory while it is still fresh in mind.

Previewing an assignment, along with asking and answering questions as you read, aid comprehension greatly. However, if you want to lock the information into memory, you must take time to review and rehearse the important information. ***Rehearsing information*** *to remember it means saying or writing the information to transfer it into long-term memory.*

Suppose you just finished reading an assignment. You previewed it, and when you read it, you asked questions. You stopped at the end of each section and answered the questions out loud, jotted the answers down, or made sketches to capture the important points. Now it's time to *check* your answers, make *corrections,* and *add* missing information. This is also the time to make vocabulary cards for key terms in the chapter.

For your brain to process and store information, you must interact with the material. This is why it is crucial that you rehearse the material by reciting or rewriting it until you can do so from memory, that is, without looking at the book. After all, that's what you're going to have to do on a test. Silently thinking through the answers isn't enough, so here's the rule: *If you can't say or write the information, you don't know it!* This is the time to find out what you know, and not while you're taking a test over the material. In effect, rehearsing lets you test yourself before the professor tests you.

If you use this three-step approach for textbook assignments, you'll be in excellent shape when it's time for a test. You will already have learned a great deal of the material. You will have created study tools (notes, sketches, vocabulary cards, etc.) to help you review further. You will have identified any material you still need help or clarification on, in plenty of time to get that help. You'll feel more relaxed and confident about the test.

A quick word about preparing for tests: The least effective way to prepare for a test is to reread textbook chapters, yet this is exactly what many students do. It's all they know to do, but unfortunately, rereading does not guarantee that you'll understand or remember the material any better the second time than you did the first. Reading and remembering are two separate things. That's why it's so important to rehearse the material by reciting or rewriting it. Strive to understand the material. The better you understand it, the easier it will be to memorize. (A few related points: The chapters in the Basic Workout and the Advanced Workout are designed to equip you with the comprehension skills you need. Second, Appendix 2 discusses preparing for tests, handling various types of test questions, and reducing test anxiety. Also, the Online Learning Center contains an excellent, comprehensive module on reading and understanding literary material, such as novels, essays, short stories, and poems. It explains how to adapt this general approach when you are assigned to read literary works.)

If you apply the prereading, "during reading," and "after reading" strategies when you read your textbook assignments, you will read them more efficiently and effectively. Give yourself a few weeks to get used to this new approach, especially if in the past you have routinely turned to the first page of an assignment and hit it cold. Think of the prereading strategies as the important warm-up that lets you perform well "during reading," and the rehearsing and reviewing as the important cooldown that lets you consolidate the gains from your "workout."

PART · ONE 1 Warm-Up

CHAPTERS IN PART ONE

Determine the Meaning of an Unfamiliar Word through Context

DETERMINE THE MEANING OF AN UNFAMILIAR WORD BY USING THE CONTEXT

College textbooks contain many words and terms that will be new to you. In addition to many general "college-level" words, you will encounter important technical terms. You're not going to want to stop and look them up in the dictionary, although there will be times when you must do that. So how can you determine the meaning of most of these words? You figure them out by using context clues. *Context clues* consist of *words in a sentence or paragraph that enable readers to reason out the meaning of unfamiliar words.* "Context" is whatever surrounds something else. In this case, the context of an unfamiliar word is the rest of the sentence and the rest of the paragraph in which it appears.

Authors build in these clues to help you understand the material you are reading. Textbook authors usually define specialized terms, and they expect you to learn those important definitions. They also expect you to know, figure out, or find out the meaning of other words that they use. When you are reading and you encounter an unfamiliar word, ask yourself, "What would this word have to mean *in order for it to make sense in this sentence*?" Then look for clues that enable you to reason out or infer the meaning of the word.

By the way, do you know that even skilled readers—including your professors—encounter unfamiliar words? When they need to determine the meaning of an unfamiliar word, the first strategy they try is to use the context. Context clues are not always perfect clues, of course, but more often than not, they enable readers to make a correct, educated guess about a word's meaning.

USE FIVE TYPES OF CONTEXT CLUES

To determine the meaning of an unfamiliar word, ask yourself, "What would this word have to mean for it to make sense in this sentence?" Authors give you a great deal of help in answering this question. There are five common types of context clues. In this section, you will learn what they are and how to use each of them. I think you'll be pleased at how straightforward and logical they are.

CLUE 1: DEFINITION OR SYNONYM CLUE

Sometimes a *definition* or *synonym* in the sentence serves as the context clue. This is the easiest type of context clue because the author simply *tells* readers what a word means. Authors often alert readers that a definition is coming by introducing it with phrases such as *is defined as, means, is known as, the term,* and *is called.* Sometimes the definition or the term is set off by punctuation marks, such as commas or dashes. The definition may also follow a colon (:) or it may be enclosed in parentheses ( ) or brackets [ ]. Sometimes the definition or term appears in quotation marks.

Because textbook authors want to make sure readers pay attention to important terms, they often put them in special print, such as **bold print,** *italics,* or color. Watch for words in special print, and take advantage of definitions and synonyms authors include for them.

These sentences illustrate how special print, clue words, and punctuation can function as definition clues. Explanations are in brackets.

- **Deceptive advertising** is defined as any ad that contains a misrepresentation, omission, or other practice that can mislead a significant number of reasonable consumers to their detriment. [The term is in bold print; the definition follows the phrase *is defined as.*]

- An important aspect of tort law involves ***product liability***—businesses' legal responsibility for any negligence in the design, production, sale, and consumption of products. [The term is in bold italics; the definition follows a dash.]

- "Victimless crimes" is the term for crimes in which the offenders' illegal actions do damage to themselves rather than to others. [The term is in quotation marks; the definition follows the clue words *is the term for.*]

- Virtually every business transaction is carried out by means of a contract, a mutual agreement between two or more parties that can be enforced in a court if one party chooses not to comply with the terms of the contract. [The term is in bold print and color; the definition follows a comma.]

- As late as the early 19th century in England, the death penalty (or *capital punishment*) was available for about 200 offenses, most of them property crimes. [The formal term is in italics in parentheses, following the more common expression *death penalty* and introduced by the clue word *or.*]

Synonyms are words or phrases that mean the same thing (such as *big* and *large*); they are similar to definitions. Authors typically introduce the synonym with *or, in other words, that is, by this we mean, that is to say,* and *also known as.* A synonym can also be an expression (such as an abbreviation, phrase or symbol) that serves as a symbolic substitute for another expression. Here are examples of synonyms as definition clues:

- A last resort for individuals or businesses that cannot fulfill their financial obligations is **bankruptcy,** or legal insolvency. [The phrase *or legal insolvency* indicates that it is equivalent in meaning to *bankruptcy.* Note that you would have to do further work if you do not know the word *insolvency.* Be sure you know what the synonyms mean!]

- Masters of business administration (MBA) programs have been shortened and businesspeople are being given credit for on-the-job experience so that completion of the program goes faster. [The abbreviation *MBA* appears in parentheses directly after the term it stands for; in the rest of the paragraph and chapter, the author would use that common abbreviation instead of writing out *master of business administration.*]

- The White House announced today that it plans to lower taxes. [Obviously, a building cannot make an announcement or lower taxes. The author uses *White House* as synonymous with the president, the person who occupies the White House.]

CLUE 2: CONTRAST CLUE

A *contrast clue* consists of a word or phrase that means the opposite of the word you are trying to figure out. Watch for words that signal a contrast: *but, however, on the other hand, nevertheless, yet, in contrast, some . . . others,* to name a few. Find the word or words in the sentence that mean the opposite of the word whose meaning you are trying to deduce, and then think of the opposite of *that* word. This sounds complicated, but the following example will make the strategy clear. Suppose you were unsure of the meaning of *unscrupulous* in this sentence:

- A few advertisers are unscrupulous, but most are honest. [Unscrupulous advertisers are contrasted with honest advertisers, so you can reason out that unscrupulous is the opposite of honest. Therefore, *unscrupulous* means *dishonest* or *not following ethical principles.*]

CLUE 3: EXAMPLE CLUE

Example clues consist of one or more examples that authors include to *illustrate* the meaning of the unfamiliar word. Examples are typically introduced by *for example, to illustrate, for instance, such as,* and *like.* Remember, though, that an example is not the same as the definition. Rather, the example is simply a clue that can help you reason out the meaning of an unknown word. If there is more than one example, try to determine what the examples have in common. Look at the examples of *carbohydrates* that are given in the following sentence:

- Many Americans include too many servings of potatoes, rice, pasta, bread, and other carbohydrates in their diet. [*Potatoes, rice, pasta,* and *bread* are given as examples of *carbohydrates.* What they have in common is that they are all starches. Therefore, carbohydrates refers to "starchy foods." Although this is not the technical, scientific definition of carbohydrates, it is enough to allow you to comprehend the general meaning and keep reading.]

CLUE 4: GENERAL SENSE OF THE SENTENCE

The *general sense* of the sentence can also help you figure out the meaning of an unknown word. In this case, you call on your own prior knowledge and experience. When readers ask themselves, "What does this word have to mean in order to make sense in this sentence?", they can usually draw on information they already know to help them answer that question. For example, you can use the general sense of the sentence to figure out the meaning of *equestrian:*

■ The equestrian center received a donation of 25 horses, as well as saddles and other new equipment for the riding team. [From the general sense of the sentence—the references to *horses, saddles,* and the *riding team*—you can deduce that *equestrian* pertains to *horseback riding* and *horseback riders.*]

CLUE 5: CLUE FROM ANOTHER SENTENCE

Sometimes authors include information in another sentence in the paragraph that allows you to determine the meaning of an unfamiliar word. The other sentence can come before or after the one with the unknown word, so it's a good idea to keep reading when you encounter an unfamiliar word. Look at the following example: In the first sentence, there are no context clues as to the meaning of the word *ribald.* The sentence that follows it, however, contains a helpful clue.

■ That comedian has a ribald sense of humor. Two television networks have canceled his show because viewers complained about his lewd language and vulgar jokes. [From the second sentence, you can conclude that *ribald* means vulgar, coarse, or off-color. The clue is that many viewers complained about his *lewd* language and his *vulgar* jokes.]

That's it. Those are the five types of context clues. How are you doing? Take a minute to stretch and yawn to get your circulation going. Drink a glass of water. All these simple actions help your brain. Look over the list of the five types of context clues, then close your eyes and try to say them out loud. (You're going to have to write them from memory in a few minutes, so take advantage of the opportunity to get ready for that. Reviewing as you go is an excellent habit to develop.)

THE TRAINER

OBSERVE THE SKILL OF USING CONTEXT CLUES

Now "peek inside the head" of an efficient reader who encounters some unfamiliar words in context to see how this person uses context clues to deduce their meaning. The efficient reader's "thoughts" appear in color.

One of the things you'll discover when you read The Trainer sections is that even skilled readers don't automatically comprehend everything instantly, accurately, or perfectly as they are reading something for the first time. They continually reassess as they read, and they sometimes have to go back and reread. Like pro athletes who monitor their performance (by keeping training records and watching tapes of their performances or games, for example), effective readers monitor their comprehension. They know when they're "getting it" and when they're not. If they are confused, they try to figure out the source of the problem so that they can take steps to correct it. In other words, they see progress as a process of making adjustments to fine-tune their skills.

By the way, when you read a difficult passage, it may help you to read it aloud and then talk your way through it aloud. In other words, say your thoughts out loud as you move through the material and mentally process it. Being aware of your own thought process is called *metacognition,* and it can be a powerful aid in helping you understand what you read.

In The Trainer section that follows, the reader reasons out the meaning of the words *injunction, nunnery, retort,* and *spurn.* Notice that the person goes down the wrong trail at first, then, as more information is obtained, is able to correct a misimpression. Read the paragraph first, and then go back and read the "thoughts."

Injunction. That's a new one to me. He's ordering Ophelia to do something, so *injunction* must mean a command or an order. That makes sense in place of the word.

Nunnery. Sounds like a place where nuns live. Perhaps it's a convent.

The ever-widening gap between Shakespeare's meaning and what audiences now take to be his meaning is well illustrated by Hamlet's famous injunction to Ophelia, "Get thee to a nunnery!" These words are Hamlet's retort when the pure, young Ophelia declares her feelings for him. Most audiences today think that *nunnery* must refer to a convent and that Hamlet is suggesting that she lock herself away in a religious institution and never marry. In reality, the audiences of Shakespeare's time knew at once that *nunnery* was Elizabethan slang for "whorehouse." Thus, in this famous rejection scene (Act III, Scene 1), the way in which Hamlet spurns Ophelia is much more cruel than modern audiences realize.

Retort. Must mean a reply because it describes the words he said to her. That fits the general sense of the sentence.

Guess the author just proved his point. I was one of those folks who thought *nunnery* meant a convent. Was I ever wrong! They give a direct definition: "Elizabethan era slang for whorehouse"—a very different meaning indeed!

Now that I see what *nunnery* means, I think a *retort* must mean not just a reply, but a hurtful, stinging reply. Hamlet clearly intends to hurt and offend Ophelia because in another sentence the author describes the words as being spoken in a "rejection scene."

Spurns. Hamlet rejected Ophelia in a very cruel way—she's an innocent, young maiden, and he tells her she belongs in a whorehouse. *Spurn* must mean "reject," but it seems to have the idea of doing it in a mean, hurtful way.

THE EDGE

POINTERS ABOUT USING CONTEXT CLUES

■ **Test your definition.**
When you think you have determined the meaning of an unfamiliar word from the context, substitute your definition in the sentence. Does it make sense? If so, then you have probably figured out its meaning. If it doesn't, then it's back to the drawing board!

■ **Some "context clues" can be misleading.**
One of the five clues described earlier will almost always help you determine the meaning of an unfamiliar word. However, context clues do not always provide perfect clues to a word's meaning. A sentence may appear to contain context clues when, in fact, it does not. These false "clues" can be misleading. Read this sentence, for example, and try to deduce the meaning of *bridled:* "The actress *bridled* at the idea that all women should be married by the time they are 30." *Bridled* may sound as if it has something to do with brides or that the woman decided to get married because she was approaching the age of 30. However, *bridled* means to take offense or to be offended by something: the actress was *offended by* the idea that all women should be married by the age of 30.

■ **Context clues may not always be complete.**
I hate to say it, but sometimes there are not sufficient context clues in a sentence to allow you to figure out the meaning of an unfamiliar word. Even if

you have to look an unfamiliar word up in the dictionary, there is still an important way that the context will help you. It can help you determine *which* dictionary definition to use: the one that makes sense in that sentence. Most words have more than one meaning, so it is important to consider all the definitions and select the one that fits the context. Look at these three sentences that contain the word *plastic:*

1. The shoe salesman had the *plastic* smile of a bored game show host.

2. That new restaurant accepts both cash and *plastic* in payment.

3. While children are young, their personalities are still quite *plastic.*

Among the definitions for *plastic,* the dictionary gives these:

1. artificial or superficial

2. slang for credit cards

3. easily influenced; impressionable

If you substitute each definition in each sentence, it is clear that only the definition with the same number as the example sentence makes sense in that sentence. The context of the sentences makes it clear which dictionary definition is appropriate.

■ **Be sure that you understand the definition or synonym given in the sentence.**

Even if you locate a definition or a synonym for an unfamiliar word, it doesn't mean that you'll automatically understand it. Suppose that you read the sentence, **"Isotonic movements** consist of concentric and eccentric muscle contractions." It's simple to find the definition of *isotonic movements:* it's the rest of the sentence. But unless you know the definition of *concentric* and *eccentric* as they are used in that sentence, you cannot understand what isotonic movements are. Sometimes, folks, you just have to go to the old dictionary.

■ **If context clues prove inadequate, you should use other ways to determine the meaning of an unfamiliar word or term.**

This is obvious, but I'm going to say it again: If there are no context clues or if the context clues are insufficient, you should pursue the meaning of the term until you understand it. If you need to go to the dictionary, do it. If you need to look up an unfamiliar word that appears in the dictionary definition, do that too. Look in the glossary in the back of your textbook. Ask someone knowledgeable. In short, do whatever you need to do to find out the meaning of the word. Then write down both the word and its definition! That's the way you learn and remember important words and terms.

■ **Use word structure clues to confirm your educated guess based on context clues.**

Combining context clues with a knowledge of roots, prefixes, and suffixes (word structure clues) is a powerful way to "attack" an unfamiliar word. (Chapter 2 is about word structure analysis. Also, Appendix 1 lists common Latin and Greek word parts, their meanings, and example words.) You might, for example, deduce from the context of this sentence that *credible* means "believable": "Because the man gave details of the crime that could only be known by someone who was present, the police felt that he was a *credible* witness." By knowing that the root word *cred* means "believe" or "belief," you can confirm that your educated guess using context clues was correct.

■ **Learning words in context helps you remember their definition.**

You will discover that learning words in context helps you remember the meaning of the words. For example, the word *travesty* means "a parody," "a badly distorted imitation," or "a debased imitation." By itself, that word might be difficult to understand. Suppose, however, that you are reading about a trial of a political prisoner in a country run by a dictator. The author describes the trial as a "travesty of justice" because the prisoner was never given a chance to defend himself, he had no attorney to represent him, and the judges had already decided he was guilty before the trial began. In other words, the trial was just an imitation or parody of a real trial, with no true justice. If you associate the word *travesty* with the phrase "a *travesty* of justice," then you will be much more likely to remember the meaning of the word.

And you will remember the definition forever if you put the word in the context of a *personally* meaningful phrase. For example, if you received a traffic ticket and felt that the judge did not give you a fair hearing, then you might make that mental association: "the way the judge handled my ticket was a *travesty* of justice." Then repeat the phrase out loud. Association and oral repetition are powerful memory tools. If you are like most people, you will discover that from now on, you will remember the meaning of *travesty* used in this example. The reason? You applied the memory devices of placing the word in context, making mental associations with your own experience or information you already know, and repeating the word or phrase out loud. Powerful stuff!

■ **Pay attention to specialized or technical terms because professors will ask you their definitions on tests.**

Every college subject has important terms that you must know. You cannot, for example, understand economics unless you learn *inflation, gross national product, recession,* and *depression.* Notice that *inflation* and *depression* have more than one definition; you would need to learn the definition specific to economics. *Depression* means something altogether different in economics than it does, say, in psychology or in a science course. Because technical, specialized terms are so important, you should make vocabulary cards for them on index cards. Writing them down helps you learn them, and at the same time, you're creating a great review tool for tests.

The chart on the next page summarizes the five types of context clues, what to look for in the sentence or paragraph, and an example of each type.

SUMMARY CHART: TYPES OF CONTEXT CLUES

Type of Clue	What to Look For	Example
Definition/Synonym Clue	A definition introduced by phrases such as *is defined as, means, is known as, refers to*; a term in special print or color. A synonym (word that means the same thing), phrases introduced by *in other words, that is, by this we mean, or,* etc. The definition or synonym may be set off by commas, parentheses, a colon, dashes, or brackets.	Among the most extreme of personality types is the **psychopath** or **sociopath,** an individual who lacks not only self-control, but also the capacity to experience guilt or a sense of caring, responsibility, or obligation to others. Psychiatrist Thomas Szasz has been arguing for years that mental illness is a **myth** or fictitious construct.
Contrast Clue	An antonym (opposite word) for the unfamiliar word; words and phrases that indicate opposites: *but, in contrast, however, on the other hand, although, instead of,* etc.	**Depressants** have the opposite effect of stimulants.
Example Clue	Examples that illustrate the meaning of the unfamiliar word, often introduced by *for example, to illustrate, such as,* and *like.*	**Opiates** (such as alcohol, morphine, codeine, and heroin and other narcotics) are extremely addictive and require regular and increasing dosage to avoid withdrawal symptoms.
General Sense of the Sentence	Based on your general knowledge and experience, determine what the word would have to mean to make sense in that sentence.	When employees in an energy-efficient, airtight building begin having headaches, nausea, and eye, nose, and throat irritation, investigators suspect **sick building syndrome** as the cause.
Clue from Another Sentence	Information in another sentence that helps explain the unfamiliar word.	Different parts of the culture change at different speeds. Half a century ago William Ogburn suggested that technological changes in a society often occur faster than social changes. He referred to this disequilibrium as **cultural lag.**

THE REPLAY

REMEMBER THE ESSENTIAL INFORMATION FROM THE CHAPTER

To remember information, you must rehearse it by saying it aloud or writing it—or preferably, doing both. Take a minute to review the five types of context clues, then try to say them out loud. When you are ready, try to write them from memory in the following space. If you prepared for this a bit earlier by reciting them (as suggested on page 6), then you should be in good shape to complete this review. Describe each type of context clue, and then tell what kinds of things you might find in the sentence that could help you determine the meaning of the unfamiliar word.

Definition of Context Clue

_____

_____

Question You Should Ask Yourself

_____

_____

Five Types of Context Clues

1. Definition or Synonym Clue

Description of the clue: _____

_____

_____

What to look for: _____

_____

_____

2. Contrast Clue

Description of the clue: _____

_____

_____

What to look for: _____

_____

_____

3. Example Clue

Description of the clue: _____

_____

_____

What to look for: _____

_____

4. General Sense of the Sentence

Description of the clue: _____

_____

_____

What to look for: _____

_____

_____

5. Clue from Another Sentence

Description of the clue: _____

_____

_____

What to look for: _____

_____

_____

If there were things you could not remember, look back at The Technique section. Use the information in it to fill in any gaps in The Replay.

How are you doing at this point? So far, so good? Take a minute and describe the extent to which you believe you understand the material in Chapter 1:

_____

_____

_____

If you feel confused, what strategies do you think you could use to help yourself? Do you need to read more carefully? Spend more time on the material? Get some help? Don't write, "I don't know." That kind of attitude invites failure, and you're a stronger person than that!

_____

_____

_____

_____

THE PRACTICE

SET 1

APPLY THE SKILL OF USING CONTEXT CLUES

Exercises: Vocabulary in Context

Ready to "lift a little weight"? You already know that to acquire or strengthen any skill, you must practice it. Now you will have an opportunity to apply the five types of context clues. As you read each item below, use the strategies to determine the meaning of the <u>underlined</u> word. (*Coach's tips:* Highlight or mark clues that help you figure out the meaning. Test your definition by substituting it in place of the underlined word or phrase. Then read the sentence aloud. Does it make sense? If not, think about what *would* make sense in the sentence.) I've worked an example to help you get started.

Example:

_____ *c* _____ The time between the computer's request for data from secondary storage and the completion of the data transfer is known as **access time.**

    a. the time it takes a computer to request data
    b. the time it takes the computer to request data from secondary storage
    c. the time between the computer's request for data from secondary storage and the completion of the data transfer
    d. the time it takes the computer to complete data transfer

Explanation: This is a direct definition. The key term, *access time,* is in bold print. In this particular sentence, the term is presented after the definition. The clue words *is known as* alert you that a formal term is being introduced. Even though the definition might seem long, a computer science instructor would still expect you to learn it.

(You just encountered the first set of directions in the practice exercise sets. Did you read *and mark* them? If not, go back and do it. Establish this good habit from the beginning. If you need to review how to mark them, see pages S-12 and S-13 in "The 'Secrets' of Success.")

_____ **1.** Introverts prefer <u>solitary</u> activities, whereas extroverts prefer activities involving other people.
    a. requiring a high level of skill
    b. pertaining to computers
    c. involving other people
    d. done alone; without anyone else

_____ **2.** Examples of common <u>allergens</u> include pollen, ragweed, dog and cat dander, and dust.
    a. pollen, ragweed, dog and cat dander, and dust
    b. substances commonly found around the house
    c. substances that cause allergic reactions
    d. allergic reactions

_____ **3.** Mean-spirited people enjoy spreading <u>malicious</u> gossip. The rumors they spread damage the victim's reputation unfairly and cause undeserved pain and embarrassment.
    a. harmful
    b. interesting
    c. cheerful
    d. uplifting

_____ 4. The <u>manic</u> pace of Saigon is evident even in the streets, where swarms of motorbikes zip through intersections.
   a. happy; upbeat
   b. excessively active; intense
   c. violent; destructive
   d. leisurely; relaxed

_____ 5. The cast of the television series is currently enjoying a three-month <u>hiatus</u>, but they will start work again in the fall.
   a. break
   b. strike
   c. call
   d. probation

_____ 6. There has been a dramatic increase in the sales of <u>cosmeceuticals</u> (cosmetics plus pharmaceuticals that are more potent than cosmetics, but not so powerful that the Food and Drug Administration needs to regulate them like drugs).
   a. cosmetics whose sales have increased dramatically
   b. cosmetics that are regulated by the Food and Drug Administration
   c. cosmetics plus pharmaceuticals that are more potent than cosmetics, but not potent enough to require regulation by the Food and Drug Administration
   d. new brands of cosmetics

_____ 7. Both twins are extremely talented and intelligent. One has <u>aspirations</u> of obtaining a master's degree and becoming a social worker; the other has <u>aspirations</u> of attending graduate school, and then becoming a concert pianist.
   a. ambitions
   b. unrealistic expectations
   c. false hopes
   d. frustrations

_____ 8. But what is most remarkable about golfer Tiger Woods is his relentless drive for what the Japanese call _kaizen_, or continuous improvement.
   a. relentless drive
   b. remarkable ability
   c. Japanese trait
   d. continuous improvement

_____ 9. Certain college courses are <u>compulsory</u> for all students who wish to receive a degree; however, there are also elective courses, and students can choose whichever of those they prefer.
   a. difficult
   b. required
   c. unpleasant
   d. enjoyable

_____ **10.** It is not lawful to practice medicine without first obtaining a <u>valid</u> medical license.
   a. received as an honor
   b. updated
   c. legal
   d. difficult to obtain

_____ **11.** At the formal dinner party, the employee made an embarrassing <u>faux pas</u> when he drank the water in the finger bowl instead of rinsing his fingertips in it.
   a. international incident
   b. illegal action
   c. grammatical error
   d. social blunder

_____ **12.** By age four-and-a-half, boys usually display better <u>spatial</u> skills than girls do. Although biology does play a role, so does nurture. In daily play, girls are not encouraged as much as boys to engage in spatially oriented activities such as playing with blocks and puzzles.
   a. pertaining to or involving space
   b. pertaining to gender differences in boys and girls
   c. pertaining to blocks and puzzles
   d. pertaining to biology and nurture

SET 2

Exercises: Vocabulary in Context

Use the fives types of context clues to reason out the meaning of the underlined words. These sentences contain slightly more challenging words, and this time there are no multiple-choice answers. However, there are *fewer* items. Write the *complete* definition on the line provided. Remember to ask yourself, "What does this word have to mean in order to make sense in *this* sentence?" (*Coach's tips:* First do the ones that seem easy, then go back and tackle the others. Look at the ones that seemed hard for you: did all of them involve the same type of context clue? If so, that's a type of clue that you need to pay special attention to. Also, continue to mark clues in the sentences if you find it helpful.)

1. The difference between a good athlete and a great one is often simple <u>tenacity</u>. The great ones are champions because of their steadfast persistence in pursuing their goals.

   Definition: _____

2. Most illnesses last for a relatively short, limited period of time, yet nearly three-quarters of all deaths among those 18 and older are the result of <u>chronic</u> diseases.

   Definition: _____

3. Economist John Maynard Keynes said that government should engage in **<u>deficit spending</u>**—spending more than it gets in taxes—which can be accomplished by the borrowing and printing of money.

   Definition: _____

   _____

4. Some criminal acts of violence are <u>premeditated</u>; others are "crimes of passion" committed on impulse or on the emotion of the moment.

   Definition: _____

5. "<u>Halfway houses</u>" often face objections from the communities in which they are located. This is understandable. Even though the offenders are considered ready to be reintroduced into society, have jobs, and are carefully supervised, no one wants these "ex-cons" living in their neighborhood.

   Definition: _____

   _____

   _____

6. Along with a rape victim's testimony, there must be <u>corroborating evidence</u>, such as semen, torn clothes, bruises, or eyewitness testimony.

   Definition: _____

   _____

7. Many communities hold <u>referendums</u> so that voters can decide local issues.

Definition: _____

8. It is hard to concentrate when there is any type of <u>interference</u> such as noise, an uncomfortably hot or cold room, a headache, even worries or daydreams.

Definition: _____

9. The fear of strangers, typically called **<u>stranger wariness,</u>** is a predictable feature of a baby's first year of life and is a major landmark of emotional development.

Definition: _____

_____

10. There are several psychological explanations of the compulsive nonstop talker's need to <u>monopolize</u> every conversation.

Definition: _____

SET 3

Exercises: Vocabulary in Context

Now that you are warmed up, try this final set of vocabulary in context exercises. They're a little more challenging, but there are only eight "reps." Use the context clues to help you determine the meaning of each <u>underlined</u> word. As always, ask yourself, "What would this word have to mean in order to make sense in *this* sentence?" The definitions of terms in college textbooks can be lengthy, so be sure you find all of the definition. (*Coach's tips:* Take a deep breath and relax if you find yourself feeling frustrated with an item. Or, skip an item that seems difficult and come back to it later. Just remember to come back to it. Otherwise, I will send you to the penalty box!)

1. Many business schools are now <u>revamping</u> their existing curriculum by integrating international examples into all of their courses and emphasizing the use of technology.

   Definition: _____

2. In Cuba and China, young adults are <u>conscripted</u> into military service and are then required to serve for a specified number of years.

   Definition: _____

3. **<u>Social movements,</u>** or political movements, as they are sometimes called, refer to broad efforts to achieve change by citizens who feel that government is not properly responsive to their interests.

   Definition: _____

   _____

   _____

4. In business a variable cost, an expense that varies directly with the quantity of the product produced and sold, is in direct contrast to a <u>fixed cost</u>.

   Definition: _____

   _____

5. After listening to a classmate's speech, you should give <u>constructive</u> criticism. Unless your criticism provides suggestions for improvement, the recipient will not be able to make progress.

   Definition: _____

6. A famous <u>adage</u> in retailing is, "Three things are crucial for the success of a business: location, location, and location."

   Definition: _____

7. The class-action lawsuit charged the securities firm with fraud after its stock suffered a <u>precipitous</u> decline and investors experienced huge financial losses.

Definition: _____

8. Although some managers empower employees by allowing them to participate in decision making, <u>autocratic</u> managers do not permit this.

Definition: _____

Analyze Word Structure

THE SKILL

ANALYZE WORD STRUCTURE

In Chapter 1, you learned how to use context clues to help you determine a word's meaning. In this chapter, you'll learn how to determine a word's meaning by analyzing its structure. **Word structure analysis** is just what it sounds like: *using the structure, or parts, of a word to figure out the meaning of the word.* If you know common Latin word parts and their meanings, you will not only be able to figure the meaning of many words, but also to remember them more easily. Moreover, you will be able to recognize families of words that are based on the same word part, and you may find that it is easier to remember how to spell the words. Word structure analysis lets you confirm the educated guess you made by using context clues. Combining context clues with word structure analysis is a powerful way to unlock and remember words' meanings.

There are three types of word parts: *prefixes, roots,* and *suffixes.* Those word parts have been put together like puzzle pieces to create tens of thousands of words in English. It is estimated that students can use word parts to figure out the meaning of 60% of the new words they encounter. That's a lot of words!

THE TECHNIQUE

USE PREFIXES, ROOTS, AND SUFFIXES TO UNLOCK WORD MEANINGS

Prefixes are word parts that are attached at the beginning of a base or root word. Prefixes have meanings, and they add their meanings to the meaning of the root word. Take, for example, the word *prefix* itself. It consists of the prefix *pre-,* meaning "before," and the root word *fix,* which means "to attach." Therefore, a prefix is a word part that is "attached before" (at the beginning) of the root word. There are many prefixes. Some common ones are *pre-, un-, non-*, and *dis-*.

Roots are base words to which other word parts are added. Each root word has a specific meaning. Once you know the meaning of a root, you will find it easier to understand and remember the meaning of words that come from it.

Suffixes are word parts that are added at the end of a base word. Some suffixes have a specific meaning, such as *–ful* ("full of" whatever the root says, such as hope*ful*) and *–or* (a person who does what the root says, such as invent*or*). Other suffixes change a word's part of speech. For example, by adding a suffix, the verb *argue* can be made into the noun argu*ment,* the adjective argument*ative,* or the adverb argu*ably*. Still other suffixes change a verb's tense, such as changing the present tense of *laugh* to the past tense, laugh*ed*.

Suffixes are not as helpful as prefixes and roots. For one thing, some suffixes have several meanings. Also, some suffixes change the spelling of the root word when they are added to it. For example, the *y* in *happy* becomes an "i" when suffixes are added: happ*i*ness, happ*i*ly, happ*i*er, and happ*i*est.

Despite their limitations, suffixes are still useful. First, they often tell you a word's part of speech. Some suffixes, for example, indicate that a word is a noun or a verb. Second, removing a suffix often lets you see what the base word is. For example, if you remove the suffix *-able* from the word *changeable,* you see immediately that the base word is the familiar word, *change*. Sometimes there may be more than one suffix. You may need to remove both (or all) of them to discover the base word.

A word can consist of a root only, a root with a prefix, a root with a suffix, or a root with both a prefix and a suffix. Regardless of how many parts there are, they always appear in this order: prefix, root, suffix. When you are reading and you encounter an unfamiliar word or term, ask yourself, *"What clues do the parts of this word give me about the meaning of the word?"*

Here are some very useful word parts that appear in tens of thousands of words. They're grouped into prefixes, roots, and suffixes. You'll be pleased to discover that you are already familiar with many of them.

PREFIXES

Some prefixes create words that mean the opposite of the base word. Others pertain to time, place or location, or indicate number or quantity. Because there are many prefixes, it's helpful to group ones that are similar and to pair ones that are opposite in meaning. Prefixes that appear in more than one section below have more than one meaning.

Some common prefixes, such as *de-,* are not included because they have several meanings. For example, *de-* can mean many things, including to do or make the opposite of (*deactivate; decode*); to remove or remove from (*deodorize; deduct*); and "out of" (*deplane; depart*).

Prefixes that Mean "Not"

Negative prefixes are among the most commonly used prefixes. When they are added to words, they create a word that means the opposite of the base word. There are four negative prefixes. Of all prefixed words, the prefix *un-* appears in roughly one-quarter of them! These four prefixes appear in an extremely large percentage of words that contain a prefix:

1. un-   unhappy, unsafe, undo, unwrap, unbutton
2. non-   nonstop, nonfiction, nondrinker, nonfat, nonverbal

3. **dis-**   disagreement, dissimilar, dislike, disable, disobey
4. **in-**   incorrect, indirect, inactive, injustice, inhuman
   also appears as il-, im-, ir-, as in illegal, immortal, impossible, irresponsible

Prefixes that Indicate Location or Spatial Relationships

Certain prefixes give you helpful clues about where something is located or occurs. The prefix *in-* means not, but it has a second meaning: *in* or *into*. Prefixes that have opposite meanings are paired (1–2, 3–4, and 5–6).

1. in-	*in, into*	inhale, include, income, ingredient
2. e-, ex-	*out, away*	exhale, exit, expire, exception, expel
3. pro-	*forward, forth*	progress, proceed, project, protrude
4. re-	*back*	return, react, refund, recede, retreat
5. sub-	*below, under*	subway, submarine, subcommittee, subdue
6. super-	*over, above*	supervise, superhighway, superior, supreme
7. inter-	*between*	interrupt, Internet, interfere, interject
8. tele-	*far, distant*	telephone, television, telemarketing
9. circum-	*around*	circumference, circumstance, circumnavigate
10. trans-	*across, through*	transfer, translate, transparent, transfusion

Prefixes that Indicate Number or Amount

1. mono-	*one, single*	monopoly, monotone, monarchy
2. bi-	*two, twice*	bicycle, bilingual, biannual
3. tri-	*three*	triangle, triathlon, triplet, trio
4. quadr-	*four*	quadrangle, quadrant, quadruplet
5. pent-	*five*	pentagon, pentathlon, pentacle
6. mini-	*small, reduced in size*	miniature, minimal, minibike, miniseries
7. micro-, micr-	*small*	microscope, microbe, microeconomics
8. multi-	*many, much*	multilingual, multiply, multitude
9. hemi-, semi-	*half, partially*	hemisphere, semicircle, semiformal
10. dec, deca-	*ten*	decade, decimal, decimate

Mono- and *micro-* are Greek prefixes. (You may also know the Greek prefixes *mega-* and *macro-*, meaning large or great.) The rest are from Latin.

Other Important Prefixes

Prefixes below that have opposite meanings are paired (1–2, 3–4, and 8–9). Notice that some prefixes have more than one spelling. Also notice that there are additional, *different* meanings of three prefixes you met earlier: *pro-*, *re-*, and *ex-*.

1. pro-	*for, in favor of*	pro-life, pro-choice, pro-war, pro-American
2. anti-, contra-	*opposed to, against*	anti-war, antibiotic, contraception, contradict
also appears as contro-, counter-		controversy, counterattack
3. mal-, mis-	*bad, wrong*	malnutrition, malpractice, misfortune, misplace
4. bene-, eu-	*good, well*	benefit, benign, eulogy, euphemism, euphoria
5. co-	*together, with*	coworker, cooperative, coauthor
also appears as col-, com-, con-		collaborate, communicate, combine, connect

6. re-	*again*	repeat, rewrite, redo, review, remarry
7. ex-	*former*	ex-wife, ex-employee, ex-president
8. pre-	*before*	predict, pretest, premature, precede
9. post-	*after, later*	posttest, postpone, postseason, postwar
10. hyper-	*too much, overly, excessive*	hyperactive, hypersensitive, hyperventilate

ROOTS

Although there are hundreds of roots that prefixes and suffixes can be added to, the following ones are very common and useful ones. Try to connect the roots and their meanings with words you already know that contain these roots.

1. aud	*hear*	audible, auditorium, audience, audiovisual
2. auto	*self*	automobile, autograph, autonomy, autocrat
3. bio	*life, living*	biology, biography, biopsy, bionic
4. cred	*belief, faith*	credit, incredible, credentials, credulous
5. dict	*say, speak, tell*	dictionary, dictate, indicate, predict
6. duc, duct	*lead, bring, take*	conduct, induce, deduction, duct
7. fac, fic	*make, do*	manufacture, factory, fictitious
8. fid, fidel	*believe, trust, faith*	confide, fidelity, fiduciary, infidel
9. flect, flex	*bend, curve, turn*	flexible, reflection, deflect, flexion
10. gam, gamy	*marriage, union*	monogamous, bigamist, polygamy,
11. gen, gene	*origin, race, type*	generation, generic, homogeneous, genre
12. ject	*throw, hurl*	reject, eject, dejected, projectile
13. junct	*join, unite*	juncture, conjunction, junction
14. leg, lex	*law*	legislature, legal, legitimate
15. man, manu, mani	*hand, make, do*	manufacture, manual, manicure, manuscript
16. mit, miss	*send, put*	remit, transmit, emission, mission
17. pel, puls	*push, drive*	repel, compel, expulsion, propeller, impulse
18. port	*carry*	portable, import, export, deport, support
19. pos, pon	*place, put*	pose, position, transpose, deposit, opponent
20. spec, spi	*see, look*	inspect, spectacle, despise, circumspect
21. tract	*pull, draw*	attract, contract, tractor, retract
22. ven, vene, vent	*come*	prevent, event, convene, intervention
23. vers, vert	*turn, twist*	convert, controversial, introvert, extrovert
24. vid, view, vis	*see, look*	visible, preview, videodisc, vision, revise
25. voc, voke	*voice, call*	vocal, vocalize, invoke, evoke, revoke

SUFFIXES

Because many suffixes have the same general meaning, it is helpful to learn them in groups. For the following example words, the base word is given in parenthesis.

A few suffixes can indicate more than one part of speech. The –*ive* and –*er* suffixes in the words *relative, narrative, computer,* and *dinner* are examples. So how can you tell which one you need? Look at the sentence in which the word appears. Do you need a word that is a "thing"? If so, you need a noun. If you need a word that describes, you need an adjective. If you need a word that shows action, you need a verb.

Notice that in the list seven suffixes appear in color: *-y, -ness, -ion, -er, -al, -able,* and *-ly*. They are some of the most useful ones, so pay special attention to them.

Suffixes that Indicate Nouns

These mean *state of, condition of,* or *quality of (what the base word indicates):*

Suffix	Example
-ance, -ence	reliance (rely), dependence (depend)
-dom	freedom (free)
-hood	adulthood (adult)
-ity, -y	maturity (mature), honesty (honest)
-ive	relative (relate)
-ment	retirement (retire)
-ness	kindness (kind)
-ship	friendship (friend)
-tion, -sion, -ion	isolation (isolate), suspension (suspend)
-tude	solitude (solitary)

These mean *a person who (does what the root indicates):*

Suffix	Example
-er, -or	reader (read), inventor (invent)
-ist	soloist (solo)

Suffixes that Indicate Verbs

These mean *to make (what the base word indicates):*

Suffix	Example
-ate	automate (automatic)
-ify	liquefy (liquid)
-ize	socialize (social)
-en	cheapen (cheap)

Suffixes that Indicate Adjectives

These suffixes mean *full of (what the base word indicates):*

Suffix	Example
-ful	colorful (color)
-ous, -ious	joyous (joy)
-ate	fortune (fortune)
-y	roomy (room)

These suffixes mean *relating to or pertaining to (what the base word indicates):*

Suffix	Example
-al	musical (music)
-ic	comic (comedy)

-ish	childish (child)
-ive	corrective (correct)

Other adjective suffixes:

<u>Suffix</u>		<u>Example</u>
-able, -ible	able to be or do (whatever the root says)	reasonable (reason); sensible (sense)
-less	without	homeless (home)

Other Helpful Suffixes

-ly, -ily	like, in the manner of	friendly (friend), sloppily (sloppy) (creates an adverb)
-ology	study or science (of whatever the root says)	biology, psychology
-ism	philosophy or belief in (whatever the root says)	terrorism, communism

Overwhelmed by these lists? Don't be. You already know and use thousands of words that contain these word parts. It's really just a matter of connecting the meaning of the prefixes, roots, and suffixes with words you know. Once you do that, you can use the meaning of the word parts to help you figure out words you *don't* know. (The appendix contains a list of these word parts, along with additional ones.)

THE TRAINER

OBSERVE THE SKILL OF ANALYZING WORD STRUCTURE

Here's our efficient reader, reading a passage that contains several words that are derived from common prefixes, suffixes, and roots. Our efficient reader has been studying word parts and is on the lookout for connections between the words and the word parts they are made from. Read the paragraph first, and then read the notations that show the efficient reader's thought processes about these connections.

They're called *video* games because the player *watches* the images and action on a screen.

The root and suffix in *credible* tell me the word means "able to be believed," or in other words, "believable."

Mind*less* means without the mind being involved — requiring no thought.

I see the word parts *dis-*, *tract*, and *-tion* in *distraction*. They tell me that the word literally means "the condition of having your attention pulled away."

Many people consider (video) games a (mindless) (distraction,) a waste of time. However, (credible) research suggests there may be (benefits) beyond increasing (manual) dexterity. Complicated video games (compel) users to try out a (multitude) of strategies. To succeed, gamers must continually (revise) their plan and (reject) ones that do not work.

The prefix in *benefits* means something that does *good*, something that is helpful. The root (*manu*) and suffix (*-al*) in *manual* indicate it's an adjective meaning "having to do with the hand."

The prefix *com-* and the root *pel* in *compel* suggest it means feeling "driven to do something." The *multi-* in *multitude* lets me know it means "many" or "lots of."

Re- plus *vise* in *revise* means "to look at again"—in other words, to rethink and change. And *re-* plus *ject* literally means to "throw back"—to throw away or refuse to use.

POINTERS ABOUT ANALYZING WORD STRUCTURE

- **Use word structure analysis to confirm guesses based on context clues.** This is important because together the two skills can enable you to nail a word's meaning.

- **You also use word structure analysis when you encounter compound words.** You do this every time you see the parts that comprise simple words such as *basketball, mailbox,* and *roommate.*

- **The *least effective* way to learn words is to try to memorize definitions.** Your brain likes to see connections between a new word and words (or information) you already know. Your brain also likes "webs" of knowledge, which is why it's helpful to learn groups of *related* words.

- **Read the etymology at the end of a dictionary entry: it gives the word's origin and history.** It tells the word parts that comprise the word. Seeing the connection between the meaning of the root word and the word's present meaning helps you remember the definition of the word.

- **Related words from the same root are called *cognates* of the root word.** You just learned that the Latin root *ject* means "to throw." From it, we get words such as e*ject* (throw out), in*ject* ("throw" or force something in), re*ject* (throw back, refuse to accept), inter*ject*ion (a sudden, short word that is "thrown" in), and pro*ject*ile (something that is thrown or propelled). You can see that the meaning of each of these is related to the idea of throwing. Once you know the root *ject,* it is easier to understand and remember the meaning of more advanced words such as *abject, subjective, dejected, conjecture,* and *trajectory.*

- **Words can consist of one word part or several various combinations of word parts.** Consider these words created from the root word *script/scribe,* which means "to write:"

root word only	*script, scribe*
prefix + root word	*prescribe (pre + scribe)*
prefix + root word + suffix	*prescription (pre + scrip + tion)*
root word + suffix	*scripted (script + ed)*

- **Word structure analysis doesn't work for every word,** but it's especially good for scientific and technical words.

- **In the dictionary, when prefixes appear as entry words, they have a hyphen at the end.** This is to remind you that something else must follow the prefix.

- **Prefixes and suffixes are usually separate syllables.** However, when you're writing and come to the end of a line, don't divide a word after only two letters. For example: dividing *pre*-vent would be fine; dividing *re*-turn would not be.

- **The only word in English that ends in *full* is the word *full.*** Knowing this will keep you from misspelling words that end in *–ful,* such as *wonderful* and *joyful.*

- **Knowing prefixes can help you with your spelling.** Take, for example, the prefix *mis-* (bad, wrong). It ends with an "s." When you add it to roots that start with "s," the new words will have two s's together:

  mis + spell = misspell

  mis + speak = misspeak

  mis + shapen = misshapen

Now you know why those words have two s's together: one ends the prefix; one starts the root word.

■ **Prefixes and suffixes are called** *affixes* because they are word parts that are "fixed" (attached) to root words.

■ **Create vocabulary cards or vocabulary cartoons to help you learn word parts.** (For more information, see the Online Learning Center.) You don't have to be an artist to draw several stick figures to accompany a sentence such as, "The City Council *convenes* once a week." *Convene = come together* or assemble for an official or public purpose.

THE REPLAY

REMEMBER THE ESSENTIAL INFORMATION FROM THE CHAPTER

You now know the three categories of word parts—prefixes, roots, and suffixes—that can help you to unlock the meaning of unfamiliar words when you read.

Question You Should Ask Yourself

Write the word parts question you should ask yourself when you are reading and you encounter an unfamiliar word or term:

_____

_____

Definitions of Key Terms

Word structure analysis: _____

_____

_____

Prefix: _____

_____

Root: _____

_____

Suffix: _____

_____

THE PRACTICE

SET 1

APPLY THE SKILL OF ANALYZING WORD STRUCTURE

This chapter is different from the others because instead of learning a *skill*, you are learning information: word parts and their meanings. Therefore, the exercises will be slightly different. Set 1 deals with suffixes, Set 2 with prefixes, and Set 3 with roots. They are slightly longer, but they are not hard.

Use the meaning of the suffixes to help you fill the correct form of the italicized word in each sentence.

Example:

If a person has an *allergy* to peanuts, he or she is _____ *allergic* _____ to them.

1. The state or condition of *arguing* is called an _____.

2. A body part that is full of *cancer* is described as _____.

3. The condition of being *governed* is termed _____.

4. A person who acts like a *fool* does things that are _____.

5. The quality of being *punctual* is called _____.

6. The condition of *violating* the law is known as a _____.

7. The condition of *resisting* something is termed _____.

8. Something that is able to be *predicted* is _____.

9. The quality of being *sharp* is _____.

10. To make water *pure* is to _____ it.

11. To do something in a *gradual* manner is to do it _____.

12. The state of being a *child* is called _____.

13. If you are without shoes, you are _____.

14. The measurement system based on *meters* is called the _____ system.

15. If you make a house more *modern*, you _____ it.

16. The state of *owning* something is termed _____.

17. To do something in a *cheerful* manner is to do it _____.

18. If the sky is full of *clouds*, the sky is _____.

19. The condition of being a movie *star* is known as _____.

20. To show *hesitation* is to _____.

SET 2

Here's a chance to practice with prefixes; the context will help you determine which prefix belongs in the blank. Try to answer these first without looking at the lists of prefixes, but then go back and check any you are unsure of. Highlight any clues in the sentence that help you determine the correct prefix. Before you begin, interlace your fingers and stretch your hands overhead, lower them, and take a couple of deep breaths.

Example:

Because the patient _____*mis*read the directions, she took the wrong number of pills. *Context clue:* "took the *wrong* number of pills"

1. If something runs _____clockwise, it runs the opposite of clockwise.

2. The _____gon building in Washington, D.C., has five sides, one for each branch of the military.

3. Before _____conferencing was available, employees often had to travel great distances to have face-to-face conferences.

4. Although the first _____atlantic flight was considered nothing less than amazing, today flights across the ocean are considered routine.

5. The crime scene investigators _____cavated the area where they thought the bodies were buried, and they examined all of the dirt and rock that was taken out.

6. My best friend _____miserated with me about not getting a salary increase, and I appreciated her sympathy.

7. The rainbow _____appeared after only a few minutes; it melted away almost as soon as it appeared.

8. The senator _____claimed that solar power was one solution to high energy costs; he put forth the idea that it is more environmentally friendly.

9. Soldiers are trained to take their rifles apart and to _____assemble them very quickly.

10. The TV news reporters interviewed the _____mayor a week after he resigned from office.

11. A figure of speech that uses exaggeration for emphasis or effect is called a _____bole.

12. The _____riceps is the large four-part extensor muscle at the front of the thigh.

13. We enjoyed hearing the sweet, _____phonious sound of the babbling stream and the chirping birds.

14. In terms of size, _____compact cars rank below compact ones.

15. An autopsy is a _____mortem examination of a dead body.

16. _____plegia refers to paralysis that affects only half of the body: there is paralysis on one side of the body.

17. Because the abused child was so _____adjusted, she was unable to adjust to the demands and stresses of daily living.

18. Working on a factory assembly line is _____tonous because employees do one task over and over again.

19. _____highways are broad highways that often have six or more lands and are used for high-speed traffic.

20. Walking around something, such as a religious structure, as part of a ritual is known as _____ambulation.

SET 3

These 25 words contain the roots you are learning. The roots appear in color. Read the sentences and use clues in them, along with the meaning of the roots, to decide which word belongs in each sentence. After you have written it, circle or underline the root to help fix it in your memory. Some of the words may be new to you. That's okay. It just means you have the opportunity to expand your vocabulary. The first one is done as an example.

abduction	credit	emit	legalize	review
abject	conjunction	fiction	manacles	spectacle
audible	deposit	genres	misogamy	tractor
automobile	dictation	genuflect	portfolio	vocation
biology	diffident	intervenes	propulsion	vertigo

1. A _____tractor_____ pulls farm implements behind it.

2. When you look back over your notes before a test, you _____re_____ your notes.

3. When stores let you buy on _____it_____, they let you take the item because they believe your promise to pay for it later.

4. Groups that want to _____alize_____ marijuana want to make it acceptable by law.

5. Distinctive styles or types of art, music, or literature are called _____res_____.

6. A _____folio_____ is a case for carrying loose materials, such as papers, photographs, or drawings.

7. If you make a _____acle_____ of yourself, everyone will stop and look at you!

8. Fire alarms _____e_____ or send out a loud, shrill sound.

9. If a child is led away by force or kidnapped, it is called an _____ab_____tion_____.

10. People who suffer from _____igo_____ feel dizzy, as if they are turning or spinning.

11. An _____mobile_____ does not require much physical effort on the part of the driver; it almost seems to run by itself.

12. Literary works that are made up rather than factual are referred to as _____tion_____.

13. Sounds that are _____ible_____ can be heard.

14. People who are _____dif_____ent_____ lack belief in themselves.

15. Handcuffs, two metal rings joined by a chain, are also called _____acles_____.

16. _____logy_____ is the study of living things.

17. If you _____genu_____, you bend your knee to the ground in reverence or worship.

18. To take _____ation_____ is to write down what someone else is saying.

19. Your calling or life's work is referred to as your _____ation_____.

20. Powerful jet _____pro_____ion_____ drives airplanes through the air at high speeds.

21. If a year of military service __inter___s__ between the time a person becomes engaged and the time the person marries, a year has come between those two events.

22. If you ___de__it___ a letter in a mailbox, you place it in the mailbox.

23. Someone who feels ___ab_____ is downcast.

24. A __con_____ion__ is a part of speech that serves to join words, phrases, clauses, or sentences.

25. Aversion to or hatred of marriage is termed ___miso_____.

Congratulations! You've now completed Part 1, The Warm-Up. Effective athletes—and students—take time to evaluate their performance. Take a minute to evaluate how well you understand the important vocabulary skills introduced in the first two chapters. Do you understand the five types of context clues? What about word structure analysis? How did you do on the practice exercises for these chapters? With regard to the vocabulary skills of using context clues and word structure analysis, what do you need to practice or learn more about? Unless your instructor directs you to use notebook paper, write your responses in the space below.

_____

_____

_____

_____

_____

_____

_____

_____

_____

_____

_____

_____

_____

_____

_____

PART·TWO

Basic Workout

CHAPTERS IN PART TWO

CHAPTER

3

Determine the Topic of a Paragraph

THE SKILL

DETERMINE THE TOPIC OF A PARAGRAPH

Every paragraph is written about something. The "something" that the author chooses to write about is called the topic. In other words, the ***topic*** is simply *who or what the author is writing about*. The topic is always a word, a phrase, or a name. (It is never written as a sentence.) You may also hear the topic called the *subject* or the *subject matter*. Determining the topic is the important first step in comprehending any paragraph that you read.

A topic can be a person's name (such as *Michael Jordan*), a place (*New York*), a thing (*sport utility vehicle*), a process (*the electoral process*), or a concept (*the right to die*). It can be a single word (such as *taxes* or *e-mail*) or a phrase (such as *how juries are selected* or *the spread of AIDS*). Again, the topic is always expressed as a word or a phrase (a group of words); it is never expressed as a sentence.

Here's a little insight from the coach: Determining the topic really isn't a new skill to you at all. When you walk up to a group of friends who are talking, you listen for a minute to figure out *who* or *what* they're talking about. In other words, you determine the topic of the conversation. The fact is, you're already good at determining the topic. In this chapter, you're going to learn to apply that very same skill to textbook paragraphs.

To determine the topic, ask yourself, "Who or what is this paragraph about?" Although the answer is often obvious, you may sometimes need a little help to answer that question or want to confirm that your hunch is correct. Fortunately, textbook authors are good about giving readers clues to the topic.

When determining the topic of a paragraph, try to be precise. Suppose a paragraph is about *Abraham Lincoln's assassination.* If you write the topic as *Abraham Lincoln,* it is not precise enough because that could refer to anything connected with Lincoln. Knowing precisely what the topic is helps your brain understand how the pieces of information in a paragraph pertain to each other. This, in turn, helps you remember the information in the paragraph.

Think about the problems that would result if paragraphs had no topic, if they were just groups of unrelated sentences written next to each other on the page. The sentences below, for example, look like a paragraph, but they are just a "topicless" collection of unrelated sentences:

> Every year, college students spend approximately $5.5 billion on alcohol—more than on books, soft drinks, coffee, juice, and milk combined. Connectivity is the microcomputer's ability to communicate with other computers and information sources. The latest U.S. Census Bureau data revealed that for the first time, the number of Americans living alone exceeds the number of married couples living with children.

Wouldn't it be hard to remember the unrelated bits of information in those sentences? Fortunately, textbook authors don't write jumbles of sentences that have no topic (although some authors write more clearly than others).

Now read these sentences. They *do* share a common topic, so together they create a paragraph.

> U.S. Census Bureau data on living patterns revealed that in 2000, for the first time, the number of Americans living alone exceeded the number of married couples living with children. Not surprisingly, the number of single-parent households also continued to rise. In addition, there was a staggering increase between 1990 and 2000 in the number of cohabiting couples.

Even though these sentences pack a lot of information, it would be easier to learn and remember because the sentences have the same topic: *year 2000 U.S. Census Bureau data on living patterns.*

Just as each paragraph has a topic, so do longer selections. Every textbook chapter, section within the chapter, essay, editorial, newspaper article, and magazine article, for example, has an *overall* topic. You will be happy to know that you can determine the overall topic by asking yourself the same general question ("Who or what is this about?") and by looking for some of the same clues to the topic that are presented in the next section. You should also look at the topics of the paragraphs that comprise the selection, and then determine the overall topic that they all have in common. For example, if each paragraph of a section in a psychology textbook describes a different reason that people forget information, then the overall topic would be *causes of forgetting.*

THE TECHNIQUE | ## USE THE FOUR STRATEGIES FOR DETERMINING THE TOPIC

After you read a paragraph, ask yourself, "Who or what is this paragraph about?" If you're unable to answer that question or are not sure you've answered it correctly, look for any of the following four clues to the topic. Every paragraph contains at least one clue, and many paragraphs have more than one.

1. LOOK FOR A HEADING OR TITLE

Textbook authors (including me!) like to let readers know in advance the topic that is going to be discussed. Consequently, they often announce the topic in the heading. Our brains like it when they get advance notice of what is coming, so take advantage of this easy clue.

A heading or a title can give you a great head start on determining the topic, but you should still read the paragraph to confirm that the entire paragraph discusses the "who or what" that appears in the heading.

Now read a paragraph from a psychology textbook that illustrates this clue. As the title suggests, the topic of the paragraph is *agoraphobia*.

AGORAPHOBIA

Agoraphobia is the most impairing of all the phobias. Literally meaning "fear of open spaces," agoraphobia involves intense fear of leaving one's home or other familiar places. In extreme cases, the agoraphobic individual is totally bound to his or her home, finding a trip to the mailbox an almost intolerable experience. Other agoraphobic individuals are able to travel freely in their neighborhood but cannot venture beyond it.

Source: Benjamin Lahey, *Psychology: An Introduction,* 8th ed., p. 546. Copyright © 2005 McGraw-Hill. Reprinted by permission of The McGraw-Hill Companies.

2. LOOK FOR WORDS IN SPECIAL PRINT, SUCH AS BOLD, ITALICS, OR COLOR

The special print can be **bold print,** *italics,* or color—or some combination, such as ***bold italics.*** Textbooks contain many important terms and concepts, so the authors spend time explaining them. When authors first introduce them, they frequently put them in special print to draw the readers' attention to them. (It's less common, but sometimes an important term appears in quotation marks.) Don't think that you can take a shortcut to the topic by picking out any words in special print. Bad strategy! Authors sometimes italicize words for emphasis, not because they are the topic of a paragraph.

Here is a sample paragraph from a health textbook. Its topic is *osteoarthritis.* Notice that the term appears in bold italics.

The most common form of arthritis (joint inflammation) is ***osteoarthritis.*** It is likely that as we age, all of us will develop osteoarthritis to some degree. Often called "wear and tear" arthritis, osteoarthritis occurs primarily in the weight-bearing joints of the knee, hip, and spine. In this form of arthritis, joint damage can occur to bone ends, cartilaginous cushions, and related structures as the years of constant friction and stress accumulate.

Source: Adapted from Wayne Payne and Dale Hahn, *Understanding Your Health,* 8th ed., p. 106. Copyright © 2005 McGraw-Hill. Reprinted by permission of The McGraw-Hill Companies.

3. LOOK FOR REPEATED WORDS OR PHRASES IN THE PARAGRAPH

Because a topic is discussed throughout the paragraph, it is only logical that the topic would be repeated several times. When you read a paragraph, be alert for the repetition of a particular word, name, or phrase. Sometimes there are also related words or words in the paragraph that mean the same thing. For example, the topic may be *anger management*, with the related words *hostility* and *rage* (referring to anger) and *control* (referring to managing anger) used in the paragraph.

Now read this sample passage from a marketing textbook. Notice that four of the six sentences in the paragraph contain the phrase *software piracy*. Moreover, the remaining sentences contain the words *software*, *pirated*, and *piracy rate*. It is obvious that *software piracy* is the topic.

It is estimated that software piracy, the unauthorized copying of business software, costs U.S. producers about $12 billion in worldwide sales annually. Software piracy has become pandemic in many countries. It has been estimated that 70% of the software in eastern Europe is pirated, followed by a piracy rate of 60% in the Middle East and 59% in Africa and Latin America. Countries with the highest software piracy rates are Vietnam (98%), China (91%), Russia (89%), and Lebanon and Oman (88%). For comparison, the piracy rate in the United States is 25% and Canada, 41%. Software piracy means lost jobs, wages, tax revenues, and a potential barrier to success for software start-up companies around the globe.

Source: Roger Kerin, Steven Hartley, and William Rudelius, *Marketing: The Core*, p. 80. Copyright © 2004 McGraw-Hill/Irwin. Reprinted by permission of The McGraw-Hill Companies.

4. LOOK FOR A NAME, WORD, OR PHRASE THAT IS MENTIONED AT THE BEGINNING OF THE PARAGRAPH AND THEN REFERRED TO THROUGHOUT THE PARAGRAPH BY PRONOUNS OR OTHER WORDS

Even though the author may not use the exact word, name, or phrase more than once in a paragraph, it will be clear that he or she is still discussing the same topic. For example, the author may mention a person's name at the beginning of a paragraph, then refer to the person throughout the paragraph using pronouns (*he* or *she*) or by other words (such as *this prominent scientist* or *the First Lady*).

Here is a paragraph from a speech textbook. Its topic is *alliteration*. Notice that the word appears only in the first sentence. The author continues to discuss alliteration, but refers to alliteration as *this device* and *it*.

Alliteration is one way you can enhance the rhythm of your speeches. The most common method is repeating the initial consonant sounds of close or adjoining words. For example: *P*eace is essential for *p*rogress, but *p*rogress is no less essential for *p*eace. Used sparingly, this device is a marvelous way to spruce up your speeches. By highlighting the sounds of words, it catches the attention of listeners and makes ideas easier to remember. Used to excess, however, it can be laughable and draw too much attention away from the content of the speech.

Source: Adapted from Stephen Lucas, *The Art of Public Speaking*, 8th ed., p. 281. Copyright © 2005 McGraw-Hill. Reprinted by permission of The McGraw-Hill Companies.

Well, those are the four clues to the topic. So how are you doing at this point? Take a minute to stretch and to take a couple of deep, slow breaths. These simple actions get your circulation moving, reduce stress, and refresh you.

Now review the definition and the four clues to the topic until you think you know them. Here's a cool tip for remembering the definition of *topic* and the four clues: put the information into the form of a rhyme and sing it to a familiar tune. I know it sounds goofy, but it works, and actually, it's a good trick for remembering information of many sorts. Because of rhythm, repetition, and rhyme, everyone remembers the words to songs that they hear or sing over and over again. You're probably familiar with the singsong "tune" that drill sergeants use when they call out (shout!) a marching cadence for recruits. The recruits "sing back" the words after the drill sergeant "sings" them. Here's what you need to know about *topic;* it's set as a "marching tune." I've put the important information in italics.

> To get the topic, shout it out:
> *"Who or what is this about?"*
>
> And I would like to proclaim
> *The topic's a word, a phrase, a name.*
>
> First look for this easy clue:
> *A title or heading to help you.*
>
> Second, it's no accident:
> *Topics appear in special print.*
>
> A third clue that's really neat:
> *Look for words that repeat.*
>
> One last clue, don't you doubt:
> *Anything discussed throughout.*

Okay, okay. I know I'm not a songwriter or a poet, but you get the idea. Feel free to create your own version using any tune you like. Whether you use yours or mine, I promise that if you "rehearse" it enough times, you *never* forget the information. (Even better: rehearse it while running or using a treadmill!)

For longer information, such as the four types of topic clues, there is also another memory strategy you can try. Make a nonsense sentence in which each word represents part of the information you need to remember. The purpose is to give your memory enough of a jog to get you started. For example, I made up this sentence to remind myself of the four clues:

> "The head printer repeatedly mentioned the beginning of the paragraph."

Here's how I use each part of the sentence to help me recall the four clues:

> head = using *head*ings or title.
>
> printer = look for words in special *print*.
>
> repeatedly = look for *repeated* words.
>
> mentioned = look for something *mentioned* at the *beginning* and then referred to by other words.

Each word gives all or part of a key word for each strategy. That single word is enough to trigger my recall of the whole strategy. (The last clue is longer, so I have to be careful not to leave off the last half of it.) There's nothing magic about my sentence. If it works for you, great—borrow it! But if you can think up a sentence of your own, go for it. Because the order of the strategies doesn't matter, you can learn them in any order. That gives you a lot more ways to create sentences. (By the way, making up your own sentence usually makes it more meaningful to you. Also, the goofier the sentence is, the more likely you are to remember it.)

When you're ready, cover the book and or close your eyes and try to say out loud the definition of topic and the four types of topic clues (*headings, words in special print, repeated words,* and *words mentioned at the beginning of the paragraph and then referred to throughout the paragraph by other words*). Stay with it until you can recite all of the information without looking. At this stage, you are laying the all-important foundation for the rest of the comprehension skills. Do yourself a favor: Learn it now. Learn it right.

THE TRAINER

OBSERVE THE SKILL OF DETERMINING THE TOPIC

Once again, the illustration gives you a peek inside an effective reader's mind as the person reads a paragraph and uses the clues to determine its topic. The reader's "thoughts" appear in color. *Read the paragraph first, then go back and read the "thoughts."*

> Maybe it's going to be about good novelists.

> Now he mentions word pictures, so maybe that's what he wants to talk about.

One sign of a good novelist is the ability to create word pictures that get you totally involved with a story. These word pictures let you "see" the haunted house, or "feel" the bite of the snow against your face, or "hear" the birds chirping on a warm spring morning, or "smell" the bacon cooking over an open campfire, or "taste" the hot enchiladas at a Mexican restaurant. Speakers can use imagery in much the same way to make their ideas come alive. Three ways to generate imagery are by using concrete words, simile, and metaphor.

Source: Stephen Lucas, *The Art of Public Speaking*, 8th ed., p. 276. Copyright © 2005 McGraw-Hill. Reprinted by permission of The McGraw-Hill Companies.

> The second sentence gives lots of examples of word pictures a writer might use.

> Oops! Now he's talking about *speakers*, and he uses the word *imagery* to describe the word pictures.

> Ahh! This is where he was going! At first it seemed he was talking about novelists using word pictures, but it was just to help me understand his real topic: *how speakers can use imagery.*

THE EDGE

POINTERS ABOUT DETERMINING THE TOPIC

■ **Be sure you know what the words in the topic mean.**
Just knowing the word or phrase that tells the topic of a paragraph or passage is not enough. You must know what the word or phrase *means*. For example, you might quickly be able to determine that the topic of a paragraph is "the influence of transcendentalism." However, unless you understand what "transcendentalism" is, you will not be able to understand the paragraph. Strategy: look up the definition of unfamiliar words and terms used as topics.

■ **Be sure that you find the entire topic: it may have more than one part.**
Sometimes you will have to combine two elements to get the complete topic. For example, a paragraph might describe long-term memory and short-term memory. Neither one by itself would be sufficient. For the complete topic, you would need *long-term and short-term memory.*

■ **Even though the heading or title is often the topic, do not assume that the heading always indicates the *exact* topic.**

The heading "A Decade of Change" is inadequate by itself. Until you read the information that follows the heading, you would not know *which* decade or changes were being referred to. The precise topic might be *changes in civil rights legislation during the 1960s*. Or consider a newspaper article entitled "An Unexpected Bonus." It could be about a couple who had quadruplets, about a "pretty painting" someone bought inexpensively that turned out to be a long lost masterpiece, or about an unanticipated salary increase for those in the military.

■ **Headings are sometimes even misleading.**

Suppose that you see the heading "The Twinkie Defense" in a criminal justice text. By itself, it sounds as if junk food is going to be used for ammunition. "The Twinkie Defense" actually refers to a legal defense offered in a highly publicized murder case in 1979. The defense attorney argued that his client committed the crime because he had indulged in a high-sugar, junk-food diet that made his behavior more and more uncontrollable. (The strategy must have worked: The jury agreed and found the defendant guilty of manslaughter rather than murder.) Also, headings are sometimes ironic; they say one thing, but mean the opposite. For example, "Pat Smith: The Perfect Candidate" could be the title of an article that actually goes on to explain why in the author's opinion this seemingly "perfect" candidate is totally unqualified to hold political office. Moral: Read the paragraph carefully!

■ **Certain clues will be especially helpful in determining the *overall* topic of longer passages.**

The clues of using a title or heading and special print are especially helpful in determining the overall topic of a chapter, section of a chapter, or other entire selection. (Remember that you should confirm by noting what the topics of the individual paragraphs have in common. That will be the overall topic.)

■ **Determining the topic is a skill that underlies certain other skills.**

Thought I'd hit you with this one last time: Determining the topic is a skill you must know in order to determine the main idea of a paragraph (Chapters 4 and 5) or the overall main idea of a longer selection. It is also a skill you must master to create an outline, write a summary, or take notes. Learning this basic skill will serve you well in many ways, so don't slide past it.

THE REPLAY

REMEMBER THE ESSENTIAL INFORMATION FROM THE CHAPTER

Here's your chance to consolidate what you've just learned and move the information into permanent memory. Review the definition of *topic* and the four clues to the *topic,* then write these from memory in the space below. I know, I know. You're thinking, "Oh, good! I can skip this part." Don't do it! (You skip it and I'll penalize you 15 yards.) *Do it now. Do it right.* That's how you strengthen your skills. (P.S. It's also a pretty good approach for a more effective *life.*)

Definition of Topic

_____

_____

Question to Ask Yourself

_____

Four Clues to the Topic

1. _____

   _____

2. _____

   _____

3. _____

   _____

4. _____

   _____

SUMMARY CHART OF BASIC COMPREHENSION SKILLS			
	Definition	Question to Ask Yourself	Clues/Other Information
Topic			
Stated Main Idea			
Supporting Details			
Implied Main Idea			
Authors' Writing Patterns			

THE PRACTICE

APPLY THE SKILL OF DETERMINING THE TOPIC OF A PARAGRAPH

SET 1

Exercises: Determining the Topic

Time once again for you to swing into action. Read each paragraph and ask yourself, *Who or what is this paragraph about?* To help you answer this question, use the four clues to the topic. Then write the letter of the answer choice that gives the topic. (*Coach's tip:* Mark any clues in the paragraph. Jot the *type* of clue in the margin beside the paragraph or beside the answer you choose.)

Crosstraining is the use of more than one aerobic activity to achieve cardiorespiratory fitness. For example, runners may use swimming, cycling, or rowing periodically to replace running in the training routines. Crosstraining allows certain muscle groups to rest and injuries to heal. In addition, crosstraining provides a refreshing change of pace for the participant. You will probably enjoy your fitness program more if you vary the activities by crosstraining.

Source: Wayne Payne, Dale Hahn, and Ellen Mauer, *Understanding Your Health,* 8th ed., pp. 115–17. Copyright © 2005 McGraw-Hill. Reprinted by permission of The McGraw-Hill Companies.

_____ 1. The topic of this paragraph is
   a. aerobic activity.
   b. crosstraining.
   c. training routines.
   d. fitness programs.

FINANCIAL MANAGERS

An accountant could be compared to a skilled laboratory technician who takes blood samples and other measures of a person's health and writes the findings on a health report. This is the equivalent of a set of financial statements in business. A financial manager of a business is the doctor who interprets the report and makes recommendations to the patient regarding changes that will improve the patient's health. In short, *financial managers* examine the financial data prepared by accountants and make recommendations for improving the health (financial strength) of the firm.

Source: William Nickels, James McHugh, and Susan McHugh, *Understanding Business,* 7th ed., p. 582. Copyright © 2005 McGraw-Hill/Irwin. Reprinted by permission of The McGraw-Hill Companies.

_____ 2. The topic of this paragraph is
   a. accountants.
   b. skilled laboratory technicians.
   c. financial managers.
   d. financial data.

A common occurrence among adults is low back pain. Four out of five adults develop this condition at least once in their lifetime, which can be so uncomfortable that they miss work, lose sleep, and generally feel incapable of engaging in daily activities. Many of the adults who have this condition will experience these effects two to three times per year.

Source: Adapted from Wayne Payne, Dale Hahn, and Ellen Mauer, *Understanding Your Health,* 8th ed., p. 113. Copyright © 2005 McGraw-Hill. Reprinted by permission of The McGraw-Hill Companies.

_____ **3.** The topic of this paragraph is
   a. a common occurrence among adults.
   b. four out of five adults with this condition.
   c. low back pain.
   d. missing work and losing sleep because of low back pain.

Blogs Many users of the Internet have fun keeping journals, or web logs—called *blogs* for short—accessible to other users. Blogs are often updated daily and reflect the personality and views of the blogger. Blog sites—for example, blogging network (www.bloggingnetwork.com) and Pyra Labs (www.blogger.com)—provide information about how you can create and maintain your own web log for a small fee.

Source: Brian Williams and Stacey Sawyer, *Using Information Technology,* 6th ed., p. 81. Copyright © 2005 McGraw-Hill. Reprinted by permission of The McGraw-Hill Companies.

_____ **4.** The topic of this paragraph is
   a. keeping journals.
   b. the Internet.
   c. blogs.
   d. updating blogs daily.

Gender roles are the behaviors, interests, attitudes, skills, and personality traits that a culture considers appropriate for males and females. All societies have gender roles. Historically, in most cultures, women have been expected to devote most of their time caring for the household and children, while men were providers and protectors. Women were expected to be compliant and nurturant; men were expected to be active, aggressive, and competitive. Today, gender roles in western cultures have become more diverse and more flexible.

Source: Sally Olds, Diane Papalia, and Ruth Feldman, *Human Development,* 9th ed., p. 275. Copyright © 2004 McGraw-Hill. Reprinted by permission of The McGraw-Hill Companies.

_____ **5.** The topic of this paragraph is
   a. men and women in all societies.
   b. gender roles.
   c. traits a culture considers appropriate.
   d. nurturant women and aggressive men.

One form of unethical competitive behavior is giving and receiving bribes and kickbacks. They are often disguised as gifts, consultant fees, and favors. The practice is more common in business-to-business and government marketing than in consumer marketing.

Source: Adapted from Eric Berkowitz, Roger Kerin, Steven Hartley, and William Rudelius, *Marketing: The Core,* p. 86. Copyright © 2004 McGraw-Hill/Irwin. Reprinted by permission of The McGraw-Hill Companies.

_____ **6.** The topic of this paragraph is
   a. unethical competitive behavior.
   b. gifts, consultant fees and favors.
   c. business-to-business and government marketing.
   d. bribes and kickbacks.

The civil rights movement of the 1960s at first did not include Native Americans. Then, in the early 1970s, militant Native Americans occupied the Bureau of Indian Affairs in Washington, D.C., and later seized control of the village of Wounded Knee on a Sioux reservation in southwestern South Dakota, exchanging gunfire with U.S. marshals. These episodes brought attention to the grievances of Native Americans and may have contributed to the passage of 1974 legislation that granted Native Americans on reservations a greater measure of control over programs that affected them. Native Americans had already benefited from the legislative climate created by the civil rights movement of the 1960s. In 1968 Congress had enacted the Indian Bill of Rights, which gives Native Americans on reservations constitutional guarantees that are similar to those held by other Americans.

Source: Adapted from Thomas E. Patterson, *The American Democracy,* 5th ed., p. 130. Copyright © 2001 McGraw-Hill. Reprinted by permission of The McGraw-Hill Companies.

_____   **7.** The topic of this paragraph is
   a. the civil rights movement of the 1960s.
   b. militant Native Americans.
   c. grievances of Native Americans.
   d. the civil rights of Native Americans.

Franklin D. Roosevelt (FDR) was president from 1933 to 1945, longer than anyone else in American history; he was elected four times. When he won the election of 1932, he took office at one of the worst points in the Great Depression, but told the American public, "The only thing we have to fear is fear itself." The early part of his presidency is remembered for the New Deal, a group of government programs designed to reverse the devastating effects of the Depression. This innovative leader used "fireside chats" over the radio to build support for his policies. In the later years of his presidency, he attempted to support the Allies in World War II without bringing the United States into the war. After the Japanese bombing of Pearl Harbor, the United States entered the war. He began the Manhattan Project, which produced the atomic bomb, a weapon that brought a quick but highly controversial end to the war.

Source: Adapted from E. D. Hirsch, Jr., Joseph Kett, and James Trefil, *The New Dictionary of Cultural Literacy: What Every American Needs to Know.* Boston: Houghton Mifflin, 2002, p. 302.

_____   **8.** The topic of this paragraph is
   a. Franklin D. Roosevelt.
   b. the election of 1932.
   c. the New Deal.
   d. Allies in World War II.

Constituency interests are also advanced by logrolling, the practice of trading one's vote with another member of Congress so that each gets what he or she most wants. The term dates to the early nineteenth century, when a settler would ask neighbors for help in rolling logs off land being cleared for farming, with the understanding that the settler would reciprocate when the neighbors were cutting trees. In Congress, logrolling occurs most often in committees where constituency interests vary. It has not been uncommon, for example, for agriculture committee members from livestock-producing states of the North to trade votes with committee members from the South where crops such as cotton, tobacco, and peanuts are grown.

Source: Adapted from Thomas E. Patterson, *The American Democracy,* 5th ed., p. 364. Copyright © 2001 McGraw-Hill. Reprinted by permission of The McGraw-Hill Companies.

_____   **9.** The topic of this paragraph is
   a. constituency interests.
   b. logrolling.
   c. a term that dates back to the 19th century.
   d. committees where constituency interests vary.

NOT CONCENTRATING AS A CAUSE OF POOR LISTENING

The brain is incredibly efficient. Although we talk at a rate of 120 to 150 words a minute, the brain can process 400 to 800 words a minute. This would seem to make listening very easy, but actually it has the opposite effect. Because we can take in a speaker's words and still have plenty of spare "brain time," we are tempted to interrupt our listening by thinking about other things. And thinking about other things is just what we do.

Source: Adapted from Stephen Lucas, *The Art of Public Speaking,* 6th ed., p. 58. Copyright © 1998 McGraw-Hill. Reprinted by permission of The McGraw-Hill Companies.

_____ **10.** The topic of this paragraph is
    a. the brain's efficiency.
    b. the rate we talked compared with brain processing time.
    c. "brain time."
    d. not concentrating as a cause of poor listening.

What does the word *drug* mean? Each of us may have different ideas about what a drug is. Although a number of definitions are available, we will consider a drug to be "any substance, natural or artificial, other than food, that by its chemical or physical nature alters structure or function in the living organism." Included in this broad definition is a variety of psychoactive drugs, medicines, and substances that many people do not usually consider to be drugs.

Source: Adapted from Wayne Payne, Dale Hahn, and Ellen Mauer, *Understanding Your Health,* 8th ed., pp. 229–30. Copyright © 2005 McGraw-Hill. Reprinted by permission of The McGraw-Hill Companies.

_____ **11.** The topic of this paragraph is
    a. different ideas about what a drug is.
    b. psychoactive drugs.
    c. the meaning of the word "drug."
    d. substances that many people do not usually consider to be drugs.

ULTRASOUND

Some parents see their baby for the first time in a sonogram, a picture of the uterus, fetus, and placenta created by *ultrasound,* high-frequency sound waves directed into the mother's abdomen. Ultrasound is used to measure fetal growth, to judge gestational age, to detect multiple pregnancies, to evaluate uterine abnormalities in the fetus, and to determine whether a fetus has died, as well as to guide other procedures, such as amniocentesis. Results from ultrasound can suggest what additional procedures may be needed. Ultrasound also can reveal the sex of the fetus.

Source: Adapted from Diane Papalia, Sally Olds, and Ruth Feldman, *Human Development,* 9th ed., pp. 100–101. Copyright © 2004 McGraw-Hill. Reprinted by permission of The McGraw-Hill Companies.

_____ **12.** The topic of this paragraph is
    a. sonograms.
    b. sound waves.
    c. ultrasound.
    d. amniocentesis.

SET 2

EXERCISES: DETERMINING THE TOPIC

Breathe. Relax. Focus. As you read each of the following paragraphs, ask yourself, *Who or what is this paragraph about?* Then use the four clues to help you determine the topic. There may be only one clue or there may be more than one. (*Coach's tip:* You may find it helpful to mark clues that you find or to jot the type of clue in the margin.) Be precise when you write the word, name, or phrase that describes the topic. Write the topic on the line beneath each paragraph.

REMAINING CHILDLESS BY CHOICE

An increasing number of couples remain childless by choice. Some of these couples want to concentrate on careers or social causes. Some feel more comfortable with adults or think that they would not make good parents. Some want to retain the intimacy of the honeymoon. Some enjoy an adult lifestyle, with freedom to travel or to make spur-of-the-moment decisions. Some women worry that pregnancy will make them less attractive and that parenthood will change their relationship with their spouse. Some people may be discouraged by the financial burdens of parenthood and the difficulty of combining parenthood with employment.

Source: Adapted from Diane Papalia, Sally Olds, and Ruth Feldman, *Human Development,* 9th ed., p. 512. Copyright © 2004 McGraw-Hill. Reprinted by permission of The McGraw-Hill Companies.

1. Topic: _____

Every recent president has had the public's confidence at the very start of the term of office. When asked in polls whether they "approve or disapprove of how the president is doing his job," a majority have expressed approval during the first months of the term. Sooner or later, however, all **presidential approval ratings** have slipped below this high point, and fewer than half of recent presidents have left office with a final-year average higher than 50 percent.

Source: Adapted from Thomas E. Patterson, *The American Democracy,* 5th ed., p. 422. Copyright © 2001 McGraw-Hill. Reprinted by permission of The McGraw-Hill Companies.

2. Topic: _____

Of all the ethical lapses a public speaker can commit, few are more serious than **plagiarism**. *Global plagiarism* is lifting a speech entirely from a single source and passing it off as your own. *Patchwork plagiarism* involves stitching a speech together by copying more or less verbatim from a few sources. Whenever you give a speech, you must be sure it represents your work, your thinking, your language. You must also take care to avoid *incremental plagiarism,* which occurs when a speaker fails to give credit for specific quotations and paraphrases that are borrowed from other people.

Source: Adapted from Stephen Lucas, *The Art of Public Speaking,* 7th ed., p. 50. Copyright © 2001 McGraw-Hill. Reprinted by permission of The McGraw-Hill Companies.

3. Topic: _____

THE TRUTH IN LENDING LAW

The **Truth in Lending Law** of 1969 was a landmark piece of legislation. For the first time, creditors were required to state the cost of borrowing as a dollar amount so that consumers would know exactly what the credit charges were and thus could compare credit costs and shop for credit.

Source: Adapted from Jack Kapoor, Les Dlabay, and Robert J. Hughes, *Personal Finance,* 7th ed., p. 202. Copyright © 2004 McGraw-Hill/Irwin. Reprinted by permission of The McGraw-Hill Companies.

4. Topic: _____

The heads of the executive departments, such as the Department of Defense and the Department of Agriculture, constitute the president's cabinet. Members of the cabinet are appointed by the president, subject to confirmation by Congress. The cabinet is a tradition but has no formal authority.

Source: Adapted from Thomas E. Patterson, *The American Democracy,* 5th ed., p. 399. Copyright © 2001 McGraw-Hill. Reprinted by permission of The McGraw-Hill Companies.

5. Topic: _____

Binge eating disorder is the newest term for what was previously referred to as compulsive overeating. Binge eaters use food to cope in the same way that bulimics do and also feel out of control and unable to stop eating during binges. People with this disorder report eating rapidly and in secret or may snack all day. They tend to eat until they feel uncomfortably full, sometimes hoarding food and eating when they aren't physically hungry. Like people with bulimia, they feel guilty and ashamed of their eating habits and have a great deal of self-loathing and body hatred. Typically, binge eaters have a long history of diet failures, feel anxious, are socially withdrawn from others, and are overweight. Heart problems, high blood pressure, joint problems, abnormal blood sugar levels, fatigue, depression, and anxiety are associated with binge eating.

Source: Adapted from Wayne Payne, Dale Hahn, and Ellen Mauer, *Understanding Your Health,* 8th ed., pp. 207–8. Copyright © 2005 McGraw-Hill. Reprinted by permission of The McGraw-Hill Companies.

6. Topic: _____

When you give a speech, you will sometimes use a visual aid. Once it gets into the hands of your listeners, you are in trouble. At least three people will be paying more attention to it than to you—the person who has just had it, the person who has it now, and the person waiting to get it next. By the time it moves on, all three may have lost track of what you are saying.

Source: Adapted from Stephen Lucas, *The Art of Public Speaking,* 8th ed., p. 337. Copyright © 2004 McGraw-Hill. Reprinted by permission of The McGraw-Hill Companies.

7. Topic: _____

EYE CONTACT AND CULTURE

Like many aspects of communication, eye contact is influenced by cultural background. When engaged in conversation, Arabs, Latin Americans, and Southern Europeans tend to look directly at the person with whom they are talking. People from Asian countries and parts of Africa tend to engage in less eye contact. In

Kenya a discussion between a woman and her son-in-law may well be conducted with each person turning her or his back to the other.

8. Topic: _____

Paul Cézanne remains one of the most enigmatic figures in modern art history, even though the details of his life are well known. A word often used to describe his personality is "difficult." Clearly, he was a man of intelligence and great sensitivity, yet he could be rude to strangers and boorish with his friends. Although this post-impressionistic painter was acquainted with most of the leading artists then working in Paris, he spent the greater part of his life in isolation in the southern French town of Aix-en-Provence, where he was born.

9. Topic: _____

AN EMPEROR'S TERRA-COTTA ARMY

In 221 B.C.E., the state of Qin (pronounced "chin") claimed victory over the other states, uniting all of China into an empire for the first time. The first emperor, Shihuangdi, was obsessed with obtaining immortality. Work on his underground burial site began even before he united China and continued until his death. The mound covering the burial itself has always been visible, but the accidental discovery in 1974 of a buried terra-cotta army guarding it was one of the most electrifying moments in 20th-century archaeology. Row upon row of life-size figures stand in the thousands—soldiers, archers, cavalrymen, and charioteers—facing east, the direction from which danger was expected to come. Time has bleached them to a ghostly gray, but when they were new, they were painted lifelike colors, for only by being as realistic as possible could they effectively protect the emperor's tomb behind them, about half a mile to the west.

10. Topic: _____

SET 3

Exercises: Determining the Topic

Last set! Ready to try the final eight passages? This set of exercises has the same format as Set 2, but these textbook passages are slightly more challenging. Once again, you'll find it helpful to mark the clues in each paragraph before you write the topic. Take a few breaths first to help you relax and focus yourself.

Economists define "saving" as that part of after-tax income which is not spent; hence, households have just two choices of what to do with their incomes after taxes—use it to consume, or save it. Saving is the portion of income which is not paid in taxes or used to purchase consumer goods but which flows into bank accounts, insurance policies, bonds and stocks, mutual funds, and other financial assets.

Source: Campbell McConnell and Stanley Brue, *Economics,* 16th ed., p. 74. Copyright © 2005 McGraw-Hill. Reprinted by permission of The McGraw-Hill Companies.

1. Topic: _____

Estimates are that between 20 percent and 60 percent of state correctional populations suffer from psychopathy. **Psychopathy**, or antisocial personality, is characterized by an inability to learn from experience, a lack of warmth, and no sense of guilt. Psychopaths lie and cheat without hesitation and engage in verbal as well as physical abuse without provocation. Theodore "Ted" Bundy is a classic example. Bundy, a former law student and former crime commission staff member, killed between 19 and 36 young women in the northwestern states and Florida. The handsome physical fitness enthusiast often brutally sexually attacked his victims before murdering them.

Source: Freda Adler, Gerhard Mueller, and William Laufer, *Criminal Justice,* 3d ed., p. 68. Copyright © 2003 McGraw-Hill. Reprinted by permission of The McGraw-Hill Companies.

2. Topic: _____

The answer to how to curb the expected increase in the world's population lies in discovering how to curb the rapid population growth of the less-developed countries. In these countries, population experts have discovered what they call the "virtuous cycle." Family planning leads to healthier women, and healthier women have healthier children, and the cycle continues. Women no longer need to have as many babies for a few to survive. More education is also helpful because better-educated people are more interested in postponing childbearing and promoting women's rights. Women who have equal rights with men tend to have fewer children.

Source: Sylvia Mader, *Biology,* 8th ed., p. 856. Copyright © 2004 McGraw-Hill. Reprinted by permission of The McGraw-Hill Companies.

3. Topic: _____

_____

Many people, including you perhaps, have invented products that are assumed to have commercial value. The question that obviously surfaces is what to do next. One step may be to apply for a patent. A **patent** is a document that gives inventors exclusive rights to their inventions for 20 years from the date they file the patent applications. The U.S. Patent and Trademark Office (USPTO) grants approximately 190,000 patents a year. In addition to filing forms, the inventor must make sure the product is truly unique. Since patent applicants are usually recommended to seek the advice of a lawyer, less than 2 percent of product inventors file on their own.

Source: William Nickels, James McHugh, and Susan McHugh, *Understanding Business,* 7th ed., p. 128. Copyright © 2005 McGraw-Hill/Irwin. Reprinted by permission of The McGraw-Hill Companies.

4. Topic: _____

DEALING WITH UNWANTED E-MAIL

The best way to deal with unwanted e-mail is to delete it. If you are tempted to send a reply indicating your disdain for the unwanted mail, think twice before answering. If the message is unwanted commercial advertising, sending a reply will tell the sender that yours is a valid e-mail address, and you may receive even more spam as a result. If you believe the unwanted e-mail is illegal, such as a mail message containing child pornographic material or other criminal activity, you can report the transmission by forwarding it to the appropriate authorities. It may help to forward the message to the postmaster at your Internet service provider, informing your ISP of the unwanted activity and asking for it to be stopped.

Source: Fred Hofstetter, *Internet Literacy,* p. 110. Copyright © 2006 McGraw-Hill/Irwin. Reprinted by permission of The McGraw-Hill Companies.

5. Topic: _____

Rites of passage of contemporary cultures include confirmations, baptisms, bar and bat mitzvahs, and fraternity hazing. Passage rites involve changes in social status, such as from boyhood to manhood and from nonmember to sorority sister. There are also rites and rituals in our business and corporate lives. Examples include promotion and retirement parties. More generally, a rite of passage may mark any change in place, condition, social position, or age.

Source: Conrad Kottak, *Cultural Anthropology,* 8th ed., pp. 311–12. Copyright © 2000 McGraw-Hill. Reprinted by permission of The McGraw-Hill Companies.

6. Topic: _____

Older adults with a history of chronic obstructive lung disease, cardiovascular disease, diabetes, or alcoholism often encounter a potentially serious mid-winter form of pneumonia known as *acute (severe) community-acquired pneumonia.* Characteristics of this condition are the sudden onset of chills, chest pain, and a cough producing sputum. In addition, a symptom-free form of pneumonia known as *walking pneumonia* is also commonly seen in adults and can become serious without warning.

Source: Wayne Payne, Dale Hahn, Ellen Mauer, *Understanding Your Health,* 8th ed., p. 441. Copyright © 2005 McGraw-Hill. Reprinted by permission of The McGraw-Hill Companies.

7. Topic: _____

_____

Judicial appointments also provide the president with opportunities to influence the judiciary's direction. When Democrat President Bill Clinton took office in 1993, more than one hundred federal judgeships were vacant. The first President Bush had expected to win reelection and had not moved quickly to fill vacancies as they arose. As it became apparent that he might lose the election, the Democrat-controlled Congress delayed action on the nominations.

This enabled Clinton to fill many of the positions with loyal Democrats. The tables were turned in 2001. Senate Republicans had slowed action on Clinton nominees, enabling George W. Bush to appoint Republicans to existing vacancies when he took office.

Source: Adapted from Thomas E. Patterson, *The American Democracy,* 7th ed., p. 466. Copyright © 2005 McGraw-Hill. Reprinted by permission of The McGraw-Hill Companies.

8. Topic: _____

_____

You did it! Congratulations—you've finished the first three chapters. I hope you're feeling "stronger" and more confident in your ability to use the context, analyze word structure and to determine the topic.

Take a minute to write about how you feel you've handled these chapters. Did you spend adequate time studying them and doing the practice exercise sets? If you missed items in the exercises, do you now understand why you missed them? Do you think you understand the concepts presented in the chapters? If you were starting these chapters again, what changes would you make in the way you approached them? Respond in the space below (unless your instructor directs you to use notebook paper).

_____
_____
_____
_____
_____
_____
_____
_____
_____
_____
_____
_____

CHAPTER 4

Identify the Stated Main Idea Sentence and the Supporting Details of a Paragraph

This chapter presents two related skills, identifying the stated main idea of a paragraph and locating the supporting details. To make it easier for you, I'm going to describe the first skill and the technique for applying it, and then do the same for the second one.

THE SKILL

IDENTIFY THE STATED MAIN IDEA SENTENCE OF A PARAGRAPH

In Chapter 3 you learned that every paragraph must have a topic. To determine the topic of a paragraph, you learned to ask yourself, "Who or what is this paragraph about?" You learned four clues that can help you determine the topic. You learned that determining the topic is the important first step in comprehending what you are reading. It is the stepping-stone to perhaps the most important reading skill: determining the main idea of a paragraph.

Just as every paragraph has a topic, every paragraph has a main idea. (You may recall that you met the word *main* in the exercises in Chapter 1: you used context clues to determine that *main* means "most important.") *When an author includes a sentence in a paragraph that tells his or her most important point about the topic, that sentence is called the* **stated main idea sentence.** Most textbook paragraphs contain stated main ideas. (In Chapter 5 you will learn about main ideas that are not stated but instead are implied.) The main idea answers the question, "What is the author's one most important point about the topic?" Ask yourself this question when you want to determine the main idea of a paragraph. (Now you can see why you must identify the topic of the paragraph before you can determine the main idea.)

The stated main idea sentence can appear anywhere in a paragraph. Authors most often place it at the beginning of a paragraph. The rest of the sentences will be details that explain more about it, give examples of it, or prove it. The end of the paragraph is the next most likely location of the stated main idea sentence. Authors know that you may need certain information *before* you can understand the main idea, so they give the details first and save the main idea for last. The third possibility is that the main idea sentence appears within the paragraph. They may start the paragraph with a question, and then answer it. Although the question itself is never the main idea, the *answer* to the question is often the main idea. For example, a paragraph might begin, "What are the key economic indicators?" In the next sentence, the main idea, the author gives the answer: "The three major indicators of economic conditions are the gross domestic product, the unemployment rate, and the price indexes." Of course, authors also start paragraphs with one or more questions just to introduce a topic or to hook the reader's attention. For example, in a speech textbook, a paragraph might begin with, "Does the thought of giving a speech make you nervous? Do you feel sick to your stomach? Does your throat go dry?"

Being able to identify the main idea will enable you to

- Know what to highlight or underline in your textbooks.
- Write correct outlines and summaries.
- Remember the information more easily.
- Make test review sheets, review cards, and study maps to help you prepare for tests.
- Make higher test grades.
- Write better paragraphs and essay test answers.
- Understand how the author organizes the information in a paragraph. (This will be discussed in Chapter 6 on organizational patterns.)

THE TECHNIQUE

FIND THE SENTENCE THAT HAS THE CHARACTERISTICS OF A MAIN IDEA SENTENCE

To determine the main idea of a paragraph, ask yourself, "What is the author's one most important point about the topic?" In addition to presenting the author's most important point, *all main idea sentences have certain other characteristics in common.* If you understand and learn these characteristics, you will always be able to identify stated main ideas in paragraphs. When you read a sentence that you think may be the stated main idea of a paragraph, you can test it to see if it meets the three criteria described next. (Think first about whether the sentence you have selected tells the author's most important point. If it does, then you're done!) If you are not sure, see if it meets these criteria. These additional characteristics are ones that *every* main idea sentence must also have:

1. THE MAIN IDEA SENTENCE *MUST ALWAYS CONTAIN THE TOPIC* (THE WORD, NAME, OR PHRASE THAT TELLS WHAT THE PARAGRAPH IS ABOUT)

Read this sample paragraph from a textbook on personal finance.

LOST OR STOLEN DEBIT CARDS

A lost or stolen debit card can be expensive. If you notify the financial institution within two days of losing the card, your liability for unauthorized use is $50. If you wait any longer, you can be liable for up to $500 of unauthorized use for up to 60 days. Beyond that, your liability is unlimited. However, some card issuers use the same rules for lost or stolen debit cards as for credit cards: a $50 maximum.

Source: Adapted from Jack Kapoor, Les Dlabay, and Robert Hughes, *Personal Finance,* 7th ed., p. 134. Copyright © 2004 McGraw-Hill. Reprinted by permission of The McGraw-Hill Companies.

As the heading and bold print suggest, the topic of this paragraph is *lost or stolen debit cards*. The phrase appears in two sentences, but only the first sentence expresses the most important point: that a lost or stolen debit card can be expensive. Therefore, the first sentence is the stated main idea. The other sentences explain more about costs cardholders may have to pay for unauthorized charges made on their lost or stolen debit cards.

2. THE MAIN IDEA SENTENCE *MUST ALWAYS MAKE COMPLETE SENSE BY ITSELF* (That is, if you read the sentence by itself without seeing the rest of the paragraph, you would still understand the authors' most important point.)

Look at the sentences from the sample paragraph.

First sentence:

A lost or stolen debit card can be expensive.

(This sentence makes complete sense because it includes the topic—*a lost or stolen debit card*—and it tells the important point about it, *that it can be expensive.*)

Second sentence:

If you notify the financial institution within two days of losing the card, your liability for unauthorized use is $50.

(This sentence does not make complete sense by itself. Unless you read the rest of the paragraph, you do not know which "card" the authors are referring to. The topic, a lost *debit* card, is incomplete, so this sentence cannot be the stated main idea sentence.)

Third sentence:

If you wait any longer, you can be liable for up to $500 of unauthorized use for up to 60 days; beyond that time, your liability is unlimited.

(This sentence does not make complete sense by itself either. Unless you read the rest of the paragraph, you do not know what it is you can be liable for. The topic, *a lost or stolen debit card,* is not mentioned at all, so this sentence cannot be the stated main idea sentence.)

Fourth sentence:

However, some card issuers use the same rules for lost or stolen debit cards as used for credit cards: a $50 maximum.

(This sentence does not make complete sense by itself. It begins with the word *however,* so we know that there was information that came before it. Also, it may not be clear to readers that the "$50 maximum" refers to the amount the cardholder has to pay for unauthorized charges made on the lost or stolen card.)

The main idea sentence in the example paragraph makes complete sense by itself. If you read only that one sentence, you would still come away with the author's most important point: losing a debit card or having it stolen can be expensive. Notice that even though the last sentence of the paragraph does contain the topic, it merely tells more about the first sentence. Also, it does not answer the question, "What is the one most important point the author wants me to understand about lost or stolen debit cards"?

3. THE MAIN IDEA SENTENCE MUST BE A *GENERAL SENTENCE* THAT *SUMS UP THE DETAILS IN THE PARAGRAPH* (All of the other sentences give specific information that explains, illustrates, proves, or tells more about the main idea.)

Look again at the sample paragraph. Notice that all the sentences after the first one explain or tell more about that important general idea. They provide details that explain and illustrate what the authors mean when they say that losing a debit card can be "expensive": It will cost the debit card holder a minimum of $50, although after 60 days, the costs could become unlimited.

LOST OR STOLEN DEBIT CARDS

A lost or stolen debit card can be expensive. If you notify the financial institution within two days of losing the card, your liability for unauthorized use is $50. If you wait any longer, you can be liable for up to $500 of unauthorized use for up to 60 days. Beyond that, your liability is unlimited. However, some card issuers use the same rules for lost or stolen debit cards as for credit cards: a $50 maximum.

Now you know how to identify the stated main idea sentence. Find the sentence the author uses to express his or her most important point about the topic. Check to see that the sentence also meets these three tests: it contains the topic, it makes complete sense by itself, and it is a general sentence that sums up the details in the rest of the paragraph.

THE TRAINER

OBSERVE THE SKILL OF IDENTIFYING THE STATED MAIN IDEA SENTENCE

Now look at this example of a simple paragraph that you might see in the newspaper. The notations around it show an effective reader's thoughts while identifying the stated main idea. You can see *why* an effective reader rules out specific sentences as the possible main idea. Read the paragraph first, and then read the effective reader's "thoughts."

Okay. I've read the paragraph. It's talking about *the best type of dog,* so that's the topic . . . Now I need to look at each of the sentences to see if one of them tells the author's most important point about the best type of dog.

Can't be this because it's a question, and the main idea is never a question.

Can't be this because it doesn't contain the topic and so it doesn't make complete sense by itself.

Nope. Doesn't contain the topic.

Which type of dog is the best one for you? It depends. You might want a small one if you live in an apartment. On the other hand, you might prefer a large, energetic one if you live in the country. Some folks just want a cute or cuddly dog to keep them company. Some need a dog that's good with children. Others want a dog that provides protection. Still others want a dog that can be trained to hunt or to serve as a companion dog for a disabled person. And, of course, there are those that choose a dog on the basis of an image they are seeking. The point is, the best type of dog is the one that meets a person's needs and lifestyle.

Nope. These don't contain the topic.

This sentence is it!
- It tells the author's most important point.
- It contains the topic, the "best type of dog."
- It's a general statement that sums up the paragraph.
- All of the other sentences explain, illustrate, or tell more about it.
- Great! It even contains an additional clue to the main idea—the phrase "The point is."

THE EDGE

POINTERS ABOUT IDENTIFYING THE STATED MAIN IDEA SENTENCE

■ **Only *one* sentence can be the stated main idea sentence of a paragraph.** When you are unsure of what you are doing, you may be tempted to mark two (or more!) sentences in a paragraph as "the" main idea. This is illogical. As noted earlier, "main" means "most important." Obviously, two sentences that contain different information cannot both be *the* one most important sentence.

There is one little bitty exception I need to tell you about. Every now and then, you will read a paragraph that begins and ends with a stated main idea sentence, *but the two sentences say the same thing.* (This is not like having two different main ideas in a paragraph!) Authors occasionally *repeat* their main idea (or restate it in slightly different words) just to be sure that the reader doesn't miss it. Look at the sample paragraph that follows. There is only one main *idea.* The very *same idea* just happens to be presented twice, in two different sentences, each of which makes complete sense by itself. (I've put the two sentences in italics.)

Water is essential for the human body to function properly. An inadequate amount of water restricts all body systems, but it also is needed to transport nutrients to cells and to remove cellular waste. It aids in regulating body temperature and helps cushion the organs of the body. Moreover, water acts as a medium for digestion. Water comprises 60 percent of the body, so it also is partly responsible for the structure of the body. *The human body cannot function properly without adequate water.*

Notice that the first and last sentences say the same thing two different ways. When authors restate the main idea, they may alert the reader to the fact that it's a restatement by using phrases such as these:

To repeat, the human body cannot function properly without adequate water.

It bears repeating: the human body cannot function properly without adequate water.

It is worth repeating: the human body cannot function properly without adequate water.

It cannot be overemphasized: the human body cannot function properly without adequate water.

It cannot be emphasized too strongly that the human body cannot function properly without adequate water.

If you read a paragraph that begins and ends with the same main idea, don't let it throw you. Far from it! Just view it as a comprehension present from the author. If you do come across an occasional paragraph that begins and ends with the same important idea, mark only one of the sentences. You don't need to mark both, and you should never get into the habit of marking more than one sentence as the stated main idea sentence.

■ **Avoid choosing a sentence as the stated main idea simply because the information in it interests you, it contains familiar information, or you think it "sounds important."**
Remember, your task is to determine the *author's* most important point.

■ **Be sure that you *understand* the information in the main idea sentence.**
Just because you locate the stated main idea sentence does not mean that you automatically understand it. For example, you might correctly identify this sentence as the main idea in a biology textbook paragraph: "Homeostasis is an important characteristic of life." You would first have to understand the meaning of "homeostasis" to understand the meaning of the sentence.

■ **Because the main idea is always a sentence, do not select a question as the stated main idea.**
You already know that authors sometimes begin a paragraph with an important question. Do, of course, look for the complete answer to the question: It's probably the main idea. (You'll learn more about this in the next chapter.) You have to be really goofing off to choose a question as the main idea sentence. (Don't make this mistake on the chapter exercise sets, or I'll *know* you weren't paying attention!)

■ **Examples are details that *support* the main idea, so examples can never be the main idea.**
When you read a sentence that contains the words "for example," "to illustrate," or "for instance," you will know immediately that the sentence is *not* the main idea of the paragraph.

■ **Watch for certain words and phrases that authors frequently use to signal their most important point, the main idea.**
These words and phrases include *To sum up, The point is, In conclusion, In general, Overall, Therefore,* and *Thus.* These clues typically introduce the main idea when it occurs at the end of the paragraph, although the main idea sentence may appear earlier in the paragraph. These words should alert you that an important general statement—the main idea—is being presented.

■ **Read the entire paragraph before you decide what the author's main point is.**
Don't make the mistake of thinking you can save time by reading only the first and last sentences of the paragraph. Dumb idea. Bad strategy. Big mistake.

■ **Longer selections, such as entire sections of textbook chapters, essays, articles, editorials, and so forth, also have an *overall* stated main idea.**
The overall main idea is just what it sounds like: one sentence that sums up the author's one, *overall* most important point about the topic of the *selection*. You will also hear it called the *thesis sentence*.

■ **Locating the stated main idea is a skill that underlies several study skills.**
In order to mark your textbooks effectively, take notes, create outlines, make concept maps, and write correct summaries, you must be able to locate the stated main idea in a paragraph. (The important study skills of note taking, outlining, making concept maps, and summarizing are presented in Chapter 14.)

THE REPLAY

REMEMBER THE ESSENTIAL INFORMATION FROM THE CHAPTER (STATED MAIN IDEA)

Now take a few minutes to review the definition of a stated main idea and the other characteristics of main idea sentences. As a help, here's my drill instructor's version of the stated main idea information. Read it out loud, record it and listen to it, sing it in the shower (don't take the book in with you!) and in the car or on the bus (sing softly on the bus, or people will stare at you). In case you're unfamiliar with "top-shelf" (third verse), it means the highest or best.

It's important that you find
The point the author has in mind.

The *main idea* is its name,
But "topic sentence" is the same.

The main idea is top-shelf:
It makes sense all by itself.

And never once should you doubt it:
Details all tell more about it.

This sentence has the topic, too.
It gives a summary or overview.

Stated main ideas you can find,
So highlight them or underline.

Once you think you know this important information, try to write it (the information, and not necessarily the verses) from memory. Stay with it until you can successfully write and say the information. Use the space below to write out the information. If you get stuck, go back and add whatever you need to make it complete and correct.

You may be tempted to skip right past this part. *Don't do it!* If you don't learn this information now, it will cause you problems later on. So take the time to do it right. Remember: you play the way you practice. Don't be sloppy or shortsighted in your preparation.

Definition of a Stated Main Idea

_____

_____

_____

_____

Question to Ask Yourself

_____

_____

Three Additional Characteristics of Main Idea Sentences

1. _____

_____

_____

_____

2. _____

_____

_____

_____

_____

3. _____

_____

_____

_____

THE SKILL

IDENTIFY THE SUPPORTING DETAILS OF A PARAGRAPH

Identifying supporting details is the other major skill presented in this chapter. I chose to discuss stated main ideas and details in the same chapter because they go together like salt and pepper, french fries and ketchup, fire and smoke, or big cities and traffic jams: where you find one, you find the other. You already know that a paragraph consists of more than a stated main idea. If it didn't, that "paragraph" would be one sentence long. In a paragraph with a stated main idea sentence, the other sentences are the supporting details.

Supporting details consist of the additional information the author provides so that the reader can understand the main idea completely. To locate the supporting details in a paragraph, first determine the topic and main idea, then ask yourself the supporting detail question: "What additional information does the author provide to help me understand the main idea completely?" Then look for specific information that tells more about the main idea or helps explain, illustrate, or prove it.

Textbooks typically have a vast number of stated main idea paragraphs. As suggested earlier, a paragraph with a stated main idea gives you a freebie: once you have found the main idea sentence, you've automatically found the supporting details. They are pretty much everything else that's left. Details consist of examples, explanations, descriptions, proof, statistics, and other bits of specific information. (In Chapter 6 you'll learn something else very cool, the various ways authors organize details into patterns such as *lists, sequences, comparisons and contrasts,* and *causes and effects.*)

You've probably already "got it," but just in case you don't, let me use a simple analogy to explain the connection between the stated main idea and the supporting details. Think of it this way:

The *paragraph* is like a *play* a football team wants to make.

The *stated main idea* is like the *quarterback,* the most important player who calls the play.

The *supporting details* are *the rest of the team;* they support the quarterback by making the play happen.

The quarterback, like the main idea, announces the most important information: He calls the play, the one most important thing everyone else must know. The rest of the team, the supporting details, need the quarterback to organize them by telling them the general play. Each player then has some specific contribution to make in executing the play, just as each detail in a paragraph contributes to the overall meaning of the paragraph. If everything goes as planned, the play is successful, or in the case of the paragraph, the paragraph is clearly organized and makes sense; the reader successfully comprehends it.

A quarterback alone on the field could never be as successful in executing a play as he could be if he had the entire team on the field. On the other hand, if all the other players are just standing around on the field with no quarterback to guide them, they're not going to be very successful either. You need both: a quarterback needs the rest of his team; a main idea needs supporting details.

Knowing about details and their supporting role enables you to comprehend more successfully. It enables you to mark your textbooks intelligently and to take better notes. Identifying supporting details enables you to grasp how textbook material in a paragraph is organized. You'll score higher on tests if you can locate and learn supporting details. Supporting details can also help you figure out the main idea when the author does not state it, but instead implies it. (Implied main ideas are discussed in the next chapter.)

IDENTIFY THE SUPPORTING DETAILS

As noted previously, you locate the supporting details in a paragraph by doing these steps: first determine the topic and main idea, then ask yourself the question, "What additional information does the author provide to help me understand the main idea completely?" The details consist of the specific information that answers that question. (Here's a nifty hint: You can also turn the main idea sentence into one or more logical questions by using *who, what, when, where, why,* or *how.* The answer will be the details.)

You should be aware that a single sentence can contain more than one detail. In other words, don't assume that there is only *one* detail per sentence. Authors often include two or more details in a *single* sentence. For example, in this paragraph the first sentence is the stated main idea. How many details are there in the remaining two sentences?

> *There are several simple strategies that will ensure you of adequate study time.* Making a study schedule can help you gain control of your time; so can making a daily "to do" list. Other ways to manage your time more productively include breaking large tasks into smaller parts so they don't seem so overwhelming and saying no to requests that would interfere with your study time.

Did you find these *four* details:

- Make a study schedule.
- Make a daily "to do" list.
- Break large tasks into smaller parts.
- Say no to requests that interfere with study time.

Your professor expects you to find all the details, even when there is more than one per sentence. (Did you notice that you could turn the main idea sentence into the question, "What are the strategies that can ensure adequate study time?" The details answer that question.)

Certain words and symbols are often used to introduce supporting details. These include words such as *first, second, next,* and *finally; also, moreover,* and *in addition.* They also include numbers (*1, 2, 3 . . .*), letters, (*a, b, c . . .*), and bullets (a dot beside each item in a list). The main idea sentence itself may also announce that a list is coming. Watch for clues in it such as *three types, four kinds, two ways, three causes, four categories,* and so forth. Examples are always details, so watch for phrases such as *for example, to illustrate, such as,* and *for instance* that introduce examples.

All details support the main idea, but some details are more important than others. *The details that directly support or explain the main idea are referred to as* **major details** *or* **primary details.** The reader can't fully understand the main idea without them. In contrast, **minor details** or **secondary details** *indirectly support the main idea because they support or explain other details.* Look at this example. The information in parentheses after each sentence explains the function of the sentence.

> In the early stages of learning a sport, it is wise not to engage in competition. (*Stated main idea.*) Beginners who compete are likely to focus on winning rather than on learning the sport properly. (*A major detail that directly explains the main idea; it explains why it isn't good for beginners to compete.*) Moreover, even though the person might win games at first, he sacrifices the chance to improve his skills for the future. (*Another major detail that directly supports the main idea and tells another reason it isn't good for*

beginners to play competitively.) For example, a beginning tennis player who is competing might avoid using a newly learned backhand shot in favor of a sure thing forehand. (*A minor detail because it illustrates the preceding detail.*)

It may be helpful to see this same information in the form of a diagram.

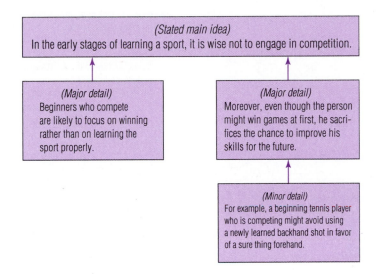

From the diagram, you can see that all of the supporting information either directly or indirectly leads back to the main idea. That's the important concept for you to understand. At this point, though, don't get hung up on the difference between a major and a minor detail. If you read a difficult textbook paragraph, though, you may find it helpful to think about how the paragraph is put together. You might even want to draw a diagram of your own.

Suppose you're having trouble deciding which sentence is the most important sentence—the stated main idea. One strategy is to ask yourself which sentence is the one all of the other sentences support. That sentence is the main idea sentence. Perhaps you've narrowed it down to two sentences. The same strategy applies. All you have to do is decide which sentence is "supported" (it will be the main idea) and which sentence does the "supporting" (it will be a detail).

THE TRAINER

OBSERVE THE SKILL OF IDENTIFYING SUPPORTING DETAILS

Here is an illustration of how an effective reader would mentally process a paragraph with a stated main idea and supporting details. As always, the reader's thoughts are the notations around the paragraph. Read the paragraph first, then the person's "thoughts."

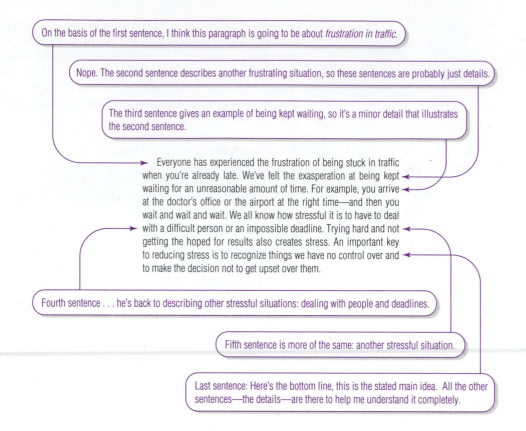

On the basis of the first sentence, I think this paragraph is going to be about *frustration in traffic.*

Nope. The second sentence describes another frustrating situation, so these sentences are probably just details.

The third sentence gives an example of being kept waiting, so it's a minor detail that illustrates the second sentence.

Everyone has experienced the frustration of being stuck in traffic when you're already late. We've felt the exasperation at being kept waiting for an unreasonable amount of time. For example, you arrive at the doctor's office or the airport at the right time—and then you wait and wait and wait. We all know how stressful it is to have to deal with a difficult person or an impossible deadline. Trying hard and not getting the hoped for results also creates stress. An important key to reducing stress is to recognize things we have no control over and to make the decision not to get upset over them.

Fourth sentence . . . he's back to describing other stressful situations: dealing with people and deadlines.

Fifth sentence is more of the same: another stressful situation.

Last sentence: Here's the bottom line, this is the stated main idea. All the other sentences—the details—are there to help me understand it completely.

THE EDGE

POINTERS ABOUT IDENTIFYING SUPPORTING DETAILS

■ **Remember that main ideas and details are two different things. Main ideas are *general;* details are *specific.***
I know, I know. I've already said this a bunch of times, but that's because it's *so* important for you to understand it. If you truly understand it, it will keep you from selecting a detail for the main idea (big mistake!) and (as you'll learn in Chapter 5), keep you from writing main idea sentences that contain details.

■ **Examples are always details.**
I know. I've said this before, too. Like all other types of details, examples are there simply to help you better understand the main idea. Watch for *to illustrate, for example, for instance,* and *such as* because they introduce details. Bottom line: Don't ever choose an example as the stated main idea. Do that, and you forfeit the game!

■ **When you mark your textbook, number the details rather than underline them.**
This is a no-brainer. If you underline the details, you'll underline practically the entire book, and that's obviously no help at all. Besides, writing a small number by each detail (or in the margin) makes it easy to see how many details there are in all. Your brain likes this, so it is especially helpful when it's time to learn the information for a test.

■ **When you take notes from your textbooks, list the details on *separate* lines.**
As you know, your brain finds it easier to comprehend and remember information that is organized. If you take notes from your textbooks (definitely a

good idea!), but you write whole paragraphs of information, you haven't helped yourself as much as you could have. Sure, it takes more paper to list the details on separate lines. So what? It makes each detail stand out clearly so that you can see at a glance how many details there are. Trust me: the extra 10 bucks you might spend on paper is going to be a tiny part of the cost of your entire college education. (By the way, you'll learn more about marking your texts and note taking in Chapter 14.)

■ **When you take notes from your textbooks, shorten or paraphrase the details.**

It's a real drag, not to mention a waste of time, to write down the important details word-for-word or sentence-for-sentence exactly as they appear in your textbooks. There's a better way: shorten the information or put it into your own words. Look back on page 74 at the example paragraph about ensuring adequate study time and the list of details from that paragraph. The last sentence was

Other ways to manage your time more productively include breaking large tasks into smaller parts so they don't seem so overwhelming and saying no to requests that would interfere with your study time.

The details in that sentence could be shortened to half the number of words yet still capture the important information:

■ Break large tasks into smaller parts.
■ Say no to requests that interfere with study time.

Besides, when it comes time to review your notes for a test, wouldn't you rather have nice, short lists to review rather than lengthy sentences or blocks of paragraphs? I would.

THE REPLAY

REMEMBER THE ESSENTIAL INFORMATION FROM THE CHAPTER (SUPPORTING DETAILS)

Here is the drill instructor chant to help you memorize what you need to know about supporting details. In the first verse, "info" is "information" and "MI" stands for "main idea," of course.

Details are the info authors supply
So you'll understand the big "MI."

Details *prove, explain,* or *illustrate*
What the main ideas state.

Details are like supporting walls:
Without 'em the main idea "roof" falls.

Definition of Major or Primary Details

_____

_____

_____

Definition of Minor or Secondary Details

_____

_____

_____

Question to Ask Yourself

_____

_____

_____

In this space, list some of the types of information that supporting details consist of.

_____

_____

_____

_____

Explain the difference between major (primary) details and minor (secondary) supporting details:

_____

_____

_____

_____

There you have it!

How are you doing at this point? Write a few words to describe how well you think you understand the material in this chapter:

_____

_____

_____

_____

_____

_____

_____

Regardless of whether you're feeling confident, confused, overwhelmed, or just plain tired, now is a good time to refresh and refocus yourself. Stand up, stretch, and take a few good deep, slow breaths to relax your muscles, get your circulation moving, and oxygenate your brain.

Something to keep in mind . . .

As you move through the text, the skills will probably feel more challenging, and the Practice Sets may seem more difficult. Don't be frustrated or discouraged if you can't apply a skill perfectly at first. What is important is that you persevere so that ultimately you understand *why* you missed an item. Then use that information to help you do better on the next set of exercises. That's the way you improve. Remember that mistakes are simply opportunities to learn. You *have* to make mistakes to make discoveries. *Mistakes are the bridge between inexperience and wisdom.* The biggest mistake you can make is to be afraid of making mistakes. Michael Jordan, perhaps the greatest athlete ever, attributes his success to his determination to learn from his mistakes: "I failed over and over again—that's why I succeeded." Baseball legend Babe Ruth advised, "Never let fear of striking out get in your way." The Babe was one of the all-time great hitters, but many people forget that he had almost twice as many strikeouts as hits. If you swing often enough (and pay attention), you'll become a better hitter.

THE PRACTICE

SET 1

APPLY THE SKILL OF IDENTIFYING THE STATED MAIN IDEA SENTENCE

Exercises: Identifying the Stated Main Idea Sentence

Ready to get into the game yourself? Read each paragraph and determine the topic by asking yourself, "Who or what is this paragraph about?" (Remember to use the four clues to the topic that you learned in the last chapter.) Once you have determined the topic, identify the main idea by asking yourself, *"What is the author's one most important point about the topic?"* (A present from your incredibly soft-hearted coach: When you find the stated main idea sentence, you are also finding the details, so *there are no separate exercise sets on supporting details.*)

What does your college education mean? One thing it means is that you have a higher likelihood of becoming an active citizen. Persons with a college education are about 40 percent more likely to vote than are persons with a grade school education. Education generates an interest in politics, confidence that one can make a difference politically, and peer pressure to participate—all of these are related to the tendency to vote. Education, in fact, is the single best predictor of voter turnout.

Source: Thomas E. Patterson, *We the People,* 6th ed., p. 238. Copyright © 2006 McGraw-Hill. Reprinted by permission of The McGraw-Hill Companies.

_____ 1. The stated main idea sentence in this paragraph is
  a. What determines who votes?
  b. Persons with a college education are about 40 percent more likely to vote than persons with a grade school education.
  c. All of these are related to the tendency to vote.
  d. Education, in fact, is the single best predictor of voter turnout.

People with learning disabilities are sometimes viewed as unintelligent. Nothing could be further from the truth. There is no relationship between learning disabilities and I.Q. For instance, dozens of well-known and highly accomplished individuals suffered from dyslexia. They include physicist Albert Einstein, U.S. General George Patton, poet William Butler Yeats, and writer John Irving.

Source: Adapted from Robert S. Feldman, *P.O.W.E.R. Learning,* 2005 ed., p. 161. Copyright © 2005 McGraw-Hill. Reprinted by permission of The McGraw-Hill Companies.

_____ 2. The stated main idea sentence in this paragraph is
  a. People with learning disabilities are sometimes viewed as unintelligent. Nothing could be further from the truth.
  b. There is no relationship between learning disabilities and I.Q.
  c. For instance, dozens of well-known and highly accomplished individuals suffered from dyslexia.
  d. They include physicist Albert Einstein, U.S. General George Patton, poet William Butler Yeats, and writer John Irving.

Ineffective messages don't get results. A reader who has to guess what the writer means may be wrong. A reader who finds a letter or memo unconvincing or insulting simply won't do what the message asks. Another story of ineffective communication is told by Yvonne Alexander, a writing consultant. Yvonne says an HMO once lost a claim in court because the judge found its policy to be "written so badly that no one could understand it."

Source: Adapted from Kitty Locker, *Business and Administrative Communication,* 7th ed., p. 10. Copyright © 2006 McGraw-Hill. Reprinted by permission of The McGraw-Hill Companies.

_____ **3.** The stated main idea sentence in this paragraph is
- **a.** Ineffective messages don't get results.
- **b.** A reader who has to guess what the writer means may be wrong.
- **c.** A reader who finds a letter or memo unconvincing or insulting simply won't do what the message asks.
- **d.** Another story of ineffective communication is told by Yvonne Alexander, a writing consultant.

Law enforcement officers are constantly faced with danger. Events go from routine to life-threatening in seconds. The risk of being shot—or having to shoot someone—is high. Each year over 50,000 police officers are assaulted. Forty-two were feloniously killed in 1999.

Source: Adapted from Freda Adler, Gerhard Mueller, and William Laufer, *Criminal Justice: An Introduction,* 3d ed., p. 192. Copyright © 2003 McGraw-Hill. Reprinted by permission of The McGraw-Hill Companies.

_____ **4.** The stated main idea sentence in this paragraph is
- **a.** Law enforcement officers are constantly faced with danger.
- **b.** Events go from routine to life-threatening in seconds.
- **c.** The risk of being shot—or having to shoot someone—is high.
- **d.** Each year over 50,000 police officers are assaulted.

More than four thousand Hispanic Americans nationwide hold public office. Hispanics have been elected to statewide office in several states, including New Mexico and Arizona. About twenty Hispanic Americans currently serve in the House of Representatives. The number of Hispanic Americans now in elected office is the highest in this country's history.

Source: Adapted from Thomas Patterson, *We the People,* 6th ed., p. 168. Copyright © 2006 McGraw-Hill. Reprinted by permission of The McGraw-Hill Companies.

_____ **5.** The stated main idea in this paragraph is
- **a.** More than four thousand Hispanic Americans nationwide hold public office.
- **b.** Hispanics have been elected to statewide office in several states, including New Mexico and Arizona.
- **c.** About twenty Hispanic Americans currently serve in the House of Representatives.
- **d.** The number of Hispanic Americans now in elected office is the highest in this country's history.

Not all relationships last a lifetime. Sometimes they just wind down, as the two people involved slowly lose interest in maintaining their partnership. At other times, they break apart, as disagreements build and there is not a strong enough bond to hold the two parties together. Or there may be an abrupt rupture if some event occurs that destroys one partner's feeling of trust.

Source: Robert S. Feldman, *P.O.W.E.R. Learning,* 2005 ed., p. 329. Copyright © 2005 McGraw-Hill. Reprinted by permission of The McGraw-Hill Companies.

_____ **6.** The stated main idea sentence in this paragraph is
- **a.** Not all relationships last a lifetime.
- **b.** Sometimes they just wind down, as the two people involved slowly lose interest in maintaining their partnership.
- **c.** At other times, they break apart, as disagreements build and there is not a strong enough bond to hold the two parties together.
- **d.** Or there may be an abrupt rupture if some event occurs that destroys one partner's feeling of trust.

Sears will not import products made by Chinese prison labor. The clothing manufacturer Phillips-Van Heusen said it would cancel orders from suppliers that violate its ethical, environmental, and human rights code. Dow Chemical expects its suppliers to conform to tough American pollution and safety laws rather than just to local laws of their respective countries. The point is, many American businesses are demanding socially responsible behavior from their international suppliers by making sure their suppliers do not violate U.S. human rights and environmental standards.

Source: William Nickels, James McHugh, and Susan McHugh, *Understanding Business,* 7th ed., p. 117. Copyright © 2005 McGraw-Hill/Irwin. Reprinted by permission of The McGraw-Hill Companies.

_____   **7.** The stated main idea in this paragraph is
- **a.** Sears will not import products made by Chinese prison labor.
- **b.** The clothing manufacturer Phillips-Van Heusen said it would cancel orders from suppliers that violate its ethical, environmental, and human rights code.
- **c.** Dow Chemical expects its suppliers to conform to tough American pollution and safety laws rather than just to local laws of their respective countries.
- **d.** The point is, many American businesses are demanding socially responsible behavior from their international suppliers by making sure their suppliers do not violate U.S. human rights and environmental standards.

Some colors seem to "advance," others to "recede." Interior designers know that if you place a bright red chair in a room, it will seem larger and farther forward than the same chair upholstered in beige or pale blue. In general, colors that create the illusion or large size and advancing are those with the warmer hues (red, orange, yellow) high intensity, and dark value. Small size and receding are suggested by colors with cooler hues (blue, green), low intensity, and light value.

Source: Adapted from Mark Getlein, *Living with Art,* p. 100. Copyright © 2005 McGraw-Hill. Reprinted by permission of The McGraw-Hill Companies.

_____   **8.** The stated main idea in this paragraph is
- **a.** Some colors seem to "advance," others to "recede."
- **b.** Interior designers know that if you place a bright red chair in a room, it will seem larger and farther forward than the same chair upholstered in beige or pale blue.
- **c.** In general, colors that create the illusion or large size and advancing are those with the warmer hues (red, orange, yellow) high intensity, and dark value.
- **d.** Small size and receding are suggested by colors with cooler hues (blue, green), low intensity, and light value.

The World Wide Web consists of more than 1 billion web pages. Moreover, the web is constantly changing. More sites are created and old ones are retired. Without a browser and various kinds of search tools, there would be no way any of us could begin to make any kind of sense of this enormous amount of data.

Source: Brian Williams and Stacey Sawyer, *Using Information Technology,* 6th ed., p. 68. Copyright © 2005 McGraw-Hill. Reprinted by permission of The McGraw-Hill Companies.

_____ **9.** The stated main idea in this paragraph is
   a. The World Wide Web consists of more than 1 billion web pages.
   b. Moreover, the web is constantly changing.
   c. More sites are created and old ones are retired.
   d. Without a browser and various kinds of search tools, there would be no way any of us could begin to make any kind of sense of this enormous amount of data.

When two people first meet, they usually try to be as explicit as possible. Even if the two share several interests, one does not assume knowledge of what the other is thinking or trying to say. This kind of insight develops only after long acquaintance. Communication style tends to change with the passage of time. Sometimes two people get to know each other so well that each anticipates what the other is trying to say—they even finish each other's sentences, so to speak. We frequently see this relationship in very close friends or in married couples.

Source: Adapted from Stewart Tubbs and Sylvia Moss, *Human Communication,* 8th ed., p. 172. Copyright © 2000 McGraw-Hill. Reprinted by permission of The McGraw-Hill Companies.

_____ **10.** The stated main idea sentence in this paragraph is
   a. When two people first meet, they usually try to be as explicit as possible.
   b. This kind of insight develops only after long acquaintance.
   c. Communication style tends to change with the passage of time.
   d. Sometimes two people get to know each other so well that each anticipates what the other is trying to say—they even finish each other's sentences, so to speak.

The marketing plan helps managers analyze and improve all company operations, including marketing and advertising programs. It dictates the role of advertising in the marketing mix. It enables better implementation, control, and continuity of advertising programs, and it ensures the most efficient allocation of advertising dollars. In short, the marketing plan has a profound effect on an organization's advertising program.

Source: Adapted from William Arens, *Contemporary Advertising,* 10th ed., p. 235. Copyright © 2006 McGraw-Hill. Reprinted by permission of The McGraw-Hill Companies.

_____ **11.** The stated main idea sentence in this paragraph is
   a. The marketing plan helps managers analyze and improve all company operations, including marketing and advertising programs.
   b. It dictates the role of advertising in the marketing mix.
   c. It enables better implementation, control, and continuity of advertising programs, and it ensures the most efficient allocation of advertising dollars.
   d. In short, the marketing plan has a profound effect on an organization's advertising program.

Carbohydrates are various combinations of sugar units, or saccharides, and are the major energy source for the body. Each gram of carbohydrate contains four calories. The average person requires approximately 2,000 calories per day. Since about 60% of our calories come from carbohydrates, it is recommended that 1,200 of our daily caloric intake come from carbohydrates.

Source: Adapted from Wayne Payne, Dale Hahn, and Ellen Mauer, *Understanding Your Health,* 8th ed., p. 131. Copyright © 2005 McGraw-Hill. Reprinted by permission of The McGraw-Hill Companies.

_____   **12.**   The stated main idea sentence in this paragraph is
   a.   Carbohydrates are various combinations of sugar units, or saccharides, and are the major source of energy for the body.
   b.   Each gram of carbohydrate contains four calories.
   c.   The average person requires approximately 2,000 calories per day.
   d.   Since about 60% of our calories come from carbohydrates, it is recommended that 1,200 of our daily caloric intake come from carbohydrates.

Congratulations! You've completed the first set. Feeling warmed up? I hope so. If you're feeling confused about anything, take a minute to write down what it is that you think you don't understand or still need to know.

_____

_____

_____

_____

_____

_____

If you need help, talk with your instructor or a sharp classmate. If those people are not available to you now (it's midnight and you're just starting your homework, for instance . . .), reread The Technique section of the chapter. The important thing is that you *take some steps to fix the problem* whenever you are confused. You're not helpless. You're not a quitter. (I'm one of your coaches; I know these things.) So here's the rest of my pep talk:

Successful athletes continually monitor their performance and make corrections. Extraordinary golfer Tiger Woods is a good example. An article in *Time* magazine ("How the Best Golfer in the World Got Even Better," August 14, 2000, vol. 156, no. 7) explains what Woods did after a string of victories that culminated with a record 12-stroke win at the 1997 Masters Tournament. He studied videotapes of his performance and concluded that his swing could be even *better*. Woods decided to completely reconstruct his golf swing, even though he was at the top of his profession. His coach, Butch Harmon, "cautioned that results wouldn't come overnight—that Woods would have to pump more iron to get stronger, especially in his forearms; that it would take months to groove the new swing; that his tournament performance would get worse before it got better. . . . But Woods didn't hesitate. He and Harmon went to work in a sequence of 1) pounding hundreds of practice balls, 2) reviewing tapes of the swing, and 3) repeating both of the above" (p. 58). Progress didn't come quickly. Woods won only *one* tournament in the next 19 months, and he often felt angry and frustrated. "But each time he lost, he declared that he was 'a better golfer' than he was when he was winning in early 1997" (p. 59). He understood that winning is not always the best measure of progress. After more than a year and a half, he hit a swing and felt for the first time that it was exactly right. The good swings began occurring more often. Then the victories began: he won 10 of 14 events during the remainder of 1999, and had 8 PGA Tour victories that same year. He is now ranked the #1 golfer in the world and holds the record for the most major professional championships, as well as the record for career prize money (which was in excess of $66.5 million at the start of 2007). If a top athlete like Tiger Woods sees the benefit of reviewing his performance and correcting errors, doesn't it stand to reason that you could—and should—do the same?

Here's how you can apply Tiger Woods' strategy: *After your instructor has checked your answers or you've gone over them in class, jot down the type of errors you made.* Did you select sentences that didn't have the topic in them? Perhaps you didn't select the most general sentence in the paragraph, the one that all the other sentences illustrate, explain, prove, or tell more about. Did you select a question as the main idea sentence? It's a very important step to pinpoint the types of mistakes you make so that you can correct them. Unless you identify them, you will continue to make them, and your goal is to do better on the next set. *Mistakes are opportunities to learn.* View them as friends who have come to tell what it is you still need to learn. Use the space below to jot down the specific types of mistakes you made in the Set 1 Exercises. What do you still need to learn?

_____

_____

_____

_____

_____

_____

_____

_____

_____

_____

_____

SET 2

Exercises: Identifying the Stated Main Idea Sentence

Did you identify and learn from any mistakes you made in Set 1? If so, you will do even better on these. For each paragraph below, determine the topic and write it on the line. Once you've determined the topic, ask yourself, *What is the one most important thing the author wants me to understand about the topic?* Then *underline* in pencil the sentence that answers the question. (Don't use a highlighter. If you change your mind, you can't "unmark" the sentence.) Be sure you *mark only one sentence* and that you *underline the complete sentence.* (The reason for finding the topic first is that the topic always appears in the main idea sentence. Check to see that the sentence you chose contains the topic. If it doesn't, then you have either identified the topic or the main idea sentence incorrectly.) Take a deep breath or two. Shake your hands and fingers to loosen up and dispel tension—then pick up your pencil and start in.

1. Scanning the newspaper for job openings and then filing an application with the company's personnel or human resources department is one way of looking for a job but often not the most effective. Many employers never advertise jobs, and one study reveals that between 75 and 85 percent of employers in typical U.S. cities did not hire any employees through want ads during an entire year.

    Source: Adapted from Ronald Adler and Jeanne Elmhorst, *Communicating at Work,* 6th ed., pp. 187–88. Copyright © 1999 McGraw-Hill. Reprinted by permission of The McGraw-Hill Companies.

    To help you identify the stated main idea sentence, first determine the topic of this paragraph:

    _____

    (*Coach's reminder:* There are *two* things to do in these exercises. Did you remember to do the second one, to mark the stated main idea sentence? Does the sentence you chose have the *topic* in it? Did you underline the *complete* sentence?)

2. Before the establishment of public schools in the 1800s, families that taught their children at home lived in isolated environments or held strict religious views that were at odds with the secular environment of public schools. Today, homeschooling is attracting a broader range of families for a variety of reasons not necessarily tied to organized religion. Poor academic quality, peer pressure, and school violence are motivating many parents to make this choice. The recent publicity given to school shooting sprees seems to have accelerated the move toward homeschooling.

    Source: Richard Schaefer, *Sociology,* 9th ed., pp. 389–90. Copyright © 2005 McGraw-Hill. Reprinted by permission of The McGraw-Hill Companies.

    To help you identify the stated main idea sentence, first determine the topic of this paragraph:

    _____

3. **Specific Goals** Employees put more effort into a task when they work toward specific goals rather than "do your best" targets. Specific goals have measurable levels of change over a specific time and a relatively short time frame, such as "reduce scrap rate by 7 percent over the next six months." Such goals communicate more precise performance expectations, so employees can direct their effort more efficiently and reliably.

    Source: Adapted from Steven McShane and Mary Ann Von Glinow, *Organizational Behavior: Essentials,* p. 98. Copyright © 2007 McGraw-Hill. Reprinted by permission of The McGraw-Hill Companies.

To help you identify the stated main idea sentence, first determine the topic of this paragraph:

_____

4.   Advertising appears on videocassettes and computer disks. Technology has spawned a host of new advertising media that can confound even the most knowledgeable media planner and buyer. Computers dial telephones and deliver messages by simulating speech or playing a prerecorded message. Computers can also put callers on hold and play prerecorded sales messages until a customer service rep answers. Business presentations are created on computer and copied to disks that are mailed to prospective customers.

Source: Adapted from William Arens, *Contemporary Advertising,* 10th ed., p. 129. Copyright © 2006 McGraw-Hill/Irwin. Reprinted by permission of the McGraw-Hill Companies.

The topic of this paragraph is:

_____

5.   Men live 8 to 10 years less than women do. They have higher rates of stress-related disorders, alcoholism, car accidents, and suicide. In sum, the male role is hazardous to men's health.

Source: Adapted from John Santrock, *Adolescence,* 8th ed., p. 347. Copyright © 2001 McGraw-Hill. Reprinted by permission of The McGraw-Hill Companies.

The topic of this paragraph is:

_____

6.   In the past the homeless population in the United States consisted primarily of unemployed, alcoholic men over 50 years of age. The homeless were less visible than they are today, living mainly in "skid-row areas of large cities or hobo villages beside the train tracks." Nowadays the homeless population is more diverse. About 46 percent are single women, 36.5 percent are families (usually mothers) with children, and 3.5 percent are children living on their own.

Source: Ronald Berger, Marvin Free, Jr., and Patricia Searles, *Crime, Justice, and Society,* p. 162. Copyright © 2001 McGraw-Hill. Reprinted by permission of The McGraw-Hill Companies.

The topic of this paragraph is:

_____

7.   A company uses **private branding,** often called private labeling or reseller branding, when it manufactures products but sells them under the brand name of a wholesaler or retailer. Radio Shack, Sears, Kmart, and Kroger are large retailers that have their own brand names. It has been estimated that one of every five items purchased at U.S. supermarkets, drugstores, and mass merchandisers bears a private brand.

Source: Adapted from Eric Berkowitz, Roger Kerin, Steven Hartley, and William Rudelius, *Marketing: The Core,* pp. 248–49. Copyright © 2004 McGraw-Hill/Irwin. Reprinted by permission of The McGraw-Hill Companies.

The topic of this paragraph is:

_____

8.   *Anorexia nervosa* (self-starvation) and *bulimia* (binge eating, alternating with self-induced vomiting and fasting) are serious illnesses involving compulsive, life-threatening behaviors. An anorexic person considers herself fat and unattractive, regardless of her actual weight. Estimates of the number of women affected vary, but studies indicate that between 4 percent and 9 percent of female college students meet the clinical criteria for diagnosis. Most individuals suffering from anorexia (85–95 percent) are women, and 12 percent of anorexics die. African American women who are overweight seem to maintain a positive body image, but dieting using unhealthy methods and eating disorders are widespread and increasing among women of color.

Source: Adapted from J. John Palen, *Social Problems for the Twenty-First Century,* pp. 127–28. Copyright © 2001 McGraw-Hill. Reprinted by permission of The McGraw-Hill Companies.

The topic of this paragraph is:

_____

_____

_____

9.   The government abolished freedom of speech, press, and assembly. An elaborate and all-powerful secret police, the Gestapo, uncovered and destroyed opposition. His power consolidated, Hitler proceeded to turn Germany into a police state. Nazi officials took over top positions in the government and pressured churches to conform to the new order. Professional organizations of doctors, teachers, lawyers, and engineers were transformed into Nazi associations. Officials even pushed people into joining Nazi leisure-time organizations.

Source: Adapted from Dennis Sherman and Joyce Salisbury, *The West in the World,* p. 770. Copyright © 2001 McGraw-Hill. Reprinted by permission of The McGraw-Hill Companies.

The topic of this paragraph is:

_____

10.   Take a look around the room you're in. How many things are powered by batteries or plugged into electrical outlets? Just as electricity drives all those appliances, lights, etc., a versatile molecule called ATP provides cells with the energy to move, build proteins, perform chemical reactions, and carry out any other necessary duties. ATP doesn't work solo in the cell, however. Assistants known as enzymes help molecules interact with each other, speeding the cell's chemistry and making it more energy-efficient. Together, ATP and enzymes govern a cell's metabolism.

Source: Sylvia Mader, *Inquiry into Life,* 9th ed., p. 104. Copyright © 2000 McGraw-Hill. Reprinted by permission of The McGraw-Hill Companies.

The topic of this paragraph is:

_____

After you have gone over this exercise set in class or had it checked, review any item you missed to determine why you missed it. Did you mark any sentences that did not contain the topic? Did you underline a question? For the stated main idea, did you underline any examples (which are always details)?

Use the lines below to write down the types of mistake you made. Pinpointing your mistakes is what will prevent you from making those same mistakes in the future. Writing them down forces you to be precise about what the problem is.

_____

_____

_____

_____

_____

_____

_____

_____

SET 3

Exercises: Identifying the Stated Main Idea Sentence

Your skills should be even stronger now. Ready to try the final eight passages? They are slightly more challenging, but there are fewer of them. Take a few full breaths to help you relax and gather your concentration. Read each paragraph and determine its topic. (*Coach's tip:* Jot the topic in the margin beside the paragraph before you try to locate the stated main idea sentence.) To locate the stated main idea, find the sentence that answers the question, *What is the one most important thing the author wants me to understand about the topic?* Then underline that sentence. Use pencil rather than a highlighter so that if you change your mind, it doesn't create a problem.

1.   Like clichés, euphemisms can confuse people who are unfamiliar with their meaning. A euphemism is a more polite, pleasant expression used in place of a socially unacceptable form. In one expert's opinion, euphemisms enter the language to "camouflage the naked truth." Most people use euphemisms in their everyday language. Euphemisms are frequently substituted for short, abrupt words, the names of physical functions, or the terms for some unpleasant social situations. Although euphemisms are frequently considered more polite than the words for which they are substituted, they distort reality. For example, you might hear people say "powder my nose," "see a man about a dog," "the little girls' room," or "go to the bathroom" instead of "urinate."

Source: Judy Pearson, Paul Nelson, Scott Titsworth, and Lynn Harter, *Human Communication,* 2d ed., p. 67. Copyright © 2006 McGraw-Hill. Reprinted by permission of The McGraw-Hill Companies.

2.   When studying the world of living things, biologists and other scientists use the scientific process. Observations along with previous data are used to formulate a hypothesis. New observations and/or experiments are carried out in order to test the hypothesis. Scientists often do controlled experiments. The control sample does not go through the step being tested, and this acts as a safeguard against a wrong conclusion.

Source: Sylvia Mader, *Inquiry into Life,* 9th ed., p. 14. Copyright © 2000 McGraw-Hill. Reprinted by permission of The McGraw-Hill Companies.

3.   Russian novelist Fyodor Dostoyevski commented that "The degree of civilization in society can be judged by entering its prisons." Anyone observing conditions in many of America's jails and lockups would question just how civilized we really are. At the Erie County Holding Center, the second largest jail in New York state, inmates are jammed in so tight sometimes 300 men must sleep on the floor. Wherever a mattress can be thrown, an inmate may be sleeping, even next to toilets. Overcrowding conditions similar to those in Erie County have given rise to a number of lawsuits in recent years, from such varied places as Kenton County, Ohio; Onondaga and Broome counties in New York; and Blount County, Tennessee.

Source: Freda Adler, Gerhard Mueller, and William Laufer, *Criminal Justice: An Introduction,* 3d ed., p. 358. Copyright © 2003 McGraw-Hill. Reprinted by permission of The McGraw-Hill Companies.

4.   **The Drug Enforcement Administration**

Established in 1973, the Drug Enforcement Administration (DEA) is the primary federal agency responsible for the enforcement of federal laws concerning the use, sale, and distribution of narcotics and other controlled substances in the United States. Of the DEA's over 9,200 staff members, nearly half are special agents. The agency is headquartered in New York; its agents are stationed throughout the United States in 21 divisional offices and 14 strike forces in major cities. Some agents are posted overseas.

Source: Freda Adler, Gerhard Mueller, and William Laufer, *Criminal Justice: An Introduction,* 3d ed., p. 121. Copyright © 2003 McGraw-Hill. Reprinted by permission of The McGraw-Hill Companies.

5.   Analysts sometimes use the words such as *liberal, conservative, populist,* and *libertarian* to describe how ordinary Americans think about politics. These are ideological terms, as are terms such as *socialism* and *communism.* An **ideology** is a consistent pattern of political attitudes that stem from a core belief. The core belief of socialism, for example, is that society should ensure that every person's basic economic needs are met. Accordingly, a socialist would support public policies that provide for economic security, such as a government-guaranteed annual income for all families.

Source: Thomas Patterson, *We the People,* 6th ed., p. 211. Copyright © 2006 McGraw-Hill. Reprinted by permission of The McGraw-Hill Companies.

6.   The stereotype of the homosexual, particularly the male, is one of promiscuity. Indeed, there is some basis for that stereotype; about half of all white males in one study reported that they had had over five hundred partners. However, Riedmann (1995) estimated that 75 percent of lesbians and 50 percent of gay men are in stable, monogamous relationships at any given time. The point is that many gays, and an even greater proportion of lesbians, try to form stable, monogamous relationships.

Source: Robert Lauer and Jeanette Lauer, *Marriage and Family,* 4th ed., p. 53. Copyright © 2000 McGraw-Hill. Reprinted by permission of The McGraw-Hill Companies.

7.   Research done by Hawken, Duncan, and Kelly (1991) shows that college students who get involved with others tend to stay in college whereas those who are uninvolved tend to drop out. These researchers point out that "socially integrated students are more likely to live in a dormitory, have a part-time job on campus, participate in clubs and social organizations, and declare an academic major earlier in their careers." Students appear to have the most difficulty establishing social integration in their first year at school, when 60 percent of the dropping out occurs.

Source: Judy Pearson and Paul Nelson, *An Introduction to Human Communication,* 8th ed., pp. 151–52. Copyright © 2000 McGraw-Hill. Reprinted by permission of The McGraw-Hill Companies.

8.   People who use computer keyboards—some of whom make as many as 21,600 keystrokes an hour—account for some RSI (repetitive strain injury) cases that result in lost work time. Before computers came along, typists would stop to make corrections or to change paper. These motions had the effect of providing many small rest breaks. Today, computer users must devise their own minibreaks to prevent excessive use of the hands and wrists that can lead to RSI injuries. People who use a mouse for more than a few hours a day—graphic designers, desktop publishing professionals, and the like—are also showing up with increased RSI injuries.

Source: Adapted from Fred Hofstetter, *Internet Literacy,* p. 272. Copyright © 2006 McGraw-Hill/Irwin. Reprinted by permission of The McGraw-Hill Companies.

Your performance on the practice exercises should give you some very helpful feedback on how well you understand the concept of a stated main idea sentence. Locating the stated main idea sentence is such a crucial skill that you need to nail it down as well as possible before moving on to other skills. Realistically, of course, you're probably not going to have it down perfectly at this point. It takes lots of practice. But do whatever you need to at this point to clear up any confusion you have. It will be well worth the effort in the long run.

C H A P T E R 5

Formulate the Implied Main Idea Sentence of a Paragraph

FORMULATE THE IMPLIED MAIN IDEA SENTENCE OF A PARAGRAPH

In Chapter 4, you learned that the main idea always answers the question, "What is the author's one most important point about the topic?" You also learned certain characteristics of main idea sentences:

- The main idea sentence always contains the topic of the paragraph.
- The main idea sentence always makes complete sense by itself.
- The main idea sentence is a general sentence that sums up the paragraph.
- The details in the paragraph explain or tell more about the information in the main idea sentence.

As you will also recall from Chapter 4, you must first determine the topic before you can determine the main idea. Further, you learned that the main idea is always expressed as a complete sentence, and the subject of that sentence is usually the topic.

Although every paragraph has a main idea, not every paragraph has the main idea stated in it. Even when authors do not state the main idea, they still imply the main idea. That is, they still provide enough information for the reader to reason out the main idea. *Imply* means to hint or suggest something rather than stating it outright. *When authors imply their main point rather than stating it as a single sentence, it is called an* **implied main idea,** *and the reader must formulate a sentence that expresses the author's main point.* You may also hear implied main ideas referred to as *formulated main ideas, unstated main ideas,* or *indirectly stated main* *ideas*. These are just different names for the same thing: an author's main idea that is put into words (as one complete sentence) by the reader.

To determine the main idea, ask yourself the question you learned in Chapter 4: "What is the author's one *most* important point about the topic?" The only difference is that when the author only implies the main idea, it is the *reader* who has to formulate it and write it as a sentence. (Even though you are the one writing the sentence, remember that you still have to tell the *author's* most important point.) When the main idea is implied, the question to ask yourself is, "What is the one most important point the author wants me to infer about the topic of this paragraph?"

As noted, the only difference between a stated main idea and an implied main idea is *who* puts the main idea into words: the author or the reader. If the author includes a stated main idea, you can locate it, then underline or highlight it exactly as it appears in the paragraph. However, when the author implies the main idea, you must formulate (create) a *single* sentence that tells the author's main point. Sometimes you can combine several words and ideas directly from the paragraph when you create this sentence; at other times, you will need to use more of your own words. Remember that the characteristics of main ideas (listed at the beginning of the chapter) also apply to implied main ideas. Check to see that any main idea sentence you write has those four characteristics.

Do you remember this paragraph from the beginning of Chapter 3, Determining the Topic of a Paragraph? Its topic is *year 2000 U.S. Census Bureau data on living patterns*. Take a minute to reread it:

> U.S. Census Bureau data on living patterns revealed that in 2000, for the first time, the number of Americans living alone exceeded the number of married couples living with children. Not surprisingly, the number of single-parent households also continued to rise. In addition, there was a staggering increase between 1990 and 2000 in the number of cohabiting couples.

Each sentence in the paragraph above is a detail; the paragraph does not have a stated main idea sentence. It would be up to you, the reader, to grasp the main point the author is making with these details: *The year 2000 U.S. Census Bureau data on living patterns revealed many significant changes.* (In fact, if you put this sentence at the beginning of the paragraph, it would work perfectly as the stated main idea.)

When you read any paragraph, look first for a stated main idea sentence. If there is not one (and most often there is), *then* think about how you, the reader, could formulate a sentence that expresses the author's most important idea.

As noted above, when authors imply the main idea rather than state it, they *always* give you all the "ingredients" you need. In this chapter, you'll learn three "recipes"—actually, three formulas—for creating implied main idea sentences. You will always be able to use one of the formulas to "formulate" the main idea. (I'm using the word *formulate* to mean "create" or "put into words.")

USE THE THREE FORMULAS FOR FORMULATING AN IMPLIED MAIN IDEA SENTENCE

To determine the implied main idea, ask yourself, "What is the one most important point the author wants me to infer about the topic of this paragraph?" Now you'll learn the three formulas (strategies) for creating implied main idea sentences. One of them should always work for you—and that should be comforting for you to know! To determine which formula to use, you will have to see what the author gives you in the paragraph to work with.

FORMULA 1: ADD ESSENTIAL INFORMATION TO A SENTENCE IN THE PARAGRAPH THAT *ALMOST* STATES THE MAIN IDEA

Sometimes a paragraph contains a sentence that *almost* states the main idea, but it lacks some essential piece of information. The "missing piece" is usually the topic. Because the entire paragraph is about the same topic, the author doesn't use it in every sentence. The author assumes you know that all of the sentences refer to the topic. (Although the missing, essential information is usually the topic, it could be something else. You have to determine what you must add to make a complete main idea sentence.) Applying Formula 1 is easy because the author has done most of the work for you—you just need to add the missing ingredient that makes the idea complete.

Here's a paragraph from a human development textbook. Its topic is *attention-deficit hyperactivity disorder (ADHD),* and its implied main idea exemplifies Formula 1.

> *Attention-deficit hyperactivity disorder (ADHD)* is the newest name applied to a complex disorder that has long puzzled professionals. It is believed to be the most common behavioral disorder in U.S. youngsters today. Some experts say it afflicts some 3.5 million youngsters, or up to 5 percent of those under age 18. It is two to three times more likely to be diagnosed in boys than in girls.

Source: Adapted from James Vander Zanden, revised by Thomas Crandell and Corinne Crandell, *Human Development,* Updated 7th ed., p. 321. Copyright © 2003 McGraw-Hill. Reprinted by permission of The McGraw-Hill Companies.

Topic: attention-deficit hyperactivity disorder (ADHD)

Implied main idea: [Attention-deficit hyperactivity disorder (ADHD)] is believed to be the most common behavioral disorder in U.S. youngsters today.

Notice that the second sentence *almost* states the main idea, but it falls short in one important way: it lacks the topic. If you read it by itself, you would wonder what "it" was. When you add the topic in place of the word "it," you create a main idea sentence that makes complete sense by itself.

You'll often be able to use Formula 1 when you read a paragraph that begins with a question. Typically, authors answer this question in the very next sentence, but they do not always repeat the topic or include enough information for the second sentence to make complete sense by itself. You have to add the topic or missing information to create a complete main idea. Read this example from a textbook on adolescence:

> Are there ways that parents can reduce parent–adolescent conflict? One of the best methods is collaborative problem solving, in which the goal is to discover a solution that satisfies both the adolescent and the parent. The process often works best when discussion is restricted to a single issue and the adolescent's agreement to try to work out a solution is secured in advance.

Source: Adapted from John Santrock, *Adolescence,* 8th ed., p. 158. Copyright © 2001 McGraw-Hill. Reprinted by permission of The McGraw-Hill Companies.

Topic: <u>reducing parent-adolescent conflict</u>

Implied main idea: <u>One of the best methods of [reducing parent-adolescent conflict] is collaborative problem solving, in which the goal is to discover a solution that satisfies both the adolescent and the parent.</u>

The second sentence *almost* tells the main idea, but it lacks the topic. If a reader reads that sentence by itself, the person would be wondering "one of the best methods to do *what?*" When you add the topic, the second sentence makes total sense and conveys the author's most important general point.

FORMULA 2: COMBINE INTO A SINGLE SENTENCE TWO SENTENCES FROM THE PARAGRAPH THAT *TOGETHER* EXPRESS THE COMPLETE MAIN IDEA

Sometimes you will read paragraphs in which there are *two* sentences that each give *part* of the main idea. If that's the case, you must combine them into a single sentence. This is because two sentences can't both be *the* most important sentence.

The two sentences can occur anywhere in a paragraph. They can be next to each other or separated by other sentences. You will usually need to use words such as *and, but, yet, nevertheless, moreover,* and so on, and/or punctuation marks when you join the two sentences.

The following psychology textbook paragraph is an example. Its topic is *tension in families with adolescents.*

In most families with adolescents, tension increases. The amount of arguing and bickering clearly rises. Most young teenagers, as part of their search for identity, experience tension between their attempts to become independent from their parents and their actual dependency on them. They may experiment with a range of behaviors, flirting with a variety of activities that their parents, and even society as a whole, find objectionable. Happily, for most families such tensions stabilize during middle adolescence and eventually decline around age 18.

Source: Adapted from Robert Feldman, *Essentials of Understanding Psychology,* 6th ed., p. 373. Copyright © 2005 McGraw-Hill. Reprinted by permission of The McGraw-Hill Companies.

Topic: <u>tension in families with adolescents</u>

Implied main idea: <u>In most families with adolescents, tension increases, but happily, for most families such tensions stabilize during middle adolescence and eventually decline around age 18.</u>

The first sentence in the paragraph contains very important information. So does the last sentence. Each tells part of the main idea, and neither by itself would be sufficient. Therefore, you must combine them to create a complete main idea sentence: *In most families with adolescents, tension increases + Happily, for most families such tensions stabilize during middle adolescence and eventually decline around age 18.* The complete main idea sentence would be, *In most families with adolescents, tension increases, but happily, for most families such tensions stabilize during middle adolescence and eventually decline around age 18.* The word *but* was added to show the relationship between the ideas in the sentences that were combined.

It is important that you learn to express the main idea as a *single* sentence, even when the author has put parts of the main idea in separate sentences in the paragraph. One reason for this is that when you aren't really sure what you're doing (or if you get tired or distracted or lazy or sloppy!), you may start underlining several sentences in every paragraph. That won't help you at all. In fact, it will confuse you and cause you to overmark your textbooks. From the beginning, you should strive to formulate implied main ideas correctly. Otherwise, it's like a tennis player who gets used to hitting sloppy shots in practice. When it's time for the real thing, that person is going to play the way he or she has practiced.

FORMULA 3: SUMMARIZE DETAILS INTO ONE *GENERAL* SENTENCE OR COMBINE *SEVERAL* IMPORTANT IDEAS INTO ONE SENTENCE

In other words,

■ Write a *general* sentence (a general inference) that is based on the details; that is, write the *general* point that the details suggest or illustrate. (Inferences will be discussed thoroughly in Chapter 9.)

—*or*—

■ Write a sentence that combines *important* ideas from *several* sentences. When you combine important information from several sentences, remember that *you are not combining details* to create the main idea. Main idea sentences do not contain details. The important information that you combine consists of parts of the main idea; it does not consist of details.

This chart shows you how to use Formula 3. The column on the left tells the "ingredients" the author gives you in the paragraph. The column on the right tells what you should do with them

If there are only details in the paragraph	→	Write a general sentence that sums them up or tells the point they are making.
If there are important *ideas* spread throughout the paragraph	→	Combine them into one sentence.

These two strategies are so similar that they can be considered the same "formula." In either case, you are summarizing or combining information.

General sentences are broad, nonspecific statements. An example of a general statement would be *Reliable information about sex can help you stay more physically and emotionally healthy.* The other sentences in the paragraph, the details, might explain what specifically is meant by "reliable information" and the ways in which it can help you stay "more physically and emotionally healthy."

This sample paragraph from a communications textbook illustrates how you can formulate a general sentence that sums up the details. Its topic is *changes that affect your relationships with others.* The whole paragraph consists of details, so you must summarize the point they "add up" to.

What kinds of changes might you expect in your own life that will affect your relationships with others? You may change your job 10 or more times. You may move your place of residence even more frequently. You probably will be married at least once, and possibly two or three times. You probably will have one child or more. You will experience loss of family members through death and dissolution of relationships. You may have a spouse whose needs conflict with your needs. Other family members may view the world differently than you and challenge your perceptions. When your life appears to be most stable and calm, unexpected changes will occur.

Source: Judy C. Pearson and Paul E. Nelson, *An Introduction to Human Communication,* 8th ed., pp. 169–70. Copyright © 2000 McGraw-Hill. Reprinted by permission of The McGraw-Hill Companies.

Topic: changes that affect your relationships with others

Implied main idea: There are many different kinds of changes in your lifetime that will affect your relationships with others.

—or— In your own life, you will experience many kinds of changes that will affect your relationships with others.

The paragraph begins with a question, "What kinds of changes might you expect in your own life that will affect your relationships with others?" The authors answer this question by giving numerous *examples* of changes that affect people's relationships: changing jobs and residences, marriage and other family changes, conflicts in needs, changes in perceptions, and so forth. They give you lots of examples so that you can reason out the general point they are making: *In your life, you will experience <u>many kinds</u> of changes that will affect your relationships.* Notice that the formulated main idea sentence does not include any of the specific examples because examples are details.

Here's a paragraph I've written to illustrate the other Formula 3 situation, combining important ideas (not details!).

American John Cage (1912–1992) is best known as a composer. His avant-garde music, which focused on pure sound, often shocked listeners. In the piece 4'33", for example, the musicians sit silently with their instruments for four minutes and 33 seconds. What many people do not realize is that Cage was also a talented artist.

Topic: John Cage

Implied main idea: John Cage is best known as an avant-garde American composer, but he was also a talented artist.

The formulated main idea combines the important ideas from the paragraph. By the way, this type of Formula 3 implied main idea sentence is a little like Formula 2 in the sense that things are being combined. In Formula 2, however, you are combining *two sentences,* each of which gives half of the main idea. In Formula 3 you are combining *three or more important ideas* into one sentence.

When you use Formula 3, you will often have to use more of your own words when you create the main idea sentence. Unlike Formula 1 (in which you can simply add information to a sentence that almost states the main idea) and Formula 2 (in which you might have to add only a word of two when you combine two sentences), you may have to use words that do not even appear in the paragraph when you use Formula 3.

THE TRAINER

OBSERVE THE SKILL OF FORMULATING THE IMPLIED MAIN IDEA SENTENCE

Once again, our "effective reader" has shown up just in time to show you how he or she would approach a paragraph that has an implied main idea. The paragraph used in the illustration is a different version of the simple paragraph that was used as an example in the last chapter. Read the paragraph first, and then read the notations that reveal the effective reader's thought processes.

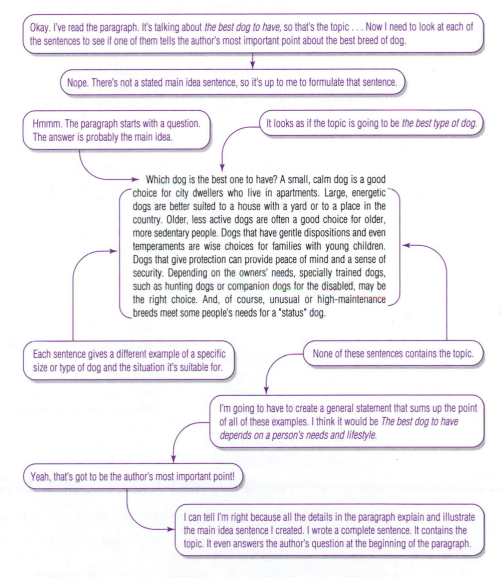

Okay. I've read the paragraph. It's talking about *the best dog to have,* so that's the topic . . . Now I need to look at each of the sentences to see if one of them tells the author's most important point about the best breed of dog.

Nope. There's not a stated main idea sentence, so it's up to me to formulate that sentence.

Hmmm. The paragraph starts with a question. The answer is probably the main idea.

It looks as if the topic is going to be *the best type of dog.*

Which dog is the best one to have? A small, calm dog is a good choice for city dwellers who live in apartments. Large, energetic dogs are better suited to a house with a yard or to a place in the country. Older, less active dogs are often a good choice for older, more sedentary people. Dogs that have gentle dispositions and even temperaments are wise choices for families with young children. Dogs that give protection can provide peace of mind and a sense of security. Depending on the owners' needs, specially trained dogs, such as hunting dogs or companion dogs for the disabled, may be the right choice. And, of course, unusual or high-maintenance breeds meet some people's needs for a "status" dog.

Each sentence gives a different example of a specific size or type of dog and the situation it's suitable for.

None of these sentences contains the topic.

I'm going to have to create a general statement that sums up the point of all of these examples. I think it would be *The best dog to have depends on a person's needs and lifestyle.*

Yeah, that's got to be the author's most important point!

I can tell I'm right because all the details in the paragraph explain and illustrate the main idea sentence I created. I wrote a complete sentence. It contains the topic. It even answers the author's question at the beginning of the paragraph.

Notice that our hypothetical reader's implied main idea sentence contains a word that wasn't even in the paragraph: *lifestyle.* Although the author did not use that word, it can be used to describe city dwellers; older, sedentary adults; families whose lifestyles include young children; and those who have a stylish, status-oriented lifestyle.

POINTERS ABOUT FORMULATING THE IMPLIED MAIN IDEA SENTENCE

■ **You must write the main idea as a *single* sentence.**
I know, I know. I've already said it a bunch of times, but it's so important that I'm saying it again! Memorize it. Tattoo it on the back of your hand. Whatever it takes. (Okay, forget the tattoo, but do remember that the main idea must always be written as one, complete sentence. Remember, too, that we consider any paragraph that doesn't have a stated main idea to have a formulated main idea.)

■ **If you are not sure how to tell if you have written a complete sentence, get help from your instructor, a tutor, or a classmate.**
Some students struggle with formulated main idea sentences because they can't tell whether they've written a complete sentence. Every sentence has to have a subject and a verb, and it has to express a complete thought. Instead, though, they often write a longer version of the topic or just a fragment that doesn't express the author's complete main point. For example, instead of writing the sentence *There are several barriers to effective reading,* they write *Barriers to effective reading* (they give just the topic; they don't include a verb). Another type of error to avoid is writing a sentence, but leaving out the topic: *There are barriers.* Don't do that either. If you need to review sentence structure, get the help you need. Otherwise, it's like practicing your golf swing without knowing exactly how to hold the golf club. You'll wear yourself out and never make any progress.

■ **When you formulate a main idea sentence, do not include *anything* else in the sentence except the author's most important point.**
Do not start your sentence with "The author's main point is . . . ," "The author says . . . ," "The author wants us to know . . . ," or "The main idea is. . . ." You do that kind of stuff, and you'll never make it across the goal line! For example, if the main idea is, *There are two types of cell division,* just write that. Do *not* write, *The author wants us to know that there are two types of cell division.*

■ **It's possible to formulate the main idea sentence in several different, but equally correct, ways.**
There's no one, right way to express the main idea of a paragraph. That may seem surprising, but as long as the meaning is correct, the exact wording doesn't matter. (You know that different people can say the same things different ways, yet the *meaning* is still the same.) For example, these sentences would all be perfectly acceptable versions of the main idea for the same paragraph:

The ability to communicate clearly is the most important skill you will ever master.

The most important skill you will ever master is the ability to communicate.

There is no more important skill to master than the ability to communicate.

Notice that although the wording is different in these three sentences, the *meaning* is the same.

■ **Even when Formula 1 or Formula 2 will work, you can put the implied main idea in your own words.**
You know that when you use Formula 3, you often have to use lots of your own words, including ones that don't appear in the paragraph. The truth is,

you can actually write *any* main idea sentence in your own words *as long as the meaning is correct*. Suppose, for example, that the implied main idea is, *Studies show that Americans spend a significant amount of time on the important activity of listening.* You could shorten this and say it this way: *Americans spend a significant amount of time listening.* Feel free to write the implied main idea sentence in your own words if it makes the sentence shorter or easier for you to understand. Just be sure that regardless of how you word the sentence, it expresses the *author's* most important point.

■ **When you formulate an implied main idea sentence, do not include details.**
One more time: When you are learning to use Formula 3, you may *think* at first that you are including details when you create a main idea sentence. However, remember that you are either (1) writing a general sentence that *sums* up the details (such as, "All children go through certain stages as they move toward adulthood") or (2) writing a sentence that *combines several important ideas* (such as, "Odd-even pricing presents prices at values just below an even amount, and marketers use it because it makes the price seem lower to consumers"). The ideas that you are combining consist of important information from the paragraph; *they are not details.*

■ **Do not include information in your formulated main idea sentence simply because the information is interesting or seems familiar.**
When you do not understand the main idea of a paragraph, you may be tempted to pick things from the paragraph just because they grabbed your attention or you already knew them. Instead, you should reread the paragraph, use the clues to help you determine the topic, look up any unfamiliar words, think about what you have read, and take any other steps that will help you understand the *author's* most important point. Then you can formulate a correct implied main idea sentence.

■ **Don't go beyond what is in the paragraph and draw a sweeping conclusion.**
Let's say that a paragraph describes several disadvantages of a high-protein diet. Examples of a correct, logical formulated main idea would be *There are disadvantages of a high-protein diet* or *High-protein diets have certain disadvantages* or *There are some disadvantages to eating a high-protein diet.* Examples of incorrect main idea sentences that go *too far beyond* the information in the paragraph would be *There are no advantages to a high-protein diet, No one should ever follow a high-protein diet, You'd have to be stupid to follow a high-protein diet,* and *High-protein diets are terrible.*

■ **To verify that the main idea sentence you have formulated is correct, test it.**
Does the sentence you wrote meet the criteria for all main idea sentences: Is it a sentence? Does it contain the topic? Does it tell the author's most important point about the topic? Does it make complete sense by itself? If the answer to all these questions is *yes,* you've formulated the correct main idea. Go to the head of the class!

■ **Be sure you understand all the words in any main idea sentence that you formulate.**
It is not enough to formulate a correct main idea sentence. You must *understand* it as well. Suppose that the implied main idea is *During the early twentieth century, the national government took on regulatory and policy responsibilities imposed by the nation's transition from an agrarian to an industrial society.* (Whew!) Unless you know what *regulatory, agrarian,* and *industrial* mean, and which years comprise the 20th century, you cannot possibly understand the author's main point.

■ **It may take you a few minutes and several tries to work out an implied main idea sentence.**

Formulating implied main idea sentences involves thinking, and thinking takes time. Don't assume there's something wrong with you if you can't come up with a complete, perfectly worded sentence on the first try. It's normal to have to start by jotting down something rough, then adding to it, rearranging words, and tweaking it until you have a clear, complete main idea sentence.

■ **Longer reading selections may have overall main ideas that are implied.**

Sometimes a longer selection (for example, a chapter section, an essay, or a newspaper editorial) has an overall main idea that is stated. But sometimes a longer selection has an overall main idea that is implied. In that case, you will have to read the entire selection and create a single sentence that tells the author's most important overall main idea. It will be a very general sentence that sums up the entire selection or tells the single, most important conclusion that the author wants readers to draw.

■ **Formulating the implied main idea is a basic skill that underlies several study skills.**

In order to mark your textbooks effectively, take notes, create outlines, make concept maps, and write correct summaries, you must first be able to determine the main idea of each paragraph. This means that you must be able to formulate the main idea when the author does not state it. (The important study skills of note taking, outlining, making concept maps, and summarizing are presented in Chapter 14.)

■ **Some "paragraphs" aren't really paragraphs at all, but you still have to deal with them.**

You know that a paragraph is a group of sentences on the same topic and that those sentences are held together by a main idea. The sentences are written together as a "block," with the first sentence indented. Okay, here's a bit of bad news I need to mention: Every now and then you'll encounter "paragraphs" in textbooks that aren't paragraphs at all. Some of them are collections of facts (details) that pertain to one topic, but they lack a main point to hold them together. A second type of poorly written "paragraph" occurs when an author mistakenly plops the main idea for a paragraph at the end of the *preceding* paragraph rather than in the paragraph in which it belongs, and thus leaves a gap in the paragraph. A third problem occurs when the author strings the main idea across several successive paragraphs. You don't get the full main idea until you've read several paragraphs. Poor writing of these sorts seems to show up more often in science texts, books on technical subjects, and in some health-related texts, such as those used in nursing courses.

The important point to know is that you will occasionally encounter funky, troublesome "paragraphs" that really aren't paragraphs at all—they are just simply poor writing—and yet *you're still going to have to deal with them.* I know it's a bummer, but when you encounter poor writing, you must compensate for it by untangling the information and organizing it in a way that makes sense to you.

■ **Use these "math formula" counterparts if they help you understand the three implied main idea formulas.**

Professor Mary Dubbé, a reading instructor at Thomas Nelson Community College (Hampton, VA), reports that she and her reading students developed these counterparts for the three implied main idea formulas in the text. (I modified their third formula a bit.) Their creative formulas are based on the simple algebraic formula of $A + B = C$, and the concept of X, an unknown. C represents the formulated main idea. Thanks to Professor Dubbé and her students for sharing. Here are the math formulas, along with the versions given in the chapter:

$$A + X = C$$

This is for Formula 1: *Add essential missing information to a sentence that almost states the main idea.* A is a sentence in the paragraph that almost states the main idea. X is the missing piece of information that will compete the main idea sentence. C is the complete, formulated main idea sentence.

$$A + B = C$$

This is for Formula 2: *Combine two sentences that each give half of the main idea.* A is one of those sentences and B is the other; together they give C, the complete main idea.

$$D + D + D = C$$

This is for Formula 3: *Write a general sentence that sums up the details or combines several piece of important information.* The Ds are details that are "summed up" to produce C, the main idea. (Remember that the details have to be summarized in a general sentence, and not just strung together as a sentence.)

■ **Experiment with the general formula, Main Idea = Topic + Focus.**
When trying to determine the implied main idea, some students find it helpful to start with the general formula, Main Idea = Topic + Focus. After you read a paragraph, ask yourself, "What's the topic?" (who or what is being discussed). Then ask yourself, "What's the focus?" (the important thing the author is saying about the topic, the most important *point* about the topic). Once you determine both the topic and the focus, you will see that one of the three implied main ideas formulas explains the way in which the information comes from the passage.

THE REPLAY

REMEMBER THE ESSENTIAL INFORMATION FROM THE CHAPTER

How can you remember the three formulas? It's as simple as 1-2-3! Here is a memory peg that works for me:

Formula 1:   Add the **1** important, missing thing (usually the topic) to a sentence from the paragraph that almost states the main idea.

Formula 2:   Combine **2** sentences from the paragraph if each contains part of the main idea.

Formula 3:   Write a general sentence that sums up the details or synthesizes the ideas from **3** or more sentences of the paragraph.

When formulating implied main ideas, you must look at the type of information the author gives in the paragraph. The chart explains what you must do to formulate the implied main idea once you determine what the author has given you to work with.

THREE WAYS TO FORMULATE IMPLIED MAIN IDEA SENTENCES	
What the author gives you in the paragraph (the "ingredients" you are given to work with)	**What you must do with the information in order to formulate the implied main idea**
If the author gives you a sentence that *almost* states the main idea, but lacks some essential piece of information (usually the topic), use Formula 1.	*Formula 1: Add* the essential piece of information that is missing to that sentence. <u>How to apply the formula:</u> Use the sentence from the paragraph and simply add or insert the information. *or* Write the main idea in your own words as long as the meaning is the same.
If the author gives you two sentences in the paragraph that each present *part* of the main idea, use Formula 2.	*Formula 2: Combine* them into one sentence (because the main idea must always be written as a single sentence). <u>How to apply the formula:</u> You will probably have to add a word or two (such as *and, but,* or *although*) to connect the two sentences. *or* Write the main idea in your own words, as long as the meaning is the same.
If the author gives you details only or parts of the main idea spread throughout the paragraph, use Formula 3.	*Formula 3:* Write a *general sentence* that "sums up" the details or combines the most important information. <u>How to apply the formula:</u> Write a *general sentence;* it can consist mostly of your own words.

Study the chart and learn the information one formula (row) at a time. Study the first row. Then cover up the second column and try to say Formula 1 out loud from memory. Uncover it to see if you were correct. Repeat the process until you know Formula 1. Then do the same thing with the second and third rows until you learn Formula 2 and Formula 3. You should be able to recite the three formulas from memory. You can't practice applying them until you first know and understand them. Once you have learned them, you are ready to start the sets of practice exercises.

In case the drill instructor "chants" work for you, here's the one for implied main ideas.

With a stated main idea, just locate it.

If it's implied, then formulate it.

Which formula to use, you can decide

By seeing what the author supplied.

When you use Formula 1,

Add the topic to a sentence and you are done.

Formula 2 works just fine

With two sentences you can combine.

With Formula 3 you must construct

A general sentence that sums things up.

Main ideas, you can see,

Are as easy as 1-2-3.

Definition of Implied Main Idea Sentence

_____

_____

_____

Question You Should Ask Yourself

_____

_____

You should now know the three formulas that will enable you to formulate implied main idea sentences of paragraphs. Test yourself by writing the formulas from memory. (Write the complete formula for each, and not the "chant" version above.) When you have written all three, go back and check them against the chart. For any you couldn't remember completely or correctly, *review* them, *recite* them, and then *write them again*. Perfect practice makes perfect.

Formula 1

_____

_____

_____

_____

Formula 2

_____

_____

_____

_____

Formula 3

_____

_____

_____

_____

Time out. I know this is a challenging chapter. In fact, you would be surprised at how much time it took me, the author, to hammer out the implied main ideas for all of the paragraphs in the sets of practice exercises. I reread the paragraphs (often several times), and then reworked many of the implied main idea sentences several times until I arrived at wording that I felt was accurate and clear. I'm not telling you this to discourage you, but to let you know that if these exercises take you more time than the ones in the previous chapters, it means you're normal. No one can do implied main ideas in a flash.

You may be looking forward to trying the practice exercises to see if you understand how to apply the formulas, to see if you "got it." But maybe you're among those who are feeling a little overwhelmed, and you're *not* looking forward to the practice exercises. Even if you're not excited about doing them, you can help yourself by focusing on the long-term benefits of the practice they provide. It's easy to get excited about the *benefits* of mastering an important comprehension skill:

- You'll have an easier time understanding your college textbooks.
- You'll make higher grades on tests.
- You'll learn more.
- You'll make better grades in your courses.

Pretty impressive benefits, right? Keep your focus on that. Remember that it is *practice* that will enable you to reach those goals.

These exercises do take more thought and effort. Lou Holtz, the former South Carolina football coach, once remarked, "*Ability* is what you are capable of doing. *Motivation* determines what you do. *Attitude* is how you do it." Decide to use your ability as fully as possible. Decide to be motivated. Decide to bring a positive attitude to the task.

I encourage you to make these decisions. Then take a few minutes to close your eyes, breathe deeply, and *visualize* yourself giving your best effort on the practice exercises, patiently rereading and reworking each paragraph, if that's what it requires. You can skip this step, but if you do, you are choosing to limit your success.

THE PRACTICE

SET 1

APPLY THE SKILL OF FORMULATING THE IMPLIED MAIN IDEA SENTENCE

Exercises: Formulating the Implied Main Idea Sentence

Read each paragraph and determine the topic. Then determine the main idea by asking yourself, "What is the author's one *most* important point about the topic?" Create a sentence in your head or write one on paper that answers that question. As you write your sentence, refer to the chart on page 107. (You will benefit significantly more if you try to write your own sentence first than if you just read through the choices and pick one.) In the margin beside each paragraph, write the number of the formula you used. Select the answer choice that has the same *meaning* as the sentence you created. (The wording may be a little different, but the meaning should be the same.) If none of the answer choices matches the meaning of the sentence you created, then your main idea sentence is not correct! You should be able to explain in class how you arrived at the answer you chose. Remember not to choose a sentence that comes directly from the paragraph: *There are no stated main ideas in these paragraphs.*

It may help you to take a break halfway through these. (Don't leave town. Just take a five-minute break.) Or, if you prefer, give all of them your best effort at one sitting. Put a small question mark beside any you're unsure of. Then go back later and look at them again with fresh eyes. See if you still think your first answer is correct. Good luck! I'm cheering for you!

You may want to break the caffeine habit because it generates dependence. You may want to break it because you don't like the headache you get when you can't find a vending machine or when nobody at the office made coffee. Perhaps you want to set a good example for your children to avoid caffeine. Or you simply may want to live as drug-free as possible.

Source: Adapted from Wayne Payne and Dale Hahn, *Understanding Your Health,* 8th ed., p. 352. Copyright © 2005 McGraw-Hill. Reprinted by permission of The McGraw-Hill Companies.

_____ **1.** The implied main idea sentence for this paragraph is
  a. You may want to break the caffeine habit because it generates dependence.
  b. There are several reasons you may want to break the caffeine habit.
  c. Caffeine is a dangerous drug.
  d. Caffeine generates dependence and causes headaches.

Imagine trying to find a book in the Library of Congress without the aid of a card catalog. It would be next to impossible. That's the problem people faced in their initial efforts to find information on the World Wide Web. And that's what created the demand for another software program: the search engine. In rapid succession, a number of programs with catchy names such as Yahoo!, Excite, and InfoSeek emerged to act as search engines for the cyberspace traveler. The user could simply type in a name, a word, or a phrase, and the search engine would scour the Net for relevant information and website addresses.

Source: William F. Arens, *Contemporary Advertising,* 10th ed., pp. 544–45. Copyright © 2006 McGraw-Hill/Irwin. Reprinted by permission of The McGraw-Hill Companies.

_____ **2.** The implied main idea sentence for this paragraph is
  a. A search engine is a necessity for anyone who wishes to use the Library of Congress.
  b. It is a software program that allows a user to type in a name, a word, or a phrase, and the search engine would scour the Net for relevant information and website addresses.

    c. Yahoo!, Excite, and InfoSeek are three programs that benefit the cyberspace traveler.

    d. A search engine is a software program that allows a World Wide Web user to type in a name, a word, or a phrase, and it then scours the Net for relevant information and website addresses.

Does working improve or undermine a couple's relationship? The answer depends on a number of things. One is the nature of the wife's job. Long hours, frequent travel, or a demanding boss can spill over into family stress. A second factor is attitudes towards the gender roles, whether traditional, egalitarian, or transitional. Employed wives tend to be happier and healthier than full-time homemakers, particularly when their husbands approve of women working; married women are most depressed when they are at home full-time but would like to be working. Not surprisingly, marital satisfaction tends to be highest among working wives with high levels of education who work out of choice, enjoy their jobs, and receive help from their husbands; marital satisfaction tends to be lower among women who have low incomes from undesirable jobs. Time together is a problem for most working couples. The less time they spend together, the less likely they are to be satisfied with their marriage.

Source: Adapted from Richard Gelles and Ann Levine, *Sociology: An Introduction,* 6th ed., pp. 424–25. Copyright © 1999 McGraw-Hill. Reprinted by permission of The McGraw-Hill Companies.

_____ **3.** The implied main idea sentence for this paragraph is

    a. The answer to whether working improves or undermines a couple's relationship depends on a number of things.

    b. The nature of a wife's job can undermine a couple's relationship.

    c. Employed wives tend to be happier and healthier than full-time homemakers are.

    d. Wives should not work outside the home.

Experiencing failure is not easy. If we take a course and fail it, it hurts, though we may pretend for a moment that it doesn't. But even if you feel tempted to shrug it off publicly, don't make that mistake privately. It's important to take responsibility for and accept failure.

Source: Robert S. Feldman, *P.O.W.E.R. Learning,* p. 287. Copyright © 2000 McGraw-Hill. Reprinted by permission of The McGraw-Hill Companies.

_____ **4.** The implied main idea sentence for this paragraph is

    a. If we take a course and fail it, it's important to take responsibility for and accept failure.

    b. Experiencing failure is not easy, but it's important to take responsibility for and accept failure.

    c. Everyone experiences failure, and it is important not to let failure get you down.

    d. If you experience failure, you should pretend it doesn't hurt and shrug it off publicly.

Written memos and reports document what was said and done and the reason for decisions. Carefully written memos and reports enable a company to use its earlier expertise without having to reinvent the wheel every time a new set of people tackles a recurring problem. Written documents also allow individuals and companies to protect themselves. If there is no written record, chaos—and expensive lawsuits—may result.

Source: Kitty Locker, *Business and Administrative Communication,* 5th ed., pp. 5–6. Copyright © 2000 McGraw-Hill. Reprinted by permission of The McGraw-Hill Companies.

_____ **5.** The implied main idea sentence for this paragraph is
    a. Written records can help companies prevent lawsuits.
    b. Written documents also allow individuals and companies to protect themselves.
    c. Written memos and documents benefit companies and individuals in several ways.
    d. It is important for employees to learn how to write clear documents and memos.

Though steroids make muscles stronger, tendons and ligaments do not proportionately increase in strength. Therefore, a strong muscle contraction can tear a tendon and/or a ligament. This is made more serious because the steroids make the injury heal more slowly. When steroids increase muscle size, the extra muscle can grow around the bones and joints, causing them to break more easily.

Source: Charles Corbin, Greg Welk, William Corbin, and Karen Welk, *Concepts of Physical Fitness,* 13th ed., p. 179. Copyright © 2006 McGraw-Hill. Reprinted by permission of The McGraw-Hill Companies.

_____ **6.** The implied main idea sentence for this paragraph is
    a. Steroids make muscles grow stronger, but they can cause injuries to happen more easily and to heal more slowly.
    b. Though steroids make muscles stronger, they can cause tears in tendons and/or ligaments.
    c. They cause slow-healing injuries.
    d. It is foolish to take steroids.

Virtual reality is also known as **VR, artificial reality,** or **virtual environments.** Virtual reality hardware includes headgear and gloves. The headgear has earphones and three-dimensional stereoscopic screens. The gloves have sensors that collect data about your hand movements. Coupled with software, this interactive sensory equipment lets you immerse yourself in a computer-generated world.

Source: Adapted from Timothy O'Leary and Linda O'Leary, *Computing Essentials, 2001–2002,* complete ed., p. 219. Copyright © 2001 McGraw-Hill. Reprinted by permission of The McGraw-Hill Companies.

_____ **7.** The implied main idea sentence for this paragraph is
    a. Virtual reality is also known as VR, artificial reality, or virtual environments.
    b. Headgear and sensory gloves are necessary for virtual reality.
    c. Coupled with software, interactive sensory equipment lets you immerse yourself in virtual reality, a computer-generated world.
    d. Virtual reality headgear has earphones and three-dimensional stereoscopic screens.

Law enforcement officers are constantly faced with danger. Events go from routine to life-threatening in seconds. The risk of being shot—or having to shoot someone—is high. Each year over 50,000 police officers are assaulted. Fifty-five were feloniously killed in 1996. Officers lawfully kill between 3,000 and 4,000 persons annually. It's not a job that brings a lot of love from the public, either. Police work subjects officers to the temptation of corruption, and although only a small percent become corrupt, widespread publicity taints all officers. The abuse of force on the part of a few police officers likewise tarnishes the reputation of entire departments.

Source: Freda Adler, Gerhard Mueller, and William Laufer, *Criminal Justice: An Introduction,* 3d ed., p. 193. Copyright © 2003 McGraw-Hill. Reprinted by permission of The McGraw-Hill Companies.

_____ **8.** The implied main idea sentence for this paragraph is
   a. Law enforcement officers are constantly faced with danger because events go from routine to life-threatening in seconds.
   b. A large part of the public views the police as corrupt and has a low opinion of all police officers.
   c. If you decide to become a law enforcement officer, you should be aware that there will be temptations to become corrupt.
   d. Law enforcement officers are constantly faced with danger, and it's not a job that brings a lot of love from the public, either.

Every student wants to succeed in school. The same qualities that get you hired and promoted can also help you succeed in this area. Your instructor will be just as impressed as your boss with good communication skills, thorough preparation, good manners, and adherence to commitments.

Source: Adapted from Sharon Ferrett, *Peak Performance,* 5th ed., pp. 3–13 and 3–14. Copyright © 2006 McGraw-Hill. Reprinted by permission of The McGraw-Hill Companies.

_____ **9.** The implied main idea sentence for this paragraph is
   a. Every student wants to succeed in school.
   b. The same qualities that get you hired and promoted can also help you succeed in school.
   c. Students should try to impress their instructors with good communication skills and good manners.
   d. Students should approach school like a job.

Arson has always been viewed as a more violent crime than burglary. In comparison with burglary, however, arson is a fairly infrequent offense. A total of 76,760 arson offenses was reported in 2001. A national survey of fire departments, however, indicates that the actual number of arson incidents is likely to be far higher than the reported figure.

Source: Freda Adler, Gerhard Mueller, and William Laufer, *Criminology,* 5th ed., p. 312. Copyright © 2004 McGraw-Hill. Reprinted by permission of The McGraw-Hill Companies.

_____ **10.** The implied main idea sentence for this paragraph is
   a. Arson has always been viewed as a more violent crime than burglary, and although the actual number of arson incidents is unknown, it occurs much less often than burglary.
   b. A national survey of fire departments indicates that the actual number of arson incidents is likely to be far higher than the figure reported in 2001.
   c. Arson is viewed as a more violent crime than burglary because more people are more likely to die in fires set by arsonists.
   d. The country has no accurate way of determining how many arson offenses are committed each year.

Verbal symbols are only the tip of the communication iceberg. On the basis of his experiments, psychologist Albert Mehrabian concluded that the total impact of a message is 7 percent verbal, 38 percent vocal, and 55 percent facial. Another specialist has suggested that no more than 30 to 35 percent of the social meaning of a conversation or an interaction is carried by its words. Nonverbal messages abound, and we "read" a good deal into them without necessarily being aware of doing so.

Source: Adapted from Michael Hughes, Carolyn Kroehler, and James Vander Zanden, *Sociology: The Core,* 6th ed., pp. 75–6. Copyright © 2002 McGraw-Hill. Reprinted by permission of The McGraw-Hill Companies.

_____ 11. The implied main idea sentence for this paragraph is
- **a.** Verbal symbols are only the tip of the communication iceberg.
- **b.** Verbal symbols are only the tip of the communication iceberg, but on the basis of his experiments, psychologist Albert Mehrabian concluded that the total impact of a message is 7 percent verbal, 38 percent vocal, and 55 percent facial.
- **c.** Considerable research has been done on nonverbal communication.
- **d.** Verbal symbols are only the tip of the communication iceberg; nonverbal messages abound, and we "read" a good deal into them without necessarily being aware of doing so.

Victims of sexual aggression, including sexual harassment, are more likely to be female than male. Rape—sexual intercourse forced upon a person by either psychological coercion or physical force—affects many more women than men. More than one in five women report that they have been forced to do something of a sexual nature. Contrary to popular myth, rape is not a crime committed in dark alleys by sexually frustrated strangers. The vast majority of rapists—as many as three-quarters or more—are known to their victims. Almost half (47 percent) of college women who are victims of rape are raped by dates or romantic partners.

Source: J. John Palen, *Social Problems of the Twenty-First Century,* pp. 134–35. Copyright © 2001 McGraw-Hill. Reprinted by permission of The McGraw-Hill Companies.

_____ 12. The implied main idea sentence for this paragraph is
- **a.** Rape affects many more women than men, with more than one in five women reporting that they have been forced to do something of a sexual nature.
- **b.** Victims of sexual aggression are more likely to be female than male, and contrary to popular myth, the vast majority of rapists are known to their victims.
- **c.** Contrary to popular myth, rape is not a crime committed in dark alleys by sexually frustrated strangers; in fact, the vast majority of rapists are known to their victims.
- **d.** Women, especially college women, need to be more selective about their dates and romantic partners because almost half of them who are rape victims are raped by those men.

Good job! You're on your way. After you go over these exercises in class or get them back after they've been graded, go through them to determine the types of errors you made. I can't emphasize strongly enough how important it is for you to understand the *types* of mistakes you've made. Did applying one particular formula cause you more difficulty than the others? Ultimately you're going to have to be able to monitor and evaluate your own comprehension once you complete your reading course. The time to begin learning to do that is now.

SET 2

Exercises: Formulating the Implied Main Idea Sentence

Because the topic of a paragraph is typically the subject of the main idea sentence, start by determining the topic of each paragraph and writing it in the space provided. Then use the formulas you learned in this chapter to help you formulate the implied main idea sentence. (You may find it helpful to refer to the chart on page 107.) Be sure that you write a complete sentence, that it includes the topic, and that it tells the author's most important point about the topic. Get out some scratch paper so that you can get each formulated main idea sentence just the way you want it before you write it in the space provided. If you have done the Set 1 Exercises, think about any errors you made on them so that you can avoid those same types of mistakes on the Set 2 Exercises.

If you discover that you are getting tired or frustrated, stop for a few minutes, stretch, and refocus your attention. If you are stumped on a particular paragraph after your best effort, write down what you think is correct, then move on to the next one. After you have done all of the items, return to any that seemed difficult.

Don't leave any items unanswered. Ice hockey superstar Wayne Gretzky said, "You miss 100 percent of the shots you never make." You leave an item blank, and you'll miss it 100 percent. Not only that, but you'll lose the opportunity to analyze any mistake you made and to learn from it. Even if you're not sure that your answer is exactly right, give it your best effort, and write it down.

What are the economic and emotional effects for children living in homes with only one parent? Single-parent families are often economically less well off, and this has an impact on children's opportunities. Over a third of single-mother families with children have incomes below the poverty line. In addition, good childcare is often hard to find. A third effect on children is that time is always at a premium in single-parent families. Furthermore, for children of divorce, the parents' separation is often a painful experience that may result in obstacles in establishing relationships later in life. Finally, children may blame themselves for the breakup or feel pressure to take sides.

Source: Adapted from Robert Feldman, *Essentials of Understanding Psychology,* 6th ed., p. 379. Copyright © 2005 McGraw-Hill. Reprinted by permission of The McGraw-Hill Companies.

1. Topic: _____

   Implied main idea: _____

   _____

By now you know that HIV/AIDS has to do with the most intimate aspects of our life, namely sexual behavior. Although HIV is tied closely to the sexual aspects of your life, it is also related to drug use, blood transfusion, pregnancy, and birth. At present there are no effective vaccines against HIV/AIDS. Your best protection against this deadly disease is establishing caring, respectful relationships and educating yourself so that you can avoid behaviors that expose you to infection.

Source: Frank D. Cox, *The AIDS Booklet,* 6th ed., p. 2. Copyright © 2000 McGraw-Hill. Reprinted by permission of The McGraw-Hill Companies.

2. Topic: _____

   Implied main idea sentence: _____

   _____

_____

_____

    The best candidate does not necessarily get the job. In most situations, *the person who knows the most about getting hired usually gets the desired position.* "Chemistry is the paramount factor in hiring," states Wilhelmus B. Bryan III, executive vice-president of William H. Clark Associates, a New York recruiting firm. Job-getting skills are not a guarantee of qualifications once the actual work begins. However, they are necessary to get hired in the first place.

Source: Adapted from Ronald Adler and Jeanne Elmhorst, *Communicating at Work,* 6th ed., p. 187. Copyright © 1999 McGraw-Hill. Reprinted by permission of The McGraw-Hill Companies.

3. Topic: _____

Implied main idea sentence: _____

_____

_____

    Interruptions and crises, minor and major, can't be eliminated. However, they can be prepared for. Try to anticipate them. Think about how you'll react to them.

Source: Adapted from Robert Feldman, *P.O.W.E.R. Learning,* p. 43. Copyright © 2005 McGraw-Hill. Reprinted by permission of The McGraw-Hill Companies.

4. Topic: _____

Implied main idea sentence: _____

_____

Playing Hard to Get

    The traditional advice that has been given to girls—by advice columnist Ann Landers and others—is that boys will be more attracted to them if they play hard to get. Is there any scientific evidence that this is true? In fact, two experiments provide no support for this kind of strategy.

Source: Adapted from Janet Hyde and John DeLamater, *Understanding Human Sexuality,* 7th ed., p. 340. Copyright © 2000 McGraw-Hill. Reprinted by permission of The McGraw-Hill Companies.

5. Topic: _____

Implied main idea sentence: _____

_____

_____

_____

    When Americans go to the polls on election day, they have in mind the choice between two individuals, the Democratic and the Republican presidential nominees. In effect, however, they are choosing a lot more than a single executive leader. They are also picking a secretary of state, the director of the FBI, the chair of the Federal Reserve Board, and a host of other executives. Each of these is a presidential appointee.

Source: Thomas E. Patterson, *We the People,* 6th ed., p. 422. Copyright © 2006 McGraw-Hill. Reprinted by permission of The McGraw-Hill Companies.

6. Topic: _____

Implied main idea sentence: _____

_____

_____

_____

Where do our notions of family come from? One way we get information is through experience. We know of our own experience and that of our friends and relatives. Another important source of information is the mass media. Consider, for instance, the family life portrayed on television. If you were a foreigner and the only thing you knew about American families came from television programs, how would you describe a typical family?

Source: Robert Lauer and Jeanette Lauer, *Marriage and Family,* 4th ed., p. 4. Copyright © 2000 McGraw-Hill. Reprinted by permission of The McGraw-Hill Companies.

7. Topic: _____

Implied main idea sentence: _____

_____

Throughout the history of the world people have characterized its existence by time periods or ages. Long ago we had the Ice Age and the Neolithic time period; in more modern times we've had the Renaissance period, the agricultural age, the age of enlightenment, and the industrial age. Today we have moved into another age that is different from any other. What is it? It is the ***information age***— a time when knowledge is power.

Source: Adapted from Stephen Haag, Maeve Cummings, and James Dawkins, *Management Information Systems for the Information Age,* 2d ed., p. 4. Copyright © 2000 McGraw-Hill. Reprinted by permission of The McGraw-Hill Companies.

8. Topic: _____

Implied main idea sentence: _____

_____

_____

Everyone needs to rest, not only through sleep but through deep relaxation. Too little of either causes irritability, depression, inability to concentrate, and memory loss. Yoga is a great way to unwind, stretch and tone the muscles, and focus energy. Many people find that meditation is essential for relaxation and renewal. You don't have to practice a certain type of meditation; just create a time for yourself when your mind is free to rest and quiet itself. Other people find that a massage relieves physical and mental tension. Visualization is another powerful technique for relaxing your body.

Source: Sharon Ferrett, *Peak Performance,* 5th ed., p. 10–23. Copyright © 2006 McGraw-Hill. Reprinted by permission of The McGraw-Hill Companies.

9. Topic: _____

Implied main idea sentence: _____

_____

Absorbent socks that fit properly should be worn during exercise. Socks that are too short can cause ingrown toenails, and loose-fitting socks can cause blisters. Not wearing socks results in blisters, abrasions, odor, and excess wear on shoes. It's important to wear the right size and the right type when you exercise.

Source: Adapted from Charles Corbin, Ruth Lindsey, and Greg Welk, *Concepts of Physical Fitness,* 10th ed., p. 37. Copyright © 2000 McGraw-Hill. Reprinted by permission of The McGraw-Hill Companies.

10. Topic: _____

Implied main idea sentence: _____

_____

How did it go? Did the items seem easier once you got into them and gained some experience? Take a minute and, on the lines below, jot down anything that confuses you about formulating implied main ideas.

_____

_____

_____

_____

_____

_____

_____

_____

_____

You've now completed the Set 2 practice exercises, but before you turn them in, look them over again. You might even want to cover up your answers and formulate the implied main ideas again. Compare your two answers to see if you still have the same idea the second time. If they're different, decide which answer is more likely to be correct.

SET 3

Exercises: Formulating the Implied Main Idea Sentence

Well, here you are at the final set of exercises on formulating the implied main idea. Congratulations! These will be more challenging, but (the good news!) there are only eight of them. Read each paragraph and think about it. Identify its topic. Then, on a piece of scratch paper, formulate an implied main idea sentence that tells the author's most important point about the topic. When you have formulated a complete sentence that clearly expresses the author's most important point, copy it in the space provided. If you start to feel fatigued or overwhelmed, follow the suggestions in the instructions for the Set 2 Exercises. Good luck!

The Constitution reflected the Framers' vision of a proper government for the American people. Its provisions addressed four broad goals. One was the creation of a national government strong enough to meet the nation's needs, particularly in the areas of defense and commerce. Another goal was to preserve the states as governing entities. The states already existed and had the loyalty of their people. Accordingly, the Framers established a system of government (federalism) in which power is divided between the national government and the states. The Framers' other goals were to establish a national government that was restricted in its lawful uses of power (limited government) and that gave the people a voice in their governance (self-government).

Source: Adapted from Thomas E. Patterson, *The American Democracy,* Alternate 7th ed., p. 50. Copyright © 2005 McGraw-Hill. Reprinted by permission of The McGraw-Hill Companies.

1. Topic: _____

Implied main idea sentence: _____

_____

_____

Polygamy is marriage involving more than one wife or husband at the same time. Most often this takes the form of *polygyny,* marriage of one man to two or more women. Polygyny was practiced in ancient China, hardly a small, primitive society. It is part of Judeo-Christian history: the ancient Hebrews (including Kings David and Solomon) were polygynists. Up until 1890, so were the Mormons of Utah. Islam, the second-largest religion in the world today, allows a man four wives (providing he treats each wife equally). Only four known societies have practiced *polyandry*—marriage of one woman to two or more men.

Source: Adapted from Richard Gelles and Ann Levine, *Sociology: An Introduction,* 6th ed., p. 405. Copyright © 1999 McGraw-Hill. Reprinted by permission of The McGraw-Hill Companies.

2. Topic: _____

Implied main idea sentence: _____

_____

In the past, every city had competing newspapers clamoring for the attention of readers who soaked up information in taxis, on commuter trains, on buses, and even in cars stuck in traffic. Gradually, however, afternoon papers failed and morning papers merged. Today, many cities have only one newspaper and circulation has plummeted. Nevertheless, newspapers remain one of the most informative, carefully edited, and insightful sources of information and analysis.

Source: Judy C. Pearson and Paul E. Nelson, *An Introduction to Human Communication,* 8th ed., p. 138. Copyright © 2000 McGraw-Hill. Reprinted by permission of The McGraw-Hill Companies.

3. Topic: _____

Implied main idea sentence: _____

_____

_____

_____

A classic study showed that Americans spend more than 40 percent of their time listening (Rankin, 1926). Weinrach and Swanda (1975) found that business personnel, including those with and without managerial responsibilities, spend nearly 33 percent of their time listening, almost 26 percent of their time speaking, nearly 23 percent of their time writing, and almost 19 percent of their time reading. When Werner (1975) investigated the communication activities of high school and college students, homemakers and employees in a variety of other occupations, she determined that they spend 55 percent of their time listening, 13 percent reading, and 8 percent writing. College students spend over half of their time (53 percent) listening either to the mass media or to other people. Studies clearly show that Americans spend a significant amount of time on this important activity.

Source: Adapted from Judy C. Pearson and Paul E. Nelson, *An Introduction to Human Communication,* 8th ed., p. 100. Copyright © 2000 McGraw-Hill. Reprinted by permission of The McGraw-Hill Companies.

4. Topic: _____

Implied main idea sentence: _____

_____

In order to develop cultural competence, it's important to identify our prejudices and stereotypes and to fight them. Sometimes they are quite subtle and difficult to detect. For instance, a wealth of data taken from observation of elementary school classrooms shows that teachers often are more responsive to boys than to girls. The teachers don't know they're doing it; it's a subtle, but very real, bias.

Source: Robert S. Feldman, *P.O.W.E.R. Learning,* p. 314. Copyright © 2005 McGraw-Hill. Reprinted by permission of The McGraw-Hill Companies.

5. Topic: _____

Implied main idea sentence: _____

_____

_____

A prototype of the abusive parent would be one who is single, is young (around 30 or less), has been married fewer than 10 years, had his or her first child before the age of 18, and is unemployed or employed part-time. Spouse abusers also are far more likely to be child abusers than are those who do not abuse their spouses. And the more times someone has abused a spouse, the more likely that person is to be a child abuser as well. Women are slightly more likely to abuse children than men, probably because women are more intensely involved with children (and rates of child abuse are higher in single-parent families which, for the most part, means single-mother families). Child abusers tend to have lower self-esteem than others, to define their children as more troublesome, to have serious financial problems, to have poorer mental health, to have lower levels of social support, and to have a large number of stressor events in their lives. Abusers are also more likely than nonabusers to have been abused themselves as children.

Source: Adapted from Robert Lauer and Jeanette Lauer, *Marriage and Family,* 6th ed., p. 332. Copyright © 2007 McGraw-Hill. Reprinted by permission of The McGraw-Hill Companies.

6. Topic: _____

_____

Implied main idea sentence: _____

_____

Until the 1980s, Japan had one of the lowest rates of divorce in the developed world. Love, however, was not the main ingredient keeping couples together. In part, strong social pressure kept couples together. Becoming divorced was shameful, a sign of individual weakness or moral failing. Marriages were also held together by a strict division of labor. Women were responsible for nearly all of the housework and childrearing. Japanese men did, and still do, much less of the housework and childcare than men in Western countries such as the United States. National studies of time use in Japan from 1965 to 1990 show that husbands do only 10 percent of the housework and childcare.

Source: Andrew Cherlin, *Public and Private Families,* 4th ed., p. 224. Copyright © 2005 McGraw-Hill. Reprinted by permission of The McGraw-Hill Companies.

7. Topic: _____

Implied main idea sentence: _____

_____

Caffeine does have pharmacological effects on the function of the cardiovascular, respiratory, renal, and nervous systems, but at the low fixed pattern of consumption that most people enjoy, caffeine is merely a mild stimulant. However, withdrawal from even a mild caffeine habit may cause headaches, fatigue, and depression. In high doses, acute effects such as restlessness, agitation, tremors, cardiac dysrhythmias (irregular heartbeat), gastric disturbance, and diarrhea have been reported.

Source: Adapted from Wayne Payne, Dale Hahn, and Ellen Mauer, *Understanding Your Health,* 8th ed., p. 252. Copyright © 2005 McGraw-Hill. Reprinted by permission of The McGraw-Hill Companies.

8. Topic: _____

Implied main idea sentence: _____

_____

_____

Now that you've finished these Set 3 Exercises, set them aside. Come back to them later to look again at any item you were unsure of. When you return to them a second time, you may discover that you have renewed clarity. When you finish them completely, give yourself a pat on the back. You've earned it!

CHAPTER 6
Recognize Authors' Writing Patterns

THE SKILL

RECOGNIZE AUTHORS' WRITING PATTERNS

Remember the analogy in Chapter 4 comparing a paragraph's main idea and details with a football team carrying out a play? The quarterback (main idea) announces the play (the author's most important point). The rest of the team (the details) help carry out that play.

No coach (no winning coach, at any rate!) ever said to his quarterback, "Tell the guys that when the play starts, they can just run wherever they want. Maybe they'll get lucky and things will turn out okay." Nor does an effective author toss out a bunch of details and leave the reader to try to figure out the connection between them and the main idea. Just as a coach chooses the best formation for a successful play, an author chooses the most logical writing pattern to present his or her main idea.

Think of the author of the paragraph as similar to the coach of a team. An effective author has a plan in mind for getting her point across to the readers, just as an effective coach has a particular plan in mind for executing a play. Once the coach decides on the play, he has his players line up in the proper formation to carry it out. The author does something similar: she organizes the details (her "players") in a pattern that helps her achieve her goal of a clear, easy-to-comprehend paragraph.

The coach uses his quarterback to let the players know how to line up; an author uses her main idea to help choose an appropriate writing pattern. Those writing patterns are the focus of this chapter.

Here's the analogy in the form of a chart:

Football	Reading
A range of possible *plays*	A range of possible *ideas*
A *coach* who decides which play to use	An *author* who decides on the main idea to be presented
A *quarterback* who announces or signals the coach's play to the team	A *main idea sentence* (stated or implied) that announces the author's most important point in a paragraph
The *rest of the team,* who help carry out the play	*Details* that *support* the main idea (make it more understandable)
The *formation* the coach uses to line up the players so they can best carry out the play	A *writing pattern* (an organizational pattern) the author uses to arrange the details in the most logical way

So how do authors decide on the way to organize the main ideas and details they present? The answer is that authors organize and present their ideas in ways that make *sense* to them, just as coaches organize their players in the way that is most likely to achieve a certain result. Authors do this by choosing from several common writing patterns. To state it plainly, **writing patterns** *are ways that authors organize material they present.* You may also hear writing patterns referred to as *organizational patterns, patterns of organization, patterns of development,* and *thinking patterns.*

Authors assume that you will recognize certain basic patterns and that you will find them helpful. These patterns are basic because they reflect the way people think. (And you probably already know that writing, like reading, is actually a form of *thinking*.) In other words, these patterns reflect the ways people—including you—naturally tend to organize information.

Recognizing these patterns helps you comprehend and remember material more easily and efficiently. It allows you to follow an author's train of thought and even anticipate where the author is going. Moreover, you will discover that your own writing improves once you become consciously aware of the patterns. You will write clearer, more organized answers on essay tests, and you will write better papers and reports. These patterns will also come in handy in the future if your job requires you to write memos and reports.

THE TECHNIQUE

LEARN THE CHARACTERISTICS OF AUTHORS' SIX WRITING PATTERNS

Textbook authors select the pattern that helps them present the material most clearly and logically, so in a way, the patterns are a gift to the reader. Take advantage of them! Each pattern reflects a certain type of relationship between the main idea and the details of a paragraph. After you read a paragraph, ask yourself, "Which pattern has the author used to organize the information in the paragraph?"

Here's lots of good news:

- Certain words in the main idea sentence itself will give you a clue to the pattern.

- Each pattern has certain clue words or signals that announce the pattern. (Not *every* paragraph contains signals words or clues, but don't panic. Even when there aren't any, you can still determine the pattern by seeing what the relationship is between the main idea and the details.)

- You use these same patterns every day of your life. Yup, every day. You use them to organize your thoughts. You use them to organize information you tell others verbally. What you're going to learn in this chapter is to become more consciously aware of them *when you are reading*.

The patterns are *list, sequence, definition, cause–effect, comparison–contrast* and *spatial order.* Some patterns have minor variations, and we'll mention them as we go. Let's look at each pattern, its clue words and signals, along with a sample paragraph that illustrates the pattern.

1. LIST PATTERN

This pattern couldn't be easier because it is exactly what it says it is. *In a **list pattern,** the author presents a group of items in no particular order because the order is not important.* The list pattern appears in nearly every textbook, but especially in science and social science textbooks such as sociology, psychology, and anthropology.

Your job as a reader is to locate *all* items on the list. Authors often make it easy because they use numbers (*1, 2, 3*), letters (*a, b, c*), or bullets (large dots or some other symbol) to make each item on the list stand out. They may start each item on a new line. Even if they don't do those things, they may use certain words to signal that items are being added to a list: *and, also, in addition, additionally, moreover, first, second, next,* and *finally.* In the main idea sentence, watch for words that suggest different categories (such as three *types,* several *kinds,* five *ways,* four *functions,* certain *features,* important *characteristics*).

Here's a sample paragraph from a human development textbook that illustrates the list pattern. I've underlined the main idea sentence in italics and put the clues in color.

Elementary schools serve many functions. First, they teach specific cognitive skills, primarily the three Rs. School curricula—such "core" subjects as mathematics, natural science, and social science—are remarkably similar throughout the world. Second, schools also inculcate more general skills, such as paying attention, sitting quietly, participating in classroom activities and completing assignments. Third, schools have come to share with the family the responsibility for transmitting society's dominant cultural goals and values. With respect to basic social norms, values, and beliefs, all education indoctrinates students with what is called the "hidden curriculum." Fourth, to one degree or another, schools function as a "sorting and sifting agency" that selects young people for upward mobility. Fifth, schools attempt to overcome gross deficits or difficulties in individual children that interfere with their adequate social functioning and participation. Often, schools work in consultation with parents as well as with school psychologists, guidance personnel, physical therapists, speech therapists, and occupational therapists. In addition, schools meet a variety of needs not directly educational.

Source: Adapted from James Vander Zanden, revised by Thomas Crandell and Corinne Crandell, *Human Development*, Updated 7th ed., pp. 356–7. Copyright © 2003 McGraw-Hill. Reprinted by permission of The McGraw-Hill Companies.

The stated main idea sentence alerts you to expect a list of the functions that elementary schools serve. The clue words *First, Second, Third, Fourth, Fifth,* and *In addition* guide you to the important details that comprise the list. (If you were marking the details, you'd want to jot a small number beside each item or, in this case, circle the clue words because each indicates a function of an elementary school.)

Variation

When a list pattern presents items grouped into categories or classifications, it may be referred to as a **division pattern** *or* **classification pattern.** The categories are named, and the parts of each group are explained. Watch for clue words such as *groups, categories, ways, types, elements, kinds,* and *classes.*

In this sample classification pattern paragraph from a criminal investigation textbook, the third sentence (underlined) is the stated main idea. Clues are in color.

It is human nature to talk. Most people cannot keep a secret. It has been estimated that 80 percent of all people will confess to a crime. There are two basic categories of people who tend to confess to crimes: (1) guilty parties who psychologically need to "get it off their chest," and (2) persons who are not guilty but who act under some urge to confess. People in the latter category of people need to be protected, so procedural safeguards, such as not basing guilt on confession alone, are provided. From the outset of the interrogation, guilty people are looking for a proper opening to communicate their guilt to the interrogator. They rarely regret confessing, for doing so gives them peace of mind.

Source: Adapted from Charles Swanson, Neil Chamelin, Leonard Territo, and Robert Taylor, *Criminal Investigation*, 9th ed., p. 161. Copyright © 2006 McGraw-Hill. Reprinted by permission of The McGraw-Hill Companies.

Notice that the main idea sentence contains the signal words *two basic categories,* as well as a number to set off each category. The first two sentences are introductory sentences. The last three sentences explain more about the people who fall in each category.

2. SEQUENCE PATTERN

This is another easy pattern because it's merely a special type of list, a list in which the order matters. *The* **sequence pattern** *presents a group of items in a specific order because the order is important.* You may hear it called a *series, chronological order,* a *process,* or *time order.* When you learn the information in a sequence, you must identify and learn all the items in the sequence *in the same order the author presented them.* Instructions and sets of directions are always sequences, so you can expect to see the sequence pattern throughout textbooks in computer science and other technical fields, as well as in medically related texts (such as nursing and EMT). History and science textbooks also contain a great deal of information presented as sequences.

What types of clues reveal a sequence pattern? Actually, some of them are the same as for the list pattern, such as *first, second, next, then,* and *finally.* But in this pattern, *first* doesn't mean just the first item on a list. It means *do this first or this happens (or happened) first.* As in the list, there may be numbers, letters, or bullets beside the item in the sequence. In the main idea sentence, watch for obvious clues such as the words *process, sequence, steps, phases,* and *series.* Watch also for dates and references to time, such as *before, while, after, soon, later,* and phrases such as *during the Middle Ages* and *during the coming decade.*

Here's a heads-up: Don't assume that there will always be only one step per sentence. A single sentence may give you two or more items in a sequence. For example, directions for administering CPR to someone who has stopped breathing might say, "Tilt the victim's head back, pinch the nostrils shut, and cover the person's mouth with your own." That one sentence tells *three* things that must be done sequentially.

Here is an example of a sequence pattern paragraph from an art history textbook. The implied main idea is, *Harlem painter Jacob Lawrence rose from poverty to become one of the most distinguished artists of his generation.* The time order or sequence clues appear in color.

> To Harlem, in about 1930, came a young teenager named Jacob Lawrence, relocating from Philadelphia with his mother, brother, and sister. The flowering of the Harlem Renaissance had passed, but there remained enough momentum to help turn the child of a poor family into one of the most distinguished American artists of his generation. He studied at the Harlem Art Workshop from 1932 to 1934 and received much encouragement from two noted black artists, Charles Alston and Augusta Savage. By the age of twenty Lawrence had begun to exhibit his work. His subject matter was from his own experience, from black experience, such as the hardship of poor people in the ghettoes. The year 1941 was significant for Lawrence's life and career: he married painter Gwendolyn Knight and he acquired his first dealer. After a major exhibition featuring his works, two important museums purchased a series of his paintings. From that point his career prospered, and for the rest of his life, his paintings were in demand. Lawrence died in 2000.
>
> *Source:* Adapted from Mark Getlein, *Living with Art,* 7th ed., p. 170. Copyright © 2005 McGraw-Hill. Reprinted by permission of The McGraw-Hill Companies.

In the example above, the main idea sentence suggests a progression. The dates, references to Lawrence's age, and other time-related words indicate a sequence.

Variation

A process is simply a type of sequence in which a series of actions or steps brings about a result. For example, registering for classes, the development of a hurricane, and how a bill becomes a law are processes. All processes are sequences, but not all sequences (such as the story of a person's life) are processes. *A **process pattern** describes a series of actions or steps designed to bring about a specific result.*

The information in the following psychology textbook passage represents a process. The stated main idea is underlined, and the clue words are in color.

> Regardless of individual ability, how does the creative process occur? The creative problem solving typically proceeds in four steps. The first step, *preparation,* includes initial attempts to formulate the problem, recall relevant facts, and think about possible solutions. The second step, *incubation,* is a period of rest. People trying to solve difficult problems that require creative solutions generally feel the need to set the problem aside for a while after the

initial preparation period. The third step, called *illumination,* refers to a sudden insight pertaining to the solution. The final step, *verification,* involves the necessary, but less anticlimactic step of testing the solution.

Source: Adapted from Benjamin Lahey, *Psychology: An Introduction,* 8th ed., p. 284. Copyright © 2004 McGraw-Hill. Reprinted by permission of The McGraw-Hill Companies.

Notice the phrases *first step, second step, third step,* and *final step* that guide the reader through the passage. Also, the author has italicized the key word that describes each step.

3. DEFINITION PATTERN

Because college textbooks contain many specialized terms, authors take special care to define them. (It's important that you learn them—and you should know by now that teachers will ask you to define them on tests.) *The* **definition pattern** *is the pattern authors use to present and discuss throughout the passage the meaning of one important term.* You'll encounter lots of paragraphs that contain a definition, of course. To be the definition *pattern,* however, the *whole* paragraph must be devoted to explaining the meaning of a term. The main idea sentence is typically the definition of the important term. The details in the paragraph explain or illustrate the term.

Definition pattern paragraphs are easy to spot. First of all, there's the definition itself. The important term may appear in *italics,* **bold print,** or color. The sentence that gives the definition (which, again, is usually the main idea sentence) will contain other clues such as *is defined as, the term, means, is known as, is called, refers to,* and *is referred to as.* Sometimes the definition itself appears in quotation marks or in italics. The words *is* and *are* often introduce definitions, but those words appear in writing constantly. Don't assume whenever you see *is* or *are* that a definition is going to follow!

To explain the meaning of an important term or concept, authors sometimes give a synonym (a word that means the same thing) for the term or concept they are defining. They often introduce the synonym by using *or, that is,* or *in other words.*

Punctuation can also help alert you to an important definition. Definitions can appear in parentheses; can be set off by a comma or commas, enclosed in brackets, or set off in dashes; or can follow a dash or a colon.

Now read a sample definition passage from a business communications textbook. The definition of "jargon" and the important point about it comprise the stated main idea.

> <u>The most significant informal communication occurs through the **grapevine,** i.e. an informal channel of communication, separate from management's formal, official communication channels</u>. Grapevines exist in all organizations. Information passed along the grapevine may relate to the job or organization, or it may be gossip and rumors unrelated to either. The accuracy of grapevine information has been of great concern to managers.
>
> *Source:* O. C. Ferrell, Geoffrey Hirt, and Linda Ferrell, *Business: A Changing World,* 5th ed., p. 248. Copyright © 2006 McGraw-Hill/Irwin. Reprinted by permission of The McGraw-Hill Companies.

The key term "grapevine" is in bold, and the definition is set off by a comma. The rest of the sentences are details that tell more about this channel of informal communication—grapevines.

Variations

When textbook authors include one or more examples to make the meaning of a term clear, the pattern is referred to as a **definition-example pattern.** In addition to the clue words for a definition, watch for words that introduce examples.

"Jargon" is the topic of this definition-example pattern paragraph from a business communications textbook. The definition is the stated main idea.

> Every profession has its own specialized vocabulary, termed **jargon.** For example, people who order office supplies talk about "NCR paper" and "three-up labels." Computer users talk about "32-bit architecture" and "image compression boards."

Source: Ronald Adler and Jeanne Elmhorst, *Communicating at Work*, 8th ed., p. 79. Copyright © 2005 McGraw-Hill. Reprinted by permission of The McGraw-Hill Companies.

Notice the clue word *termed* and bold italics for the term "jargon." The definition is followed by two examples of jargon: jargon used by people who order office supplies and computer users.

Sometimes, instead of a definition and an example, an author presents a general statement and a description or examples. *A general statement—a key concept, rule, or principle—along with a description or examples is called a* **generalization-and-example pattern.** (You learned the difference between general and specific when you learned about topic. A *generalization* is a statement, idea, or principle that applies broadly; that is, it applies to many people, situation, or things, or in many circumstances.) As with the definition-example pattern, watch for signal words that introduce examples, such as *to illustrate, for example, for instance,* and *that is.* The following paragraph, which you might see in a biology text, uses this pattern.

> Life comes only from life; every living thing reproduces. For example, at the simplest level, even one-cell organisms multiply by dividing in two. In more complex organisms, such as human beings, reproduction occurs by a sperm fertilizing an egg, followed by innumerable cell divisions and differentiations.

The first sentence presents a general principle. The words *For example* introduce the two examples of simple organisms and more complex organisms.

4. CAUSE–EFFECT PATTERN

Causes are reasons that things happen; effects are results or outcomes. *Authors use the* **cause–effect pattern** *to present cause(s), effect(s) or both.* This pattern, like the sequence pattern, appears frequently in history and science textbooks, as well as social science textbooks. (I find it easier to think in terms of *reasons* and *results,* rather than causes and effects. Try this to see if it helps you, too.)

Some clue words that indicate *causes* are *reason(s), cause(s), because, is due to, caused by,* and *resulted from.* Clues that indicate *effects* include *the result(s), the outcome(s), the effect(s), the final product, therefore, thus, consequences, consequently, as a consequence, on that account, for that reason, hence, so, result(ed) in,* and *lead to.* These important words frequently show up in the main idea sentence. When you spot them, see whether the cause–effect pattern is being used. (Be sure you look at the important relationship in the paragraph. The word *because* in a paragraph doesn't automatically mean there is a cause–effect pattern.) Watch for this pattern, though, when the author asks an important question that includes the word *why* or phrases such as *What happens if . . . ?*

When an author uses the cause–effect pattern, it's your job to sort out the causes from the effects. There may be one cause and one effect, such as a specific virus that causes one particular disease. The author may present several causes that all lead to one effect (such as poor diet, inadequate rest, insufficient rest, and lack of exercise causing a weakened immune system). There may be one cause that leads to several effects (such as poor interpersonal skills resulting in strained family relationships, a lack of friends and a fulfilling social life, and lack of advancement in a career). Sometimes the author even presents a chain-reaction set of causes and effects: one thing leads to another, and that, in turn, becomes the cause of something else. For example: A student learns computer programming; because she has acquired these skills, she obtains a high-paying part-time job; because of the job, she is able to buy a car.

Keep in mind that in reality, causes always happen *before* results. That's only logical. So don't let it confuse you if an author tells the effect first, and then tells the cause. In the sentence, "John took an aspirin because he had a headache," the effect is given first (John took an aspirin), then the cause or reason (he had a headache). The order in which the events would actually have occurred is that John had the headache first, and then he took an aspirin.

Now read this cause–effect effect paragraph from a social psychology textbook. (Social psychology is the scientific study of how people think about, influence, and relate to one another.) The clue words are in color to make them stand out. The stated main idea is underlined to give you an ongoing review of main ideas and to illustrate that the main idea typically gives clues to the author's writing pattern.

> <u>Marriage enhances happiness for at least two reasons</u>. First, married people are more likely to enjoy an enduring, supportive, intimate relationship, and are less likely to suffer loneliness. A good marriage gives each partner a dependable companion, a lover, a friend. There is a second, more prosaic, reason why marriage promotes happiness, or at least buffers us from misery. Marriage offers the roles of spouse and parent, which can provide additional sources of self-esteem. Our personal identity then depends on several roles and, as a result, it holds up under the loss of any one. For example, if I mess up at work, well, I can tell myself I'm still a good husband and father, and, in the final analysis, these parts of me are what matter most.
>
> *Source:* David Myers, *Social Psychology*, 7th ed., p. 591. Copyright © 2002 McGraw-Hill. Reprinted by permission of The McGraw-Hill Companies.

The main idea sentence alerts readers to expect to be told two reasons marriage makes people happier. The details, which are identified with *first* and *second*, explain those reasons. The clue words are *reason, why,* and *as a result.*

Variation

A variation of the cause–effect pattern is the *problem-solution* pattern, which appears more often in textbooks in science, history, and technical fields, such as computer science and nursing. *Authors use the **problem-solution pattern** to present the causes of a problem and its unpleasant or unwanted effects, and they typically present one or more solutions that are keyed to the causes.* The inclusion of solutions is what makes this pattern slightly different from an ordinary cause–effect pattern. In addition to the clue words *cause* and *effect,* watch for ones such as *problem, solve, solution, answer,* and *remedy.*

The following paragraph is from an anthropology textbook. (Anthropology is the scientific study of the origin, the behavior, and the physical, social, and cultural development of humans.) The topic is *global deforestation* (cutting down and clearing away of forests), and the first sentence states the main idea.

> To address the global deforestation problem, we need conservation strategies that work. Laws and enforcement may help reduce commercially driven deforestation, but local people also use and abuse forested lands. We must find ways to make forest preservation attractive to local people and to ensure their cooperation. Solutions must be based on culturally appropriate policies that are based on anthropological knowledge of each affected area. Governments and international agencies are likely to fail if they try to impose their goals without considering the practices, customs, rules, laws, beliefs, and values of the people who will be affected by them.
>
> *Source:* Adapted from Conrad Kottak, *Physical Anthropology and Archaeology*, p. 141. Copyright © 2004 McGraw-Hill. Reprinted by permission of The McGraw-Hill Companies.

The details of the paragraph discuss factors that must be taken into consideration when trying to solve the problem of deforestation. The clue words are *problem* and *solutions*. Notice, too, that in the second sentence "commercially driven deforestation" means deforestation *caused by* companies who are doing it to make money. In the third sentence, "find ways" means find *solutions*.

5. COMPARISON–CONTRAST PATTERN

A ***comparison–contrast pattern*** *presents similarities (comparisons) between two or more things, differences (contrasts) between two or more things, or both similarities and differences.* Authors use it when they want to explain or describe how two or more things are alike or different. They use it when they want to present opposing sides of an issue (such as the issue of gun control or capital punishment). For this reason, you may also hear the pattern referred to as *ideas in opposition*. Your job as a reader is to determine what is being compared or contrasted, and the ways in which they are similar or different.

Clue words and signals that can indicate a comparison are *similarly, likewise, both, same, also, resembles, parallels, in the same manner, in the same way,* and words that describe comparisons (such as *safer, slower, less productive, more expensive*). Words that indicate a contrast include *in contrast, however, on the one hand . . . on the other hand, while, although, whereas, nevertheless, instead (of), difference, unlike, notwithstanding, conversely, rather than, as opposed to, some . . . others,* and words that have opposite meanings (such as *the employed* and *the unemployed, barbiturates* and *stimulants,* etc.).

Read this sample comparison–contrast passage from a communications textbook. I've put in color the words that signal this type of pattern. The second sentence is the stated main idea, a general sentence that sums up the rest of the paragraph.

> For students of communication, the distinction between high- and low-context cultures is among the most fascinating. High- and low-context cultures have several important differences in the way information is coded. Members of **high-context cultures** are *more skilled in reading nonverbal*

behaviors, and they assume that other people will also be able to do so. They speak less than members of low-context cultures and they listen more. In general, their communication tends to be indirect and less explicit. Members of **low-context cultures,** on the other hand, *stress direct and explicit communication.* They emphasize verbal messages and the shared information they encode.

Source: Adapted from Stewart Tubbs and Sylvia Moss, *Human Communication,* 10th ed., p. 317. Copyright © 2006 McGraw-Hill. Reprinted by permission of The McGraw-Hill Companies.

This paragraph is filled with clue words: *distinction* (meaning difference), the opposites *high- and low-context cultures, differences,* and *on the other hand.* In addition, there are comparative words, such as *more, less than,* and *less.* Notice that this paragraph presents only contrasts (differences).

6. SPATIAL ORDER PATTERN

The **spatial order pattern***, or place order pattern, describes something's location or layout.* Authors would use this pattern, for example, to describe the position of armies in a battle, the elements in a painting, tree trunk growth rings, the location of parts of a computer CPU, lobes of the brain, or the layout of an ancient city. Information in spatial order patterns is often accompanied by a figure or diagram. Watch for signal words such as *above, below, behind, in front of, beside, near, farther from, within, outside of, north/south/east/west (of), facing, opposite, to the left/right,* and other words that indicate the position of one object relative to another. The following passage from a criminal investigation textbook discusses impact bloodstains, those produced with more force than gravity (stains from blood that falls freely due to gravity). The first sentence is the stated main idea.

The directionality of an impact bloodstain can be determined by analyzing the shape of the bloodstain. When a blood droplet impacts a flat surface at a low angle, the resultant stain will have an elliptical shape and an extension called a spine. The extension will be on the side opposite the stain's origin. When a blood droplet impacts a surface, the resultant bloodstain has a shape that is characteristic of the angle described by the path of the droplet and the plane of the surface impact. The determination of the area of origin of a bloodstain pattern will establish the specific location or position of the victim at the time the wound was made.

Source: Adapted from Charles Swanson, Neil Chamelin, Leonard Territo, and Robert Taylor, *Criminal Investigation,* 9th ed., p. 270. Copyright © 2006 McGraw-Hill. Reprinted by permission of The McGraw-Hill Companies.

A spatial order pattern is signaled by the terms *directionality, shape, elliptical shape,* and *on the side opposite.* The terms *flat surface, low angle, extension, characteristic of the angle,* and *plane of the surface impact* also describe position. In addition, the paragraph states that understanding the origin of the bloodstain helps investigators establish the victim's location or position when the person was wounded.

These are the six primary patterns authors use to present information. The Edge includes the description pattern and summary pattern (page 137). Both are so obvious that they do not require special attention here.

SUMMARY CHART

Here's a present to you from me: a chart that summarizes many of the clue words associated with each pattern. Don't think that you must memorize all of the clue words and signals that go with each pattern. Remember that there is a logical connection between them and the pattern in which they are used. Besides, you use these words to organize your thoughts every day when you speak and write. (*Suggestion from your coach:* Refer to this chart as you do the exercise sets in this chapter. Notice that alternate names, along with variations of the patterns, are given. You don't need to memorize them.)

1. List Pattern   (Variation: Division or Classification Pattern)

and	1, 2, 3 . . .
also, too	a, b, c . . .
another	bullets (•)
moreover, besides	asterisks (*)
in addition	words that announce lists (such as
first, second, third . . .	*categories, kinds, types, ways, classes,*
further	*groups, parts, elements, characteristics,*
finally	*features,* etc.)

2. Sequence Pattern   (Variation: Process Pattern)

first, second, third . . .	*progression*
now, then, next, finally	*series*
dates	*stages*
words that refer to time	*when, while*
1, 2, 3 . . .	*before, prior to, during, after*
a, b, c . . .	*last, at last*
steps	*process, spectrum, continuum*
phases	instructions and directions

3. Definition Pattern   (Variations: Definition-Example Pattern and Generalization-and-Example Pattern)

words in bold print	*refers to, is referred to as*
words in italics	*the term*
words in color	*is called*
is defined as	*by this we mean*
means	*or* (followed by a synonym)
in other words	punctuation that sets off a definition
is, is known as	or synonym , : ( ) [ ] —
that is (i.e.)	examples that illustrate the definition or meaning of a term

4. Cause–Effect Pattern   (Variation: Problem–Solution Pattern)

Cause:	Effect:	
the reason(s)	*thus*	*hence*
the causes(s)	*the result(s)*	*as a consequence*
because, since	*the effect(s)*	*on that account*

(Continued)

SUMMARY CHART (CONTINUED)

is due to [cause]	*the outcome*	[effect] *was caused by*
was caused by [cause]	*consequently*	*resulted in, results in* [effect]
[cause] *led to*	*the final product*	[effect] *is due to*
resulted from [cause]	*therefore*	[effect] *resulted from*

Questions that indicate cause–effect:

- *What causes* [effect]? (Answer will be the cause.)
- *Why does* [effect] *occur?* (Answer will be the cause.)
- *What is the reason for* [effect]? (Answer will be the cause.)
- *How can* [effect] *be explained?* (Answer will be the cause.)
- *What does* [cause] *lead to?* (Answer will be the effect.)

Problem–Solution:

problem	*answer*
solution; solve	*remedy*

5. Comparison–Contrast Pattern

Comparison:	Contrast:	
similarly	*in contrast*	*some; others*
likewise	*however*	*nonetheless*
both	*as opposed to*	*conversely*
same; alike	*whereas*	words that have opposite meanings *(such as* men *and* women, ancient *and* modern, *etc.)*
also	*while*	
resembles	*although*	
parallels	*nevertheless*	
in the same manner	*instead (of)*	
in the same way	*different; difference*	
words that compare (adjectives that describe comparisons, such as *safer, slower, lighter, more valuable, less toxic,* etc.)	*unlike; dissimilar* *conversely* *rather than* *on the one hand; on the other hand*	

6. Spatial Order Pattern

positioned, placed, located, situated	*site, location*
above, below	*opposite, facing*
in front of, behind	*to the left/right* (of)
beside	*within, outside* (of)
farther from	*near, close to, adjacent to*
north/south/east/west (of)	

THE TRAINER

OBSERVE THE SKILL OF RECOGNIZING AUTHORS' WRITING PATTERNS

Let's look at the thoughts that might go through an effective reader's mind as he or she determines the author's writing pattern in a paragraph. Read the paragraph in the illustration first, then go back and read the comments in color that represent the thoughts of our imaginary reader.

> Okay, I've read the first sentence. At this point, it seems as if it could be the stated main idea. I expect the rest of the paragraph to tell me what the "series" of mistakes is. That word "series" makes me think this is going to be a sequence.

> I think I was right! Big clue: the word "first" at the beginning of the next sentence.

Companies that experience a crisis for which they are ill prepared seem to make a series of mistakes. First, warnings about possible problems are ignored at one or several management levels. Then the crisis hits. Under pressure, the company does the worst thing it could do: It denies the severity of the problem or it denies its own role in the problem. Finally, when the company is forced to face reality, it takes hasty, poorly conceived action.

Source: David Rachman, Michael Mescon, Courtland Bovée, and John Thill, *Business Today,* p. 170. Copyright © 1993 McGraw-Hill. Reprinted by permission of The McGraw-Hill Companies.

> Aha! Look at these other clues. As I read the rest of the paragraph, I see the words "Then" and "Finally." I'm right. The first sentence is the main idea and it gave me the clue about a "series." There are four steps, and all of them except the one about the company's denial are introduced by clue words. It's definitely a *sequence*!

THE EDGE

POINTERS ABOUT RECOGNIZING AUTHORS' WRITING PATTERNS

■ **There won't *always* be clue words or signals for the pattern in a paragraph.**
An author can introduce every part of a pattern, some parts of a pattern, or none of the parts with clue words or signals. Here is a sample paragraph that uses the definition pattern. The only clue to the pattern is that the word *sleepwalking* is in bold print. The second sentence gives the rest of the definition.

Sleepwalking is another interesting phenomenon that occurs primarily during the deepest parts of non-REM sleep. Sleepwalkers rise from the bed and carry on complicated activities, such as walking from one room to another, even though they are sound asleep. Sleepwalking is most common in children before the age of puberty but is not particularly unusual in adults. Sleepwalking usually reappears in adults only during periods of stress, but except for the danger of accidents while wandering around in the dark, it's not an abnormal behavior.

Source: Benjamin Lahey, *Psychology: An Introduction,* 8th ed., p. 175. Copyright © 2004 McGraw-Hill. Reprinted by permission of The McGraw-Hill Companies.

The complete main idea (which must be formulated) is, *In sleepwalking, people rise from bed and carry on complicated activities, even though they are in the deepest parts of non-REM sleep.* The last two sentences in the paragraph are details that provide additional information. Note that *none* of the details is introduced by a clue word.

■ **Some paragraphs and longer selections have a *combination* of patterns. This is known as a *mixed pattern*.**

Let me show you an example of a mixed-pattern paragraph. The technology education textbook excerpt that follows presents contrasts in the average volume of emails sent at various points during the last several years. The author also compares the impact of email with other major advances in communication history. In addition, the author tells the effect of the explosion in emails. The paragraph is a *mixed pattern* because it contains more than one pattern: the comparison–contrast pattern and a cause–effect pattern. It could also be argued that it contains a sequence pattern because it presents the volume for three different years. With mixed patterns, be sure you identify all the patterns that are used so that you understand the relationships the author is presenting.

In 1998 the volume of email in the United States surpassed the volume of hand-delivered mail. In 2002, an estimated average of 8 billion messages a day were zipping back and forth across the United States, whereas 3.5 billion were being sent daily three years earlier! By 2006, the total number of email messages sent daily will probably exceed 60 billion worldwide, compared with 31 billion worldwide in 2002. Already, in fact, email is the leading use of PCs. Because of this explosion in usage, suggests a *Business Week* report, "email ranks with such pivotal advances as the printing press, the telephone, and television in mass impact."

Source: Adapted from Brian Williams and Stacey Sawyer, *Using Information Technology*, 4th ed., p. 4. Copyright © 2006 McGraw-Hill/Irwin. Reprinted by permission of The McGraw-Hill Companies.

In order for a paragraph to have a mixed pattern, there must actually be two or more complete patterns. Just because an author includes a minor definition in a cause–effect paragraph doesn't make the paragraph a mixed-pattern paragraph.

■ **Avoid viewing every paragraph pattern as a list pattern.**

When you are first working with patterns, you may be tempted to view everything as a list. But if you see every paragraph as having the same pattern, there is no value in knowing the pattern. When you *think* a paragraph has a list pattern, you should always ask yourself one additional question, "A list of *what?*" If your answer is

■ a list of *items or events in a specific order,* call it a *sequence* (or process) pattern.
■ a list of *causes or effects,* call it a *cause–effect* pattern.
■ a list of *similarities or differences,* call it a *comparison–contrast* pattern.

You should consider a paragraph as having a list pattern *only* when the paragraph presents a group of items or events in no particular order and you have ruled out all the other patterns as possibilities.

■ **Take advantage of clues in the main idea sentence (whether stated or implied) that indicate the author's writing pattern.**

Look carefully at the main idea sentence: there are often clue words in it. If there are, take advantage of them!

■ **Different readers may view the same paragraph as having a different pattern, but what matters is that each reader *sees* a pattern and has logical *reasons* for choosing that pattern.**

I know this sounds goofy, but it's true. Suppose, for example, you read a paragraph that explains why men absorb less alcohol into their bloodstream than women who have the same body weight and who drink the same number of drinks. You might view the paragraph as a comparison–contrast on alcohol absorption in men and women. Someone else might remember the information more easily by viewing it as a cause–effect pattern about the *reasons* for the difference. (Of course, one pattern is usually a little more logical than the other, and many paragraphs clearly have only one possible pattern.) The important point: Look for a pattern and know why you think it's that pattern.

■ **In certain disciplines, some patterns show up more often.**

Textbooks in history, science, computer science, and many technical fields frequently present information that is organized with a sequence pattern. The cause–effect pattern and problem-solution pattern also often appear in science, history, and textbooks for technical courses. Comparison–contrast is a pattern you'd expect to see used in social science texts, such as psychology, sociology, and political science.

■ **Longer selections often have an *overall* pattern.**

Just as individual paragraphs typically have a pattern, so do longer selections. A longer selection may have one of the six patterns described in this chapter, or it may have a mixed pattern.

■ **When you need to learn information presented in a comparison–contrast paragraph, make a chart.**

To make it easier to learn information in a comparison–contrast paragraph, you should organize the information on paper. A good way to do that is to draw a chart. Research shows that simply *creating* a chart helps you transfer information into your long-term (permanent) memory. To create a chart write the items that are being compared and contrasted, and then list the types or categories of similarities or differences. Finally, fill in the specific similarities and differences. For example, a chart on the differences between communication styles in high-context and low-context cultures (described in the sample paragraph on pages 133–134) could be set up this way:

COMMUNICATION DIFFERENCES IN HIGH-CONTEXT AND LOW-CONTEXT CULTURES		
	High-Context Cultures	**Low-Context Cultures**
Nonverbal behaviors	Better at interpreting these; assume others can do this	(Less skilled at interpreting nonverbal messages)
Speaking	Speak less	(Speak more)
Listening	Listen more	(Listen less)
Communication style	Indirect, less explicit	Direct, explicit Emphasize verbal messages

The information in parentheses in the right column was not directly stated in the paragraph, but it was clear from what was said about high-context cultures that there were differences.

■ **Two additional patterns are the *description pattern* and the *summary pattern*.**

Good news: Both of these patterns are common, obvious, and exactly what they sound like. *Authors use the **description pattern** to describe something: to tell what it is like or give its characteristics.* In an art history textbook, the author might describe a famous statue—the subject matter, the material used, the size, and what makes the statue special or unusual. The details give the characteristics or specific description. Watch for signal words such as *could be described as, characterized by,* and *like* and *as.*

In this sample paragraph, the author of a fitness textbook describes heatstroke. Although the entire paragraph describes heatstroke, only one sentence contains clue words.

Heatstroke is a serious, life-threatening emergency. The specific cause of heatstroke is unknown; however, there is a breakdown of the sweating mechanism, and the body loses the ability to sweat. It is characterized by sudden collapse with loss of consciousness; red, relatively dry skin; and most important, a very high body temperature. Heatstroke can occur suddenly and without warning. Usually, the victim will not experience signs of heat cramps or heat exhaustion. Every first-aid effort should be directed to lowering body temperature. It is imperative that the victim be transported to a hospital as quickly as possible. The possibility of death from heatstroke can be significantly reduced if body temperature is lowered to normal within 45 minutes.

Source: William Prentice, *Get Fit, Stay Fit,* 3d ed., p. 259. Copyright © 2004 McGraw-Hill. Reprinted by permission of The McGraw-Hill Companies.

*The **summary pattern** is typically used in a concluding paragraph at the end of a selection, article, or section of a textbook to present the overall main idea or conclusion.* (You were introduced to overall main idea in Chapter 4, remember? You'll learn more about conclusions in Chapter 9.) Pay special attention to summary paragraphs: you can expect to be asked test questions about the information in them. Because overall main ideas and conclusions are so important, authors are usually great about announcing them with clue words. These include *In summary, To sum up, In sum, In short, In brief, In a nutshell, In general, The point is,* and *Overall.* Conclusions are often announced with *Thus, Therefore, Consequently,* and *In conclusion.* These clue words often appear at the beginning of the sentence or paragraph, but they do not have to. Sometimes they appear in the middle of a sentence or they start the final sentence of a paragraph. Here's a marriage and family textbook passage that illustrates the summary pattern. Notice the use of the phrase *in sum.*

Life in the black family, in sum, is likely to have certain problematic aspects primarily because of the effects of discrimination and deprivation in American society, But many black families are strong and viable and in some areas even have an advantage over white families.

Source: Robert Lauer and Jeanette Lauer, *Marriage and Family,* 6th ed., p. 39. Copyright © 2007 McGraw-Hill. Reprinted by permission of The McGraw-Hill Companies.

TRANSITION WORDS, RELATIONSHIPS AMONG IDEAS, AND METACOMPREHENSION

You can increase your comprehension if you (1) understand the *function* of each paragraph in a longer selection and (2) recognize the transition words that authors use to move you from one idea or paragraph to the next. These two things logically go together. ***Transition words** are words and phrases that show relationships among ideas within paragraphs and within longer selections.* (These words can also help you see the organizational pattern the author is using.)

When you read material that is written with clear transitions, you will generally know "where you are," "how you got there," and the type of information the author is giving you (such as an example, a new idea, a conclusion, etc.). However, if the author does not use very many transitions, you may have to go back through the material after you have finished reading it and think about how it was organized. This important step not only helps you understand the material, but it will also help you remember the material more easily.

Authors also use many of the same clue words to indicate the relationship between information in a single sentence or to show the connection between information in two consecutive sentences. Because you use these same transition words every day of your life, you may not be consciously aware of them. Although there seem to be many types of relationships described below, you will be pleased to discover that you are already familiar with them and that they are commonsense.

On a standardized reading test or state-mandated basic skills test, you may be asked about the relationship of ideas in two parts of the *same* sentence or between two *different* sentences. Such questions are usually worded, "What is the relationship between . . ." or "Identify the relationship between. . . ." You will be asked to identify the way in which two ideas relate to each other; in other words, how the ideas are connected to each other. Watch for clue words and transition words because they will help you determine the connection. If there are two sentences, the transition word often appears at the beginning of the second sentence, such as the word *therefore* in *It takes time to review for a test. Therefore, you should start early.* Sometimes, though, you may have to supply the transition word. For example, in the sentence, *It takes times to review for a test; start early,* you would mentally supply the word *so: It takes time to review for a test, so start early.*

Recognizing the function of a sentence or paragraph in a *longer passage or selection is a process known as **metacomprehension**.* In other words, you're comprehending the big picture, seeing how each part contributes to the whole.

Now read about various types of relationships between ideas within sentences, between sentences, and among paragraphs in a longer selection. We'll also look at the transition words authors use to signal them. They're commonsense, and they'll look very familiar to you. You've already met most of them in the list, sequence, comparison–contrast, cause–effect, spatial order, and summary paragraph patterns.

Here are some common functions that sentences and paragraphs can serve:

- *To introduce a topic.* Many paragraphs and selections begin with a sentence or paragraph that is designed to get the reader's attention or to introduce the topic. For example, an author might begin with a surprising or controversial statement, or perhaps a question. The author might begin with some background information or even the overall main idea (called the *thesis*).

- *To add information.* This relationship among ideas is also known as *elaboration.* Authors use the clue words for lists to indicate that information is being added. That is, they use words such as *and, also, further, in addition, equally, besides, next, moreover, furthermore,* and *finally.* (For example, "Driving a hybrid or fuel efficient car is one way to reduce fuel costs. *Another* is to ride with others by carpooling or taking public transportation. *Besides,* there are motorcycles, bicycling, *and* even walking.")

- *To clarify information.* Authors use certain words to let you know they are trying to make information in a sentence clearer or easier to understand. These include *in other words, clearly, it is obvious, that is, as a matter of fact, in fact, evidently,* and *of course.* A new or complex concept is usually followed by a clarification. The clarification can come in the sentence itself: "A form of marriage that has been widely practiced throughout the world is polygyny, *that is,* marriage that consists of one husband and several wives." Or clarification might be given in the following sentence: "A form of marriage that has been widely practiced throughout the world is polygyny. *In other words,* marriage that consists of one husband and several wives has been found worldwide."

■ *To change directions.* Some sentences or paragraphs alert you that the author is making a detour or even a U-turn. That is, the author presents a contrast, an opposing view, or an exception. Some transition words that signal a direction change are *in contrast, but, on the other hand, unlike,* and *although.*

■ *To continue with an earlier train of thought.* The author is returning to the original train of thought after a detour and is now "going forward" again. The author lets you know this is happening by using transition words such as *and yet, nevertheless, in spite of, despite,* and *regardless.*

■ *To move ahead with new information.* Certain transition words indicate that the author is "back on the main highway" and once again "moving ahead." That is, the author begins presenting new or additional information. Signals include *moreover, in addition, also, first, second, next,* and so forth. (If items or events are presented in a specific order you'll see transition words such as *first, second, next, later, then, finally,* and *last.*) This is the same as adding information (second bullet in this list).

■ *To present causes or effects (or problems and solutions).* Some transition words signal that the author is presenting causes or effects. Watch for transitions such as *resulted in, led to, caused, due to, because, caused by, consequently, therefore,* and *thus.*

■ *To present proof.* There may be one or more paragraphs that present evidence or proof that supports the overall main idea. Watch for clues such as *one reason, another reason,* and *because.*

■ *To present examples.* It is easy to identify examples because authors introduce them with signal words such as *to illustrate, such as, for instance,* and *for example.*

■ *To present a conclusion or summary.* Conclusions and summary statements (often the main idea of the paragraph or the selection) typically appear at the end of a paragraph or selection. Authors emphasize this important information by using transitions such as *in conclusion, to summarize, in summary, thus, therefore, consequently, the point is,* and *remember.*

When you are reading material that seems difficult or confusing, stop and ask yourself, "What is the relationship between the ideas in this sentence?" and "What is the relationship between the ideas in these sentences?" As you know, the brain is a born pattern seeker and problem solver. Sometimes you just need to ask it the right questions.

As you read, ask yourself, What is the *function* of this paragraph? (To present an introduction? Give examples? Exceptions? Proof? A conclusion?) Watch for transition words because they can help you determine the function. For a longer selection or section of a chapter, jot the function of each paragraph in the margin beside it. (You may also want to jot down the topic or main idea as well.) Suppose, for example, you read a textbook passage about the problem of the increasing number of homeless families in America. You might make these metacomprehension marginal annotations about the function of each paragraph:

Function

Paragraph 1:   Introduction—attention grabber

Paragraph 2:   Problem

Paragraph 3:   Background (history of problem)

Paragraph 4:   First major cause

Paragraph 5:   Second major cause

Paragraph 6:   Third major cause

Paragraph 7:   One possible solution

Paragraph 8:   A second possible solution

Paragraph 9:   A third possible solution

Paragraph 10:   Conclusion (recommendation of which solution to choose)

Unless a passage is very clearly written, you may not be able to determine the pattern until after you have finished reading it and have reflected for a moment. Writing out the functions of the paragraphs helps you see how the author has organized the information. It enables you to comprehend and remember the information more easily. Plug in the main idea for each paragraph and you've got it made.

THE REPLAY

▷◁

REMEMBERING THE ESSENTIAL INFORMATION FROM THE CHAPTER

Bravo! You now know the six common writing patterns authors use. To recognize these writing patterns, you can call on your common sense and on knowledge you already possess. When you are reading a paragraph or a longer selection, ask yourself, "What pattern has the author used to organize the information?"

Here is the drill sergeant's "chant" for patterns. Read it aloud. View it as a rap song and sing it! Use it in whatever way helps you learn the information.

Paragraph patterns conceptualize
Ways that authors organize.

Order's not important in a *list;*
Just be sure no items are missed.

In *sequence,* the order must be correct;
From first to last, make things connect.

Definition always defines a term
That the author wants you to learn.

Compare/contrast presents with ease
Differences and similarities.

Cause–effect helps all adults
Understand reasons and results.

Spatial, whether near or far,
Indicates where things are.

These patterns help you analyze
The ways that authors organize.

Now complete The Replay. Write out the definition of "writing patterns" and the question to ask yourself. Then write the *names* and *definitions* of the six patterns on the lines below. (*Coach's tip:* Highlight the names of the writing patterns to make them stand out.) Try first to write them from memory. If you get stuck, go back and look them up. After you have finished writing, read the information aloud, then try to say it aloud without looking. Finally, add at least three or four clue words or signals that go with each pattern. Again, if you get stuck, look back at the summary chart on pages 135–136. Taking a few minutes to do these extra steps will be a powerful key to learning this information.

Definition of Writing Pattern

_____

_____

Question to Ask Yourself

_____

_____

_____

First writing pattern: _____

Definition: _____

_____

_____

Clue words and signals: _____

_____

_____

_____

_____

Second writing pattern: _____

Definition: _____

_____

_____

Clue words and signals: _____

_____

_____

_____

Third writing pattern: _____

Definition: _____

_____

_____

Clue words and signals: _____

_____

_____

_____

_____

_____

Fourth writing pattern: _____

Definition: _____

_____

Clue words and signals: *Causes:* _____

_____

Effect: _____

_____

_____

Fifth writing pattern: _____

Definition: _____

_____

_____

Clue words and signals: *Comparisons:* _____

_____

_____

Contrasts: _____

_____

_____

_____

Sixth writing pattern: _____

Definition: _____

Clue words and signals: _____

_____

_____

_____

How are you doing at this point? Do you realize what a long way you've come since you began this book? Take a minute to reflect on where you are. How do you feel about what you've accomplished? At this point is there anything that confuses you? Write your responses here:

_____

_____

_____

_____

_____

_____

_____

_____

THE PRACTICE

SET 1

APPLY THE SKILL OF RECOGNIZING AUTHORS' WRITING PATTERNS

Exercises: Recognizing Authors' Writing Patterns

Read each paragraph below. Think about its main idea and how the author has organized the details in relation to the main idea. Look for clue words and signals that suggest the pattern. I've helped you out a little: All the paragraphs contain clue words or signals. Mark the clue words and signals because they will help you identify the pattern. Only paragraphs with a single *list, sequence, definition, cause–effect, comparison–contrast* or *spatial* pattern have been used: None of the paragraphs has a mixed pattern. You will probably need to read some of the paragraphs more than once. Use the list of clue words and signals on pages 135–136 to help you as you work through this exercise. Before you begin, take some deep, relaxing breaths.

CAMPAIGN DEVELOPMENT

Public relations practitioners use a systematic approach to developing their campaigns. One such approach, developed by Bernays, is called "the engineering of consent" and consists of the following eight steps:

1. Define goals or objectives.
2. Research publics to find out whether goals are realistic and attainable, and how.
3. Modify goals if research finds them unrealistic.
4. Determine a strategy to reach goals.
5. Plan actions, themes, and appeals to publics.
6. Plan the organization to meet goals.
7. Time and plan tactics to meet goals.
8. Set up a budget.

Source: James R. Wilson and S. Roy Wilson, *Mass Media, Mass Culture,* 5th ed., pp. 382–83. Copyright © 2001 McGraw-Hill. Reprinted by permission of The McGraw-Hill Companies.

_____   1.   The writing pattern in this paragraph is
        a.   list.
        b.   sequence.
        c.   comparison–contrast.
        d.   cause–effect.

Words are the tools of a speaker's craft. They have special uses just like the tools of any other profession. Have you ever watched a carpenter at work? The job that would take you or me a couple of hours is done by the carpenter in 10 minutes—with the right tools. You can't drive a nail with a screwdriver or turn a screw with a hammer. It is the same with public speaking. You must choose the right words for the job you want to do.

Source: Stephen Lucas, *The Art of Public Speaking,* 8th ed., p. 267. Copyright © 2004 McGraw-Hill. Reprinted by permission of The McGraw-Hill Companies.

_____   2.   The writing pattern in this paragraph is
        a.   definition.
        b.   list.
        c.   sequence.
        d.   comparison–contrast.

The consequences of America's high adolescent pregnancy rate are cause for great concern. Adolescent pregnancy creates health risks for both the offspring and the mother. Infants born to adolescent mothers are more likely to have low birth weights—a prominent factor in infant mortality—as well as neurological problems and childhood illness. Adolescent mothers often drop out of school. Although many adolescent mothers resume their education later in life, they generally do not catch up with women who postpone childbearing.

Source: Adapted from John Santrock, *Adolescence,* 8th ed., p. 369. Copyright © 2001 McGraw-Hill. Reprinted by permission of The McGraw-Hill Companies.

_____   **3.** The writing pattern in this paragraph is
     a. definition.
     b. sequence.
     c. list.
     d. cause–effect.

Condominiums are individually owned housing units in a building with several such units. Individual ownership does not include the common areas, such as hallways, outside grounds, and recreational facilities. These areas are owned by the condominium association, which is run by the people who own the housing units. The condominium association oversees the management and operation of the housing complex. Condominium owners are charged a monthly fee to cover the maintenance, repairs, improvements, and insurance for the building and the common areas. A condominium is not a type of building or structure; it is a legal form of home ownership.

Source: Adapted from Jack Kapoor, Les Dlabay, and Robert J. Hughes, *Personal Finance,* 7th ed., p. 291. Copyright © 2004 McGraw-Hill. Reprinted by permission of The McGraw-Hill Companies.

_____   **4.** The writing pattern in this paragraph is
     a. list.
     b. sequence.
     c. definition.
     d. comparison–contrast.

Back problems account for more than 20% of work injuries. Many of these could be prevented through proper lifting technique:

- First, avoid bending at the waist. Remain in an upright position and crouch down if you need to lower yourself to grasp the object. Bend at the knees and hips.

- Next, place feet securely about shoulder-width apart; grip the object firmly.

- Then lift gradually, with straight arms. Avoid quick, jerky motions. Lift by standing up or pushing with your leg muscles. Keep the object close to your body.

- If you have to turn, change the position of your feet. Twisting is a common and dangerous cause of injury. Plan ahead so that your pathway is clear and turning can be minimized.

- Finally, put the object down gently, reversing the rules for lifting.

Source: Paul Insel and Walton Roth, *Core Concepts in Health,* 9th ed., Brief, p. 377. Copyright © 2002 McGraw-Hill. Reprinted by permission of The McGraw-Hill Companies.

_____   **5.** The writing pattern in this paragraph is
     a. list.
     b. sequence.
     c. comparison–contrast.
     d. cause–effect.

PAYING FOR COLLEGE

Tuition costs vary greatly from one school to another, but they are substantial everywhere. It costs just over $1,627 per year in tuition at the average public community college; the average four-year public college costs $3,356; and the average private college costs $15,380. If you live on campus, count on another five or six thousand dollars for room and board.

Source: Robert S. Feldman, *P.O.W.E.R. Learning,* 2005 ed., p. 350. Copyright © 2005 McGraw-Hill. Reprinted by permission of The McGraw-Hill Companies.

_____   **6.** The writing pattern in this paragraph is
    a. comparison–contrast.
    b. sequence.
    c. cause–effect.
    d. definition.

ADVERTISING DEFINED

Advertising is the activity consumers most associate with the term *marketing.* **Advertising** is a marketing communications element that is persuasive, nonpersonal, paid for by an identified sponsor, and disseminated through mass channels of communications to promote the adoption of goods, services, persons or ideas.

Source: William Bearden, Thomas Ingram, and Raymond LaForge, *Marketing,* 3d ed., p. 393. Copyright © 2001 McGraw-Hill. Reprinted by permission of The McGraw-Hill Companies.

_____   **7.** The writing pattern in this paragraph is
    a. list.
    b. sequence.
    c. definition.
    d. cause–effect.

Why do women stay with men who abuse them? Some cannot bring themselves to face and admit what is happening. Some have low self-esteem and feel they deserve to be beaten. Constant ridicule, criticism, threats, punishment, and psychological manipulation may destroy their self-confidence and overwhelm them with self-doubt. Some women feel they have nowhere to turn. Their abusive partners isolate them from family and friends. They are often financially dependent and lack outside social support. If they try to end the relationship or call the police, they get more abuse. Some women are afraid to leave—a realistic fear, since some abusive husbands later track down and beat or even kill their estranged wives.

Source: Adapted from Sally Olds, Diane Papalia and Ruth Feldman, *Human Development,* 9th ed., p. 511. Copyright © 2004 McGraw-Hill. Reprinted by permission of The McGraw-Hill Companies.

_____   **8.** The writing pattern in this paragraph is
    a. comparison–contrast.
    b. sequence.
    c. definition.
    d. cause–effect.

The known part of the cavern in the Chauvet Cave near Ardèche, France, consists of four great halls, up to 70 yards long and 40 yards wide. They are connected by smaller galleries that are roughly five by four yards. The more than 300 prehistoric cave paintings and engravings vary in size between 2 feet and 12 feet long. Some stand alone, while others are clustered in panels or painted with some cohesion, such as two rhinos head-to-head as if in a fight.

Source: Adapted from Conrad Kottak, *Physical Anthropology and Archaeology*, p. 215. Copyright © 2004 McGraw-Hill. Reprinted by permission of The McGraw-Hill Companies.

_____ **9.** The writing pattern in this paragraph is
  a. list.
  b. cause–effect.
  c. definition.
  d. spatial.

STRESS REDUCTION

Prolonged stress is a problem for many college students. It can wear you down and produce burnout. It can lead to physical problems, such as migraine headaches, ulcers, high blood pressure, or serious illnesses. Research has indicated that constant change over a long period of time can cause excessive levels of stress. Too many negative or positive changes stimulate the production of certain hormones and chemicals that affect the body. The solution is not to avoid stress but to acknowledge it directly and learn to manage and channel it.

Source: Adapted from Sharon Ferrett, *Peak Performance*, 5th ed., pp. 10–22. Copyright © 2006 McGraw-Hill. Reprinted by permission of The McGraw-Hill Companies.

_____ **10.** The writing pattern in this paragraph is
  a. comparison–contrast.
  b. sequence.
  c. problem–solution.
  d. definition.

Under ordinary conditions, laboratory examination of blood evidence can determine the following about the source of the blood:

1. The species (human, dog, horse, etc.).
2. The sex.
3. The blood type and the DNA profile.
4. Whether drugs or alcohol have been used by the source of the blood.
5. The presence of certain types of illnesses (e.g., venereal disease).
6. The presence of carbon monoxide.
7. Whether the source was a smoker.

Source: Charles Swanson, Neil Chamelin, Leonard Territo, and Robert Taylor, *Criminal Investigation*, 9th ed., p. 124. Copyright © 2006 McGraw-Hill. Reprinted by permission of The McGraw-Hill Companies.

_____ **11.** The writing pattern in this paragraph is
  a. list.
  b. sequence.
  c. definition.
  d. comparison–contrast.

A mountain of data reveal that most people are happier attached than unattached. Compared to those single or widowed, and especially compared to those divorced or separated, married people report being happier and more satisfied with life. In representative surveys of more than 35,000 Americans since 1972, for example, 23 percent of never-married adults, but 40 percent of married adults, have reported being very happy. This marriage-happiness link occurs across ethnic groups. Moreover, satisfaction with marriage predicts overall happiness much better than does satisfaction with job, finances, or community. And among the nonmarried, rates of suicide and depression run higher. Indeed, there are few stronger predictors of happiness than a close, nurturing, equitable, intimate, life-long companionship with one's best friend.

Source: Adapted from David Myers, *Social Psychology*, 7th ed., p. 590. Copyright © 2002 McGraw-Hill. Reprinted by permission of The McGraw-Hill Companies.

_____ **12.** The writing pattern in this paragraph is
   a. problem–solution.
   b. sequence.
   c. definition.
   d. comparison–contrast.

That wasn't as hard as you thought it was going to be, was it? Determining an author's organizational pattern is a little like solving a puzzle. There are lots of clues, but you have to be alert and take advantage of them.

Did any particular pattern seem to cause you difficulty? Were you able to locate most of the clue words and signals? Take a minute to respond to these questions. Then jot down anything about patterns that you need to ask about in class.

_____

_____

_____

_____

_____

_____

_____

SET 2

Exercises: Recognizing Authors' Writing Patterns

For this set of exercises, read each paragraph. Then do these three things:

1. Mark any clue words or signals.

2. Write the name of the pattern used in the paragraph.

3. Tell the information that is organized by the pattern. That is, tell specifically *what* is being listed, sequenced, defined, or compared or contrasted. For a cause–effect paragraph, tell the cause and the effect. For problem–solution, identify the problem and the solution. For a spatial pattern, tell what is being described. Examples of answers would be *a list (of the characteristics of deciduous trees), a sequence (of steps for preparing a microscopic slide), the causes (of pneumonia), a contrast (between boys' and girls' achievement in math), the definition (of gerrymandering), the problem (of gang violence),* or *spatial (the layout of a basketball court).* Refer to the list of clue words and signals on pages 135–136 to help you as you work though this exercise.

Part of being a successful student is following directions. Don't lose points on assignments or tests because you fail to read or follow the directions.

1.   CAUSES OF OBESITY

There is still an ongoing debate as to the causes of obesity. Genetic, physiological, metabolic, environmental, psychological, and other factors may all play a part. Genetics, dietary practice, and activity level seem to all play a role in the dramatic increase in obesity in Americans during the last 20 years. There are four additional factors that seem to play a significant role in the prevalence of obesity: sex, age, socioeconomic status, and race. As biology only accounts for 33% of the variation in body weight, the environment can also exert an enormous influence. Among women, obesity is strongly associated with socioeconomic status. While the precise cause of obesity remains unclear, we do know that obesity is a complex condition caused by a variety of factors. Until we are sure what causes obesity, it makes sense that it is difficult to develop effective ways of managing weight.

Source: Adapted from Wayne Payne, Dale Hahn, and Ellen Mauer, *Understanding Your Health,* 8th ed., p. 185. Copyright © 2005 McGraw-Hill. Reprinted by permission of The McGraw-Hill Companies.

Pattern: _____

_____

(Did you remember to tell the *type* of information organized by the pattern?)

2.   SUICIDE

Suicide is the third leading cause of death for young adults 15 to 24 years old and the eleventh leading cause of all deaths in the United States. Men commit suicide four times more often than women do, and 72% of all suicides are committed by white men. Suicide occurs most often among Americans age 65 and older. However, women are three times more likely than men to attempt suicide. Men tend to employ more lethal methods such as using firearms, hanging, or jumping from high places, while women tend to use methods of suicide such as overdosing with pills or cutting their wrists, which are slower methods and allow more time for medical attention. Twice as many Caucasians complete suicide as African Americans, with Asian Americans being one of the lowest risk groups in terms of ethnicity. The suicide rate for the Hispanic population is lower than for Caucasians but higher than for African Americans.

Source: Wayne Payne, Dale Hahn, and Ellen Mauer, *Understanding Your Health,* 8th ed., p. 45. Copyright © 2005 McGraw-Hill. Reprinted by permission of The McGraw-Hill Companies.

Pattern: _____

_____

_____

3. A political party can legally give $10,000 directly to a House candidate and $37,500 to a Senate candidate. This funding, along with the money a candidate receives from individual contributors ($2,000 maximum per contributor) and interest groups ($5,000 maximum per group), is termed **hard money.** It goes directly to the candidate and can be spent as he or she chooses.

Source: Adapted from Thomas E. Patterson, *The American Democracy,* Alternate 7th ed., p. 262. Copyright © 2005 McGraw-Hill. Reprinted by permission of The McGraw-Hill Companies.

Pattern: _____

4. ### PRESERVING FOOTWEAR PRINTS

Footwear prints at a crime scene may or may not be readily visible. If they are not immediately apparent, turn off the lights and search for prints using a flashlight held close to, but obliquely from, the surface you are examining. When you find prints:

1. Take general crime scene photos showing the location of the footwear prints.
2. Take photos from directly overhead using lighting and a tripod. Before you take photos, place a linear scale next to, and on the same plane as, the footwear prints. Also place a label in the area being photographed to correlate photos with crime scene and photo log records.

Source: Adapted from Charles Swanson, Neil Chamelin, Leonard Territo, and Robert Taylor, *Criminal Investigation,* 9th ed., p. 98. Copyright © 2006 McGraw-Hill. Reprinted by permission of The McGraw-Hill Companies.

Pattern: _____

_____

5. Manufacturers lose hundreds of millions of dollars annually on fraudulent coupon submissions. Some coupons are counterfeited; others are submitted for products that were never purchased. To fight this problem, some companies have developed computerized systems to detect fraudulent submissions and charge them back to the retailers who made them.

Source: William Arens, *Contemporary Advertising,* 10th ed., p. 330. Copyright © 2006 McGraw-Hill/ Irwin. Reprinted by permission of The McGraw-Hill Companies.

Pattern: _____

_____

6. With so much information available everywhere all the time, what will this do to us as human beings? We can already see the outlines of the future. *One* *result is information overload:* By 2005 more than 36 billion person-to-person emails were being sent daily. Already, the average business user reportedly spends more than 2 hours a day just dealing with email. *Another is less use of our brains for memorizing:* Familiar phone numbers and other facts are being stored on speed-dial cellphones, pocket computers, and electronic databases, increasing our dependence on technology. *A third result is a surge in "multitasking" activity:* People have become highly skilled in performing several tasks at once, such as doing homework while talking on the phone or watching TV; answering email and surfing the World Wide Web. *A fourth is that smart mobile devices could produce "smart mobs"*—groups of people who can do things together (in business, politics, and journalism, for example) even if they don't know each other. These four trends pose unique challenges to how you learn and manage information.

Source: Adapted from Brian Williams and Stacey Sawyer, *Using Information Technology*, 4th ed., p. 2. Copyright © 2006 McGraw-Hill/Irwin. Reprinted by permission of The McGraw-Hill Companies.

Pattern: _____

_____

_____

7.   A person's dominant mode can often be determined by watching his or her eyes. Generally speaking, left-brained individuals—about 90 percent of the population—display the predictable eye movements when searching their memories. Visually-oriented people look up and to the left at a 45-degree angle. People with an auditory dominant mode look directly left. "Feeling" people look down and to the right at a 45-degree angle. People in the other 10 percent of the population are right-brained and will display a mirror image of the eye movements of their left-brained counterparts.

Source: Charles Swanson, Neil Chamelin, Leonard Territo, and Robert Taylor, *Criminal Investigation*, 9th ed., p. 159. Copyright © 2006 McGraw-Hill. Reprinted by permission of The McGraw-Hill Companies.

Pattern: _____

_____

8.   Here are some tips for keeping your motivation alive, so that you can work with your full energy behind you.

- **Take responsibility for your failures—and successes.** When you do poorly on a test, don't blame the teacher, the textbook, or a job that kept you from studying. Analyze the situation, and see how you could have changed what you did to be more successful in the future. At the same time, when you're successful, think of the things you did to bring about that success.

- **Think positively.** Assume that the strengths that you have will allow you to succeed and that, if you have difficulty, you can figure out what to do.

- **Accept that you can't control everything.** Seek to understand which things can be changed and which cannot. You might be able to get an extension on a paper due date, but you are probably not going to be excused from a collegewide requirement.

Source: Robert S. Feldman, *P.O.W.E.R. Learning*, 2005 ed. p. 14. Copyright © 2005 McGraw-Hill. Reprinted by permission of The McGraw-Hill Companies.

Pattern: _____

_____

9. Passive listening is a habit, but so is active listening. Active listeners give their undivided attention to the speaker in a genuine effort to understand his or her point of view. In conversation, they do not interrupt the speaker or finish his or her sentences. When listening to a speech, they do not allow themselves to be distracted by internal or external interference, and they do not prejudge the speaker. They take listening seriously and do the best they can to stay focused on the speaker and his or her message.

Source: Stephen Lucas, *The Art of Public Speaking,* 8th ed., pp. 63–4. Copyright © 2004 McGraw-Hill. Reprinted by permission of The McGraw-Hill Companies.

Pattern: _____

_____

_____

10. Although you may always be a little nervous about public speaking, it's important to keep several points in mind:

- Audiences are generally sympathetic. They've all been where you are and probably share your fears about public speaking. They're on your side and are rooting for you to succeed.

- Once you start speaking, it will become easier. Anxiety tends to be highest before you start talking. Most people find that after they start a talk, their nervousness declines.

- Practice helps. Practice and preparation for the talk will go a long way toward easing your tension.

Source: Robert S. Feldman, *P.O.W.E.R. Learning,* 2005 Ed., p. 189. Copyright © 2005 McGraw-Hill. Reprinted by permission of The McGraw-Hill Companies.

Pattern: _____

_____

_____

SET 3

Exercises: Recognizing Authors' Writing Patterns

Last set! Read each paragraph carefully because these are a little harder than the previous ones. Mark any clue words or signals, and then write the name of the pattern used in the paragraph. Just as you did in the previous set of exercises, tell specifically *what* is being listed or classified, sequenced, defined, or compared or contrasted. For a cause–effect paragraph, tell the cause and the effect. For a spatial pattern, tell what is being described. (Yawn and stretch for a minute, then start in.)

1. Criminologists have looked closely at situations in which assaults are committed. One researcher identified six stages of a confrontational situation that leads to an assault:

    1. One person insults another.
    2. The insulted person perceives the significance of the insult, often by noting the reactions of others present, and becomes angry.
    3. The insulted person contemplates a response: fight, flight or conciliation. If the response chosen is fight, the insultee assaults the insulter then and there. If another response is chosen, the situation advances to stage 4.
    4. The original insulter, now reprimanded, shamed, or embarrassed, makes a countermove: fight or flight.
    5. If the choice is a fight, the insulter assaults (and possibly kills) the insultee.
    6. The "triumphant" party flees or awaits the consequences (for example, police response).

    Source: Freda Adler, Gerhard Mueller, and William Laufer, *Criminology,* 5th ed., pp. 247–48. Copyright © 2004 McGraw-Hill. Reprinted by permission of The McGraw-Hill Companies.

    Pattern: _____

    _____

    _____

2. ### THE IMPORTANCE OF EFFECTIVE DESIGN

    When document design is poor, both organizations and society suffer. The *Challenger* space shuttle blew up because its o-rings failed in the excessive cold. Poor communication—including charts that hid, rather than emphasized, the data—contributed to the decision to launch. The *Columbia* space shuttle disintegrated during reentry, and poor communication was again implicated in NASA's failure to ensure the spacecraft was safe. After studying transcripts of meetings, Edward R. Tufte, who specializes in visual presentations of evidence, concluded that engineers did offer their concerns and supporting statistics, but they did so using visuals that obscured the seriousness, and that the piece of foam striking the shuttle was far larger than anything they had tested. In 2000, the badly designed "butterfly ballot" confused enough voters to change the outcome of the U.S. presidential election.

    Source: Kitty Locker, *Business and Administrative Communication,* 7th ed., p. 128. Copyright © 2006 McGraw-Hill/Irwin. Reprinted by permission of The McGraw-Hill Companies.

    Pattern: _____

    _____

3. The great Roman orator Cicero (106–43 b.c.) wrote that the Romans were like other people except in their religious fervor: "In reference for the gods, we are far superior." Perhaps more than any other ancient civilizations, the Romans

saw the world as infused with spirits; in their view, almost every space was governed by some divinity. Rome itself was guarded by three deities that protected the state—Jupiter, Juno, and Minerva—but there were gods for even smaller spaces. There were goddesses for the countryside, for the hills, and for the valleys. There were three gods to guard entrances—one for the door, one for the hinges, and a third for the lintel, the door's upper supporting beam. The remaining spaces within the home were equally inhabited by spirits that demanded worship and sacrifice.

Source: Dennis Sherman and Joyce Salisbury, *The West in the World,* pp. 120–21. Copyright © 2001 McGraw-Hill. Reprinted by permission of The McGraw-Hill Companies.

Pattern: _____

_____

4.   Today millions of buyers and sellers are linking up at online auctions, where everything is available from comic books to wines. There are generally two types of auction sites: (1) person-to-person auctions, such as eBay (www.ebay.com), that connect buyers and sellers for a listing fee and a commission on sold items, and (2) vendor-based auctions, such as OnSale (www.onsale.com), that buy merchandise and sell it at discount. Some auctions are specialized, such as Priceline (www.priceline.com), an auction site for airline tickets and other items.

Source: Adapted from Fred Hofstetter, *Internet Literacy,* 4th ed., p. 83. Copyright © 2005 McGraw-Hill/Irwin. Reprinted by permission of The McGraw-Hill Companies.

Pattern: _____

_____

_____

5.   At first encounter with *Guernica,* Picasso's 1937 mural protesting the brutality of war, the viewer is overwhelmed by its presence. The painting is huge—more than 25 feet long and nearly 12 feet high—and its stark, powerful imagery seems to reach out and engulf the observer. Picasso used no colors; the whole painting is done in white and black and shades of gray. We cannot misunderstand the scenes of extreme pain and anguish throughout the canvas. At far left a shrieking mother holds her dead child, and at far right another woman, in a burning house, screams in agony. The gaping mouths and clenched hands speak of disbelief at such mindless cruelty.

Source: Adapted from Mark Getlein, *Living with Art,* 7th ed., p. 59. Copyright © 2005 McGraw-Hill. Reprinted by permission of The McGraw-Hill Companies.

Pattern: _____

_____

6.   **COMMITTEE CHAIRS: THE SENIORITY PRINCIPLE**

Most of the work of Congress takes place in the meetings of its thirty-five standing (permanent) committees and their numerous subcommittees, each of which is headed by a chairperson. Committee chairs are always members of the majority party, and they usually have the most *seniority* (the most consecutive years of service on a particular committee). Seniority is based strictly on time served on a committee, not on time spent in Congress. If a member switches committees, the years spent on the first committee do not count toward seniority on the second one.

Source: Adapted from Thomas Patterson, *The American Democracy*, Alternate 7th ed., p. 350. Copyright © 2005 McGraw-Hill. Reprinted by permission of The McGraw-Hill Companies.

Pattern: _____

_____

7.   In one particular instance, Ben & Jerry's received a large number of complaints that its Cherry Garcia Ice Cream didn't have enough cherries. The complaints were coming in from all over the country, so it wasn't a regional problem. Employees determined that the manufacturing process (from the supplies of raw materials to the mixing) was satisfactory and had no anomalies. Eventually the problem was determined to be that the ice cream container for Cherry Garcia Ice Cream had on it a photo of frozen yogurt, a product with more cherries than ice cream. Simply changing the photo on the carton solved the problem.

Source: Stephen Haag, Maeve Cummings, and Amy Phillips, *Management Information Systems*, 6th ed., pp. 150–51. Copyright © 2007 McGraw-Hill/Irwin. Reprinted by permission of The McGraw-Hill Companies.

Pattern: _____

_____

8.   On the basis of observations and previous data, a scientist formulates a hypothesis. The hypothesis is tested by further observations or a controlled experiment, and new data either support or falsify the hypothesis. The scientist may then choose to retest the same hypothesis or to test a related hypothesis.

Source: Adapted from Sylvia Mader, *Inquiry into Life,* 9th ed., p. 6. Copyright © 2001 McGraw-Hill. Reprinted by permission of The McGraw-Hill Companies.

Pattern: _____

_____

Congratulations on completing all the instructional chapters in the Basic Workout. The next section, Part 3: Basic Stretching, will give you a chance to "reach" a bit by having you apply *all* the skills you've learned so far. If you've been training steadily, you should be able to do it. Good luck!

PART·THREE 3 Basic Stretching

CHAPTER IN PART THREE

7 Apply All the Basic Skills to Paragraphs

CHAPTER

Apply All the Basic Skills to Paragraphs

APPLY ALL THE BASIC SKILLS TO PARAGRAPHS

Here you are! Do you realize at this point that you've completed all the chapters that comprise the Basic Workout? You've learned how to

- determine the topic of a paragraph.
- locate the stated main idea.
- formulate the main idea when the author does not state it as a single sentence.
- identify the supporting details.
- recognize the writing pattern the author uses to organize and present the information.

Not only that, but you've had lots of practice applying each of these skills!

Practicing reading skills one at a time, however, is like isolating a particular muscle or athletic skill in order to strengthen it. It's important to do that, but just as you don't use one muscle at a time when you're actually playing a sport or doing an aerobic workout, you don't use one skill at a time when you read. Whether you are doing physical activity or reading your textbooks, you have to use all the skills together. That's what this section is all about. It's called "Basic Stretching" because applying several skills to a paragraph may feel like a bit of a "stretch" after practicing the skills in isolation in the preceding chapters.

This chapter is different from the preceding ones because no new skills are introduced. (I know you'll be happy about that!) You won't find the regular chapter sections, such as The Technique, The Trainer, and The Edge. Instead, this chapter consists of three sets of practice exercises that require you to apply *all* the skills you've learned so far. The exercises themselves also differ slightly from those in the preceding chapters. There are still 12 paragraphs in Set 1, 10 paragraphs in Set 2, and 8 paragraphs in Set 3. However, *there is more than one question per paragraph.* In other words, in this chapter the "12-10-8 reps" pyramid describes the number of *paragraphs* per set rather than the total number of questions.

You may be rolling your eyes and thinking, "What!?!" But the extended practice will help you consolidate your learning. It's like gymnasts who work on separate moves, but who still need to go through the whole routine repeatedly to make their performance smooth and automatic. As you repeatedly apply all the basic reading skills to sets of paragraphs, you too will develop more ease and fluidity in your comprehension.

I'm going to talk to you now as a coach, and I'm going to remind you again about the value of practicing what you're learning. My examples come from sports, but keep in mind that what is important are the *principles* they illustrate—not the athletes' abilities or accomplishments. An article in *Newsweek* (June 18, 2001, pp. 42–47) entitled "The Dominator," focused on the "secrets" of Tiger Woods' dominance in professional golf. Even though Woods, then age 25, is considered the world's greatest golfer, he seems to get better and better. *Newsweek* asked Woods and other top athletes (including Michael Jordan, Jackie Joyner-Kersee, Wayne Gretzky, Joe Montana, and Martina Navratilova), what sets apart truly elite athletes such as themselves from other, less-successful professional athletes. It's a given that Woods, like other elite athletes, has extraordinary physical talent, uncommon emotional control, and boundless enthusiasm for the sport. The first rule of success that all of the champion athletes identified was—you guessed it—good old-fashioned *hard work.* Woods practices more than any other golfer; he's even been known to practice during tournaments after the day's round is over. Martina Navratilova has won more singles titles than any other tennis player (male or female), including a record nine Wimbledon tournaments. Navratilova commented, "For every great shot you hit, you've already hit a bunch of times in practice." Former San Francisco 49ers superstar Joe Montana was blunt about practicing. He noted that it can be just plain boring and that lesser athletes simply aren't willing to put in the long hours—or else they deceive themselves into thinking that they are working harder than they really are. The top athletes agreed that practice pays off in pressure situations. As hockey's leading scorer and four-time Stanley Cup winner Wayne Gretzky put it, "No matter who you are, no matter how good an athlete you are, we're creatures of habit. The better your habits are, the better they'll be in pressure situations."

What does this suggest about you and your reading skills? It suggests that practice, even if it takes long hours, hard work, and at times seems boring, will pay off for you in the long run. You'll find that you have the reading skills to perform well under the pressure of a test or in a difficult course. Moreover, you'll already be accustomed to working hard and preparing carefully. This will foster success throughout your life in all areas of endeavor.

The top athletes mentioned another rule of success: "Never, ever be satisfied." Tiger Woods and the other great athletes worked hard to make it to the top. Most athletes try to do that. The difference is that the great ones are committed to improving their game even after they *reach* the top of their profession. You should approach your reading skills the same way. There's no limit on how good a reader you can become. Why stop at average? Why stop at above-average?

When Tiger Woods was interviewed before the start of the U.S. Open golf tournament in 2001, he had already won four major tournaments in a row that year. The interviewer asked him if his goal was to win five tournaments in a row. Woods replied no, his goal was to win *one* tournament, the one that was coming up. In other words, Woods was saying that he wasn't thinking about the past or the future (about the pressure or the prestige of winning five major tournaments in a single year). Instead, he was focusing on the task at hand: the tournament that was happening right then. It makes sense for you, as a student, to adopt that same attitude: focus on the here and now. Focus on each individual reading exercise, not on how many items there are in all, how hard they are, or how many there are left to go. As it turned out, Tiger didn't win the tournament, but he undoubtedly learned a great deal from it that he used to improve his future performance. In 2002, he won the U.S. Open and his third Masters, pushing his number of major titles to eight. By the beginning of 2007, he had won 15 amateur and professional championships. He had won 12 major (professional) championships. He is ranked the best golfer in the world.

One last example illustrates the rules of success that great athletes mentioned. He's a mountain climber named Erik Weihenmayer (pronounced WINE-mayor), who in 2002 and by the age of 34 had summited (climbed to the top of) the "seven summits." (He's pictured on page 165.) The seven summits consist of the tallest peak on each of the world's seven continents. By continent and height, these peaks are Asia: Mount Everest in Nepal (29,035 feet); South America: Aconcagua in Argentina (22,840); North America: Mount McKinley in Alaska (20,320); Africa: Mount Kilimanjaro in Tanzania (19,339); Europe: Mount Elbrus in Russia (18,481); Antarctica: Vinson Massif in the Sentinel Range (16,067); and Australia: Mount Kosciusko in New South Wales (7,310). (Indonesia's 16,023-foot Puncak Jaya is sometimes included as one of the tallest mountains.) Weihenmayer's achievement is impressive by any standard. Fewer than 100 people have summited all seven peaks. Weihenmayer exemplifies the great athlete: extraordinary physical talent, uncommon emotional control, boundless enthusiasm, unlimited hard work, and never, ever being satisfied with the status quo. (He is also a skier, biker, marathoner, skydiver, and he is a certified open-water scuba diver. When he was younger, he won wrestling championships and was an avid dirt biker. After summiting the seven highest mountains, he announced his intention to try parasailing.)

Of the "big seven" mountains, Everest is the highest and most difficult to climb. Nearly 90 percent of those who attempt to climb Mount Everest never make it to the top, and many of those who do manage to make it to the top never make it back down. To get conditioned to the altitude and to take adequate supplies to the first base camp on Everest, however, climbers must make several treks across the Khumbu Icefall, an enormous glacier. It is treacherous because it is constantly changing, and it is laced with stretches of crumbly ice as well as large and small crevasses (long, narrow openings in the ice that can be very deep). Weihenmayer's team leader calculated that team members needed to be able to cross the icefall in seven hours. Weihenmayer's first pass took him 13 hours. Weihenmayer ended up traversing it 10 times for practice. By the last trip, he had whittled his time to five hours. That's hard work. That's patience. That's persistent practice.

The final assault near the top of Everest's South Summit is the point at which many climbers turn back. There is a 656-foot-long knife-edge ridge that can only be crossed by taking baby steps and anchoring the way with a pickaxe. The dropoff on one side of this narrow ridge is a 10,000-foot vertical fall into Tibet; on the other side is a 7,000-foot fall into Nepal (China). If climbers make it past the ridge, they face a 39-foot rock face, then a 45-minute walk up a steep snow slope to reach the summit. That's what Weihenmayer faced, and *Weihenmayer is blind*. He has been blind since he was 13, when he lost his vision to a rare hereditary disease of the retina. His achievement would have been phenomenal if he were sighted. The fact that he summited Everest blind is truly astonishing.

Why am I telling you about Weihenmayer? Undeniably, his story and his triumphs are fascinating. But more than that, it's to inspire you to give your best, to encourage you not to get stalled out at the bottom of the "mountain" because it looks high or because there's a long, challenging path before you. You don't have to get to the summit in a day or a week or even a semester (although you very well may accomplish the latter). What you do need to do is to take the next step. Then the one after that. Take it step by step, exercise by exercise. What matters is that you *keep moving*.

At this point, you've moved your supplies to the first base camp of the mountain— you've learned and practiced a set of basic vocabulary and comprehension skills. Now you're ready to see what you can do with them. You're going to be applying *several* skills to each of the paragraphs in the three exercise sets that follow. Some passages have appeared before. However, you will be applying different skills to them besides the one for which the paragraph was originally used. If you've been working hard, you should be stronger in all of these skills now than you were when you began this book. Good luck! See you at the summit!

THE PRACTICE

SET 1

APPLY ALL THE BASIC SKILLS TO PARAGRAPHS

Exercises: Applying All the Basic Skills to Paragraphs

Read each paragraph, and then mark the answers to the questions that follow. Because determining the main idea is such an essential skill, you will be asked the main idea of each paragraph. However, you will not be asked to apply every skill to every passage. Circle any clue words, number the details, read the passage aloud, reread it if you need to—do whatever helps you be successful. There are 12 paragraphs, but there are 50 questions. Your instructor will give you specific instructions for doing them. You should be able to explain the *reason* for each answer choice you make. It's especially important that you take a minute to breathe deeply, relax your muscles, and focus your concentration. When you've done that, start in.

Paragraph 1

More than four thousand Hispanic Americans nationwide hold public office. Hispanics have been elected to statewide office in several states, including New Mexico and Arizona. About twenty Hispanic Americans currently serve in the House of Representatives. The number of Hispanic Americans now in elected office is the highest in this country's history.

Source: Adapted from Thomas Patterson, *We the People*, 6th ed., p. 168. Copyright © 2006 McGraw-Hill. Reprinted by permission of The McGraw-Hill Companies.

_____ 1. The topic of this paragraph is
  a. Hispanic Americans.
  b. Hispanic Americans in elected office.
  c. Hispanic governors.
  d. Americans who hold public office.

_____ 2. The main idea of this paragraph is:
  a. In 1974 Arizona and New Mexico elected governors of Spanish-speaking background.
  b. About 20 Hispanic Americans currently serve in the House of Representatives.
  c. More than four thousand Hispanic Americans nationwide hold public office.
  d. The number of Hispanic Americans now in elected office is the highest in our country's history.

_____ 3. How many supporting details are given in this paragraph?
  a. one
  b. two
  c. three
  d. four

_____ 4. What is the meaning of *background* as it is used in this paragraph?
  a. ethnic heritage
  b. area of relative unimportance
  c. scenery located behind something
  d. subdued music that accompanies an event

_____ **5.** The writing pattern used in this paragraph is
   a. cause–effect.
   b. list.
   c. definition.
   d. comparison–contrast.

Paragraph 2

Not concentrating is a cause of poor listening. The brain is incredibly efficient. Although we talk at a rate of 120 to 150 words a minute, the brain can process 400 to 800 words a minute. This would seem to make listening very easy, but actually it has the opposite effect. Because we can take in a speaker's words and still have plenty of spare "brain time," we are tempted to interrupt our listening by thinking about other things. And thinking about other things is just what we do.

Source: Adapted from Stephen Lucas, *The Art of Public Speaking,* 8th ed., p. 58. Copyright © 2004 McGraw-Hill. Reprinted by permission of The McGraw-Hill Companies.

_____ **6.** The topic of this paragraph is
   a. the brain.
   b. how fast we think and talk.
   c. not concentrating.
   d. not concentrating and poor listening.

_____ **7.** The main idea of this paragraph is:
   a. Not concentrating is a cause of poor listening.
   b. The brain is incredibly efficient. Although we talk at a rate of 120 to 150 words a minute, the brain can process 400 to 800 words a minute.
   c. This would seem to make listening very easy, but actually it has the opposite effect.
   d. Because we can take in a speaker's words and still have plenty of spare "brain time," we are tempted to interrupt our listening by thinking about other things.

_____ **8.** How many supporting details are given in this paragraph?
   a. two
   b. three
   c. four
   d. five

_____ **9.** The writing pattern used in this paragraph is
   a. sequence.
   b. definition.
   c. comparison–contrast.
   d. cause–effect.

_____ **10.** The root in the word *incredibly* indicates that the word has to do with
   a. believing.
   b. carrying.
   c. speaking.
   d. sending.

Paragraph 3

Of all the ethical lapses a public speaker can commit, few are more serious than plagiarism. *Global plagiarism* is lifting a speech entirely from a single source and passing it off as your own. *Patchwork plagiarism* involves stitching a speech together by copying more or less verbatim from a few sources. Whenever you give a speech, you must be sure it represents your work, your thinking, your language. You must also take care to avoid *incremental plagiarism,* which occurs when a speaker fails to give credit for specific quotations and paraphrases that are borrowed from other people.

Source: Stephen Lucas, *The Art of Public Speaking,* 8th ed., p. 50. Copyright © 2004 McGraw-Hill. Reprinted by permission of The McGraw-Hill Companies.

_____ **11.** The topic of this paragraph is
    a. ethical lapses.
    b. public speaking.
    c. plagiarism.
    d. incremental plagiarism.

_____ **12.** The main idea of this paragraph is:
    a. Plagiarism is a serious ethical lapse.
    b. Plagiarism is a serious ethical lapse, so as a public speaker, you should avoid all forms of it.
    c. Public speakers should educate themselves about plagiarism.
    d. You must also take care to avoid *incremental plagiarism,* which occurs when a speaker fails to give credit for specific quotations and paraphrases that are borrowed from other people.

_____ **13.** What is the meaning of *lifting* as it is used in this paragraph?
    a. stealing
    b. raising
    c. ceasing
    d. rescinding

_____ **14.** The writing pattern used in this paragraph is
    a. list.
    b. sequence.
    c. spatial.
    d. cause–effect.

Paragraph 4

Skilled performances look easy and effortless. In reality, as every dancer, musician, and athlete knows, they're the products of hard work, hours of practice, attention to detail, and intense concentration. Like skilled performances in other arts, writing rests on a base of work.

Source: Adapted from Kitty Locker, *Business and Administrative Communication,* 5th ed., p. 116. Copyright © 2000 McGraw-Hill. Reprinted by permission of The McGraw-Hill Companies.

_____ **15.** The topic of this paragraph is
    a. hard work and attention to detail.
    b. easy, effortless performances.
    c. skilled performances and writing.
    d. dancers, musicians, and athletes.

_____ **16.** The main idea of this paragraph is:
    a. Skilled performances look easy and effortless.
    b. Why some things are harder than they look.
    c. In reality, as every dancer, musician, and athlete knows, they're the products of hard work, hours of practice, attention to detail, and intense concentration.
    d. Skilled performances look easy and effortless, but like all skilled performances, writing rests on a base of work.

_____ **17.** The writing pattern used in this paragraph is
   a. definition.
   b. comparison–contrast.
   c. list.
   d. sequence.

_____ **18.** The suffixes in the words *performances* and *concentration* indicate that the words are
   a. adjectives.
   b. adverbs.
   c. nouns.
   d. verbs.

Paragraph 5

THE IMPORTANCE OF EXPERTISE

Most of the policy problems that the federal government confronts do not lend themselves to simple solutions. Whether the issue is space travel or hunger in America, expert knowledge is essential to the development of effective public policy. Much of this expertise is held by bureaucrats. They spend their careers working in a particular policy area, and many of them have had scientific, technical, or other specialized training.

Source: Adapted from Thomas E. Patterson, *The American Democracy,* Alternate 7th ed., p. 427. Copyright © 2005 McGraw-Hill. Reprinted by permission of The McGraw-Hill Companies.

_____ **19.** The topic of this paragraph is
   a. bureaucrats' expertise in policy areas.
   b. policy problems.
   c. expertise.
   d. the federal government.

_____ **20.** The main idea of this paragraph is:
   a. Most of the policy problems that the federal government confronts do not lend themselves to simple solutions, such as the issues of space travel and hunger in America.
   b. Most of the policy problems that the federal government confronts do not lend themselves to simple solutions so the government relies on bureaucrats to provide expertise.
   c. Bureaucrats spend their careers working in a particular policy area, and many of them have had scientific, technical, or other specialized training.
   d. Much of this expertise is held by bureaucrats who spend their careers working in a particular policy area, and many of them have had scientific, technical, or other specialized training.

_____ **21.** What is the meaning of *confronts* as it is used in this paragraph?
   a. disagrees with
   b. defies
   c. is baffled by
   d. deals with

_____ **22.** The writing pattern used in this paragraph is
   a. list.
   b. sequence.
   c. comparison–contrast.
   d. cause–effect.

Paragraph 6

Readers who have already made up their minds are highly resistant to change. Therefore, when you must write to readers who oppose what you have to say, you need to

■ Start your message with any areas of agreement or common ground that you share with your reader.

■ Make a special effort to be clear and unambiguous. Points that might be clear to a neutral reader can be misread by someone with a chip on his or her shoulder.

■ Make a special effort to avoid statements that will anger the reader.

■ Limit your statement or request to the smallest possible area. If parts of your message could be delivered later, postpone them.

■ Show that your solution is the best solution currently available, even though it isn't perfect.

Source: Adapted from Kitty Locker, *Business and Administrative Communication,* 5th ed., p. 68. Copyright © 2000 McGraw-Hill. Reprinted by permission of The McGraw-Hill Companies.

_____ **23.** The topic of this paragraph is
   a. showing that your solution is the best one currently available.
   b. readers who have already made up their minds.
   c. how to write to readers who oppose what you have to say.
   d. making an effort to write in a clear, unambiguous way.

_____ **24.** The main idea of this paragraph is:
   a. It is difficult to write to readers who have already made up their minds.
   b. Readers who have already made up their minds are highly resistant to change, and therefore, you need to do certain things when you write to readers who oppose what you have to say.
   c. Show that your solution is the best solution currently available, even though it isn't perfect.
   d. Make a special effort to be clear and unambiguous.

_____ **25.** How many supporting details are given in this paragraph?
   a. three
   b. four
   c. five
   d. six

_____ **26.** What is the meaning of *neutral* as it is used in this paragraph?
   a. not favoring either side of an issue
   b. hostile; angry
   c. not having any interest in
   d. unsophisticated

_____ **27.** The writing pattern used in this paragraph is
   a. sequence.
   b. cause–effect.
   c. comparison–contrast.
   d. definition.

_____ **28.** The prefix *op-* in *oppose* means "against." The root word in it means to
   a. come.
   b. place, put.
   c. say, speak.
   d. turn, twist.

_____ **29.** The word parts in *postpone* literally mean to
   a. "say later."
   b. "send later."
   c. "believe later."
   d. "put later."

_____ **30.** The suffixes in *ambiguous*, *neutral*, and *available* indicate that these words are
   a. adjectives.
   b. adverbs.
   c. nouns.
   d. verbs.

Paragraph 7

   Night terrors are a less common, but perhaps even more upsetting nocturnal experience than nightmares. The individual awakens suddenly in a state of panic, sometimes screaming, and usually with no clear recollection of an accompanying dream. A sense of calm usually returns within a few minutes, but these are terrifying experiences. Unlike nightmares, they do not occur during REM sleep but occur during the deepest phases of non-REM sleep. Night terrors are most common in preschool-age children, but sometimes adults experience them.

   Source: Adapted from Benjamin Lahey, *Psychology: An Introduction*, 8th ed., p. 175. Copyright © 2004 McGraw-Hill. Reprinted by permission of The McGraw-Hill Companies.

_____ **31.** The topic of this paragraph is
   a. night terrors.
   b. nightmares.
   c. panic attacks.
   d. REM and non-REM sleep.

_____ **32.** The main idea of this paragraph is:
   a. Night terrors are a less common, but perhaps even more upsetting nocturnal experience than nightmares.
   b. The individual awakens suddenly in a state of panic, sometimes screaming, and usually with no clear recollection of an accompanying dream.
   c. A sense of calm usually returns within a few minutes, but these are terrifying experiences.
   d. Night terrors are most common in preschool-age children, but sometimes adults experience them.

_____ **33.** What is the meaning of *nocturnal* as it is used in this paragraph?
   a. frightening
   b. pertaining to childhood
   c. happening frequently
   d. occurring at night

Paragraph 8

Language is what lets us communicate with one another far more precisely than any other animals can. It lets us lay joint plans, teach one another, and learn from what others experienced elsewhere or in the past. With it, we can mentally store precise representations of the world and hence encode and process information far more efficiently than can any animals.

Source: Adapted from Jared Diamond, "Reinventions of Human Language," in Lee Cronk and Vaughn Bryant, eds., *Through the Looking Glass: Readings in General Anthropology,* 2d ed., p. 28. Copyright © 2000 McGraw-Hill. Reprinted by permission of The McGraw-Hill Companies.

_____ **34.** The topic of this paragraph is
    a. functions of language.
    b. humans and other animals.
    c. learning from the past.
    d. mentally storing representations of the world.

_____ **35.** The main idea of this paragraph is:
    a. Language is what lets us communicate with one another far more precisely than any other animals can.
    b. Without language we could not learn from the past.
    c. Language serves a variety of important functions for human beings.
    d. Language allows us to store precise representations and learn from the past.

_____ **36.** How many supporting details are given in this paragraph?
    a. two
    b. four
    c. six
    d. eight

_____ **37.** What is the meaning of *joint* as it is used in this paragraph?
    a. shared
    b. evenly distributed
    c. segmented
    d. point of connection between two bones

Paragraph 9

Chat groups are becoming a very popular type of discussion group. They allow direct live communication. They typically connect individuals who have never met face-to-face. To participate, you join a chat group, select a channel or topic, and communicate live with others by typing words on your computer. Other members of your channel immediately see those words on their computers and can respond in the same manner.

Source: Timothy O'Leary and Linda O'Leary, *Computing Essentials, 2007,* p. 37. Copyright © 2007 McGraw-Hill. Reprinted by permission of The McGraw-Hill Companies.

_____ **38.** The topic of this paragraph is
    a. chat groups.
    b. mailing lists.
    c. newsgroups.
    d. channels.

_____ **39.** The main idea of this paragraph is:
  a. Chat groups are becoming a very popular type of discussion group.
  b. They allow direct live communication.
  c. To participate, you join a chat group, select a channel or topic, and communicate live with others by typing words on your computer.
  d. Other members of your channel immediately see those words on their computers and can respond in the same manner.

Paragraph 10

What does the process of leadership emergence tell you about how to *not* become a leader? The following rules, if followed, will probably result in low status and if followed well, will get you out of being a leader. Miss as many group meetings as possible. Say very little. Jump to be the group's secretary. Do what you are told. When you do contribute be dogmatic, verbally aggressive, and act like you know it all—do so early in the group's history. When you can, play the role of the joker. Finally, show a disdain for leadership.

Source: John Brilhart, Gloria Galanes, and Katherine Adams, *Effective Group Discussion,* 10th ed., p. 197. Copyright © 2001 McGraw-Hill. Reprinted by permission of The McGraw-Hill Companies.

_____ **40.** The topic of this paragraph is
  a. leadership emergence.
  b. how not to become a leader.
  c. rules to follow.
  d. being dogmatic, verbally aggressive, and acting like you know it all.

_____ **41.** The main idea of this paragraph is:
  a. What does the process of leadership emergence tell you about how to not become a leader?
  b. Certain "rules," if followed, will prevent you from becoming a leader.
  c. When you do contribute be dogmatic, verbally aggressive, and act like you know it all—do so early in the group's history.
  d. The process of leadership emergence tells us that if you show a disdain for leadership, you will *not* become a leader.

_____ **42.** How many supporting details are given in this paragraph?
  a. three
  b. five
  c. seven
  d. nine

_____ **43.** The writing pattern used in this paragraph is
  a. cause–effect.
  b. sequence.
  c. definition.
  d. comparison–contrast.

Paragraph 11

The procedure for proper check writing consists of the following steps:
1. Record the current date.
2. Write the name of the person or organization receiving the payment.

3. Record the amount of the check in figures.

4. Write the amount of the check in words; checks for less than a dollar should be written as "only 79 cents," for example, with the word *dollars* on the check crossed out.

5. Sign the check in the same way you signed the signature card when you opened your account.

6. Make a note of the reason for payment to assist with budget and tax preparation.

Source: Adapted from Jack Kapoor, Les Dlabay, and Robert Hughes, *Personal Finance,* 7th ed., p. 158. Copyright © 2004 McGraw-Hill. Reprinted by permission of The McGraw-Hill Companies.

_____ **44.** The topic of this paragraph is
    a. the procedure for proper check writing.
    b. recording the current date.
    c. why it is important to record checks correctly.
    d. writing checks to assist with budget and tax preparation.

_____ **45.** The main idea of this paragraph is:
    a. There is a procedure to follow for proper check writing.
    b. You should always record the current date on a check.
    c. To prevent fraud, you should follow the proper procedure for writing checks.
    d. the reason for payment can assist with budget and tax preparation.

_____ **46.** How many supporting details are given in this paragraph?
    a. three
    b. four
    c. five
    d. six

_____ **47.** The writing pattern used in this paragraph is
    a. list.
    b. sequence.
    c. cause–effect.
    d. definition.

Paragraph 12

The most common injuries incurred in physical activity are sprains and strains. A *strain* occurs when the fibers in a muscle are injured. Common activity-related injuries are hamstring strains that occur after a vigorous sprint. A good example would be the occasional athlete who sprints to first base without warming up and after not playing in a long time. Other commonly strained muscles include the muscles in the front of the thigh, the low back, and the calf muscles. A *sprain* is an injury to a ligament—the connective tissue that connects bones to bones. The most common sprain is to the ankle; frequently the ankle is rolled to the outside when jumping or running. Evidence suggests that lace-up ankle braces made of non-elastic material are effective in reducing ankle sprains. Other common sprains are to the knee, the shoulder, and the wrist.

Source: Charles Corbin, Ruth Lindsey, Greg Welk, William Corbin, and Karen Welk, *Concepts of Physical Fitness,* p. 43. Copyright © 2006 McGraw-Hill. Reprinted by permission of The McGraw-Hill Companies.

_____ **48.** The topic of this paragraph is
   a. the most common injuries.
   b. strains and sprains.
   c. common activity-related injuries.
   d. knee, shoulder, and wrist sprains.

_____ **49.** The main idea of this paragraph is
   a. The most common injuries incurred in physical activity are sprains and strains.
   b. Common activity-related injuries are hamstring strains that occur after a vigorous sprint.
   c. Athletes should be especially careful to avoid sprains and strains, the most common injuries incurred in physical activity.
   d. Evidence suggests that lace-up ankle braces made of non-elastic material are effective in reducing ankle sprains.

_____ **50.** What is the meaning of *incurred* as it is used in this paragraph?
   a. acquired
   b. avoided
   c. counteracted
   d. prevented

How did you do? Take a minute to evaluate your effort and success with these exercises and to describe how you're feeling at this point.

_____

_____

_____

_____

_____

_____

Were there certain types of questions that seemed harder than others? If so, which types? What do you think you can you do to strengthen those skills further?

_____

_____

_____

_____

_____

_____

_____

SET 2

Exercises: Applying All the Basic Skills to Paragraphs

For these exercises, you will write out the answers. The individual items are numbered. Here are some reminders and hints to get you started on the right track:

- Remember that the topic has to appear in the main idea sentence, regardless of whether the main idea is stated or you have to formulate it.

- Not every paragraph will contain clues to its pattern.

- There are no mixed-pattern paragraphs; only paragraphs with *list, sequence, definition, cause–effect/problem-solution, comparison–contrast*, and *spatial* patterns have been used.

- When you tell the pattern type, tell *what* is being listed, sequenced, defined, compared or contrasted, what the cause and the effect are, or what is being described spatially.

- Reread the paragraphs if you need to.

- Read them aloud if you need to.

- THINK about what the paragraphs are saying and how the information is organized.

If, even after your best effort, you're stumped on a paragraph or a question, go on to the next one. Then come back later to the one that seemed hard. Resist the temptation to give up on it! Resist the temptation to scribble down anything just so that you'll have an "answer." YOU CAN DO IT! Even if your answer isn't perfect, you'll have a chance to learn what you need to do next time. Stretch, relax, focus, and then start in.

Paragraph 1

On a hill, the Acropolis, overlooking the city of Athens, stands the shell of what many consider the most splendid building ever conceived: the *Parthenon.* It was erected in the 5th century b.c. as a temple to the goddess Athena, patroness of the city, and at one time its core held a colossal statue of the goddess. Rising proudly on a hill, visible from almost every corner of the city and for miles around, the Parthenon made it possible for all literally to "fix their eyes every day on the greatness of Athens." All four walls of the exterior were decorated with sculptures high up under the roof, and originally portions of the marble façade were painted a vivid blue and red.

Source: Adapted from Rita Gilbert and William McCarter, *Living with Art,* 2d ed., p. 67. Copyright © 1988 McGraw-Hill. Reprinted by permission of The McGraw-Hill Companies.

1. The topic of this paragraph is _____

2. The main idea of this paragraph is _____

   _____

   _____

   _____

3. In this paragraph *façade* means _____

4. The writing pattern and type of information organized is _____

   _____

5. Some clues to the pattern are _____

_____

Paragraph 2

    Probably the most direct and nastiest form of organizational politics is attacking and blaming others. This includes giving rivals a bad image in the eyes of decision-makers. A subtle tactic occurs when people disassociate themselves from undesirable situations or use excuses to form an external attribute of the cause of the problem. For example, you might explain to your boss that a report is late because of lack of support from another work unit or other conditions beyond your control.

Source: Steven McShane and Mary Ann Von Glinow, *Organizational Behavior,* p. 384. Copyright © 2000 McGraw-Hill. Reprinted by permission of The McGraw-Hill Companies.

6. The topic of this paragraph is_____

_____

7. The main idea of this paragraph is _____

_____

8. In this paragraph *subtle* means _____

_____

_____

Paragraph 3

    Black couples are more egalitarian than white couples in the sharing of household tasks. There is a high degree of cooperation and shared decision making among African American couples. And a higher proportion of black wives (70.3 percent) than of white wives (56.6 percent) report that their husbands or partners act as child-care providers. Compared to white couples, black couples have a greater amount of equality.

Source: Adapted from Robert Lauer and Jeanette Lauer, *Marriage and Family,* 6th ed., p. 39. Copyright © 2007 McGraw-Hill. Reprinted by permission of The McGraw-Hill Companies.

9. The topic of this paragraph is_____

10. The main idea of the paragraph is_____

_____

11. On separate lines, list the supporting details given in this paragraph.

_____

_____

_____

_____

12. In this paragraph *egalitarian* means _____

_____

13. The writing pattern and type of information organized is _____

_____

14. Some clues to the pattern are _____

_____

Paragraph 4

The key actors in today's global economic system are ***multinational corporations:*** companies with holdings and subsidiaries in several different nations. Multinationals organize human, natural, and technological resources from all over the globe into single economic units. For example, International Harvester has factories in Turkey, where it assembles chassis built in the United States with engines made in Germany. From its headquarters in Canada, Massey-Ferguson directs plants in Detroit that assemble components from France, Mexico, and Britain. American car manufacturers use parts made in other nations, and they own assembly plants abroad. Toyota and Honda both have manufacturing plants in the United States and import many of their vehicles into Japan. Almost 70 percent of the color televisions made by Japanese companies are manufactured elsewhere.

Source: Adapted from Richard Gelles and Ann Levine, *Sociology: An Introduction,* 6th ed., p. 553. Copyright © 1999 McGraw-Hill. Reprinted by permission of The McGraw-Hill Companies.

15. The topic of this paragraph is _____

16. The main idea of this paragraph is _____

_____

_____

_____

_____

17. The writing pattern and type of information organized is _____

_____

18. Some clues to the pattern are _____

_____

Paragraph 5

At the middle of the last century, for most young adults, dating and courtship led directly to marriage. Today, many will live with a partner before marrying. Others will have a child prior to marrying and then live with or marry someone else. There has also been an increase in cohabitation and in births to teenagers outside marriage. It is still the case, however, that about 90 percent of whites and 70 to 75 percent of African Americans are projected to marry eventually.

Source: Adapted from Andrew Cherlin, *Public and Private Families,* 2d ed., p. 248. Copyright © 1999 McGraw-Hill. Reprinted by permission of The McGraw-Hill Companies.

19. The topic of this paragraph is _____

_____

20. The main idea of this paragraph is _____

_____

_____

_____

21. The writing pattern used in this paragraph is _____

_____

22. Some clues to the pattern are _____

_____

_____

Paragraph 6

There could hardly be a more challenging or interesting task for the environmental designer than planning a college campus. After all, it is much like designing a city from the ground up, and few people in history have had the chance to do that. The campus will, presumably, endure for many hundreds of years. It will serve as a working environment and home away from home for a constantly changing population of students and professors. It must be comfortable and efficient, but above all, it must express the special personality of the college. It must say through its design: This is who we are.

Source: Adapted from Rita Gilbert, *Living with Art,* 5th ed., p. 340. Copyright © 1998 McGraw-Hill. Reprinted by permission of The McGraw-Hill Companies.

23. The topic of this paragraph is _____

_____

24. The main idea of this paragraph is _____

_____

25. In this paragraph *from the ground up* means _____

_____

26. The writing pattern and type of information organized is_____

_____

_____

_____

_____

_____

_____

27. Some clues to the pattern are _____

_____

Paragraph 7

    Although creativity is highly valued in our culture, it is a difficult concept to define. No specific scientific definition has been widely accepted among researchers, and a wide gulf exists between the ways in which scientists define creativity and the way it's thought of by those in the arts. We can define *creativity* in general terms, however, as the ability to produce "products" that are both novel and socially valued. Examples of products would be plays, solutions to social problems, poems, sources of energy, and symphonies. "Socially valued" means a product is useful, aesthetically beautiful, informative, and so on.

Source: Adapted from Benjamin Lahey, *Psychology: An Introduction*, 8th ed., p. 283. Copyright © 2004 McGraw-Hill. Reprinted by permission of The McGraw-Hill Companies.

28. The topic of this paragraph is_____

29. The main idea of the paragraph is_____

_____

30. On separate lines, list the supporting details given in this paragraph.

_____

_____

_____

_____

_____

_____

31. In this paragraph *gulf* means _____

32. The writing pattern and type of information organized is_____

_____

33. Some clues to the pattern are _____

_____

Paragraph 8

Which company's effective use of technology has skyrocketed it to the top in online retailing? Amazon.com. It was one of the first sites to take advantage of the Internet's computing power to allow consumers to search easily for any book in print, read thousands of reviews, and make purchases with a few clicks of a mouse. Customers' shipping and credit card information are stored securely after their first purchase. Subsequent purchases require only a single click to send the requested titles on their way. E-mail confirmations are sent to purchasers, and shipping is often upgraded for free. Amazon was also the first commercial site to incorporate the technology necessary to analyze a customer's purchases and make recommendations for other books. The technology also allows Amazon to gather instant feedback on customer preferences and other items they might want to buy.

Source: Adapted from O. C. Ferrell and Geoffrey Hirt, *Business: A Changing World,* 3d ed., p. 18. Copyright © 2000 McGraw-Hill. Reprinted by permission of The McGraw-Hill Companies.

34. The topic of this paragraph is_____

35. The main idea of this paragraph is_____

_____

_____

36. In this paragraph *subsequent* means _____

37. The writing pattern and type of information organized is_____

_____

_____

38. Some clues to the pattern are _____

Paragraph 9

Decades of weak leadership ended when a dynamic new leader ascended the Russian throne. Catherine the Great (reigned 1762–1796) grew up an obscure princess from one of the little German states. For political reasons, her family married her to young Peter III (reigned 1762), the tyrannical and intellectually limited grandson of Peter the Great and heir to the Russian crown. He soon rejected her in all ways, and once he became tsar he quickly lost most of his supporters as well. "I did not care about Peter," she later wrote, "but I did care about the crown." Less than a year after he took the throne, Catherine conspired with a group of aristocratic army officers, who assassinated him and declared Catherine tsarina of Russia. The new empress used her striking intelligence, charm, and political talent to assert her own power and expand Russian territory and might.

Source: Adapted from Dennis Sherman and Joyce Salisbury, *The West in the World,* p. 502. Copyright © 2001 McGraw-Hill. Reprinted by permission of The McGraw-Hill Companies.

39. The topic of this paragraph is _____

40. The main idea of this paragraph is _____

_____

_____

_____

41. In this paragraph *ascended the Russian throne* means _____

_____

42. Write the detail that explains what happened to Peter III._____

_____

_____

Paragraph 10

The general problem of group cohesiveness, a desirable characteristic of groups, is that it can lead to groupthink (the desire for agreement prevents critical analysis and discussion). To protect the group from groupthink while still maintaining cohesiveness, groups are encouraged to appoint a "devil's advocate." The role of that person (or persons) is to raise reasoned objections, to express countering viewpoints, and to provide a "reality check." Another solution to groupthink is to stress to group members the importance of supporting their opinions with evidence. Furthermore, emphasizing commitment to the task rather than just commitment to the group can help members overcome the tendency to hold back differing opinions.

Source: Adapted from Judy Pearson, Paul Nelson, Scott Titsworth, and Lynn Harter, *Human Communication,* 2d ed., p. 227. Copyright © 2006 McGraw-Hill. Reprinted by permission of The McGraw-Hill Companies.

43. The topic of this paragraph is _____

44. The main idea of the paragraph is _____

_____

_____

45. On separate lines, list the supporting details given in this paragraph.

_____

_____

_____

_____

_____

_____

46. In this paragraph *cohesiveness* means _____

_____

47. The writing pattern and type of information organized is _____

_____

48. Some clues to the pattern are _____

49. The root in *advocate* is_____ and means_____

50. The root is *objection* is_____and means_____

I know these were more challenging exercises, but they serve an important purpose. Be sure when you go over them in class or get your score on them that you understand any item you missed. Cyclist Lance Armstrong's training coach, Chris Carmichael, understood the importance of getting the basics down. He said, "I truly believe that athletes achieve greatness through their mastery of the most fundamental elements of their sports. . . . Training the fundamentals involves a great deal of repetition. You have to perform the same movements over and over again until your body learns to consider them second nature. . . . Athletes of all experience levels need to spend time focusing on fundamental skills and techniques. Take a cue from downhill skiers, swimmers, tennis players, golfers, and soccer players. *Even the best and most experienced professionals constantly practice fundamental skills because their success at the elite level is based on their mastery of the most basic elements of their sports.*"

Just as the success of top athletes rests on their mastery of the fundamentals, your success as a student rests on your mastering the fundamentals of reading comprehension. Just as top athletes must practice constantly, so must you. You should feel good about having completed the entire Basic Workout and the Set 2 Basic Stretching Exercises. The skills you've learned will continue to be important throughout the rest of the book, the rest of your college years, and the rest of your life.

SET 3

Exercises: Applying All the Basic Skills to Paragraphs

Last set! These are challenging, so shake your hands and fingers to release tension and loosen yourself up. Take a few slow, deep breaths to clear your head and relax you further.

A couple of pointers: Some of these paragraphs have a mixed pattern. For those, write "mixed pattern," and then tell *which* patterns have been used. Continue to mark key words, write topics in the margin, number details, read paragraphs aloud, draw diagrams, and reread the paragraphs—whatever helps you. There are only eight paragraphs. As in Set 2, the individual items are numbered, and you must write out your answers.

Paragraph 1

Unjustified, unexcused killings are **criminal homicides.** They are subdivided into three categories: murder, manslaughter, and negligent homicide (a lesser form of involuntary manslaughter). A premeditated and deliberate, intentional and malicious (with malice aforethought—meaning the perpetrator had no justification or excuse) killing is *murder in the first degree.* Without premeditation or deliberation, it is *murder in the second degree. Voluntary manslaughter* is a killing committed intentionally but without malice, as in the heat of passion or in response to strong provocation without an opportunity to cool off. A crime is called an *involuntary manslaughter* when a person causes the death of another unintentionally but recklessly by consciously disregarding a substantial and unjustifiable risk that endangers the person's life. In some jurisdictions there exists a lesser form of involuntary manslaughter, called *negligent homicide,* a killing usually in conjunction with automobile or industrial accidents.

Source: Adapted from Freda Adler, Gerhard Mueller, and William Laufer, *Criminal Justice: An Introduction,* 3d ed., p. 40. Copyright © 2003 McGraw-Hill. Reprinted by permission of The McGraw-Hill Companies.

1. The topic of this paragraph is _____

2. The main idea of this paragraph is _____

_____

_____

_____

3. In this paragraph *premeditated* means _____

4. On separate lines, list the supporting details that explain the two types of murder, the two types of manslaughter, and negligent homicide.

_____

_____

_____

_____

_____

_____

_____

_____

_____

_____

_____

_____

_____

5. The writing pattern and type of information organized is _____

_____

_____

_____

6. Some clues to the pattern are _____

_____

_____

_____

Paragraph 2

One of the most striking contrasts between the United States and Brazil, the two most populous nations of the Western Hemisphere, is in the meaning and role of the family. Contemporary North American adults usually define their families as consisting of their husbands or wives and their children. However, when middle-class Brazilians talk about their families, they mean their parents, siblings, aunts, uncles, grandparents, and cousins. Later they add their children, but rarely the husband or wife, who has his or her own family. The children are shared by the two families. Because middle-class Americans lack an extended family support system, marriage assumes more importance. The husband–wife relationship is supposed to take precedence over either spouse's relationship with his or her own parents. This places a significant strain on North American marriages.

Source: Conrad Kottak, _Cultural Anthropology,_ 11th ed., p. 195. Copyright © 2006 McGraw-Hill. Reprinted by permission of The McGraw-Hill Companies.

7. The topic of this paragraph is_____

_____

8. The main idea of this paragraph is _____

_____

_____

_____

_____

9. In this paragraph *precedence* means _____

_____

10. On separate lines, list supporting details that describe North American families and Brazilian families.

_____

_____

_____

_____

_____

_____

11. The writing pattern and type of information organized is _____

_____

_____

_____

_____

12. Some clues to the pattern are _____

_____

_____

_____

Paragraph 3

Contemporary surveys indicate that a strong majority of the U.S. public believes that criminal punishments are not sufficiently severe, although this sentiment is stronger among men, whites, political conservatives, and religious fundamentalists. Over the last two decades, however, we have not been weak-kneed in our resolve to punish criminals. Use of the death penalty has been on the rise, sentences have been getting longer, and the number of people under correctional supervision has been skyrocketing. In fact, the number of adults under correctional supervision increased from 1,840,421 in 1980 to 5,690,695 in 1997, a rise of over 200 percent. Those incarcerated in jails and prisons increased nearly 250 percent. The current per capita prison population is 445 per 100,000, a rate that ranks with Russia's as the highest in the world. The state of California has been leading the way, now incarcerating more people than France, Great Britain, Germany, Singapore, and the Netherlands combined.

Source: Adapted from Ronald Berger, Marvin Free, and Patricia Searles, *Crime, Justice, and Society,* p. 399. Copyright © 2001 McGraw-Hill. Reprinted by permission of The McGraw-Hill Companies.

13. The topic of this paragraph is _____

14. The main idea of this paragraph is _____

_____

_____

_____

_____

15. In this paragraph *weak-kneed* means _____

_____

16. On separate lines, list the three supporting details that prove that criminal punishments have increased dramatically.

_____

_____

_____

17. The writing pattern and type of information organized is _____

_____

_____

18. Some clues to the pattern are _____

_____

Paragraph 4

TROPICAL RAIN FOREST, A TERRESTRIAL ECOSYSTEM

Tropical rain forests are the most complex ecosystems in the world. They are found near the equator where there is plentiful sun and rainfall the entire year. Major rain forests are located in South America, central and west Africa, and Southeast Asia. Rain forests have a multilayered canopy which consists of broad-leaved evergreen trees of different heights. Most animal populations live in the canopy where they interact with each other. Brightly colored birds, such as toucans and macaws, fly around eating fruits, buds, and pollen. Other birds, such as long-billed hummingbirds feed on nectar often taken from small plants that grow independently on the trees. Tree sloths and spider monkeys are mammals that live in the canopy and are preyed upon by jaguars. Other canopy animals include butterflies, tree frogs, and dart-poison frogs. Many canopy animals, such as bats, are active only at night. Snakes, spiders, and ants are animals that live on or near the ground and not in the canopy.

Source: Sylvia Mader, *Inquiry into Life,* 9th ed., p. 11. Copyright © 2000 McGraw-Hill. Reprinted by permission of The McGraw-Hill Companies.

19. The topic of this paragraph is _____

_____

20. The main idea of this paragraph is _____

_____

21. In this paragraph *canopy* means _____

_____

22. The writing pattern and type of information organized is_____

_____

_____

23. Some clues to the pattern are _____

_____

_____

_____

Paragraph 5

RACE AS A BIOLOGICAL CONSTRUCT

In the biological construction of race, people belonging to a given race are said to share distinctive gene characteristics that produce specific physical traits. People are defined as either Caucasoid, Negroid, or Mongoloid (Asian) on the basis of skin color, nasal index, hair texture, hair color, eye color, head form, lip form, facial index, stature, and blood group. Sometimes even intellectual characteristics were claimed to vary by race. Scientifically, however, the idea of a pure race is nonsense because the world's gene pools are mixed to the point where only general groupings can be distinguished. Moreover, differences within a supposed race sometimes are greater than those between races. Many residents of south India, for example, have darker skin pigment than most African Americans. In the United States we often speak as if whites and blacks belong to distinct genetic groups, but virtually all African Americans have some white ancestry, and just under a tenth of "whites" have some African American ancestry.

Source: J. John Palen, *Social Problems for the Twenty-First Century,* p. 63. Copyright © 2001 McGraw-Hill. Reprinted by permission of The McGraw-Hill Companies.

24. The topic of this paragraph is _____

_____

25. The main idea of this paragraph is _____

_____

_____

_____

_____

_____

26. In the title of this paragraph *construct* means _____

_____

27. The writing pattern and type of information organized is _____

_____

_____

_____

28. Some clues to the pattern are _____

_____

_____

Paragraph 6

Fish provide the main source of protein for the population of some 40 countries. The problem is that the world fish catch reached a peak in 1970 and has been declining since. Sophisticated radar-guided huge net-fishing fleets and the floating fish-processing factories used by Japan, Russia, Taiwan, Spain, and others have resulted in overfishing to the point where the present catches of many kinds of table fish exceed the regenerative capacity of the species. Once-common varieties have become listed as endangered species. Commercial fishing from Maine to Florida has declined dramatically because increased pollution runoff and the building of homes along the coastline have destroyed spawning habitats. With increasing competition for the remaining species, world fish harvests are declining both in quality and quantity.

Source: Adapted from John Palen, *Social Problems for the Twenty-First Century*, pp. 161–62. Copyright © 2001 McGraw-Hill. Reprinted by permission of The McGraw-Hill Companies.

29. The topic of this paragraph is _____

_____

30. The main idea of the paragraph is _____

_____

31. On separate lines, list the supporting details given in this paragraph.

_____

_____

_____

_____

_____

_____

32. In this paragraph *regenerative* means _____

_____

33. The writing pattern and type of information organized is _____

_____

_____

_____

_____

34. Some clues to the pattern are_____

Paragraph 7

A **gland** is a tissue that secretes a substance within or from the body. The glands of the body can be divided into *exocrine* or *endocrine*. Exocrine glands secrete substances from the body, and are further divided into *apocrine* and *eccrine* glands. Both apocrine and eccrine glands have ducts through which the apocrine gland secretes sebaceous fluid, like the oil that is secreted to the surface of the skin, or the bile ducts of the liver. The eccrine gland secretes sweat. The endocrine gland is ductless and secretes a substance directly into the blood. Traditionally, the substances secreted from endocrine glands were known as **hormones.** . . . Research during the last decade has revealed that the traditional definition of a hormone may not be appropriate. It is now known that tissues other than true endocrine glands secrete substances that act as hormones. For example, the hypothalamus, heart, kidney, liver, gastrointestinal tract, lymphocytes, and endothelial cells all secrete substances that exert regulatory effects on other tissues.

Source: Adapted from Robert Robergs and Scott Roberts, *Exercise Physiology for Fitness, Performance, and Health,* p. 185. Copyright © 2000 McGraw-Hill. Reprinted by permission of The McGraw-Hill Companies.

35. The topic of this paragraph is _____

_____

36. The main idea of this paragraph is _____

_____

_____

_____

_____

37. In this paragraph *secrete* means _____

38. On separate lines, list supporting details that explain the types of glands.

_____

_____

_____

_____

_____

_____

Paragraph 8

A major division in Islam was created by a dispute over the succession to the caliphate (the political and religious leadership of the community). As a result, two major divisions, the Sunnis and the Shiites, were formed. Although the Shiites and Sunnis agree on the fundamentals of Islam, they differ in other respects. The Sunnis are an austere sect that is less authoritarian and more pragmatic than the Shiites. In their view, as long as Muslims accept Allah, they are free to interpret their religion as they like. The Shiites, in contrast, insist that those claiming to be Muslim must put themselves under the authority of a holy man (*ayatollah*).

Source: Donald Ball, Wendell McCullough, Paul Frantz, Michael Geringer, and Michael Minor, *International Business,* 8th ed., p. 315. Copyright © 2002 Irwin/McGraw-Hill. Reprinted by permission of The McGraw-Hill Companies.

39. The topic of this paragraph is _____

40. The main idea of this paragraph is _____

_____

_____

41. In this paragraph *succession* means _____

_____

42. On separate lines, list supporting details in this paragraph that describe the two major sects (types) of Muslims.

_____

_____

_____

_____

_____

_____

_____

_____

43. The writing pattern and type of information organized is_____

_____

_____

44. Some clues to the pattern are_____

_____

Paragraph 9

Sociologist Edwin Burgess's concentric zonal hypothesis suggested that cities grow from the center to the periphery through a series of circular zones. Each zone has distinct social and housing features. Different land users—owners of single-family homes, apartment buildings, stores, factories, and warehouses—sort themselves out through the ecological processes of competition, segregation, invasion, and succession in such a way that similar-use zones arise. The zones reflect ecological competition, especially economic costs, rather than planning, zoning, or the efforts of government. Thus, downtown land usage went to the department stores and business offices that were most willing to pay the costs in terms of money, congestion, and pollution. Burgess and others also noted that each zone had distinctive social characteristics, with different kinds of social problems. Crime, mental illness, family breakdown, and other social problems were non-randomly distributed throughout the metropolitan area. The Burgess hypothesis helps us understand why most American cities look so similar.

Source: Adapted from John Palen, *Social Problems for the Twenty-First Century,* p. 182. Copyright © 2001 McGraw-Hill. Reprinted by permission of The McGraw-Hill Companies.

45. The topic of this paragraph is_____

_____

_____

46. The main idea of this paragraph is _____

_____

_____

_____

47. In this selection the word *congestion* means _____

48. On separate lines, list at least three details that tell about the zones

_____

_____

_____

_____

_____

_____

_____

_____

_____

_____

_____

49. The type of writing pattern used to organize the information in the paragraph is

_____

_____

_____

_____

50. The root in the word *factories* indicates that the word's meaning has to do with

_____

You've reached a milestone—congratulations! How do you think you did on these exercises? How are you feeling at this point?

_____

_____

_____

_____

_____

_____

Were there certain types of questions that seemed harder than others? What can you do to strengthen those skills further?

_____

_____

_____

_____

_____

_____

_____

PART·FOUR

4 Advanced Workout

the Advanced Workout

If you've been "working out" diligently in this book, then you're probably already feeling a lot stronger in your basic reading skills. You have a clearer idea of what the basic reading skills are (topic, main idea, supporting details, and author's writing pattern) and how to apply them to a paragraph. You know how they are related to each other (for example, the topic must always appear in the main idea sentence; details support the main idea). You know that there are certain questions you can ask yourself and specific steps you can follow to determine each of these important elements of basic comprehension. You know that there are also clues, characteristics, and formulas to help you apply the comprehension skills correctly and to check to see if you applied them correctly. You know that if you use these strategies, you will comprehend accurately the basic information in material you read.

Now we're ready to "raise the bar" a little and increase the challenge. In this part of the book, you'll be learning and practicing advanced comprehension skills. In other words, these are critical skills that go *beyond* the basic comprehension skills. Because they are advanced, you may often need to reread all or part of a paragraph, and you're definitely going to have to think about it once you've read it. The skills in the advanced workout include:

- Distinguishing facts from opinions. (Chapter 8)

- Making inferences and drawing conclusions. (Chapter 9)

- Determining the author's purpose, tone, point of view, and intended audience. (Chapter 10)

- Evaluating an author's argument. (Chapter 11)

Because these skills are more challenging—it's like lifting more weight—and because you will not always need to apply each of these skills to every paragraph, the three exercise sets are shorter. In Chapters 8, 9, and 10, Set 1 Exercises contain 10 multiple-choice items (not 12); open-ended Set 2 Exercises contain only 8 items (rather than 10), and Set 3 Exercises consist of only 6 items (rather than 8). Each of the Chapter 11 exercise sets contains 7 items. Give your best effort on every exercise set; they're all preparation for the Advanced Stretching section (Chapter 12). At that point, you'll be applying several of the skills to single- and multiparagraph selections.

It's still important for you to continue to practice, and to practice mindfully. If you need some inspiration, just think about Baltimore Orioles baseball great Cal Ripken, Jr., who retired in 2001 after 21 seasons. Ripken, who was known as "The Iron Man," broke Lou Gehrig's record of playing in 2,130 *consecutive* games. In fact, Ripken went on to play in 2,632 consecutive games. In 17 seasons, Ripken never missed a game and never missed a day of work. Besides his astounding record of consecutive games, Ripken was in 7 playoffs and 19 All-Star games. In his career, he had more than 3,000 hits, including 400 home runs, a feat accomplished by only 7 players. And one year, he made only *three* errors. In 2001 he played in his last All-Star Game—and hit a home run. Talk about giving your best up to the very last. Do you suppose there's a connection between his success and his work ethic? What would your seasons—your semesters—be like if you showed up for every single practice (did every single homework assignment), played in every game (attended every class session), and gave your best in every playoff (gave your best on every test)? Your record might look a lot like the Iron Man's.

CHAPTER 8

Distinguish Facts from Opinions

DISTINGUISH FACTS FROM OPINIONS

Up to this point, the comprehension skills you've learned have been basic ones. They are skills that you can—and should—apply to virtually all of your college textbook reading. In this chapter you'll learn the first of several critical reading skills. *Critical reading skills are skills that go beyond basic comprehension to gain additional insights.* They require you to do some additional thinking *after* you have read a passage.

In college, you'll read thousands of facts as well as thousands of opinions of experts. Your textbooks are written by experts, of course, but your college reading assignments will include more than just textbooks. At various times, you'll probably have to obtain information from the Internet, newspapers, journals, magazines, essays, and so forth. Not all of the information will be written by experts, nor will all of it be factual. For these reasons, it's going to be important for you to be able to distinguish facts from opinions. Moreover, you need to use this critical thinking skill in order to be a discriminating citizen and consumer.

You already know that not everything you hear or read is true. *Information that can be verified (proved true) is called a **fact**.* Information can be verified by research, observation, experimentation, or experience. (By the way, the opposite of a fact is information that can be disproved. In other words, it is simply incorrect information, and it is of no value. Many students mistakenly think that the opposite of a fact is an opinion.)

Some things, however, cannot be proved or disproved (for example, "The United States would be better off if a woman were president"). *Information that cannot be proved or disproved is called an* **opinion;** *it is a statement that represents someone's judgment or belief.* Let's say, for example, it is your opinion (that is, it is your belief) that love is the most powerful emotion. There is no way to prove or disprove your belief, so it will always be an opinion. Others might ague that fear, guilt, or anger is the most powerful emotion—and those would also be opinions.

Now let's say, for example, that you think "Studying more than 20 hours a week causes insanity." If that statement can be researched and tested, it will either turn out to be true (in which case, it is a fact) or it will be proved incorrect (in which case, it is wrong information). Either way, it will not be an opinion. (Sorry about that, but you can't dodge studying more than 20 hours a week by declaring that it causes insanity.)

Because opinions represent judgments and beliefs, not everyone will share the same opinion on an issue. For example, some students would accept the opinion that "Computer science is the best major in college," but others would disagree. That's another important characteristic of opinions: people disagree about them.

In college you may be asked to write papers on controversial issues. For instance, a government professor might ask you to select an issue and gather information from various sources. As you are reading the material, you will have to decide whether the authors are presenting facts or opinions. If you think information is a fact when it's actually an opinion, you can be misled. Moreover, writers sometimes try to make their opinions sound as if they were facts so that the reader will accept what they say. You don't want to be manipulated, so it's important for you to be able distinguish facts from opinions. When you read an opinion, you will have to decide how well supported the opinion is. That means you must determine whether the opinion is supported by relevant facts and/or by expert opinions that pertain directly to the topic or issue.

THE TECHNIQUE

APPLY THE CHARACTERISTICS OF FACTS AND OPINIONS

Ask yourself, "Can the information the author presents be proved, or does it represent a judgment?" Fortunately, there is a short series of questions you can ask to help you answer it. In addition, there will often be extra clues that you're reading an opinion. First, though, here's the process:

Ask yourself, *Can the information in the statement be verified (by you or someone else) through research, observation, experimentation, or experience?*
There are three possible answers:

1. If the answer is *yes,* the statement represents a *fact.*
   (It's a fact, and you're done!)

2. If the answer is *no,* the statement represents *incorrect information.*
   (It's neither a fact nor an opinion. It's wrong information, and you're done.)

3. *If it cannot be determined whether the answer is yes or no,* the information represents an *opinion.* This time, though, you're not quite done. There's one more step: you need to decide whether or not the opinion is well supported. There are two possibilities:

   (a) The opinion is *well supported,* so it is a *valuable* opinion.

   (b) The opinion is *not supported* or is *poorly supported,* so it is of *no value.*

"Well supported" means that the author backs up the opinion with the testimony of experts or presents facts or other logical reasons for the opinion. If an author presents no reasons or presents illogical or irrelevant reasons, then the opinion is of no value. Here's an example of an opinion with hypothetical examples of good support and poor support.

Opinion: *Children should not watch more than one hour of television each day.*

Examples of good support (with the type of support in italics) would be:

■ According to child development specialist Marvin Laidback, "Children need to spend less time watching television and more time playing with other children so they develop their social skills, build their muscles, and develop their coordination. Rather than watch television they should be doing activities that foster creativity (such as drawing) and doing activities that develop their minds (such as reading)." (a quote from an expert)

■ The Council on Childhood Aggression and Violence reports that the amount of violence children exhibit directly correlates with the amount of violence they watch on television. (research finding)

■ A survey of 500 elementary school teachers revealed that the children who watched the most television were the ones who were most disruptive and least attentive in class. (research results from a survey)

Examples of poor support (with the reason it is poor support explained in italics) would be:

■ Parents can't watch the programs they want if the children are using the television. (irrelevant)

■ There's nothing worthwhile on television for children anyway. (the author's personal opinion, which others would disagree with)

■ Watching television more than one hour a day might ruin their eyes. (no proof is offered)

■ My four-year-old nephew broke his arm when he jumped off a chair imitating a wrestling stunt he saw on TV. (a single incident from the author's personal experience that is not, by itself, convincing)

Clearly, the first set of reasons presents logical, valid support for limiting children's television watching. The support is convincing. In contrast, the second set of reasons is weak. If poor support is the only support an author offers, the reader should not accept the author's opinion because the opinion is not valid (well reasoned, logical).

Here are extra clues about opinions: first, watch for "judgment words." These are words that can be interpreted several ways. They mean different things to different people. For example, consider the words *better, sad, successful, disappointing, beautiful, effective, unappealing,* and *remarkable.* In the statement, "James Lee Burke is today's most talented mystery writer," the words *most talented* will mean different things to different people. Does *most talented* mean he invents clever plots? Creates fascinating characters? Describes things vividly and realistically? Perhaps it means all of these things—or something else altogether. Whenever different people can interpret something in different ways, it's a major tip-off you're getting an opinion.

The second clue is even more obvious. Authors use words and phrases such as these to alert you to an opinion: *In our opinion, It seems to us, It appears that, It seems likely that, Experts interpret this to mean, In our view, Perhaps, It could be that, It seems, Presumably, Arguably, One interpretation is that, It seems possible that,* and *Apparently.*

The third clue to an opinion is when an author speaks of something that is going to happen in the future. Obviously, you can't prove something that hasn't happened yet. If an author says, "Someday stem cell research will offer the cure to dozens of illnesses we cannot currently cure," *someday* and *will offer* (future tense) alert you that the statement is an opinion.

OBSERVE THE SKILL OF DISTINGUISHING FACTS FROM OPINIONS

To see how an effective reader might apply this skill, read the sample paragraph in the illustration. Then read the imaginary reader's thoughts, which appear in color. The main idea, an opinion, is stated as the first sentence. The rest of the paragraph presents the writer's reasons for the opinion.

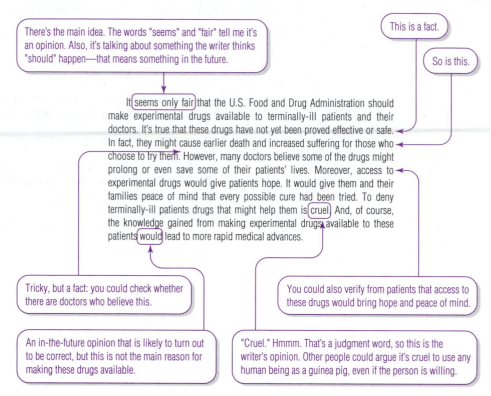

There's the main idea. The words "seems" and "fair" tell me it's an opinion. Also, it's talking about something the writer thinks "should" happen—that means something in the future.

This is a fact.

So is this.

It seems only fair that the U.S. Food and Drug Administration should make experimental drugs available to terminally-ill patients and their doctors. It's true that these drugs have not yet been proved effective or safe. In fact, they might cause earlier death and increased suffering for those who choose to try them. However, many doctors believe some of the drugs might prolong or even save some of their patients' lives. Moreover, access to experimental drugs would give patients hope. It would give them and their families peace of mind that every possible cure had been tried. To deny terminally-ill patients drugs that might help them is cruel. And, of course, the knowledge gained from making experimental drugs available to these patients would lead to more rapid medical advances.

Tricky, but a fact: you could check whether there are doctors who believe this.

You could also verify from patients that access to these drugs would bring hope and peace of mind.

An in-the-future opinion that is likely to turn out to be correct, but this is not the main reason for making these drugs available.

"Cruel." Hmmm. That's a judgment word, so this is the writer's opinion. Other people could argue it's cruel to use any human being as a guinea pig, even if the person is willing.

Bottom line: The author supports the main idea, which is an opinion, with several relevant facts and a reasonable opinion about more rapid medical advances, so the opinion is well supported.

POINTERS ABOUT DISTINGUISHING FACTS FROM OPINIONS

■ **Facts are not "better" than opinions.**
Many students mistakenly believe that facts are important and that opinions are unimportant. Nothing could be further from the truth. *A well-supported opinion is every bit as valuable as a fact.* Scientific theories, for example, are expert opinions that have not yet been proved or may never be provable through ways currently known to us. Also, college textbook authors are typically experts in their fields. In their books, they often give their opinions and the opinions of other experts. Those opinions can be very valuable, so don't dismiss them because they're "just opinions"!

■ **College textbooks contain both facts and opinions.**

Some students believe that everything they read, especially everything in their textbooks, is a fact. This is not the case. As noted above, college textbooks contain many opinions. Because something appears in print does not mean it's a fact. I could write, "Janet Elder scored the winning touchdown in the last Super Bowl." It obviously isn't a fact, even if I put it in print and you just read it.

■ **Just because a writer makes something *sound* like a fact doesn't mean it *is* a fact.**

As noted earlier, when writers try to persuade readers to believe something they have written, they may present their opinions as if they're facts. To make an opinion appear to be a fact, writers may introduce the opinion with phrases such as

Everyone knows that . . .

It's a fact that . . .

It's obvious that . . .

For example, just because I write, "It's a fact that I'm eight feet tall" does not make it true. (I'm not!) You must still *think* for yourself and evaluate what the author has written.

■ **Speculation about events that haven't happened yet are opinions.**

I want to emphasize this again, in case you missed it before: Predictions about what might happen in the future are *opinions*. For example, the statement "Our newly elected governor is going to enact more environmental protection legislation than any previous governor" is an opinion. Only after the person has served as governor could his or her performance in this regard be evaluated.

■ **A single paragraph can consist of facts only, opinions only, or can contain both facts and opinions.**

For that matter, a single sentence can contain both facts and opinions. Here's an example: "Approximately 60 percent of the higher-education institutions in the United States now have open admissions, and the number of students they graduate will increase during this decade." The first part of the sentence contains information that could be verified by research and is, therefore, a fact: "Approximately 60 percent of the higher-education institutions in the United States have open admissions." The information in the last half of the sentence describes what the author expects to happen in the future: "the number of students they graduate will increase during this decade." Because there is no way to prove something before it happens, it represents an opinion—an opinion that might become a fact once the decade is over, but at this point it's still an opinion.

■ **When you evaluate a statement, you must evaluate it as a *whole*.**

Some statements are clearly facts or opinions:

  ■ "The term 'database' is perhaps one of the most overused and misunderstood terms in today's business environment." This is clearly an *opinion* because of the word "perhaps" and the judgment words "overused" and "misunderstood."

  ■ "When you create a database, you first create the data dictionary." This is a *fact* because you could do research to verify that this is the first step in building a computerized database.

Some statements can seem tricky. Consider these, for example:

■ "Some doctors believe a high-protein, low-carbohydrate diet is the healthiest diet." This statement may appear to be an opinion; however, it is a fact. That's right, a fact, because you could do a survey to determine whether some doctors have that opinion. It is a fact that some doctors have the opinion that "a high-protein, low-carbohydrate diet is the healthiest diet."

■ "Shakespeare is considered by many critics to be the greatest playwright of all times." This is also information that could be verified and, therefore, represents a fact. In other words, it is a fact that some critics have that opinion about Shakespeare. However, if the statement simply said, "Shakespeare is the greatest playwright of all times," then it would be an opinion because the word "greatest" is a judgment word, and there is no way to prove this to everyone's satisfaction. Remember that you must evaluate a statement *as a whole*. If any part of it is an opinion, you must consider the entire statement to be an opinion.

■ **Verification can be done by you, or it can come from some other source.** In order to be considered a fact, information must be verifiable by research, experimentation, observation, or experience. This doesn't mean you have to go out and conduct an experiment or do the research yourself. You can find out about experiments and research done by others, and use that information as verification. Also, you can ask yourself whether it would be possible for someone to *do* such research, even if no one has already done it. If so, then the information would not represent an opinion. It would either be a fact or incorrect information.

THE REPLAY

REMEMBER THE ESSENTIAL INFORMATION FROM THE CHAPTER

You know that distinguishing facts from opinions is a critical reading skill, that is, a skill that goes beyond basic comprehension to give you additional insights. Review the definitions of *fact* and *opinion* until you can write them from memory. To fix in your mind the process of evaluating whether a statement represents a fact or an opinion, review the steps outlined in The Technique section. Then jot down the definitions, the extra clues to an opinion, and the steps that show the process. If you prefer, you can sketch a flowchart of the process like the one you saw earlier in the chapter. Feel free to use your own words and symbols, of course. Writing down the information will help you remember it. (But you knew that.)

Definition of a Fact

_____

_____

Definition of an Opinion

_____

_____

_____

Question to Ask Yourself

_____

_____

Describe the process for distinguishing whether a statement represents a fact or an opinion.

_____

_____

_____

_____

_____

_____

_____

List three clues that you are reading an opinion.

_____

_____

_____

_____

_____

_____

_____

_____

THE PRACTICE

APPLY THE SKILL OF DISTINGUISHING FACTS FROM OPINIONS

SET 1

Exercises: Distinguishing Facts from Opinions

Read each paragraph below. Decide whether the information in the quoted statement can be verified some way. If it can, mark "fact" as the answer. If the information cannot be proved *or* disproved, mark it an opinion. (*A tip from your coach:* Watch for judgment words and the other clues that signal opinions.)

Remember there are now only 10 exercises in Set 1 and that these particular exercises have only two answer choices. Not only that, but the paragraphs are used more than once because several sentences are used from the same paragraph. The paragraphs come from college textbooks. Take a couple of deep, relaxing breaths to clear your mind. Ready?

Paragraph 1

Current American divorce rates are far higher than those of previous generations. The number of divorced individuals nearly quadrupled between 1970 and the mid-1990s. While American divorce rates are no longer increasing, they remain the highest of any industrial nation in the world. Children today have a greater chance of growing up in a family split by divorce than in any other period in American history. As recently as 1960 four-fifths of all American children were living with both their natural parents, but today's children have only a 50–50 chance of getting through childhood with both parents. Fatherless families now constitute one-quarter of all white families with children, two-thirds of black families with children, and over one-third of Hispanic families with children. Daniel Patrick Moynihan observes that we "may be the first society in history where children are worse off than adults."

Source: Adapted from J. John Palen, *Social Problems for the Twenty-First Century*, p. 268. Copyright © 2001 McGraw-Hill. Reprinted by permission of The McGraw-Hill Companies.

_____ 1. "Current American divorce rates are far higher than those of previous generations."

This statement represents
a. a fact.
b. an opinion.

_____ 2. "While American divorce rates are no longer increasing, they remain the highest of any industrial nation in the world."

This statement represents
a. a fact.
b. an opinion.

_____ 3. "Daniel Patrick Moynihan observes that we 'may be the first society in history where children are worse off than adults.'"

This statement represents
a. a fact.
b. an opinion.

Paragraph 2

In estimating their chances for success on a task such as a major exam, people's confidence runs highest when removed in time from "the moment of truth." By exam day, the possibility of failure looms larger and confidence typically drops (Gilovich & others, 1993). Roger Buehler and his colleagues (1994) report that most students also confidently underestimate how long it will take them to complete papers and other major assignments.

Source: David Myers, *Exploring Social Psychology,* 2d ed., p. 36. Copyright © 2000 McGraw-Hill. Reprinted by permission of The McGraw-Hill Companies.

_____ **4.** "In estimating their chances for success on a task such as a major exam, people's confidence runs highest when removed in time from 'the moment of truth.'"

This statement represents
a. a fact.
b. an opinion.

_____ **5.** "Roger Buehler and his colleagues (1994) report that most students also confidently underestimate how long it will take them to complete papers and other major assignments."

This statement represents
a. a fact.
b. an opinion.

Paragraph 3

With regard to variations within groups, the Hmong, an ethnic subgroup from Vietnam, have clung more persistently to their traditional pattern. This pattern includes male dominance, early marriage for females, and early and frequent childbearing. Interestingly, at the same time, the Hmong maintain high educational expectations for their women, which will increase pressures to change the traditional pattern.

Source: Robert Lauer and Jeanette Lauer, *Marriage and Family,* 6th ed., p. 42. Copyright © 2007 McGraw-Hill. Reprinted by permission of The McGraw-Hill Companies.

_____ **6.** This pattern includes male dominance, early marriage for females, and early and frequent childbearing.

This statement represents
a. a fact.
b. an opinion.

_____ **7.** Interestingly, at the same time, the Hmong maintain high educational expectations for their women, which will increase pressures to change the traditional pattern.

This statement represents
a. a fact.
b. an opinion.

Paragraph 4

Under the Ptolemies, the port city of Alexandria became the premier city of the Hellenistic world. It was a dynamic cosmopolitan city that by the end of the first century B.C. boasted almost one million inhabitants. Alexandria was a bustling port city where the main enterprise was the pursuit of wealth. The harbors were busy and the markets thronging, and international banks grew to serve the people. To make sure ships could enter the port safely, Hellenistic scientists built a huge lighthouse on an island (Pharos) outside the harbor. The structure was 440 feet high, and the light from the lantern at the top was intensified by a system of reflectors. Ships approaching the harbor were guided by the beam of the lighthouse that was looked on as one of the seven wonders of the ancient world.

Source: Adapted from Dennis Sherman and Joyce Salisbury, *The West in the World,* p. 90. Copyright © 2001 McGraw-Hill. Reprinted by permission of The McGraw-Hill Companies.

_____ **8.** "Alexandria was a bustling port city where the main enterprise was the pursuit of wealth."

This statement represents
a. a fact.
b. an opinion.

_____ **9.** "The structure was 440 feet high, and the light from the lantern at the top was intensified by a system of reflectors."

This statement represents
a. a fact.
b. an opinion.

_____ **10.** "Ships approaching the harbor were guided by the beam of the lighthouse that was looked on as one of the seven wonders of the ancient world."

This statement represents
a. a fact.
b. an opinion.

SET 2

Exercises: Distinguishing Facts from Opinions

Read each of the following eight paragraphs. Decide whether the sentence from it is a fact or an opinion. Write your answer in the space provided. Then explain *why* that sentence can be considered a fact or an opinion. More than one sentence may be used from a single paragraph. (*A tip from your coach:* To help you identify opinions, watch for judgment words and the other clue words and phrases mentioned earlier in the chapter.)

Now stretch your hands high above your head. After you lower them, yawn (yes, yawn), and then shake your hands and fingers to loosen up and dissipate tension. You're ready to go!

Paragraph 1

Good character is the most essential personal quality for true success in school, work, and life. Recent surveys of business leaders indicate that dishonesty and lying are the number one reason for on-the-job difficulties. If a company believes that an employee lacks integrity, all of that person's positive qualities—from skill and experience to productivity and intelligence—are meaningless. Employers usually list honesty or good character as an essential personal quality, followed by the ability to relate to and get along with others. In short, they want people who have integrity and civility. Also, a number of books have been written by successful top executives who claim that good character, honesty, and a strong value system are what make you an effective leader. All the corporate scandals seen in the news lately are testimonials that business leaders with poor ethics and values will eventually meet their demise.

Source: Sharon Ferrett, *Peak Performance*, 5th ed., p. 2–3. Copyright © 2006 McGraw-Hill. Reprinted by permission of The McGraw-Hill Companies.

1. Good character is the most essential personal quality for true success in school, work, and life.

   Does this statement represent a *fact* or an *opinion?*_____

   Why?_____

   _____

   _____

Paragraph 2

THE EMPLOYMENT INTERVIEW

An employment interview is designed to explore how well a candidate might fit a job. The exploration of fit works both ways: Employers certainly measure prospective candidates during this conversation, and prospective employees can decide whether the job in question is right for them. The short time spent in an employment interview can have major consequences. Consider the stakes: Most workers spend the greatest part of their adult lives on the job—roughly 2,000 hours per year or upward of 80,000 hours during a career. The financial difference between a well-paid position and an unrewarding one can also be staggering. Even without considering the effects of inflation, a gap of only $200 per month can amount to almost $100,000 over the course of a career. Finally, the emotional results of having the right job are considerable. A frustrating job not only makes for unhappiness at work but these dissatisfactions also have a way of leaking into nonworking hours as well.

Source: Ronald Adler and Jeanne Elmhorst, *Communicating at Work*, 8th ed., p. 203. Copyright © 2005 McGraw-Hill. Reprinted by permission of The McGraw-Hill Companies.

2. Most workers spend the greatest part of their adult lives on the job—roughly 2,000 hours per year or upward of 80,000 hours during a career.

   Does this statement represent a *fact* or an *opinion?*_____

   Why?_____

3. The financial difference between a well-paid position and an unrewarding one can also be staggering.

   Does this statement represent a *fact* or an *opinion?*_____

   Why?_____

Paragraph 3

SHIFT WORK AND CHILDCARE

One surprisingly common way in which dual-earner couples manage childcare is to work different shifts. In one study, one-third of all dual-earner couples with preschool-aged children had at least one spouse working an evening, night, or rotating shift. Husbands who were home when their wives were working did more cooking, cleaning, and washing than husbands who were never home when their wives were working. The increase in nonday-shift and weekend work isn't due solely to couples' childcare needs. The growth of the service sector of the economy is also responsible. Nevertheless, when asked why they were working evening or night shifts, a majority of married women in a Census Bureau survey said the main reason was that their hours made it easier to care for their children or other relatives.

Source: Andrew Cherlin, *Public and Private Families*, 4th ed., p. 281. Copyright © 2005 McGraw-Hill. Reprinted by permission of The McGraw-Hill Companies.

4. One surprisingly common way in which dual-earner couples manage childcare is to work different shifts.

   Does this statement represent a *fact* or an *opinion?*_____

   Why?_____

5. In one study, one-third of all dual-earner couples with preschool-aged children had at least one spouse working an evening, night, or rotating shift.

   Does this statement represent a *fact* or an *opinion?*_____

   Why?_____

Paragraph 4

When I first began to work in the New Guinea highlands, I often became enraged when I saw how grossly women were abused. Along jungle trails I encountered married couples, the woman typically bent under a huge load of firewood and vegetables, carrying an infant, while her husband sauntered along, bearing nothing more than his bow and arrow. Men's hunting trips seemed to be little more than male-bonding opportunities, yielding only a few prey animals consumed on the spot by the hunters. Wives were bought, sold, and discarded without their consent.

Source: Jared Diamond, "What Are Men Good For?" in Lee Cronk and Vaughn Bryant, eds., *Through the Looking Glass: Readings in General Anthropology*, 2d ed., p. 171. Copyright © 2000 McGraw-Hill. Reprinted by permission of The McGraw-Hill Companies.

6. "Along jungle trails I encountered married couples, the woman typically bent under a huge load of firewood and vegetables, carrying an infant, while her husband sauntered along, bearing nothing more than his bow and arrow."

   Does this sentence represent a *fact* or an *opinion?* _____

   Why? _____

   _____

7. "Men's hunting trips seemed to be little more than male-bonding opportunities, yielding only a few prey animals consumed on the spot by the hunters."

   Does this sentence represent a *fact* or an *opinion?* _____

   Why? _____

   _____

   _____

   _____

   _____

8. "Wives were bought, sold, and discarded without their consent."

   Does this sentence represent a *fact* or an *opinion?* _____

   Why? _____

   _____

How did you do? Did you feel confident about your answers? Take a minute to evaluate your understanding of facts and opinions. Is there anything that still confuses you? If so, try to be very specific about what you think the problem might be.

_____

_____

_____

_____

_____

_____

_____

SET 3

Exercises: Distinguishing Facts from Opinions

Read the following two paragraphs. Yes, there are only two, and there are only six questions. Although you will be doing the same thing as in Set 2, these are more challenging. Decide whether each of the three sentences taken from a paragraph represents a fact or an opinion. Write your answer in the space provided. Then explain *why* that sentence can be considered a fact or an opinion. (Remember to watch for clues that help you identify opinions: judgment words and the other clue words and phrases mentioned earlier in the chapter.) Use a few of the techniques you know to help you relax and focus before you begin working on these.

Paragraph 1

THE CONSTITUTION AND ITS INTERPRETATION

The Constitution of the United States is the nation's highest law, and judges and justices are sworn to uphold it. When a case raises a constitutional issue, a court has the duty to apply the Constitution to the case. For example, the Constitution prohibits the states from printing their own currency. If a state decided that it would do so anyway, a federal judge would be obligated to rule against the practice. Nevertheless, constitutional provisions are open to interpretation in some cases. For example, the Fourth Amendment of the Constitution protects individuals against "unreasonable searches and seizures," but the meaning of "unreasonable" is not specified. Judges must decide on its meaning in particular situations. Take, for example, the question of whether wiretapping, which was not invented until 150 years after ratification of the Fourth Amendment, is included in the prohibition on unreasonable searches and seizures. Reasoning that the Fourth Amendment was intended to protect individuals from government intrusion in their private lives, judges have ruled that indiscriminate wiretapping is unconstitutional.

Source: Thomas Patterson, *We the People*, 6th ed., p. 501. Copyright © 2006 McGraw-Hill. Reprinted by permission of The McGraw-Hill Companies.

1. The Constitution of the United States is the nation's highest law, and judges and justices are sworn to uphold it.

   Does this statement represent a *fact* or an *opinion?* _____

   Why? _____

2. Nevertheless, constitutional provisions are open to interpretation in some cases.

   Does this statement represent a *fact* or an *opinion?* _____

   Why? _____

3. Reasoning that the Fourth Amendment was intended to protect individuals from government intrusion in their private lives, judges have ruled that indiscriminate wiretapping is unconstitutional.

   Does this statement represent a *fact* or an *opinion?* _____

   Why? _____

Paragraph 2

Interracial marriages are more challenging and more fragile than marriages that are racially homogamous. A comparison of black, white non-Hispanic, and interracial couples showed that the latter focused more on their emotional attachments to each other and also on the amount of work needed to maintain the marriage. In some cases, the stability of the marriage depends on which spouse is of which race. For example, marriages with a black husband and white wife are more stable than those with a white husband and black wife. The probability of an interracial marriage lasting depends on a number of factors. As with other marriages, interracial unions are more likely to last when there are children and when the couple marry at a relatively later age. And they are more likely to be satisfying when each spouse has pride in, and identifies with, his or her own race while at the same time being accepting of other races.

Source: Robert Lauer and Jeanette Lauer, *Marriage and Family*, 6th ed., p. 44. Copyright © 2007 McGraw-Hill. Reprinted by permission of The McGraw-Hill Companies.

4. Interracial marriages are more challenging and more fragile than marriages that are racially homogamous.

   Does this statement represent a *fact* or an *opinion?*_____

   Why?_____

   _____

5. A comparison of black, white non-Hispanic, and interracial couples showed that the latter focused more on their emotional attachments to each other and also on the amount of work needed to maintain the marriage.

   Does this statement represent a *fact* or an *opinion?*_____

   Why?_____

6. The probability of an interracial marriage lasting depends on a number of factors.

   Does this statement represent a *fact* or an *opinion?*_____

   Why?_____

   Congratulations! You've lifted more weight—and that's a fact! Now that you've finished the first chapter in the Advanced Workout, take a minute to assess your experience and your progress.

   _____

   _____

   _____

   _____

CHAPTER

Make Inferences and Draw Conclusions

THE SKILL

MAKE INFERENCES AND DRAW CONCLUSIONS

In the previous chapter, you learned the first advanced skill: distinguishing facts from opinions. In this chapter, you'll add a second advanced skill: making inferences and drawing conclusions. Making inferences and drawing conclusions are so closely related that we're going to consider them together, and for our purposes, you can think of them as essentially the same thing.

An inference is a logical conclusion that is based on evidence or information that is known or presumed to be true. In reading, *an **inference** is a logical conclusion that is based on what an author has stated.* For example, suppose you read a newspaper article that describes a political candidate's qualifications. They include an undergraduate degree in American history from Harvard, a stint as a volunteer in the Peace Corps in a Third World country, and a law degree from Yale. As you are reading the article, you might infer that the candidate is well educated (degrees in American history and law), smart (earned degrees from Harvard and Yale), and has a desire to help others (served as a Peace Corps volunteer helping people in a developing country).

*A **conclusion** is a decision, opinion, or judgment reached after thoughtful consideration of material you have read.* It must be based on information you have read, but must go beyond what the author states. To continue with the example above, your conclusion about the candidate would very likely be that he is qualified to hold political office. (You might also conclude that you are going to vote for him.) A conclusion typically comes after *all* of the information has been considered. There may be one major inference or conclusion an author expects readers to make, or there may be several.

219

Fortunately, making inferences and drawing conclusions is a thinking process you use every day of your life. You laugh at jokes and cartoons because you've made the correct inference. You constantly make inferences based on people's expressions, body language, and tone of voice to help you understand what they are saying and how they feel about it. You may "read between the lines" in a note a friend sends you and pick up on a different message from the one the words seem to be saying.

Both college professors and textbook authors—including me—expect you to make logical inferences and draw conclusions as you read. In a political science class, you might read about both sides of a controversial issue such as gun control, and then draw a conclusion as to which argument was more logical and convincing. In a literature class, you will have to infer what characters are like based on their actions, their words, and how other characters react to them. You may have to infer why certain characters did what they did or said what they said.

Are you aware that you've already been using inferences in a variety of ways in this book? Consider these skills that often involve making inferences: deducing the meaning of a word from context, determining the topic of a paragraph, formulating implied main ideas by inferring what all the details "add up to," and identifying an author's writing pattern.

Sometimes there are no inferences to make or conclusions to draw when you are reading, but often there are. Moreover, authors may actually state their own conclusions. When they do this, they usually present the conclusion at the end of a paragraph or section. In fact, the conclusion is often the main idea of the paragraph or even the overall main idea of an entire section. To get your attention, authors may announce the important conclusion with *Thus, Therefore, The point is, In conclusion, As a consequence, Consequently,* and so forth. By the way, when authors state their conclusions, there is nothing for you to infer or conclude, but pay attention to their stated conclusions. The reason they *tell* you their important conclusions is to be sure you don't miss them on your own.

THE TECHNIQUE

BASE INFERENCES AND CONCLUSIONS ON THE PASSAGE

After you read a paragraph, ask yourself, "What logical inference or conclusion does the author expect me to make?" You must always *base* your inference or conclusion on the information the author provides. Your inference or conclusion must go *beyond* what the author states. Sometimes there is no inference or conclusion for you to make; at other times, there will be one or more.

Because inferences and conclusions must go beyond the information the author presents, you cannot use as an inference or a conclusion anything that the author states. For example, if the author states that a certain government program was a failure, then you cannot infer or conclude that the program was failure. You don't *need* to infer it because the author states it outright. However, if the author talked only about how expensive the program was and how few people actually benefited from it, then you could logically conclude that the program was a failure. (As you can see, the verbs for this reasoning process are to *infer* and to *conclude*.)

THE TRAINER

OBSERVE THE SKILL OF MAKING INFERENCES AND DRAWING CONCLUSIONS

Let's see this skill in action. The paragraph in the illustration serves as the basis for several logical inferences. The words in color tell you the effective reader's thoughts as he or she goes back through and analyzes the paragraph. You know the drill: read the paragraph and then the reader's "thoughts." The reader's conclusions appear in the thought bubble at the bottom right because the conclusions can only be reached *after* reflecting on the *entire* paragraph.

> This is about heroin addiction and an experiment in which the Swiss *gave* heroin addicts the drug.

> The third and fourth sentences are telling some of the results: Crime went down and addicts were eventually able to get jobs. Many got off welfare.

Other countries have dealt with heroin addiction differently than the United States. In 1994 Switzerland began the first large-scale controlled experiment in *heroin maintenance*, a three-year program under the supervision of the World Health Organization and the Swiss Academy of Medical Science that provided heroin to a thousand regular users. Evaluation of the program indicated that crime among the addicted subjects declined by 60 percent. Half of the formerly unemployed users were now working, and a third who had been on welfare were self-supporting. Homelessness was eliminated and improvements in participants' health were noted. About 8 percent of the users gave up heroin altogether.

Source: Adapted from Ronald Berger, Marvin Free, and Patricia Searles, *Crime, Justice, and Society,* p. 445. Copyright © 2001 McGraw-Hill. Reprinted by permission of The McGraw-Hill Companies.

> The last two sentences tell even more results:
> --Homelessness was eliminated.
> --Addicts' health got better.
> --A small percentage even stopped using heroin.

> Can I conclude that other countries deal with heroin addiction differently from the way the U.S. does? No. The author *states* that, so I can't infer it.

> The authors don't mention any negative effects of the program. Based on the positive results they reported, it seems logical for me to conclude that (1) the program was a success, (2) this approach should be researched further or even tried on a larger scale, (3) heroin addicts can be better citizens and lead happier, healthier lives if they do not have to contend daily with trying to obtain heroin illegally, (4) society as a whole benefits when heroin users are supplied with heroin in a supervised program.

THE EDGE

POINTERS ABOUT MAKING INFERENCES AND DRAWING CONCLUSIONS

■ **Simply putting information in the paragraph into your own words does *not* make that information an inference or conclusion.**

This is so important that I'm going to say it one more time: If information appears in a paragraph, then it cannot also be an inference that you, the reader, make. For example, if the author states that "improvements in participants' health were noted," you cannot infer that "participants became healthier." You've just said the same thing, but in different words. You could, however, go beyond what the author has stated and logically infer that because participants' health improved, they

   ■ had lower medical costs;

   ■ needed to see the doctor less often;

   ■ missed fewer days at work because of health problems;

   ■ enjoyed a better quality of life.

■ *Imply* **and** *infer* **are related, but they are two different things.**
Imply and *infer* are really just two parts of a process. Imply has to do with sending a message. Infer has to do with receiving it. If you *imply* something, you *hint* or *suggest* it without coming out directly and stating it. For example,

you could imply that you do not like someone by making a face when you hear the person's name. You could imply that you'd like the rest of your friend's french fries by asking, "Are you going to eat the rest of those?" instead of just asking directly if you can have them. When a person infers (picks up on or correctly understands) a message that someone else has implied, then that person infers the sender's meaning. If your friend replies, "I'm too full to eat one more bite!" then you infer (understand) that you're welcome to eat the rest of the fries!

The *sender implies*   ➜   The *receiver infers* (understands
(hints or suggests)   or correctly interprets the hint or
                                                         suggestion)

■ **Interpreting figurative language, such as simile, metaphor, and hyperbole, involves making inferences.**
Because many figures of speech are designed to paint a picture in the reader's mind, the words don't mean what they literally seem to say. Suppose for example, you tell a friend, "I'm dying to hear about your trip" or you read Nelson Mandela's comment that "Resentment is like drinking poison and waiting for it to kill our enemy." You don't literally mean that you're dying, but rather that you're excited or eager. Mandela's point is that resentment destroys the person who harbors it, and not the person's enemy. (Appendix 6 presents four common figures of speech. The Online Learning Center has complete module on common figures of speech.)

THE REPLAY

REMEMBER THE ESSENTIAL INFORMATION FROM THE CHAPTER

Here is the drill sergeant's chant for inferences. It was created by Professor Kathleen Riley, Polk Community College (Winter Haven, Florida) to help her students. You'll find it helpful, too! Read it aloud a few times, and you're on your way to remembering the important points about inferences.

> *Making inferences* is one name;
> *Drawing conclusions* means the same.
>
> Details are things that authors write
> Inferences are out of sight.
>
> Details: underline in ink.
> Inferences: you've got to think.
>
> Inferences make you a star.
> Don't pick a choice that goes too far!
>
> Base inferences on what you've read,
> Not on the ideas in your head!

Review the material in this chapter, including the definition and questions for inference and conclusion. Then write them in the spaces provided.

Definition of Inference

_____

_____

Definition of Conclusion

_____

_____

_____

Question to Ask Yourself

_____

_____

Explain why you cannot use as your own inference or conclusion information the author states in the paragraph, even if you paraphrase it.

_____

_____

Explain the difference between *imply* and *infer*.

_____

_____

THE PRACTICE

APPLY THE SKILL OF MAKING INFERENCES AND DRAWING CONCLUSIONS

SET 1

Exercises: Making Inferences and Drawing Conclusions

Read each paragraph below. Decide whether each answer choice represents a logical inference (conclusion) based on the information presented in the paragraph. *There may be more than one correct inference per paragraph.* Be sure to mark *all* of the statements that represent logical inferences or conclusions. When there is more than one, write the letter of *all* of the correct choices on the line provided. You should be able to explain which information in the paragraph you based your answer choice on. These excerpts are from college textbooks. Take a deep breath or two, gather your concentration, and then start in.

Increasing your reading comprehension is an essential job skill. The amount of your on-the-job reading increases throughout your career. Besides a mountain of memos, professional journals, letters, forms, manuals, annual reports, legal documents, government requirements, and codes, you will be reading community items, newspapers, and magazines. The employee who reads quickly, has the ability to concentrate, and comprehends accurately has an advantage over an employee who dislikes reading or has difficulty concentrating or comprehending.

Source: Adapted from Sharon Ferrett, *Peak Performance,* 3d ed., p. 5–17. Copyright © 2000 McGraw-Hill. Reprinted by permission of The McGraw-Hill Companies.

_____ 1. Identify any logical inferences or conclusions:
   a. Employees who continue to improve their reading comprehension skills are more likely to get ahead than employees who don't develop their reading skills.
   b. A successful career is not possible without strong reading skills.
   c. Speed reading is the most important reading skill an employee can possess.
   d. A college reading improvement course could be very helpful to students who plan to have a career.

"Shopaholics" and young adults are most vulnerable to misusing credit. College students are a prime target for credit card issuers, and issuers make it very easy for students to get credit cards. Wendy Leright, a 25-year-old teacher in Detroit, knows all too well. As a college freshman, she applied for and got seven credit cards, all bearing at least an 18.9 percent interest rate and a $20 annual fee. Although unemployed, she used the cards freely, buying expensive clothes for herself, extravagant Christmas presents for friends and family, and even a one-week vacation in the Bahamas. "It got to a point where I didn't even look at the price tag," she said. By her senior year, Wendy had amassed $9,000 in credit card debt and couldn't make the monthly payments of nearly $200. She eventually turned to her parents to bail her out. "Until my mother sat me down and showed me how much interest I had to pay, I hadn't even given it a thought. I was shocked," Wendy said. "I would have had to pay it off for years."

Source: Adapted from Jack Kapoor, Les Dlabay, and Robert J. Hughes, *Personal Finance,* 7th ed., p. 165. Copyright © 2004 McGraw-Hill. Reprinted by permission of The McGraw-Hill Companies.

_____   2. Identify any logical inferences or conclusions:
   a. College students should not use credit cards.
   b. College students should educate themselves about using credit cards wisely.
   c. Having multiple credit cards makes it easier for college students to overspend.
   d. Credit card companies are unethical.

How important is an interview in getting the right job? The Bureau of National Affairs, a private research firm that serves both government and industry, conducted a survey to answer this question. It polled 196 personnel executives, seeking the factors that were most important in hiring applicants. The results showed that the employment interview is the single most important factor in landing a job. Further research revealed that the most important factor during these critically decisive interviews was communication skills. Employers identified the ability to communicate effectively as more important in shaping a hiring decision than grade-point average, work experience, extracurricular activities, appearance, and preference for job location.

Source: Adapted from Ronald Adler and Jeanne Elmhorst, *Communicating at Work,* 8th ed., p. 203. Copyright © 2005 McGraw-Hill. Reprinted by permission of The McGraw-Hill Companies.

_____   3. Identify any logical inferences or conclusions:
   a. It's important to get the right job.
   b. The employment interview is the single most important factor in landing a job.
   c. Job applicants are likely to be more successful if they have taken steps to strengthen their communication skills.
   d. Communication skills are overrated.

A series of well-controlled laboratory studies by psychologist Michael Bock examined the relationship between emotional arousal and memory. When individuals were shown a list of words and asked to recall them later, they were better able to recall words with positive emotional impact (such as *kiss* and *prize*) than words with negative emotional impact (such as *disease* and *loss*). However, words with a neutral impact were recalled least well in Bock's studies. This suggests that, although Freud was correct in saying that negative events are recalled less well than positive events, experiences with any type of emotional impact appear to be easier to recall than neutral experiences.

Source: Benjamin Lahey, *Psychology,* 8th ed., p. 255. Copyright © 2004 McGraw-Hill. Reprinted by permission of The McGraw-Hill Companies.

_____   4. Identify any logical inferences or conclusions:
   a. Psychologist Michael Bock conducted a series of well-controlled laboratory studies.
   b. A person recalling a car wreck he or she witnessed would probably remember it less clearly than a ceremony at which the person was presented with an award.
   c. More research is needed on memory and how it functions.
   d. Deliberately attaching a positive emotion to something you want to remember could help you recall it more easily.

MEDIA AVAILABILITY AND ECONOMICS: THE GLOBAL MARKETER'S HEADACHE

Every country has communications media, but they are not always available for commercial use (especially radio and television) and coverage may be limited. Lower literacy rates and education levels in some countries restrict coverage of print media. Where income levels are low, TV ownership is also low. These factors tend to segment markets by media coverage.

Source: Adapted from William Arens, *Contemporary Advertising,* 7th ed., pp. 263–64. Copyright © 2000 McGraw-Hill. Reprinted by permission of The McGraw-Hill Companies.

_____ 5. Identify any logical inferences or conclusions:
   a. International companies have to adjust their marketing efforts to the conditions in various countries in which they wish to sell their products or services.
   b. Print media are of limited usefulness in countries where literacy and education levels are substandard.
   c. Television would be a more effective advertising medium in the United States than in Cuba, India, or Nepal.
   d. Companies that want to have more effective marketing campaigns should sponsor literacy training in countries with low literacy levels.

Emergencies are never expected, but when they do arise, they often demand performance that requires good fitness. For example, flood victims may need to fill sandbags for hours without rest, and accident victims may be required to walk or run long instances for help. Also, good fitness is required for such simple tasks as safely changing a spare tire or loading a moving van without injury.

Source: Adapted from Charles Corbin, Ruth Lindsey, Greg Welk, and William Corbin, *Fundamental Concepts of Fitness and Wellness,* p. 88. Copyright © 2001 McGraw-Hill. Reprinted by permission of The McGraw-Hill Companies.

_____ 6. Identify any logical inferences or conclusions:
   a. The most important reason for working out is to be able to handle emergencies when they arise.
   b. All emergencies require physical fitness in the person who is trying to deal with them.
   c. If you suffer an injury while changing a spare tire or loading a moving van, it is because you are not in good enough physical condition.
   d. In case of an emergency, being physically fit could save your life or help you save someone else's life.

In the early 1990s, after eight years of unprecedented growth, the United States and Canada experienced the first throes of a recession. Interest rates rose, real estate sales dropped, construction of new homes slowed, defense spending was cut, and unemployment began to rise. To make matters worse, threats of war in the Persian Gulf caused fear of higher fuel prices. Consumer confidence declined, and with it sales sank. As sales dropped, many executives cut back their marketing communication budgets, some to zero. Two years later, when the recession was over, these executives wondered why sales were still down and how their companies had lost so much market share.

Source: William Arens, *Contemporary Advertising,* 10th ed., p. 255. Copyright © 2006 McGraw-Hill/Irwin. Reprinted by permission of The McGraw-Hill Companies.

_____ **7.** Identify any logical inferences or conclusions:
  a. In order not to lose even more market share during a recession, companies should continue to spend money on marketing.
  b. Threats of war cause fear that fuel prices will rise.
  c. Recessions last two years.
  d. In the early 1990s, the United States and Canada experienced the initial phases of a recession.

Overall, Americans are only moderately involved in politics. While they are concerned with political affairs, they are mostly immersed in their private pursuits, a reflection in part of the culture's emphasis on individualism. The lower level of participation among low-income citizens has particular significance in that it works to reduce their influence on public policy and leadership.

Source: Adapted from Thomas E. Patterson, *We the People,* 6th ed., p. 254. Copyright © 2006 McGraw-Hill. Reprinted by permission of The McGraw-Hill Companies.

_____ **8.** Identify any logical inferences or conclusions:
  a. Americans should become more involved in politics.
  b. If more low-income citizens participated in the political process, that segment of the population could increase its influence on public policy and leadership.
  c. Every American citizen has an obligation to vote in every election.
  d. Politicians should work harder to motivate Americans to get involved in political activities.

If you are a visual learner, you can draw pictures, charts, and diagrams and highlight illustrations as you read. Develop mental pictures in your head. If you are primarily an auditory learner, read out loud or into a tape recorder and then listen to the tapes. If you are a kinesthetic learner, write out information, build models, do experiments, and so forth. You may find it helpful to integrate techniques for different learning styles. Write your vocabulary, formulas, and key words on note cards. Visualize key words and main ideas, and read them to yourself. Read while standing up. Recite and summarize your material with your study team.

Source: Adapted from Sharon Ferrett, *Peak Performance,* 5th ed., p. 5–10. Copyright © 2006 McGraw-Hill. Reprinted by permission of The McGraw-Hill Companies.

_____ **9.** Identify any logical inferences or conclusions:
  a. You can be a more effective student and reader if you use techniques that work with your learning style.
  b. Students should study only with students whose learning is the same as theirs.
  c. A visual learning style works better for students than an auditory learning style.
  d. It can be an advantage to a student to know his or her learning style.

You can probably buy a good used computer of some sort for under $300 and a printer for under $50. On the other hand, you might spend $1,000 to $2,500 on a new state-of-the-art system. When upgraded, this computer could meet your needs for the next five years. There is nothing wrong with getting a used system if you have a way of checking it out. For a reasonable fee, a computer-repair shop can examine it prior to your purchase. Look at newspaper ads and notices on campus bulletin boards for good buys on used equipment. Also try the Internet. If you stay with recognized brands, such as Apple, IBM, Compaq, or Dell, you probably won't have any difficulties. If you're buying new equipment, be sure to look for student discounts. Most college bookstores, for instance, offer special prices to students. Also check the Web. There are numerous sites specializing in discounted computer systems.

Source: Adapted from Timothy O'Leary and Linda O'Leary, *Computer Essentials 2007,* Introductory ed., p. 353. Copyright © 2007 McGraw-Hill. Reprinted by permission of The McGraw-Hill Companies.

_____ 10. Identify any logical inferences or conclusions:
  a. Students should buy a used computer because it is much less expensive than a new, state-of-the-art one.
  b. Regardless of whether you buy a used or new computer, you should check several sources to get a good machine at the best price.
  c. Students should buy a new computer so that they will have a warranty.
  d. College students who own computers will have problems with other students wanting to use them.

SET 2

Exercises: Making Inferences and Drawing Conclusions

All warmed up? Read these eight paragraphs. Then write at least one logical inference. (Of course, you can write more than one if you feel inspired!) You are free to write *any logical inference* that is based on the information in the selection. (*Hint from your coach:* "Logical" is a very important word in that last sentence.) If you need a bit of help, however, there is a statement to guide you as to what you might make an inference about. You should be able to explain which information in the paragraph you based your inference on. (*A reminder from your coach:* Remember not to use information straight from the paragraph as an inference, even if you put it into your own words first. Unless your inference goes *beyond* what is stated in the paragraph, you're going to get a flag on the play!)

Everyone makes slips occasionally. During an interview with the director of admissions at Lafayette, a candidate was asked why he thought that particular college would be suitable for him. His response was, "Well, I don't want to go to a real big college or a real small college. I just want a mediocre college like Lafayette."

Source: Stewart Tubbs and Sylvia Moss, *Human Communication,* 10th ed., p. 13. Copyright © 2006 McGraw-Hill. Reprinted by permission of The McGraw-Hill Companies.

1. Write an inference you could make about *the candidate who was applying for admission to Lafayette College.*

_____

_____

_____

_____

_____

_____

_____

_____

When women talk about what seems obviously interesting to them, their conversations often include reports of conversations. Tone of voice, timing, intonation, and wording are all re-created in the telling in order to explain—dramatize, really—the experience that is being reported. If men tell about an incident and give a brief summary instead of recreating what was said and how, the women often feel that the essence of the experience is being omitted. If the woman asks, "What exactly did he say?" and "How did he say it?," the man probably can't remember. If she continues to press him, he may feel as if he's being grilled.

Source: Deborah Tannen, "Talk in the Intimate Relationships: His and Hers," in Santi Buscemi and Charlotte Smith, eds., *75 Readings: An Anthology,* 8th ed., p. 205. Copyright © 2001 McGraw-Hill. Reprinted by permission of The McGraw-Hill Companies.

2. Write an inference about *men*, *women*, and *how they report conversations*.

_____

_____

_____

_____

_____

_____

_____

_____

_____

_____

_____

_____

_____

_____

_____

_____

From studies by cultural anthropologists we acquire data about the incredible range of variation in gender identity and gender roles among the world's cultures. The variable factors include such things as the roles of each gender in economic activities, differences in political and other decision-making power and influence, and expected norms of behavior. For example, in the United States only a century ago, men were seen as the gender that properly had political, economic, and social power and that, therefore, should be educated. Women were far less likely to receive a college education, seldom held any sort of management position (if they did work outside the home at all), and, until 1920, were not even allowed to vote. Women were sometimes thought of as the weaker sex. Obviously, things are different now, at least to a degree. As our culture has changed, our gender roles and identities have changed to fit our evolving cultural system.

Source: Michael Park, *Introducing Anthropology,* 2d ed., p. 123. Copyright © 2003 McGraw-Hill. Reprinted by permission of The McGraw-Hill Companies.

3. Write an inference about *men, women, and gender roles.*

_____

_____

_____

_____

_____

_____

_____

Sixty-five percent of older persons requiring long-term care rely on family and friends as caregivers. An additional 30% make use of paid providers in addition to family and friends. The average caregiver is 46 years old and female, and has the added responsibilities of being married and working outside the home. Our nation has come to rely on families, rather than social service agencies, nursing homes, or other health care providers, to provide long-term care for the chronically ill. It is estimated that the combined economic value of these unpaid caregivers exceeds $257 billion each year.

Source: Wayne Payne, Dale Hahn, and Ellen Mauer, *Understanding Your Health,* 8th ed., p. 423. Copyright © 2005 McGraw-Hill. Reprinted by permission of The McGraw-Hill Companies.

4. Write an inference about *the physical and emotional health of average caretaker,* a married 46-year-old female who also works outside the home.

_____

_____

_____

_____

Primates long ago learned not to stare at unfamiliar or threatening creatures. Most people glance quickly, then look away, when a troop of bikers cruises the street—unless they are willing to face a confrontation. But people do enjoy staring unnoticed; Americans are a nation of voyeurs, who take a perverse delight in almost anything outside everyday experience. I am fortunate that my own voyeuristic impulses are professionalized. I am an anthropologist, and my job is to stare, or as we in the field prefer to think of it, to observe.

Source: Alan M. Klein, "Of Muscles and Men," in Lee Cronk and Vaughn Bryant, eds., *Through the Looking Glass: Readings in General Anthropology,* 2d ed., p. 236. Copyright © 2000 McGraw-Hill. Reprinted by permission of The McGraw-Hill Companies.

5. Write an inference about *staring*.

_____

_____

_____

_____

_____

_____

The Internal Revenue Service (IRS) of the United States is seldom seen as anyone's friend. IRS CIO Tom Grams wants to change that and has supervised numerous efforts over the past several years to become a "friend" to the taxpayer. Most notably, Tom has led in several efforts to create customer self-service systems for taxpayers. In 2004 alone, the IRS Web site drew more than 800 million page visits, or approximately three visits for every man, woman, and child in the United States. In 2004, there were a total of 136.2 million individual tax returns filed with the IRS. Would you care to guess how many of those were filed online with the IRS's new self-service tax filing system? It may surprise you to learn that 52.7 million individual tax returns were filed online in 2004 (approximately 40 percent of all individual tax returns). Of that 52.7 million, 14.5 million were self-prepared by people with personal computers, with the remainder being filed by tax professionals. Tom hopes that percentage will top 80 percent in the year 2007. Those are astounding numbers, especially considering that tax filing online is still voluntary and will be so through 2007.

Source: Stephen Haag, Maeve Cummings, and Amy Phillips, *Management Information Systems,* 6th ed., p. 19. Copyright © 2007 McGraw-Hill/Irwin. Reprinted by permission of The McGraw-Hill Companies.

6. Write an inference about *the public's perception of the Internal Revenue Service (IRS)*.

_____

_____

_____

_____

_____

_____

_____

For years, The Jerry Springer Show had featured warped behavior on the part of the guests, with a raucous mix of screaming, obscenities, and fist fights, finished off by a closing comment from Springer who attempted to show that there was some sort of socially redeeming value to what had just taken place on the program. But representatives of the producer and distributor of the Springer show, Studios USA, agreed to completely eliminate the violence and even to go back and edit out any fights in programs that had been taped but not yet aired. It didn't take long for the public to register its position in the controversy—the ratings for The Jerry Springer Show began to decline. A short time later, Springer announced that the fights would be back.

Source: James R. Wilson and S. Roy Wilson, *Mass Media, Mass Culture,* 5th ed., p. 320. Copyright © 2001 McGraw-Hill. Reprinted by permission of The McGraw-Hill Companies.

7. Write an inference about *The Jerry Springer Show, the people who produce the show,* or *the people who watch it.*

_____

_____

_____

_____

_____

_____

_____

If they do have heart-to-heart talks, the meaning of those talks may be opposite for men and women. To many women, the relationship is working as long as they can talk things out. To many men, the relationship isn't working out if they have to keep working it over. She keeps trying to get talks going to save the relationship, and he keeps trying to avoid them because he sees them as weakening it.

Source: Adapted from Deborah Tannen, "Talk in the Intimate Relationship: His and Hers," from *That's Not What I Meant* by Deborah Tannen. Copyright © 1986 by Deborah Tannen, as excerpted in *75 Readings Plus,* 7th ed., Santi Buscemi and Charlotte Smith, eds., p. 216. Copyright © 2004 McGraw-Hill/Irwin. Reprinted by permission of The McGraw-Hill Companies.

8. Write an inference about *heart-to-heart talks between men and women.*

_____

_____

_____

_____

_____

_____

_____

_____

_____

How did it go? Take a minute to reflect on your performance on the Set 2 Exercises. What specifically do you need to do differently, better, or more consistently? Write your conclusions here.

_____

_____

_____

_____

_____

_____

_____

_____

SET 3

Exercises: Making Inferences and Drawing Conclusions

Read each of the following six paragraphs. You will be doing the same thing as in Set 2, but this time *there is no statement to guide you as to what to include in your inference*. Write at least one *logical* (there's that word again!) inference. (It will often be possible to make more than one inference, and you are welcome to do so.) You should be able to explain which information in the paragraph you based your inference on. There are two "bonus items" at the end. Take a minute to take a couple of deep, full breaths. Stretch and yawn (gets the oxygen to your brain), then pick up your pen and get rolling.

Monasteries always served as both havens during stormy political times and as outlets for those who sought a highly spiritual life. For centuries, these communities rejuvenated the Christian world and helped the church meet people's changing spiritual needs. Men and women in search of personal spiritual perfection would ultimately become powerful social forces for the medieval world.

Source: Dennis Sherman and Joyce Salisbury, *The West in the World,* p. 179. Copyright © 2001 McGraw-Hill. Reprinted by permission of The McGraw-Hill Companies.

1. Write an inference based on the paragraph above:

_____

_____

_____

_____

_____

_____

_____

_____

_____

_____

_____

_____

VALUES, BELIEFS, AND PRACTICES

Values and beliefs, often unconscious, affect our response to people and situations. Most North Americans, for example, value "fairness." "You're not playing fair" is a sharp criticism calling for changed behavior. In some countries, however, people expect certain groups to receive preferential treatment. Most North Americans accept competition and believe that it produces better performance. The Japanese, however, believe that competition leads to disharmony. U.S. business people believe that success is based on individual achievement and is open to anyone who excels. In England and in France, success is more obviously linked to social class. And in some countries, people of some castes or races are prohibited by law from full participation in society.

Source: Kitty Locker, *Business and Administrative Communication,* 5th ed., p. 315. Copyright © 2000 McGraw-Hill. Reprinted by permission of The McGraw-Hill Companies.

2. Write an inference based on the paragraph above:

_____

_____

_____

_____

_____

_____

_____

_____

_____

Only a minority of citizens engages in the more demanding forms of political activity, such as work on community affairs or on behalf of a candidate during a political campaign. The proportion of Americans who engage in these more demanding forms of activity exceeds the proportion of Europeans who do so. Nevertheless, only about one in every four Americans will take an active part in a political organization at some point in their lives. Most political activists are individuals of higher income and education; they have the skills and material resources to participate effectively and tend to take greater interest in politics. More than in any other Western democracy, political participation in the United States is related to economic status.

Source: Adapted from Thomas E. Patterson, *We the People,* 6th ed., p. 254. Copyright © 2006 McGraw-Hill. Reprinted by permission of The McGraw-Hill Companies.

3. Write an inference based on the paragraph above:

_____

_____

_____

_____

_____

_____

_____

_____

A healthy cell has a characteristic shape, with a boundary that allows entry to some substances, yet blocks others. Not so the misshapen cancer cell, with its fluid surface and less discriminating boundaries. The cancer cell breaches the controls that hold the cells in place, squeezing into spaces where other cells do not, secreting biochemicals that blast pathways through healthy tissue. The cancer even creates its own personal blood supply. The renegade cell's genetic controls differ from those of healthy cells and it transmits these differences when it divides. Cancer cells disregard the "rules" of normal cell division that enable the body to develop and maintain distinct organs. To defy that many biological traditions, the cancer cell uses up tremendous amounts of energy, causing further disruptions.

Source: Ricki Lewis, Douglas Gaffin, Mariëlle Hoefnagels, and Bruce Parker, *Life,* 4th ed., p. 41. Copyright © 2002 McGraw-Hill. Reprinted by permission of The McGraw-Hill Companies.

4. Write an inference based on the paragraph above:

_____

_____

_____

_____

_____

_____

_____

_____

_____

_____

_____

Global warming increases the environmental temperature and will bring about other effects, which computer models attempt to forecast. It is predicted that, as the oceans warm, temperatures in the polar regions will rise to a greater degree than in other regions. If so, glaciers will melt, and sea levels will rise, not only due to this melting but also because water expands as it warms. Water evaporation will increase, and most likely there will be increased rainfall along the coasts and dryer conditions inland. The occurrence of droughts will reduce agricultural yields and also cause trees to die off. Expansion of forests into arctic areas might not offset the loss of forests in the temperate zones. Coastal agricultural lands, such as the deltas of Bangladesh and China, will be inundated, and billions of dollars will have to be spent to keep coastal cities such as New York, Boston, Miami, and Galveston from disappearing into the sea. Species extinction is also likely.

Source: Adapted from Sylvia Mader, *Biology*, 8th ed., p. 889. Copyright © 2004 McGraw-Hill. Reprinted by permission of The McGraw-Hill Companies.

5. Write an inference based on the paragraph above.

_____

_____

_____

_____

_____

_____

"Meet the Typical American," announced a 1954 *Reader's Digest* article. "The average American male stands five feet nine inches tall, weighs 158 pounds, prefers brunettes, baseball, beefsteak, and French fried potatoes, and thinks the ability to run a home smoothly and efficiently is the most important quality in a wife." The average American woman, the article continued, "is five feet four, weighs 132, can't stand an unshaven face." This typical female preferred marriage to a career.

Source: Larry Madaras, *Taking Sides: Clashing Views on Controversial Issues in American History Since 1945,* 2d ed., p. 89. Copyright © 2003 McGraw-Hill. Reprinted by permission of The McGraw-Hill Companies.

6. Write an inference based on the paragraph above.

_____

_____

_____

_____

_____

_____

Bonus Set

Now relax and try these four bonus items.

Item 1

There was a merchant in Baghdad who sent his servant to market to buy provisions, and in a little while the servant came back, white and trembling, and said, "Master, just now when I was in the marketplace I was jostled by a woman in the crowd and when I turned I saw it was Death that jostled me. She looked at me and made a threatening gesture. Now lend me your horse and I will ride away from this city and avoid my fate. I will go to Samarra and there death will not find me." The merchant lent him his horse, and the servant mounted it. He dug his spurs into its flanks and as fast as the horse could gallop, he went. Then the merchant went down to the marketplace and he saw Death standing in the crowd and he came to Death and said, "Why did you make a threatening gesture to my servant when you saw him this morning?" "That was not a threatening gesture," Death said. "It was only a start of surprise. I was astonished to see him in Baghdad, for I had an appointment with him tonight in Samarra."

Source: "Appointment in Samarra," retelling of a folktale by W. Somerset Maugham, 1933.

Based on this selection, what inference can you make about death (or fate)?

_____

_____

What do you base your inference on?

_____

_____

_____

_____

_____

Item 2

CLOSE TO HOME   By John McPherson

Source: CLOSE TO HOME © 2001 John McPherson. Reprinted with permission of Universal Press Syndicate. All rights reserved.

The man in the cartoon is calling the Zartech Computer Company for tech support (help with his computer). How does he know that he is going to be on hold for a *very* long time before a Zartech representative comes on the line? In other words, explain the inference that makes this cartoon funny:

_____

_____

_____

_____

Item 3

These are warnings and directions from actual products. They are unintentionally funny because there is something illogical about each of them. If you make the correct inferences, you understand why they are funny. For each one, identify what is illogical.

Example:

On a hairdryer: "Do not use while sleeping."

Why it's funny: *If you're asleep, you couldn't be using a hairdryer at the*

same time.

1. On a package front: "You could be a winner! No purchase necessary. Details inside."

   Why it's funny: _____

   _____

2. On sleeping pills: "Warning: May cause drowsiness."

   Why it's funny: _____

   _____

3. On a bag of peanuts: "Warning: Contains nuts."

   Why it's funny: _____

   _____

4. On children's cough medicine: "Do not drive a car or operate machinery after taking this medicine."

   Why it's funny: _____

5. On a frozen dinner entrée: "Serving Suggestion: Defrost."

   Why it's funny: _____

6. On a snack package of airline peanuts: "Instructions: Open packet, eat nuts."

   Why it's funny: _____

   _____

   _____

7. On a chainsaw: "Do not attempt to stop chain with your hands."

   Why it's funny: _____

8. On a heat-and-serve pudding: "Product will be hot after heating."

   Why it's funny: _____

9. Printed on the bottom of a cake package: "Do not turn upside down."

   Why it's funny: _____

   _____

10. On Christmas lights: "For indoor or outdoor use only."

    Why it's funny: _____

11. On the label of an iron: "Do not iron clothes on body."

    Why it's funny: _____

    _____

Item 4

This short story was first published in 1950 in *Ellery Queen's Mystery Magazine*. The author is able to present an entire story in 77 words because he leaves it to the reader as to infer what is going on and what has happened.

CONVERSATION PIECE

By Ned Guymon

"No!"

"Yes!"

"You didn't!"

"I did."

"When?"

"Just now."

"Where?"

"Bedroom?"

"Dead?"

"Yes."

"Why?"

"You know."

"I don't!"

"You do."

"Unfaithful?"

"Yes."

"With whom?"

"With you."

"No!"

"Yes."

"She didn't . . ."

"She did."

"We didn't . . ."

"You did."

"You knew?"

"I knew."

"How long?"

"Long enough."

"What now?"

"Guess."

"Police?"

"Later." → why later.

"Guess again."

"Tell me!"

"Look."

"Oh, no!"

"Oh, yes."

"You can't!"

"I can."

"Please!"

"Don't beg."

"Forgive me!"

"Too late."

"Good God!"

"Good-bye."

. . .

"Operator?"

"Yes, sir?"

"The police."

Source: Ned Guymon, "Conversation Piece," *Ellery Queen's Mystery Magazine,* 1950.

What has happened right before conversation begins?

_____

_____

Who is the conversation between?

_____

_____

Where does the conversation take place?

_____

_____

What does the speaker mean by the word "Later"?

_____

_____

One speaker says, "You can't!" Can't do what?

_____

_____

Who calls the police and why?

_____

_____

Why is this short story entitled "Conversation Piece"?

_____

_____

Now you've completed another entire chapter in the Advanced Workout. Congratulations! Do you think this chapter was easier or harder than the one on facts and opinions? Do you think you understand the concepts of inference and conclusion? Be sure to note, too, any point of confusion you may still have.

_____

_____

_____

_____

_____

_____

_____

_____

CHAPTER 10

Determine an Author's Purpose, Tone, Point of View, and Intended Audience

THE SKILL

DETERMINE AN AUTHOR'S PURPOSE, TONE, POINT OF VIEW, AND INTENDED AUDIENCE

In the previous two chapters, you learned the advanced critical reading skills of distinguishing facts from opinions and making logical inferences and drawing conclusions. In this chapter, you'll add several more advanced skills: determining an author's tone, purpose, point of view, and intended audience. As with the other critical reading skills, you will often have to apply these after you have read (or reread) a paragraph or selection. Let's look at each of the four skills featured in this chapter.

AUTHOR'S PURPOSE

When authors write, they have a purpose, something that they want to accomplish. *An author's **purpose** is simply his or her reason for writing*. At any given time, an author is usually writing for one of these four purposes:

■ To *inform*—to give *inform*ation.

■ To *instruct*—to explain how to do something (that is, to give *instruct*ions).

■ To *persuade*—to convince readers to do or believe something.

■ To *entertain*—to present humor or other enjoyable material.

Textbook authors, of course, do more informing and instructing. Textbooks are filled with information, as well as sets of directions. Sets of directions always have the purpose of instructing (that's why they're called "*instruct*ions") because they are designed to explain how to do something. Needless to say, you will also read some material for your college courses that is designed to persuade (for example, when reading various opinions on a political issue) and to entertain (such as a humorous short story in a literature class). Of course, all nontextbook material is also written for a purpose. You'll see examples of the four purposes every day in any newspaper. For example, a travel columnist might write to *inform* readers about a particular travel destination, to *instruct* them how to compare online airline ticket prices, to *persuade* them to try a cruise, or to *entertain* with a funny or enjoyable experience he or she had on a recent trip. (If you think about it for a minute, you'll realize that whenever *you* write something, you have purpose for doing it.)

After you have read something, determine the author's purpose by asking yourself, *What is the author's reason for writing this?*

AUTHOR'S TONE

To help them accomplish their purpose, authors choose an appropriate tone. *Tone refers to the author's use of words and writing style to convey his or her attitude toward a topic.* For example, an author who wants to persuade readers might use an enthusiastic tone, a concerned tone, or even an angry, indignant tone.

Authors use tone in much the same way that speakers use tone of voice. If you could hear the author saying the words he or she has written, what would the person's tone of voice sound like? Sarcastic? Excited? Optimistic? Angry? Apologetic? Enthusiastic? Sincere?

It is important to understand the author's tone, or you may misinterpret the meaning. If the author is sarcastic or is joking, and you think the writer is serious, you will completely misunderstand the message. Tone can be especially important in a piece of writing in which the author expresses an opinion, such as a newspaper editorial or a letter written to a newspaper or magazine by a reader. Tone helps you understand *the author's **intended meaning:** what the author wants readers to understand, even if the words appear to be saying something different.* To determine the author's intended meaning, ask yourself, "What is the author's real meaning?" (As the OLC module on interpreting literature explains, tone is also important in understanding literary works.)

Authors choose words that help convey their tone. For example, a writer might choose the word *pushy* rather than *assertive* to describe someone he or she dislikes. The author might use a flippant, offhand writing style to give readers a further clue about his or her negative attitude toward the person (his topic). "After you have read something (especially about a controversial topic), determine the author's tone by asking yourself, *What do the author's word choice and writing style convey about his or her attitude toward the topic?*

AUTHOR'S POINT OF VIEW

*An author's **point of view** refers to his or her position on an issue or, in other words, the author's opinion or belief regarding an issue.* If an issue (topic) is controversial, people have conflicting opinions about it. When authors present a controversial issue, they may take a position in favor of one side of the issue (and, therefore, against the other side). In other words, they have a *bias*. Biases aren't necessarily bad or unfair, but you need to be aware of a writer's bias so that you aren't manipulated by the author. Sometimes writers simply tell you their bias; at other times, you must figure it out by looking at the information they present (and leave out!) and the way they present that information. (In Chapter 11, you will learn more about author's bias.)

Sometimes authors take a neutral, unbiased position and present both sides of an issue objectively. For example, various writers would have different points of view on environmental issues, health issues, political issues, social issues, and so forth. If you read carefully and then think about what you have read, you should be able to figure out the author's point of view. Here's some good news: Authors often *tell* the reader what their position is. And here's more good news: the author's point of view is often the main idea. After you have read a selection, determine the author's point of view by asking yourself, *What is the author's position or belief regarding the issue?*

AUTHOR'S INTENDED AUDIENCE

Authors not only write for specific purposes, use an appropriate tone, and have a point of view on an issue, they also have an intended audience in mind when they write. *Intended audience means the people the writer has in mind as the readers.* There are three categories of intended audiences. First, the intended audience might be a *specific person* (for example, when someone writes a letter to the editor of a newspaper or to his or her state legislator, that recipient is the intended audience). Second, the intended audience might be a *particular group of people* (registered voters, bass fishing enthusiasts, country music lovers, vegetarians, nurses, preteen girls, etc.). For example, magazines such as *Fortune, Yoga Journal, Wired,* and *Sports Illustrated* target specific "group" audiences. Finally, the intended audience might be the *general public.* Most newspapers and many magazines (*USA Today, Reader's Digest,* and *Time* magazine, for example) are written for the public at large. These publications are ones that practically any adult would have an interest in and that require no special knowledge for readers to understand them. The source of printed information will often give you a major clue about who the intended audience is. For example, if the source is a medical journal, the intended audience is physicians. Or, if it is an instruction manual that comes with a DVD player, then the DVD user would be the intended audience.

Writers take into consideration how much their intended audience is likely to already know about a topic. The author of an introductory-level sociology textbook assumes the intended audience will be college freshmen or sophomores who have little or no prior knowledge of sociology. Consequently, the author tries to present basic concepts and explain them clearly and completely. A neurosurgeon writing an article for a medical journal, however, has other surgeons in mind as the audience and knows that they will be familiar with the medical terminology in the article. For the writer of a column of child development, the audience might be parents of young children, and would present the information in a way that the typical parent could easily understand. After you read a selection, determine the author's intended audience by asking yourself, *Who did the author have in mind as readers? Was it a particular person (who?), a certain group of people (which group?), or the general public?*

| THE TECHNIQUE | **ASK THE PURPOSE, TONE, POINT OF VIEW, AND INTENDED AUDIENCE QUESTIONS** |

The skills presented in this chapter are complementary skills: understanding one helps you understand the others because they go together. As noted above, a writer starts out with a specific purpose in mind for writing something. To help get the point across, the author chooses an appropriate tone. If the author is presenting a controversial issue, he or she typically presents his or her point of view or position on this issue. The writer also has in mind an intended audience for whom he or she is writing, and that influences the author's choice of words and style of writing (tone).

Use the following questions to help you determine each of these elements of critical reading:

- Determine the *author's purpose* by asking yourself, *What is the author's reason for writing this?*
- Determine the *author's tone* by asking yourself, *What do the author's word choice and writing style convey about his or her attitude toward the topic?*
- Determine the *author's point of view* by asking yourself, *What is the author's position or belief regarding the issue?*
- Determine the *author's intended audience* by asking yourself, *Who did the author have in mind as readers?*

THE TRAINER

OBSERVE THE SKILLS OF AUTHOR'S PURPOSE, TONE, POINT OF VIEW, AND INTENDED AUDIENCE

Time for our effective reader to hop into action and model the application of these skills. This illustration shows our reader applying the four skills presented in this chapter. Read the passage first, then read the "thoughts" of the effective reader that appear in color.

> Okay—here's the topic: reckless jet skiers who pose a danger to themselves and others.

> Ah! The *intended audience*: homeowners who live on lakefront property.

Soon it will be summer, and once again our beautiful lake will be overrun with reckless jet skiers who pose a danger to themselves and the rest of us. Jet skis are an increasing hazard on our lakes. Irresponsible jet skiers are not only injuring themselves in record numbers, they are injuring and killing innocent people who are simply out to enjoy a day at the lake. Enough is enough! It's time to take action. As homeowners who live on lakefront property, we must insist on stringent regulations to curb the excessive speed of jet skiers. In addition, no one under the age of 16 should be allowed to use a jet ski. Furthermore, all jet skiers should be required to take safety courses. Finally, we must lobby for a restriction on the number of jet skiers who can be on the water at any given time. Jet skiers who violate the rules should be made to pay heavy fines or be banned from future use of the lake. Call our city council members today! Tell them it's time for a change—a change for the better.

> The writer's *point of view* is that it's time to create regulations for jet skiers.

> The writer is trying to get readers to "take action," to call their city council members, so the author's *purpose* must be to persuade.

> The author's *tone* . . . let's see. Well, the author feels very strongly about the matter and the purpose was to persuade. The writer uses exclamation points, words such as *should, must,* and *insist,* and is urging readers to take action. I'd say the tone could be described as urgent, concerned, impassioned.

THE EDGE

POINTERS ABOUT AUTHOR'S PURPOSE, TONE, POINT OF VIEW, AND INTENDED AUDIENCE

■ **If you think the author's purpose is to inform, think a minute more about whether there could be some other purpose.**
At first, it may seem to you as if everything you read has the purpose of informing. In a sense, you're right, of course. But ask yourself what the author is trying to inform you about. If the author is trying to inform you about *how to do something,* then the purpose is to *instruct.* If the author is informing you about something in order *to get you to do it or believe it,* then the author's purpose is to *persuade.* If the author is informing you about *something funny, pleasant,* or *enjoyable,* then the purpose is to *entertain.* The purpose is to *inform* only when the author is simply *presenting information.*

■ **Sometimes the author *states* the purpose or indicates who the intended audience is.**
When this is the case, the author has done your work for you! For example, a biology textbook author might write, "This chapter explains the organization of ecosystems" or "In this section you will learn the proper procedure for preparing a slide for the microscope." Clearly, the purpose of the first is to *inform,* and the purpose of the later is to *instruct.*

The author of a study skills textbook might write, "Like every college freshman, you will have many exciting—and sometimes frustrating and confusing—experiences." From the first words of that sentence, you can tell that the intended audience is *college freshmen.* A computer science textbook author might write, "As a computer network manager, you will often be called upon to resolve complex problems as quickly as possible." The intended audience is obviously students who are considering becoming *computer network managers.*

Watch for authors' own indications of their purpose for writing and their intended audience.

■ **On standardized tests, recognize "purpose words" that mean the same thing.**
With regard to authors' purposes, keep in mind that there is more than one way to say the same thing. If you must take a standardized test, such as a course exit test or a state-mandated basic reading skills test, remember that these other words can be used to describe the four common purposes:

To inform: to tell, explain (about), describe, discuss

To instruct: to describe how to, explain how to, tells how to, give steps in order to

To persuade: to convince, make people believe, encourage people to, motivate people to, inspire people to (do or believe something)

To entertain: to amuse readers, make readers laugh, tell a funny story

Suppose, for example, that on a reading test there is a passage about how to identify poison ivy. The author's purpose is to instruct. You are asked the question, "The author wrote this selection in order to . . . " When you look at the answer choices, you do not see the word *instruct.* However, you do see one that says, "*explain how to* identify poison ivy." "Explain how to" means the same thing as "to instruct." That's the answer you'd want to choose.

■ **In addition to the four most common purposes for writing, authors may write for other purposes or a combination of purposes.**
Sometimes authors write to *describe a scene.* It might be the scene of a battle, for instance, or the scene at a royal coronation. It might be a scene in a

work of fiction, such as a description of the desert or of a bizarre landscape in a science fiction world. At other times, the writer's purpose is to *narrate (tell) a story.* It might be an account of an actual experience, such as a soldier's experience in a war-torn country, or it might be a fictional story, the sort found in a novel or short story. Authors occasionally have other, more specialized purposes, such as to *explore, investigate, evaluate, criticize,* or *praise.* (Don't get all hung up in these. It's just good to know they exist.)

There will always be one primary purpose, but there may be a secondary purpose. For instance, an author might want to persuade readers (primary purpose), but he or she might also want to entertain readers by using a humorous tone or poking fun whoever or whatever is being written about. Some well-known political writers, such as the late Molly Ivins, use this approach. (Again, don't get hung up on this. It's just helpful to know authors sometimes have a second, less-important purpose.)

■ **The author's point of view may also be referred to as the "author's argument."**
You know that lawyers "argue" a client's case in court. That means they present the facts and evidence that are likely to help their client have a favorable outcome. An author's argument is similar: it refers to the position (opinion) the author wants to persuade you to believe. (In other words, the author "argues the case" to readers). In a paragraph in which the main idea is the author's opinion, you will often hear that main idea referred to as the author's point of view or the author's argument. For example, an author's argument (main idea, point of view) might be: "The federal government must take the lead in raising educational standards in public schools across the nation."

■ **In literature, "point of view" has another meaning: the person through whose eyes the story is being told.**
In literature, *point of view* is a term used to describe the way in which readers are presented with the story, that is, through whose eyes the story is being told. The narrator (storyteller) might be a first-person narrator, which means that one of the characters in the story is telling the story. Or, it might be an omniscient (all-knowing) narrator who tells the story. (You can learn more about this in the OLC module, Achieving Basic Comprehension of Literary Works.)

■ **Pay attention to the author's tone because it helps you understand his or her real (intended) meaning.**
Sometimes an author's words appear to be saying one thing, yet the author's meaning is actually something else. In fact, it may be the *opposite* of what the words seem to be saying. This is true when authors use sarcasm: They say one thing, but mean the other. For example, a writer might sarcastically state what a "great idea" it is to allow all children to have unlimited access to the Internet and how "silly" it is for parents to monitor the websites their children visit. A reader who misses the sarcasm would think the writer was serious, when in reality, the writer's point is that children should *not* have unlimited access to the Internet and parents *should* monitor the websites their children visit.

■ **There are many words that can be used to describe an author's tone.**
You saw an illustration of this in The Trainer section earlier. *Urgent, concerned,* and *impassioned,* for example, all have a similar meaning, so any of them could describe the author's tone. Don't think that there is always one specific word that correctly describes an author's tone in a paragraph.

Here are some words that can be used to describe tone. You already know some of them. I'm including the definitions so that you can learn any that are new to you. (These are all words that you, as a college student, should have in your vocabulary.) To make them easier to learn, they are grouped into categories.

1. **Words that describe a *neutral* tone**
   (typically used in textbooks, reference material, sets of directions, instructional manuals, most newspaper and magazine articles, and other factual, objective material that is presented in a straightforward manner)

dispassionate	devoid of or unaffected by passion, emotion, or bias
indifferent	appearing to have no preference or concern
matter-of-fact	straightforward; unemotional
neutral	unemotional; not indicating a preference for either side in a dispute or controversy
objective	uninfluenced by emotions or personal prejudices
unemotional	involving little or no emotion or feeling

2. **Words that describe a *serious* tone**
   (typically used in important formal announcements such as obituaries, for example)

reserved	marked by self-restraint and reticence
serious	grave, earnest, not trifling or jesting; deeply interested or involved
solemn	deeply earnest, serious, and sober

3. **Words that describe an *emotional* tone**
   (typically found in personal articles, political writing, and some persuasive writing, such as editorials)

celebratory	done with festivity or rejoicing
cheerful	glad, merry, reflecting good humor
compassionate	showing kindness, mercy, or compassion; sympathetic
concerned	caring deeply about an issue or person
defiant	resisting authority or force; intentionally contemptuous
distressed	showing anxiety, strain, or suffering
emotional	showing strong feeling
impassioned	characterized by passion or zeal
intense	deeply felt, profound
nostalgic	feeling bittersweet longing for things, persons, or situations in the past
remorseful	feeling regret
self-pitying	feeling sorry for oneself
sentimental	based on emotions rather than reason
urgent	calling for immediate attention; instantly important

4. **Words that describe a *hostile, critical,* or *disapproving* tone**
   (typically found in movie and book reviews, editorials, and some magazine articles)

angry	feeling or showing anger; incensed or enraged
caustic	causing a burning or stinging sensation from intense emotion

condescending	patronizing; dealing with others as if they are inferior
critical	inclined to criticize or find fault
derogatory	intended to belittle, disparage, or diminish
disapproving	passing unfavorable judgment upon; condemning
disgusted	filled with disgust or irritated impatience
hostile	antagonistic; showing ill will
indignant	angered by something unjust, mean, or unworthy; irate
insulting	treated with gross insensitivity, insolence, or contemptuous rudeness
intolerant	not allowing difference of opinion or sentiment
negative	marked by hostility, opposition, or resistance
pessimistic	expecting the worst; having a negative attitude or gloomy outlook
righteous	morally upright; morally justifiable
threatening	intended to give a warning
vindictive	spiteful; revengeful

5. **Words that describe a *humorous, sarcastic, ironic,* or *satiric* tone**
   (can appear in writing of many sorts, including literature and social criticism, and some newspaper and magazine columns and articles)

amused	feeling entertained or occupied in a pleasant manner
bitter	characterized by sharpness, severity, or cruelty
comical	humorous; amusing
contemptuous	openly disrespectful; showing haughty disdain
cynical	scornful of the motives, virtue, or integrity of others expressing scorn and bitter mockery
disbelieving	not believing; refusing to believe
disdainful	contemptuous; scornful
farcical	characterized by broad or ludicrous humor
humorous	funny; amusing
ironic	humorously sarcastic or mocking
irreverent	disrespectful; critical of what is generally accepted or respected; showing a lack of reverence
lighthearted	not burdened by trouble, worry, or care; happy and carefree
malicious	intended to cause harm or suffering; having wicked or mischievous intentions or motives
mocking	treating with scorn or contempt
playful	full of sun and high spirits
ridiculing	making fun of; evoking contemptuous feelings or laughter at a person or thing
sarcastic	characterized by the desire to show scorn or contempt; making cutting remarks to show scorn or contempt
satirical	using sarcasm, irony, or caustic wit to expose or ridicule human folly, vice, or stupidity
scornful	treating someone or something as despicable or unworthy; showing utter contempt
skeptical	reluctant to believe; doubting or questioning everything

6. **Words that describe a *supportive* tone**
   (found in many types of writing, such as certain textbooks, inspirational writing, some magazine articles, and personal correspondence)

approving	expressing approval or agreement
conciliatory	willing to compromise or give in on some matters
encouraging	showing support
enthusiastic	showing excitement
gentle	kind; considerate; tender
hopeful	inspiring hope
optimistic	expecting the best; having a positive outlook
positive	in favor of, supportive; optimistic
respectful	showing proper respect, regard, or esteem
sincere	genuine; without hypocrisy or pretense
supportive	showing support or assistance
sympathetic	inclined to sympathy; showing pity; empathic
tolerant	showing respect for the fights, opinions, or practices of others

7. **Some *other* words that can be used to describe tone**

ambivalent	having opposite feelings or attitudes at the same time
apologetic	self-deprecating; humble; offering or expressing an apology or excuse
arrogant	giving oneself an undue degree of importance; haughty
authoritative	speaking in a definite and confident manner
cautious	careful; not wanting to take chances
conciliatory	willing to give in on some matters
evasive	intentionally vague or ambiguous; not giving a direct answer
gloomy	depressing; dismal
grim	gloomy; stern; forbidding; unnerving
humble	marked by meekness or modesty; not arrogant or prideful
hypocritical	professing beliefs, feelings, or virtues that one does not actually hold or possess
obsequious	trying to flatter or please by being submissive; servile; fawning
self-righteous	piously sure of one's own morality or virtue

You may get a clue that an author is using an emotional tone (*concerned, urgent, impassioned, angry,* etc.) if the author uses words that elicit an emotional response from readers, uses exclamation points, or uses italics, bold print, or capital letters for emphasis. As you might expect, emotional language typically appears in passages that are written to *persuade* the reader to do or believe something. To help "hear" the author's tone, try reading a passage aloud.

■ **Do not confuse a description of the topic with a description of the tone.**
An author might write about a sad topic, but present the information in a neutral, unemotional tone. Look at the following two paragraphs, both of which describe a sad event, a tornado's destruction of a small town. The purpose of

each of them is to inform readers about what happened. Read the first passage, which is factual, and notice that it has a neutral, unemotional tone.

> Yesterday a category 4 tornado swept through Pineville, a town with a population of 1,500. Winds in excess of 140 miles per hour lifted structures off their foundations. The entire town was destroyed and debris was scattered as far as 50 miles. Thirty people lost their lives and another one hundred were injured. Damage is estimated at 1 million dollars.

Now read this description of the same event:

> Yesterday will go down in history as a horribly tragic nightmare for Pineville, a friendly little town of 1,500. A vicious category 4 tornado smashed the town with winds of more than 140 miles per hour and flung debris for more than 50 miles. Thirty unlucky citizens perished and an additional one hundred suffered injuries from the killer storm. And as if that were not enough, this monster of mother nature inflicted more than 1 million dollars' worth of damage on hapless Pineville.

The second passage uses emotional language, such as *horribly tragic nightmare, vicious, smashed, perished, killer, monster, inflicted,* and *hapless.* The author's word choice indicates how sorry and sad the writer feels about what has happened, so the tone could be described as *sympathetic, compassionate,* or just *emotional.*

■ **Be specific about who the intended audience is.**
Sometimes students say the intended audience is "readers" or "the readers," but how helpful are responses such as those? Tell *who* those "readers" are likely to be.

THE REPLAY

REMEMBER THE ESSENTIAL INFORMATION FROM THE CHAPTER

Take a minute to try to write out from memory what each of these skills is. Then write the question you should ask yourself to determine each of them. (Review them first, if you need to.) After you have written them, check what you have written and make any corrections or additions. Do this *now*. Do it *right*. You'll be glad you did.

1. Author's Purpose

Definition:_____

_____

Question to Ask Yourself:_____

_____

List authors' four main purposes for writing. _____

_____

2. Author's Tone

Definition:_____

_____

Question to Ask Yourself:_____

_____

Give five examples of words that can be used to describe an author's tone._____

_____

3. Author's Point of View

Definition:_____

_____

Question to Ask Yourself:_____

_____

_____

Explain the difference between a *neutral* point of view and a *biased* point of view.

_____

_____

_____

_____

_____

_____

4. Author's Intended Audience

Definition: _____

_____

Question to Ask Yourself: _____

_____

List the three general categories of intended audiences. _____

_____

_____

THE PRACTICE

SET 1

APPLY THE SKILL OF DETERMING AN AUTHOR'S PURPOSE, TONE, POINT OF VIEW, AND INTENDED AUDIENCE

Exercises: Determining an Author's Purpose, Tone, Point of View, and Intended Audience

Read each of the 10 excerpts below. Most are from textbooks, but a couple are from nontextbook sources. Then select the answer choice that correctly identifies the author's *purpose, tone* (refer to "tone words" and their definitions on pages 253–255) *point of view,* or *intended audience.* Remember that these are complementary skills: Each one can help you understand the others. Stretch your arms. Shrug your shoulders. Yawn. Then get going!

Excerpt 1

I meant to write this piece earlier, but I had to go to the supermarket and buy more fruit. By the time I got back, I still hadn't worked out. I didn't wake up early this morning to get a headstart because it would have cut into my eight hours of dream time. Then, when I finally got to the computer today, bottle of water at my side, I got right up again to go to the bathroom.

Staying healthy is practically a full-time job.

The thing is, I already have a full-time job.

As it happens, most of us have full-time jobs. And families. And households. And hobbies. Trying to shoehorn into our schedules all the health advice we're given is enough to make us give up and drown our frustrations in a pint of Ben and Jerry's Chubby Hubby.

Source: Melissa Morrison, "Exercise. Eat Right. Drink Water. Get a Full Night's Rest. Who Has Time for Health?" *The Dallas Morning News,* June 22, 2001, p. 7C. Reprinted by permission of the author.

_____ **1.** The author's *point of view* is:
   a. It's important to eat fresh fruit every day.
   b. Staying healthy is practically a full-time job, and most of us don't have the time it requires.
   c. Most of us already have full-time jobs.
   d. It is easy to make poor food choices when we feel frustrated.

_____ **2.** The author's *tone* is
   a. humorous.
   b. sarcastic.
   c. angry.
   d. intolerant.

Excerpt 2

The writer posted the following message as a remembrance at www.virtualwall.org, an extraordinary website dedicated to those Americans in the military who gave their lives during the Vietnam War. Their names, more than 58,000 of them, are inscribed on the black granite Vietnam Memorial ("The Wall") in Washington, D.C. In his remembrance, the writer refers to *Saving Private Ryan,* a movie in which Capt. Miller (played by Tom Hanks) is sent to find and bring home young Private Ryan. All of Ryan's brothers have been killed in the war, and he is the only remaining son. Capt. Miller dies saving Private Ryan.

To all those who paid the ultimate sacrifice for their country, their loved ones, their friends, their enemies, and those they never knew and will never know for generations to come, I thank you.

I am not a "vet." I have never served in any branch of the military or for any government entity. I can never know the pain, anger, frustration, or fear you experienced. Indeed, I cannot possibly imagine it. I only know that I am able to write this remembrance today because you *did* suffer through those inhumanities. Words alone can never express the sadness I feel knowing you had to make those sacrifices. Words alone can never express the anger I feel knowing you had to make those sacrifices. And words alone can never express the pride I feel knowing that you *did* make those sacrifices for people, including those like me whom you never knew. Even though I do not stand in front of that granite monolith and caress each and every name inscribed thereon, know that, in spirit, I already have. In one of the final scenes of *Saving Private Ryan,* Capt. Miller tells Ryan to "earn this," meaning the sacrifice they made for him. I hope I can "earn this" for you. You will not be forgotten.

Source: Veteran's essay posted on the www.virtualwall.org, May 22, 2000. Reprinted by permission of Jeffrey A. Sexton.

_____   3.   The author's primary *purpose* is to
   a.   inform others of his guilt about not having served in the military service and become a "vet."
   b.   persuade others that they should feel anger about Americans having to give their lives to defend the country.
   c.   persuade others of the importance of the movie *Saving Private Ryan.*
   d.   inform those in the military who sacrificed their lives for our country of his gratitude to them and his intention to honor their sacrifice by becoming worthy of it.

_____   4.   The author's *intended audience* is primarily those who have
   a.   visited the "granite monolith" (the Vietnam Memorial).
   b.   seen the movie *Saving Private Ryan.*
   c.   died in military service to our country.
   d.   served in the military or who are considering enlisting in the military.

Excerpt 3

PREVENTION! EDUCATION! PROTECTION! Avoid unsafe sex practices; avoid intravenous drug use. This advice has become the formula for surviving in the world of AIDS. *Controlling your own behavior can help prevent human immunodeficiency virus (HIV) infection.* It has been more than two decades since Luc Montagnier of the Pasteur Institute (in France) published the first report on the virus (HIV) that is now known to cause AIDS. Despite the high-powered arsenal of contemporary biology and media hype, there is nothing on the horizon resembling a cure for AIDS. Nor is science anywhere near a workable vaccine against HIV.

Source: Frank Cox, *The AIDS Booklet,* 6th ed., p. 2. Copyright © 2000 McGraw-Hill. Reprinted by permission of The McGraw-Hill Companies.

_____   5.   The author's *tone* is
   a.   urgent.
   b.   optimistic.
   c.   indifferent.
   d.   sentimental.

_____ 6. The author's *purpose* is to
   a. persuade readers to take precautions to prevent HIV infection, which ultimately becomes AIDS.
   b. inform readers why AIDS treatments have been largely unsuccessful.
   c. persuade scientists to redouble their efforts to develop a vaccine against AIDS.
   d. inform readers about the background and history of HIV and AIDS.

_____ 7. The *intended audience* is
   a. medical personnel who deal with AIDS patients.
   b. high school and college students.
   c. health and sex education teachers.
   d. anyone who is sexually active, who uses intravenous drugs, or who may be considering becoming sexually active or using intravenous drugs.

Excerpt 4

ARE YOU A READER, A LISTENER, OR A DOER?

One way to explore how you learn best is to ask yourself if you are a reader, a listener, or a doer. Do you get more information from *reading and seeing, talking and listening,* or *doing?* Of course, you do all these things, but your learning strength or style may be in one of these areas. A person who learns better by reading possesses a visual learning style. Someone who learns better by listening is considered an auditory learner. A kinesthetic learner learns by touch.

Source: Adapted from Sharon Ferrett, *Peak Performance,* 5th ed., p. 1–8. Copyright © 2006 McGraw-Hill. Reprinted by permission of The McGraw-Hill Companies.

_____ 8. The author's *tone* is
   a. remorseful.
   b. emotional.
   c. matter-of-fact.
   d. disbelieving.

_____ 9. The author's *intended audience* is
   a. teachers; educators.
   b. students; learners.
   c. administrators.
   d. college students who plan to become teachers.

Excerpt 5

As many speakers have discovered, it is easy to overestimate the audience's stock of information. In most informative speeches, your listeners will be only vaguely knowledgeable (at best) about the details of your topic. (Otherwise, there would not be much need for an informative speech!) Therefore, you must lead your listeners step by step, without any shortcuts. You cannot assume they will know what you mean. Rather, you must be sure to explain everything so thoroughly that they cannot help but understand. As you work on your speech, always consider whether it will be clear to someone who is hearing about the topic for the first time.

Source: Stephen Lucas, *The Art of Public Speaking,* 8th ed., p. 377. Copyright © 2004 McGraw-Hill. Reprinted by permission of The McGraw-Hill Companies.

_____ **10.** The *intended audience* is
   a. speech teachers.
   b. politicians and other public officials who must often make public appearances.
   c. professional speech makers.
   d. people who are learning how to give speeches; students in a speech class.

_____ **11.** The author's *point of view* is:
   a. Most audiences are incapable of understanding informative speeches.
   b. When giving an informative speech, explain everything thoroughly enough so that it will be clear even to someone who is hearing about the topic for the first time.
   c. It is important to research your topic thoroughly so that you can explain it clearly.
   d. Giving a successful informative speech requires both skill and patience.

_____ **12.** The author's *purpose* is to
   a. instruct readers about how to give an effective informative speech.
   b. persuade readers not to go into an informative speech underprepared.
   c. inform readers about the parts of an informative speech.
   d. entertain readers with an example of an informative speech.

Excerpt 6

Social Security is one of the few welfare programs run entirely by the federal government. Washington collects the payroll taxes that fund the program and sends monthly checks directly to the nearly forty million Social Security recipients, who receive on average about $900 a month. Although people qualify for Social Security by paying payroll taxes during their working years, the money they receive upon retirement is funded by payroll taxes on current workers' salaries. This arrangement poses a long-term threat to the viability of the Social Security program because people today live longer than they once did. Roughly one in five Americans will be over age sixty-five in the year 2037, and there will not be enough workers then to pay for retirees' Social Security benefits. Some kind of adjustment in the current program will be required.

Source: Thomas Patterson, *We the People,* 6th ed., p. 572. Copyright © 2006 McGraw-Hill. Reprinted by permission of The McGraw-Hill Companies.

_____ **13.** The author's *tone* is:
   a. malicious.
   b. encouraging.
   c. amused.
   d. authoritative.

_____ **14.** The author's *point of view* is that:
   a. Social Security should be done away with.
   b. Taxes should be raised to cover Social Security's long-term funding.
   c. Because people today live longer, an adjustment must be made in Social Security now in order for retirees to receive benefits in 2037 and beyond.
   d. Because people are now living longer, there are no solutions to the long-term funding shortage that threatens the Social Security program.

Excerpt 7

Unfortunately, there are even fewer vocational opportunities for women in prisons than for men. Those that do exist are often in stereotypic female occupations (e.g., cosmetology, hairdressing, food service, clerical, housekeeping) that do not reflect the wide array of jobs available to women in today's world of work.

Source: Adapted from Ronald Berger, Marvin Free, and Patricia Searles, *Crime, Justice, and Society,* p. 420. Copyright © 2001 McGraw-Hill. Reprinted by permission of The McGraw-Hill Companies.

_____ **15.** The author's *tone* is:
    a. arrogant.
    b. disapproving.
    c. mocking.
    d. nostalgic.

Excerpt 8

Recommendations to protect yourself from identity theft include the following:

- Shred or burn financial information containing account or Social Security numbers.
- Use passwords other than maiden names.
- Don't put your Social Security number on any document unless it is legally required.
- Check your credit report once or twice a year to make sure it is correct.
- Have your name removed from mailing lists operated by credit agencies and companies offering credit promotions.
- If you become a victim, notify the credit card company and other businesses with specific details. Also, file a police report to provide documentation of the scam.

Websites with additional information on financial privacy and identity theft include www.identitytheft.org, www.idfraud.org, www.privacyrights.org, and www.pirg.org/calpirg/consumer/privacy.

Source: Adapted from Jack Kapoor, Les Dlabay, and Robert J. Hughes, *Personal Finance,* 7th ed., p. 150. Copyright © 2004 McGraw-Hill. Reprinted by permission of The McGraw-Hill Companies.

_____ **16.** The authors' *purpose* is to
    a. inform readers how identity theft occurs.
    b. persuade readers to report identity theft as soon as they become aware of it.
    c. entertain readers with information about how an identity theft was foiled.
    d. instruct readers about ways to protect themselves from identity fraud.

_____ **17.** The authors' *point of view* is that:
    a. People should take steps to protect themselves against identity theft.
    b. Identity theft is a rapidly growing crime.
    c. There are no effective ways for people to prevent identity theft.
    d. Identity theft is an easy crime for criminals to commit.

Excerpt 9

There truly will come a time when knobs and dials are no longer present on any home appliance. Instead, people will simply speak commands and the appliance will respond appropriately. For couch potatoes, this represents a real problem. The only exercise for most couch potatoes occurs while operating the remote control—with automatic speech recognition, their thumbs won't even get a workout.

Source: Adapted from Stephen Haag, Maeve Cummings, and James Dawkins, *Management Information Systems for the Information Age,* 2d ed., p. 284. Copyright © 2000 Irwin/McGraw-Hill. Reprinted by permission of The McGraw-Hill Companies.

_____ **18.** The authors' *purpose* is to
   a. inform.
   b. instruct.
   c. persuade.
   d. entertain.

_____ **19.** The authors' *intended audience* is
   a. computer specialists.
   b. the general public.
   c. couch potatoes.
   d. elementary school–age children.

Excerpt 10

The three leading causes of death in adolescence are accidents, suicide, and homicide (Takanishi, 1993). More than half of all deaths in adolescents ages 10 to 19 are due to accidents, and most of those involve motor vehicles, especially for older adolescents. Risky driving habits, such as speeding, tailgating, and driving under the influence of alcohol or other drugs, might be more important causes of these accidents than lack of driving experience. In about 50 percent of the motor vehicle fatalities involving an adolescent, the driver has a blood alcohol level of 0.10 percent, twice the level needed to be "under the influence" in some states. A high rate of intoxication is often present in adolescents who die as pedestrians or while using recreational vehicles.

Source: Adapted from John Santrock, *Adolescence,* 8th ed., pp. 92–93. Copyright © 2001 McGraw-Hill. Reprinted by permission of The McGraw-Hill Companies.

_____ **20.** The author's *purpose* is to
   a. inform readers about one of the leading causes of adolescent deaths, accidents involving motor vehicles.
   b. instruct adolescents how to increase their chances of surviving adolescence.
   c. persuade adolescents to drive more responsibly.
   d. persuade parents to monitor their adolescent children more closely.

_____ **21.** The author's *point of view* is that:
   a. The high number of adolescent deaths dues to motor vehicle accidents suggests that both the legal driving age and drinking age should be raised.
   b. Adolescent deaths from suicide and homicide outnumber the deaths from accidents.
   c. The primary cause of adolescent deaths is accidents, especially motor vehicle, pedestrian, and recreational vehicle accidents involving alcohol.
   d. Alcohol is implicated not only in motor vehicle accidents that kill adolescents, but in deaths to adolescent pedestrians and recreational vehicle users.

So far, so good? I hope so. Stand up and stretch again. You've earned it!

How's it going at this point? Do you feel that you are able to apply the skills in this chapter? If you are having difficulty, try to pinpoint and describe the nature of the problem and write a description of it on the lines below. Be sure to ask about it the next time you attend class. (Remember that one of the secrets of success is monitoring—evaluating—your progress on an ongoing basis so that you can take steps to make necessary changes. Just as successful athletes do this, so do effective students.)

_____

_____

_____

_____

_____

_____

_____

_____

SET 2

Exercises: Determining an Author's Purpose, Tone, Point of View, and Intended Audience

Ready for round 2? Read each of the following paragraphs. Then provide the information asked for in the items beneath each paragraph: the author's *purpose* (inform, instruct, persuade, and entertain), *tone* (refer to pages 253–255), *point of view,* or *intended audience.* Notice that the numbers are beside the questions, not the paragraphs. To help you relax, alternate tilting your head gently to the left and the right, a couple of times to each side. Then close your eyes and look up, down, left, and right. Open your mouth wide, and then close it again. These simple actions will help release tension from the muscles in the face, and that, in turn, helps relax you all over. All done? Let's roll.

Paragraph 1

It is too soon to determine the ultimate impact Jean Piaget's theory will have on our understanding of cognitive development. Yet we must recognize that we would not know as much as we do about children's intellectual development without the monumental contributions of Piaget. He noted many ways in which children seem to differ from adults, and he shed light on how adults acquire fundamental concepts such as the concepts of space, time, morality, and causality. Contemporary researchers have attempted to integrate aspects of Piaget's theory into cognitive learning and information–processing theories.

Source: James Vander Zanden, Thomas Crandell, and Corinne Crandell, *Human Development,* Updated 7th ed., p. 49. Copyright © 2003 McGraw-Hill. Reprinted by permission of The McGraw-Hill Companies.

1. The authors' *point of view* is: _____

_____

_____

_____

_____

_____

Paragraph 2

Dirty Harry, the 1971 film that spawned several sequels, best illustrates the popular media image of the crime fighter. In that film Clint Eastwood plays Harry, a maverick police officer who is not constrained by standard police procedures. Harry is a man of action who has no patience for the Bill of Rights, the constitutionally protected liberties he holds responsible for letting scores of dangerous criminals go free. In *Dirty Harry* the qualities that have made Eastwood a Hollywood icon—"the quiet one with the painfully bottled-up capacity for violence"—break loose. Harry is in pursuit of a vicious killer, Scorpio, who has hijacked a school bus. When forcefully apprehended by Harry, Scorpio shouts, "I have a right to a lawyer!" But Harry kills Scorpio in cold blood, and in the final scene he removes his police badge and throws it into a gravel pit.

Source: Adapted from Ronald Berger, Marvin Free, and Patricia Searles, *Crime, Justice, and Society,* p. 9. Copyright © 2001 McGraw-Hill. Reprinted by permission of The McGraw-Hill Companies.

2. The authors' *purpose* is to _____

_____

_____

_____

Paragraph 3

Sometimes, inconsistent nonverbal signals result from the sender's internal confusion or uncertainty. For example, a group member may both like and dislike different elements of someone's proposal; this genuine confusion may appear as mixed signals in the form of a positive head nod with a frowning face. To avoid sending mixed messages, be honest and clear. If you as a speaker are confused, help other members interpret your remarks by honestly revealing your confusion. If you are confused or puzzled by the mixed messages of another, say so, and help the other person clarify his or her intent.

Source: John Brilhart, Gloria Galanes, and Katherine Adams, *Effective Group Discussion,* 10th ed., p. 76. Copyright © 2001 McGraw-Hill. Reprinted by permission of The McGraw-Hill Companies.

3. The authors' *purpose* is to _____

_____

_____

4. The authors' *intended audience* is _____

_____

_____

_____

Paragraph 4

JUST-IN-TIME INVENTORY MANAGEMENT

An increasingly popular technique is **just-in-time (JIT) inventory management,** which eliminates waste by using smaller quantities of materials that arrive "just in time" for use in the transformation process and therefore require less storage space and other inventory management expense. JIT minimizes inventory by providing an almost continuous flow of items from suppliers to the production facility. Many U.S. companies, including General Motors, Hewlett-Packard, IBM, and Harley Davidson, have adopted JIT to reduce costs and boost efficiency.

Source: O. C. Ferrell, Geoffrey Hirt, and Linda Ferrell, *Business: A Changing World,* 3d ed., p. 269. Copyright © 2006 McGraw-Hill. Reprinted by permission of The McGraw-Hill Companies.

5. The authors' *intended audience* is _____

_____

_____

6. The authors' *purpose* is to _____

_____

_____

_____

Paragraph 5

Our language has changed to reflect and give meaning to the influence of computer technology on our world. A bit of computer humor recently passed along on the Internet pokes fun at this change. Remember when a "window" was something you hated to clean and a "ram" was the cousin of a goat? "Meg" was the name of your girlfriend and "gig" was a job for the night. "Memory" was something that you lost with age, a "CD" was a bank account, "log on" was adding fuel to the fire, "hard drive" was a long trip, "mouse pad" was where a mouse lived, and "backup" happened in your commode. Now they all mean different things and that really "mega bytes"!

Source: John Brilhart, Gloria Galanes, and Katherine Adams, *Effective Group Discussion,* 10th ed., p. 67. Copyright © 2001 McGraw-Hill. Reprinted by permission of The McGraw-Hill Companies.

7. The authors' *tone* is _____

_____

8. The authors' *purpose* is to _____

_____

Stop at this point to assess your understanding of the skills in Chapter 10. Of the four skills (author's purpose, tone, point of view, and intended audience), are there any that you feel unclear about? If so, which ones? What specifically is the source or nature of your confusion?

_____

_____

_____

_____

_____

_____

_____

SET 3

Exercises: Determining an Author's Purpose, Tone, Point of View, and Intended Audience

Here's the final set! Read each of the following paragraphs. Then provide the information asked for beneath each paragraph: the author's *purpose, tone, point of view,* or *intended audience*. To relax yourself, roll your head in a slow circle once or twice in either direction. Then relax the muscles in your face, especially your jaw muscles (a place many people unconsciously carry considerable tension). Once you've done this, tackle this last, brief set of exercises.

Paragraph 1

REACHING NEW HEIGHTS IN MUSIC

Of all the eighteenth-century arts, music left the most profound legacy. Much of it reflected the tastes of its royal, aristocratic, and ecclesiastical patrons. Composers and musicians, therefore, usually stuck to established forms and music was typically heard as pleasing background to conversations, balls, and other social occasions in the bastions of the aristocracy. Increasingly, however, music was played in public halls to a larger audience. Opera houses opened everywhere, and composers could now hope to make money from paying audiences as well as from court and aristocratic patronage. Several cities became well known as musical centers, but Vienna topped them all. This Austrian city became the musical heart of Europe, drawing hundreds of musicians who competed for favor there.

Source: Adapted from Dennis Sherman and Joyce Salisbury, *The West in the World,* pp. 524–25. Copyright © 2001 McGraw-Hill. Reprinted by permission of The McGraw-Hill Companies.

1. The authors' *purpose* is to _____

_____

2. The authors' *intended audience* is _____

_____

Paragraph 2

SQUARING THE ECONOMIC CIRCLE: HUMORIST ART BUCHWALD EXAMINES THE MULTIPLIER

The recession hit so fast that nobody knows exactly how it happened. One day we were the land of milk and honey and the next day we were the land of sour cream and food stamps.

Source: From Art Buchwald, "Squaring the Economic Circle," *Cleveland Plain Dealer,* February 22, 1975, in Campbell McConnell and Stanley Brue, *Economics,* 16th ed., p. 167. Copyright © 2005 McGraw-Hill/Irwin. Reprinted by permission of The McGraw-Hill Companies.

3. The author's *tone* _____

_____

_____

_____

4. The author's *intended audience* is _____

_____

_____

[*Coach's tip:* Look at the source of the material.]

Paragraph 3

SHOULD CONGRESS BE SUBJECT TO TERM LIMITS?

The terms of Members of Congress are already limited. We face the voters every other year. We are given only a two-year term in the House. If the voters do not like what we are doing, they can easily kick us out. Elections are the best term limits ever invented. Term limits are also unconstitutional. They were specifically considered by our Founding Fathers and specifically rejected, for a whole host of good reasons. They would prohibit voters from voting for a candidate who might otherwise be their first choice. They would prohibit good people from running for office. Also, very few Members of Congress would be able to develop experience and expertise about important matters on which they were expected to legislate. Term limits solve a problem that does not exist. We should let the voters decide, and not just arbitrarily limit their choices.

—Congressman John J. Duncan Jr. (R-Tenn.)

Source: Adapted from Thomas E. Patterson, *The American Democracy,* 5th ed., p. 55. Copyright © 2001 McGraw-Hill. Reprinted by permission of The McGraw-Hill Companies.

[*Coach's tip:* First determine the topic and the intended audience.]

5. The author is Congressman John Duncan. His *point of view* is _____

_____

_____

_____

_____

6. The author's *purpose* is _____

_____

_____

_____

_____

Congratulations! You've completed another chapter in the Advanced Workout.

11

Evaluate an Author's Argument

THE SKILL

EVALUATE AN AUTHOR'S ARGUMENT

So far, in the advanced workout you have learned the critical reading skills of distinguishing facts from opinions, making logical inferences and drawing conclusions, and determining the author's purpose, tone, point of view, and intended audience. In this chapter, you'll use those advanced skills and some additional ones in order to evaluate critically an author's argument (the author's position on a controversial issue). Unless you critically evaluate controversial material that you read, the author may manipulate or mislead you on the issue. There are several steps in evaluating an author's argument. Let's look at them.

THE TECHNIQUE

IDENTIFY THE ISSUE AND THE AUTHOR'S ARGUMENT, THEN ASK THE EVALUATION QUESTIONS

Before you can evaluate an author's argument, you have to first identify the issue the writer is presenting. *Issue means the controversial topic the author is discussing.* Every day, newspapers, magazines, and radio and television news shows and talk shows present people's views on controversial issues. (These are issues on which people disagree, such as capital punishment, abortion, health care, the country's foreign policy, the environment, and tax reform.) After you have read something, ask yourself, "Is the author writing about a controversial issue?" If the answer is yes, then you'll need to determine precisely what the author's argument is.

*The **author's argument** is his or her point of view on an issue.* (Point of view is the term you learned in the last chapter that means the author's position or opinion on an issue.) In other words, it is the opinion or belief that the author wants to persuade readers to believe. Suppose the issue is congressional age limits (setting the age at which a member of Congress must retire). One author's argument might be, "Members of Congress should not be allowed to serve past the age of 65." You would expect the author to argue (explain and defend) his or her reasons for this belief. To determine the author's argument, ask yourself, "What is the author's position or belief regarding the issue?"

You should note whether the author has a bias. As explained in Chapter 10, bias means that the author favors one side of the issue over the other. (In the example above, the writer's bias is in favor of an age limit for members of Congress.) Typically, authors take a position in favor of an issue (they support it) or against it (they oppose it). Less often, they present both sides of an issue objectively (they remain neutral and present evidence and support for both sides), so that readers can make an informed decision on their own. We describe someone as being "pro" or "con" on an issue. When authors favor something, we often say they are "pro" whatever the issue is: pro-environment, pro-election reform, pro-war. "Con" means the person holds a *contrary* or opposing point of view. When authors oppose something, they are often described as "anti" whatever the issue is: anti-environment, anti-election reform, anti-war. Before you can evaluate the material an author is presenting, you must know which side of the issue the author favors.

Once you know what the author's argument is, you're ready to proceed with these additional steps to evaluate how accurately and convincingly the author has presented the issue. The first thing you should do is determine the assumptions the author makes about the issue. *An **author's assumptions** consist of things the author takes for granted without presenting any proof.* In other words, they are things the author assumes to be true. After you have read what an author has to say about an issue and have identified the author's argument (which typically reflects the author's bias), ask yourself the first evaluation question, "What does the author take for granted?" This is an important question to ask because sometimes authors assume things that are incorrect or illogical, and then base their argument on them. Authors may state their assumptions, but more often they leave them unstated—you must figure them out for yourself. For example, in the argument, "Members of Congress should not be allowed to serve past the age of 65," the author assumes that members of Congress who are under the age of 65 are more effective than those who are past 65. (This is also an example of an assumption that should be questioned, incidentally.) The author also assumes that (1) members of Congress are incapable of judging for themselves when it is time to retire, and (2) age is a critical factor in the person's effectiveness. It's easy to be taken in by authors if you do not question the assumptions they base their arguments on.

The second step is to check out the types of support authors present to "make their case." Look at the details the author includes because they give the reasons for the author's side argument. ***Types of support** refers to the kind of evidence the author uses to back up the argument.* Support can include research findings, case studies, personal experience or observation, examples, facts, comparisons, and expert testimony or opinion. In the latter case, the author may be an expert on the topic or may quote or present research findings and opinions of other experts. Be leery, however, when authors make vague claims (such as "Research proves . . . ," "Studies show . . . ," and "Many authorities believe . . . "), yet never give the specifics. Ask yourself, "What kind of support does the author present to back the argument?"

Now you need to *evaluate* the support itself. Ask yourself this third question, "Is the support directly related to the argument?" If so, the support is *relevant. In other words, the support has **relevance** if it is directly related to the argument.* Suppose the writer who is proposing age limits on members of Congress mentions that there were several people in his family who had serious health problems after age 65. This support would not be particularly relevant (and, therefore, not very persuasive). If, on the other hand, the author could present the results of a large medical study on the decreased mental and physical health after age 65, that support would be more convincing. When the author presents personal experience as evidence, you will have to evaluate it very carefully. (To do that, you must determine whether the author possesses any true expertise on the topic.)

Once you've determined the relevance of the support, you must evaluate how objective the argument is. *The author's argument has **objectivity** when the support consists of facts and other clear evidence.* When authors are experts on their topic, they can generally give strong, verifiable support for their opinions and beliefs. However, you should be wary of support that is *subjective,* that is based only on the writer's personal feelings, on emotions, unsupported opinions, or limited personal experience. Remember, though, that if the author is an expert on the topic, his or her opinion matters. Ask yourself the fourth question, "Does the author present facts and clear evidence as support?"

You must also assess whether the author's argument is complete. *An argument has **completeness** if the author presents adequate support and overcomes opposing points.* Sometimes authors simply do not give enough "evidence" to make their argument convincing. One form of incompleteness occurs when authors deliberately leave out information that weakens their argument. They do this, of course, to sway unthinking readers to accept their argument. (This is a lot like the strategy some teenagers use when they want to do something that they know their parents would object to: they just leave out certain information. For example, the teenager says, "I'd like to go to a party at Pat's house Saturday night. There's nothing to worry about. Pat's parents are very strict." Pat's parents may indeed be very strict, but what the teenager leaves out is that Pat's parents are going to be out of town and they have no clue Pat is planning to throw a party.) Examine the support authors present to see if they have left out information that would weaken (or even disprove) their argument. For example, the author arguing for age limits on members of Congress might deliberately leave out facts that would weaken his or her case: older members generally have extensive experience; they understand thoroughly the legislative procedures and political process; they tend to have high standing on important committees; they are influential in Congress and in their political party; they are known to the public and can get media coverage; and they have been reelected many times because they have earned the trust, loyalty, and respect of their constituents. Wise authors, whenever possible, include and refute information that seems to support the other side of the argument. For example, they will introduce opposing points by saying, "Although it might appear that . . . " or "Critics might argue that. . . . " Then they refute those points. To assess the completeness of an argument, ask yourself the fifth question, "Has the author included adequate support and overcome points that might weaken the case?"

Almost done. (Whew!) Put together everything that you have done to decide if the author's argument is *valid* (logical) and *credible* (believable). *The author's argument has **validity** if it is logical (well reasoned). The author's argument has **credibility** if it is believable (convincing).* Keep in mind that authors do not have to *prove* that their argument is correct. After all, not everything can be proved. To be credible, an argument simply needs to be well supported and well reasoned. You can see that both the validity and the credibility hinge on everything you've evaluated up to this point. An argument cannot be valid and credible unless the author has made appropriate assumptions and presented relevant, objective, and complete support. Also, when evaluating the credibility of an author's argument, determine whether the author has given precise sources of the information, rather than just vague references. Look for information that reveals anything about the author's credentials. For example, an author taking a position on a controversial prescription drug might be a doctor, a researcher for a pharmaceutical company, or a patient who had an unpleasant, life-threatening experience with the drug. (Needless to say, authors' backgrounds shape their positions or biases.) As noted earlier, the author is often an authority on the topic being discussed. Of course, this is not to say that equally eminent authorities might not have opposing views. That's one reason you must read critically: to evaluate and decide for yourself the correct position on an issue. Be sure you complete your evaluation of written material by asking the last two, very important questions. To determine the validity, ask yourself, "Is the author's argument logical (well reasoned)?" To determine the credibility, ask yourself, "Is the author's argument believable (convincing)?"

To summarize: After you read a passage about a controversial issue, reread it, identify the *issue* (controversial topic) and the author's *argument* (point of view, position, or bias on the issue). Then ask yourself these seven questions. Each question is related to the others, so answering one can help you answer the others.

1. What are the author's *assumptions* (things the author takes for granted and presents without proof)?

2. What *type of support* (facts, experts' opinions, research, observations, personal experiences, etc.) does the author present?

3. How *relevant* (directly related to the issue) is the support?

4. Is the author's argument *objective* (based on facts and other pertinent evidence)?

5. Is the author's argument *complete* (the author includes and addresses information that could weaken or refute his or her position)?

6. Based on all of the above, is the author's argument *valid* (logical)?

7. Based on all of the above, is the author's argument *credible* (believable)?

Your answers to these questions will enable you to critically evaluate an author's argument. The author's assumptions, types of support, relevance of support, objectivity, and completeness determine whether or not the argument has validity. A thoughtful reader will not accept illogical arguments because they have no credibility (are not convincing).

Incidentally, when you read about a controversial issue, you will find it helpful to note in the margin information of the following sort: When you identify the issue and the author's argument, mark them. As you come across each piece of support, label it "Support 1" or "Support 2," and so on, in the margin. You'll help yourself even more if you write the *type* of support: "Support 1—research study" or "Support 2—expert opinion." Finally, jot "relevant" or "irrelevant" beside each piece of support, or use "+" and "−" signs to indicate strong or weak support. When it's time to evaluate the entire selection, you will have an overview right before your eyes.

Is your head spinning at this point? I know that evaluating material critically can seem incredibly complicated at first, but the parts of the process fit together logically. As you practice applying these skills, you'll gain competence and confidence in your ability to evaluate material you read.

THE TRAINER

APPLY THE SKILL OF EVALUATING AN AUTHOR'S ARGUMENT

In the illustration is a passage on the issue of whether or not public high schools should start their classes at 10:00 A.M., a controversial issue that is gaining increasing national attention. I wrote the passage, although the specific research studies cited are real and the other factual information is correct. Read the selection, and then read the "thoughts" of the effective reader who is analyzing the author's argument.

The title suggests that the author favors starting something later, but I'm not sure what.

The first paragraph seems to give background information: how much sleep teens get and how much they need, the ways lack of sleep affects them in school and how school hours are out of sync with teens' sleep/awake cycles.

Okay—here it is in paragraph 2, the writer's argument: Start school at 10:00 A.M. The author even puts it in italics to make it stand out. The author tells how a later start would (1) give teens more rest, (2) fit their body rhythms, (3) allow time to eat breakfast, (4) reduce their stress, (5) improve concentration, and (6) lead to better school performance.

A Later Start Is a Better Start

Studies by sleep researchers agree that teenagers need approximately 9 to 10 hours of sleep a night—and that most of them don't get enough rest. A survey of more than 3,000 students revealed that the adolescents' total sleep time decreased by 40 to 50 minutes between the ages of 13 and 19, and that students who got the least sleep made the lowest grades (Wolfson & Carskadon, 1998). Researchers also found that adolescents undergo a shift in the brain's natural sleep cycle that causes them to go to sleep later and get up later than when they were younger. Ironically, most secondary schools start earlier than elementary schools, creating a schedule that is out of sync with adolescents' biological rhythms.

In order to squeeze in a little extra sleep, many teens get up too late to eat breakfast. Then they've compounded their problem: they're sleepy, tired, irritable, hungry, and undernourished for the demands school will make on their bodies and minds. Is there a solution to the problem of sleep-deprived teens? Fortunately, yes. *Start high school classes at 10:00 A.M.* This would allow students to get the rest they need and not work against their natural biological rhythms. Starting school later in the morning would allow them time to eat a good breakfast. Moreover, research has shown that teens tend to be least alert and most stressed early in the morning. Starting school later in the morning would enable them to start their day in a calmer fashion. Finally, according to researchers Crouter and Larson (1998), "Starting school later would maximize students' ability to concentrate." Being more alert and able to concentrate means better performance in school and higher grades.

There is yet another advantage of a delayed start to the school day. Most students sleep later on the weekends, so starting classes at 10:00 A.M. on weekdays would allow them to keep a more consistent schedule seven days a week. Since sleep doesn't average out, this is a simple way to help ensure adequate rest for teens.

Finally, the time of day that most teens are likely to get in trouble is between the time they get home from school and dinnertime (the time when working parents arrive home). With the shift in the school day, teens would still be in school during the late afternoon. Having teens start and end the school later would have the added bonus of providing supervision during the time when most kids get in trouble.

Let's see. In the third paragraph, the author tells another advantage: (7) better rest because the weekday and weekend sleep schedule would be more consistent.

And, the final reason, (8) as a by-product, teens would still be in school at the time of day that they are most likely to get into trouble.

The author makes the *assumptions* that being rested is a key factor for teenagers' success in school (which might be correct) and that there aren't other solutions to the problem of teenagers' inadequate rest (which is incorrect).

The author gave logical, convincing reasons and cited research to support several of them. What did the author leave out, though? What are some possible problems with shifting secondary school hours to later in the day? Well, what about parents who have to leave for work before their teens have to leave for school? What about families who have children of different ages? Would elementary, middle school, and secondary school students all be starting and ending at different times? What about afterschool sports and extracurricular activities? Would students be going home in the dark during the winter? Also, some teens have to work part-time. Would those who now work in the afternoon be forced to change to evening hours? The author doesn't mention any possible negative aspects.

Okay, my overall evaluation: The author has a *bias* (for starting secondary school classes later in the mornings) and makes a *valid* argument for it by presenting logical, *objective* reasons and backing several of them with research findings and experts' opinions (the *types of support*). The final reason, it would reduce the amount of time after school when teens usually get in trouble, might be an added bonus, but it doesn't seem as relevant as the other reasons for shifting the entire school day. But the overall support is relevant. Also, the author doesn't address any of the drawbacks of a later start to teens' school day, so the argument *isn't complete*. On balance, I would say that the author presents a strong argument, with the one drawback being the lack of completeness. The argument is *credible*.

In case you're wondering what this paragraph might look like with the type of marginal notations I mentioned a minute ago, here it is:

A LATER START IS A BETTER START

Studies by sleep researchers agree that teenagers need approximately 9 to 10 hours of sleep a night—and that most of them don't get enough rest. A survey of more than 3,000 students revealed that the adolescents' total sleep time decreased by 40 to 50 minutes between the ages of 13 and 19, and that students who got the least sleep made the lowest grades (Wolfson & Carskadon, 1998). Researchers also found that adolescents undergo a shift in the brain's natural sleep cycle that causes them to go to sleep later and get up later than when they were younger. Ironically, most secondary schools start earlier than elementary schools, creating a schedule that is out of sync with adolescents' biological rhythms.

In order to squeeze in a little extra sleep, many teens get up too late to eat breakfast. Then they've compounded their problem: they're sleepy, tired, irritable, hungry, and undernourished for the demands school will make on their bodies and minds. Is there a solution to the problem of sleep-deprived teens? Fortunately, yes. *Start high school classes at 10:00 A.M.* This would allow students to get the rest they need and not work against their natural biological rhythms. Starting school later in the morning would allow them time to eat a good breakfast. Moreover, research has shown that teens tend to be least alert and most stressed early in the morning. Starting school later in the morning would enable them to start their day in a calmer fashion. Finally, according to researchers Crouter and Larson (1998), "Starting school later would maximize students' ability to concentrate." Being more alert and able to concentrate means better performance in school and higher grades.

There is yet another advantage of a delayed start to the school day. Most students sleep later on the weekends, so starting classes at 10:00 A.M. on weekdays would allow them to keep a more consistent schedule seven days a week. Since sleep doesn't average out, this is a simple way to help ensure adequate rest for teens.

Finally, the time of day that most teens are likely to get in trouble is between the time they get home from school and dinnertime (the time when working parents arrive home). With the shift in the school day, teens would still be in school during the late afternoon. Having teens start and end the school later would have the added bonus of providing supervision during the time when most kids get in trouble.

Margin annotations:
- Problem
- Effect
- Cause 1
- Cause 2
- Effect
- Author's argument (also the solution)
- Support 1 (relevant)
- Support 2 (relevant)
- Support 3 (relevant)
- Support 4 (relevant)
- Support 5 (relevant; research)
- Support 6 (relevant)
- Support 7 (relevant)
- Support 8 (weaker; less relevant)

THE EDGE | **POINTERS ABOUT EVALUATING AN AUTHOR'S ARGUMENT**

■ **Don't let yourself become overwhelmed just because there are several steps in evaluating an author's argument.**

I want to emphasize again how important it is to take it *step-by-step*. (It's like the old joke, "How do you eat an elephant?" Answer: "One bite at a time.") Challenge that brain of yours, and avoid the temptation to throw in the towel. You don't want to get in the habit of walking away from things that seem hard because this can become a pattern, one that can deprive you of some of life's most meaningful experiences.

■ **Watch out for your own biases when you evaluate an author's argument.**

All of us have our own biases. Unless you are aware of yours, they can unfairly influence your evaluation of an author's argument. If you feel strongly about one side of an issue, and the author takes the opposing view, you may dismiss the argument without giving it serious, honest consideration. On the other hand, if you agree strongly with the author's position, you might not notice obvious flaws in the argument. Don't fall into either of these traps. (*A word of warning:* On standardized reading tests, you may be asked to identify the author's "argument," "position," or "point of view." You will miss these questions if instead you select what you think the author's position *should* be—in other words, what *you* believe.)

■ **There are several propaganda techniques and fallacies authors can use to manipulate readers into buying their argument.**

Authors sometimes present flawed reasoning in their arguments or use propaganda techniques that appeal to readers' emotions rather than to their logic. They do this because they know that noncritical readers are not likely to notice, which makes it easy to persuade them and take them in. There isn't space to discuss all of them here, but Appendix 3 and the Student Online Learning Center both have information and activities on propaganda techniques and fallacies.

■ **Arguments can be *inductive* or *deductive*.**

This has to do with how the information in the argument is organized or structured. When you read an author's argument, it will be helpful to you to decide which approach the author has taken, and whether the author presents accurate, logical support.

An ***inductive argument*** *presents several specific observations, reasons, or facts that lead to a logical generalization based on them.* An inductive argument will be convincing if the specific pieces of support logically lead to the conclusion. Here is an example that consists of three observations followed by the conclusion based on them: "The size of computers has decreased dramatically during the last several years. Cell phones have also become more significantly smaller. Even video games that once had to be played on large monitors are available now on handheld units. It is clear that as technology has improved, technological devices have become smaller."

In contrast, deductive arguments start at the opposite end. A ***deductive argument*** *opens with a general statement or rule, followed by the premises on which it is based. Premises* are the specific examples, reasons, cases, or other details that support (prove or explain) the general statement. This is the type of reasoning used in geometry and law in which a general rule is applied to the facts of a certain math problem or legal case. For the general statement to be true, the premises must be true. It they are faulty, the deductive argument will be false. Here is an example of a deductive argument that consists of a general statement followed by three reasons: "College students should participate in at least one campus organization. It provides a way to make new friends and become part of the college community. It also provides them with opportunities to hold leadership positions. Moreover, it can be helpful to be able to list the experience on their résumé."

When you write persuasive papers in your college courses, think about whether an inductive or a deductive approach would work better. Be sure that the support you include is accurate, specific, and logically connected to the general statement or conclusion.

Information in Appendix 3 and the Online Learning Center describes ways authors sometimes try to manipulate readers into "buying their argument." They do this by using forms of flawed reasoning called *fallacies* and about *propaganda techniques,* which appeal to emotion rather than the intellect. Becoming a more critical reader can prevent you from being tricked into accepting or believing a flawed or inappropriately emotional argument.

THE REPLAY

▷◁

REMEMBER THE ESSENTIAL INFORMATION FROM THE CHAPTER

These are the key elements in evaluating material critically. Review the material in this chapter; there's a lot, so it may take 10 or 15 minutes. Then try to write from memory the definition of each important term. You may want to do the first five items, and then do the last four a little while later. When you've finished, check your answers by consulting the chapter. Finally, make any corrections and additions. (Remember what I just mentioned about not tossing in the towel because something seems challenging.)

Definition of Issue

_____

_____

Definition of Author's Argument

_____

_____

Steps in Evaluating an Author's Argument (define each term)

1. Authors' assumptions _____

_____

2. Type of support _____

_____

3. Relevance of the support _____

_____

4. Ojectivity of the author's argument _____

_____

5. Completeness of the author's argument _____

_____

6. Validity of the author's argument _____

_____

7. Credibility of the author's argument: _____

_____

THE PRACTICE

APPLY THE SKILL OF EVALUATING AN AUTHOR'S ARGUMENT

The Chapter 11 practice exercise sets are different from the earlier ones in the Advanced Workout. The Set 1 Exercises are not multiple choice. Also, there is only *one* passage per set. The passage is followed by questions about the *seven* elements involved in critically evaluating the argument. There are actually fewer total questions in the three sets. The passage in Set 2 is longer, but it is not hard. The passage in Set 3 is challenging, but short.

Take these step-by-step. Breathe, stretch, and relax if you find yourself getting tense. To help you get started, I've included an introduction to each selection. Don't forget to mark the passage or write in the margin when you find information that will help you evaluate the author's argument.

SET 1

Exercises: Evaluating an Author's Argument

This essay is from a debate-style reader that presents controversies in health and contemporary society. The readings represent the arguments of leading social scientists, health-care professionals, and social commentators. One author of this selection below, Marion Nestle, is a professor of nutrition; Michael Jacobson is director of the Center for Science in the Public Interest.

As long ago as 1974, an editorial in *The Lancet,* a respected medical journal, identified obesity as the most important nutritional disease in the affluent countries of the world. In the intervening years, the problem has done nothing but increase—dramatically. The government has taken action to help reduce deaths related to smoking by passing laws that affect the sale, taxation, and advertising of tobacco products. Should the government take similar steps regarding obesity? Read the selection below to find out these writers' point of view.

SHOULD THE GOVERNMENT REGULATE JUNK FOOD? YES, PUBLIC HEALTH POLICY SHOULD BE USED TO HALT THE OBESITY EPIDEMIC

1   Anti-obesity measures need to address television watching, a major sedentary activity as well as one that exposes viewers to countless commercials for high-calorie foods. The average American child between the ages of 8 and 18 spends more than three hours daily watching television and another three or four hours with other media. Television is an increasingly well-established risk factor for obesity and its health consequences in both adults and children. At least one study now shows that reducing the number of hours spent watching television or playing video games is a promising approach to preventing obesity in children. Government and private organizations could sponsor an annual "No TV Week" to remind people that life is possible, even better, with little or no television and that watching television could well be replaced by physical and social activities that expend more energy. The Department of Education and DHHS [Department of Health and Human Services] could sponsor a national campaign, building on previous work by the nonprofit TV-Free America.

2   Advertisements for candy, snacks, fast foods, and soft drinks should not be allowed on television shows commonly watched by children younger than age 10. Researchers have shown that younger children do not understand the concept of advertising—that it differs from program content and is designed to sell, not inform—and that children of all ages are highly influenced by television commercials to buy or demand the products that they see advertised. It makes no sense for a society to allow private interests to misshape the eating habits of the next generation, and it is time for Congress to repeal the law that blocks the Federal Trade Commission from promulgating industry-wide rules to control advertising during children's television programs.

3   Federal and state government agencies could do more to make physical activity more attractive and convenient. They could provide incentives to communities to develop safe bicycle paths and jogging trails; to build more public swimming pools, tennis courts, and ball fields; to pass zoning rules favoring sidewalks in residential and commercial areas, traffic-free areas, and traffic patterns that encourage people to walk to school, work, and shopping; and safety protection for streets, parks, and playgrounds. Government could also provide incentives to use mass transit, and disincentives to drive private cars, thereby encouraging people to walk to bus stops and train stations.

4   State boards of education and local school boards have an obligation to promote healthful lifestyles. Physical education should again be required, preferably on a daily basis, to encourage students to expend energy and to help them develop lifelong enjoyment of jogging, ball games, swimming, and other low-cost activities. School boards should be encouraged to resist efforts of marketers to sell soda and high-calorie, low nutrient snack foods in hallways and cafeterias. Congress could support more healthful school meals by insisting that the US Department of Agriculture (USDA) set stricter limits on sales of foods high in energy (calories), fat, and sugar that compete with the sale of balanced breakfasts and lunches.

Source: Adapted from Marion Nestle and Michael Jacobson, "Halting the Obesity Epidemic: A Public Health Policy Approach," in Eileen Daniel, ed., *Taking Sides: Clashing Views in Health and Society,* 7th ed., pp. 112–13. Copyright © 2006 McGraw-Hill. Reprinted by permission of The McGraw-Hill Companies.

1. What *issue* (controversial topic) is presented? _____

_____

_____

2. What is the authors' *argument* (bias or position on the issue)? (Remember to write this as a complete sentence that contains the topic.) _____

_____

_____

_____

3. What are some of the authors' assumptions (things the authors take for granted and presents without proof)? _____

_____

_____

_____

_____

_____

_____

_____

_____

_____

4. What *type of support* (facts, experts' opinions, research, observations, personal experiences, etc.) do the authors present? _____

_____

_____

_____

_____

5. How *relevant* (directly related to the issue) is the support? _____

_____

_____

6. Is the authors' argument *objective* (based on facts and other pertinent evidence) and *complete* (information that would weaken or disprove the case has not been left out)? _____

_____

_____

_____

_____

_____

_____

_____

7. Is the authors' argument *valid* (logical) and *credible* (believable)? _____

_____

_____

_____

_____

Feeling overwhelmed? Worried that you've made lots of mistakes in the Set 1 Exercises? Keep in mind what I said at the beginning of the book: Mistakes are the bridge between inexperience and wisdom. At this point, you're inexperienced at critically evaluating written material. (If every college student could already do this perfectly, there would be no need for this chapter.) You're still learning, and taking on challenging experiences *builds* brain power.

Take a minute to assess your understanding of the material in this chapter. What confuses you? What steps can you take to clear up the confusion?

_____

_____

_____

_____

_____

_____

_____

_____

_____

_____

SET 2

Exercises: Evaluating an Author's Argument

Don't get nervous—this selection is longer, but it's interesting and not particularly difficult. Just think about what you're reading and follow the author's argument as he builds his case. The author is Canadian, so you will see several references to things in Canada and you will see the British spelling used for some words, such as *fibre* for *fiber,* and *tonnes* for *tons.* The words are so similar, however, that it will not be a problem. You will also encounter the word *kilogram,* a metric measure equivalent to 2.2 pounds. (*Coach's tip:* As you read, remember to note in the margin the aspects of the author's argument and your evaluation.)

As always, take a minute to clear your head and dissipate tension before you begin. Close your eyes and then look up, down, left and right. Relax the muscles in your face, especially your jaw muscles. Tilt your head gently too either side a couple of times. Stretch your hands as high as you can and hold the stretch for a few seconds before lowering them. Feel better? Great! You're ready to start in!

LET'S GO VEGGIE!

1　　If there was a single act that would improve your health, cut your risk of food-borne illnesses, and help preserve the environment and the welfare of millions of animals, would you do it?

2　　The act I'm referring to is the choice you make every time you sit down to a meal.

3　　More than a million Canadians have already acted: They have chosen to not eat meat. And the pace of change has been dramatic. Vegetarian food sales are showing unparalleled growth. Especially popular are meat-free burgers and hot dogs, and the plant-based cuisines of India, China, Mexico, Italy and Japan. Even fast food chains are getting in on the act. Subway reports that its Number 1–selling sub worldwide is the Veggie Delite.

4　　Fuelling the shift toward vegetarianism have been the health recommendations of medical research. Study after study has uncovered the same basic truth: Plant foods lower your risk of chronic disease; animal foods increase it. The American Dietetic Association says: "Scientific data suggest positive relationships between a vegetarian diet and reduced risk for several chronic degenerative diseases." In the fall of 1997, after reviewing 4,500 studies on diet and cancer, the World Cancer Research Fund flatly stated: "We've been running the human biological engine on the wrong fuel." This "wrong fuel" has helped boost the cost of degenerative disease in Canada to an estimated $400 billion a year, according to Bruce Holub, a professor of nutritional science at the University of Guelph.

5　　Animal foods have serious nutritional drawbacks: They are devoid of fibre, contain far too much saturated fat and cholesterol, and may even carry traces of hormones, steroids and antibiotics. It makes little difference whether you eat beef, pork, chicken or fish.

6　　Animal foods are also gaining notoriety as breeding grounds for E. coli, campylobacter and other bacteria that cause illness. According to the Canadian Food Inspection Agency, six out of ten chickens are infected with salmonella. It's like playing Russian roulette with your health. . . .

7　　While health and food safety are compelling reasons for choosing a vegetarian lifestyle, there are also larger issues to consider. Animal-based agriculture is one of the most environmentally destructive industries on the face of the Earth.

8　　Think for a moment about the vast resources required to raise, feed, shelter, transport, process and package the 500 million Canadian farm animals slaughtered each year. Water and energy are used at every step of the way. Alberta Agriculture calculates that it takes 10 to 20 times more energy to produce meat than to produce grain.

9   Less than a quarter of our agricultural land is used to feed people directly. The rest is devoted to grazing and growing food for animals. Ecosystems of forest, wetland and grassland have been decimated to fuel the demand for land. Using so much land heightens topsoil loss, the use of harsh fertilizers and pesticides, and the need for irrigation water from dammed rivers. If people can shift away from meat, much of this land could be converted back to wilderness.

10   The problem is that animals are inefficient at converting plants to edible flesh. It takes, for example, 8.4 kilograms of grain to produce one kilogram of pork, the U.S. government estimates. After putting so many resources into animals, what do we get out? Manure—at a rate of over 10,000 kilograms per second in Canada alone, according to the government. Environment Canada says cattle excrete 40 kilograms of manure for every kilogram of edible beef. A large egg factory can produce 50 to 100 tonnes of waste per week, the Ontario Ministry of Agriculture estimates. . . .

11   And then there is methane, a primary contributing gas in global warming and ozone layer depletion. Excluding natural sources, 27 percent of Canada's and 20 percent of the world's methane comes from livestock.

12   John Robbins, author of the Pulitzer prize–nominated book *Diet for a New America* (Group West), said it best when he stated: "Eating lower on the food chain is perhaps the most potent single act we can take to halt the destruction of our environment and preserve our natural resources."

13   Our environment also includes the animals killed for their meat. It has become an accepted fact that today's factory-farmed animals live short, miserable, unnatural lives. . . .

14   Because it can cost hundreds of dollars per minute to stop the conveyor line, animal welfare comes second to profit. Over 150,000 animals are "processed" every hour of every working day in Canada, according to Agriculture Canada. The picture gets uglier still. En route to slaughter, farm animals may legally spend anywhere from 36 to 72 hours without food, water or rest. They're not even afforded the "luxury" of temperature controlled trucks in extreme summer heat or sub-zero cold. Agriculture Canada has estimated that more than 3 million Canadian farm animals die slow and painful deaths en route to slaughter each year. . . .

15   Although it is difficult to face these harsh realities, it is even more difficult to ignore them. Three times a day, you make a decision that not only affects the quality of your life, but the rest of the living world. We hold in our knives and forks the power to change this world.

16   Consider the words of Albert Einstein: "Nothing will benefit human health and increase the chances for survival of life on Earth as the evolution to a vegetarian diet."

17   Bon appétit.

Source: Adapted from Joseph Pace, "Let's Go Veggie!," *The Toronto Star,* May 27, 1998. Reprinted by permission of the author.

1. What *issue* (controversial topic) is presented?

_____

2. What is the author's *argument* (bias or position on the issue)? (Remember to write this as a complete sentence that contains the topic.)

_____

_____

3. What are some of the author's *assumptions* (things the author takes for granted and presents without proof)?

_____

_____

_____

_____

_____

_____

_____

_____

_____

_____

_____

4. What *type of support* (facts, experts' opinions, research, observations, personal experiences, etc.) does the author present?

_____

_____

_____

_____

_____

_____

_____

_____

_____

_____

5. How *relevant* (directly related to the issue) is the support?

_____

6. How *objective* (based on facts and other pertinent evidence) and *complete* (information that would weaken or disprove the case has not been left out) is the author's argument?

_____

_____

_____

_____

_____

_____

_____

_____

_____

_____

_____

_____

_____

_____

_____

_____

_____

_____

_____

_____

_____

7. Is the author's argument *valid* (logical) and *credible* (believable)?

_____

_____

_____

_____

_____

Time once again to reflect on your performance. How accurately were you able to evaluate the author's argument? List any skills (identifying the issue and argument, or any of the seven evaluation items) that seemed hard for you. What specific steps can you take to improve your ability to evaluate authors' arguments critically?

_____

_____

_____

_____

_____

_____

_____

_____

_____

_____

_____

SET 3

Exercises: Evaluating an Author's Argument

The following selection deals with the same issue as the selection in the Set 1 Exercises. It is from a textbook on controversial issues in health and contemporary society and is typical of material you might be assigned to read in a political science, ethics, or health course. It contains some words that may be new to you. Try to use the context to figure them out, and then look up any you are still unsure of. After you have read the selection, read it a second time. At that point, note in the margin the aspects of the author's argument. For example, as you locate each element of the author's support (reasons she gives for her position of the issue), label them "support 1," "support 2," etc., in the margin. (See example on page 278.) Set aside enough time to do the Set 3 Exercises. This set requires thought and patience. It will seem challenging, but give it your best effort—and keep in mind that items you miss are opportunities to learn.

HEAVY DUTY: NO, THE GOVERNMENT SHOULD NOT REGULATE JUNK FOOD

1   Just a few years back the only people suggesting a parallel between cigarettes and Big Macs were tobacco-industry reps seeking to discredit the anti-smoking movement—and their slippery-slope arguments generally elicited jeers. In April 1998, as Congress squabbled over a tobacco bill, a *Washington Post* editorial denounced the fatty-foods analogy as an effort "to change the subject." "Tobacco," the *Post* assured its readers, "is a unique product. Its disastrous effect on public health and the duplicitous history of the industry both make it so. What happens to it is not a threat to other industries."

2   But the *Post* (among many others) may soon owe those tobacco executives an apology. As early as 1998 Kelly Brownell, head of Yale's Center for Eating and Weight Disorders and popularizer of the "Twinkie tax," caused a stir by informing multiple media outlets, "To me, there is no difference between Ronald McDonald and Joe Camel." By last year the U.S. government was coming around to a similar view. In his obesity "Call to Action," Surgeon General David Satcher cautioned, "Overweight"—anti-fat advocates use the word as a noun as well as an adjective—"and obesity may soon cause as much preventable disease and death as cigarette smoking." Making an oft-cited comparison, the statement noted: "Approximately 300,000 U.S. deaths a year currently are associated with obesity and overweight (compared to more than 400,000 deaths a year associated with cigarette smoking)."

3   Taking another page from the tobacco playbook, anti-fat advocates deny that eating is purely a matter of personal choice—highlighting fat merchants' aggressive and dishonest sales tactics. Nestle, whose 2002 book *Food Politics* details how the food industry manipulates America's eating habits, explained in a recent phone interview that "where the similarities are really unnerving is in the marketing: The use of targeted messages to children, for example. The use of targeted messages to minorities." The unsuspecting fatties who, under relentless marketing pressure and often at an early age, develop a Hostess habit are—at least in part—victims of forces beyond their control.

4   But here's where the tobacco-fat analogy begins to fall apart. While the industries' marketing strategies may be similar, and the resulting health costs comparable, the products being marketed are not. Nicotine, as the *Post* rightly implied in its 1998 editorial, is a poisonous, highly addictive substance—addictive in the clinical sense, not in the I-can't-stop-noshing-on-these-Pringles sense. For decades tobacco executives knew this and blatantly lied about it (under oath), even as they worked to hook as many people as possible. McDonald's by contrast may irresponsibly, even intentionally, downplay the unhealthfulness of its fries; but, as even anti-fat warriors admit, those fries are not inherently toxic.

And while Keebler tries to entice kids with cartoon pitchmen, no one has accused the company of manipulating the chemistry of Fudge Sticks to ensure clinical addiction.

5   Most anti-fat warriors admit that their new crusade is trickier than the one against smoking—in no small part because the food industry's argument that any food or drink can be enjoyed in moderation without compromising your health is (though self-interested) basically true. Nonetheless, say anti-fatties, most Americans are either too naïve or too weak to resist the persuasive power of fat merchants. "It's not fair," Nestle told ABC in January. "People are confronted with food in every possible way to eat more. The function of the food industry is to get people to eat more, not less." And, she insisted in our interview, the notion that parents should be responsible for what their kids eat is increasingly unrealistic: "Most parents I know aren't that strong. They're fighting a nine hundred billion dollar a year industry by themselves." Thus, government must level the playing field. CSPI (perhaps the foremost anti-fat organization) has long advocated a restriction on ads for soda and snack food during kids' TV shows. But for better or worse—OK, worse—whipping your target audience into a gotta-have-it frenzy is what advertising is all about. And while using clowns and elves to peddle supercaloric treats to tots may be hardball, it's pretty much par for the course in the jungles of American capitalism. As even Nestle admits, "The seduction of food companies is no different than that of any other companies."

6   Which is precisely the argument against a government-sponsored war on fat. Does the food industry spend billions each year to make us crave goodies we don't need? Absolutely. So does the fashion industry, the auto industry, and the toy industry. Any number of the products we buy—motorcycles, string bikinis, stiletto heels—can be hazardous to our health when used irresponsibly. There's little doubt that lives and health care dollars would be saved if the government prodded Americans to drop 15 to 50 pounds. We could also reduce skin cancer rates if we taxed flesh-exposing swimsuits and prevent auto accidents if we taxed Corvettes (or teenage drivers). Americans do all kinds of things that are bad for them, and for the most part the government lets us, unless there's a strong likelihood that we will hurt someone other than ourselves.

7   Which is, incidentally, another important distinction between fatty foods and cigarettes. It's hard to believe the war on tobacco would have gotten out of the barracks were it not for mountains of research demonstrating the health impact of smoking on nonsmokers—innocent bystanders who happened to get in the way of a stray puff in a restaurant or at work. To date, there's no scientific evidence of the dangers of second-hand cholesterol: Watching a co-worker wolf down that Filet-o-Fish may make you want to gag, but it's not going to give you heart disease.

8   None of this is to say that Americans—especially children—wouldn't benefit from better dietary education. If HHS, state health agencies, or even the American Medical Association want to run public service ads singing the praises of cantaloupe, fantastic. There is also a compelling case that, during school hours, when kids are under government supervision, every effort should be made to provide a healthful environment. Many states are considering prohibiting or restricting vending machines on school grounds. Nutrition professor Marion Nestle and CSPI's [Center for Science in the Public Interest] Michael Jacobson advocate banning junk food ads from the in-class network CHANNEL ONE. And a quick survey of school cafeteria fare—frequently laden with nachos, pizza, burgers, and Tater Tots—suggests that more attention could be paid to the dietary messages we're sending. For that matter, a little classroom time on the ABCs of nutrition and exercise wouldn't hurt either.

9   But when you move from school to home, and from suggestion to intervention, you quickly enter intellectual quicksand. While anti-tobacco advocates had a clear target, figuring out where to draw the boundary in the fat wars, could prove impossibly complicated. As Nestle writes in *Food Politics:* "Unlike the straightforward 'don't smoke' advice, the dietary message can never be 'don't eat.' Instead, it has to be the more complicated and ambiguous 'eat this instead of that,' 'eat this more often than that' and the overall prescription 'eat less.' " The upshot is that it's almost impossible to draw clear, bright lines about which foods merit sanctions such as fat taxes or ad restrictions and which ones don't. One approach is simply to create a broad, amorphous category of "junk food," which is more or less what California did when it created a snack tax in 1991 (aimed primarily at dosing its budget gap, not improving health). As a result, California's law was filled with nonsensical distinctions. For instance, Twinkies were taxable; doughnuts weren't. (The following year voters repealed the wildly confusing, highly unpopular measure.) Of course, given the massive economic implications, it's likely that, if implemented nationally, such distinctions would quickly become the focus of intense lobbying—meaning that politics, not merely nutrition, would determine which foods took a hit. To avoid such subjectivity, some anti-fat crusaders have suggested levying taxes according to fat content instead. But that would leave out countless crummy, fattening-yet virtually fat-free-foods (such as Skittles and chocolate syrup), while penalizing relatively healthful foods (think nuts and granola) that are high in fat.

10   At present the anti-fat movement's most popular target seems to be America's soda habit. But a tax that applies to Pepsi ONE and Diet Coke but not to Yoo-hoo, Gatorade, lemonade, Mocha Frappuccino, or any of the countless sugary fruit "juices" on the market seems decidedly unjust. Now, you could argue—and the anti-fat warriors do—that Diet Coke, while not fattening, has absolutely no nutritional value. But if we're going to expand our list of socially unacceptable products to anything that isn't actively healthy (as opposed to unhealthily fat-promoting), then we are wading deep into Huxleyan territory.

11   And the quicksand isn't simply intellectual; it's cultural as well. The United States is overwhelmingly fat, but it is not uniformly fat. Poor folks tend to be fatter than rich folks. Minorities tend to be fatter than whites—and not simply because inner-city blacks and Latinos can't afford to eat well. As Ann Thacher, chief of health promotion and disease prevention for Rhode Island, and others point out, some of the food traditions woven into Hispanic culture contribute to obesity. In some Latino communities, being plump is still a sign of affluence and is therefore considered desirable. It's one thing for anti-fat warriors to attack a global conglomerate like McDonald's for trying to make people porky; it's quite another to tell an entire community to rethink its culture.

12   What it comes down to, ultimately, is that our relationships to food are simply too complex for the government to oversee. People eat differently in New Orleans than they do in Berkeley. And they do so, for the most part, because they want to. Sure, we would be a healthier society if everyone ate what they eat in Berkeley. But do we really want to live in a country where the government pressures us to do so? Health is only one measure of a good life, and government is far too crude a mechanism to effectively—or humanely—calibrate its importance for millions of different people. Slippery-slope arguments are usually specious, and until recently the fat-tobacco analogy offered by tobacco execs seemed so as well. But, in fact, we are on the exact slope they claimed, and we are picking up speed. Somewhere, Joe Camel is laughing.

Source: Excerpted and adapted from Michelle Cottle, "Heavy Duty," in Eileen Daniel, ed., *Taking Sides: Clashing Views in Health and Society,* 7th ed., pp. 122–25. Copyright © 2006 McGraw-Hill. Reprinted by permission of The McGraw-Hill Companies.

1. What *issue* (controversial topic) is presented? _____

_____

_____

2. What is the author's *argument* (bias or position on the issue)? (Remember to write this as a complete sentence that contains the topic.) _____

_____

_____

3. What are some of the author's assumptions (things the author takes for granted and presents without proof)? _____

_____

_____

_____

_____

_____

_____

_____

_____

_____

4. What *type of support* (facts, experts' opinions, research, observations, personal experiences, etc.) does the author present? _____

_____

_____

_____

_____

_____

_____

_____

_____

_____

_____

_____

_____

_____

5. How *relevant* (directly related to the issue) is the support? _____

_____

_____

_____

_____

_____

6. Is the author's argument *objective* (based on facts and other pertinent evidence) and *complete* (information that would weaken or disprove the case has not been left out)? _____

_____

_____

_____

_____

_____

_____

_____

_____

_____

7. Is the author's argument *valid* (logical) and *credible* (believable)? _____

_____

_____

_____

_____

_____

_____

_____

_____

Bravo! You have the satisfaction of knowing that you took on a challenging chapter and completed it! Take a minute to process your experience with this chapter. What do you think you need to work on further in evaluating an author's argument? Include any questions that you still have about the skills presented in this chapter.

_____

_____

_____

_____

_____

_____

_____

5

PART · FIVE

Advanced Stretching

CHAPTER 12

Apply All the Advanced Skills to Single- and Multiple- Paragraph Selections

THE PRACTICE

APPLY ALL THE ADVANCED SKILLS TO SINGLE- AND MULTIPLE-PARAGRAPH SELECTIONS

Congratulations! Do you realize that at this point you've completed *all* the skills that comprise the Advanced Workout? You've learned to go beyond what is given in the passage by using these skills:

■ Distinguishing facts from opinions.

■ Making logical inferences and drawing conclusions.

■ Determining the author's tone, purpose, point of view, and intended audience.

■ Critically evaluating an author's argument.

By now, you've had quite a bit of practice applying each of these skills, but (as you know) perfect practice makes perfect. I hope that as you did the exercise sets in the previous four chapters, you learned from the items you missed. The items you miss are the ones you can learn from. Each time you miss something *and understand why,* you improve your skills: You know what to do differently next time; you know the types of mistakes to avoid in the future. That's how you refine your skills. (See #14, "Monitor Your Workouts and Evaluate Your Progress" in the "'Secrets' of Success" section, pages S-11–S-12.) In this chapter you'll get additional opportunities to practice, practice, practice! Take a mindful approach to doing these exercises and to learning from the items you miss. It will pay off.

Let's see what you can do at this point. In Chapter 7 in Part 3, Basic Stretching, I stated that you'd moved your supplies to the first base camp of the mountain—you learned and practiced a set of basic vocabulary and comprehension skills and were ready to apply all the basic skills. In this chapter, you're much higher up the mountain: you're ready to apply advanced skills to the selections in the three exercise sets that follow. Some of the passages you may have seen before (depending on whether you were assigned every set of practice exercises in the preceding chapters). However, you will be applying *different skills* to those passages than the skills you applied earlier. Even though the "air may be a little thinner" and your climbing gear might seem a little heavier, you're stronger, more experienced, and more skilled than when you began. Keep trekking! See you at the summit!

SET 1

Exercises: Applying All the Advanced Skills

Read each passage, and then answer each question that follows it. You will not be asked to apply every advanced skill to every passage. Before you begin, take a minute to use any of the techniques you've learned for putting yourself into a more relaxed, but alert state of mind.

Passage 1

People who marry as teenagers have a higher likelihood of divorce than people who wait until their twenties. Teenagers probably cannot choose partners as well as older persons can. In part, they are not mature enough. Compared with people in their twenties, teenagers may not know as well what kinds of persons they will be as adults and what their needs in a partner will be. Even if they do have a good sense of their emerging selves, they will have a more difficult time picking an appropriate partner because it is hard to know what kind of spouse an 18-year-old will prove to be over the long run. Moreover, teenage marriages are sometimes precipitated by an accidental pregnancy, and it is known that a premarital birth raises the likelihood of divorce. It does so partly because it brings together a couple who might not otherwise have chosen to marry each other. It also may be more difficult, on a practical level, for a couple to make a marriage work if a young child is present from day one. Still, earlier marriage cannot be an explanation for the post-1960 rise in divorce because age at marriage increased after 1960.

Source: Adapted from Andrew Cherlin, *Public and Private Families,* 4th ed., pp. 412–13. Copyright © 2005 McGraw-Hill. Reprinted by permission of The McGraw-Hill Companies.

_____   **1.** The author's *purpose* is
   a. to instruct readers how to evaluate their readiness for marriage.
   b. to inform readers of the reasons teenagers have a higher likelihood of divorce than people who wait until their twenties to marry.
   c. to inform readers how marriage trends have changed between 1960 and now.
   d. to persuade readers to wait until they are at least in their twenties before they marry.

_____   **2.** The author's *tone* is
   a. angry.
   b. sarcastic.
   c. humorous.
   d. neutral.

_____   **3.** Which of the following represents a *logical conclusion* based on the information in the passage?
   a. There are several reasons teenage marriages are more likely to fail.
   b. With proper counseling, teenagers can have as successful marriages as older couples do.
   c. A marriage between a teenager and an older person will be more successful than a marriage between two teenagers.
   d. The older a couple is when they marry, the more successful the marriage is likely to be.

_____ **4.** An *assumption* the author makes is:
  a. Teenagers would not marry if they knew the high risk of divorce for their age group.
  b. Nothing can be done to reduce the divorce rate.
  c. It is important to try to understand which marriages fail and why.
  d. Divorce should be prohibited except in cases of abuse, addiction, or adultery.

Passage 2

To understand this selection, there are some things you need to know. A *cult* is a community of obsessive religious worship and ritual. Heaven's Gate was a cult whose members viewed their bodies merely as "containers" and committed mass suicide. David Koresh was a leader of another religious cult who died along with its members in a violent standoff with federal agents. Jim Jones was also a religious cult leader who convinced his followers to commit mass suicide by drinking poison. "New Religious movements" (paragraph 4) is the term social scientists use for cults.

1   Contrary to the idea that cults turn hapless people into mindless robots, these techniques—increasing behavioral commitments, persuasion, and group isolation—do not have unlimited power. The Unification Church has successfully recruited fewer than 1 in 10 people who attend its workshops (Ennis & Verrilli, 1989). Most who had joined Heaven's Gate had left before that fateful day of "container shedding" [mass suicide]. David Koresh ruled with a mix of persuasion, intimidation, and violence. As Jim Jones made his demands more extreme, he, too, increasingly had to control people with intimidation. He used threats of harm to those who fled the community, beatings for noncompliance, and drugs to neutralize disagreeable members. By the end, he was as much an arm twister as a mind bender.

2   Moreover, cult influence techniques are in some ways similar to techniques used by groups more familiar to us. Fraternity and sorority members have reported that the initial "love bombing" of potential cult recruits is not unlike their own "rush" period. Members lavish attention on prospective pledges and make them feel special. During the pledge period, new members are somewhat isolated, cut off from old friends who did not pledge. They spend time studying the history and rules of their new group. They suffer and spend time on its behalf. They are expected to comply with all its demands. Not surprisingly, the result is usually a committed new member.

3   Much the same is true of some therapeutic communities for recovering drug and alcohol abusers. Zealous self-help groups form a cohesive "social cocoon," have intense beliefs, and exert a profound influence on members' behavior (Galanter, 1989, 1990).

4   I chose the examples of fraternities, sororities, and self-help groups not to disparage them but to illustrate two concluding observations. First, if we attribute the pull of New Religious movements to the leader's mystical force or to the followers' peculiar weaknesses, we might delude ourselves into thinking we are immune to social control techniques. In truth, our own groups—and countless salespeople, political leaders, and other persuaders—successfully use many of these tactics on us. Between education and indoctrination, enlightenment and propaganda, conversion and coercion, therapy and mind control, there is but a blurry line.

5   Second, that Jim Jones abused the power of persuasion does not mean persuasion is intrinsically bad. Nuclear power enables us to light up homes or wipe out cities. Sexual power enables us to express and celebrate committed love or

exploit people for selfish gratification. Persuasive power enables us to enlighten or deceive. Knowing that these powers can be harnessed for evil purposes should alert us, as scientists and citizens, to guard against their immoral use. But the powers themselves are neither inherently evil nor inherently good; how we use them determines whether their effect is destructive or constructive.

Source: David Myers, *Exploring Social Psychology,* 3d ed., pp. 166–67. Copyright © 2004 McGraw-Hill. Reprinted by permission of The McGraw-Hill Companies.

_____ 5. The author's *argument* is:
  a. What we think of as cult techniques do not have the power to turn people into mindless robots and, moreover, the techniques many familiar groups use to recruit and retain members are similar in some ways to cult techniques.
  b. Cult leaders have mystical powers that enable them to identify weak individuals and persuade them to become and remain cult members.
  c. In order to recruit and keep followers, David Koresh and Jim Jones combined cult techniques with persuasion, intimidation, and violence.
  d. There is nothing wrong with cult influence techniques or else fraternities, sororities, and other familiar groups would not use them.

_____ 6. What *type of support* does the author present to back his argument?
  a. a case study of one sorority
  b. the general examples of fraternities, sororities, self-help groups, salespeople, political leaders, and other "persuasive people"
  c. experiments conducted with members of self-help groups
  d. his personal observations and experience as a fraternity member

_____ 7. How *relevant* (directly related to the issue) is the support?
  a. of no relevance
  b. slightly relevant
  c. relevant
  d. relevance cannot be determined

_____ 8. How *objective* (based on facts and pertinent evidence) is the author's argument?
  a. not objective at all
  b. not objective because the support presented consists of personal opinions
  c. objective because the support consists of a pertinent, real-life illustrations
  d. objectivity cannot be determined

_____ 9. How *credible* (believable) is the author's argument in the second paragraph?
  a. has no credibility because no support was provided
  b. has limited credibility because the support that was presented was not completely relevant
  c. is credible because the support backs the author's argument
  d. credibility cannot be evaluated

_____ **10.** An *assumption* the author makes is:
   a. Cult leaders use special techniques that are known only to them.
   b. The general public has many misperceptions about cults and their techniques.
   c. Cult membership is going to increase dramatically during the next decade.
   d. Sororities and fraternities should be viewed as cults.

_____ **11.** Which of the following statements from paragraph 4 represents an *opinion* rather than a fact?
   a. I chose the examples of fraternities, sororities, and self-help groups not to disparage them but to illustrate two concluding observations.
   b. If we attribute the pull of New Religious movements to the leader's mystical force or to the followers' peculiar weaknesses, we might delude ourselves into thinking we are immune to social control techniques.
   c. In truth, our own groups—and countless salespeople, political leaders, and other persuaders—successfully use many of these tactics on us.
   d. Between education and indoctrination, enlightenment and propaganda, conversion and coercion, therapy and mind control, there is but a blurry line.

SET 2

Exercises: Applying All the Advanced Skills

Read each passage, and then write the answers to the questions that follow. You will not be asked to apply every skill to both passages. The first passage is a short one. The next two, which are longer, deal with the same topic: online intimacy/dating (developing relationships with people over the Internet; using the Internet to find people to date.) Before you start, use one or more of the relaxation techniques to put yourself in a calm, relaxed, focused state of mind. (As you remember to do this, it will eventually become a helpful habit.)

Passage 1

Luckily, from the start of my project in 1987, some Datoga families had been kind to me, inviting me to live in their homesteads. They nevertheless took pleasure in criticizing everything I did. My feeble attempts to make a cow, terrified at the sight of a white person, yield milk deserved such ridicule. But I found it harder to take criticism for skills of which I was more proud, such as driving across rocky river beds or taking notes in almost pitch-dark huts, particularly since no Datoga in the community knew how to do either of these things. I had already learned to live with my apparent ineptitude (anthropologists do well to wear thick skin), but I increasingly sensed a need to upgrade my image. By visiting a sacred site deep in the country of the forsworn enemy neighboring tribe, the Maasai, with a group of respected Datoga elders, albeit in the relative safety and comfort of a Land Rover, I might gain just a little respect, especially if we did everything right.

Source: Monique Mulder, "Gitangda Is Great," in Lee Cronk and Vaughn Bryant, eds., *Through the Looking Glass: Readings in General Anthropology,* 2d ed., pp. 8–9. Copyright © 2000 McGraw-Hill. Reprinted by permission of The McGraw-Hill Companies.

1. "Luckily, from the start of my project in 1987, some Datoga families had been kind to me, inviting me to live in their homesteads."

   Fact or opinion? _____

   _____

   _____

2. "My feeble attempts to make a cow, terrified at the sight of a white person, yield milk deserved such ridicule."

   Fact or opinion? _____

   _____

3. "But I found it harder to take criticism for skills of which I was more proud, such as driving across rocky river beds or taking notes in almost pitch-dark huts, particularly since no Datoga in the community knew how to do either of these things."

   Fact or opinion? _____

   _____

4. Write one logical *inference* a reader could make about the author *and tell what in the paragraph you based it on:*

_____

_____

_____

_____

_____

_____

_____

5. Is the author's *tone* humorous or serious? _____

_____

6. Is the author's primary *purpose* to instruct, persuade, or entertain the reader?

_____

_____

Passage 2

THE RISKS OF ONLINE INTIMACY

1   Relationship websites give one the opportunity to meet a partner online. Examples are personals.yahoo.com, date.com, americansingles.com, and match.com.

2   Relationship websites may expose you to a wider variety of potential partners than is possible in more conventional ways, as through school, church, or club activities. In addition, you may get to know someone for qualities other than looks or physical attractiveness—the very qualities (such as intellectual interests) that may help to support a relationship over the long term. But how effective is the Internet as a means of finding the perfect mate? "When it comes to the search for lasting love," says one report, "psychologists are finding that chat rooms, message boards, and especially online dating services may have built-in mechanisms that make any off-screen romance very likely to fail. Some reasons:

- *Online life and real life aren't the same:* Psychologists say there is little similarity between "disembodied email consciousness" and a real-life encounter. Thus, it's impossible to say whether two people who get along well online will get along in the real world.

- *Online connections can be emotionally intense:* "Most people you encounter, online or off, are those you will not be emotionally interested in," says Joseph Walter, a professor at Rensselaer Polytechnic Institute who studies online relationships. "What's different about the Internet is surprise" at how quickly feelings bloom. "The medium sucks you in."

- *Online text communication doesn't allow nonverbal communication:* Motion and activity—gestures, smiles, eye contact, and other nonverbal communication—are not available with email. Yet it is these nuances that transcend words and that, of course, are missing from online text-based relationships. One Hawaii man developed an email romance with a woman in Michigan that he met through an online bulletin board. When they finally met in person, he discovered she wore heavy eye mascara—a turnoff to a man who considered himself a hippie.

- *People meeting online showcase their good points:* With a burgeoning online romance, "you get the sensitivity and thoughtfulness," says Walter. "If you meet [offline] spontaneously, you build your impression from real data, not from an idealized basis. It is nearly impossible for people to live up to such an artificially high, idealized range of expectations" as can be built up by online correspondence.

3   Still, the Internet does allow the possibility that a couple may develop real rather than false intimacy. "In real life," says psychologist Storm King, "you don't talk to strangers. Online, you are encouraged to talk to strangers. The Internet lets people have relationships they could not have any other way."

Source: Brian Williams and Stacey Sawyer, *Using Information Technology,* 6th ed., p. 82. Copyright © 2005 McGraw-Hill. Reprinted by permission of The McGraw-Hill Companies.

7. "Relationship websites may expose you to a wider variety of potential partners than is possible in more conventional ways, as through school, church, or club activities."

   Fact or *opinion?* _____

8. "The medium sucks you in."

   Fact or *opinion?* _____

   _____

9. Write the logical *inference* readers could make about whether people are likely to find lasting love via a relationship that begins on the Internet. Tell what in the selection you base your answer on.

   _____

   _____

   _____

   _____

   _____

10. What type of *evidence* (sources of support) do the authors present?

   _____

   _____

   _____

11. Is the authors' primary *purpose* to inform, instruct, persuade, or entertain the reader?

_____

_____

Passage 3

FINDING PEOPLE TO DATE

1   Another possibility for finding someone to date is to go online. A romance can develop online through continued meetings in the chat room or by e-mail. Eventually, the couple may decide to telephone each other and/or meet face-to-face. One young woman who met a man on the Internet and married him five months later told us, "As soon as we started e-mailing, we knew we had so much in common that we wanted to meet. And at our first face-to-face meeting he proposed marriage and I accepted."

2   There are both advantages and disadvantages to meeting someone on the Internet and then pursuing the relationship further. A major disadvantage is that you miss the nonverbal signals that can provide so much information about a person. If you decide to meet face-to-face, you may find that you have started a relationship with someone who is disturbed or even dangerous; it is important to know how to protect yourself before getting involved online (Gwinnell 1998). Another disadvantage is that you may want to pursue a relationship with someone who lives at a great distance from you. We heard an online account of a Canadian woman who met and fell in love with a Swedish man via the Internet. They now were engaged and struggling with the logistics of where to live.

3   On the other hand, it is an advantage that you get to know something about each other before being distracted by physical appearance. Your feelings about someone, including your evaluation of that person's attractiveness, can change considerably as you get to know the person. Perhaps many potentially fulfilling relationships never develop because there is no initial physical attraction.

4   One other advantage to Internet meetings is that they provide an opportunity to meet and pursue a relationship with someone when other avenues seem to be closed or less accessible. In a word, many people have found love through Internet meetings. There are even books available to guide people on the proper use of the Internet to locate a potential life partner.

Source: Adapted from Robert Lauer and Jeanette Lauer, *Marriage and Family,* 6th ed., pp. 127–28. Copyright © 2007 McGraw-Hill. Reprinted by permission of The McGraw-Hill Companies.

12. "There are both advantages and disadvantages to meeting someone on the Internet and then pursuing the relationship further."

Fact or *opinion?* _____

13. "Perhaps many potentially fulfilling relationships never develop because there is no initial physical attraction."

Fact or *opinion?* _____

14. Write the logical *inference* readers could make about whether people are likely to find lasting love via a relationship that begins on the Internet. Tell what in the selection you base your answer on.

15. Describe the authors' *tone*. _____

16. Is the authors' primary *purpose* to inform, instruct, persuade, or entertain the reader?

_____

17. What type of *support* do the authors give?

_____

_____

18. Based on the statement, "There are even books available to guide people on the proper use of the Internet to locate a potential life partner," what is one *inference* the reader could make?

_____

_____

_____

How did you do on the Set 2 Exercises? Was there any particular *type* of question that caused you difficulty? If so, which one(s)? What steps could you take to improve your ability to apply that skill?

_____

_____

_____

_____

_____

_____

_____

_____

SET 3

Exercises: Applying All the Advanced Skills

The first selection was written by Judy Brady, an essayist and political activist. First published in *Ms.* magazine more than three decades ago, it has become one of the most famous essays of modern times. Read the article and then answer the questions about it.

Passage 1

WHY I WANT A WIFE

1   I belong to that classification of people known as wives. I am A Wife. And, not altogether incidentally, I am a mother.

2   Not too long ago a male friend of mine appeared on the scene fresh from a recent divorce. He had one child, who is, of course, with his ex-wife. He is looking for another wife. As I thought about him while I was ironing one evening, it suddenly occurred to me that I, too, would like to have a wife. Why do I want a wife?

3   I would like to go back to school so that I can become economically independent, support myself, and, if need be, support those dependent upon me. I want a wife who will work and send me to school. And while I am going to school I want a wife to take care of my children. I want a wife to keep track of the children's doctor and dentist appointments. And to keep track of mine, too. I want a wife to make sure my children eat properly and are kept clean. I want a wife who will wash the children's clothes and keep them mended. I want a wife who is a good nurturant attendant to my children, who arranges for their schooling, makes sure that they have an adequate social life with their peers, takes them to the park, the zoo, etc. I want a wife who takes care of the children when they are sick, a wife who arranges to be around when the children need special care, because, of course, I cannot miss classes at school. My wife must arrange to lose time at work and not lose the job. It may mean a small cut in my wife's income from time to time, but I guess I can tolerate that. Needless to say, my wife will arrange and pay for the care of the children while my wife is working.

4   I want a wife who will take care of *my* physical needs. I want a wife who will keep my house clean. A wife who will pick up after me. I want a wife who will keep my clothes clean, ironed, mended, replaced when need be, and who will see to it that my personal things are kept in their proper place so that I can find what I need the minute I need it. I want a wife who cooks the meals, a wife who is a good cook. I want a wife who will plan the menus, do the necessary grocery shopping, prepare the meals, serve them pleasantly, and then do the cleaning up while I do my studying. I want a wife who will care for me when I am sick and sympathize with my pain and loss of time from school. I want a wife to go along when our family takes a vacation so that someone can continue to care for me and my children when I need a rest and change of scene.

5   I want a wife who will not bother me with rambling complaints about a wife's duties. But I want a wife who will listen to me when I feel the need to explain a rather difficult point I have come across in my course of studies. And I want a wife who will type my papers for me when I have written them.

6   I want a wife who will take care of the details of my social life. When my wife and I are invited out by friends, I want a wife who will take care of the babysitting arrangements. When I meet people at school that I like and want to entertain, I want a wife who will have the house clean, will prepare a special meal, serve it to me and my friends, and not interrupt when I talk about the things that interest me and my friends. I want a wife who will have arranged that the children are fed and ready for bed before my guests arrive so that the children do not bother us. I want a wife who takes care of the needs of my guests so that they feel comfortable, who makes sure that they have an ashtray,

that they are passed the hors d'oeuvres, that they are offered a second helping of the food, that their wine glasses are replenished when necessary, that their coffee is served to them as they like it. And I want a wife who knows that sometimes I need a night out by myself.

. . .

7   When I am through with school and have a job, I want my wife to quit working and remain at home so that my wife can more fully and completely take care of a wife's duties.

8   My God, who *wouldn't* want a wife?

Source: Abridged from Judy Brady, "Why I Want a Wife," *Ms.,* Spring, 1972. Copyright 1970 by Judy Brady.

1. What is the author's *point of view* regarding the roles of husbands and wives? (Be sure to write a sentence.)

_____

_____

_____

2. What is the author's *purpose?*

_____

_____

_____

3. What is the author's *tone?* _____

4. What is the author's *intended audience?* _____

_____

_____

5. What *conclusion* does the author want the reader to draw?

_____

_____

Passage 2

Read this lengthier passage, and then answer the six questions about it. This excerpt is taken from Jessica Mitford's now-famous *The American Way of Death,* an exposé of the funeral industry that was first published in 1963. The passage is about embalming, the procedure funeral homes use to prepare bodies for "public viewing" by those attending the funeral. It isn't a topic that's discussed very much, and I need to warn you that some of the information may be a little troubling, or even shocking.

The selection contains some specialized terms and many other words that may be new to you. Use context clues and, if necessary, the dictionary. The word *formaldehyde* in the title refers to a chemical that is used to preserve the bodies.

"Alas, poor Yorick!" (paragraph 2) is a line from Shakespeare's *Hamlet*. Yorick has died during the years Hamlet has been away, and all that remains of Yorick is his skull. Hamlet picks it up and speaks those words.

This time, you really do need to take a couple of minutes to close your eyes, breathe deeply, and relax your muscles. Clear your mind of any distractions, and then tackle this last set.

BEHIND THE FORMALDEHYDE CURTAIN

1   The drama begins to unfold with the arrival of the corpse at the mortuary.

2   Alas, poor Yorick! How surprised he would be to see how his counterpart of today is whisked off to a funeral parlor and is in short order sprayed, sliced, pierced, pickled, trussed, trimmed, creamed, waxed, painted, rouged and neatly dressed—transformed from a common corpse into a Beautiful Memory Picture. This process is known in the trade as embalming and restorative art, and is so universally employed in the United States and Canada that the funeral director does it routinely, without consulting corpse or kin. He regards as eccentric those few who are hardy enough to suggest that it might be dispensed with. Yet no law requires embalming, no religious doctrine commends it, nor is it dictated by considerations of health, sanitation, or even of personal daintiness. In no part of the world but in Northern America is it widely used. The purpose of embalming is to make the corpse presentable for viewing in a suitably costly container; and here too the funeral director routinely, without first consulting the family, prepares the body for public display. . . .

3   Embalming is indeed a most extraordinary procedure, and one must wonder at the docility of Americans who each year pay hundreds of millions of dollars for its perpetuation, blissfully ignorant of what it is all about, what is done, how it is done. Not one in ten thousand has any idea of what actually takes place. Books on the subject are extremely hard to come by. They are not to be found in most libraries or bookshops. . . .

4   A close look at what does actually take place may explain in large measure the undertaker's intractable reticence concerning a procedure that has become his major *raison d'être*. Is it possible he fears that public information about embalming might lead patrons to wonder if they really want this service? If the funeral men are loath to discuss the subject outside the trade, the reader may, understandably, be equally loath to go on reading at this point. For those who have the stomach for it, let us part the formaldehyde curtain. . . .

5   The body is first laid out in the undertaker's morgue—or rather, Mr. Jones is reposing in the preparation room—to be readied to bid the world farewell.

6   The preparation room in any of the better funeral establishments has the tiled and sterile look of a surgery, and indeed the embalmer–restorative artist who does his chores there is beginning to adopt the term "dermasurgeon" (appropriately corrupted by some mortician–writers as "demi-surgeon") to describe his calling. His equipment, consisting of scalpels, scissors, augers, forceps, clamps, needles, pumps, tubes, bowls, and basins, is crudely imitative of the surgeon's, as is his technique, acquired in a nine or twelve-month post-high school course in an embalming school. He is supplied by an advanced chemical industry with a bewildering array of fluids, sprays, pastes, oils, powders, creams, to fix or soften tissue, shrink or distend it as needed, dry it here, restore the moisture there. There are cosmetics, waxes and paints to fill and cover features, even plaster of Paris to replace entire limbs. There are ingenious aids to prop and stabilize the cadaver:

A VariPose Head Rest, the Edwards Arm and Hand Positioner, the Repose Block (to support the shoulders during the embalming), and the Throop Foot Positioner, which resembles an old-fashioned stock.

7   Mr. John H. Eckels, president of the Eckels College of Mortuary Science, thus describes the first part of the embalming procedure: "In the hands of a skilled practitioner, this work may be done in a comparatively short time and without mutilating the body other than by slight incision—so slight that it scarcely would cause serious inconvenience if made upon a living person. It is necessary to remove the blood, and doing this not only helps in the disinfecting, but removes the principal cause of disfigurements due to discoloration."

8   Another textbook discusses the all-important time element: "The earlier this is done, the better, for every hour that elapses between death and embalming will add to the problems and complications encountered. . . ." Just how soon should one get going on the embalming? The author tells us, "On the basis of such scanty information made available to this profession through its rudimentary and haphazard system of technical research, we must conclude that the best results are to be obtained if the subject is embalmed before life is completely extinct—that is, before cellular death has occurred. In the average case, this would mean within an hour after somatic death." For those who feel that there is something a little rudimentary, not to say haphazard, about this advice, a comforting thought is offered by another writer. Speaking of fears entertained in early days of premature burial, he points out, "One of the effects of embalming by chemical injection, however, has been to dispel fears of live burial." How true; once the blood is removed, chances of live burial are indeed remote. . . .

9   About three to six gallons of a dyed and perfumed solution of formaldehyde, glycerin, borax, phenol, alcohol and water is soon circulating through Mr. Jones, whose mouth has been sewn together with a "needle directed upward between the upper lip and gum and brought out through the left nostril," with the corners raised slightly "for a more pleasant expression." If he should be bucktoothed, his teeth are cleaned with Bon Ami and coated with colorless nail polish. His eyes, meanwhile, are closed with flesh-tinted eye caps and eye cement.

10   The next step is to have at Mr. Jones with a thing called a trocar. This is a long, hollow needle attached to a tube. It is jabbed into the abdomen, poked around the entrails and chest cavity, the contents of which are pumped out and replaced with "cavity fluid." This done, and the hole in the abdomen sewn up, Mr. Jones's face is heavily creamed (to protect the skin from burns which may be caused by leakage of the chemicals), and he is covered with a sheet and left unmolested for a while. But not for long—there is more, much more, in store for him. He has been embalmed, but not yet restored, and the best time to start the restorative work is eight to ten hours after embalming, when the tissues have become firm and dry.

11   The object of all this attention to the corpse, it must be remembered, is to make it presentable for viewing in an attitude of healthy repose. "Our customs require the presentation of our dead in the semblance of normality . . . unmarred by the ravages of illness, disease or mutilation," says Mr. J. Sheridan Mayer in his *Restorative Art*. This is rather a large order since few people die in the full bloom of health, unravaged by illness and unmarked by some disfigurement. The funeral industry is equal to the challenge: "In some cases the gruesome appearance of a mutilated or disease-ridden subject may be quite discouraging. The task of restoration may seem impossible and shake the confidence of the embalmer. This is the time for intestinal fortitude and determination. Once the formative work is begun and affected tissues are cleaned or removed, all doubts about success

vanish. It is surprising and gratifying to discover the results which may be obtained."

Source: Jessica Mitford, *The American Way of Death.* Copyright © 1963, 1978 by Jessica Mitford. All Rights Reserved. Reprinted by permission of the Estate of Jessica Mitford.

6. What is the author's *point of view* regarding embalming? (Be sure that you write a sentence and that it contains the topic.)

_____

_____

_____

7. What is the author's *purpose?*

_____

_____

_____

8. What is the author's *tone?*

_____

_____

_____

_____

_____

9. Who is the author's *intended audience?*

_____

_____

_____

10. Indicate whether each of these sentences from the passage represents a *fact* or an *opinion:*

He is supplied by an advanced chemical industry with a bewildering array of fluids, sprays, pastes, oils, powders, creams, to fix or soften tissue, shrink or distend it as needed, dry it here, restore the moisture there.

Fact or *opinion?* _____

There are cosmetics, waxes and paints to fill and cover features, even plaster of Paris to replace entire limbs.

Fact or *opinion?* _____

_____

11. On the basis of the information in the selection, write a logical *inference* about readers' attitudes toward embalming after they have read the article.

_____

_____

_____

_____

_____

_____

Kick this "field goal" for an extra point:

What is the author's *intended meaning* of the title of the selection, "Behind the Formaldehyde Curtain"?

_____

_____

_____

_____

_____

How well do you think you understand the skills in the Advanced Stretching section? Are there any that you still need to work on? If so, tell which skill and specifically what it is that confuses you. The more precisely you can define the problem, the easier it will be for your instructor to help you clear it up.

_____

_____

_____

_____

PART · SIX

Cooldown

The Cooldown

Can you believe you've reached this section of the book? I'm proud of you for having come so far, and you should be proud of yourself, too. The skills in the Cool Down finish out what you need to know about college-level reading and study skills. The Cool Down chapters focus on

- interpreting graphic aids (bar graphs, line graphs, pie charts, flowcharts, and tables). (Chapter 13)
- organizing information for study (underlining, highlighting, and annotating textbooks; taking notes from textbooks; making outlines and maps; and summarizing). (Chapter 14)

These skills are really just special applications of the basic and advanced skills you learned in Parts 2 and 3.

Some Thoughts as You Begin the "Fourth Quarter" of This Book

You may be feeling a little tired at this point in the semester and at this point in *Exercise Your College Reading Skills.* That's normal. But the fact is, you still have to keep moving. Former South Carolina football coach Lou Holtz believes, "How you respond to the challenge in the second half will determine what you become after the game, whether you are a winner or a loser." So keep your head in the game, even if the game seems hard.

Let me tell you about something I saw on TV during the 1968 Summer Olympics in Mexico City. I was a college student then, but I've never forgotten the scene. The event was the marathon. It was so late at night that they had already turned on the stadium lights. Hardly any spectators were still in the stadium because every competitor had completed the race at least an hour earlier—that is, all except one. Out of the darkness emerged one lone runner, a runner from Tanzania (Africa) named John Stephen Akhwari.

"Runner" really isn't an accurate description: he was hobbling badly; one leg was bloody and bandaged; his knee was dislocated. Each step caused him obvious pain. Still he struggled toward the stadium. As he neared the stadium, word of the lone straggler began to spread quickly. He was so far behind the other competitors that it was a shock to everyone that there was still a runner on the course. A small group of spectators, other Olympians, and members of the press headed back into the stadium to see how this strange spectacle was going to end. Akhwari paused at the stadium entrance and after a moment began the final, lone lap toward the finish line. Everyone there wondered why a man who was obviously going to come in dead last would still struggle so fiercely for the finish line.

As Akhwari took his final, slow, painful step across the finish line, the spectators went wild with appreciation for his effort. Afterward, a reporter asked him why he hadn't quit a race that he had absolutely no chance of winning. Although I've forgotten all the rest of the winners of the 1968 Olympics, I've never forgotten John Stephen Akhwari or his reply to the reporter. "My country did not send me to Mexico City to start the race," he said. "They sent me to finish." His answer, which reflects so much courage, determination, and dignity, indelibly etched Akhwari in my mind as the real winner of those Olympics.

Apparently I wasn't the only one who has never forgotten Akhwari. He was honored at the 2000 Olympic Games in Sydney, Australia. Although more than three decades had elapsed since his "loss" in Mexico City, so many people still remembered and admired this courageous man that the 2000 Olympics Committee invited him to Sydney to honor him in a special ceremony. You are nearing the final lap of your reading course and this text. I hope that you, like John Stephen Akhwari, came not just to start the race, but to finish it.

13

CHAPTER

Interpret Graphic Aids

THE SKILL

INTERPRET GRAPHIC AIDS

Batter up! Even though this chapter is part of the Cool Down, get ready to "go to bat" once again. In this chapter you'll learn to interpret graphic material, with the emphasis on the types of visual aids that appear most frequently in textbooks.

As you read your college textbooks you will continually encounter graphic aids. *Graphic aids present information in pictorial form or in other specific formats to consolidate, clarify, or prove the written material they go with.* Graphic aids, which are also called visual aids or graphics, include diagrams, maps, photographs, sketches, and cartoons, as well as *bar graphs, line graphs, pie charts, flowcharts,* and *tables.* The last five types of graphic aids are the ones we're going to focus on. There are two reasons: first, you are probably already reasonably skilled at interpreting diagrams, photographs, sketches, and cartoons, but less practiced in interpreting the others; second, these are the graphic aids that appear most often in college texts.

You may also have noticed that newspapers and news magazines are filled with graphics. Pick up any copy of *Business Week, Newsweek, Time, The Wall Street Journal,* or *USA Today,* and you'll see dozens of them in every print and online issue. The same is true for publications in the arts, the sciences, and technology. Publishers know the wisdom of the adage, "One picture is worth a thousand words." That's why they include so many pictures and other graphics. They know it can help readers see at a glance the point an author is making. I mention the abundance of graphics in news publications because you will frequently use such publications as resources in your college courses. Being able to interpret graphics will enable you to comprehend both textbooks and resource materials more effectively.

Let's look at each of the following five types of graphics. If the definitions don't make complete sense at this point, don't be concerned. Any confusion should clear up when you see an example of each type of graphic and an explanation of it.

bar graph	A chart that compares the relative amount of items by using parallel rectangular bars of varying lengths
line graph	A diagram whose points are connected to show the relationship between two or more variables (that is, it shows how one thing changes in relation to a change in something else)
pie chart	A circle graph that uses various sized "slices" to represent relative parts of the whole
flowchart	A diagram that uses connected boxes, circles, and other shapes to show the steps in a process or a procedure
table	Facts and figures arranged in rows and columns to show relationships among the data

How do you interpret graphics? How do you apply the study techniques? Let's get started!

THE TECHNIQUE   **INTERPRET BAR GRAPHS, LINE GRAPHS, PIE CHARTS, FLOWCHARTS, AND TABLES**

GENERAL GUIDELINES FOR INTERPRETING GRAPHICS

Interpreting graphic aids involves using the comprehension skills you've learned earlier in this book: You'll still have to determine the topic, infer the "main idea" if it isn't included in the explanation that accompanies the graphic, examine the "details" that comprise the graphic, and draw appropriate, reasonable conclusions based on the graphic.

Now let's look at a general approach that you can use to interpret all five of the graphs featured in this chapter.

- Read the *title*. This is the logical place to start because it usually tells you the topic.

- Look at the *source* of the information. Is it current? Is the source reliable? Outdated information or information from unreliable sources will be of little or no value.

- Read any *explanation* that accompanies the graphic. It often gives the main point.

- If there is a legend, read it. A *legend* is a small explanatory table or list of symbols that accompanies a graph, chart, or map. For example, a legend on a line graph would indicate what is represented by lines of various colors and types (smooth lines, dashed lines, dotted lines, etc.). A legend on a bar graph would tell what is represented by various types of bars (e.g., bars that are solid, striped, shaded to various degrees, of various colors, etc.).

- Read the *labels*. If there is not a legend, you should be able to determine what is being measured or compared by reading the labels. These appear on the side and bottom of the graph (the vertical and horizontal axes), at the tops of columns and at the beginnings of rows, and on the "slices" of a pie chart.

- Determine *what is being measured or compared* and *the units of measurement*. For example, a bar graph designed to compare the number of tuberculosis (TB) cases reported in Third World countries might have the vertical axis labeled "Reported TB Cases, 1985–2005" and a horizontal axis labeled

"Country." The numbers used for "Reported TB Cases" might be in thousands, with the number "50" used to represent 50,000. Be especially careful when numbers are used for measurement. If you do not pay attention to the unit of measurement, you will misunderstand the graphic. (There is a big difference between 50 cases of TB and 50,000 cases!) Units of measurement can be almost anything: time (milliseconds, seconds, minutes, hours, decades, centuries); percents; units of any size (a hundred, a thousand, a million, a billion). You should also understand what those units (such as billions and milliseconds) mean. You must not only know *what* is being measured—temperatures, populations, dollars, ozone levels—you must know the *unit* of measurement.

■ Look for *trends* and patterns. A *trend* means there is a general direction in which something tends to move. In other words, there is a consistent increase or decrease. For example, a line graph might reveal that, overall, the number of smokers is decreasing (the line representing smokers angles down), but that smoking is increasing among females in their teens and twenties (the line representing them angles up). Jagged, erratic lines tell another story—that there was great instability or continuous change. Take notice, too, of any "extreme" on a graph: a bar on a bar graph that is considerably taller or shorter than the rest; a point on a line graph that shoots far above or below the rest of the line; numbers in a table that are much smaller or larger than the rest; or an extremely large or small "slice" on a pie chart. Watch for any pattern that recurs in the data (such as an inverse relationship between interest rates and bond prices).

■ Think about how the graphic might *illustrate, clarify, or prove a point the author makes* in the accompanying text material.

■ Determine whether there are other important *conclusions* you can draw from information in the graphic. Paying attention to trends and patterns can be especially valuable in this regard. The conclusions you draw will go *beyond* the information that appears in the graphic, but should be logically based on it.

THE TRAINER   OBSERVE THE SKILL OF INTERPRETING GRAPHIC AIDS

Instead of showing an effective reader's "thoughts" as I've been doing, I'm going to give you an example of each of the five types of graphics. Examine each one first without reading the explanation. See if you can answer the questions yourself. Then look at the explanation beneath each graphic to see if your answers match the effective reader's answers. The information in color explains where in the graphic our effective reader found the information that answers each question or on which the answer is based. These graphics come from college textbooks, but they also show the original source (unless the graphic was created by the author or authors of the textbook). For the source and date of the graphic, use the original source.

BAR GRAPH

A **bar graph** *is a chart that compares the relative amount of items by using parallel rectangular bars of varying lengths.* The bars may be vertical or horizontal. There may be one set of bars or several, depending on how many things are being compared. The following bar graph is an example of a vertical bar graph because the *height* of the rectangular bars indicates the amount of what is being measured. (In a horizontal bar graph, the *length* of the bar indicates the amount.)

**Percentages of American High School Seniors
Who Have Ever Used Various Drugs**
(*Source:* L. Johnston, G. Bachman, and P. O'Malley (2002). *Monitoring the
Future.* Ann Arbor, MI: Institute for Social Research.)

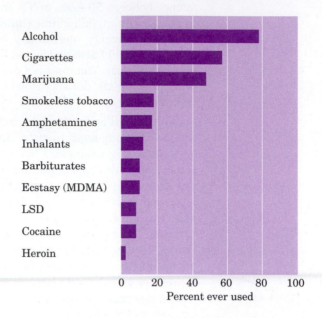

Source: Lawrence Steinberg, *Adolesence,* 7th ed., p. 447. Copyright © 2005
McGraw-Hill. Reprinted by permission of The McGraw-Hill Companies.

Title or Explanation: "Percentages of American High School Seniors Who
Have Ever Used Various Drugs" (title given at the top of the graphic)

Source and Date: Monitoring the Future, published by the Institute for Social
Research, 2002. (Original source appears beneath title.)

Headings and Levels: Vertical axis: types of drugs; horizontal axis: percent
ever used (Information comes from the title and the numbers along each
axis.)

Units of Measurement: horizontal axis—percent in increments of 20; vertical
axis—none (Information comes from the numbers along the horizontal axis.)

Important information or conclusions:

- Alcohol, cigarettes and marijuana are the three drugs most tried/used by
  high school seniors—used by approximately 50 percent or more.
- All other drugs have been used by less than 20 percent of seniors, with
  heroin the lowest.

LINE GRAPH

A ***line graph*** *is a diagram whose points are connected to show the relationship
between two or more variables* (that is, it shows how one thing changes in relation
to a change in something else).

Rising Media Costs: Super Bowl, Super Dollars

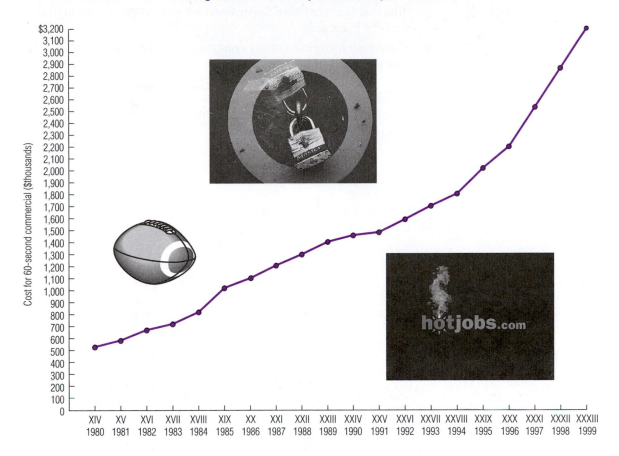

Source: Eric Berkowitz, Roger Kerin, Steven Hartley, and William Rudelius *Marketing,* 6th ed., p. 521. Copyright © 2000 Irwin/McGraw-Hill. Reprinted by permission of The McGraw-Hill Companies.

Title or Explanation: "Rising Media Costs: Super Bowl, Super Dollars" (title given at the top of the graphic)

Source and Date: None given, other than from a marketing text published in 2000.

Headings and Levels: Costs for 60-second commercials; Super Bowl numbers and corresponding years from 1980–1999 (Information comes from the labels/information along each axis.)

Units of Measurement: Vertical axis: dollars, in *thousands* of dollars ("$thousands") between 0 and 3,200; horizontal axis: single years, from 1980–1999 (Information comes from the labels/information along each axis.)

Important information or conclusions:

■ The cost for 60-second ads during the Super Bowl have increased from $500,000 per minute in 1980 to $3.2 million in 1999. (determined by looking at the lowest number and highest number shown by the line; remember that each number represents *thousands*)

■ Trend: a steady increase. There has never been a drop in the cost for advertisements during the Super Bowl. (The line angles steadily upward; also the title, "*Rising* Media Costs," indicates this.)

■ Advertising costs increased most sharply since the mid-1990s. (from seeing that this was the point at which the line began to angle up more sharply)

- Because advertisers continue to pay increasingly high prices, they must find that the benefits of Super Bowl advertising justify the high cost. (logical inference)

- Only very financially strong companies with large advertising budgets can afford Super Bowl advertisements. (logical inference because the cost of a Super Bowl commercial is so high)

- Careful thought and planning, as well as expense, go into making Super Bowl ads. (logical inference because the cost of a Super Bowl commercial is so high)

PIE CHART

A **pie chart** is a circle graph that uses various sized "slices" to represent relative parts of the whole.

The Federal Budget Dollar, Fiscal Year 2005
(*Source:* Office of Management and Budget)

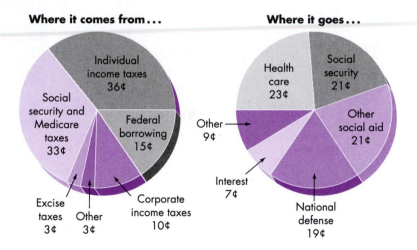

Source: Thomas E. Patterson, *We the People*, 6th ed., p. 540. Copyright © 2006 McGraw-Hill. Reprinted by permission of The McGraw-Hill Companies.

Title or Explanation: "The Federal Budget Dollar, Fiscal Year 2005" (given at the top of the graphic)

Source and Date: Office of Management and Budget (given at the top of the graphic)

Headings and Levels: "Where It Comes From . . . " and "Where It Goes . . . " (given above each pie chart)

Units of Measurement: Cents, representing percent of each federal dollar collected and spent (numbers are written with the ¢ sign)

Important information or conclusions:

- 69% of the government's money comes from individual income taxes (36¢) and social security and Medicare taxes (33¢). (determined by adding up the two largest numbers for sources of the government's money—left pie chart)

- 65% of the government's expenditures go for health care (23%), social security (21%), and other social aid (21%). (determined by adding up the numbers for the biggest expenditures—right pie chart)

- Most of the government's revenue comes from taxes; most expenditures go to individuals (although those paying and receiving are not exactly the same people). (from comparing the two totals)

FLOWCHART

*A **flowchart** is a diagram that uses connected boxes, circles and other shapes to show the steps in a process or a procedure.*

Consumer Buying Influences and Financial Implications

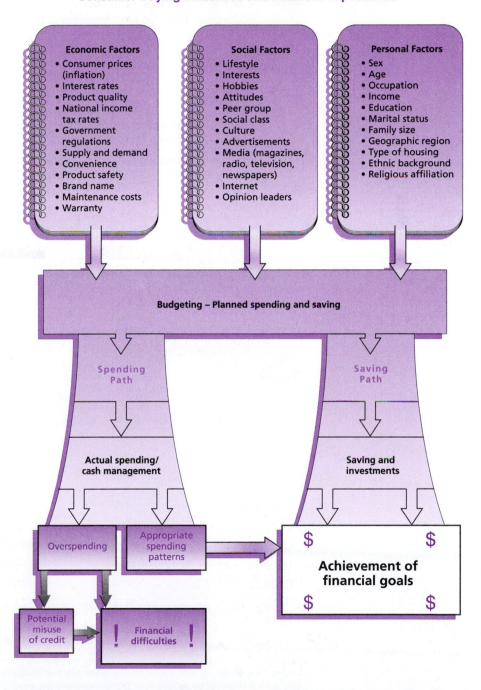

Source: Jack Kapoor, Les Dlabay, and Robert Hughes, *Personal Finance,* 7th ed., p. 240. Copyright © 2004 McGraw-Hill/Irwin. Reprinted by permission of The McGraw-Hill Companies.

Title or Explanation: "Consumer Buying Influences and Financial Implications" (title given at top of graphic)

Source and Date: None given, so we must assume the authors of the textbook created the flowchart.

Headings and Levels: None given (other than ones that appear in the "boxes")

Units of Measurement: None given (since none were used)

Important information or conclusions:

- Three sets of factors (economic, social, and personal) shape consumers' budgeting. (from the three headings in the boxes at the top of the flowchart)

- The two major components of budgeting are spending and saving. (from the middle bar and the labels on the two columns that descend from it, "Spending Path" and "Saving Path")

- Savings and spending will either be appropriate and lead to the achievement of financial goals, or there will be overspending, which leads to potential credit abuse and financial problems. (from following the arrows to the ends of both "paths")

- If there is overspending *or* too little saving and investing, financial goals cannot be met. (flowchart shows that *both* planned spending and saving must happen in order to achieve financial goals)

TABLE

A **table** shows relationships between facts and figures by arranging information in rows and columns.

"WOULD YOU MARRY SOMEONE YOU DIDN'T LOVE?" (*Source:* Hatfield, Elaine, *Passionate Love and Sexual Desire: A Cross-Cultural Perspective.* Paper presented at the Annual Meeting, Society for the Scientific Study of Sexuality, Miami, 1994.)			
	Responses (Percent)		
Cultural Group	**Yes**	**Undecided**	**No**
Australia	4.8%	15.2%	80.0%
Brazil	4.3	10.0	85.7
England	7.3	9.1	83.6
Hong Kong	5.8	16.7	77.6
India	49.0	26.9	24.0
Japan	2.3	35.7	62.0
Mexico	10.2	9.3	80.5
Pakistan	50.4	10.4	39.1
Philippines	11.4	25.0	63.6
Thailand	18.8	47.5	33.8
United States	3.5	10.6	85.9

Source: Janet Hyde and John DeLamater, *Understanding Human Sexuality,* 9th ed., p. 332. Copyright © 2006 McGraw-Hill. Reprinted by permission of The McGraw-Hill Companies.

Title or Explanation: "Would You Marry Someone You Didn't Love?" (top of table)

Source and Date: Paper presented at the 1994 Annual Meeting of the Society for the Scientific Study of Sexuality (indicated above the table)

Headings and Levels: Cultural Group; Responses (percent for Yes, Undecided, No) (from looking at column labels)

Units of Measurement: percentages (of those surveyed who responded Yes, Undecided, and No) (from the use of the % sign beside the first number in each column)

Important information or conclusions:

■ In Australia, Brazil, England, Mexico, and the United States, at least 80% of those surveyed responded No. (by comparing the figures in the last column and identifying the highest ones)

■ In cultures that value individualism, more respondents replied No. (logical conclusion)

■ The highest number of yesses was recorded in cultures that place less value on individualism and have more rigid class systems (roughly half the respondents in India and Pakistan indicated they would marry someone they did not love; in Thailand nearly half of those surveyed were undecided). (logical conclusion)

THE EDGE

POINTERS ABOUT INTERPRETING GRAPHIC AIDS

■ **Stop and look at a graphic aid when the author first refers to it.**
When you are reading a textbook or an article that contains a graphic, be sure to look at it *when the author first mentions it.* Authors refer to a graphic at the exact point they believe the graphic will be most helpful. To direct your attention to a related graphic, authors might say, for instance, "See Figure 2.1" or they put "Table 4.2" in parenthesis at the point they want you to stop and refer to the table. Don't keep reading and ignore their instruction to look at the graphic. Even if you remember to go back and look at the graphic later, it will not make as much sense to you or be as helpful.

■ **Watch for trends and patterns.**
I want to emphasize again the importance of looking for trends and patterns because they reveal a consistent increase or decrease in something. They can also indicate a correlation (relationship) between things. For example, a chart might show that personal income rises as a person's number of years of education increases. A table might indicate that as the number of hours children watch TV per week increases, their level of physical fitness declines. A trend is often the *most* important piece of information a graphic aid shows.

■ **To help you organize and learn information, create graphics of your own.**
There's no law that says *you* can't put information you want to learn into the form of a graph, a flowchart, or a table. Creating these helps you transfer information into your long-term memory and leaves you with a great study aid when it's time to review for a test. Especially if you are a visual learner, make a point of putting information in your notes into graphic form. Of course, you are not restricted to the five types of graphics featured in this chapter. You should include sketches, charts, diagrams—whatever works for you.

THE REPLAY

REMEMBER THE ESSENTIAL INFORMATION FROM THE CHAPTER

Define graphic aids and each of these five common graphic aids. In the margin, *draw a small sketch* to show what the visual aid looks like.

Definition of Graphic Aids

_____

_____

_____

1. Bar Graph

_____

_____

2. Line Graph

_____

_____

_____

_____

3. Pie Chart

_____

_____

4. Flowchart

_____

_____

_____

5. Table

_____

_____

_____

THE PRACTICE

SET 1

APPLY THE SKILL OF INTERPRETING GRAPHIC AIDS

Exercises: Interpreting Graphic Aids

In these exercises you will apply the general approach to obtaining information from graphics aids. For each graphic, identify the title and/or explanation, the source and date, the headings and levels, the units of measurement, and the important information or conclusions. Of course, not every graphic will have an explanation, source, date, or units of measurement. (For example, a pie chart might simply show relative amounts; a flowchart does not have units of measurement.) For the source and date of the graphic, use the *original* source (given on the graphic) rather than the name and publication date of the textbook in which the graphic appeared (which is given beneath the graphic). If no source is given on the graphic itself, it means the textbook author created the graphic. In that case, you *should* use the name of the textbook and its publication date for the source and date. If information of a particular type is missing, simply write "not given."

Before you begin, close your eyes for a minute as you rotate your head in gentle circles in both directions. Open your mouth as wide as possible to release tension from your jaw muscles. (While you're at it, you might as well yawn and get some extra oxygen to your brain!) Feel better? Then let's go!

1. Bar Graph

Number of Americans Living Alone
(*Source:* U.S. Bureau of the Census 1987:45; Saluter 1994:xi; and U.S. Census Bureau 2004/2005:49)

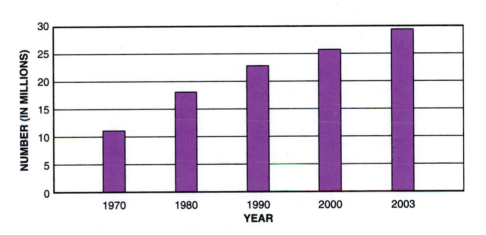

Source: Robert Lauer and Jeanette Lauer, *Marriage and Family,* 6th ed., p. 9. Copyright © 2007 McGraw-Hill. Reprinted by permission of The McGraw-Hill Companies.

Title or Explanation: _____

Source and Date: _____

_____

Headings and Levels: _____

Units of Measurement: _____

_____

Important information or conclusions:

_____

_____

_____

_____

_____

2. Line Graph

Birth Rate per 1,000 Population: 1910–2002
(*Source:* U.S. Bureau of the Census 1989:59 and 2004/2005:60)

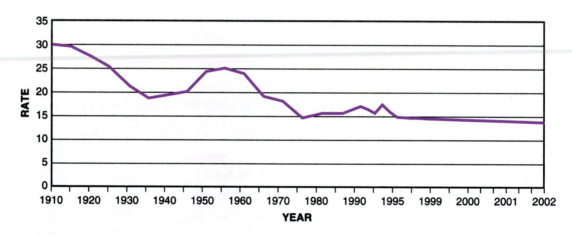

Source: Robert Lauer and Jeanette Lauer, *Marriage and Family,* 6th ed., p. 11. Copyright © 2007 McGraw-Hill. Reprinted by permission of The McGraw-Hill Companies.

Title or Explanation: _____

Source and Date: _____

Headings and Levels: _____

Units of Measurement: _____

_____

Important information or conclusions:

_____

_____

_____

_____

_____

_____

_____

_____

_____

_____

_____

_____

3. Pie Chart

Regional Distribution of People with HIV/AIDS
(*Source:* United Nations.)

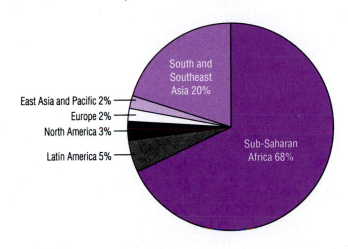

Source: J. John Palen, *Social Problems for the Twenty-First Century*, p. 407.
Copyright © 2001 McGraw-Hill. Reprinted by permission of The McGraw-Hill
Companies.

Title or Explanation: _____

_____

Source and Date: _____

Headings and Levels: _____

Units of Measurement: _____

_____

Important information or conclusions:

_____

_____

_____

_____

_____

_____

_____

4. Table

NUMBER OF PEOPLE ONLINE (MILLIONS) *(Data compiled from the July 2004 United Nations sources.)*			
Region	**Population**	**Internet users**	**Penetration (%)**
Africa	893.2	12.8	1.4%
Asia	3,607.5	256.5	7.1
Europe	730.9	224.5	30.7
Middle East	259.0	168.4	6.5
North America	325.2	223.0	68.6
Latin America/Caribbean	541.8	50.8	9.4
Oceania	32.5	15.8	48.5
World total	6,390.1	800.0	12.5

Source: William Arens and David Schaefer, *Essentials of Contemporary Advertising,* p. 355. Copyright © 2007 McGraw-Hill/Irwin. Reproduced by permission of The McGraw-Hill Companies.

Title or Explanation: _____

Source and Date: _____

Headings and Levels: _____

Units of Measurement: _____

_____

Important information or conclusions:

_____

_____

_____

_____

_____

_____

5. Flowchart

The Marketing Process with the 4 Ps

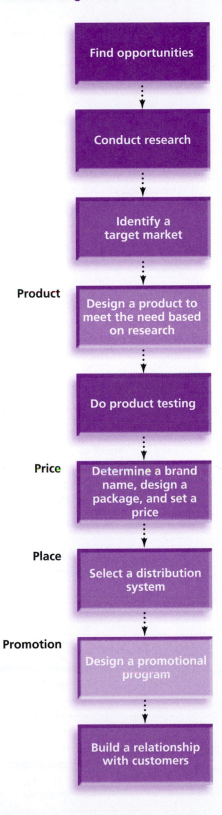

Product

Price

Place

Promotion

Source: William Nickels, James McHugh, and Susan McHugh, *Understanding Business,* 7th ed., p. 403. Copyright © 2005 McGraw-Hill/Irwin. Reprinted by permission of The McGraw-Hill Companies.

Title or Explanation: _____

Source and Date: _____

_____

_____

Headings and Levels: _____

Units of Measurement: _____

Important information or conclusions:

_____

_____

_____

_____

_____

_____

_____

Take a moment to assess how easily and accurately you were able to find and interpret information in the five graphic aids. Is there any part of the process that seems confusing? Do any of the types of graphic aids seem more difficult than the others? Write your thoughts here:

_____

_____

_____

_____

_____

_____

_____

_____

SET 2

Exercises: Interpreting Graphs

For these exercises, follow the general approach for studying each graph, and then answer the questions. Take a minute first to relax and refocus. Some of these questions require a bit more concentration and take extra thought, but you can do it. Don't be tempted to give up just because an answer might not be immediately obvious.

1. Bar Graph

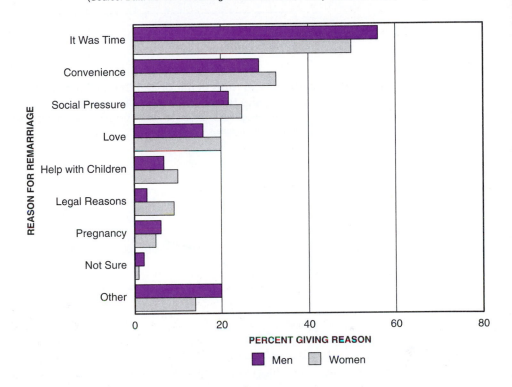

Reasons for Remarriage Offered by 205 Men and Women
(*Source:* Data from L. H. Ganong and M. Coleman, *Family Relations* 38:30, 1989.)

Source: Robert Laver and Jeanette Laver, *Marriage and Family,* 6th ed., p. 372. Copyright © 2007 McGraw-Hill. Reprinted by permission of The McGraw-Hill Companies.

1. Which reasons did a greater number of women than men give for remarriage?

_____

_____

2. Did more men or women identify pregnancy as the reason for remarriage?

_____

3. Are people more likely to remarry for convenience or because of social pressure?

_____

4. Approximately what percentage of men identified love as the reason for remarriage? Women?

_____

5. For which two reasons did approximately the same percentage of women give as the reason for remarriage?

_____

6. In which categories, besides "Other," did men and women vary most in the percentages given by each?

_____

---

2. Line Graph

Number of Deaths due to AIDS in the United States, for Non-Hispanic Whites, Non-Hispanic Blacks, and Hispanics, from 1985 and before to 2000.
(_Source:_ For 1985 and before, and through 1990, U.S. Bureau of the Census [1996]; for 1991–1996, U.S. Centers for Disease Control and Prevention, various reports.)

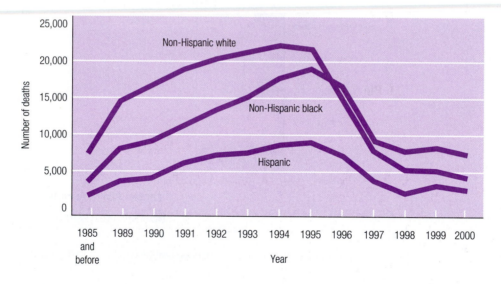

Source: Andrew Cherlin, _Public and Private Families,_ 4th ed., p. 213. Copyright © 2005 McGraw-Hill. Reprinted by permission of The McGraw-Hill Companies.

7. What is the topic of this graph?

_____

_____

_____

8. What are the labels on this graph? What is the unit of measurement?

_____

_____

_____

9. Prior to 1994, what trend is reflected in the data in the graph?

_____

_____

10. What significant change occurred in all groups in 1995 and 1996?

_____

_____

11. Overall, which group has had the highest number of AIDS deaths?

_____

_____

12. In 1996, which group had the highest number of AIDS deaths, and what was the approximate number of deaths?

_____

_____

_____

3. Pie Chart

U.S. Population by Race and Ethnicity, 1995 and 2020
(*Source:* U.S. Bureau of the Census, *Current Population Reports*, P25-1104: middle series projections. Washington, DC.)

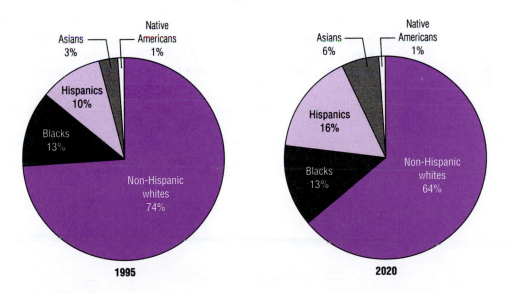

Source: J. John Palen, *Social Problems for the Twenty-First Century*, p. 67. Copyright © 2001 McGraw-Hill. Reprinted by permission of The McGraw-Hill Companies.

13. Which racial/ethnic group is projected to have the greatest population increase by 2020, and by what percent?

_____

_____

14. Is the percentage of any group expected to decline between 1995 and 2020? If so, which one(s) and by what percent?

_____

_____

15. Which group is expected to double its percentage of the population by 2020?

_____

_____

_____

16. Which groups are expected to stay the same in terms of the percent of the population it comprises?

_____

_____

17. The largest minority group will change between 1995 and 2020. What group was the largest minority group in 1995, and which group is projected to replace it by 2020 as the largest minority?

_____

_____

_____

_____

18. What might be some of the reasons that the Hispanic percent of the population is projected to increase by 2020? (This goes beyond the information in the graph, but you should be able to come up with some reasons.)

_____

_____

_____

_____

_____

_____

_____

4. Table

	C (mg)	**Beta Carotene (mg)**	**E (mg)**	**Folacin (mg)**
		TOP TEN ANTIOXIDANT ALL-STARS		
		(Source: University of California at Berkeley Wellness Letter, 1994.)		
Broccoli (1/2 cup cooked)	49	0.7	0.9	53
Cantaloupe (1 cup cubed)	68	3.1	0.3	17
Carrot (1 medium)	7	12.2	0.3	10
Kale (1/2 cup cooked)	27	2.9	3.7	9
Mango (1 medium)	57	4.8	2.3	31
Pumpkin (1/2 cup canned)	5	10.5	1.1	15
Red bell pepper (1/2 cup raw)	95	1.7	0.3	8
Spinach (1/2 cup cooked)	9	4.4	2.0	131
Strawberries (1 cup)	86	—	0.3	26
Sweet potato (1 medium, cooked)	28	14.9	5.5	26
Adult RDA or suggested intake	60	5–6	8–10	180–200

Runners-up: Brussels sprouts, all citrus fruits, tomatoes, potatoes, other berries, other leafy greens (dandelion, turnip, and mustard greens, swiss chard, arugula), cauliflower, green pepper, asparagus, peas, beets, and winter squash.

Source: Charles Corbin, Gregory Welk, William Corbin, and Karen Welk, *Concepts of Physical Fitness,* 13th ed., p. 318. Copyright © 2006 McGraw-Hill. Reprinted by permission of The McGraw-Hill Companies.

19. What is the unit of measurement for the vitamins?

_____

_____

20. Which food contains the most mg of vitamin C per serving?

_____

_____

21. Which contains more beta carotene per serving: sweet potatoes or carrots?

_____

_____

_____

22. Would a serving of strawberries meet the adult RDA or suggested intake of vitamin C?

_____

_____

_____

_____

_____

_____

23. Which three foods contain the highest amounts of folacin per serving?

_____

_____

24. Would one serving each of sweet potatoes and kale supply the adult RDA of vitamin E? Explain why or why not.

_____

_____

_____

_____

_____

_____

5. Flowchart

Computing Taxable Income and Your Tax Liability

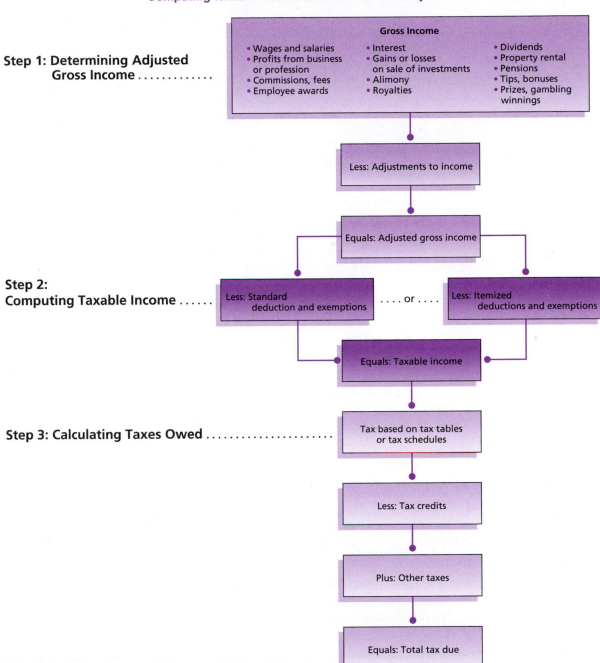

Step 1: Determining Adjusted Gross Income . . . .

Step 2: Computing Taxable Income . . . . . .

Step 3: Calculating Taxes Owed . . . .

Gross Income
- Wages and salaries
- Profits from business or profession
- Commissions, fees
- Employee awards
- Interest
- Gains or losses on sale of investments
- Alimony
- Royalties
- Dividends
- Property rental
- Pensions
- Tips, bonuses
- Prizes, gambling winnings

Less: Adjustments to income

Equals: Adjusted gross income

Less: Standard deduction and exemptions . . . . or . . . . Less: Itemized deductions and exemptions

Equals: Taxable income

Tax based on tax tables or tax schedules

Less: Tax credits

Plus: Other taxes

Equals: Total tax due

Source: Jack Kapoor, Les Dlabay, Robert Hughes, *Focus on Personal Finance*, p. 64. Copyright © 2006 McGraw-Hill/Irwin. Reprinted by permission of The McGraw-Hill Companies.

25. What is the topic of this flowchart?

_____

26. How many general steps are there in the process?

_____

_____

_____

27. What must be deducted from the gross income?

_____

_____

_____

28. What decision must be made in Step 2?

_____

_____

_____

29. What must be deducted in Step 3 and what must be added to the tax based on tax tables or tax schedules?

_____

_____

_____

30. If you win money gambling, is it considered part of your gross income?

_____

These items were more challenging. How did you do on them? If you were stumped on an item, how did you go about figuring it out? What type of graph do you need the most additional practice on?

_____

_____

_____

_____

_____

SET 3

Exercises: Interpreting Graphs

In these exercises on graphs, you'll again be answering questions based on the graphs. Think about how you did on the last set. Is there anything you need to do differently? Do you need to spend more time on the exercises? Think about them more carefully?

Relax and refocus by taking a couple of deep breaths. Open and close your hands a few times, then shake them out. Close your eyes and look up, down, right and left. (It's good to do this periodically whenever you must do a lot of reading at one time.) Okay. Jump in, but be aware that these graphic aids require careful thought and that interpreting them requires more time—perhaps considerably more—than those in the previous exercise sets.

1. Bar Graph

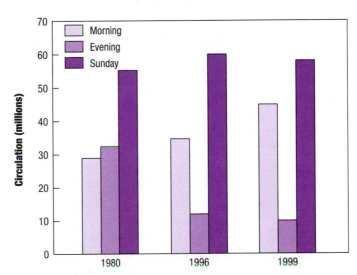

Daily-Newspaper Circulation, 1980–1999
(Compiled by author)

Source: Joseph Dominick, *The Dynamics of Mass Communication: Media in the Digital Age,* 7th ed., p. 99. Copyright © 2002 McGraw-Hill. Reprinted by permission of The McGraw-Hill Companies.

1. What is the topic of this bar graph, and what is being compared?

2. Which type of circulation consistently had the highest circulation, and to what do you think this might be attributable?

3. What trend is evident in morning circulation between 1980 and 1999? Why do you think this occurred?

_____

_____

_____

_____

_____

_____

_____

_____

4. In which category of circulation and in which time period did the sharpest decline occur?

_____

5. What was the approximate daily-newspaper circulation for the Sunday edition in 1999?

_____

6. In 1996, what was the approximate total circulation in millions?

_____

2. Line Graph

Past Month Drug Use by High School Seniors, by Drug Type: 1975 to 2001

(_Source:_ The National Institute on Drug Abuse, _Monitoring the Future Study,_ Washington, DC: U.S. Department of Justice, 2002, p. 10.)

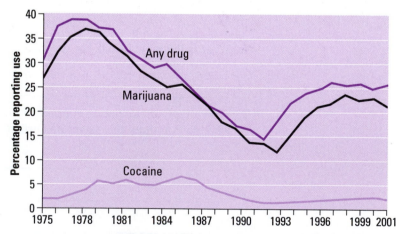

Source: Freda Adler, Gerhard Mueller, and William Laufer, _Criminal Justice: An Introduction,_ 4th ed., p. 72. Copyright © 2006 McGraw-Hill. Reprinted by permission of the McGraw-Hill Companies.

7. Approximately which year did the fewest high school seniors report using any drug during the past month?

_____

8. In 1975 approximately what percent of high school seniors reported having used cocaine during the past month??

_____

9. During which year did reported use of marijuana during the past month begin a sharp increase?

_____

10. Approximately which year did the "Any Drug" category and "Marijuana" category diverge (go in different directions)?

_____

11. What was the overall trend for "Any drug" and "Marijuana" usage categories between 1981 and 1992?

_____

12. What are some possible reasons that reported cocaine use is significantly and consistently lower than marijuana between 1975 and 2001?

_____

_____

_____

_____

_____

3. Pie Chart

Amount of Contact Between Children and Fathers, for Children Who Were Living with Their Mothers and Whose Fathers Were Living Elsewhere, According to the National Survey of Families and Households, 1987–1988.
(*Source:* Seltzer [1991].)

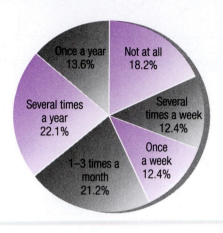

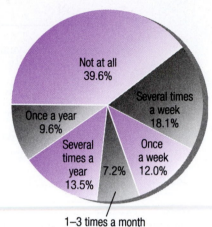

Parents were married when child
was born

Parents were not married when
child was born

Source: Andrew Cherlin, *Public and Private Families,* 4th ed., p. 420. Copyright © 2005 McGraw-Hill. Reprinted by permission of The McGraw-Hill Companies.

13. What is the topic of this pie chart?

_____

_____

_____

_____

14. What is the predominant pattern of contact with their fathers for children living with their mothers and who were born to unmarried parents? How does that compare with the data for children born to parents who were married?

_____

_____

_____

_____

15. How current are the data used in these pie charts?

_____

_____

16. What percentage of children born to previously married parents had seen their fathers either once or not at all during the preceding year?

_____

_____

_____

_____

17. What percentage of children born to never-married parents had seen their fathers either once or not at all during the preceding year?

_____

_____

_____

_____

18. What might be some of the reasons that 43 percent of children born to previously married parents see their fathers 1 to 3 times a month compared to the nearly 40 percent of children born to never-married parents who never see their fathers? (This information is not included in the graph, but you should be able to reason it out.)

_____

_____

_____

_____

_____

_____

_____

4. Table

FACTORS RELATED TO VOTER TURNOUT
(*Source:* Percentages obtained from multiple sources and are the averages for the past decade.)

Country	Approximate Voter Turnout	Automatic Registration?	Social Democrat, Socialist, or Labor Party?	Election Day a Holiday or Weekend Day?
Belgium	90%	Yes	Yes	Yes
Germany	85%	Yes	Yes	Yes
Denmark	85%	Yes	Yes	No
Italy	80%	Yes	Yes	Yes
Austria	80%	Yes	Yes	Yes
France	80%	No	Yes	Yes
Great Britain	60%	Yes	Yes	No
Canada	60%	Yes	No	No
Japan	60%	Yes	Yes	Yes
United States	55%	No	No	No

Source: Thomas Patterson, *We the People*, 6th ed., p.232. Copyright © 2006 McGraw-Hill. Reprinted by permission of McGraw-Hill Companies.

19. Does automatic voter registration seem to be correlated with voter turnout? If so, in what way?

_____

_____

_____

20. Is having a socialist or labor party correlated with voter turnout? If so, in what way?

_____

_____

_____

21. Of the nations included in the survey, how many have voter turnout of 80% or higher, and where (on which continent) are those countries located?

_____

22. How many countries hold elections on a weekend day or give election day as a holiday?

_____

23. What are some reasons having an election on a weekend day or declaring it a holiday make a difference in voter turnout?

_____

_____

24. The absence of which significant factors seem to be correlated with the voter turnout in the United States?

_____

_____

_____

5. Flowchart

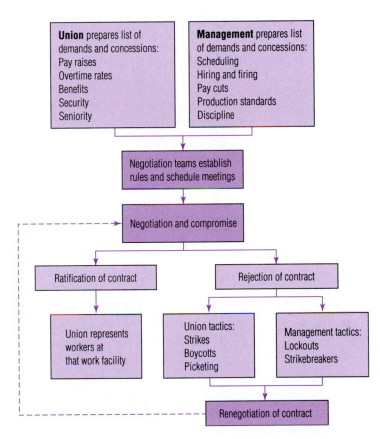

The Collective Bargaining Process

Source: O. C. Ferrell and Geoffrey Hirt, *Business: A Changing World,* 5th ed., p. 327.
Copyright © 2006 McGraw-Hill. Reprinted by permission of The McGraw-Hill Companies.

25. What is the topic of this flowchart?

_____

26. Which two groups initially prepare lists of demands and concessions?

_____

_____

27. What happens if a contract is rejected?

_____

_____

_____

_____

_____

28. Are lockouts a union tactic or a management tactic?

_____

_____

29. What things typically comprise a union's demands and concessions?

_____

_____

30. What two things can happen immediately after the negotiation and compromise step?

_____

_____

_____

That's it! Is your head spinning? Take a minute to stand up and stretch. Then assess your understanding of the material in this chapter and your experience with the exercise sets.

_____

_____

_____

_____

_____

_____

_____

_____

CHAPTER 14

Organize Information for Study

THE SKILL

ORGANIZE INFORMATION FOR STUDY

Last chapter in the Cooldown—hats off to you! In this chapter you'll learn to utilize the skills you acquired in the comprehension chapters to organize textbook material so that you can learn it as efficiently as possible. Organizing textbook information makes it easier to memorize the information when you prepare for tests. This chapter targets these six important study skills: *marking* and *annotating* your textbooks, *note taking* from texts, *outlining* and *mapping,* and *summarizing.*

The goal is to give you a variety of techniques to choose from. That way, you can experiment to see which techniques or combination of techniques works best for you. You may find that you prefer to use different techniques in different courses. For example, in a history course in which the professor gives essay tests, you may find it especially advantageous to prepare for tests by writing summaries.

Here's a brief description of each of these study skills. Some of them have been mentioned previously in this book, and you probably are already familiar with some (or even all) of them. If that's the case, great! This chapter will make you even better at them.

marking textbooks	Making the topics, main ideas, and definitions stand out in textbooks by underlining or highlighting them and drawing boxes or circles around important terms.
annotating textbooks	Writing explanatory notes and symbols in the margin to help you see how the information is organized and to make it easier to remember.
note taking from texts	On separate paper, creating your personal record of the textbook information (main ideas and details) you need to learn and remember; notes can be organized on the page in several ways, including outlining and mapping.
outlining	A specific way of organizing main ideas and details on the page to show the relationships between them. Outlines can be formal or informal.
mapping	An informal way of organizing main ideas and details by using boxes, circles, lines, arrows, and so forth to show relationships. A map is also called a *study map, learning map,* or *concept map.*
summarizing	A condensation of the main ideas presented in a longer selection written in your own words.

As you can see, main ideas and details are the keys to these essential study skills. That's why they are presented early in this book and the study skills are left until the end. You can't utilize these study techniques unless you first have a solid grasp of main ideas (both stated and implied) and details.

It's been estimated that 8 out of every 10 questions on college tests come directly from information in your textbooks, so it's critical that you be able to identify and organize the important textbook information. Now here's something you've probably discovered from your own experience: Reading—even reading carefully and rereading material—isn't enough to learn the material for tests. Learning (remembering) the information involves taking some extra steps. This chapter will equip you with great techniques for organizing information—and you *know* how much your brain loves information that's organized!

THE TECHNIQUE

MARK AND ANNOTATE TEXTBOOKS, TAKE NOTES, MAKE OUTLINES AND STUDY MAPS, AND WRITE SUMMARIES

In this section, I'm going to explain and illustrate the application of each of these skills. Consequently, there isn't a separate "Trainer" section in this chapter. (As in Chapter 13, our "effective reader" gets to take a rest. Our reader is probably at Starbucks at this very moment, kicking back and enjoying a latte.) To illustrate the six study skills, I'm going to use the same selection each time. That makes it easy for you to see the differences and similarities among the techniques. The selection comes from a sociology text and its topic is Asian-Americans' economic success.

MARKING AND ANNOTATING

Students typically use the skills of marking and annotating together because they complement each other. ***Marking*** *consists of techniques for making topics, main ideas, and important definitions stand out in your textbooks.* (Notice that you *don't* mark details.) Marking includes underlining, highlighting, and drawing boxes or circles around important terms. ***Annotations*** *are explanatory notes and symbols that you* *write in the margins to help you organize and remember the information.* Of course, if your handwriting is large or the margins in your textbook are narrow, you may prefer to take notes on separate paper. (Note taking is discussed in the next section.)

You know what underlining and highlighting are, and in fact, you probably use them to mark your textbooks. But are you as skillful at them as you could be? If you're like most college students, you *overmark* your books. There are two likely reasons for this. First, you're trying to mark the book *as you read it.* (Set your pen, pencil, or highlighter down until *after* you've read a paragraph or section. Then, once you've determined what's important, you can pick up a marker.) Second, you may be marking the details. (You may recall in Chapter 4, Identify the Stated Main Idea Sentence and the Supporting Details of a Paragraph, the suggestion to *number* the supporting details or *list* them on separate paper. *Never underline or highlight details*—if you do, you'll mark everything, and that's of no help at all.) Overmarking actually makes it harder for you when it is time to review for a test: Everything is marked, the wrong things are marked, and the pages look confusing. The whole point of marking texts is to make the important information easy to locate when it's time to go back and review for a test.

By the way, don't make the mistake of believing that just because you've underlined lots of sentences and spattered highlighter on the pages that you've understood what you read. Making lots of marks isn't a substitute for reading the material carefully and thinking about it.

Read, think, and then *follow these guidelines* for marking and annotating your textbooks. You will have to experiment to see which techniques or combination of techniques works best for you.

Marking Textbooks

- Underline or highlight stated main idea sentences and important definitions. (Often, an important definition *is* the stated main idea of a paragraph.)

- Box or circle important terms. (Remember the earlier pointer: on tests, expect to be asked the definition of important terms.)

- Place a number beside each supporting detail in a paragraph and beside each item in an unnumbered list.

Annotating Textbooks

- Write the topics beside the paragraphs.

- Formulate implied main ideas and write them in the margin.

- Write out important definitions in your own words or write *def* in the margin beside a paragraph that contains a definition.

- Place a question mark beside information you do not understand. That way, you can identify information you need to get clarification on before the next test.

- Use an asterisk (*) to signal important overall main ideas, summary statements, and conclusions. (Save these for the very most important points.)

- Write *ex* beside examples if they are critical to your understanding the material or if you think you may be asked to give examples on a test.

- If a textbook chapter has headings and subheadings in different sizes or colors to show the relationships among the topics (such as this text, for example), you can pencil in Roman numerals, letters, or numbers beside them, creating your own outline right in the book. (Outlining is explained in the next section.)

Now read this excerpt on the economic success of Asian Americans. It comes from a sociology textbook. Notice what has been marked, and then look at the annotations. Notice that in the first paragraph the main idea can be formulated by combining two sentences that each give half of the main idea. For that reason, the halves have been underlined and linked together.

Economically, Asian Americans are doing well. The median Asian American family income is more than $18,000 above the median for Hispanics and $20,000 above that for blacks. (The *median* is the middle value in a distribution, above and below which lie an equal number of values.) The Asian figure is bolstered by having a number of family members working in the household. However, high average incomes mask substantial populations of the poor. As of 1998 some 14 percent of Asians were below the poverty line as compared to 13 percent of the overall population. Asian income differences reflect ethnic backgrounds, with Japanese Americans having the highest incomes and more recent immigrant Cambodians, Laotians, and Vietnamese the lowest. Asian American minority status is expected by some to erode and disappear in a couple of generations.

The relative economic success of Asian Americans can be linked to their success in using all family resources. For some, these resources include ①strong educational backgrounds, ②strong family systems, and ③family investment funds. ④Family support networks allow members to draw on capital from a household with several workers. ⑤The pooling of wages provides funds for investment or education. ⑥For poor newcomers lacking these resources (and often not speaking English), the metropolitan ethnic enclave economy provides at least entry-level jobs.

Ironically, doing well sometimes creates social problems. The open hostility directed against Asian immigrants during the first half of the twentieth century has sometimes been replaced with ①more subtle manifestations of prejudice. Being a so-called "model minority" has a price. Asian Americans ②may encounter a glass ceiling because they are seen as a "super minority." ③The hard work and success of Asian immigrants sometimes results in others who are less successful viewing the newcomers as unfair competitors.

Source: Adapted from J. John Palen, *Social Problems for the Twenty-First Century,* pp. 103–04. Copyright © 2000 McGraw-Hill. Reprinted by permission of The McGraw-Hill Companies.

Notice how much easier it would be to learn this material for a test from a text marked and annotated in this way. Also, the student can use the question marks to quickly identify the two things that need clarification ("enclave" and "glass ceiling").

TAKING NOTES FROM TEXTBOOKS BY OUTLINING AND MAPPING

There are many different note-taking formats. (*Formats* are ways to organize the information on the page.) Perhaps the best-known and most widely advocated note-taking system is the Cornell method (which, incidentally, was named for Cornell University). The reason this method and variations of it are so popular is because the format includes a built-in review column. Although note taking from a lecture is not our focus here, the Cornell note-taking system can be used just as effectively in the classroom. Taking notes in class helps you concentrate; taking notes from your texts helps you comprehend the material and prepare effectively for class and for tests.

To create the review column, simply rule off a 2″ to 3″–wide review column on the left side of clean notebook paper pages. Leave the column blank while you are taking notes from the text (or lecture). On the main part of the page, take your notes in an organized manner by using either a formal or an informal outline. When you have finished taking notes, go back and fill in the review column. Write either a question or a clue word or phrase beside each major section in your notes. When you are ready to review for a test, cover the main body of the notes and look at each question or clue word. Read each question or clue word and use it to trigger your recall of the corresponding information. If you cannot answer the question or say the information *out loud, without looking at the material,* uncover it and read it. Then cover it up and say it aloud *without looking.* After rehearsing the information this way, you will eventually be able to say the material from memory simply by looking at the questions or clue words. *Until you can say it without looking, you don't know it.*

When you use this technique, you help yourself several ways. First, you incorporate reading, writing, reciting, and hearing into your learning. Combined, they are more powerful than any single one by itself. Second, you cannot remember material without rehearsing it (saying it or writing it). Finally, using the Cornell format to record the information followed by oral recitation from the recall column allows you to test yourself on the material *before* you take the actual test. If you are trying to answer a question aloud and no sound is coming out of your mouth, that's a major tip-off that you need to continue working on the material. (*Coach's observation:* The time to discover that you don't know the material is *before* you take the test—not while you're actually taking it.) After an explanation of outlining, I'll show you an outline of the excerpt on Asian-Americans' economic success in Cornell format.

OUTLINING

Outlining *is a formal way of organizing main ideas and supporting details to show the relationships among them.* Outlining can be especially beneficial when you are dealing with complex material, when you want to condense material to get an overview of the parts, or when you are dealing with material that isn't well organized to begin with. (Unfortunately, not all textbooks are equally well written.) When taking a test that includes essay questions, you should take a minute to make a quick outline of the points (and perhaps examples) you want to include in your answer. You will write a more logical, coherent, and complete answer—and receive more points as a result. When teachers assign you a paper to write, they will often require you to turn in an outline. (Sometimes they ask you to turn in a preliminary outline to make sure you know where you are going and to see that you are headed in the right direction before you start writing.)

The terrific advantage of outlines is that they reveal at a glance the relative importance of each part of the material: The most important points are aligned to the left, with the less important material listed beneath the more important points and indented to the right. The farther to the right a set of points is indented, the less important the information is. Items that are indented the same amount are of equal importance.

Outlines can be formal or informal. *Formal outlines* use a strict system of Roman numerals, upper- and lowercase letters, and Arabic numbers (the type of numbers you see and write every day). *Informal outlines* typically use Arabic numbers; details listed beneath the main points may be set off with simple dashes or alphabet letters. Regardless of the type of outline, however, indentation is important, and points (details) are listed on separate lines beneath the main point they support. With both types of outline, you should give the outline the same title as the material you are outlining: do not title your outline "Outline." (It is unnecessary because it will be obvious that it is an outline. It's like naming your dog "Dog.") Regardless of the type of outline, you can paraphrase the material (put it in your own words) or use the wording from the text.

Let's look at formal outlines. These can be either *sentence outlines* or *topic outlines,* but sentence outlines are more valuable as study tools. When you outline a paragraph, the main idea is the most important point, of course, so it is written beside Roman numeral "I" (one) and placed against the left margin. (If a paragraph has a stated main idea, use it. Otherwise, you will have to formulate the main idea.) Details are indented *on separate lines* beneath the main point they support. Each detail is designated by a letter, and there will be as many of them as there are details. If there are minor details that support a major detail, they are indented beneath it. To make the levels of outlines clear, alternate using numbers and letters.

When an item is longer than one line in length and must be continued on the line below it, align it with the *first letter of the first word above it.* (See the example that follows.) If you go all the way back to the left margin, the levels of indentation will be obscured. A correct outline of a paragraph with five supporting details would look like this:

I.   Main idea sentence; if the sentence is more than one line long, indent the "spillover" and align it with the first letter of the first word on the line above.

   A.   Supporting detail 1; if the sentence is more than one line long, indent the "spillover" and align it with the first letter of the first word on the line above.

   B.   Supporting detail 2

   C.   Supporting detail 3

   D.   Supporting detail 4

   E.   Supporting detail 5

Note the examples of how long "sentences" (beside Roman numeral I and A) are carried over and indented on the next line.

For multiparagraph selections, the process is repeated paragraph by paragraph, like this:

I. First main idea sentence

   A. Major supporting detail

      1.   Minor supporting detail

      2.   Minor supporting detail

      3.   Minor supporting detail

   B. Major supporting detail

   C. Major supporting detail

II. Second main idea sentence

   A. Major supporting detail

   B. Major supporting detail

      1.   Minor supporting detail

      2.   Minor supporting detail

   C. Major supporting detail

   D. Major supporting detail

III. Third main idea sentence

   A. Major supporting detail

   B. Major supporting detail

Notice that in the outline above, some of the major (primary) details are supported by minor (secondary) details. Those minor details are written on separate lines and indented even farther to the right than the major details. Because it is a sentence outline, each detail—major or minor—is also written as a sentence. There will be as many Roman numerals as there are paragraphs (main ideas). The number of letters beneath each Roman numeral will depend on the number of details in the particular paragraph.

Here's the outline of the excerpt on Asian-Americans' economic success. I've placed the outline in a set of notes taken in the Cornell note-taking format. To show you where the information came from in the selection, I've used many of the exact words that appear in the selection, although some of the information has been paraphrased and condensed. Notice that the Review Column (on the left) has been filled in with questions and that they contain several abbreviations. Notice also that under Roman numeral II the minor details are set off with numbers rather than letters and they are indented farther to the right than the major details.

Review Column ↓	Notes Outlined from the Text ↓
	Asian-Americans' Economic Success
Current econ status?	I. Economically, Asian Americans are doing well; however, high average incomes mask the substantial populations of poor Asians.
◯ —compared w/other groups?	A. The median Asian American family income is well above that of both Hispanics and blacks.
	B. Incomes are high because of the number of family members working in the household.
	C. The number of Asians who are below the poverty line (14 percent) is roughly the same as for the overall population.
—diffs w/in Asian group itself?	D. Asian income differences reflect ethnic backgrounds, with Japanese Americans having the highest incomes and more recent immigrant groups the lowest.
	E. Asian-American minority status is expected by some to erode and disappear in a couple of generations.
Reasons for econ success?	II. The relative economic success of Asian Americans can be linked to their success in using all family resources.
	A. They have strong educational backgrounds.
	B. They have strong family systems.
◯	C. They have strong family investment funds.
	D. Family support networks allow members to draw on capital from a household with several workers.
	E. They pool their wages.
	1. This provides funds for investment.
	2. This provides funds for education.
	F. For poor newcomers lacking these resources (and often not speaking English), the metropolitan ethnic enclave economy provides at least entry-level jobs.
Problems created by their success?	III. Doing well sometimes creates social problems for Asians.
	A. There are subtle manifestations of prejudice against the so-called "model minority."
	B. Asian Americans may encounter a "glass ceiling" because they are seen as a "super minority."
◯	C. Less successful nonimmigrants may view Asian newcomers as unfair competitors.

MAPPING

Some students prefer mapping to outlining. In particular, those who are more "right-brained" (artistic, intuitive, creative) may find it easier to visualize and remember the information when it's captured on the page in boxes or circles that are linked together in a meaningful way. That's what **mapping** is: *organizing main ideas and details in an informal way by using boxes, circles, lines, arrows, and so on, to show relationships.* As with outlining, mapping must be done on notebook paper because it requires more space than textbook margins provide. Flowcharts, which you learned about in Chapter 13, are one type of map.

Study maps can be simple or complex; it depends on the nature of the material. The simplest ones consist of a main idea set off in the center of a page with the details radiating out from it like spokes of a bicycle wheel. There is no one correct way to create a map, however. This is an advantage because it allows you to construct each map in the way that is most personally meaningful to you.

Colin Rose and Malcolm Nicholl, authors of a wonderful book entitled *Accelerated Learning for the 21st Century* (New York: Dell, 1997), refer to these maps as "learning maps" or "visual note taking." Here is my version of some of their suggestions for creating effective maps, along with some suggestions of my own.

- Start with the topic in the center of the page. You can put it inside any shape you like. (It doesn't have to be a circle or a box. Depending on the subject matter, you might draw it in the shape of a fish, an egg, or a lightbulb.)

- Use key words (mainly key nouns and verbs) that will sufficiently jog your memory so that you can recite the rest of the information when you review.

- Work outward—radiate in all directions from the main topic in the center of the page, but use no more than seven branches.

- Use symbols, pictures, and other images in your map. You're not limited to using just words.

- Vary the word size, but write key words and phrases in bold capital letters.

- Keep words to a minimum. Use easily identifiable and meaningful symbols, such as exclamation points, question marks, hearts, stick figures, check marks, and so forth. You don't have to be an artist.

- Leave plenty of white space between the words and images so that they stand out. Clutter is confusing.

- Use color. The more vivid the better. You can also put related items in the same color.

- Practice and be patient. Don't be frustrated if you don't get it right the first time. Redrawing your learning map actually helps you remember the material more clearly. It helps transfer the information into long-term memory.

The illustration at the top of the next page shows a learning map of the type recommended in *Accelerated Learning for the 21st Century.* Its topic? How to make a learning map! The map on the bottom half of the page is for the example passage on Asian-Americans' economic success. (A hand-drawn map would be in full color and take lots more space, of course.)

START IN THE CENTER
(TOPIC)

"BRANCH OUT" using only
KEY WORDS or PHRASES

LINK IDEAS THAT
ARE RELATED

THESE HELP:

➡ ☆ ✓ SYMBOLS

CAPITAL LETTERS

🕷 🖱 ✍ PICTURES

COLOR

LOTS OF WHITE S P A C E

Creating a
STUDY MAP

• FILL IN MISSING
INFORMATION

• MAKE REVISIONS
AND CORRECTIONS

• REDRAW THE MAP
IF IT LOOKS MESSY

• REDRAWING ALSO
AIDS RECALL

Here is a study map of the selection on Asian-Americans' economic success:

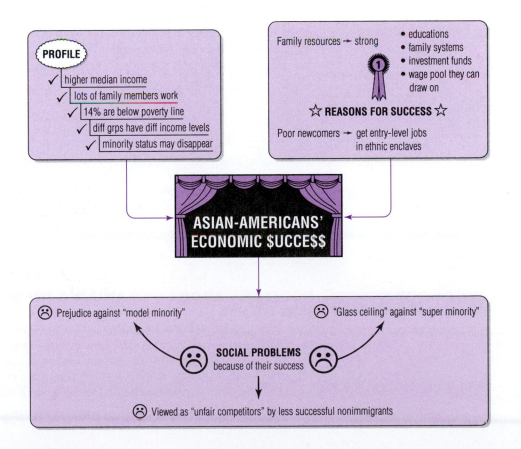

PROFILE

✓ higher median income
✓ lots of family members work
✓ 14% are below poverty line
✓ diff grps have diff income levels
✓ minority status may disappear

Family resources → strong
• educations
• family systems
• investment funds
• wage pool they can
draw on

☆ **REASONS FOR SUCCESS** ☆

Poor newcomers → get entry-level jobs
in ethnic enclaves

**ASIAN-AMERICANS'
ECONOMIC $UCCE$$**

☹ Prejudice against "model minority"   ☹ "Glass ceiling" against "super minority"

☹ **SOCIAL PROBLEMS** ☹
because of their success

☹ Viewed as "unfair competitors" by less successful nonimmigrants

SUMMARIZING

Summarizing is another useful type of textbook note-taking skill. A *summary is a condensation of all the main ideas an author has presented in a longer selection.* The longer selection might be a textbook chapter or section, a newspaper or magazine article, or an editorial.

Because a summary captures only the most important information, it is an excellent way to prepare for essay tests. Some students like to write a summary at the end of each section of the notes they take in the Cornell format, regardless of whether they are taking notes from a textbook or lecture notes. It's an extremely reinforcing way to rehearse and learn material. It makes you be specific and also pay attention to the spelling of important words and names, dates, terms, and so forth. (The time to discover that you don't know how to *spell* an important word or name is not while you are taking a test. Misspellings make a poor impression on your professor, the person who is grading the test.)

To write a summary, follow this game plan:

■ Use the title of the section or the title of the *original material* as the title of your summary. Don't title it "Summary." That isn't helpful to you or to anyone else who may read your summary.

■ Present all the main ideas (regardless of whether they were stated or implied) in the *same order* the author did. (If there is an introductory paragraph that is simply an "attention-getter" that contains no important information, you should leave it out.)

■ Do not include a detail unless it is impossible to understand the material without it (such as a detail that gives the meaning of a key term).

■ Don't add your own opinions or any information from other sources.

■ Paraphrase the information and add transition words and phrases to make the meaning clear and the flow of ideas smooth.

Here's some good news: If you have made an outline of a selection or excerpt, you have already identified the information (the main ideas) you need for a summary. Here is a summary of the excerpt on Asian Americans we have been using to illustrate the study tools. Notice that it is comprised of the main ideas from the outline and notice how brief it is in comparison to the original excerpt.

Asian-Americans' Economic Success

Economically, Asian Americans are doing well, yet there are still many Asians who are poor. A wide range of family resources and ethnic enclave support are keys to their economic success. However, their very success has caused some social problems for them.

THE EDGE

POINTERS ABOUT ORGANIZING INFORMATION FOR STUDY

■ **Experiment with various study techniques and tools.**
You need to find what works for you. If you're not sure whether outlines or study maps would be more helpful to you, put a study map on the back of a left-hand page in your notebook. On the front of the right-hand page, make

an outline of the same material. When you go back later to study the material, notice which one your eyes go to first. That's probably the one your brain prefers. Be sure that you give yourself ample time and opportunity to experiment. You will get better with every map, outline, and summary. Research tells us that there is as much value in *making* the study aid as there is in having the finished product to use for test review.

■ **Developing study skills takes time and practice.**
Remember that no one is born knowing these skills. They come with practice, and even skilled students have to spend some time creating these study aids. It may go slowly while you are learning the techniques, but don't let that discourage you. Keep in mind that when the first Indianapolis 500 race was held in 1911, the average speed was 74.59 mph. (No, you didn't misread that. It was just *under* 75 mph.) The point is, things will get better and go faster as you make progress. Practice, practice, practice.

■ **To polish your skills, team up with a classmate.**
Find a classmate who is serious about learning the study skills presented in this chapter. You can work together on taking notes and making summaries or outlines. Discuss and decide together what you think should be included and then write it down. Or, you can each make your notes, summary, or outline independently, and then get together to compare what you each wrote. Did you both include the same things? If not, discuss the reasons each of you included what you did and how you each organized the material.

In your other classes (sociology, history, etc.), find someone who already seems to be good at these study skills. Ask them if you can compare your notes, summaries, and outlines with theirs. Ask your instructor to look at your notes and make suggestions for improving them. If your college or university has a learning skills center or tutoring center, take your textbook and your notes and have a tutor evaluate them and make suggestions.

■ **In courses that are difficult for you, form a study group with other students.**
If you enroll in a course that is difficult for you, find three or four classmates who are willing to form a study group. (This is obvious, but I'll say it anyway: pick serious, motivated students for your study group. Don't waste time with those who just want to get together socially and chat.) Plan to meet with your study group members outside of class once or twice a week. Use the time to go over the chapters and homework assignments. (One of the benefits of a study group is that you are saying the material out loud as well as hearing it. Involving several senses makes for stronger learning.) Compare your class notes to see if there was anything important you failed to write down. Seek clarification on any material that confuses you. Get together for review sessions before each test. Research shows that adult students learn well from each other. Participating in a study group can be not only a great source of academic support, but also a valuable source of moral and emotional support.

■ **Understand the way each study aid handles main ideas and details.**
The following chart shows the format for organizing main ideas and supporting details using the various study aids. You can see that determining main ideas and locating details are at the heart of all these techniques.

Study Aid	What Is Done with Main Ideas	What Is Done with Supporting Details
Marking and annotating	• Underline stated main ideas. • Jot formulated main ideas in margins beside paragraphs.	• Write a small number in the paragraph beside each detail. —*or*— • List details in shortened form in the margin beside a paragraph.
Outline (formal)	• Write each main idea *in order* beside a Roman numeral. Write these next to the left margin. (For an informal outline, use Arabic numbers.)	• Indent and write them *in order* on separate lines beneath the main idea they support. • Write a capital letter beside each major detail. (For informal outlines, use numbers, asterisks, letters, etc., to set off each detail.)
Map (of main ideas and major details)	• Place the main idea in the middle of the page inside a box or circle or some other shape. (To make a topic and main idea map, place the topic in the box and branch the main ideas off it.)	• Write details on lines radiating out from the main idea box or in boxes connected to it. • If you include minor details, branch them off the major detail they support. (*Note:* Including these can sometimes make a map too cluttered.)
Note taking (Cornell format)	• Write main ideas in the central portion of the page, next to the line that separates them from the review column on the left side of the page.	• Indent details on separate lines beneath the main idea they support. • Put a number, bullet, or dash in front of each detail to set it off.
Summary	• Using your own words, write a paragraph that presents the main ideas in the same order as they appear in the original selection. • Use transition words and phrases as needed for clarity and flow of ideas.	(Summaries generally contain no details. A detail may be included, however, if it is essential for understanding a main idea.)

■ **Review cards are a variation on note taking that many students find helpful.**

Review cards are a study tool created by writing questions and answers on index cards as a way of selecting, organizing, and reviewing the most important information in a textbook chapter. They provide a way of giving yourself a private test before the instructor gives you the actual one. The cards reveal what you know and what you still need to learn. When you master the information on them, you will feel more confident and relaxed at test time, and you will make a higher grade.

Here are the steps for making review cards.

1. On the *front* of an index card, write a question. Use questions you create from the section headings in a chapter, questions included in the chapter, questions from your instructor, or a combination of these. You can also write things such as "List three ways . . . " or "Describe how . . . ", or "Explain the steps in. . . ."

2. On the *back* of the card, write the answer to the question or write the information called for. Write the answers in words that are the same or similar to those you are likely to see or use on a test. The purpose of these cards, however, is to help you learn, so include a sketch or a memory peg if you like.

3. After you have made your review cards, turn through the stack, one card at a time. Answer each question aloud. Then turn the card over to see if you answered it completely and correctly.

4. When you can consistently answer a question correctly, remove the card from the stack.

5. For questions you stumble on or cannot answer, turn the card over, and read the correct answer aloud. Then say it aloud from memory. Keep those cards in the stack until you master the information on them.

Each time you work through the stack, you will learn more of the information on the cards. You can review the cards whenever you have a few free minutes. You can review them by yourself, with a partner, or with members of a study group.

Here is an example of what the front and back of a review card looks like:

Front

What are the six basic emotions?

Back

1. joy
2. surprise
3. fear   F
4. anger   A
5. disgust   D
6. sadness   S

Memory peg: <u>Joy</u> was <u>surprised</u> by <u>fads</u>.

Notice that in the example review card, the student has included two memory pegs: the word "fads," an acronym to recall four of the emotions, along with a sentence that provides a way to remember them and the other two emotions.

THE REPLAY

REMEMBER THE ESSENTIAL INFORMATION FROM THE CHAPTER

Review the first section of this chapter, and then describe each of these techniques that can be used to organize the information you need to study and learn.

Marking Textbooks

_____

_____

_____

_____

Annotating Textbooks

_____

_____

_____

_____

Note taking from texts

_____

_____

_____

_____

_____

Outlining

_____

_____

_____

_____

Mapping

_____

_____

_____

_____

_____

Summarizing

_____

_____

_____

_____

THE PRACTICE

APPLY THE SKILL OF ORGANIZING INFORMATION FOR STUDY

In Sets 1 and 2, the excerpts are only a few paragraphs long. In real life, your textbook assignments would be much longer, so the excerpt in Set 3 is lengthier. Because there are several skills to apply in each set, your instructor may assign you only certain ones or only a few at a time. With thought, patience, and practice, you will become better and better at these study skills. Give yourself a block of uninterrupted time when you do these exercises. If you need to take some notes on scratch paper first, that's fine. No one can turn out a perfect version on the initial attempt.

SET 1

Exercises: Organizing Information for Study

First read the excerpt, and then follow your instructor's directions as to which study skills to apply. You may be asked to *underline* and *annotate* it, to make an *outline* or a *map*, to take *notes* in Cornell format, to write a *summary*, or some combination of these.

This excerpt is from a "strategies for success in college and life" textbook and it contains useful information. Notice that the author has used bullets to make the main points stand out. (Take advantage of any help that authors give you!) The excerpt focuses on strategies that can help you make a decision when you just can't seem to make up your mind on an important matter. Relax and refocus yourself before beginning—you know what to do!

Exercise 1: Underlining and Annotating

After you have read the selection, go through it again. Underline the stated main ideas. (One reason I chose this selection is because every paragraph has a stated main idea.) Mark any other important information. In the left margin, jot key words for each paragraph. There is no single "correct" way to mark the selection. At this stage, the goal is to identify the most important information and to avoid overmarking.

CHOOSING AMONG ALTERNATIVES

What if you still can't make up your mind on an important matter? Try these strategies:

- **Give the decision time.** Sometimes waiting helps. Time can be an ally by giving you a chance to think of additional alternatives. Sometimes the situation will change, or you'll have a change in viewpoint.

- **Make a mental movie, acting out the various alternatives.** Many of us have difficulty seeing ourselves in the future and envisioning how various options would play out. One way to get around this difficulty is to cast yourself into a series of "mental movies" that have different endings depending on the decision you make. Working through the different scripts in your head makes potential outcomes far more real and less abstract than they would be if you simply left them as items on a list of various options.

- **Toss a coin.** This isn't always as crazy as it sounds. If each alternative seems equally positive or negative to you, pull out a coin—make option A "heads" and B "tails." Then flip it.

 The real power of the coin-toss strategy is that it might help you discover your true feelings. It may happen while the coin is in the air, or it may be that when you see the result of the coin toss, you won't like the outcome and will say to yourself, "No way." In such a case, you've just found out how you really feel.

■ **Learn to view indecision as a decision.** Sometimes we spend so much time making a decision that our indecision becomes a decision. It works like this: Suppose a friend asks you to help her work on a student government task force that is studying the use of alcohol on campus. You'd like to participate, but, because you'll have to commit to a term-long series of meetings, you're worried about the expenditure of time it will take.

Because the first meeting isn't going to occur for a few weeks, you have some time to make up your mind. But you just can't seem to decide, even though you think about the pros and cons every once in a while. Finally, it's the day of the meeting, and you still don't know what to do.

The truth is, you've made the decision: You don't really want to be on the committee. Your indecision is telling you that—bottom line—you don't have sufficient interest to make the commitment. In some cases, then, viewing your own behavior gives you the response to your question.

■ **Go with your gut feeling.** Call it what you like—gut feeling, intuition, superstition—but sometimes we need to go with our hearts and not our minds. If you've thought rationally about a decision and have been unable to determine the best course of action but have a gut feeling that one choice is better than another, then follow your feelings.

Following a gut feeling does not mean that you don't need to consider the pros and cons of a decision rationally and carefully. In fact, generally our "intuitions" are best when informed by the thoughtfulness of a more rational process.

Source: Adapted from Robert Feldman, *P.O.W.E.R. Learning,* pp. 288–91. Copyright © 2005 McGraw-Hill. Reprinted by permission of The McGraw-Hill Companies.

Exercise 2: Outline

On notebook paper, prepare a formal outline of the main ideas in the selection. Give your outline the same title as the selection itself. You can use the main ideas exactly as they are in the selection or you can write them in your own words. Pay special attention to the format (Roman numerals, indentation, etc.). If you like, use the following space to write a draft of your outline.

_____

_____

_____

_____

_____

_____

_____

_____

_____

_____

_____

_____

_____

_____

_____

_____

_____

_____

Exercise 3: Map

On notebook paper, create a study map for the selection. The overall main idea for the selection can be formulated as *When you are having trouble making up your mind, there are several techniques you can use to help you choose among alternatives.* Write this in a box in the center of the page, and then branch the main ideas out from it on separate lines. If you like, use the following space to make a draft of your map.

Exercise 4: Note Taking in Cornell Format

On notebook paper rule off a 2" to 3"–wide review column on the left side of the page. Fill in the central portion of the page with your notes, and then beside each main point, write a key word or phrase in the review column. If you like, use the following space to plan your notes.

Exercise 5: Summary

On notebook paper, write a one-paragraph summary of the selection. Give your summary the same title as the original selection. Include only main ideas in your summary and keep them in the same order that appear in the selection. Use your own words, and add transitional words and phrases as needed to make the flow of ideas clear and smooth. If you like, use the following lines to write a draft of your summary.

_____

_____

_____

_____

_____

_____

_____

_____

_____

_____

_____

_____

_____

_____

SET 2

Exercises: Organizing Information for Study

Read the excerpt, and then follow your instructor's directions as to which study skills to apply. You may be asked to *underline* and *annotate* the excerpt, to make an *outline* or a *map*, to take *notes*, or to write a *summary*. The topic of this excerpt, which comes from a book on marriage and family life, is "myths about singles." You'll find it quite interesting. Even if you are married, you undoubtedly have many friends who are single. Once again, the authors have given you a head start by using numbers to make the organization very clear. Before you begin an exercise, be sure that you have allowed enough time to complete it without interruption.

Take a few deep breaths, stretch your hands high over your head, and relax the muscles in your face, neck, and shoulders. Once you're focused, start in.

Exercise 1: Underlining and Annotating

Read the entire selection first, and then go back through it paragraph by paragraph. Underline the stated main ideas. (Other than the first paragraph, all the paragraphs in this selection have stated main ideas.) Mark any other important information. (Notice that this selection presents myths—incorrect stereotypes—about singles, and then presents accurate information.) In the margin, jot key words for each paragraph. There is no single "correct" way to mark the selection. At this stage, the goal is still to identify the most important information and to avoid overmarking. Remember not to underline details, the major cause of overmarking.

MYTHS ABOUT SINGLES

Who are the people who are single? The unmarried category includes the divorced, the widowed, and the never-married. There is a popular stereotype of the never-married as being either "swingers—the beautiful people who are constantly going to parties, who have uncommitted lives and a lot of uncommitted sex—or "lonely losers," who are depressed a good deal of the time. But most singles fall into neither of those categories. Like other groups who have been subjected to something of a social stigma, singles have had to battle stereotypes and myths. Cargan and Melko (1982) surveyed four hundred people in Dayton, Ohio, including some married, never-married, divorced, and remarried individuals. They used their data to counter seven myths about the never-married:

1. *They are still tied to their mothers' apron strings.* In fact, the researchers found little difference between the never-married and others in their perceptions of parents and other relatives.

2. *They are selfish.* Some people believe that singles do not get married simply because they are too centered on themselves, leading lives of self-indulgence and pursuing self-interests. But Cargan and Melko found that they value friends more highly than do the married and contribute more to community service.

3. *They are financially well-off.* The married people in the researchers' sample were better off economically than the never-married. Indeed, in the society as a whole, married people are likely to be better off than singles. There are a sufficient number of affluent, single professionals to lend credibility to the myth. But when compared to families, a far greater proportion of singles are in poverty.

4. *They are happier.* This is a myth held by singles themselves, many of whom tend to think that they are happier than married people. Married people think otherwise. The evidence suggests that marrieds have an advantage in the area of well-being.

5. *There are more singles now than ever.* There are far more singles than there were in 1970. But the proportion in 1987 was not as high as it was in the first four decades of the century.

6. *Being and staying single is an acceptable way of life.* This is another myth of singles themselves, who like to assert it but don't practice it for the most part. Most singles plan on getting married at some point. In the Cargan and Melko study, most believed that they would be married within about five years.

7. *Something is wrong with those who never marry.* Evidence also belies this myth. An individual who postpones or even decides against marriage is not suffering from some disorder. Singles have greater problems with loneliness and with maintaining their happiness. But there are advantages as well as disadvantages to their status, and they may decide that the former outweigh the latter.

Source: Adapted from Robert Lauer and Jeanette Lauer, *Marriage and Family,* 4th ed., pp. 198, 200, 201. Copyright © 2000 McGraw-Hill. Reprinted by permission of The McGraw-Hill Companies.

Exercise 2: Outline

On notebook paper, prepare an informal study outline of the main ideas and details in the selection. Give your outline the same title as the selection itself. You can put the information in your own words. You don't need to use Roman numerals, but you should still make the main points stand out and indent each detail on a separate line beneath the main idea it supports. For each myth, be sure to give the accurate information that counters it. If you like, use the following space to plan your outline.

_____

_____

_____

_____

_____

_____

_____

_____

_____

_____

_____

_____

_____

_____

_____

_____

_____

_____

_____

_____

_____

_____

_____

_____

Exercise 3: Map

On notebook paper, create a study map for the selection. Remember to use color and include symbols and pictures. The authors use the opening paragraph to present their overall main idea. (*Coach's tip:* You must formulate it.) Include it in a box in the center of the page, and then link the main ideas to the center box. If you like, you can use the following space to plan your map.

Exercise 4: Note Taking in Cornell Format

On notebook paper, rule off a 2" to 3"–wide review column on the left side of the page. Fill in the central portion of the page with your notes and then, beside each main point, write a key word or phrase in the review column. If you like, use the following space to plan your outline.

Exercise 5: Summary

On notebook paper, write a one-paragraph summary of the selection. Give your summary the same title as the original selection. Include only main ideas in your summary and keep them in the same order that appear in the selection. Use your own words, and add numbers and transitional words and phrases as needed to make the flow of ideas clear and smooth. If you like, you can use the following space to write a rough draft of your summary.

_____

_____

_____

_____

_____

SET 3

Exercises: Organizing Information for Study

Because this selection is longer, your instructor may direct you to mark and annotate only certain sections of it. Also, you may be directed to outline a particular section in detail rather than to outline the entire selection. If you are directed to outline the whole selection, it will probably be a main idea outline that excludes the details.

In this selection you will encounter the acronym BAC, which stands for blood alcohol concentration. BAC, the percentage of alcohol in a measured quantity of blood, indicates a person's degree of intoxication. It can be determined directly, through analysis of a blood sample, or indirectly, through analysis of exhaled air ("breathalyzer" test).

Exercise 1: Marked and Annotated Text

ALCOHOL-RELATED SOCIAL PROBLEMS

Alcohol abuse is related to a variety of social problems. These problems affect the quality of interpersonal relationships, employment stability, and the financial security of both the individual and family. Clearly, alcohol's negative social consequences damage our quality of life. In financial terms the annual cost of alcohol abuse and dependence has been estimated at $185 billion.

Accidents

The four leading causes of accidental death in the United States (motor vehicle collisions, falls, drownings, and fires and burns) have significant statistical connections to alcohol use.

Motor Vehicle Collisions

Data from the National Highway Traffic Safety Administration (NHTSA) indicate that in 2001 more than 17,000 alcohol-related vehicular crash deaths occurred. This figure represented 41% of all the total traffic fatalities for 2001. Although seventeen thousand remains an unacceptably high figure, this total represented a 13% reduction from the 20,000 alcohol-related fatalities reported in 1991.

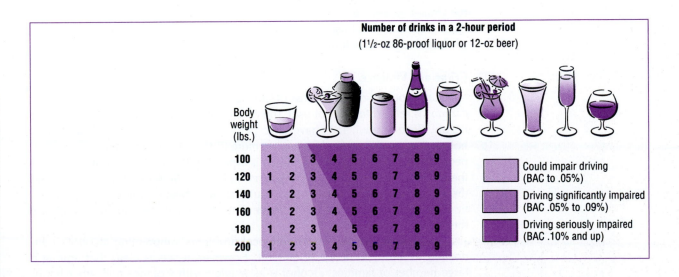

Number of drinks in a 2-hour period
(1½-oz 86-proof liquor or 12-oz beer)

Body weight (lbs.)									
100	1	2	3	4	5	6	7	8	9
120	1	2	3	4	5	6	7	8	9
140	1	2	3	4	5	6	7	8	9
160	1	2	3	4	5	6	7	8	9
180	1	2	3	4	5	6	7	8	9
200	1	2	3	4	5	6	7	8	9

Could impair driving (BAC to .05%)

Driving significantly impaired (BAC .05% to .09%)

Driving seriously impaired (BAC .10% and up)

Presently in the United States, an alcohol-related car crash fatality occurs every 30 minute. Every 2 minutes, an alcohol-related car crash injury happens. More than 275,000 people were injured in such crashes in 2001. In 2000, the NHTSA reported that approximately 1.5 million drivers were arrested for drunk driving, reflecting an arrest rate of 1 for every 130 licensed drivers in the United States.

One response to drunk driving has been for all states to raise the legal drinking age to 21 years. This was accomplished in the mid-1980s. In October 2000, President Bill Clinton signed into law a federal bill that requires all states to lower the legal BAC to .08% by the year 2003 or risk losing federal highway funds. Has your state enacted this .08% BAC limit? You can search the MADD (Mothers Against Drunk Driving) website at www.madd.org to find out current .08% BAC law information.

Other programs and policies are being implemented that are designed to prevent intoxicated people from driving. Many states have enacted zero tolerance laws to help prevent underage drinking and driving. Also included have been efforts to educate bartenders to recognize intoxicated customers, to use off-duty police officers as observers in bars, to place police roadblocks, and to develop mechanical devices that prevent intoxicated drivers from starting their cars, and to encourage people to establish designated drivers.

Falls

Many people are surprised to learn that falls are the second leading cause of accidental death in the United States. Alcohol use increases the risk for falls. Various studies suggest that alcohol is involved in between 21% and 77% of deadly falls and 18% to 53% percent of nonfatal falls.

Drownings

Drownings are the third leading cause of accidental death in the United States. Studies have shown that alcohol use is implicated in 21% to 47% of these deaths. More than one-third of boaters have been found to drink alcohol while boating.

Fires and Burns

Fires and burns are responsible for an estimated 5,000 deaths each year in the United States, the fourth leading cause of accidental death. This cause is also connected to alcohol use: Studies indicate that nearly half of burn victims have BACs above the legal limit.

Crime and Violence

Have you noticed that most of the violent behavior and vandalism on your campus is related to alcohol use? The connection of alcohol to crime has a long history. Prison populations have large percentages of alcohol abusers and alcoholics. People who commit crimes are more likely to have alcohol problems than people in the general population. This is especially true for young criminals. Furthermore, alcohol use has been reported in 53% to 66% of all homicides, with the victim, the perpetrator, or both found to have been drinking. In rape situations, rapists are intoxicated 50% of the time and victims are intoxicated 30% of the time.

Because of research methodological problems, pinpointing alcohol's connection to family violence is difficult. However, it seems clear that among a large number of families, alcohol is associated with violence and other harmful behavior, including physical abuse, child abuse, psychological abuse, and abandonment.

The difficult question that arises when discussing the relationship between alcohol use and violence is whether a cause-effect link can be proved. Obviously, not everyone who drinks becomes violent, but in many violent crimes at least one person involved has been drinking. The answer is perhaps that alcohol by itself is not enough to cause violence, but use of alcohol may be one of several factors that act in combination to cause violent behavior in some instances.

Suicide

Alcohol use has been related to large percentages of suicides. Alcoholism plays a large role in 30% of completed suicides. In addition, alcohol use is associated with impulsive suicides rather than with premeditated ones. Drinking is also connected with more violent and lethal means of suicide, such as the use of firearms.

For many of these social problems, alcohol use impairs critical judgment and allows a person's behavior to quickly become reckless, antisocial, and deadly.

Source: Wayne Payne, Dale Hahn, and Ellen Mauer, *Understanding Your Health,* 8th ed., pp. 271–74. Copyright © 2005 McGraw-Hill. Reprinted by permission of The McGraw-Hill Companies.

Exercise 2: Outline

On notebook paper, prepare a formal outline of the main ideas in the selection. Give your outline the correct title. Formulate the *overall* main idea, and write it at the beginning of your outline, that is, after the title, but before Roman numeral I. Reread the selection if you need to. Use the headings to help you see the big picture and how the parts fit together. Pay special attention to the format (Roman numerals and indentation) as you create your outline. Allow yourself enough time to complete this exercise.

_____

_____

_____

_____

_____

_____

_____

_____

_____

_____

_____

_____

_____

_____

_____

_____

_____

_____

_____

_____

_____

_____

_____

_____

_____

_____

_____

_____

_____

_____

_____

_____

_____

_____

_____

_____

_____

_____

_____

_____

_____

_____

_____

Exercise 3: Map

On notebook paper, create a study map for the selection. Formulate the overall main idea and write it in the middle of the page. Branch the main ideas out from it on separate lines. (If your handwriting is large or if you prefer, you can draw a separate map for each paragraph. Before doing this, check your instructor.)

Exercise 4: Note Taking in Cornell Format

On notebook paper, rule off a 2"–3" Review Column on the left side of the page. Fill in the central portion of the page with your notes, and then beside each main point, write a key word or phrase in the review column. Many students like to put the overall main idea for a section at the end of their notes for that section. It helps them draw together the important points in the material. If you like, use the following space to plan your outline.

Exercise 5: Summary

   On notebook paper, write a one-paragraph summary of the selection. Give your summary the correct title. Include only main ideas in your summary and keep them in the same order that appear in the selection. Use your own words and add transitional words and phrases as needed to make the flow of ideas clear and smooth. If you like, use the following space to write a draft of your summary.

_____

_____

_____

_____

_____

_____

_____

_____

_____

_____

_____

PART·SEVEN

7

Grand Slam: Playing in the Big Leagues

The Grand Slam

I've called this section the "Grand Slam" because in professional sports circuits, a grand slam means an athlete has won *all* the major events or titles in a sport (such as winning all the major tennis titles for that year). Obviously, this is a significant achievement, one that can be accomplished only if the player has built skill through consistent, diligent practice. Now is your chance to see what *you* can do. (By the way, in baseball, a grand slam refers to a home run hit when three runners are on base. That's an accomplishment that also requires skill!)

Chapter 15, "Apply All the Skills You Have Learned" is subtitled "Playing in the Big Leagues" because the selections represent a broad cross section of the types of materials you're likely to encounter in college. The selections come from computer science, criminology, psychology, popular culture, human development, personal finance, political science, and geography textbooks. There are also an excerpt from a book on accelerated learning, a scientific article, and a newspaper article. Moreover, they are all longer selections.

There are twelve selections. The first six are accompanied by reading and vocabulary skills questions. The last six, however, are accompanied by a set of ten comprehension questions, ten vocabulary-in-context questions, writing prompts, and Web resources on the topic of the selection. The comprehension questions are the type that a content area professor might ask you on a test. It's a great opportunity to see what you can do.

Give each selection your best effort. The results will tell you which skills you've mastered and which ones you need to practice further. Good luck!

The bulk of this chapter consists of lengthier reading selections that are typical of the sort you might be assigned to read in your college courses. It's "big league" not only because of that, but also because you're going to be applying *all* the skills you've learned in *Exercise Your College Reading Skills*. (Breathe easy. You won't apply every skill to every selection.)

READING SELECTIONS

When you do any of the following exercises, allow enough time to complete it without interruption. Each time you are interrupted, you lose your concentration. When you are trying to get started again, you lose time trying to figure out where you were and what the author's train of thought was. In short, you lose both focus and momentum. (You know what happens when athletes lose their concentration and momentum: It can be disastrous. The negative impact is great enough that football teams often try to use it to their advantage: They call for a time-out just as the opposition is ready to begin a play.) Getting refocused is especially difficult if the interruption in your reading and studying is a long one—for example, you leave to run an errand or you get involved in a lengthy phone conversation. Here's your game strategy for success:

- Block out enough time for your study session.
- Find a quiet place to work.
- Study at a desk or table in a place with good lighting.
- Turn off the TV, CD player, and so forth.
- Tell others not to disturb you.
- Don't answer the phone.

(*Coach's tip:* An easy way to accomplish nearly all of the above is to study in the library!)

Before you begin a selection, use the techniques you have learned for putting yourself in a state of relaxed concentration. Reading the introduction to the selection and looking through the selection will give you an overview and help you focus your concentration. Even a brief preview (overview) will give you an idea of what the selection is about and how it is organized—and your brain likes seeing the big picture in advance. Make each exercise one of mindful practice. Remember, you'll get out of it what you put into it. Give it your best shot.

SELECTION 1

This selection, from an introductory computer science text, discusses threats to computer security. Although everyone is familiar with computers, not everyone realizes the range of computer security threats.

Crashes can result in lost data

THREATS TO COMPUTER SECURITY

1   We are all concerned with having a safe and secure environment to live in. We are careful to lock our car doors and our homes. We are careful about where we walk at night and whom we talk to. This is personal security. What about computer security? What if someone gains unauthorized access to our computer or other computers that contain information about us? What if someone steals our computer or other computers that contain information about us? What are the major threats to computer security?

2   Keeping information private depends on keeping computer systems safe from criminals, natural hazards, and other threats.

Computer Criminals

3   Computer criminals are of five types:

- **Employees:** The largest category of computer criminals consists of those with the easiest access to computers—namely, employees. Sometimes the employee is simply trying to steal something from the employer—equipment, software, electronic funds, proprietary information, or computer time. Sometimes the employee is acting out of resentment and is trying to get back at the company.

- **Outside users:** Not only employees but also some suppliers or clients may have access to a company's computer system. Examples are bank customers who use an automated teller machine. Like employees, these authorized users may be able to obtain confidential passwords or find other ways of committing computer crimes.

- **Hackers and crackers:** Some people think of these two groups as being the same, but they are not. *Hackers* are people who gain unauthorized access to a computer system for the fun and challenge of it. *Crackers* do the same thing but for malicious purposes. They may intend to steal technical information or to introduce what they call a *bomb*—a destructive computer program—into the system.

- **Organized crime:** Members of organized crime groups have discovered that they can use computers just as people in legitimate businesses do, but for illegal purposes. For example, computers are useful for keeping track of stolen goods or illegal gambling debts. In addition, counterfeiters and forgers use microcomputers and printers to produce sophisticated-looking documents such as checks and driver's licenses.

- **Terrorists:** Knowledgeable terrorist groups and hostile governments could potentially crash satellites and wage economic warfare by disrupting navigation and communication systems. The Department of Defense reports that its computer systems are probed approximately 250,000 times a year by unknown sources.

Computer Crime

4   A **computer crime** is an illegal action in which the perpetrator uses special knowledge of computer technology. The FBI estimates that businesses lost $1.5 trillion in the past year from computer crimes. The number of these crimes has tripled in the past two years. Computer crime can take various forms including the creation of malicious programs, denial of service attacks, Internet scams, theft, and data manipulation.

Malicious Programs

5   Hackers and crackers are notorious for creating and distributing malicious programs. These programs are called **malware,** which is short for **mal**icious soft**ware.** They are specifically designed to damage or disrupt a computer system. The three most common types of malware are viruses, worms, and Trojan horses.

6   - **Viruses** are programs that migrate through networks and operating systems, and most attach themselves to different programs and databases. While most viruses are relatively harmless, some can be quite destructive. Once activated, these destructive viruses can alter and/or delete files. Some delete all files on the hard disk and can damage system components. Creating and knowingly spreading a virus is a very serious crime and a federal offense punishable under the Computer Abuse Amendments Act of 1994.

7   •   **Worms** are a special type of virus that does not attach itself to programs and databases. Rather it fills a computer system with self-replicating information, clogging the system so that its operations are slowed or stopped. A recent worm traveled across the world within hours, stopping tens of thousands of computers along its way. Internet worms also can be carriers of more traditional viruses. Once the traditional virus has been deposited by a worm onto an unsuspecting computer system, the virus will either activate immediately or lie dormant until some future time.

8   Viruses and worms typically find their way into microcomputers through e-mail attachments, copied floppy disks, or programs downloaded from the Internet. Because viruses can be so serious—certain "disk-killer" viruses can destroy all the information on a person's system—computer users are advised to exercise care in accepting new programs and data from other sources.

9   Detection programs called **virus checkers** are available to alert users when certain kinds of viruses and worms enter their system. Four of the most widely used virus checkers are Dr. Solomon's AntiVirus, McAfee VirusScan, eSafe, and Norton AntiVirus. Unfortunately, new viruses are developed all the time, and not all viruses can be detected.

10   •   **Trojan horses** are programs that come into a computer system disguised as something else. Trojan horses are not viruses. Like worms, however, they are carriers of viruses. The most common types of Trojan horses appear as free computer games and free screen saver programs that can be downloaded from the Internet. Once the Trojan horse is downloaded onto a computer system, the viruses are deposited and ready to activate. One of the most dangerous types of Trojan horse claims to provide free antivirus programs. These programs begin by locating and disabling any existing virus protection programs and then deposit the virus.

Denial of Service

11   Like a worm, a **denial of service (DoS) attack** attempts to slow down or stop a computer system or network. Unlike a worm that self-replicates, a DoS attack floods a computer or network with requests for information and data. The targets of these attacks are usually Internet service providers (ISP) and specific Web sites. Once under attack, the servers at the ISP or the Web site become overwhelmed with these requests for service and are unable to respond to legitimate users. As a result, the ISP or Web site is effectively shut down.

Internet Scams

12   A scam is a fraudulent or deceptive act or operation designed to trick individuals into spending their time and money for little or no return. An **Internet scam** is simply a scam using the Internet. Internet scams are becoming a serious problem and have created financial and legal problems for tens of thousands of people. Almost all of the scams are initiated by a mass mailing to unsuspecting individuals.

Theft

13   Theft can take many forms—of hardware, of software, of data, of computer time. Thieves steal equipment and programs, of course, but there are also white-collar crimes. These crimes include the theft of data in the form of confidential information such as preferred-client lists. Another common crime is the use (theft) of a company's computer time by an employee to run another business.

14   Unauthorized copying of programs for personal gain is a form of theft called **software piracy.** According to the Software Copyright Act of 1980, it is legal for a program owner to make only his or her own backup copies of that program. *It's important to note that none of these copies may be legally resold or given away. This may*

come as a surprise to those who copy software from a friend, but that's the law. It is also illegal to download copyright-protected music and videos from the Internet.

15 Pirated software accounts for over 40 percent of software used in the United States. The incidence of pirated software is even higher overseas in such countries as Italy (82 percent) and Thailand (92 percent). Penalties for violating this law are up to $250,000 in fines and five years in prison.

Data Manipulation

16 Finding entry into someone's computer network and leaving a prankster's message may seem like fun, which is why hackers do it. It is still against the law. Moreover, even if the manipulation seems harmless, it may cause a great deal of anxiety and wasted time among network users.

17 The **Computer Fraud and Abuse Act of 1986** makes it a crime for unauthorized persons even to view—let alone copy or damage—data using any computer across state lines. It also prohibits unauthorized use of any government computer or a computer used by any federally insured financial institution. Offenders can be sentenced to up to 20 years in prison and fined up to $100,000.

Other Threats and Hazards

18 There are plenty of other hazards to computer systems and data besides criminals. They include the following:

- **Natural disasters:** Natural forces include fires, floods, wind, hurricanes, tornadoes, and earthquakes. Even home computer users should store backup disks of programs and data in safe locations in case of fire or storm damage.

- **Civil strife and terrorism:** Wars, riots, and terrorist activities are real risks in all parts of the world. Even people in developed countries must be mindful of these acts.

- **Technological failures:** Hardware and software don't always do what they are supposed to do. For instance, too little electricity, caused by a brownout or blackout, may cause the loss of data in primary storage. Too much electricity, as when lightning or some other electrical disturbance affects a power line, may cause a voltage surge, or spike. This excess of electricity may destroy chips or other electronic components of a computer.

19 Another technological catastrophe occurs when a hard-disk drive suddenly crashes, or fails, perhaps because it has been bumped inadvertently. If the user has forgotten to make backup copies of data on the hard disk, data may be lost.

20 - **Human errors:** Human mistakes are inevitable. Data-entry errors are probably the most commonplace and they can lead to mistaken identity. Programmer errors also occur frequently. Some mistakes may result from faulty design, as when a software manufacturer makes a deletion command closely resembling another command. Some errors may be the result of sloppy procedures. One such example occurs when office workers save important documents under file names that are not descriptive and not recognizable by others.

Source: Adapted from Timothy O'Leary and Linda O'Leary, *Computing Essentials 2007,* Introductory Ed., pp. 295–300. Copyright © 2007 McGraw-Hill/Irwin. Reprinted by permission of The McGraw-Hill Companies.

1. Based on the *context*, what is the meaning of the word *proprietary* in paragraph 3, first bullet?

_____

_____

2. Write the *main idea* for paragraph 3, bullet 1.

_____

_____

_____

3. Write the *overall main idea* for the entire selection.

_____

_____

_____

_____

4. According to the *details* in the selection, besides criminals, what are other hazards to computer security?

_____

_____

5. Based on the information in paragraphs 5–10, complete this chart about malware, malicious programs. (Your instructor may direct you to use notebook paper.)

TYPES OF MALWARE (MALICIOUS PROGRAMS)			
Type	**What It Is**	**How It Works**	**Other Information**
viruses			
worms			

TYPES OF MALWARE (MALICIOUS PROGRAMS) (CONTINUED)			
Type	**What It Is**	**How It Works**	**Other Information**
Trojan horses			

6. What is the *overall organizational pattern* of the selection? (In other words, how is the information arranged?)

_____

7. What *inference(s)* could you make about threats to computer security?

_____

_____

_____

_____

_____

_____

_____

_____

_____

_____

8. Does each of the following statements represent a *fact* or an *opinion*?

_____ "It's important to note that none of these copies may be legally resold or given away."

_____ "These programs are called *malware,* which is short for *malicious software.*"

9. What is the *authors' purpose* in writing this selection?

_____

_____

10. Who is the *intended audience*?

_____

_____

11. On notebook paper create a *concept map* for paragraph 18 of the selection. Use the space below to plan your map.

12. On notebook paper, write a *formal outline* of the major and minor *topics* of the selection. Use the space below to plan your outline or write a draft of it.

_____

_____

_____

_____

_____

_____

_____

_____

_____

_____

_____

_____

_____

_____

_____

_____

_____

_____

_____

_____

_____

13. On notebook paper, write a *summary* of the selection. Use the space below to plan your summary or write a draft of it.

_____

_____

_____

_____

_____

_____

_____

_____

_____

_____

_____

_____

SELECTION 2

The following excerpt is from a book on accelerated learning. It presents techniques that can be used not only to make you a more efficient, effective student, but also a more effective person in every area of your life. The selection consists of four sections, but it is easy to read, and interesting. You'll find that it's filled with valuable information about setting goals, daring to imagine, mobilizing willpower, and creating your own vision.

ACHIEVING WHAT YOU REALLY WANT IN LIFE

1   You won't hit a target you can't see. Learning is like setting out on a journey. You need to know your final destination. And you need to know how you're going to get there.

2   What is it you really want in life? To achieve it you must:

1.   Have a clear vision of what it is you want to achieve.

2.   Have a firm belief that you can achieve that vision.

3   Researchers have proven that one of the common denominators of peak performers is that they possess an above average ability to consciously practice a task in their minds, using imagery or visualization. They "start with the end in mind."

4   A university study of two groups of basketball players showed that one group who split their time evenly between the physical practice of free throws and mental imagery outperformed a second group who used physical practice only. Not surprisingly, both groups did better than a control group who did not practice at all.

5   Imagery can include all of the senses. It can mean seeing images, hearing sounds, experiencing feelings, and even smelling or tasting in the mind. Deliberately invoking all the senses becomes a powerful and effective learning tool.

6   If you have not previously used imagery, it can be a bit of a culture shock. But surely you have imagined something in your head that you wanted to happen? And surely you worry about things? If you worry—you are good at imagery. Because worry is imagining and acting as if something you don't want to happen has actually happened. If you can worry, you can visualize. So let's use it positively to learn.

7   Imagery/visualization works because the mind cannot distinguish between an actual event and one that is "only imagined." This is because the same electrochemical neural pathways in the brain are activated.

8   Let us give you a practical example of what we mean:

9   Imagine you are in the kitchen of your home. You take a fresh lemon from the fruit bowl. It is cool in your hand. The yellow dimpled skin feels waxy. The lemon comes to a small green conical point at either end. As you look at it in the palm of your hand you realize it is firm and quite heavy for its size.

10   You raise the lemon to your nose. It gives off such a characteristic, unmistakable citrus smell, doesn't it? You take a sharp knife and cut the lemon in half. The two halves fall apart—the white pulpy inner skin contrasting with the drops of pale lemon-colored juice that gently ooze out. The lemon smell is slightly stronger.

11   Now you bite deeply into the lemon and let the juice swirl around in your mouth. That sharp sour lemon flavor is unmistakable.

12   Stop a minute! Is your mouth watering? Did you purse your lips? Maybe you winced a little? If so, you have achieved synesthesia, because you imagined the feel, sight, smell, and taste of the lemon. You have used your imagination well.

13   The implications are fascinating because, of course, nothing actually happened—except in your imagination! Yet your mind communicated directly to your salivary glands and told them to wash away the sour taste. You puckered your lips and grimaced.

14   The words you read were not reality. But they created reality. *The subconscious mind cannot differentiate between what is real and what it believes is real.*

15   Yet it directly controls your actions in a very tangible way.

The Will to Succeed

16   We talk about people having the willpower to succeed. Ask most people to define *willpower* and you will find that they use expressions such as "grim determination" or "gritting your teeth and sticking with it." There is an interesting implication in such a definition. It implies a struggle. And presumably that struggle could only be with yourself. Does that sound like a healthy state of mind?

17   We prefer to define willpower in this way.

WILLPOWER = A CLEAR VISION + BELIEF IN YOUR ABILITY

18   A vision is important because if you don't stand for something—you can fall for anything. You need to create in your mind a successful outcome. Napoleon, for instance, played out all of his battles in his mind before they took place. He expressed it well: "Imagination is stronger than willpower."

19   The power of determination was vividly illustrated in a five-year study of 120 of America's top artists, athletes, and scholars, led by University of Chicago education professor Benjamin Bloom.

20   The key element that all the peak performers had in common was not an innate talent but an extraordinary drive and determination that came from a vision of what they would become.

21   Says Dr. Bloom, "We expected to find tales of great natural gifts. We didn't find that at all. Their mothers often said it was their other child who had the greater gift." But what the high achievers had was vision.

Dare to Imagine

22   At her "Dare to Imagine" project Marilyn King seeks to inspire her youngsters by promoting what she feels are the three traits shared by most successful people.

1.   They are motivated by something that really matters to them, something they really want to do or be. King calls this "Passion."

2.   They can see a goal really clearly, and they can imagine taking all the steps to achieve it: "Vision."

3.   They are willing to do something each day, according to a plan, that will bring them one step closer to their dream: "Action."

Passion + Vision + Action = Success!

23   To help youngsters achieve success, King, a former Olympic champion, has them identify their passion and create the vision in their mind. Then they put a photograph or make a drawing of it in the center of a piece of paper. The students draw lines radiating from the image and they write down the traits or skills needed to achieve their vision, rating them from one to ten. The most important skill is circled. The students' success maps also include action steps needed, names of advisers and cheerleaders, obstacles that must be overcome and ways to overcome them, resources available, accomplishments and awards, and creation of a success statement. King suggests reading the statement in front of a mirror ten times, morning and evening, for ten days.

24   Many of her students have experienced dramatic improvement both in their schoolwork and behavior, and the program is enthusiastically supported by the mayor and local realtors. King is now training mentors for the at-risk kids and expanding the program to include many more students.

Creating Your Own Vision

25   Your involvement in a learning program is clear evidence that you have a desire to improve yourself and/or help others to do so. You know the rewards of learning and the penalties of ignorance.

26   It's essential, however, that you are now specific in the goals you wish to attain. It is simply not good enough to want to "do better." It's important to have a life plan of which your educational and career goals form an integral part.

27   As Gus Tuberville, president of William Penn College, puts it, "For learning to take place with any kind of efficiency, students must be motivated. To be motivated they must become interested. And they become interested when they are actively working on projects which they can relate to their values and goals in life."

28   What are your values and goals in life? What do you want in your relationships with the people who matter most to you—your spouse, partner, parents, children, relatives, friends, close business associates? What do you want your state of health to be? What action do you need to take to accomplish that? Do you need to change your eating and exercise habits?

29   What do you want to do to grow as a well-balanced person? What hobbies and sports would you like to pursue? Do you want to travel? Write? Paint? Hang-glide? Learn to play a musical instrument? What would make you feel proud? Concentrate on what you *feel* is right, rather than what you think you *ought* to do.

30   Your first step is to create the vision. You need to decide exactly what you want to be. You need a vision you can see clearly, a goal you can actually see yourself reaching. Beware of words such as *wish* and *try*.

31   When people say, "I wish I could . . . " what they really mean is "I'd like to . . . but it's too much trouble and hard work." When they say, "I'll try to . . . " what they usually mean is "I'm warning you now that I may fail."

32   *Wish* and *try* lack conviction. The only words to use are **"I will . . . !"**

33   Once you have your vision, your ultimate long-term goal, you need to be specific and you need to organize the steps to get you there. Write it down. It's a simple thing to do, but very powerful. Just the act of committing to paper the goal you aim to achieve makes it "real." When you put it in writing, you can't be vague. You are clearly stating your intentions.

34   If it's a really important goal, write it on a Post-it sticker and place it where you will see it every day.

35   So—you want to put together a step-by-step action plan. What do you need:

- Money? How much? Where do you get it?

- Time? How do you take time out of your already busy schedule?

- Knowledge? Where do you acquire it?

- Skills? Where do you get them?

- Support? Who, from among your family, friends, colleagues, and superiors, can and will help you?

Source: Colin Rose and Malcolm Nicholl, *Accelerated Learning for the 21st Century,* 1997, pp. 76–81. Copyright © 1998 by Colin Rose and Malcolm J. Nicholl. Used by permission of Dell Publishing, a division of Random House, Inc.

1. Based on the *context*, what is the meaning of *purse* as it is used in paragraph 12?

_____

_____

_____

2. Write the *main idea* for paragraph 23.

_____

_____

3. Which *organizational pattern* is used in paragraph 23?

_____

_____

_____

4. What is the authors' *purpose* in writing the material in selection 2?

_____

_____

5. Who is the authors' *intended audience?*

_____

_____

6. Identify each of the following sentences as either a *fact* or an *opinion:*

_____ "A university study of two groups of basketball players showed that one group who split their time evenly between the physical practice of free throws and mental imagery outperformed a second group who used physical practice only."

_____ "Not surprisingly, both groups did better than a control group who did not practice at all."

_____ "The subconscious mind cannot differentiate between what is real and what it believes is real."

_____ "A vision is important because if you don't stand for something — you can fall for anything."

7. Based on information in the selection what can you conclude about the type of person Marilyn King is?

_____

_____

8. On the basis of the information in the selection, what *inference* could you make about a person who does not have a clear vision?

_____

_____

_____

9. What is the authors' *point of view* about the role of innate ability in a person's success?

_____

_____

_____

_____

_____

10. Write at least one *assumption* that underlies the authors' argument in this selection that people can achieve what they really want in life if they have a clear vision and a firm belief that they can achieve that vision.

_____

_____

_____

_____

11. Evaluate the *authors' credibility.* (In other words, were they convincing? Did you believe the case they were making for having a vision and believing that it can be accomplished? Why or why not?)

_____

_____

_____

_____

12. On notebook paper, write a one-paragraph *summary* of each section. Use the four headings for the summary titles. If you like, use the space below to plan your answers.

_____

_____

_____

_____

13. On notebook paper, create a *concept map* of the major points in the section, "Dare to Imagine" (paragraphs 22–24). If you like, first use the planning space below.

SELECTION 3

Stem cell research is a highly controversial and divisive topic. The following information, from the Public Broadcast System's Innovation *series, gives background information on stem cells, describes two types of stem cells, and presents each side of the argument. There are some technical words in the selection, but you will be able to follow the reasoning if you read carefully. You will probably have to read all or part of the article a second time, and you will find it helpful to jot down key terms and the arguments on either side of the issue.*

THE STEM CELL CONTROVERSY

1   Stem cells constitute one of the most fascinating—and controversial—areas of biology today. Researchers, who are still learning how the body uses these cells to restore or regenerate tissue, hope to harness the power of stem cells and make them a human "repair kit." But there is also a deep division over how safe—or

how ethical—using these cells will be. While stem cells could revolutionize medicine, they also raise profound ethical questions about what steps should be taken to restore health or save lives.

What Are Stem Cells?

2   Stem cells, the building blocks of the body, have two essential characteristics that make them unique. They are unspecialized cells that can renew themselves for long periods through cell division. In addition, under the right conditions, they can develop, or "differentiate," to become cells with more specialized functions. Although there are three major types of stem cells—embryonic stem cells, embryonic "fetal" germ cells, and adult stem cells—scientists mainly work with adult and embryonic stem cells from animals and humans. (Embryonic germ cells are found in a specific part of the embryo/fetus; they normally develop into mature gametes—eggs and sperm.) The labels "adult" and "embryonic" relate to the stem cells' place of origin.

Adult Stem Cells

3   Adult stem cells are unspecialized, undifferentiated cells that exist in very small numbers among specialized cells in an adult organ or tissue. Their main function is to maintain and periodically repair the tissues in which they are found. Adult stem cells are rare and hard to detect, but so far researchers have found them in a number of places, including the brain, the bone marrow, peripheral blood, blood vessels, skeletal muscle, skin, and liver. One adult stem cell, the hematopoietic stem cell, has been used for decades to treat diseases, including leukemia, lymphoma, and inherited blood disorders, and to replace cells destroyed by cancer chemotherapy. Researchers are investigating whether it is possible to expand adult stem cells, increasing their numbers in either a cell culture or within the body so that more diseases might be treated.

4   Researchers long assumed that adult stem cells could yield only those specialized cells of the tissue or organ where they were located—for example a skin stem cell could only give rise to a skin cell. But the last few years has brought provocative evidence that some adult stem cells may have "plasticity" and may be able to transform into different cell types, a process known as transdifferentiation.

Embryonic Stem Cells

5   Embryonic stem cells, as their name implies, are taken from embryos. These cells are "pluripotent," or capable of differentiating into any cell type derived from the three embryonic germ layers (the three initial tissue layers arising in an embryo)—mesoderm, endoderm, and ectoderm. Under the right conditions, human embryonic stem cells will proliferate indefinitely without specializing or differentiating into specific cell types, to form an embryonic stem cell line. Embryonic stem cells were first isolated in mice more than 20 years ago, but it was not until 1998 that James Thomson of the University of Wisconsin managed to derive and grow the first stable line of human cells.

6   The embryos from which these stem cells are derived form under two different conditions. Until very recently, these cells were always taken from surplus eggs left over from in vitro fertilization procedures and contributed with the informed consent of the donors. In vitro fertilization (IVF) is a technique used to assist women who are experiencing difficulty in conceiving a child. A woman's eggs are removed from her ovary and then fertilized in a laboratory culture dish. The fertilized eggs are maintained in a laboratory dish and allowed to develop into pre-implantation embryos, or pre-embryos. A little over two days later, they are delivered to a healthy uterus to continue development.

7   Many times, surplus embryos remain after the in vitro procedure. These can be donated to other couples or discarded, but they can also be frozen and stored for future IVF attempts or donated for research. The best estimate, by the RAND Institute in May 2003, is that nearly 400,000 embryos are frozen and stored in the U.S. alone, with about 11,000 such embryos designated for research.

8   In February 2004, scientists in South Korea became the first to derive human stem cells from embryos using a second method called somatic cell nuclear transfer (SCNT)—a procedure often referred to as therapeutic cloning.

9   Whether the embryonic stem cells are isolated from surplus IVF embryos or through SCNT, the embryo is destroyed in the process. This fact is the root of the controversy over using these cells in research.

10   Researchers think human embryonic stem cells could be a boon to medical research and treatment. "Embryonic stem cells could serve as replacement cells for those that have been lost or destroyed because of disease," says Robert Goldstein, Chief Scientific Officer of the Juvenile Diabetes Research Foundation. "If we can discover the biological cues that make an embryonic stem cell develop into a specialized cell—like an insulin-secreting cell in the pancreas—we could try to reproduce these signals in the lab and create a source of replacement cells for many afflictions."

11   Embryonic stem cells have other potential uses: as tools for studying early events in human development (shedding light on birth defects), as test systems for new drug therapies, to screen potential toxins, and as vehicles or "vectors" to deliver genes that could correct defects. These applications remain theoretical— the field is too new for any of these treatments to have reached human stages. But various animal studies have demonstrated "proof of principle" that these approaches can work. For example, mouse embryonic stem cells have been converted into specialized cell types and transplanted into animals to relieve symptoms of spinal cord injury and Parkinson's disease.

The Controversy

12   The isolation of human embryonic stem cells in 1998 thrust stem cell research into a volatile national debate tied to the fight over abortion. Deriving embryonic stem cells, and destroying an embryo in the process, raised profound ethical questions. Most revolve around the question of when life begins. Is an embryo a person? Should we forego embryonic stem cell research to protect the embryo? Is it right to negate a potential life for benefits that are unproven? Should researchers avoid this ethical minefield and redouble their efforts with adult stem cells?

The Case Against Using Embryonic Stem Cells

13   Objections to deriving human embryonic stem cells arise from the contention that human embryos are nothing less than individual beings in the earliest stages of life. As some members of a bioethics council appointed by President Bush put it in 2002, "We find it disquieting, even somewhat ignoble, to treat what are in fact the seeds of the next generation as mere raw material for satisfying the needs of our own."

14   Those opposed to using embryonic stem cells contend that the benefits from the cells are speculative today, while the medical applications of adult stem cells have been shown for years. "Embryonic stem cells have not helped a single human patient or demonstrated any therapeutic benefit," reads a statement by the United States Conference of Catholic Bishops. "By contrast, adult stem cells and other ethically acceptable alternatives have already helped hundreds of thousands of patients, and new clinical uses expand almost weekly."

15   Many on this side of the argument cite the recent studies suggesting that adult stem cells can change type, or transdifferentiate. If researchers could isolate enough adult stem cells, couldn't they, instead of embryonic stem cells, be used as replacement tissue? Some scientists even think it might be possible to "reprogram" adult stem cells back to an embryonic-cell-like state again, providing a source for replacement tissue without the moral objections. An added benefit of this technique would be that the cells come from the patient's own body and thus are less likely to be rejected.

16   Another issue with using embryonic stem cells concerns their ability to divide indefinitely. Studies in animals have shown that embryonic stem cells sometimes form tumors called "teratomas" or develop into a mixed collection of partially formed tissue. This could make injecting them into human patients risky. Adult stem cells, on the other hand, are not thought to pose such risks.

The Case for Using Embryonic Stem Cells

17   Many scientists do not think adult stem cells offer the same therapeutic and research potential as embryonic stem cells. Adult stem cells are difficult to isolate, and they do not proliferate well in culture. There's little proof, researchers argue, of a wide array of human adult stem cells that can differentiate into multiple tissue types. Some studies that appeared to show adult stem cells transforming into other cell types have been called into question by more recent findings, and evidence seems to indicate that adult stem cells may not possess the same capacity to give rise to any cell type as embryonic stem cells do.

18   But despite the questions, the consensus among most scientists is that research on both stem cell types should continue on parallel tracks. Even those who have made their mark working with adult stem cells, such as Catherine Verfaillie of the University of Minnesota, hold this view. "We will not know which stem cells, adult or embryonic, are most useful in treating a particular disease without side by side comparison of adult and embryonic stem cells," Verfaillie wrote on February 4, 2002, in a letter submitted to Pennsylvania Senator Arlen Specter.

19   And in 2001, a letter from 40 Nobel Laureates to President Bush stated: "It is premature to conclude that adult stem cells have the same potential as embryonic stem cells—and that potential will almost certainly vary from disease to disease. . . . Therefore, for disorders that prove not to be treatable with adult stem cells, impeding human pluripotent stem cell research risks unnecessary delay for millions of patients who may die or endure needless suffering while the effectiveness of adult stem cells is evaluated."

20   Many disease sufferers consider embryonic stem cells to be their only lifeline. Karen Miner, 52, has been paralyzed from the shoulders down after her car went into a ravine during a rainstorm 11 years ago. In 1998, she co-founded Californians for Cure, which advocates for spinal cord and embryonic stem cell research in California. Miner doesn't understand why "pro-life" forces are aligned against her cause.

21   "They really don't understand that it's not destroying a life, it's saving a life," she says. "I do not believe these cells are children. Blood cells are alive, and so are skin cells. We cut into them during surgery, but no one considers that murder. They make it sound like there are people growing out in warehouses that we take body parts from."

22   Finally, in answer to those who consider destruction of an embryo unjustified even if it saves a life, those favoring embryonic stem cell research point out that IVF-created embryos often get discarded, so they should be put to use rather than wasted.

Source: Innovation, Episode 6: "Miracle Cell," produced by Thirteen/WNET New York © 2004 Educational Broadcasting Corporation. Accessed at http://www.pbs.org/wnet/innovation/print/essay6.html

1. Which organizational pattern is used in paragraph 12?

_____

_____

_____

2. List the reasons given *for* using embryonic stem cells.

_____

_____

_____

_____

_____

_____

_____

_____

_____

_____

_____

_____

_____

_____

_____

3. Is information in this article presented in a *biased or unbiased* manner? Explain your answer.

_____

_____

4. What support is given *in opposition to* embryonic stem cell research?

_____

_____

_____

_____

_____

_____

_____

_____

_____

_____

_____

_____

_____

_____

_____

_____

_____

_____

_____

5. What *types of support* are given in support of both sides of the argument?

_____

_____

_____

_____

_____

6. What is the *main idea* of paragraph 5?

_____

_____

_____

7. What is the *author's purpose* in writing this article?

_____

_____

8. Based on the context, what is the meaning of *boon* as used in this sentence in paragraph 10: "Researchers think human embryonic stem cells could be a *boon* to medical research and treatment"?

_____

9. Based on your knowledge of word parts, what is the meaning of *disquieting* in paragraph 13?

_____

_____

10. Identify each of the following statements as either a *fact* or an *opinion*.

_____ Stem cells constitute one of the most fascinating—and controversial—areas of biology today.

_____ Embryonic stem cells have other potential uses: as tools for studying early events in human development (shedding light on birth defects), as test systems for new drug therapies, to screen potential toxins, and as vehicles or "vectors" to deliver genes that could correct defects.

_____ Miner doesn't understand why "pro-life" forces are aligned against her cause.

_____ In February 2004, scientists in South Korea became the first to derive human stem cells from embryos using a second method called somatic cell nuclear transfer (SCNT)—a procedure often referred to as therapeutic cloning.

SELECTION 4

Perhaps you have already had the experience of having something stolen from you, but if not, the probability is high that it will happen at some point during your lifetime. This selection, which comes from a criminology text, focuses on the factors that go into the decision to burglarize one place rather than another, how robbers choose victims and businesses to rob, and how thieves decide what to steal.

BURGLARS AND BURGLARY, ROBBERS AND ROBBERIES, AND HOT PRODUCTS

Burglars and Burglary

1   Criminologists are increasingly interested in the factors that go into a decision to burglarize: the location or setting of the building, the presence of guards or dogs, the type of burglar alarms and external lighting, and so forth. Does a car in the driveway or a radio playing music in the house have a significant impact on the choice of home to burglarize? George Rengert and John Wasilchick conducted extensive interviews with suburban burglars in an effort to understand their techniques. They found significant differences with respect to several factors:

• The *amount of planning* that precedes a burglary. Professional burglars plan more than do amateurs.

• The extent to which a burglar engages in *systematic selection of a home*. Some burglars examine the obvious clues, such as presence of a burglar alarm, a watchdog, mail piled up in the mailbox, newspapers on a doorstep. More experienced burglars look for subtle clues, for example, closed windows coupled with air conditioners that are turned off.

- The extent to which a burglar pays *attention to situational cues.* Some burglars routinely choose a corner property because it offers more avenues of escape, has fewer adjoining properties, and offers visibility.

2 Rengert and Wasilchick have also examined the use of time and place in burglary. Time is a critical factor to burglars, for three reasons:

- They must minimize the time spent in targeted places so as not to reveal their intention to burglarize.

- Opportunities for burglary occur only when a dwelling is unguarded or unoccupied, that is, during daytime. (Many burglars would call in sick so often that they would be fired from their legitimate jobs; others simply quit their jobs because they interfered with their burglaries.)

- Burglars have "working hours"; that is, they have time available only during a limited number of hours (if they have a legitimate job).

3 Before committing their offenses, burglars take into account familiarity with the area, fear of recognition, concern over standing out as somebody who does not belong, and the possibility (following some successful burglaries) that a particular area is no longer cost-beneficial. Season, too, plays an important role. One experienced burglar stated that because neighborhoods are populated with children in the summer, he opted for winter months: "The best time to do crime out here is between 8:00 and 9:00 A.M. All the mothers are taking the kids to school. I wait until I see the car leave. By the time she gets back, I've come and gone."

4 Recent research demonstrates how important it is for burglars to have prior knowledge of their targets. They obtain such knowledge by knowing the occupants, by being tipped off about the occupants or by observing the potential target. Some burglars even acquire jobs that afford them the opportunity to observe their potential victims' daily activities; others gain access to the interior of a house, search for valuable goods, and steal them at a later date.

Robbers and Robberies

5 Richard Wright and Scott Decker conducted in-depth interviews with street robbers and found that they frequently victimize other street-involved individuals—drug dealers, drug users, and gang members—people who, because they are criminals themselves, are unlikely to go to the police. These people are also targeted because they are believed to have a lot of money, jewelry, and other desirable items. Street robbers report that they sometimes specifically target people whom they do not like, or people who have hurt or offended them in the past. When women are targeted, it is because robbers believe they will not resist and are not armed. On the other hand, women are not the desirable targets men are because robbers think women do not carry as much money.

6 Criminologists also study whether commercial robbers operate the same way as street robbers in their selection of targets. Robbers who target business establishments are interested in some of the same factors that concern burglars. Perpetrators carefully examine the location of the potential robbery, the potential gain, the capability of security personnel, the possibility of intervention by bystanders, and the presence of guards, cameras, and alarms.

7 Criminologists have found that potential victims and establishments can do quite a bit to decrease the likelihood of being robbed. Following a series of convenience-store robberies in Gainesville, Florida, in 1985, a city ordinance required store owners to clear their windows of signs that obstructed the view of the interior, to position cash registers where they would be visible from the street, and to install approved electronic cameras. Within a little over a year, convenience-store robberies had decreased 64 percent.

Hot Products

8   Why do thieves decide to steal some things and not others? What makes targets attractive? We have examined how burglars select which homes to burglarize, but once they have broken into a residence, how do they decide what to steal? When robbers target victims, they do so believing their chances of making off with something valuable are greater than their chances of not being successful in the robbery attempt. But what is it about things that makes them valuable to robbers? Cohen and Felson argued that items are attractive if they are visible, easy to take away, valuable, and accessible. Twenty years later, Ronald Clarke expanded this idea with his discussion of hot products—those consumer goods that are attractive to thieves. Using an acronym (CRAVED) to organize this idea, Clarke claims that goods are attractive if they are concealable, removable, available, valuable, enjoyable, and disposable (i.e., can be easily fenced). This approach takes into account what thieves do with goods after they are stolen, because that factor figures into their decisions about the attractiveness of items.

Source: Freda Adler, Gerhard Mueller, and William Laufer, *Criminology,* 5th ed., pp. 219–22. Copyright © 2004 McGraw-Hill. Reprinted by permission of The McGraw-Hill Companies.

1. Write the *main idea* for paragraph 4:

_____

_____

_____

_____

2. Write the *main idea* for paragraph 5:

_____

_____

_____

_____

3. Write the *main idea* for paragraph 7:

_____

_____

4. Write the *main idea* for paragraph 8:

_____

_____

_____

_____

_____

5. On separate lines, list the *details* in paragraph 4:

_____

_____

_____

_____

_____

_____

_____

6. Which *organizational pattern* is used in each of the following paragraphs?

Paragraph 2: _____

_____

_____

Paragraph 6: _____

_____

Paragraph 8: _____

_____

7. Identify each statement as either an *opinion* or a *fact:*

_____ "Some burglars routinely choose a corner property because it offers more avenues of escape, has fewer adjoining properties, and offers visibility."

_____ "Many burglars would call in sick so often that they would be fired from their legitimate jobs; others simply quit their jobs because they interfered with their burglaries."

_____ "Cohen and Felson argued that items are attractive if they are visible, easy to take away, valuable, and accessible."

8. On the basis of the selection, write at least one logical *inference* about what a person could do to minimize the likelihood of being burglarized.

_____

_____

_____

_____

_____

9. Who is the authors' *intended audience?*

_____

_____

10. What is the authors' *purpose* for writing this selection?

_____

_____

11. On the basis of the information about "hot products," make an *inference* as to why a thief would be more likely to steal a pearl necklace than a PC (computer) of comparable worth.

_____

_____

12. *Underline* and *annotate* the section "Robbers and Robberies" (paragraphs 5–7).

ROBBERS AND ROBBERIES

Richard Wright and Scott Decker conducted in-depth interviews with street robbers and found that they frequently victimize other street-involved individuals—drug dealers, drug users, and gang members—people who, because they are criminals themselves, are unlikely to go to the police. These people are also targeted because they are believed to have a lot of money, jewelry, and other desirable items. Street robbers report that they sometimes specifically target people whom they do not like, or people who have hurt or offended them in the past. When women are targeted, it is because robbers believe they will not resist and are not armed. On the other hand, women are not the desirable targets men are because robbers think women do not carry as much money.

Criminologists also study whether commercial robbers operate the same way as street robbers in their selection of targets. Robbers who target business establishments are interested in some of the same factors that concern burglars. Perpetrators carefully examine the location of the potential robbery, the potential gain, the capability of security personnel, the possibility of intervention by bystanders, and the presence of guards, cameras, and alarms.

Criminologists have found that potential victims and establishments can do quite a bit to decrease the likelihood of being robbed. Following a series of convenience-store robberies in Gainesville, Florida, in 1985, a city ordinance required store owners to clear their windows of signs that obstructed the view of the interior, to position cash registers where they would be visible from the street, and to install approved electronic cameras. Within a little over a year, convenience-store robberies had decreased 64 percent.

SELECTION 5

This psychology textbook selection discusses the controversial issue of repressed memories.

REPRESSED MEMORIES: TRUTH OR FICTION?

1   Guilty of murder in the first degree.

2   That was the jury's verdict in the case of George Franklin, Sr., who was charged with murdering his daughter's playmate. But this case was different from most other murder cases: It was based on memories that had been repressed for twenty years. Franklin's daughter claimed that she had forgotten everything she had once known about her father's crime until two years earlier, when she began to have flashbacks of the event. Gradually, though, the memories became clearer in her mind, until she recalled her father lifting a rock over his head and then seeing her friend lying on the ground, covered with blood. On the basis of her memories, her father was convicted—and later cleared of the crime after an appeal of the conviction.

3   Although the prosecutor and jury clearly believed Franklin's daughter, there is good reason to question the validity of *repressed memories,* recollections of events that are initially so shocking that the mind responds by pushing them into the unconscious. Supporters of the notion of repressed memory (who draw on Freud's psychoanalytic approach) suggest that such memories may remain hidden, possibly throughout a person's lifetime, unless they are triggered by some current circumstance, such as the probing that occurs during psychological therapy.

4   However, memory researcher Elizabeth Loftus maintains that so-called repressed memories may well be inaccurate or even wholly false—representing *false memory.* For example, false memories develop when people are unable to recall the source of a memory of a particular event about which they have only vague recollections. When the source of the memory becomes unclear or ambiguous, people may begin to confuse whether they actually experienced the event or whether it was imagined. Ultimately, people come to believe that the event actually occurred.

5   In fact, some therapists have been accused of accidentally encouraging people who come to them with psychological difficulties to re-create false chronicles of childhood sexual experiences. Furthermore, the publicity surrounding well-publicized declarations of supposed repressed memories, such as those of people who claim to be the victims of satanic rituals, makes the possibility of repressed memories seem more legitimate and ultimately may prime people to recall memories of events that never happened.

6   The controversy regarding the legitimacy of repressed memories is unlikely to be resolved soon. Many psychologists, particularly those who provide therapy, give great weight to the reality of repressed memories. On the other side of the issue are memory researchers who maintain that there is no scientific support for the existence of such memories. There is also a middle ground: memory researchers who suggest that false memories are a result of normal information processing. The challenge for those on all sides of the issue is to distinguish truth from fiction.

Source: Adapted from Robert Feldman, *Essentials of Understanding Psychology,* 6th ed., p. 236. Copyright © 2005 McGraw-Hill. Reprinted by permission of The McGraw-Hill Companies.

1. Write the *overall main idea* of the selection.

_____

_____

_____

2. What is the meaning of *chronicles* as it is used in paragraph 5?

_____

3. Identify each of the following statements as a *fact* or an *opinion:*

_____ "Supporters of the notion of repressed memory suggest that such memories may remain hidden, possibly throughout a person's lifetime, unless they are triggered by some current circumstance, such as the probing that occurs during psychological therapy."

_____ "However, memory researcher Elizabeth Loftus maintains that so-called repressed memories may well be inaccurate or even wholly false—representing *false memory*."

_____ "In fact, some therapists have been accused of inadvertently encouraging people who come to them with psychological difficulties to recreate false chronicles of childhood sexual experiences."

4. What is the author's *purpose* in writing this selection?

_____

_____

5. Write at least one logical *inference* about what George Franklin's position is likely to be with regard to the issue of repressed memories.

_____

_____

_____

_____

_____

_____

6. Does the author of this selection have a *bias* on the issue of repressed memories?

_____

_____

_____

_____

7. *Annotate* the selection by writing the *topic* beside each paragraph and/or the *function* of the paragraph.

SELECTION 6

This was written by Pamela Eakes, founder of Mothers Against Violence in America.

DO YOU KNOW WHAT VIDEO GAMES YOUR CHILDREN ARE PLAYING?

1   It's a tireless task parents have keeping their kids safe. Graphic TV programs, sexually explicit magazines and alcohol all must be kept out of reach. Unfortunately, parents must add another pop culture challenge to their list: video games. A recent study by the American Academy of Pediatrics (AAP) shows that more than 90 percent of parents don't monitor ratings on the video games played by their kids. Many are unaware that a ratings system for video games even exists, and children probably know more about the rating system than their parents do. Worse yet, parents may not know that the content of certain games could affect the social and emotional development of their child, and may even be hazardous to children's health.

2   Violence is the most prevalent health risk for children and adolescents. Homicide, suicide, and accidents are the top causes of death for 15- to 24-year-olds. Each year, more than 150,000 adolescents are arrested for violent crimes; more than 300,000 are seriously assaulted; and 3,500 are murdered. Violence done to and by America's young people is a public health emergency that must be addressed by parents, physicians and policymakers.

3   More than 3,500 research studies have examined the association between media violence and violent behavior. All but 18 of the studies have shown that the more violence one sees, the more likely one is to be violent. According to the AAP, depictions of violence that are realistic, portrayed without pain and suffering, and experienced in the context of good feelings are more likely to be emulated.

4   On April 20, 1999, two heavily armed adolescent boys walked into Columbine High School in Littleton, Colorado, and shot 12 of their classmates and a teacher to death. Then they killed themselves. When authorities investigated, they discovered that the boys had played thousands of hours of a "first-person shooter" video game that had been modified to occur in a layout identical to that of their high school, with yearbook pictures electronically pasted onto the game's imaginary victims. What led these boys to deliberately kill their fellow students is complicated, and no single reason has been identified as the cause.

5   One of the questions parents asked after the Columbine shooting was: "How could it be that the parents did not know their children were playing such heinous video games?" The answer is that parents are not familiar with video games because they don't play them.

6   Parents *don't know* that video games that have a mature rating may contain content that is entirely inappropriate for children under the age of 17. They *don't know* that a child playing an M-rated game can actively participate in the simulated murder of police officers, women, minorities and innocent bystanders. These acts are graphically depicted and include victims being shot, beaten to death, decapitated, burned alive, and urinated on. These games may also present favorable depictions of prostitution, racism, misogyny, and drug use.

7   Parents *do know* that children learn by observing, imitating what they observe, and acting on the world around them. According to child psychologist Michael Rich, children develop what psychologists call "behavioral scripts." They interpret their experiences and respond to others using those scripts.

8   One can easily see how repeated exposure to violent behavioral scripts can lead to increased feelings of hostility, expectation that others will behave aggressively, desensitization to the pain of others, and an increased likelihood of interacting and responding to others with violence.

9   Violent video games are an ideal environment in which to learn violence. Violent video games:

- place the player in the role of the aggressor and reward him or her for violent behavior.
- allow the player to rehearse an entire behavioral script from provocation to choosing a violent resolution of conflict.
- are addictive—kids want to play them for hours to improve their playing skills, and repetition increases learning.

10   Parents already know they must be aware of the television and movies their children watch. Now they must be aware of the content of the video games their children play at home and in the homes of their friends.

11   To educate parents and guardians about the content of video games, Mothers Against Violence in America invites parents to join the Campaign for a Game Smart Community and learn about the content and rating system. There are hundreds of video games available, and selecting the right game for your child is very important.

Source: Pamela Eakes, "Do You Know What Video Games Your Children Are Playing?" http://www.pbs.org/kcts/videogamerevolution/impact/violence.html

1. What is the author's *point of view* regarding video game violence and children?

   _____

   _____

2. What does the author propose parents do in order to keep their children safe?

   _____

   _____

   _____

   _____

3. List at least three *types of support* the author presents to support her point of view.

   _____

   _____

   _____

   _____

   _____

4. Does each of the following statements represent a *fact* or an *opinion*?

   _____ Homicide, suicide, and accidents are the top causes of death for 15- to 24-year olds.

_____ It's a tireless task parents have keeping their kids safe.

_____ "One can easily see how repeated exposure to violent behavioral scripts can lead to increased feelings of hostility, expectation that others will behave aggressively, desensitization to the pain of others, and an increased likelihood of interacting and responding to others with violence."

5. Which type of *organization pattern* is used in paragraphs 7 and 8?

_____

_____

_____

6. What is the meaning of *emulated* as used in the sentence, "According to the AAP, depictions of violence that are realistic, portrayed without pain and suffering, and experienced in the context of good feelings are more likely to be *emulated*."

_____

7. Based on your knowledge of prefixes and knowing that the root *gyn* means "women," what is the meaning of *misogyny* in the sentence, "These games may also present favorable depictions of prostitution, racism, *misogyny,* and drug use"?

_____

8. Parents who read and accept the author's points of view would be likely to *conclude* that they should do what?

_____

_____

9. Who does the author say must address the public health emergency of violence done to and by America's young people? Write that *supporting detail* below.

_____

10. Who is the *intended audience* of this article?

_____

Unlike Selections 1–6, which are accompanied by skills questions, Selections 7–12 are accompanied by objective comprehension questions (the type a content area professor might ask on a test), vocabulary-in-context items, and writing prompts.

SELECTION 7

The author, Henry Jenkins, is a professor at MIT (Massachusetts Institute of Technology). In this selection, he seeks to explode eight widely held misperceptions about video games.

REALITY BYTES: EIGHT MYTHS ABOUT VIDEO GAMES DEBUNKED

1   A large gap exists between the public's perception of video games and what the research actually shows. The following is an attempt to separate fact from fiction.

2   **1.   The availability of video games has led to an epidemic of youth violence.**

According to federal crime statistics, the rate of juvenile violent crime in the United States is at a 30-year low. Researchers find that people serving time for violent crimes typically consume less media before committing their crimes than the average person in the general population. It's true that young offenders who have committed school shootings in America have also been game players. But young people in general are more likely to be gamers—90 percent of boys and 40 percent of girls play. The overwhelming majority of kids who play do NOT commit antisocial acts. According to a 2001 U.S. Surgeon General's report, the strongest risk factors for school shootings centered on mental stability and the quality of home life, not media exposure. The moral panic over violent video games is doubly harmful. It has led adult authorities to be more suspicious and hostile to many kids who already feel cut off from the system. It also misdirects energy away from eliminating the actual causes of youth violence and allows problems to continue to fester.

3   **2.   Scientific evidence links violent game play with youth aggression.**

Claims like this are based on the work of researchers who represent one relatively narrow school of research, "media effects." This research includes some 300 studies of media violence. But most of those studies are inconclusive and many have been criticized on methodological grounds. In these studies, media images are removed from any narrative context. Subjects are asked to engage with content that they would not normally consume and may not understand. Finally, the laboratory context is radically different from the environments where games would normally be played. Most studies found a correlation, not a causal relationship, which means the research could simply show that aggressive people like aggressive entertainment. That's why the vague term "links" is used here. If there is a consensus emerging around this research, it is that violent video games may be one risk factor—when coupled with other more immediate, real-world influences—which can contribute to anti-social behavior. But no research has found that video games are a primary factor or that violent video game play could turn an otherwise normal person into a killer.

4   **3.   Children are the primary market for video games.**

While most American kids do play video games, the center of the video game market has shifted older as the first generation of gamers continues to play into adulthood. Already 62 percent of the console market and 66 percent of the PC market is age 18 or older. The game industry caters to adult tastes. Meanwhile, a sizable number of parents ignore game ratings because they assume that games are for kids. One quarter of children ages 11 to 16 identify an M-Rated (Mature Content) game as among their favorites. Clearly, more should be done to restrict advertising and marketing that targets young consumers with mature content, and to educate parents about the media choices they are facing. But parents need to share some of the responsibility for making decisions about what is appropriate for their children. The news on this front is not all bad. The Federal Trade Commission has found that 83 percent of game purchases for underage consumers are made by parents or by parents and children together.

5   **4.   Almost no girls play computer games.**

Historically, the video game market has been predominantly male. However, the percentage of women playing games has steadily increased over the past decade.

Women now slightly outnumber men playing Web-based games. Spurred by the belief that games were an important gateway into other kinds of digital literacy, efforts were made in the mid-90s to build games that appealed to girls. More recent games such as *The Sims* were huge crossover successes that attracted many women who had never played games before. Given the historic imbalance in the game market (and among people working inside the game industry), the presence of sexist stereotyping in games is hardly surprising. Yet it's also important to note that female game characters are often portrayed as powerful and independent. In his book *Killing Monsters,* Gerard Jones argues that young girls often build upon these representations of strong women warriors as a means of building up their self confidence in confronting challenges in their everyday lives.

6   **5.   Because games are used to train soldiers to kill, they have the same impact on the kids who play them.**

Former military psychologist and moral reformer David Grossman argues that because the military uses games in training (including, he claims, training soldiers to shoot and kill), the generation of young people who play such games are similarly being brutalized and conditioned to be aggressive in their everyday social interactions.

7   Grossman's model only works if:

- we remove training and education from a meaningful cultural context.
- we assume learners have no conscious goals and that they show no resistance to what they are being taught.
- we assume that they unwittingly apply what they learn in a fantasy environment to real world spaces.

8   The military uses games as part of a specific curriculum, with clearly defined goals, in a context where students actively want to learn and have a need for the information being transmitted. There are consequences for not mastering those skills. That being said, a growing body of research does suggest that games can enhance learning. In his recent book, *What Video Games Have to Teach Us About Learning and Literacy,* James Gee describes game players as active problem solvers who do not see mistakes as errors, but as opportunities for improvement. Players search for newer, better solutions to problems and challenges, he says. And they are encouraged to constantly form and test hypotheses. This research points to a fundamentally different model of how and what players learn from games.

9   **6.   Video games are not a meaningful form of expression.**

On April 19, 2002, U.S. District Judge Stephen N. Limbaugh Sr. ruled that video games do not convey ideas and thus enjoy no constitutional protection. As evidence, Saint Louis County presented the judge with videotaped excerpts from four games, all within a narrow range of genres, and all the subject of previous controversy. Overturning a similar decision in Indianapolis, Federal Court of Appeals Judge Richard Posner noted: "Violence has always been and remains a central interest of humankind and a recurrent, even obsessive theme of culture both high and low. It engages the interest of children from an early age, as anyone familiar with the classic fairy tales collected by Grimm, Andersen, and Perrault are aware." Posner adds, "To shield children right up to the age of 18 from exposure to violent descriptions and images would not only be quixotic, but deforming; it would leave them unequipped to cope with the world as we know it." Many early games were little more than shooting galleries where players were encouraged to blast everything that moved. Many current games are designed to be ethical testing grounds. They allow players to navigate an expansive and open-ended world, make their own choices and witness their consequences. *The Sims* designer Will Wright argues that games are perhaps the only medium that allows us to experience guilt over the actions of fictional characters. In a movie, one can always pull back and condemn the character or the artist when they cross certain social boundaries. But in playing a game, we choose what happens to the characters. In the right circumstances, we can be encouraged to examine our own values by seeing how we behave within virtual space.

10   ### 7.   Video game play is socially isolating.

Much video game play is social. Almost 60 percent of frequent gamers play with friends. Thirty-three percent play with siblings and 25 percent play with spouses or parents. Even games designed for single players are often played socially, with one person giving advice to another holding a joystick. A growing number of games are designed for multiple players—for either cooperative play in the same space or online play with distributed players. Sociologist Talmadge Wright has logged many hours observing online communities interact with and react to violent video games, concluding that meta-gaming (conversation about game content) provides a context for thinking about rules and rule-breaking. In this way there are really two games taking place simultaneously: one, the explicit conflict and combat on the screen; the other, the implicit cooperation and comradeship between the players. Two players may be fighting to death on screen and growing closer as friends off screen. Social expectations are reaffirmed through the social contract governing play, even as they are symbolically cast aside within the transgressive fantasies represented onscreen.

11   ### 8.   Video game play is desensitizing.

Classic studies of play behavior among primates suggest that apes make basic distinctions between play fighting and actual combat. In some circumstances, they seem to take pleasure wrestling and tussling with each other. In others, they might rip each other apart in mortal combat. Game designer and play theorist Eric Zimmerman describes the ways we understand play as distinctive from reality as entering the "magic circle." The same action—say, sweeping a floor—may take on different meanings in play (as in playing house) than in reality (housework). Play allows kids to express feelings and impulses that have to be carefully held in check in their real-world interactions. Media reformers argue that playing violent video games can cause a lack of empathy for real-world victims. Yet, a child who responds to a video game the same way he or she responds to a real-world tragedy could be showing symptoms of being severely emotionally disturbed. Here's where the media effects research, which often uses punching rubber dolls as a marker of real-world aggression, becomes problematic. The kid who is punching a toy designed for this purpose is still within the "magic circle" of play and understands her actions on those terms. Such research shows us only that violent play leads to more violent play.

Source: Henry Jenkins, "Reality Bytes: Eight Myths About Video Games Debunked," http://www.pbs.org/kcts/videogamerevolution/impact/myths.html

Comprehension Check

True-False

_____   1.   Only slightly more men than women play Web-based games.

_____   2.   With regard to school shootings, a student's exposure to media is not as significant a factor as quality of home life and mental stability.

_____ **3.** Some video games provide players opportunities in virtual space to examine their values.

_____ **4.** Extensive video game playing leads to aggression and violence because video games are socially isolating.

_____ **5.** U.S. courts have ruled that games are not a meaningful form of expression and, therefore, that they have no constitutional protection.

Multiple-Choice

_____ **6.** The primary video game market is
- **a.** children under 11 years.
- **b.** children 11–16 years of age.
- **c.** adults 18 or older.
- **d.** young girls.

_____ **7.** Which of the following is NOT a way in which games can enhance learning?
- **a.** Active problem solving is encouraged.
- **b.** Mistakes are viewed as opportunities for improvement.
- **c.** No specific goals are presented.
- **d.** Hypotheses are continually formed and tested.

_____ **8.** Of frequent gamers who play video games with others, the highest percent play with
- **a.** friends.
- **b.** siblings.
- **c.** spouses.
- **d.** parents.

_____ **9.** Meta-gaming refers to
- **a.** playing in online communities.
- **b.** conversation about the content of a game.
- **c.** thinking about rules and rule-breaking.
- **d.** implicit cooperation and comradeship between players.

_____ **10.** Research on the desensitizing effects of video game playing on children may be flawed because children
- **a.** perceive play fighting and actual combat as the same.
- **b.** take pleasure in wrestling and tussling.
- **c.** who play violent video games have a lack of empathy for real-world problems.
- **d.** understand the "magic circle" of play is different from real life.

Vocabulary-in-Context Check

The first sentence comes from the selection and contains a word that is italicized (_like this_). The second sentence uses the word in the same sense, but in a different context. _Choose the meaning that fits the context of both sentences._ You will often be able to use your knowledge of word parts to confirm your educated guess.

_____ 1. Reality Bytes: Eight Myths About Video Games *Debunked* (title)

Television ads for the *debunked* diet drug were removed from the air.

Debunked means
a. proved true.
b. widely written about.
c. highly praised.
d. exposed as false.

_____ 2. But most of those studies are *inconclusive* and many have been criticized on methodological grounds. (paragraph 3)

The results of the first tests were *inconclusive,* so the doctor ordered additional tests before making a diagnosis.

Inconclusive means
a. incorrect; wrong.
b. not definite; questionable.
c. argued about; disputed.
d. accurate.

_____ 3. The game industry *caters* to adult tastes. (paragraph 4)

The citizen's group charged that the legislature *caters* to special-interest groups.

Caters means
a. attends to the wants of.
b. provides food for.
c. approves of.
d. takes advantage of.

_____ 4. Historically, the video game market has been *predominantly* male. (paragraph 5)

That neighborhood is *predominantly* homeowners above the age of sixty, with a few younger couples.

Predominantly means
a. exclusively.
b. partially.
c. mainly.
d. completely.

_____ 5. Former military psychologist and moral reformer David Grossman argues that because the military uses games in training (including, he claims, training soldiers to shoot and kill), the generation of young people who play such games are similarly being *brutalized* and conditioned to be aggressive in their everyday social interactions. (paragraph 6)

Being in combat can leave soldiers *brutalized* and unable to relate appropriately to others after their return home.

Brutalized means
a. treated cruelly.
b. treated kindly.
c. made stronger.
d. made cruel or unfeeling.

_____ **6.** As evidence, Saint Louis County presented the judge with video-taped excerpts from four games, all within a narrow range of *genres,* and all the subject of previous controversy. (paragraph 9)

There are many *genres* of literature; for example, there are novels, short stories, poems, and plays.

Genres means
a. types; categories.
b. popular forms.
c. types of literature.
d. types of video games.

_____ **7.** Posner adds, "To shield children right up to the age of 18 from exposure to violent descriptions and images would not only be *quixotic,* but deforming; it would leave them unequipped to cope with the world as we know it." (paragraph 9)

His behavior was so *quixotic* that we never knew what to expect.

Quixotic means.
a. unreasonable.
b. impulsive; capricious.
c. predictable; unchanging.
d. unacceptable.

_____ **8.** Posner adds, "To shield children right up to the age of 18 from exposure to violent descriptions and images would not only be quixotic, but *deforming;* it would leave them unequipped to cope with the world as we know it." (paragraph 9)

Being raised in an abusive home is *deforming* to a child's character and development.

Deforming means
a. ruining the appearance of.
b. exaggerating the characteristics of.
c. causing the loss of desirable qualities.
d. changing the physical shape of.

_____ **9.** Social expectations are reaffirmed through the social contract governing play, even as they are symbolically cast aside within the *transgressive* fantasies represented onscreen. (paragraph 10)

The bizarre, *transgressive* nature of their child's behavior caused the parents to seek professional help for their son.

Transgressive means
a. sinful.
b. imaginative.
c. exceeding a limit or boundary.
d. based on truth or evidence.

_____ **10.** In others, they might rip each other apart in *mortal* combat. (paragraph 11)

The passenger suffered a *mortal* injury in the car wreck and died a few hours later.

Mortal means
a. eternal.
b. causing death; fatal.
c. painful.
d. serious; severe.

Writing Prompts

Your instructor may assign you some or all of the following questions. For items marked with the collaborative icon, your instructor may ask you to work in small groups (three or four students) to come up with an answer. *Everyone* in the group should be able to explain the group's answer.

1. Which, if any, of the myths did you believe prior to reading the article? In what way were your beliefs strengthened or changed as a result of reading this article?

_____

_____

_____

_____

2. Did the author present a convincing argument with regard to whether video games have been misperceived? Why or why not?

_____

_____

_____

_____

3. Psychologists and other researchers do not agree on the influence of violent video games on aggression and violence in those who play them. In light of that, what steps could or should be taken until more is known about the effects?

_____

_____

_____

_____

4. Today, the typical young adult will have spent 10,000 hours playing video games before reaching college age. If you are a video game player, describe your experience with them. Which types of games do you play? How often? What effects do you think playing them has had on you? If you do not play video games, describe a friend's experience with video games.

_____

_____

_____

_____

Web Resources

If a URL has become inactive or if you need more information, use "video game myths" or a similar descriptor with an Internet search engine such as Google.

http://www.apa.org/science/psa/sb-anderson.html

This 2003 article "Violent Video Games: Myths, Facts, and Unanswered Questions" was written by a psychologist and is presented by the American Psychological Association. It presents a very different view from "Reality Bytes."

SELECTION 8

Frederick M. Hess is director of education policy studies at the American Enterprise Institute and is working on Emancipating Education, *a book that examines why American schools look like they do and how we might reinvent them for the 21st century.*

SUMMER VACATION OF OUR DISCONTENT

1   Can our kids afford to take summer vacation? Right now, about 50 million children are on summer vacation across the United States. Many are discovering new interests at summer camp, playing ball at the Y, or traveling with Mom and Dad. But millions of others are loitering in parking lots and shopping malls, cruising iffy websites, and slouching toward academic disaster. For this second group, it's time to take a fresh look at the traditional summer break.

2   Summer vacation once made good sense—back when we lived in a brawn-based economy, academic achievement mattered less, an absence of air conditioning or modern hygiene turned crowded schools into health risks, and children had moms who were home every day.

3   Historian Kenneth Gold has noted that summer vacation, as we know it, was an invention of the mid-19th-century belief that "too much schooling impaired a child's and a teacher's health." Community leaders fretted that summer was a "period of epidemics, and most fruitful of diseases generally," and sought to keep children at home or send them to the countryside.

4   In that era, the nation's first professional educators believed that too much schooling would exhaust both teacher and student. They thought that placid summers under parental supervision would be more beneficial than time spent in humid, crowded schools.

5   Today, things have changed. We know that for today's children, knowledge and academic skills will be critical to their future success and happiness. In many communities, children are safer in well-run schools than they are at home alone.

6   Other advanced nations don't provide an American-style summer vacation. Most industrialized nations offer no more than seven consecutive weeks of vacation. Meanwhile, American school districts offer up to thirteen.

7   In a long-gone world of plentiful manufacturing jobs and self-contained economies, such comparisons mattered less. Today, however, our children will find themselves competing with peers from Europe, India, and China for lucrative and rewarding brain-based jobs.

8   Summer vacation can also be a massive inconvenience for today's middle-class families. In the 1960s, reports the Population Resource Center, more than

60% of families consisted of a father working out of the house, a stay-at-home mother, and multiple children. Now, as U.S. Census data show, two-thirds of American children live in households where two parents work or with a single working parent, meaning no one is home to supervise children during the summer. For these families, summer vacation can be more an obstacle than a break. Parents must find ways to occupy their children's time and to monitor their socializing and Web usage from work.

9   The Urban Institute reports that, at most, just 30% of school-aged children in families with an employed primary caretaker are cared for by a parent during the summer. The Urban Institute study also notes that forty-one percent of working families with school-age children pay for childcare during the summer, typically spending about 8% of their summertime earnings. Meanwhile, expensive school facilities, computers, texts, and transportation sit idle.

10   But the biggest problem with summer vacation today may be its impact on the academic achievement of low-income kids. In scores of studies, researchers—including scholars at places like the Johns Hopkins Center for Summer Learning and the Northwest Regional Educational Laboratory—have reported that these students lose significant academic ground in the summertime, while their more advantaged peers—those more likely to read and attend pricey summer camps—do not.

11   This has been a big factor in aggravating the "achievement gap" for urban and minority children. Programs with extended school years have had much success in boosting the achievement of these kids. The widely praised KIPP Academies, for instance, have employed a lengthened school year and a mandatory 3–4 week summer school session to boost achievement among their predominantly minority and urban students.

12   Today, "modified-calendar" schools exist in 46 states but enroll barely two million kids—about 5% of all K–12 students. Why aren't more schools offering an extended academic calendar?

13   One fierce opponent is the "summer activity industry." The nation's golf courses, amusement parks, and beachside resorts depend heavily on a cheap teen workforce. Movie theaters want teens with spending money, and the summer camp industry depends on families needing a place for their kids.

14   Teachers unions, too, are reluctant to see the school year extended. Efforts to add even two or three days to the academic year typically provoke objections from teachers and angry opposition from union officials.

15   Let's be clear: This is not a "national problem" or a uniform one. Summer vacations are still a wonderful time for many families and communities. Legislators need not pursue one-size-fits-all solutions to "fix" the school calendar.

16   Rather, it's time to acknowledge that 19th-century school practices may be a poor fit for many of today's families. It should be much easier for interested families to find schools that operate into or through the summer.

17   State officials should strike down laws—often supported by the summer recreation industry—that restrict the permissible school year for most schools. They should also help provide the operational funds necessary to support schools that operate through the summer.

18   School boards and superintendents should encourage more of their schools to move in this direction and appropriately compensate teachers and staff. Extending the school year will have the added benefit of helping to make teaching a full-time, more lucrative profession for educators who choose to work in these schools.

19   Additional schooling should not be an invitation to drudgery or an attack on childhood. It would allow schools to include more recess and athletics throughout the year, give teachers more time to conduct rich and imaginative lessons, and provide more time for music and the arts, all without compromising academic instruction.

20   Summer vacation can be a grand thing. But in the 21st century, for many children and families, it may also be an anachronism.

Source: Frederick Hess, "Summer Vacation of Our Discontent," July 12, 2006.
http://www.washingtonpost.com/wpdyn/content/article/2006/07/11/AR2006071100871_pf.html
© Washingtonpost.Newsweek Interactive

Comprehension Check

True-False

_____   1.   Not having school during the summer began during the mid-1800s because diseases and epidemics occurred more often during those months.

_____   2.   Today, "modified-calendar" schools exist in 46 states but enroll barely one million kids.

_____   3.   School during the summer would make it possible to have more time throughout the year for art, music, and athletics.

_____   4.   Summer programs have been effective in increasing achievement in urban and minority students.

_____   5.   The number of U.S. children on vacation during the summer is approximately 50 million.

Multiple-Choice

_____   6.   Which of the following in NOT mentioned as part of the "summer activity industry"?
a.   movie theaters
b.   summer camps
c.   karate classes
d.   amusement parks

_____   7.   Resistance to offering an extended academic calendar has come from
a.   governors.
b.   teachers unions.
c.   the Urban Institute.
d.   historian Kenneth Gold.

_____   8.   Nationally, the percent of K–12 students who enroll in "modified-calendar" schools is
a.   5%
b.   12%
c.   19%
d.   30%

_____   9.   How many consecutive weeks of vacation do other advanced nations typically give students?
a.   no more than 13
b.   no more than 11
c.   no more than 9
d.   no more than 7

_____ **10.** The biggest problem caused by summer vacation may be
   a. kids surfing the net unsupervised.
   b. kinds from low-income families lose significant academic ground.
   c. kids hanging out in malls.
   d. parents having to spend too much for childcare during those months.

Vocabulary-in-Context Check

The first sentence comes from the selection and contains a word that is italicized (*like this*). The second sentence uses the word in the same sense, but in a different context. *Choose the meaning that fits the context of both sentences.* You will often be able to use your knowledge of word parts to confirm your educated guess.

_____ **1.** Summer Vacation of Our *Discontent* (title)

The employees' level of *discontent* was so high that they decided to go on strike.

Discontent means
   a. rebellion.
   b. dissatisfaction.
   c. pleasure; enjoyment.
   d. hostility.

_____ **2.** But millions of others are *loitering* in parking lots and shopping malls, cruising iffy websites, and slouching toward academic disaster. (paragraph 1)

The unemployed men spent their days *loitering* on the street corner, chatting and passing the time.

Loitering means
   a. lingering aimlessly.
   b. lying down.
   c. sleeping.
   d. committing petty crimes.

_____ **3.** Summer vacation once made good sense—back when we lived in a *brawn*-based economy, academic achievement mattered less, an absence of air conditioning or modern hygiene turned crowded schools into health risks, and children had moms who were home every day. (paragraph 2)

Wrestlers and professional football players are often accused of being "all *brawn* and no brains."

Brawn means
   a. muscular strength and power.
   b. good looks.
   c. skill; talent.
   d. intellectual ability.

_____ **4.** Historian Kenneth Gold has noted that summer vacation, as we know it, was an invention of the mid-19th-century belief that "too much schooling *impaired* a child's and a teacher's health." (paragraph 4)

Listening to extremely loud music permanently *impaired* his hearing.

Impaired means
a. affected.
b. improved.
c. changed.
d. diminished.

_____ 5. They thought that *placid* summers under parental supervision would be more beneficial than time spent in humid, crowded schools. (paragraph 4)

The child had such a happy, *placid* nature that she rarely cried or became upset.

Placid means
a. beautiful.
b. calm, peaceful.
c. cheerful.
d. dull.

_____ 6. Today, however, our children will find themselves competing with peers from Europe, India, and China for *lucrative* and rewarding brain-based jobs. (paragraph 7)

Because of their *lucrative* marketing strategy, the company made millions of dollars.

Lucrative means
a. clever.
b. highly technical.
c. profitable; producing wealth.
d. unethical; dishonest.

_____ 7. The widely praised KIPP Academies, for instance, have employed a lengthened school year and a *mandatory* 3–4 week summer school session to boost achievement among their predominantly minority and urban students. (paragraph 11)

In order to graduate, high school seniors must pass a *mandatory* state exam.

Mandatory means
a. difficult; challenging.
b. required.
c. interesting.
d. exhausting.

_____ 8. Let's be clear: This is not a "national problem" or a *uniform* one. (paragraph 15)

The *uniform* legal code in this country applies equally to all citizens.

Uniform means
a. difficult to understand.
b. ever-changing.
c. the same everywhere.
d. complicated; complex.

_____ 9. Additional schooling should not be an invitation to *drudgery* or an attack on childhood. (paragraph 19)

Pat hated the *drudgery* of working in a factory, but it was the only job she was able to get.

Drudgery means
a. academic work.
b. tedious unpleasant work.
c. prestige.
d. shame; humiliation.

_____ **10.** But in the 21st century, for many children and families, it may also be an *anachronism*. (paragraph 20)

The idea that women should not work outside the home is now an *anachronism*.

Anachronism means
a. a helpful idea.
b. a new approach.
c. a solution to a difficult problem.
d. something that belongs to an earlier time.

Writing Prompts

Your instructor may assign you some or all of the following questions. For items marked with the collaborative icon, your instructor may ask you to work in small groups (three or four students) to come up with an answer. *Everyone* in the group should be able to explain the group's answer.

1. List at least three of the reasons the author says long summer vacations from school no longer make sense for all students.

_____

_____

_____

_____

_____

_____

_____

_____

2. Do you think the traditional summer vacation from school is an idea that no longer makes sense in all school districts? Explain your position.

_____

_____

_____

_____

3. What does the author recommend as solutions to the problem of summer vacations in areas where it creates more problems than benefits?

_____

_____

_____

_____

_____

_____

_____

4. In the past, how have you spent your summers? How would you have responded to being in school (or some form of it) during part or all of that time? Would it have helped or hurt you? In what ways?

_____

_____

_____

_____

Web Resources

If a URL has become inactive or if you need more information, use "summer vacation from school" or a similar descriptor with an Internet search engine such as Google.

http://www.infoplease.com/spot/schoolyear1.html

This gives the history of the summer vacation, as well as what works and what doesn't.

http://www.cato.org/research/education/articles/cansumvac.html

"Canceling Summer Vacation," a 2000 _Washington Times_ article, opposes decreasing the length of summer vacation from school.

SELECTION 9

Are you a Twentysomething? A baby boomer who may be somewhat puzzled by them? According to the authors of this human development textbook selection, "Today in American society, there is a less clear–cut line between adolescence and adulthood than a few decades ago. Some social scientists have suggested that adolescence extends into the twenties, with more young adults living at home with parents during their expensive college years and when launching a career, or returning home after a short-lived marriage or as a single parent. Many middle-class young adults expect to maintain a lifestyle equivalent to or better than that of their parents *while struggling through these early adult years." The following selection discusses the meaning of "adulthood" and presents demographics on adulthood as background for a discussion of Generation X, the young adults of today.*

ADULTHOOD: BABY BOOMERS AND GENERATION XERS

DEVELOPMENTAL PERSPECTIVES

1   The category adulthood lacks the concrete boundaries of infancy, childhood, and adolescence. Even in the scientific literature it has functioned as a kind of catchall category for everything that happens to individuals after they "grow up." Sigmund Freud, for instance, viewed adult life as merely a ripple on the surface of an already set personality structure; Jean Piaget assumed that no additional cognitive changes occur after adolescence; and Lawrence Kohlberg saw moral development as reaching a lifetime plateau after early adulthood. Many middle-aged American parents are asking themselves: *When is my son or daughter going to be an adult, capable of working and living independently of our resources?* There is no firm answer to their question today, and it seems to be quite an individual matter.

2   In the United States, adulthood generally begins when a person leaves high school, attends college, takes a full-time job, enters the military, or gets married. Yet, becoming an adult is a rather different matter for various segments of each society. In Western societies, men have traditionally emphasized such issues in development as autonomy, independence, and identity. In contrast, women, some ethnic minorities, and non-Western societies have typically assigned greater importance to issues of relatedness, such as closeness within a family. Recently, Arnett (2000) proposed a distinct developmental stage from about ages 18 to 25 called *emerging adulthood,* a time that for many allows greater exploration of life's possibilities in work, love, and worldviews and lays a foundation for the remainder of adult life.

Demographic Aspects of Adulthood

3   People's feelings, attitudes, and beliefs about adulthood are influenced by the relative proportion of individuals who are adults. In the United States, major population or demographic changes are under way that will have important social consequences. The *baby-boom generation* (those born between 1946 and 1964) represents a huge "age lump" passing through the population, a sort of demographic tidal-wave. This age cohort—more than 79 million Americans—was responsible for the 70 percent jump in the number of school-age children from 1950 to 1970.

4   In the 1950s the baby boomers made the United States a child-oriented society full of new schools, suburbs, and station wagons. The baby boomers born before 1955 provided the nation with rock and roll, went to Vietnam and Woodstock, attended college in masses, and fueled the student, civil rights, women's movement, and peace movements of the 1960s to 1970s. Later, as the baby boomers entered into middle age, the contemplation—even celebration—of the middle years found expression in popular culture. It is hardly a coincidence that family sitcoms such as "The Mary Tyler Moore Show" of the 1970s focused on single life and work and played to what was then a younger audience. Or that "All in the Family" sharply contrasted the views of young boomers "Meathead" and Gloria with middle-aged Edith and Archie. Similarly, family situation comedy was popular in "The Cosby Show" and "Family Ties," which dominated the TV ratings in the 1980s. Television sitcoms about singles such as "Murphy Brown," "Seinfeld," and "Friends" were popular in the 1990s.

5   The baby boomers have brought about a rapid expansion of the nation's labor force. In the early 1970s there were about 52 million Americans between 20 and

39 years of age (one-fourth of the population). By 1980 the number had risen to 72 million (one-third of the population). The bumper crop of baby boomers were 35 to 54 years old in 2000 and constituted about 28 percent of the total U.S. population (U.S. Census Bureau, 2001a).

6   As the boomers have moved into their middle-years, they have become more productive (many having attended college and acquired additional skills). Additionally, they earn more money and save more money—all of which will likely give a competitive edge to the United States in the world economic arenas in the 2000s. As the baby boom generation moves into middle adulthood, their children—the next generation of young adults—have come of age.

Generation X or Twentysomethings

7   Today's young adults in the cohort aged 20 to 27, who are more ethnically diverse than previous generations, are sandwiched between the baby-boom and "little boom" generation. They are variously labeled by others, or by themselves, as the "Baby-Busters," "Generation X," "Twentysomethings" or "Boomerang Generation." These vague labels reflect the fact that in many ways the image of this generation has not as yet fully evolved, and there are various subgroups within this generation. Nonetheless, from opinion polls, research surveys, and anecdotal evidence, some characteristics of this cohort are emerging (see Table 1).

8   Generation X has been raised in a variety of family structures with many of their fathers and mothers working, and they share an appreciation for individuality and an acceptance of diversity in race, ethnicity, family structure, sexual orientation, and lifestyle. More than 40 percent of today's young adults spent time in a single-parent home by the age of 16 because the divorce rate doubled between the years 1965 and 1977. The *National Survey of Children,* a longitudinal study of people born in the late 1960s, found that one-fourth of this generation had received psychological treatment for emotional, learning, or behavioral problems by the time they reached adulthood.

9   Other surveys and research suggest the following about Generation X:

- Having grown up with both parents working/furthering their education, Xers are used to getting things done on their own. Hence, they tend to be independent problem solvers and self-starters. They want support and feedback, but they don't want to be controlled.

TABLE 1 COMPONENTS OF THE AMERICAN DREAM, BY THREE GENERATIONS, 1996

	Percentage Saying This Is Part of Their American Dream		
	Elderly %	Baby-Boom Generation %	Generation X %
Having a happy marriage	77	74	70
Living in a decent, secure community	75	81	71
Owning own home	74	79	81
Having children	64	59	51
Unlimited opportunity to pursue dreams	63	71	70
College education for self	50	56	63
Being a winner	45	40	50
Living where everyone else shares my values	41	38	28
Becoming wealthy	33	37	46

Reprinted from *American Demographics* magazine, May 1998. Courtesy of Intertec Publishing Corp., Stamford, Connecticut. All Rights Reserved.

- Because many of them grew up with computers, Generation Xers are technologically literate. They are familiar with computer technology and prefer quick access to the Internet, CD-ROMs, DVDs, palm-pilots, cell phones, and the World Wide Web as their sources for locating information.

- Conditioned to expect immediate gratification, Generation Xers are focused. As learners, they don't want to waste time doing quantities of schoolwork; they want their work to be meaningful to them.

- Knowing that they must keep learning to be marketable, Generation Xers are lifelong learners. They do not expect to grow old working for the same company, so they view their job environments as places to grow. They seek continuing education and training opportunities; if they don't get them, they seek new jobs where they can.

- Craving success on their own terms, Generation Xers are ambitious. They are "flocking to technology start-ups, founding small businesses, and even taking up causes—all in their own way."

- As illustrated by their involvement in extreme sports such as bungee jumping and sky surfing, Generation Xers are fearless. "Indeed, adversity, far from discouraging youths, has given them a harder, even ruthless edge. Most believe 'I have to take what I can get in this world because no one is going to give me anything.' "

- They are more likely to get along with their parents, siblings, and stepparents, to live with their parents longer, and to marry later. The percentage of women aged 25 to 29 who had never married more than tripled from 11 percent in 1970 to nearly 40 percent in 2000, males in their twenties who have never married increased from 19 percent in 1970 to 52 percent in 2000.

- They are more likely to be cohabitating before marriage. The number of cohabiting couples rose from 500,000 in 1970 to 3.8 million in 2000.

10   The process of leaving home remains an important part of the transition for today's young adults (Generation X or the Millennials). Whereas in the past leaving home was frequently associated with the event of marriage, now moving out of the parental home comes from a desire to be independent.

11   According to the U.S. Census (2001b), 56 percent of men aged 18 to 24 (73 million) lived at home with one or both parents. For women of this age, 43 percent lived at home with one or both parents. Although in general the median marriage age is rising in the United States, Arnett (2000) points out that marriage age is better understood as a factor of cultural practices and is influenced by socioeconomic status as well. For example, the Mormons encourage early marriage. Figure 1 (page 441) shows the difference of median marriage age among different countries.

12   Note that the more industrialized countries have higher medians, although the trend in the less prosperous countries is also on the rise, especially for men whose employment opportunities have been diminishing.

Comprehension Check

True-False

_____   1.   There are clear-cut boundaries to adulthood that are the same in all segments of society.

Figure 1   Differing Perspectives on Growing Old

With the number of people age 100 years or older doubling every decade since 1950 in the industrialized world, it is of interest to note differences in attitudes toward old age. Younger Americans are more likely than older Americans to indicate that they wish to live to be 100. However, older Americans are more likely to believe they will live to an older age.

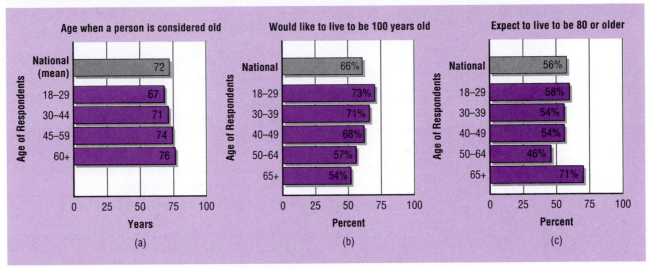

Source: This article is from *The American Enterprise,* a national magazine of politics, business and culture.

_____ **2.** "Baby boomers" is a term that refers to people born between 1950 and 1970.

_____ **3.** There is greater ethnic diversity in Generation X than in earlier generations.

_____ **4.** Baby boomers are more likely to be technologically literate than Generation Xers are.

_____ **5.** Generation Xers are more likely to get along with siblings, parents, and stepparents than baby boomers were.

Multiple-Choice

_____ **6.** What is the median marriage age of women in the United States?
a. 21.9
b. 25.2
c. 26.0
d. 26.2

_____ **7.** "Generation X" refers to the
a. children of baby boomers.
b. parents of baby boomers.
c. generation that came before the "Boomerang Generation."
d. generation that came after the "Twentysomethings."

_____ 8. The largest percent of which generation identifies wealth as being part of their American dream?
   a. the elderly
   b. the baby boom generation
   c. Generation X
   d. cannot be determined

_____ 9. What percentage of Generation Xers spent time living in a single-parent home by the age of 16?
   a. more than 70 percent
   b. more than 62 percent
   c. more than 40 percent
   d. more than 43 percent

_____ 10. Generation Xers are more likely than previous generations to
   a. create a rapid expansion in the labor force.
   b. be interested in having a happy marriage.
   c. have children.
   d. be lifelong learners who go where the job opportunities are.

Vocabulary-in-Context Check

The first sentence comes from the selection and contains a word that is italicized (*like this*). The second sentence uses the word in the same sense, but in a different context. *Choose the meaning that fits the context of both sentences.* You will often be able to use your knowledge of word parts to confirm your educated guess.

_____ 1. Lawrence Kohlberg saw moral development as reaching a lifetime *plateau* after early adulthood. (paragraph 1)

Dieters often lose weight, hit a *plateau,* and then start to lose weight again.

Plateau means
   a. the highest point.
   b. a steep decline.
   c. a stable state.
   d. fluctuation; change.

_____ 2. This age *cohort*—more than 79 million Americans—was responsible for the 70 percent jump in the number of school-age children from 1950 to 1970. (paragraph 3)

The *cohort* of voters aged 60 and older tend to vote in greater numbers.

Cohort means
   a. companion or associate.
   b. a generational group.
   c. factor.
   d. limit.

_____ 3. Later, as the baby boomers entered into middle age, the *contemplation*—even celebration—of the middle years found expression in popular culture. (paragraph 4)

Most religious leaders spend time in *contemplation* of spiritual matters.

Contemplation means
a. lack of acceptance.
b. meditation about.
c. thoughtful consideration.
d. hostility toward.

_____ 4. The *bumper crop* of baby boomers were 35 to 54 years old in 2000 and constituted about 28 percent of the total U.S. population. (paragraph 5)

Because we had a *bumper crop* of apples this year, there was enough to make 15 gallons of apple cider and to dry 10 bushels of apples.

Bumper crop means
a. an extraordinarily abundant quantity.
b. a ruined or damaged group.
c. an unknown amount.
d. a smaller than normal quantity.

_____ 5. Nonetheless, from opinion polls, research surveys, and *anecdotal* evidence, some characteristics of this cohort are emerging. (paragraph 7)

There were *anecdotal* reports from several mothers that the children became ill after eating that brand of cereal, but this hasn't been confirmed.

Anecdotal means
a. based on careful analysis.
b. based on scientific research.
c. based on gossip.
d. based on casual observations.

_____ 6. The *National Survey of Children*, a *longitudinal* study of people born in the late 1960s, found that one-fourth of this generation had received psychological treatment for emotional, learning, or behavioral problems by the time they reached adulthood. (paragraph 8)

The *longitudinal* research on 20 sets of twins spanned three decades.

Longitudinal means
a. concerned with the development of persons or groups over time.
b. related to length.
c. placed lengthwise.
d. concerned with longitude.

_____ 7. Conditioned to expect immediate *gratification*, Generation Xers are focused. (paragraph 9, bullet 3)

Because young children are unable to delay *gratification*, they pitch tantrums if they do not immediately get what they want.

Gratification means
a. pleasing others.
b. being displeased.
c. satisfaction.
d. sadness.

_____ 8. "Indeed, *adversity,* far from discouraging youths, has given them a harder, even ruthless edge." (paragraph 9, bullet 6)

The pioneers who settled the American West had to endure and overcome great *adversity.*

Adversity means
a. adventure.
b. challenge; competition.
c. misfortune; hardship.
d. danger.

_____ 9. "Indeed, adversity, far from discouraging youths, has given them a harder, even *ruthless* edge." (paragraph 9, bullet 6)

The *ruthless* serial killer tortured his victims before killing them.

Ruthless means
a. having no pity; merciless.
b. determined.
c. psychologically disturbed.
d. showing sympathy.

_____ 10. They are more likely to be *cohabitating* before marriage. (paragraph 9, bullet 8)

Because of their religious beliefs, they do not think *cohabiting* is moral.

Cohabiting means
a. living together in the same dwelling.
b. living together in a sexual relationship when not legally married.
c. living together as friends.
d. living with relatives.

Writing Prompts

Your instructor may assign you some or all of the following questions. For items marked with the collaborative icon, your instructor may ask you to work in small groups (three or four students) to come up with an answer. *Everyone* in the group should be able to explain the group's answer.

1. Generation Xers bring attitudes and skills to the workplace that are different from those of previous generations. What are some of these differences, and what impact do you think they will have on the companies and businesses that Gen Xers work for?

_____

_____

_____

_____

_____

_____

_____

_____

_____

_____

_____

_____

_____

_____

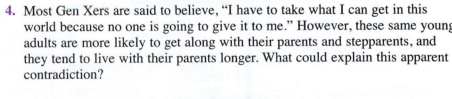

2. How do you think Gen Xers view marriage? Support your answer with evidence from the selection.

_____

_____

_____

_____

_____

_____

3. To which generational group do you belong? Does the description of it seem accurate? Explain the ways in which the description and characteristics do or do not apply to you.

_____

_____

_____

_____

4. Most Gen Xers are said to believe, "I have to take what I can get in this world because no one is going to give it to me." However, these same young adults are more likely to get along with their parents and stepparents, and they tend to live with their parents longer. What could explain this apparent contradiction?

_____

_____

Web Resources

If a URL has become inactive or if you need more information, use "Generation X" or a similar descriptor with an Internet search engine such as Google.

http://en.wikipedia.org/wiki/Generation_X

This is the Wikipedia (free encyclopedia) description of Generation X. Contains an interesting list of names of all of the American generations, including ones after Generation X (Boomerang Generation, Generation Y, Internet Generation, and New Silent Generation).

http://www.jour.unr.edu/outpost/specials/genx.overvw1.html

Information about the book from which Generation X got its name. Also click on "Myths and Reality" and "Facts and Figures" about Generation X. The facts and figures are from a 1996 *Wall Street Journal* article about Gen Xers; the statistics are interestingly different from what they might be today.

SELECTION 10

A STRATEGY FOR MANAGING CASH

1   More than 20,000 banks, savings and loan associations, credit unions, and other financial institutions provide a variety of services for your payment and savings needs. Today a trip to "the bank" may mean a visit to a credit union, an automatic teller machine in a shopping mall, or transferring funds on the Web.

2   While some financial decisions relate directly to goals, your daily activities require various financial services. Exhibit 1 provides an overview of financial services for managing cash flows and moving toward specific financial goals.

Exhibit 1   Financial Services for Managing Cash Flow

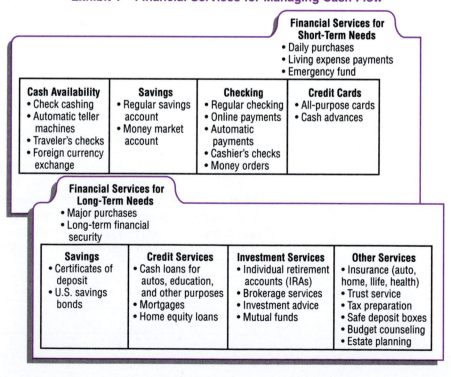

Meeting Daily Money Needs

3   Buying groceries, paying the rent, and other routine spending activities require a cash management plan.

4   **MANAGING CASH** Cash, check, credit card, or automatic teller machine (ATM) card are the common payment choices. While most people desire ease of payment, they must also consider fees and the potential for impulse buying and overspending. For example, in recent years ATM fees have risen from nothing to $1 or $2 per cash withdrawal and even higher charges for balance inquiries. If you are charged two $1 transaction fees a week and could invest your money at 5 percent, this convenience will cost you more than $570 over a five-year period.

5   Common mistakes made when managing current cash needs include

- Overspending as a result of impulse buying and using credit cards.
- Having insufficient liquid assets (cash, checking account) to pay current bills.
- Using savings or borrowing to pay for current expenses.
- Failing to put unneeded funds in an interest-earning savings account or investment plan to achieve long-term goals.

6   **SOURCES OF QUICK CASH** No matter how carefully you manage your money, there may be times when you will need more cash than you currently have available. To cope with that situation, you have two basic choices: liquidate savings or borrow. A savings account, certificate of deposit, mutual fund, or other investment may be accessed when you need funds. Or a credit card cash advance or a personal loan may be appropriate. Remember, however, that both using savings and increasing borrowing reduce your net worth and your potential to achieve long-term financial security.

Types of Financial Services

7   Banks and other financial institutions offer services to meet a variety of needs. These services fall into four main categories.

8   **1. SAVINGS** Safe storage of funds for future use is a basic need for everyone. These services, commonly referred to as *time deposits,* include money in savings accounts and certificates of deposit. Selection of a savings plan is commonly based on the interest rate earned, liquidity, safety, and convenience.

9   **2. PAYMENT SERVICES** The ability to transfer money to other parties is a necessary part of daily business activities. This can be done using a checking account (a regular checking account, activity account, or interest-earning account) or through other payment methods that are commonly called *demand deposits* (certified check, cashier's check, money order, and traveler's check).

10   **3. BORROWING** Most people use credit at sometime during their lives. Credit alternatives range from short-term accounts, such as credit cards and cash loans, to long-term borrowing, such as a home mortgage.

11   **4. OTHER FINANCIAL SERVICES** Insurance protection, investment for the future, real estate purchases, tax assistance, and financial planning are additional services you may need for successful financial management. With some financial plans, someone else manages your funds. A **trust** is a legal agreement that provides for the management and control of assets by one party for the benefit of another. This type of arrangement is most commonly created through a commercial bank or a lawyer. Parents who want to set aside certain funds for their children's education may use a trust. The investments and money in the trust are managed by a bank, and the necessary amounts go to the children for their educational expenses.

12   To simplify the maze of financial services and to attract customers, many financial institutions offer all-in-one accounts. An **asset management account,** also called a *cash management account,* provides a complete financial services program for a single fee. Investment brokers and other financial institutions offer this all-purpose account, which usually includes a checking account, an ATM card, a credit card, online banking, as well as a line of credit for obtaining quick cash loans. These accounts also provide access to stock, bond, mutual fund, and other types of investments. Asset management accounts are offered by companies such as American Express (www.americanexpress.com) and Charles Schwab (www.schwab.com).

13   **5.   ELECTRONIC BANKING** Banking by telephone, home computer, and other online services continues to expand, with 24-hour access to various transactions (see Exhibit 2). Most banks and other financial institutions have "cyber" branches that provide the following:

- *Direct deposit* of paychecks and government payments is used by a major portion of our society. Funds are deposited electronically and available automatically for your use.

- *Automatic payments* transfer funds for rent, mortgage, utilities, loan payment, and investment deposits without writing a check. Be sure to check your bank statement regularly to ensure that correct amounts have been deducted.

- Access to an **automatic teller machine (ATM),** more commonly called a cash machine, allows banking and other types of transactions such as buying bus passes, postage stamps, and gift certificates. To minimize ATM fees, compare several financial institutions, use your bank's ATM to avoid surcharges, and withdraw larger amounts to avoid fees on several small transactions.

- A **debit card,** or *cash card,* activates ATM transactions and may also be used to make purchases. A debit card is in contrast to a *credit card,* since you are spending your own funds rather than borrowing additional money.

Exhibit 2   Electronic Banking Transactions

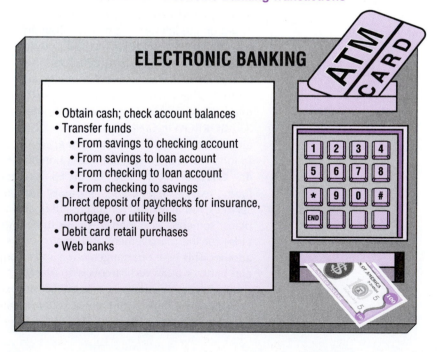

14   A lost or stolen debit card can be expensive. If you notify the financial institution within two days of the lost card, your liability for unauthorized use is $50. After that, you can be liable for up to $500 of unauthorized use for up to 60 days. Beyond that, your liability is unlimited. However, some card issuers use the same rules for lost or stolen debit cards as for credit cards: a $50 maximum. Of course, you are not liable for unauthorized use, such as a con artist using your account number to make a purchase. Remember to report the fraud within 60 days of receiving your statement to protect your right not to be charged for the transaction.

15   While most traditional financial institutions also offer online banking services, Web-only banks have also started. For example, E*Trade Bank (www.etradebank.com) operates online while also providing customers with access to ATMs. Many of today's best checking and savings deals come from Web-based branchless banks.

Source: Jack Kapoor, Les Dlabay, and Robert Hughes, *Personal Finance,* 7th ed., pp. 132–35, 148, 151. Copyright © 2004 McGraw-Hill/Irwin. Reprinted by permission of The McGraw-Hill Companies.

Comprehension Check

True-False

_____   1.   A majority of people use direct electronic deposit of paychecks and government checks.

_____   2.   Some ATMs offer transactions such as buying postage stamps, bus passes, and gift certificates.

_____   3.   Electronic banking customers can preauthorize payments for insurance, mortgage, and utility bills.

_____   4.   A debit card differs from a credit card because the person is spending his or her own funds rather than borrowing additional money.

_____   5.   When more cash than is available is needed quickly, a person can either liquidate savings or write a check.

Multiple-Choice

_____   6.   An asset management account would appeal to primarily to banking customers who
    a.   want complete financial services and prefer the simplicity of paying a single fee.
    b.   are extremely wealthy.
    c.   live in an area in which a bank is not conveniently located for them.
    d.   do not invest in stocks, bonds, or mutual funds.

_____   7.   An advantage of electronic banking is
    a.   reduced fees for transactions.
    b.   e-mails confirming all transactions.
    c.   a monthly printout of transactions.
    d.   24-hour access to various transactions.

_____ 8. A trust is
   a. a legal agreement that provides for the management and control of assets by one party for the benefit of another.
   b. an all-purpose account, which usually includes a checking account, an ATM card, a credit card, online banking, as well as a line of credit for obtaining quick cash loans.
   c. the safe storage of funds for future use.
   d. a cash management account.

_____ 9. Which of the following is NOT a short-term financial need?
   a. daily purchases
   b. buying a car.
   c. living expense payments
   d. emergencies

_____ 10. Electronic banking by telephone, home computer, and other online services would probably be especially appealing to people who
   a. travel a great deal.
   b. have mobility or transportation problems.
   c. have limited time.
   d. all of the above

Vocabulary-in-Context Check

The first sentence comes from the selection and contains a word that is italicized (*like this*). The second sentence uses the word in the same sense, but in a different context. *Choose the meaning that fits the context of both sentences.* You will often be able to use your knowledge of word parts to confirm your educated guess.

_____ 1. While most people desire *ease* of payment, they must also consider fees and the potential for impulse buying and overspending. (paragraph 4)

   Although adults typically struggle to learn a second language, young children do it with *ease*.

   Ease means
   a. speed.
   b. extended amount of time.
   c. freedom from difficulty or effort.
   d. freedom from fear.

_____ 2. For example, in recent years ATM fees have risen from nothing to $1 or $2 per cash withdrawal and even higher charges for *balance* inquiries. (paragraph 4)

   After I paid my bills, the *balance* in my checking account was only two-hundred dollars.

   Balance means
   a. amount of money available in an account.
   b. a state of equilibrium.
   c. total amount of money owed.
   d. a weighing device.

_____ **3.** To cope with that situation, you have two basic choices: *liquidate* savings or borrow. (paragraph 6)

To avoid bankruptcy, the storeowner had to *liquidate* his inventory and pay off creditors.

Liquidate means
a. to sell at low prices.
b. to convert into cash.
c. to invest earnings in additional shares of stock.
d. to change into a liquid.

_____ **4.** Remember, however, that both using savings and increasing borrowing reduce your *net* worth and your potential to achieve long-term financial security. (paragraph 6)

Our company's *net* profit was up six percent last year.

Net means
a. pertaining to a device made of meshwork.
b. pertaining to a network.
c. remaining after all deductions have been made for expenses and debts.
d. at the time of death.

_____ **5.** A trust is a legal agreement that provides for the management and control of *assets* by one party for the benefit of another. (paragraph 11)

My grandfather's *assets* include a house, a rental property, some shares of stocks, and a valuable stamp collection.

Assets means
a. valuable qualities or characteristics.
b. property owned by a person at the time of his or her death.
c. the entire property owned by a person that can be used to settle debts.
d. advantages.

_____ **6.** To simplify the *maze* of financial services and to attract customers, many financial institutions offer all-in-one accounts. (paragraph 12)

Before I was finally able to talk with a manager who could help me, I spent ten minutes working my way through a *maze* of automated telephone options and unhelpful customer service representatives.

Maze means
a. a graphic puzzle of a path through an intricate pattern.
b. something made up of many confusing elements.
c. a set of interconnecting pathways.
d. challenge.

_____ **7.** Most banks and other financial institutions have "*cyber*" branches that provide the following [banking services]. (paragraph 13)

Many people find it more convenient to go *cyber* shopping on the Internet than to go to actual stores.

Cyber means
a. neighborhood.
b. existing on computers.
c. pertaining to shopping.
d. related to banking.

_____ 8. To minimize ATM fees, compare several financial institutions, use your bank's ATM to avoid *surcharges,* and withdraw larger amounts to avoid fees on several small transactions. (paragraph 13, bullet 3)

Consumers protested the *surcharges* added to their bills by the utility company.

Surcharges means
a. illegal charges made by a company or institution.
b. amounts charged for services that were not requested.
c. unfair fees.
d. additional sums added to the usual cost.

_____ 9. Beyond that, your *liability* is unlimited. (paragraph 14)

To avoid *liability,* you should be careful about co-signing a loan for someone else; if that person fails to repay the loan, then you must do it.

Liability means
a. financial responsibility; debt.
b. bankruptcy.
c. ability to plan financially.
d. disappointment.

_____ 10. Many of today's best checking and savings deals come from Web-based *branchless* banks. (paragraph 15)

Although the mortgage company was *branchless* and had only one office for the first six years, today it has branch offices in every part of the city.

Branchless means
a. offering high demand services.
b. having no other business divisions.
c. charging excessive fees.
d. available to only a select few.

Writing Prompts

Your instructor may assign you some or all of the following questions. For items marked with the collaborative icon, your instructor may ask you to work in small groups (three or four students) to come up with an answer. *Everyone* in the group should be able to explain the group's answer.

1. Do you have a plan for managing cash? Which financial services described in the selection are ones you currently use? Which additional ones would be helpful to you?

_____

_____

_____

_____

_____

2. In light of advances in technology and the increasing use of it by more people, in what ways do you thinking banking and customer transactions are likely to change in the future?

_____

_____

_____

_____

_____

_____

3. List at least three new things you learned from the selection.

_____

_____

_____

_____

_____

_____

Web Resources

If a URL has become inactive or if you need more information, use "college students managing cash" or a similar descriptor with an Internet search engine such as Google.

http://www.bankrate.com/brm/news/financial-birthdays/twenties/early20s-cash.asp

This bankrate.com section is entitled "Invest in Yourself: 20s" and contains links to dozens of financial tips and articles of interest to young adults and college students.

http://www.nysscpa.org/sound_advice/money_7.4.05.htm

Sponsored by the New York State Society of CPAs, this readable, informative selection lays out what college students need to know about managing credit.

http://www.youngmoney.com/credit_debt/credit_basics

Youngmoney.com offers a wealth of articles on credit basics for college students.

SELECTION 11

The following selection is from a U.S. government textbook. It gives a historical perspective of the legal rights of gays and lesbians, including the highly charged issue of same-sex marriage and civil unions.

LEGAL RIGHTS OF GAYS AND LESBIANS

1   A group that until very recently has not received substantial legal protection is gays and lesbians. In 2000, for example, the Supreme Court ruled that Boy Scouts, as a private organization that has a right to freedom of association, can ban gays because the Scout creed prohibits homosexuality.

2   Research has not identified the full extent of discrimination against gays and lesbians, but fragmentary evidence indicates that it is substantial. A disproportionate number of hate crimes—including assaults—are directed at gay men. A poll found that nearly 40 percent of the members of the Los Angeles Bar Association had witnessed overt discrimination in their firm and that more than 50 percent thought their firm's work environment was antagonistic to lawyers who were gay or lesbian. A survey of New York State gays and lesbians found that half had experienced gender-based discrimination at a restaurant, store, hotel, or other public place.

3   Historically, gays and lesbians fought discrimination by trying to keep their sexual orientation a secret. Many still do so, but gays and lesbians now also comprise a powerful political group. One of the first indications was when Democratic presidential nominee Bill Clinton in 1992 promised to change the military's ban on homosexuals. The resulting "don't ask, don't tell" policy allows gays and lesbians to remain in the military as long as they do not by words or actions openly reveal their sexual preference. Nevertheless, the "don't ask, don't tell" policy was a hollow victory to many gays and lesbians, who had wanted the ban to be lifted completely.

4   Gays and lesbians gained a significant legal victory when the Supreme Court in *Romer v. Evans* (1996) struck down a Colorado constitutional amendment that nullified all existing and any new legal protections for homosexuals. In a 6–3 ruling, the Court said that the Colorado law violated the Constitution's guarantee of equal protection because it subjected individuals to employment and other forms of discrimination simply because of their sexual preference The Court concluded that the law had no reasonable purpose but was instead motivated by hostility toward homosexuals. In *Lawrence v. Texas* (2003), the Court handed gays and lesbians another victory by invalidating state laws that prohibit sexual relations between consenting adults of the same sex.

5   Recently, a major issue for gays and lesbians has been securing the same legal status that the law extends to married opposite-sex couples. During the past decade or so, same-sex couples have succeeded in getting some states and many cities and firms to extend employee benefits, such as health care, to employees' same-sex partners. These arrangements, however, do not apply to things such as inheritance and hospital visitation rights, which are granted by state law to married couples and their families. There is also the issue of the social validation

Figure 1   Opinions on Gay and Lesbian Lifestyles
Americans are less likely than Western Europeans to believe that society should accept gay and lesbian lifestyles.

Percentage agreeing that "homosexuality is a way
of life that should be accepted by society."

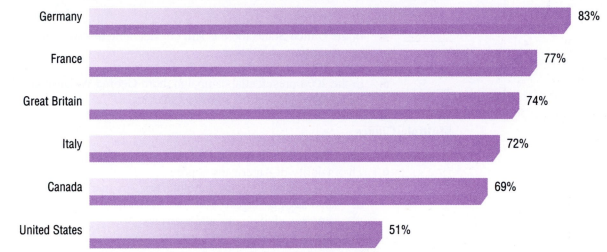

Germany — 83%
France — 77%
Great Britain — 74%
Italy — 72%
Canada — 69%
United States — 51%

Source: Global Attitudes Survey (2002) by the Pew Research Center for the People and the Press.

accorded to couples who are married as opposed to those who are not. For these reasons, gay and lesbian couples have pressed for legal recognition of their relationships. In 2000, the state of Vermont legalized the civil union of same-sex couples, thereby granting them the same legal rights as those held by opposite-sex married couples. In 2004, upon order of the state's high court, Massachusetts instituted same-sex marriage, giving same-sex married couples the same social and legal status as opposite-sex married couples.

6   This issue spilled over to the 2004 presidential campaign when President George W. Bush reacted to the Massachusetts high court decision by claiming that marriage should be reserved for "a man and a woman." The Democratic party's nominee, John Kerry, also came out against same-sex marriage, but, unlike Bush, he endorsed civil unions.

7   For their part, a majority of Americans oppose same-sex marriage, although they are divided almost evenly on the issue of civil unions. Nevertheless, attitudes toward same-sex relationships have moderated substantially in recent decades. Most Americans, for example, now believe that partners in same-sex relationships should receive the same employee health benefits as spouses. Yet Americans, perhaps because of their deeper religious beliefs, are less supportive of gay and lesbian lifestyles than are Europeans (see Figure 1). One thing is sure: issues of gay and lesbian rights, including same-sex marriage and civil union, will be a focus of political action and controversy for the foreseeable future.

Source: Thomas E. Patterson, *The American Democracy,* 7th Alternate ed., pp. 158–61. Copyright © 2005 McGraw-Hill. Reprinted by permission of the The McGraw-Hill Companies.

Comprehension Check

True-False

_____   **1.**   Because of recent legislation in the United States, the issues of same-sex marriage and civil union finally seem to be resolved.

_____ **2.** Some states, cities, and firms have extended employee benefits to employees' same-sex partners.

_____ **3.** In 2002 the state of Vermont recognized same-sex marriages.

_____ **4.** In the United States there is still considerable discrimination against gays and lesbians.

_____ **5.** In the 2004 presidential campaign, both George W. Bush and John Kerry came out against same-sex marriages.

Multiple-Choice

_____ **6.** The majority of Americans oppose
  a. same-sex civil unions, but not same-sex marriages.
  b. same-sex marriages.
  c. same-sex civil unions and marriages.
  d. same-sex marriages, but have less opposition to civil unions.

_____ **7.** A disproportionate number of hate crimes have been directed at
  a. lesbians.
  b. gay men.
  c. members of the Los Angeles Bar Association.
  d. New York State gays and lesbians.

_____ **8.** A "don't ask, don't tell" policy is used in
  a. law firms.
  b. the military.
  c. hotels.
  d. public places.

_____ **9.** In the Global Attitudes Survey (2002), which country had the highest percent agreeing that homosexuality should be acceptable as a lifestyle?
  a. France
  b. Germany
  c. Great Britain
  d. Italy

_____ **10.** Americans may be less accepting than Europeans are of gay and lesbian lifestyles because of Americans'
  a. deeper religious beliefs.
  b. willingness to file lawsuits.
  c. love of political controversy.
  d. fear of any lifestyle than differs from a traditional one.

Vocabulary-in-Context Check

The first sentence comes from the selection and contains a word that is italicized (*like this*). The second sentence uses the word in the same sense, but in a different context. *Choose the meaning that fits the context of both sentences.* You will often be able to use your knowledge of word parts to confirm your educated guess.

_____ **1.** A group that until very recently has not received *substantial* legal protection is gays and lesbians. (paragraph 1)

Since September 11, 2001, the issue of terrorism has received *substantial* coverage in the media.

Substantial means
a. permanent; lasting.
b. official.
c. widely accepted by the public.
d. considerable in importance, value, or extent.

_____ **2.** In 2000, for example, the Supreme Court ruled that Boy Scouts, as a private organization that has a right to freedom of association, can ban gays because the Scout *creed* prohibits homosexuality. (paragraph 1)

At the beginning of every meeting, club members stand and recite its *creed* in unison.

Creed means
a. secret pledge.
b. formal statement of beliefs.
c. personal statement of values.
d. special motto known only to certain members of a group.

_____ **3.** A *disproportionate* number of hate crimes—including assaults—are directed at gay men. (paragraph 4)

Despite modest increases in recent years, the number of women in chief executive positions is still *disproportionate*.

Disproportionate means
a. surprising.
b. smaller in quantity.
c. larger in quantity.
d. out of proportion in relation to the whole.

_____ **4.** A poll found that nearly 40 percent of the members of the Los Angeles Bar Association had witnessed *overt* discrimination in their firm and that more than 50 percent thought their firm's work environment was antagonistic to lawyers who were gay or lesbian. (paragraph 2)

The gambler's cheating was so *overt* that he was quickly caught and escorted out of the casino by security guards.

Overt means
a. skillful; clever.
b. open and observable.
c. intelligently done.
d. hidden.

_____ **5.** A poll found that nearly 40 percent of the members of the Los Angeles Bar Association had witnessed overt discrimination in their firm and that more than 50 percent thought their firm's work environment was *antagonistic* to lawyers who were gay or lesbian. (paragraph 2)

The divorcing couple were so *antagonistic* toward each other that they spoke to each other only through their lawyers.

***Antagonistic* means**
a. hostile.
b. confusing; puzzling.
c. dependent upon.
d. welcoming.

_____ 6. One of the first indications was when Democratic presidential nominee Bill Clinton in 1992 promised to change the military's *ban* on homosexuals. (paragraph 3)

The city government's *ban* on smoking in restaurants angered many smokers' rights groups.

***Ban* means**
a. limit.
b. public statement.
c. a prohibition imposed by law.
d. strong disapproval.

_____ 7. Nevertheless, the "don't ask, don't tell" policy was a *hollow* victory to many gays and lesbians, who had wanted the ban to be lifted completely. (paragraph 3)

Although the coach said nice things about the opposing team, it was clear from the way he said it that it was *hollow* flattery.

***Hollow* means**
a. meaningful.
b. not having true value or meaning.
c. sudden; unexpected.
d. making an echoing sound.

_____ 8. Gays and lesbians gained a significant legal victory when the Supreme Court in *Romer v. Evans* (1996) struck down a Colorado constitutional amendment that *nullified* all existing and any new legal protections for homosexuals. (paragraph 4)

Because of voting irregularities, city officials *nullified* the election results and scheduled a revote a month later.

***Nullified* means**
a. changed in accordance with newer laws.
b. published in newspapers.
c. filed in a court of law.
d. declared to have no legal force.

_____ 9. There is also the issue of the social *validation* accorded to couples who are married as opposed to those who are not. (paragraph 5)

To adolescents, the *validation* by their peers means everything.

***Validation* means**
a. approval or acceptance.
b. isolation.
c. legal approval.
d. rejection.

_____ **10.** The Democratic party's nominee, John Kerry, also came out against same-sex marriage, but, unlike Bush, he endorsed *civil* unions. (paragraph 6)

Rather than having a large church wedding, the couple decided to be married in a simple *civil* ceremony at the courthouse.

Civil means
  a. courteous; polite.
  b. related to the military.
  c. pertaining to ordinary life as opposed to religious life.
  d. formal and lengthy.

Writing Prompts

Your instructor may assign you some or all of the following questions. For items marked with the collaborative icon, your instructor may ask you to work in small groups (three or four students) to come up with an answer. *Everyone* in the group should be able to explain the group's answer.

1. List at least three new things you learned or that you found interesting.

_____

_____

_____

_____

2. Does the military's "don't ask, don't tell" policy make sense? If not, how could this problem be handled instead? Explain your position.

_____

_____

_____

_____

3. If gay couples are allowed to be legally married, what implications might that have for American society?

_____

_____

_____

_____

Web Resources

If a URL has become inactive or if you need more information, use "gay and lesbian rights" or a similar descriptor with an Internet search engine such as Google.

http://gaylife.about.com/cs/mentalhealth1/a/samesexmarriage.htm

This about.com page about marriage rights for gays and lesbians includes links to other relevant sites, including ones that pertain to similar rights in other countries.

http://www.publicagenda.org/issues/overview.cfm?issue_type=gay_rights

"Gay Rights: Overview," sponsored by Public Agenda, "a nonpartisan opinion research and civic engagement organization." The Understanding the Issue guide includes a fact file.

SELECTION 12

The following geography textbook excerpt explores terrorism and political geography. It describes and illustrates different forms of terrorism and explores ways the problem of terrorism can addressed. The word "terrorism" instantly became part of everyone's vocabulary after the 2001 World Trade Center attacks, and it is still virtually impossible to find a national newscast that does not mention terroism. Political geography *is a branch of human geography concerned with the spatial analysis of political phenomena. Its primary interest is in country units, or states, and spatial patterns that reflect the exercise of central governmental control.*

TERRORISM AND POLITICAL GEOGRAPHY

1   "Where were you when the world stopped turning?" asks Alan Jackson in his song about the September 11, 2001, terrorist attacks on the United States. You probably know the answer to his question, and you probably always will. Of course, the world didn't really stop turning, but that's how it felt to millions of Americans with no previous exposure to terrorism.

2   What is terrorism? How does it relate to political geography? Do all countries experience terrorism? Is terrorism new? Is there a way to prevent it? Attempting to answer these questions, difficult as they are, may help us understand the phenomenon.

3   **Terrorism** is the calculated use of violent acts against civilians and symbolic targets to publicize a cause, intimidate or coerce a civilian population, or affect the conduct of a government. *International terrorism,* such as the attacks of September 11, 2001, includes acts that transcend national boundaries. International terrorism is intended to intimidate people in other countries. *Domestic terrorism* consists of acts by individuals or groups against the citizens or government of their own country. *State terrorism* is committed by the agents of a government. *Subnational terrorism* is committed by groups outside a government.

4   Terrorism, thus, is a weapon. It is a weapon whose aim is intimidation and whose victims are usually civilians.

State Terrorism

5   State terrorism is probably as old as the concept of a state. As early as 146 B.C., for example, Roman forces sacked and completely destroyed the city of Carthage, burning it to the ground, killing men, women, and children, and sowing salt on the fields so that no crops could grow. Governments have used systematic policies of violence and intimidation to further dominate and control their own populations. Nazi Germany, the Pol Pot regime in Cambodia, and Stalinist Russia are 20th-century examples of state terrorism. Heads of state ordered

the murder, imprisonment, or exile of enemies of the state—politicians, intellectuals, dissidents—anyone who dared to criticize the government. In Rwanda, the former Yugoslavia, and Saddam Hussein's Iraq, state terrorism aimed against ethnic and religious minorities provided the government with a method of consolidating power; in each case, genocide, or mass murder of ethnic minority groups, was the result. The government or its agencies waged full-fledged military campaigns against minority groups.

Subnational Terrorism

6   Subnational terrorism began much later, at the same time as the rise of the nation-state. Subnational terrorism can be perpetrated by those who feel wronged by their own or another government. For example, ethnic groups in a minority who feel that the national government has taken their territory and absorbed them into a larger political entity, such as the Basques in Spain, have used terrorist acts to resist the government. Ethnic and religious groups that have been split by national boundaries imposed by others, such as Palestinian Arabs in the Middle East, have used terrorism to make governance impossible. Political, ethnic, or religious groups that feel oppressed by their own government, such as the Oklahoma City bombers in the United States, have committed acts of domestic terrorism.

7   Nearly every country has experienced some form of terrorism at some point since the mid-19th century. These acts have been as various as the anarchist assassinations of political leaders in Europe during the 1840s and in the United States in the late 19th century, the abduction of Canadian government officials by the Front Liberation du Quebec (FLQ) in 1970, and the release of sarin gas in the Tokyo subways in 1995 by the group Aum Shinrikyo.

8   The political and religious aims of these attackers, however, can cause confusion on the world stage. In 2001, the Reuters News Agency told its reporters to stop using the word terrorism, because "one person's terrorist is another's freedom fighter." The definition of terrorism rests on the ability to identify motives.

9   Although it may be difficult to distinguish among types of terrorism, it is even more difficult to prevent it. Generally speaking, there are four common responses to terrorism on the part of governments and international bodies:

1.   *Reducing or addressing the causes of terrorism.* In some cases, political change can reduce a terrorist threat. For example, the 1998 Good Friday Agreement in Northern Ireland led to a reduction in terrorist acts; the Spanish government's granting of some regional autonomy to the Basques helped quiet the actions of the ETA and reduced the support of many Basque people for such acts.

2.   *Increasing international cooperation in the surveillance of subnational groups.* Spurred by terrorist crimes in Bahrain and Saudi Arabia, the Arab Gulf States agreed in 1998 to exchange intelligence regarding terrorist groups, to share intelligence regarding the prevention of an anticipated terrorist act, and to assist each other in investigating terrorist crimes.

3.   *Increasing security measures in a country.* In the United States, following September 11, 2001, the government organized a Department of Homeland Security, federalized air traffic screening, and increased efforts to reduce financial support for foreign terrorist organizations. In concert, the European Union froze the assets of any group on its list of terrorist organizations.

4.   *Using military means, either unilaterally or multilaterally, against terrorists or governments that sponsor terrorists.* Following the September 11 attacks, the United States led a coalition of countries in attacking the government of Afghanistan, which had harbored Osama bin Laden's al-Queda terrorist organization.

10   Each response to terrorism is expensive, politically difficult, and/or potentially harmful to the life and liberty of civilians. Governments must decide which
response or combination of responses is likely to have the most beneficial effect.

Source: Arthur Getis, Judith Getis, Jerome Feldmann, Victoria Getis, and Jon Malinowski, *Introduction to Geography,* 10th ed., pp. 322–23. Copyright © 2006, McGraw-Hill. Reprinted by permission of The McGraw-Hill Companies.

Comprehension Check

True-False

_____ 1. Terrorism can be conducted by an individual or a group.

_____ 2. It is more difficult to distinguish between forms of terrorism than it is to prevent it.

_____ 3. The victims of terrorism are usually citizens.

_____ 4. The earliest form of terrorism was subnational terrorism.

_____ 5. At some point since the mid-19th century, nearly every country has experienced some form of terrorism.

Multiple-Choice

_____ 6. Acts of terrorism committed by groups outside a government is termed
   a. domestic terrorism.
   b. international terrorism.
   c. state terrorism.
   d. subnational terrorism.

_____ 7. Which of the following is NOT a common response by govern-ments or international bodies to terrorism?
   a. increasing security measures in a country
   b. negotiating with terrorists
   c. reducing or addressing the causes of terrorism
   d. increasing international cooperation in the surveillance of subnational groups

_____ 8. Genocide, the mass murder of ethnic minority groups by a gov-ernment's military troops, has occurred in
   a. Iraq.
   b. Spain.
   c. Canada.
   d. Bahrain.

_____ 9. Nazi Germany is an example of
   a. domestic terrorism.
   b. international terrorism.
   c. state terrorism.
   d. subnational terrorism.

_____ **10.** The September 11, 2001, attacks on the World Trade Center
would be classified as

   a. domestic terrorism.
   b. international terrorism.
   c. state terrorism.
   d. subnational terrorism.

Vocabulary-in-Context Check

The first sentence comes from the selection and contains a word that is italicized (*like this*). The second sentence uses the word in the same sense, but in a different context. *Choose the meaning that fits the context of both sentences.* You will often be able to use your knowledge of word parts to confirm your educated guess.

_____ **1.** Terrorism is the *calculated* use of violent acts against civilians
and symbolic targets to publicize a cause, intimidate or coerce
a civilian population, or affect the conduct of a government.
(paragraph 3)

The rescuers took a *calculated* risk that they would be able to get
to the climbers before darkness.

Calculated means
   a. spontaneous; unplanned.
   b. involving numbers.
   c. made for a deliberate purpose.
   d. daring or bold.

_____ **2.** International terrorism is intended to *intimidate* people in other
countries. (paragraph 3)

Bullies *intimidate* others in order to maintain their power.

Intimidate means
   a. to inspire admiration and awe.
   b. to fill with fear; coerce by threats.
   c. to ease the anger or agitation of.
   d. to become close allies or friends.

_____ **3.** Nazi Germany, the Pol Pot *regime* in Cambodia, and Stalinist
Russia are 20th-century examples of state terrorism. (paragraph 5)

Fidel Castro's Communist *regime* in Cuba has lasted for more
than four decades.

Regime means
   a. cruel dictatorship.
   b. period during which a particular administration prevails.
   c. merger; union.
   d. term of elected office.

_____ **4.** In Rwanda, the former Yugoslavia, and Saddam Hussein's Iraq,
state terrorism aimed against ethnic and religious minorities provided the government with a method of *consolidating* power; in
each case, genocide, or mass murder of ethnic minority groups,
was the result. (paragraph 5)

By *consolidating* his hold on the company's finances, he was
eventually able to gain control of the company.

Consolidating means
a. sharing mutually.
b. relinquishing; giving up.
c. abandoning.
d. strengthening; making secure.

_____ 5. The government or its agencies waged *full-fledged* military campaigns against minority groups. (paragraph 5)

After initiation, they were considered *full-fledged* members of the club who could hold office and vote.

Full-fledged means
a. having insufficient support.
b. having an unclear purpose.
c. having reached full development.
d. having no final goal.

_____ 6. Political, ethnic, or religious groups that feel *oppressed* by their own government, such as the Oklahoma City bombers in the United States, have committed acts of domestic terrorism. (paragraph 6)

The American Revolution came about because colonists felt increasingly *oppressed* by the British monarchy.

Oppressed means
a. annoyed.
b. not understood or misunderstood.
c. punished.
d. kept down by severe and unjust use of force or authority.

_____ 7. These acts have been as various as the *anarchist* assassinations of political leaders in Europe during the 1840s and in the United States in the late 19th century. (paragraph 7)

The *anarchist* philosophy holds that all forms of government or rulership are undesirable and should be abolished.

Anarchist means
a. pertaining to the absence of any form of political authority.
b. pertaining to 20th-century politics.
c. pertaining to the rights of the middle class.
d. pertaining to Eastern Europe.

_____ 8. . . . the Spanish government's granting of some regional *autonomy* to the Basques helped quiet the actions of the ETA and reduced the support of many Basque people for such acts. (paragraph 9, item 1)

India, once a colony ruled by the British Empire, eventually gained *autonomy* and became an independent nation in 1947.

Autonomy means
a. self-government.
b. partial control.
c. unlimited power.
d. widespread respect.

_____ **9.** Using military means, either *unilaterally* or multilaterally, against terrorists or governments that sponsor terrorists. (heading, paragraph 9, item 4)

France *unilaterally* changed its position on the issue and abruptly withdrew from the negotiations with the other countries.

Unilaterally means
a. without notice.
b. done at the same time.
c. involving only one nation.
d. with formal approval.

_____ **10.** Following the September 11 attacks, the United States led a *coalition* of countries in attacking the government of Afghanistan, which had harbored Osama bin Laden's al-Queda terrorist organization. (paragraph 9, item 4)

After the tornado devastated the town, several state organizations formed a *coalition* to get aid to those who had lost their homes.

Coalition means
a. permanent council.
b. partnership comprised of religious groups.
c. an alliance, especially a temporary one.
d. lengthy conference or meeting.

Writing Prompts

Your instructor may assign you some or all of the following questions. For items marked with the collaborative icon, your instructor may ask you to work in small groups (three or four students) to come up with an answer. *Everyone* in the group should be able to explain the group's answer.

1. The selection mentions that "in 2001, the Reuters News Agency told its reporters to stop using the word terrorism, because 'one person's terrorist is another's freedom fighter'" and that "the definition of terrorism rests on the ability to identify motives." Explain the meaning of the statement "one person's terrorist is another's freedom fighter."

_____

_____

_____

_____

2. The September 11, 2001, terrorist attacks have had a profound effect on the United States. List at least three changes in American life or change in the way the United States perceives itself after those attacks.

_____

_____

_____

Web Resources

If a URL has become inactive or if you need more information, use "terrorism" or variations of that descriptor with an Internet search engine such as Google.

http://www.tkb.org/Home.jsp

The TKB (terrorism knowledge base) Website is a comprehensive databank regarding global terrorist incidents and organizations. It is sponsored by the National Memorial Institute for the Prevention of Terrorism. Start with the two-minute virtual tour of this outstanding website (requires speakers to hear the narrative). Users can look up terrorist groups by location, ideology, or groups. Interactive terrorism trends map and download.

http://en.wikipedia.org/wiki/Terrorism

The Wikipedia (free encyclopedia) entry on terrorism. Among other things, includes definitions, the War on Terrorism, types, and tactics.

Kudos to You from Your Coach! (Kudos Means Praise for Exceptional Achievement.)

Well, here you are at the end of the *entire* "workout" that comprises *Exercise Your College Reading Skills!* Did you occasionally have some sore "muscles"? Did you think at certain points that the "weight" was a little too heavy to lift? Probably so, but the important thing is that you've completed what you set out to do. And you should feel good about yourself for staying in the game. In mountaineering terms, you've reached the summit, and I'm so proud of you. Yes, there are skills you probably need additional practice on, but if you've given a full effort, then you are already a much stronger, more skilled reader than you were when you began this book.

I hope that you will see additional progress in your reading and study techniques as you continue to apply these skills in your college courses. Did you know, though, that simply finishing this book, your reading course, and a college semester places you in an elite group? The majority of the people in the world cannot read or write, and most of them will never have the opportunity to learn. Even if you never have another day of college, you are already better educated than most of the world's population. My belief is that because you have this advantage, you have a unique opportunity—and a responsibility—to give something back to the world. My hope is that you be a force for good, that you will use your education to help others. I hope that you will do something every day, no matter how small it might seem, to make the world a better place. Over a lifetime, even small acts of kindness and courtesy make a difference.

Baltimore Orioles pitching coach Mike Flanagan observed, "You can't compete from the dugout." So stay out on the field and keep pitching. My hope, too, is that you take away even more from this book than greatly strengthened reading skills, and that is the confidence and knowledge that through your own motivated effort, self-discipline, and mindful practice, *you can accomplish whatever goals you set for yourself.* My best wishes for your continued success.

A List of Word Parts

Understanding the meaning of various word parts can help you define many unfamiliar words, especially in context. Most word parts listed in this appendix are Latin or Greek. Try to associate each word part (left column) and its meaning (middle column) with the example (example). Associating the part and its definition with an example will help you remember word parts that are new to you (but you already knew that from Chapter 1 on using context clues and Chapter 2 on analyzing word structure).

	Word Part	Definition	Example
1.	a	without, not	amoral
2.	ab	from	abstain
3.	acou	hear	acoustic
4.	acro	high	acrobat
5.	alter	another	alternate
6.	ambi	both; around	ambivalent
7.	ambul	walk; go	ambulatory
8.	andr	man (human)	android
9.	annu, anni	year	annual, anniversary
10.	ante	before, forward	antebellum, antecedent
11.	anthrop	humankind	anthropology
12.	anti	against	antifreeze
13.	aqua	water	aquarium
14.	arch	ruler; chief, highest	archbishop, archenemy
15.	astro	star	astronomy
16.	aud	hear	auditory
17.	auto	self	automatic
18.	avi	bird	aviary
19.	belli	war	belligerent
20.	bene	well, good	beneficial
21.	bi	two	bicycle
22.	bio	life	biology
23.	bov	cattle	bovine
24.	by	secondarily	by-product
25.	camera	chamber	bicameral

	Word Part	Definition	Example
26.	cani	dog	canine
27.	capit	head	decapitate
28.	card	heart	cardiac
29.	carn	flesh	carnivorous
30.	caust, caut	burn	caustic, cauterize
31.	cav	hollow	cavity
32.	cent	hundred	century
33.	chromo	color	monochromatic
34.	chrono	time	chronology
35.	cide	kill	homicide
36.	contra	against	contraceptive
37.	cosm	universe	microcosm
38.	counter	against	counteract
39.	crat, cracy	rule	democratic
40.	cred, creed	belief	credibility, creed
41.	crypt	secret, hidden	cryptography
42.	cycl	circle	tricycle
43.	deca	ten	decade
44.	dei	god	deity
45.	demo	people	democracy
46.	dent	tooth	dentist
47.	derm	skin	dermatology
48.	di	two, double	dichotomy
49.	dict	speak	diction
50.	dorm	sleep	dormitory
51.	dyna	power	dynamo
52.	dys	bad, difficult	dysfunctional
53.	enni	year	centennial
54.	epi	upon, outer	epidermis
55.	equ	horse	equine
56.	esque	like, resembling	statuesque
57.	ethn	race, nation	ethnic
58.	eu	good, well	eulogy
59.	ex	out	exit
60.	extra	beyond, over	extravagant
61.	fer	carry, bear	transfer, conifer
62.	ferr	iron	ferrous
63.	fid	faith, trust	fidelity
64.	fini	limit	finite
65.	flagr	burn	conflagration
66.	flect, flex	bend	reflect, flexible
67.	fore	before	forewarn
68.	fort	strong	fortress
69.	frater	brother	fraternity
70.	gamy	marriage	monogamy

	Word Part	Definition	Example
71.	gastr	stomach	gastric
72.	gene, gen	origin, race, type	genesis, genocide, genre
73.	geo	earth	geography
74.	geronto	old	gerontology
75.	grad, gress	go, step	regress
76.	graph, gram	write, record	telegraph
77.	gyne	woman	gynecology
78.	helio	sun	heliocentric
79.	hemi	half	hemisphere
80.	hemo	blood	hemophilia
81.	hetero	other, different	heterosexual
82.	homo	same	homosexual
83.	hydr	water	hydrant
84.	hyper	over, above	hyperactive
85.	hypo	under, less than	hypodermic
86.	ign	fire	ignite
87.	in, il, im, ir	not	inactive
88.	inter	between	intercept
89.	intra	within	intravenous
90.	itis	inflammation	tonsilitis
91.	ject	throw	eject
92.	junct	join	junction
93.	kilo	thousand	kilometer
94.	later	side	lateral
95.	leg	law	legal
96.	liber	free	liberate
97.	libr	book	library
98.	lingua	tongue, language	bilingual
99.	lith	stone	lithograph
100.	locu, loqu, log	speak	elocution, colloquial, dialogue
101.	logy	study of	psychology
102.	luc	light, clear	lucid
103.	macro	large	macrocosm
104.	magn	great	magnify
105.	mal	bad, ill	malfunction
106.	mamma	breast	mammal
107.	mania	craving for	kleptomania
108.	manu	hand	manual
109.	matri, mater	mother	maternal
110.	mega	large	megaphone
111.	meter, metr	measure	thermometer, metric
112.	micro	small	microscope
113.	milli	thousand, thousandth	millennium, millimeter
114.	mini	less	minimal

	Word Part	Definition	Example
115.	miso	hatred of	misogamy
116.	miss, mit	send	dismiss, transmit
117.	mob, mov, mot	to move	mobile, movable, motion
118.	mono	one	monotone
119.	morph	form	amorphous
120.	mort	death	mortal
121.	multi	many	multitude
122.	nat	born, birth	prenatal
123.	naut	sail	nautical
124.	neo	new	neophyte
125.	noct	night	nocturnal
126.	nox	harmful	noxious
127.	ob, oc, of, op	against	object, occlude, offend, oppress
128.	oct	eight	octopus, octagon
129.	ocul	eye	oculist
130.	oid	resembling	humanoid
131.	omni	all	omnipotent
132.	onym	name, word	pseudonym
133.	ortho	correct, straight	orthodontist
134.	osis	condition	psychosis
135.	osteo, ost	bone	osteopath
136.	out	better than	outrun
137.	pac, pax	peace	pacifist
138.	pan	all	panorama
139.	para	beside	parallel, parapsychology
140.	path	feeling, illness	sympathy, pathology
141.	patri, pater	father	paternity
142.	ped, pod	foot	pedal, tripod
143.	pel	drive	repel
144.	pend	hang	pendulum, pending
145.	penta	five	pentagon, pentathlon
146.	per	through	perspire
147.	peri	around	perimeter
148.	petr	rock	petrified
149.	philo	love	philosophy
150.	phobia	fear of	acrophobia
151.	phono	sound	phonics, phonograph
152.	photo	light	photograph
153.	pneum	air	pneumatic
154.	poly	many	polygon
155.	port	carry	portable
156.	pos	place	position
157.	post	after	postwar

	Word Part	Definition	Example
158.	pre	before	prewar
159.	primo	first	primitive, primordial
160.	pro	forward, in favor of	progress, pro-American
161.	pseud	false	pseudoscience
162.	psych	mind	psychic
163.	pugn	fight	pugnacious
164.	punct	point	puncture
165.	purg	cleanse	purge
166.	pyre	fire	pyromania
167.	quad, quart	four	quadruplets, quartet
168.	quint	five	quintet
169.	re	back, again	return, repeat
170.	reg	guide, rule; king	regulate, regal
171.	rupt	break	rupture, disrupt
172.	scend	climb	descend
173.	scope	see; view	telescope
174.	scribe, scrip	write	scribble, prescription
175.	sequ	follow	sequence, sequel
176.	semi	half	semicircle
177.	seni	old	senile
178.	simil	like	similar
179.	sol	sun	solar
180.	soli	alone	solitude
181.	somni	sleep	insomnia
182.	soph	wise	sophomore, sophisticated
183.	spect	see	spectator
184.	spir	breathe	respiratory
185.	strict	tighten	constrict
186.	sub	under	submarine
187.	super, sur	over	supervisor, surpass
188.	surg	rise	surge, resurgent
189.	tang, tact	touch	tangible, tactile
190.	tech, tect	skill	technician
191.	tele	far	telepathy
192.	tend, tens	stretch	tendon, tension
193.	terri	earth	territory
194.	tert	third	tertiary
195.	theo	god	theology
196.	therm	heat	thermometer
197.	tomy	cut	vasectomy
198.	tors, tort	twist	distort
199.	toxi	poison	toxic
200.	tract	pull, drag	tractor, extract, distract
201.	tri	three	trio

	Word Part	Definition	Example
202.	ultra	beyond, over	ultramodern
203.	unct, ung	oil	unctuous, unguent
204.	uni	one	unity
205.	vacu	empty	vacuum
206.	veni, vent	come	convene, convention
207.	verd	green	verdant
208.	vers, vert	turn	reverse
209.	vid, vis	see	video, vision
210.	vinc	conquer	invincible
211.	vit, viv	life	vitality, vivacious
212.	voc, voke	voice, call	vocal, evoke
213.	voli, volunt	wish	volition, volunteer
214.	volv	roll, to turn	revolve
215.	zoo	animal	zoology

There are countless vocabulary-related websites. Here are some that I like. They're fascinating, informative, and some are downright fun (unless you happen to be logophobic).

www.wordfocus.com	Latin and Greek word parts and the thousands of words derived from them are the focus here.
www.phobialist.com	Lists and defines more than 500 phobias. (Who knew there were so many?! Dazzle your friends!)
www.wordspy.com	Keeps track of newly coined words (neologisms) that are entering our language, such as *puggle, advertecture, carckberry, frankenfood cup-holder cuisine, celeblogs, shoefiti, gaydar, earworm, nicoteen,* and *al desko.* (Think how up-to-date you'll sound!) Also offers a "word of the day."
www.vocabulary.com	Called Vocabulary University, this website features a wealth of information, activities, and games at all levels.

READYING YOUR TEST-TAKING STRATEGIES

Preparation for tests requires a number of strategies. Among the most important are the following:

Remember: Everything You Do in a Course Is Preparation for a Test

All the things you do during a course help to prepare you for a test. There is no surer way to get good grades on tests than to attend class faithfully and to complete all class assignments seriously and on time.

Preparing for tests is a long-term proposition. It's not a matter of "giving your all" the night before the test. Instead, it's a matter of giving your all to every aspect of the course.

Know What You Are Preparing For

Determine as much as you can about the test *before* you begin to study for it. The more you know about a test beforehand, the more efficient your studying will be.

To find out about an upcoming test, ask these questions:

- What material will the test cover?
- How many questions will be on it?
- How much time is it expected to take? A full class period? Only part of a period?
- What kinds of questions will be on the test?
- How will it be graded?
- Will sample questions be provided?
- Are tests from previous terms available?

Match Test Preparation to Question Types

Test questions come in different types, and each requires a somewhat different style of preparation.

- **Essay questions.** Essay tests focus on the big picture—ways in which the various pieces of information being tested fit together. You'll need to know not just a series of facts, but also the connections between them, and you will have to be able to discuss these ideas in an organized and logical way.

The best approach to studying for an essay test involves four steps:

1. Carefully reread your class notes and any notes you've made on assigned readings that will be covered on the upcoming exam. Also go through the readings themselves, reviewing underlined or highlighted material and marginal notes.

2. Play professor: Think of likely exam questions. To do this, you can use the key words, phrases, concepts, and questions that come up in your class notes or in your text. Some instructors give out lists of possible essay topics; if yours does, focus on this list, but don't ignore other possibilities.

3. Without looking at your notes or your readings, answer each potential essay question—aloud. Don't feel embarrassed about doing this. Talking aloud is often more useful than answering the question in your head.

   You can also write down the main points that any answer should cover. (Don't write out *complete* answers to the questions unless your instructor tells you in advance exactly what is going to be on the test. Your time is probably better spent learning the material than rehearsing precisely formulated responses.)

4. After you've answered the questions, check yourself by looking at the notes and readings once again. If you feel confident that you've answered particular questions adequately, check them off. You can go back later for a quick review.

   But if there are questions that you had trouble with, review that material immediately. Then repeat the third step above, answering the questions again.

■ **Multiple-choice, true–false, and matching questions.** While the focus of review for essay questions should be on major issues and controversies, studying for multiple-choice, true–false, and matching questions requires more attention to the details.

   Almost anything is fair game for multiple-choice, true–false, and matching questions, so you can't afford to overlook anything when studying. True, these kinds of questions put the material right there on the page for you to react to—Did Columbus land in 1492, or not?—rather than asking you to provide the names and dates yourself (as in the case of the essay question). Nevertheless, to do well on these tests you must put your memory into high gear and master a great many facts.

   It's a particularly good idea to write down important facts on index cards like those on page A–9. Remember the advantages of these cards: They're portable and available all the time, and the act of creating them helps drive the material into your memory. Furthermore, you can shuffle them and test yourself repeatedly until you've mastered the material.

■ **Short-answer and fill-in questions.** Short-answer and fill-in questions are similar to essays in that they require you to recall key pieces of information rather than, as is the case with multiple-choice, true–false, and matching questions, finding it on the page in front of you. However, short-answer and fill-in questions—unlike essay questions—typically don't demand that you integrate or compare different types of information. Consequently, the focus of your study should be on the recall of specific, detailed information.

Political reforms of progressive age:
-direct primaries: people vote for whom they want to run; not appointed
-initiative: people propose laws on their own
-referendum: gov. proposes; people say yes or no
-recall: people can remove politicians from office before they finish term

Endoplasmic reticulum (ER):
Smooth ER—makes fats (lipids)
Rough ER—has ribosomes which make proteins
Together, they make membranes for whole cell (for plasma membrane, mitochondrion, etc.) Also make more of themselves.

Test Yourself

Once you feel you've mastered the material, test yourself on it. There are several ways to do this. One is to create a complete test for yourself, in writing, making its form as close as possible to what you expect the actual test to be. For instance, if your instructor has told you the classroom test will be primarily made up of short-answer questions, your test should be, too.

You might also construct a test and administer it to a classmate or a member of your study group. In turn, you could take a test that someone else has constructed. Constructing and taking practice tests are excellent ways of studying the material and cementing it into memory.

Deal with Test Anxiety

What does the anticipation of a test do to you? Do you feel shaky? Frantic, like there's not enough time to get it all done? Do you feel as if there's a knot in your stomach? Do you grit your teeth?

Test anxiety is a temporary condition characterized by fears and concerns about test-taking. Almost everyone experiences it to some degree, although for some people it's more of a problem than for others. The real danger with test anxiety is that it can become so overwhelming that it can hurt test performance.

You'll never eliminate test anxiety completely, nor do you want to. A little bit of nervousness can energize us, making us more attentive and vigilant. Like any competitive event, testing can motivate us to do our best. You might think of moderate test anxiety as a desire to perform at your peak—a useful quality at test time.

On the other hand, for some, anxiety can spiral into the kind of paralyzing fear that makes their mind go blank. There are several ways to keep this from happening to you:

1. *Prepare thoroughly.* The more you prepare, the less test anxiety you'll feel. Good preparation can give you a sense of control and mastery, and it will prevent test anxiety from overwhelming you.

2. *Take a realistic view of the test.* Remember that your future success does not hinge on your performance on any single exam. Think of the big picture: put the task ahead in context, and remind yourself of all the hurdles you've passed so far.

3. *Learn relaxation techniques.* You can learn to reduce or even eliminate the jittery physical symptoms of test anxiety by using relaxation techniques. Breathe evenly, gently inhaling and exhaling. Focus your mind on a pleasant,

relaxing scene such as a beautiful forest or a peaceful farm, or on a restful sound such as that of ocean waves breaking on the beach.

4. *Visualize success.* Think of an image of your instructor handing back your test marked with a big fat "A." Or imagine your instructor congratulating you on your fine performance the day after the test. Positive visualizations that highlight your potential success can help replace images of failure that may fuel test anxiety.

Form a Study Group

Study groups are small, informal groups of students who work together to learn course material and study for a test. Forming such a group can be an excellent way to prepare for any kind of test. Some study groups are formed for particular tests, while others meet consistently throughout the term.

The typical study group meets a week or two before a test and plans a strategy for studying. Members share their understanding of what will be on the test, based on what an instructor has said in class and on their review of notes and text material. Together, they develop a list of review questions to guide their individual study. The group then breaks up, and the members study on their own.

A few days before the test, members of the study group meet again. They discuss answers to the review questions, go over the material, and share any new insights they may have about the upcoming test. They may also quiz one another about the material to identify any weaknesses or gaps in their knowledge.

Study groups can be extremely powerful tools because they help accomplish several things:

- They help members organize and structure the material to approach their studying in a systematic and logical way.

- They allow students to share different perspectives on the material.

- They make it more likely that students will not overlook any potentially important information.

- They force members to rethink the course material, explaining it in words that other group members will understand. This helps both understanding and recall of the information when it is needed on the test.

- Finally, they help motivate members to do their best. When you're part of a study group, you're no longer working just for yourself; your studying also benefits the other study group members. Not wanting to let down your classmates in a study group may encourage you to work harder.

There are some potential drawbacks to keep in mind. Study groups don't always work well for students with learning styles that favor working independently. In addition, "problem" members—those who don't pull their weight—may cause difficulties for the group. In general, though, the advantages of study groups far outweigh their disadvantages.

Cramming: You Shouldn't, But . . .

You know, of course, that **cramming**, hurried, last-minute studying, is not the way to go. You know that you're likely to forget the material the moment the test is over because long-term retention is nearly impossible without thoughtful study. But . . .

. . . it's been one of those weeks where everything went wrong.

. . . the instructor sprang the test on you at the last minute.

. . . you forgot about the test until the night before it was scheduled.

Whatever the reason, there may be times when you can't study properly. What do you do if you *have* to cram for an exam?

Don't spend a lot of time on what you're unable to do. Beating yourself up about your failings as a student will only hinder your efforts. Instead, admit you're human and imperfect like everyone else. Then spend a few minutes developing a plan about what you can accomplish in the limited time you've got.

The first thing to do is choose what you really need to study. You won't be able to learn everything, so you have to make choices. Figure out the main focus of the course, and concentrate on it.

Once you have a strategy, prepare a one-page summary sheet with hard-to-remember information. Just writing the material down will help you remember it, and you can refer to the summary sheet frequently over the limited time you do have to study.

Next, read through your class notes, concentrating on the material you've underlined and the key concepts and ideas that you've already noted. Forget about reading all the material in the books and articles you're being tested on. Instead, only read the passages that you've underlined and the notes you've taken on the readings. Finally, maximize your study time. Using your notes, note cards, and concept maps, go over the information. Read it. Say it aloud. Think about it and the way it relates to other information. In short, use all the techniques we've talked about for learning and recalling information.

Just remember: When the exam is over, material that you have crammed into your head is destined to leave your mind as quickly as it entered. If you've crammed for a midterm, don't assume that the information will still be there when you study for the final. In the end, cramming often ends up taking more time for worse results than does studying with appropriate techniques.

FACING THE DAY OF THE TEST

You've studied a lot, and you're happy with your level of mastery. Or perhaps you have the nagging feeling that there's something you haven't quite gotten to. Or maybe you know you haven't had enough time to study as much as you'd like, and you're expecting a disaster.

Whatever your frame of mind, it will help to organize your plan of attack on the day of the test. What's included on the test is out of your hands, but you can control what you bring to it.

For starters, bring the right tools to the test. Have at least two pens and two pencils with you. It's usually best to write in pen because, in general, writing tends to be easier to read in pen than pencil. But you also might want to have pencils on hand. Sometimes instructors will use machine-scored tests, which require the use of pencil. Or there may be test questions that involve computations, and solving them may entail frequent reworking of calculations.

You should also be sure to bring a watch to the test, even if there will be a clock on the wall of the classroom. You will want to be able to pace yourself properly during the test. Just having your own watch will help you feel more in control of your time during the test.

Sometimes instructors permit you to use notes and books during the test. If you haven't brought them with you, they're not going to be of much help. So make sure you bring them if they're permitted. Even for closed-book tests, having such material available before the test actually starts may allow you a few minutes of review after you arrive in the classroom.

On the day of a test, avoid the temptation to compare notes with your friends about how much they've studied. Yes, you might end up feeling good because many of your fellow classmates studied less than you did. But chances are you'll find others who seem to have spent significantly *more* time studying than you, and this will do little to encourage you.

In addition, you might want to *plan on panicking*. Although it sounds like the worst possible approach, permitting yourself the option of spending a minute feeling panicky will help you to recover from your initial fears.

Finally, listen carefully to what an instructor says before the test is handed out. The instructor may tell you about a question that is optional or worth more points or inform you of a typographical error on the test. Whatever the instructor says just before the test, you can be sure it's information that you don't want to ignore.

TACKLING THE TEST

Take a deep breath—literally.

There's no better way to start work on a test than by taking a deep breath, followed by several others. The deep breaths will help you to overcome any initial panic and anxiety you may be experiencing. It's OK to give yourself over for a moment to panic and anxiety, but, to work at your best, use relaxation techniques to displace those initial feelings. Tell yourself, "It's OK. I am going to do my best on this."

Read the test instructions and then *skim through the entire exam*. Look at the kinds of questions and pay attention to the way they will be scored. If the point weighting of the various parts of the exam is not clear, ask the instructor to clarify it.

Knowing the point weighting is critical because it will help you to allocate your time. You don't want to spend 90 percent of your time on an essay that's worth only 10 percent of the points, and you want to be sure to leave time at the end of the test to check your answers. An initial read-through also helps you verify that you have every page of the exam and that there is no other physical problem with it, such as badly copied pages or ink marks that partially obscure some of the questions.

If there are any lists, formulas, or other key facts that you're concerned you may forget, jot them down now on the back of a test page or on a piece of scrap paper. You may want to refer to this material later during the test.

Once this background work is out of the way, you'll be ready to proceed to actually answering the questions. These principles will help you to do your best on the test:

- **Answer the easiest questions first.** By initially getting the questions out of the way that are easiest for you, you accomplish several important things. First, you'll be leaving yourself more time to think about the tougher questions later. In addition, moving through a series of questions without a struggle will build your confidence. Finally, working through a number of questions will build up a base of points that may be enough to earn you at least a minimally acceptable grade.

- **Write legibly on one side of the paper.** If an instructor can't read what you've written, you're not going to get credit for it, no matter how brilliant your answer. So be sure to keep your handwriting legible.

  It's also a good idea to write your answers to essay questions on only one side of a page. This will allow you to go back later and add or revise information.

- **Master machine-scored tests.** Tests will sometimes be scored, in part, by computer. In such cases, you'll usually have to indicate your answers by filling in—with a pencil—circles or squares on a computer answer sheet.

  Be careful! A stray mark or smudge can cause the computer scanner to misread your answer sheet, producing errors in grading. Be sure to bring a good eraser in addition to a pencil; the biggest source of mistakes in machine grading is incomplete erasing.

It's best to write your answers not only on the answer sheet but also on the test itself (if the test is not intended for future re-use). That way you can go back and check your answers easily—a step you should take frequently.

Use Strategies Targeted to Answering Specific Types of Test Items

Every type of item requires a particular approach. Use these strategies to tailor your approach to specific kinds of questions:

■ **Essay Questions.** Essay questions, with their emphasis on description and analysis, often present challenges because they are relatively unstructured. Unless you're careful, it's easy to wander off and begin to answer questions that were never asked. To prevent that problem, the first thing to do is read the question carefully, noting what specifically is being asked. If your essay will be lengthy, you might even want to write a short outline.

Pay attention to key words that indicate what, specifically, the instructor is looking for in an answer. Certain action words are commonly used in essays, and you should understand them fully. For instance, knowing the distinction between "compare" and "contrast" can spell the difference between success and failure. The table defines common action words.

ACTION WORDS FOR ESSAYS

These words are commonly used in essay questions. Learning the distinctions among them will help you during tests.

Analyze: Examine and break into component parts.

Clarify: Explain with significant detail.

Compare: Describe similarities and differences.

Compare and contrast: Describe and distinguish similarities and differences.

Contrast: Explain and distinguish differences.

Critique: Judge and analyze, explaining what is wrong—and right—about a concept.

Define: Provide the meaning.

Discuss: Explain, review, and consider.

Enumerate: Provide a listing of ideas, concepts, reasons, items, etc.

Evaluate: Provide pros and cons of something; provide an opinion, and justify it.

Explain: Give reasons why or how; clarify, justify, and illustrate.

Illustrate: Provide examples; show instances.

Interpret: Explain the meaning of something.

Justify: Explain why a concept can be supported, typically by using examples and other types of support.

Outline: Provide a framework or explanation—usually in narrative form—of a concept, idea, event, or phenomenon.

Prove: Using evidence and arguments, convince the reader of a particular point.

Relate: Show how things fit together; provide analogies.

Review: Describe or summarize, often with an evaluation.

State: Assert or explain.

Summarize: Provide a condensed, precise list or narrative.

Trace: Track or sketch out how events or circumstances have evolved; provide a history or time line.

Use the right language in essays. Be brief and to the point in your essay. Avoid flowery introductory language. Compare these two sentences:

"In our study of world literature, it may be useful to ponder how *The Canterbury Tales* came to represent such an important milestone in the field, and it will be seen that there are several critical reasons why it did have such an impact."

"The Canterbury Tales were groundbreaking for several reasons."

This second sentence says the same thing much more effectively and economically.

Essays are improved when they include examples and point out differences. Your response should follow a logical sequence, moving from major points to minor ones, or following a time sequence. Above all, your answer should address every aspect of the question posed on the test. Because essays often contain several different, embedded questions, you have to be certain that you have answered every part, in order to receive full credit.

■ **Multiple-Choice Questions.** If you've ever looked at a multiple-choice question and said to yourself, "But every choice seems right," you understand what can be tricky about this type of question. However, there are some simple strategies that can help you deal with multiple-choice questions.

First, read the instructions carefully to determine whether only one response choice will be correct, or whether more than one of the choices may be correct. Almost always only one choice is right, but in some cases instructors may permit you to check off more than one answer.

Turn to the first question and read the question part—the part before the response choices. *Before you look at the choices, try to answer the question in your head.* This can help you avoid being confused by inappropriate choices.

Next, *carefully read through every choice.* Even if you come to one that you think is right, keep reading—there may be a subsequent answer that is better.

Look for absolutes like "every," "always," "only," "none," and "never." Choices that contain such absolute words are rarely correct. On the other hand, less-absolute words, such as "generally," "usually," "often," "rarely," "seldom," and "typically" may indicate a correct response.

Be especially on guard for the word "not," which negates the sentence ("The one key concept that is not embodied in the U.S. Constitution is . . . "). It's easy to gloss over "not," and if you have the misfortune of doing so, it will be nearly impossible to answer the item correctly.

If you're having trouble understanding a question, underline key words or phrases, or try to break the question into different short sections. Sometimes it is helpful to work backwards, *Jeopardy* style, and look at the response choices first to see if you can find one that is clearly accurate or clearly inaccurate.

Use an educated guessing strategy—which is very different from wild or random guessing. Unless you are penalized for wrong answers (a scoring rule by which wrong answers are deducted from the points you have earned on other questions, rather than merely not counting at all toward your score), it always pays to guess.

The first step in educated guessing is to eliminate any obviously false answers. The next step is to examine the remaining choices closely. Does one response choice include a qualifier that makes it unlikely ("the probability of war always increases when a U.S. president is facing political difficulties")? Does one choice include a subtle factual error ("when Columbus began his journey to the New World in 1492, he went with the support of the French monarchy")? In such cases, you may be able to figure out the correct response by eliminating the others.

■ **True–False Questions.** Although most of the principles we've already discussed apply equally well to true–false questions, a few additional tricks of the trade may help you with this question type.

Begin a set of true–false questions by marking the items you're sure you know the answer to. But don't rush; it's important to read every part of a true–false question, because key words such as "never," "always," and "sometimes" often determine the appropriate response.

If you don't have a clue about whether a statement is true or false, here's another last-resort principle: Choose "true." In general, more statements on a true–false test are likely to be true than false.

■ **Matching Questions.** Matching questions typically present you with two columns of related information, which you must link using a process of elimination. For example, a list of terms or concepts may be presented in one column, along with a list of corresponding definitions or explanations in the second column. The best strategy is to reduce the size of both columns by matching the items you're most confident about first; this will leave a short list in each column, and the final matching may become apparent.

■ **Short-Answer and Fill-In Questions.** Short-answer and fill-in questions basically require you to *generate and supply* specific information in your own words. Unlike essays, which are more free-form and may have several possible answers, short-answer and fill-in questions are quite specific, requiring only one answer.

Use both the instructions for the questions and the questions themselves to determine the level of specificity that is needed in an answer. Try not to provide too much or too little information. Usually, brevity is best.

TAKING YOUR OWN FINAL EXAMINATION

The last few minutes of a test may feel like the final moments of a marathon. You need to focus your energy and push forward harder. It can be make-or-break time.

Save some time at the end of a test so you can check your work. You should have been keeping track of your time all along, so plan on stopping a few minutes before the end of the test period to review what you've done. It's a critical step, and it can make the difference between a terrific grade and a mediocre one. It's a rare person who can work for an uninterrupted period of time on a test and commit absolutely no errors—even if he or she knows the material backward and forward. Consequently, checking what you've done is crucial.

Start evaluating your test by looking for obvious mistakes. Make sure you've answered every question and haven't skipped any parts of questions. If there is a separate answer sheet, check to see that all your answers have been recorded on the answer sheet and in the right spot.

If the test has included essay and short-answer questions, proofread your responses. Check for obvious errors—misspellings, missing words, and repetitions. Make sure you've responded to every part of each question and that each essay, as a whole, makes sense.

Check over your responses to multiple-choice, true–false, and matching questions. If there are some items that you haven't yet answered because you couldn't remember the necessary information, now is the time to take a stab at them. As we discussed earlier, it usually pays to guess, even randomly if you must. On most tests, no answer and a wrong answer are worth the same amount—nothing!

What about items that you initially were genuinely unsure about, and you guessed at the answer? Unless you have a good reason to change your original answer—such as a new insight or a sudden recollection of some key information—your first guess is likely your best guess.

Know When to Stop

After evaluating and checking your answers, you may reach a point when there is still some time left. What to do? If you're satisfied with your responses, it's simply time to tell yourself, "Let it go."

Permit yourself the luxury of knowing that you've done your best and it's time to hand the test to your instructor. You don't have to review your work over and over just because there is time remaining in the class period and some of your classmates are still working on their tests. In fact, such behavior is often counterproductive, because it may lead you to start overinterpreting test items and reading things into questions that really aren't there.

Disaster! I've run out of time! It's a nightmarish feeling: The clock is ticking relentlessly, and it's clear that you don't have enough time to finish the test. What should you do?

Stop working! Although this advice may sound foolish, in fact the most important thing you can do is to take a minute to calm yourself. Take some deep breaths to replace the feelings of panic that are likely welling up inside you. Collect your thoughts, and plan a strategy for the last moments of the test.

If there are essays that remain undone, consider how you'd answer them if you had more time. Then write an outline of each answer. If you don't have time even for that, write a few key words. Writing anything is better than handing in a blank page, and you may get at least some credit for your response. The key principle here: Something is better than nothing, and even one point is worth more than zero points.

The same principle holds for other types of questions. Even wild guesses are almost always better than not responding at all to an item. So rather than telling yourself you've certainly failed and giving up, do as much as you can in the remaining moments of the exam.

REFLECTING ON THE REAL TEST OF LEARNING

Most of us focus on the evaluative aspects of tests. We look at the grade we've received on a test as an end in itself. It's a natural reaction.

But there's another way to look at test results: They can help guide us toward future success. By looking at what we've learned (and haven't learned) about a given subject, we'll be in a better position to know what to focus on when we take future exams. Furthermore, by examining the kinds of mistakes we make, we can learn to do better in the future.

When you get your test back, you have the opportunity to reflect on what you've learned and to consider your performance. Begin by looking at your mistakes. Chances are they'll jump out at you because they will be marked incorrect. Did you misunderstand or misapply some principle? Was there a certain aspect of the material covered on the test that you missed? Were there particular kinds of information that you didn't realize you needed to know? Or did you lose some points because of your test-taking skills? Did you make careless errors, such as forgetting to fill in a question or misreading the directions? Was your handwriting so sloppy that your instructor had trouble reading it?

Once you have a good idea of what material you didn't fully understand or remember, get the correct answers to the items you missed—from your instructor, fellow classmates, or your book. If it's a math exam, rework problems you've missed. Finally, summarize—in writing—the material you had trouble with. This will help you study for future exams that cover the same material.

Finally, if you're dissatisfied with your performance, talk to your instructor—not to complain, but to seek help. Instructors don't like to give bad grades, and they may be able to point out problems in your test that you can address readily so you can do better in the future. Demonstrate to your instructor that you want to do better and are willing to put in the work to get there. The worst thing to do is crumple up the test and quickly leave the class in embarrassment. Remember, you're not the first person to get a bad grade, and the power to improve your test-taking performance lies within you.

Source: Adapted from Robert Feldman, *P.O.W.E.R. Learning,* pp. 119–137. Copyright © 2005 McGraw-Hill. Reprinted by permission of The McGraw-Hill Companies.

HANDLING READING TESTS BY USING SKIM, SCAN, READ: SEEING THE FOREST, THE TREES AND THE SPACES BETWEEN THEM

Introduction

There may be several times when you must pass a reading test or a reading section of a longer test. College entrance tests, reading course exit exams, state-mandated basic skills tests, and graduate school admission exams are examples. Or, you may need to pass a reading test when you apply for government jobs, certain other jobs, or the military.

When you read passages on a reading test, it is important to tell the difference between the Forest (Main Idea and Topic), the Trees (Details), and the Spaces between them (Conclusions/Inferences). To see them all more clearly, you need to

SKIM the passage to get the "Big Picture" skills of main idea and topic/subject matter.

SCAN to get the "Close-Up" skills of supporting detail and vocabulary.

READ the entire passage to answer the "In-Between" conclusion/inference questions and confirm your other answers.

The Technique

Skim

Think of reading a passage as similar to viewing a forest. The best way to get an overall picture of a forest is to hop into an airplane and view it from the air. Reading the entire passage first is like walking through the forest. You will be overwhelmed with trees/details and possibly lose sight of the "big picture" of the forest. ***Skimming*** is like being in a plane that takes you out of the tree/detail level, and it is the ideal way to answer the main idea and topic questions. To skim, follow these steps:

1. Read the title.
2. Read any unusual print.
3. Read the first paragraph or two to locate the main idea if it is stated.
4. Read the first sentence of the rest of the paragraphs.
5. Read all of the last paragraph.

Once you have skimmed the passage, look at the choices for main idea. They are very similar to a key element in the "Goldilocks" story:

- One choice is likely to be too *broad* or too *big* for the passage. It contains ideas beyond the ones in the passage.
- One choice is likely to be too *narrow* or too *small* for the passage. It is a detail in the passage, and it does not convey the content of the entire selection.
- One choice is the *main idea.* It is *just right,* and it covers all the content of the passage—no more and no less.

Take a guess at the right answer. Mark it on your test, but not on your answer sheet (if you are using one).

Next, you have to choose the topic/subject matter of the passage. You will have two clues:

1. The title of the passage will be an important clue.
2. The topic is always part of the main idea. The topic answers the question, "Who or what is the passage about?"

Again, take another guess and mark it on your test.

Scan

Scanning is like landing in your plane and looking for individual trees; that is, seeking particular information about the meaning of a word or about a detail in the passage. Once you have skimmed, you will have a better idea where to scan for the details. This information will save you time in finding what you need. Follow these steps to scan:

1. Focus in your mind the idea that you are looking for.
2. If you have already read the answer, scan the parts of the passage you have skimmed. If not, scan what you have not already skimmed.
3. Pace yourself so you move quickly through the material.
4. Stop when you find the answer to the question.

Use this method to make educated guesses about answers to detail and vocabulary questions. Be sure to read the entire context of any vocabulary word in the question. Again, mark your test.

Read

Only after you have seen the Big Picture of the forest and have found the particular details and vocabulary you were asked about, the trees, should you *read the entire passage* to confirm your other choices and answer conclusion/inference questions. The inference question requires that you examine the space between the trees to find what *isn't* there. Remember,

1. You MUST read the entire passage at some point. Do it *after* skimming and scanning. This way, you will be confident that your guesses are right.
2. Answers to inference questions will not be stated in the passage. Ideas that are stated in a passage are answers to detail questions. Details are always wrong answers to inference questions. For inference questions, read the entire passage and select the choice that you can figure out *based on the clues* in the passage.

Now, answer any conclusion/inference questions on the test and go over all your other guesses to check that they are correct.

Congratulations! You have successfully found the forest, the trees, and the spaces between them!

Source: Adapted from material developed by Prof. Kathleen Riley, Polk Community College, September 4, 2005. Used with permission.

Recognizing Propaganda and Fallacies

In Chapter 11, you learned the criteria for evaluating an author's argument, and you were introduced to propaganda techniques and fallacies in The Edge. Some authors use these techniques in an attempt to persuade readers unfairly, and you will learn how to evaluate the sources on which authors base their arguments.

There are dozens of types of erroneous reasoning authors can use to persuade unthinking readers into believing their argument. One way is simply not to use reason. Instead, the authors rely on ***propaganda techniques,*** *techniques that sell points of view (or products) by appealing to emotion rather than reason.* Just as there is a range of emotions, there are dozens of forms of propaganda.

Another way authors manipulate noncritical readers is by using ***fallacies***, *statements or arguments based on faulty reasoning.* There are more than 125 types of fallacies, but we'll look only at the most common ones.

Every day you see and hear advertisements that employ propaganda techniques and flawed reasoning. Authors, like advertisers, use them for a very good reason: They often work! Critical readers, like critical consumers, however, don't get taken in. When you read a persuasive material—an author's argument—you must think critically whether the basis of the appeal is emotional. You must think critically to determine whether the reasoning is flawed. (You must also evaluate the source of the author's support: If it comes from unreliable sources, you should reject the argument. Appendix 4 explains how to evaluate websites.)

Being aware of propaganda techniques and fallacies can also make you a better writer (and speechmaker) because you can avoid flawed reasoning that would hurt your credibility and cause your audience to reject your argument.

PROPAGANDA TECHNIQUES

Propaganda techniques play on readers' emotions rather than appeal to their reason. Authors use devices to appeal to the reader's fears, vanity or status, sense of pity or compassion, sense of tradition, guilt, greed, and so forth. When you read an author's argument, ask yourself, *"Is the author trying to manipulate me by appealing to emotion rather than reason?"*

Here are some examples of ads that employ some of these propaganda techniques.

- ***Appeal to fear:*** "There are lots of crime scenes, but your home doesn't have to be one of them. Enjoy the peace of mind a Clinks security system can provide."

- ***Appeal to vanity:*** "Only Beautiful People drink Kissoff vodka."

- ***Appeal to pride:*** "Patriotic Americans will feel proud to display this beautiful, miniature set of flags that represent all 50 states of this great nation."

- *Appeal to compassion:* "Abandoned pets are just waiting for a loving home. Please open your heart and give a kitten or puppy a chance for a happy life."
- *Appeal to guilt:* "Your children won't go to bed hungry tonight. Doesn't every child deserve the same? Donate today to the XYZ Children's Fund."
- *Appeal to anger:* "America's Social Security system is going broke, and millions of hardworking Americans will not receive the benefits they've worked all their lives for. This is outrageous! Tell Congress that you're no longer willing to put up with a broken system and their empty promises!"

FALLACIES

Fallacies represent various sorts of errors in reasoning. When you read persuasive writing, ask yourself, *"Is the author's argument based on faulty reasoning?"* You do not have to learn all of these types of fallacies by name. The first three are among the most important, though, because they are used so often. What matters is (1) that you become aware of the many ways readers can be manipulated by authors' fallacious reasoning, and (2) that you do not accept any argument without thinking critically about the author's reasoning in it. For each type of fallacy, there is a definition and an example. Many examples are typical of advertisements you encounter daily.

1. *Hasty generalization*—the author jumps to a conclusion without providing adequate proof or evidence.
   - "I grew up in a small town, and so did my parents. Small towns are the best place to raise children."
   - "SUVs use lots of gas, and they get poor mileage. The government should not allow car manufacturers to produce them."

In Chapter 11 you learned about inductive arguments in which the reasoning moves from specific facts to a general conclusion. Authors who provide relevant statistics or testimony from experts make their case stronger. Authors who make hasty generalizations jump to conclusions without presenting adequate support or by presenting support that is unfair, unbiased, or not representative. This weakens their case.

2. *False cause*—the author assumes that because one thing happens after another, the second event must be caused by the first event. (In a logic course, this will be called by its Latin name, *post hoc, ergo propter hoc,* which means "after this, therefore because of this.") It is incorrect to assume that one event caused another simply because that event happened first. Moreover, most events, whether divorces, terrorism, or rising gasoline prices, have more than a single cause.
   - "We never had any problem with crime in this neighborhood until we did away with the Neighborhood Watch Program."
   - "Last year voters rejected funding to create new schools, and this year students' test scores are the lowest ever."
   - "Every time I run into Alice, something bad happens the next day."

3. *False analogy*—the author makes a comparison that is misleading because it is inappropriate or inaccurate. The author acts as if two cases or situations are similar and wants readers to infer that because something was true in one situation, it must also be true in the other. This is also called an *invalid analogy.*
   - "Bob Smith is a decorated war hero, so he would be an excellent president of the company."

- "If you like saving money, you'll love owning a hybrid car."
- "Sleeping on an Air Loft mattress is like sleeping on a cloud."

4. *Ad hominem*—the author attacks the opponent personally (the person's character, actions, etc.) rather than addressing the person's actual views. "Ad hominem" is Latin for "to the man"; the author attacks the person rather than the real issue, person's ideas. (*Name-calling* is a form of this. This is just what it sounds like, and the author does it to distract attention from the real issue or to damage the person's credibility.)

- "Maria Sangria used to have a drinking problem. I don't think this is the kind of person we want to serve on our school board."
- "My opponent comes from a very wealthy family. Why should expect him to work hard if he is elected?"

5. *Either-or*—in this trap, the author puts everything into one of two mutually exclusive categories, leaving the impression that there is nothing else and nothing in between the two positions. The author tries to make readers believe that they must accept "either this or that," as if they were the only two choices. This is also referred to as a *false dilemma* because there are almost always more than two alternatives to solving a problem.

- Voters should approve the proposed bond issue or just forget the entire highway improvement project.
- "It's your choice: you can either vote for a new community youth center or watch gang violence increase."
- "Wouldn't you rather spend a couple of dollars for EZ Glide Oil instead of paying hundreds of dollars in costly engine repairs?"

6. *Bandwagon*—the author says that because everyone is doing something, it must be a good thing or the right thing. In other words, the author wants readers to "jump on the bandwagon" and go along with everyone else.

- "Join the millions who now enjoy a good night's rest with Moonesta sleep aid."
- "Twenty million satisfied users of Meltaway Diet Aid can't be wrong. Isn't it time you joined them?"

7. *Plain folks*—the author presents himself or herself as being just like the readers (rather than being an authority who is superior to them) and suggests that because they're alike (have similar values), readers should automatically accept the author's argument.

- "At Palmer's Café, our food isn't fancy, just good. Come taste the 'down home' difference."
- "I may only be a housewife, but I know how to keep my family healthy. We take Golly-Gee vitamins every day."

8. *Sweeping generalization*—the author goes beyond the support or evidence presented and makes overly broad, all-encompassing statements ("All _____ are _____").

- "All teenagers are reckless drivers."
- "Women don't make effective executives."

9. *Straw man*—first the author distorts the opponent's position (that is, the other side of the argument) and then attacks the distorted position instead of the opponent's actual one.

- "My opponent owns a farm, so he obviously doesn't care what happens in our state's cities. Not caring about the future of our cities spells disaster for our state."

10. *Appeal to authority*—the author tries to persuade the reader to accept an argument by saying that some authority believes it or because the author is an "authority" (which may not be the case at all!).

   ■ "Doctors overwhelmingly recommend Nasosniff for their allergy patients."

   ■ "High school math teachers know that Whiz Bang Math software gives students a competitive edge."

11. *Testimonial*—the author mentions a famous person who endorses the author's viewpoint, cause, or product. The famous person, however, may have no particular knowledge or direct experience with what he or she is endorsing. (This is also called *endorsement* and is similar to an appeal to authority.)

   ■ "Rodeo star Buck Off drives a truck as rugged as he is. Shouldn't Dodge be your brand, too?"

   ■ The "Got millk?" ads are an example. Various celebrities adorned with milk mustaches endorse milk.

12. *Transfer*—the author shifts qualities (good or bad) from one person or issue to another as a way of influencing the reader's perception of the original person or issue.

   ■ "The mayor has been associated in business with two men who took bankruptcy, so he is clearly unfit to handle our city's economic affairs."

   ■ "Princess Diana would have worked on behalf of this cause."

13. *Circular reasoning*—the author goes in a circle by restating the argument or conclusion instead of providing any relevant support.

   ■ "Big-Oh brand televisions are the best because there's none better."

   ■ "The inner city is rundown because the buildings haven't been maintained."

14. *Begging the question*—the author presents as a certainty something that is open to debate (because it is *not* a certainty).

   ■ "It is obvious that leather sofas are more beautiful and last longer."

   ■ "There's no question that home schooling is better for children than attending public school."

15. *Red herring*—the author introduces unrelated, irrelevant information to divert attention from the real issue. The odd name derives from English farmers' trick of dragging a smoked herring (a type of fish) around the edges of their crops to keep fox hunters' horses and hounds from running through their fields and damaging their crops. The fish smell obliterated the scent of the fox that the hounds were chasing. Consider this example in which the real issue is raising the minimum wage:

   ■ "How can the governor worry about increasing the minimum wage in this state when our cities have such terrible problems with air pollution?"

   ■ The mayor has come under attack for his handling of the city's finances. But his efforts to promote literacy have been admirable. Unless we address the literacy problem, our city's workforce will become increasingly less qualified.

16. *Slippery slope*—the author argues that taking one step will inevitably lead to other steps that cannot be stopped until it ends in disaster.

   ■ "If we negotiate with employees on their insurance coverage, then before we know it, they'll be demanding additional things in their retirement packages, and eventually the company will go broke."

   ■ If you give teenagers any freedom, they'll start hanging out with the wrong crowd, Then they'll be doing drugs and dropping out of school.

17. *Glittering generalities*—the author uses broad, widely accepted ideals and righteous words in hopes that readers accept or approve something without examining it closely. Words and phrases such as *the best, the greatest, truth, liberty, justice, freedom, America's favorite,* and the *people's choice* are examples of the type of language used in glittering generalities.

   ■ "You'll love Tea-Riffic, the country's favorite brand of flavored ice tea."

   ■ "Americans who value freedom and justice will want to buy several of these limited edition medallions commemorating the nation's first president."

18. *Card stacking*—the author presents carefully chosen facts, statistics, and illustrations that may be misleading.

   ■ "Nine out of ten doctors approve of the active ingredient in Quench heartburn tablets."

   ■ "Surveys show that four out of five dentists recommend sugarless gum."

   In the preceding examples, readers aren't told how many doctors and dentists were surveyed. It may have been a very small number. Also, the doctors may approve of the active ingredient, but what about the rest of the ingredients or the quantity of the active ingredient? Dentists may recommend patients not chew any gum, but for those who do, they recommend sugarless gum.

19. *Appeal to tradition*—the author appeals to readers on the basis that what has been done should continue to be done in the present and future.

   ■ "Three generations of pride go into every Smith Family smoked ham."

   ■ "It just wouldn't be Thanksgiving without Pilgrim Brand cranberry sauce."

Propaganda and fallacies are part of our everyday life. Being aware of them can make you a better thinker, reader, writer, and consumer. (The Online Learning Center has practice exercises on identifying propaganda techniques and fallacies.)

The Online Learning Center has exercises on recognizing propaganda and fallacies.

APPENDIX 4

Conducting Research Using the Internet and Evaluating Websites

USING INTERNET SEARCH ENGINES TO LOCATE RELEVANT SITES

Because there are millions of Web pages, finding appropriate, accurate information on the Internet can be a confusing, daunting task. As a starting point, you can conduct a *search* using a **search engine,** a specialized program to help locate—search out—information on the Internet and the Web. Each search engine has a website, and you first must go to one of those. Among the best known and most popular are Google (www.google.com), Yahoo! (www.yahoo.com), Ask.com (www.ask.com), Windows Live Search (www.live.com) (formerly MSN Search), and Alta Vista (www.altavista.com).

The preceding search engines are general ones, but there are also specialized ones for topics related to law, medicine, history, and fashion, for example. To find specialized search engines, enter the topic plus the word *search* into any general search engine (example: *law search*). See below for more detailed instructions. In addition, there are *metasearch engines*, programs that automatically submit a search request to several search engines simultaneously. An example is WebCrawler, (webcrawler.com). Academic search engines are also available; they focus on books, theses, peer-reviewed papers, abstracts, and articles. Examples are Google Scholar (scholar.google.com) and Windows Live Academic (academic.live.com). To search for sources in libraries near you, use WorldCat (www.worldcat.org).

Once at a search engine's website, you will see a "search" box. In it, you type a keyword or phrase that describes the type of information you are seeking. (Misspelled words are a common error, so check your spelling.) The more specific your description, the more accurate results you will receive. You can limit your search by including the word "and" between each word or putting quotation marks around a phrase. For example, suppose you want information about the Dallas Cowboys (the football team). Typing in all four words or typing "Dallas Cowboys football team" will result in the search engine list of relevant Web pages. However, if you simply type in *Dallas Cowboys* in Google, it brings up 21.5 *million* results that include ones about Dallas (any cities of that name, the TV show, and so forth), as well as websites about cowboys. (If you type *Dallas AND Cowboys,* it will list only sites that contain both words. Typing OR between the words will bring up any website that contains either word, which generates even more results. The word NOT can be used to exclude information, such as Dallas Cowboys NOT cowboys. The words AND, OR, and NOT are referred to as *Boolean operators.*) If you enclose the search phrase with quotation marks [*"Dallas Cowboys"*] using Google, it will return approximately six million results, and almost all will pertain to the football team.)

Once you have typed in a keyword or phrase, the search engine scours its database for Web pages that contain the word or phrase. It then displays a partial list (usually 10 at a time) of the matches, or **hits**, that it locates. In general, look only at the first page of results. If the sites do not appear to have the information you need, move on. Use other keywords or another search engine. In fact, to locate the information you need, you will typically have to conduct multiple searches using several search engines or keywords and phrases. The hits themselves sometimes contain terms and information that can help you in your search. So that you don't duplicate your effort on subsequent searches, keep a list of the search engines and keywords you use. (Most colleges and universities offer informal training sessions on how to conduct Internet and Web research. Check with your school's library.)

NAVIGATING TO A WEBSITE

Browsers, such as Mozilla Firefox, Microsoft Internet Explorer, and Netscape, are programs that provide access to Web resources. They make it possible to *surf* (explore) the Web by moving easily from one site to another. Browsers connect users to remote computers, open and transfer files, and display the text and images on Web pages.

Browsers use URLs (uniform resource locators) to connect you to resources on the Web. A **URL (Uniform Resource Locator)** gives the location or address of a Web page or website. Each Web page and website has its own distinct URL. Every URL address consists of certain elements that appear is a set order, and every URL has at least two basic parts: a protocol and domain name. The general order of information in an address is:

http://www.domain name.domain suffix/folder name/filename

Addresses that consist of only the two basic parts take users to the website's **home page**, a first page that usually contains a menu for the rest of the website, information about who sponsors it, and its purpose. Here is an example of a basic URL (home page URL), consisting of the protocol and domain name. It is the home page for the Public Broadcasting Service, commonly referred to as "public television." (The complete *domain name* consists of the server name plus the top-level domain or domain suffix, which is indicated by the letters following the dot.)

Example URL: **http://www.pbs.org**

Many URLs have additional parts indicating directory paths, file names, and pointers. These are added to the home page address because they take you from the home page to other parts of the website. The following example is the more detailed URL for a specific episode of the Public Broadcasting Service's *Frontline* series entitled, "Inside the Teenage Brain." The additional parts after the basic URL lead to specific information accessed through a home page:

| ① | ② | ③ | ④ | ⑤ | ⑥ |

http://www.pbs.org/wgbh/pages/frontline/shows/teenbrain/work/anatomy.html

The numbers in the example correspond to these parts of the URL:

1. **Protocol:** Protocols are rules for exchanging data between computers. Web addresses usually begin with "http://" to indicate the language (*hypertext transfer protocol*) by which computers communicate via the Internet.

2. **Subdomain name:** This part of the domain name designates the part of the domain to which the URL refers.

3. **Domain name:** This is a name registered by the website owner. It designates the server on which the resource is located.

4. **Domain suffix:** The letters following the dot (.) indicate the type of organization, institution, or information or the country of origin (e.g. *.org* = nonprofit organization, *.com* = commercial organization, *.edu* = educational institution, *.gov* = government organization, *.mil* = military institution, *.net* = Internet service provider, .mobi = mobile content provider, .name = individuals, .travel = travel and tourism, .uk = United Kingdom, .br = Brazil)). (When a web address is read or said aloud, every "." is pronounced "dot.")

5. **Directory path:** This identifies the specific location in the website's host computer.

6. **File name:** This identifies the specific file in the website's host computer.

When you reach a website, a document file (Web page) is sent back to your computer. The letters *HTML* at the end of an address are an abbreviation for *Hypertext Markup Language*, the computer language of the WWW. Web pages viewed with browsers are created in this language, and the letters HTML at the end of the URL address tells your computer to display it as a Web page.

A home page gives information about the site and typically includes highlighted words or images, *hyperlinks* or *links* you can click on to connect to other related information such as additional text, graphics, or video clips. Some links take you to other parts of a website; other links take you to different websites.

Be careful to type in URLs accurately. Any changes you make in the address's punctuation, spelling, or capitalization, regardless of whether it is a mistake or if you are trying to "correct" one of those elements, will cause the URL to be misread. You will receive an error message saying the address cannot be found.

NAVIGATING AMONG AND WITHIN WEBSITES

Browsers include toolbar commands that make it easy to return to previous websites or to a home page if you have left it by accessing links from it.

■ Each click on the *triangle or arrow pointing to the left* (◀) takes you back to the screen viewed prior to one the user is currently on.

■ Each click on the *triangle or arrow pointing to the right* (▶) takes you to the screen viewed after the one you are currently on; it is inactive if you are at the last screen you have gone to.

■ There may be a *stop command* (X) that instantly ends downloading. This is handy if you inadvertently click a link to another screen or change your mind.

■ The *refresh or reload button* (↺) can be used if there are problems downloading, as indicated by an unusually slow download, an incomplete page, or distorted text or graphics.

■ The *home button* (an icon that looks like the outline of a house) takes you to the Internet service provider's home page or any page of your own choosing, depending on your browser's settings.

On the Internet Explorer screen graphic below, locate the arrows and other command icons described in the list. They appear on the second, third and fourth lines of the sample window.

Internet Explorer

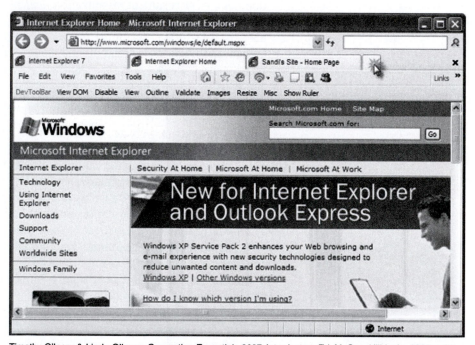

Timothy O'leary & Linda O'leary, *Computing Essentials 2007,* Introductory Ed. McGrawHill Irwin, 2007, p.32.

PREVIEWING A WEBSITE

Just as it's wise to preview a reading assignment, it's a good idea to preview a website when you first go to it. To get an overview of the website's organization and contents, look at the title or headlines, introductory or descriptive information about the website, table of contents, category headings, buttons or links, and graphics. See if there is a search feature that lets you seek specific information on the website. Look for a sitemap link. Clicking it will take you to a single Web page that lists all the links to content in the website.

For example, suppose you are studying Greek architectural styles in an art history course. If you go to www.greatbuildings.com, you will see the website's title, "The Great Buildings Collection" (see graphic below). Major headings at this architecture reference site include Search, Buildings, Architects, and Places. (There are also photos of a few buildings, and clicking on any of them shows the type of information that is displayed, such as architect, location, date, building type, construction system, style, along with other views, drawings, 3-D models, discussion, print resources. There are links for architecture books, 3-D models, architectural types, and advanced search.) There is a search box, where you could type in the name of a specific Greek building, such as the Parthenon. At the bottom of the page are additional links, including ones to information about the site's privacy policy, photo licensing, and so forth.

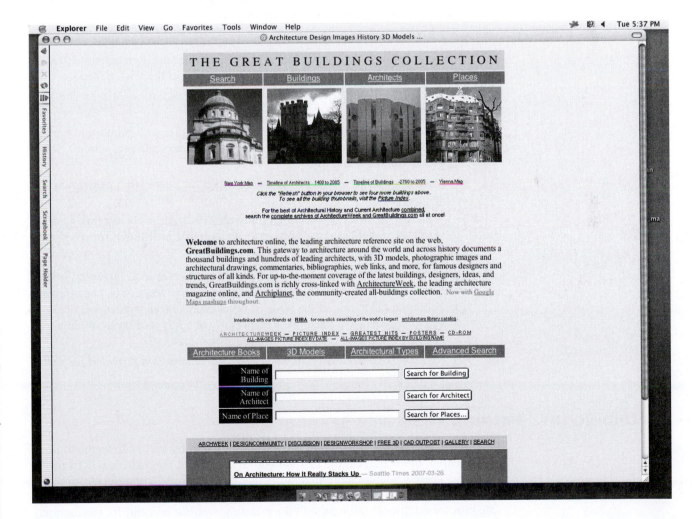

EVALUATING INTERNET SOURCES

Before you decide to use information from a website, especially for a paper or presentation, you should evaluate the website. Unlike college libraries where librarians screen materials the college purchases, there is no screening of Internet websites. The fact is that nearly anyone can post anything. There are millions of self-proclaimed "experts," so you must thoughtfully evaluate the validity, reliability, and credibility of information that appears on the Internet. (See Chapter 11 for information about validity, reliability, and credibility.)

It's always a good idea to write down information related to your evaluation of a website, especially if you are examining several of them. If a website fails to meet basic evaluation standards (for example, you are unable to determine who sponsors it or the information is poorly written or out of date), your evaluation will take only a few minutes. Red flags such as those are indications you do not need to go any further.

Much of the criteria for evaluating books and journal articles applies to evaluating information from Internet sites, but there are special considerations as well. You may not be able to find all of the following information, but find all that you can.

- *How recent is the information? When was the website last updated?*
  This information is usually included on the website. If it's badly out of date, you may not want to proceed further in your evaluation.

- *Find the name of the author or organization that sponsors (pays for) the website, and something about the person or organization.*

  - Click on homepage or "About [name of organization or author]."

  - Go to the basic URL by deleting everything after the domain name (that is, everything after .org, .edu, .gov, .mil, or .com) in the URL address.

  - Does the person seem qualified? Is the organization established and well respected?

  - What is the purpose of the website? (For example, is its purpose to present information? Provide a forum? Persuade readers to take action? Sell a product or service?)

  - Does the website tell readers how to contact the person or organization that sponsors it?

  - What do the links reveal about the website? Some websites link to other sites that are more biased or have an agenda that is different from what the first one's appears to be.

- *What is the basic orientation or point of view expressed at the website, and on what do you base this? Does it reflect a bias? In other words, has information about the other side of the issue or other points of view been left out? What assumptions have been made, especially unsupported ones? What about the tone? (Is it factual? Sarcastic? Angry? Inflammatory?)*

- *Are claims documented with facts? Is there documentation provided for facts that are presented?*

RECORDING INFORMATION FROM WEB SEARCHES

When you are preparing paper or presentation, start by jotting down the topic of your search, the search engine that led you to a site, and the address (URL) of the website. There's nothing more frustrating than to have found good information, but not be able to use it because you can't locate it again. (See www.studygs.net/evaluate.htm for additional information on evaluating website content. Its bibliography includes other sources of information for evaluating websites.)

If you decide to use the information from a website, you will undoubtedly want to go back to the website. Many students find it helpful to print out the information they think they might use. It not only gives an accurate version of what appears on the site, but also has the URL at the top of the page. A second option is to write down the URL along with a brief description of what the website contains that is of interest to you. *Bookmarking* the site, which may be called *Add to Favorites* or something similar, is another option. While you are at the website, click on that icon in your browser's menu bar. Bookmarking serves the same purpose as putting a marker in a book. It enables you to return to a website without having to type in the URL again. A list of bookmarks gives you a convenient record of them.

Do not make the mistake of "writing" a paper by merely cutting and pasting together information from various websites without crediting the sources. It's a form of plagiarism—cheating—that professors spot very quickly. Be meticulous about giving the sources of information that comes from others or is not common knowledge. You must give the source regardless of whether you synthesize, summarize, or directly quote the information. Handbooks for writers tell the proper form for citations, and you can also find the information online. For example, see www.mhhe.com/catalyst, an online writing and research tool. Click on Research, and then on Bibliomaker (scroll down; there are samples of citations for various types of online material). The Research section of *Catalyst* also contains a wealth of information on using the Internet and research techniques, along with discipline specific resources. You may access the Catalyst academic research tutorial directly using the following link: http://maimon-auth.mhhe.com/research/index.html.

The Internet can be a wonderful source of information on almost any topic, whether it is research for a course you are taking or information for your personal use, such as shopping, movie reviews, maps, weather information, travel information, or health information. With a little knowledge and practice, you can become an efficient, savvy user.

5 Learning Style Tips

You may already know how you learn best. If not, take the learning styles assessment that is also included in the OLC or go to any of these websites:

- http://www.vark-learn.com/documents/general.pdf (learning style inventory)
- http://ttc.coe.uga.edu/surveys (learning style inventory and intelligences survey)
- http://www.ulc.arizona.edu/assessments.htm (also includes study skills suggestions)

After you have read the descriptions of various learning styles, find your learning style below and discover ways to make your style work for you in your college classes. Don't get hung up on the learning styles labels. The important thing is to experiment to find out *what works for you*. The great thing about being an adult college student is that you can take control of how you learn best!

VISUAL LEARNERS

- Seek out courses in which professors use textbooks, give handouts, present information in PowerPoint presentations, use overhead projectors, show films, do demonstrations, write notes on the board or on a computer-linked Smartboard, incorporate online resources such as an online learning center that accompanies the text, related websites, etc.
- Sit near the front of the class so that you can see well and take advantage of any visual aids used in class. This will also enable you to see the professor's face and body language. It will cut down on other visual distractions and help you stay focused.
- Create concept maps, diagrams, sketches, etc., to capture important information; include color if you find it helpful. (See Ch. 14, Organize Information for Study.)
- Create review cards and summary sheets. Make flash cards for important terms, concepts, names, formulas, etc. (See Ch. 14, Organize Information for Study.)
- Consider taking courses offered in an online format.
- Before you read an assignment, preview it. Turn through it and look at any visual aids or organizers (illustrations, graphs, diagrams; the sizes of headings and subheadings; special print such as bold, color, or italics).
- Close your eyes and visualize a difficult-to-spell word, paying special attention to the tricky part of the word. Visualize that part in color, in capital letters, etc., to create a mental image of a word (or a picture, for

that matter); then close your eyes and move them up and to the right. Move only your eyes, and not your face or head.

■ Try writing the word with different spellings to see which spelling "looks right." Look for familiar affixes and roots. (See Ch. 2, Analyze Word Structure.) You may also want to consider buying a handheld Franklin electronic dictionary, PDA, or other handheld device that uses dictionary software.

■ Study in a study carrel or somewhere there are few visual distractions (don't study facing a window, for example). You may also find that you study better alone since listening in not a way you prefer to learn.

■ Find a place where the light is right. Some learners like bright light; others prefer less bright.

■ When you can anticipate some of the essay test questions, practice writing out answers ahead of time. Making an outline may also be helpful. (See Ch. 14, Organize Information for Study.)

■ In math classes, when appropriate, draw a "picture" of the problem before you start. List the information that is given (known) and what is unknown. Write down the steps to follow in solving the problem.

■ To aid in the recall of a stored image of a word (access picture memories), close your eyes and look up and to the left. Move only your eyes, and not your face or head.

VISUAL-SPATIAL LEARNERS

In addition to the suggestions above,

■ When you are reading and you come to a punctuation mark, stop and visualize what you are reading about.

■ Make a schedule; time management probably isn't a strength of yours.

■ Keep an assignment notebook; update it daily. Write down the assignment and the due date. Then set deadlines for yourself for completing each assignment.

■ If handwriting is problem for you, learn to type. Keyboarding (typing) may be easier for you than handwriting. If handwriting and typing are both difficult for you, consider using voice-activated (speech recognition) software that "types" what you say aloud. (*Dragon Naturally Speaking* software seems to be a good one. Besides being able to dictate to the computer, this software can read e-mails, etc., aloud to you. Go to a website such as VoiceRecognition.com for descriptions of various speech-recognition software programs.)

■ When you must use handwriting, write on graph paper rather than regular notebook paper if it helps you make your writing more uniform and easy to read. Choose graph paper that has big enough squares and pale lines. If you have trouble lining up numbers when you do basic operations (add, subtract, multiply, divide) in math problems, use graph paper. You can also turn notebook paper sideways and use the lines to help you line up the numbers.

■ Once you have finished writing, use the spell-checker and grammar checker features of your word-processing program. If seeing wavy red or green "error" lines beneath words interferes with your concentration, simply turn off the monitor while you are typing the first draft. Then turn it on and check it.

■ Look for relationships among concepts and in the material you are learning. (See Ch. 6, Recognize Authors' Writing Patterns.)

■ Pay attention to details; you may tend to focus on the big picture and miss the details. (See Ch. 4, Identify Main Ideas and Supporting Details.)

■ Picture important terms and difficult-to-spell words in your mind. Visualize certain letters being in color or in huge letters. "Look" at the picture of the word in your mind, and then spell the word from back to front by looking at the picture. When you can do that, you have a clear image of the word in mind. You know how to spell it. You can also create a picture to go with the word or the letters of "spelling demon" words.

■ Use color (pens, highlighters) to color code ideas or information of various types in your textbooks. You might use purple for information related to one topic and green for another, or you might use one color for major concepts and another for the details that go with it. You might use color to show where one section of material ends and another starts. You can also record information on different color vocabulary cards.

■ Use your imagination: create a story, make a mental videotape you can watch in your head, draw a picture, make a three-dimensional model or object to represent a concept; create a game to help you learn and remember the material.

■ If you usually need more time on tests, ask if you can take the test in your college test center (if it has one), or see if you can sit outside the professor's office and take it (or finish it).

■ If you have difficulty creating outlines, use *Inspiration* software to help you organize your ideas visually. You can move information around as you organize your thoughts. (Go to www.inspiration.com for information and for examples of how the software can be used. There is also a good section on visual learners.) (See Ch. 14, Organize Information for Study.)

■ Experiment to see which fonts are easier for you to read. It may help you to make enlarged copies of pages or to use a larger point size when you print out pages from your computer. You may also find it helpful to print the pages on colored paper, such as light yellow or green.

■ If reading is difficult for you, find a simpler book on a subject (preferably one with lots of pictures and illustrations) and read it first. Then go back to your textbook.

■ If you type up your notes or papers, turn off the hyphenation. Leave the right margin unjustified. In other words, do not set the right margin so that all the lines end at the same place. It makes paragraphs into hard-to-read blocks of print.

■ If it helps you, use your finger to guide you when you are reading. You can also place an index card beneath the line you are reading or even cut out a frame that allows you to see only one line of print as a time.

■ Try using a picture dictionary, such as *The Macmillan Visual Desk Reference,* or a simpler dictionary that includes lots of pictures.

AUDITORY LEARNERS

■ Sit near the front of the class so that you can see and hear well.

■ Whenever possible, write out information in your own words. Then read it aloud.

■ Repeat important information and definitions out loud.

■ Read your textbook assignments, or even just especially difficult passages, aloud.

■ Set information to a familiar tune; create a rap or rhyme you can say aloud.

■ Find or form a study group so you can hear material being discussed. Be sure that you are prepared ahead of time so that you are ready to contribute to the group.

■ Record class lectures on a tape recorder. Remember that you must use the tape once you've recorded it!

■ When reviewing for a test, record information in your own voice. Listen to the tape in your car or on a Walkman when you are walking, jogging, commuting, or doing household activities that do not require full concentration (such as washing dishes).

■ When you look up a word in the dictionary, pay attention to its pronunciation; say it out loud. Buy a handheld Franklin electronic dictionary, PDA, or other handheld device that uses dictionary software.

■ Pronounce a word aloud or in your mind before you try to spell it. Sound out the parts of the word or recite the letters aloud when you are learning to spell a difficult word.

■ If noise bothers you when you study, find a quiet place to study. Turn off the iPod, CD player, TV, radio, cell phone, etc. Use earplugs if you cannot find in a quiet place.

■ If you like background music, try some of the slower classical music by Handel, Bach, or Mozart. Music with 50–70 beats per minute, such as Baroque music, seems to help the brain focus when it does certain types of thinking tasks. Use instrumental music only—no songs with lyrics.

■ Have someone call out key terms or questions to you when you are reviewing for a test.

■ Look for professors who emphasize lecture, discussion, collaborative (small-group) learning, and question-and-answer review sessions.

■ Work with a tutor through your college's tutoring center; you will benefit from discussing material with a knowledgeable person and from hearing your questions answered aloud. Tutor someone else; you will learn by explaining the material to another person.

■ Create questions and answer them aloud as a way to review for tests.

■ When you encounter a picture, graph, or any other visual in a textbook, describe aloud to yourself the information it is designed to convey.

■ To lock a word in auditory memory, say the letters while looking to the right.

■ To help recall something that you said or heard, look to the left. Move only your eyes, and not your face or head.

TACTILE/ KINESTHETIC LEARNERS

- Write down important information. The motion of writing it is the important aspect. Keyboarding (typing) may also work for you.
- Mark your textbooks because this is a form of physical involvement. Underline, annotate, etc.
- Consider taking courses that have a hands-on component, such as technical courses, science courses that have a lab component, drama classes, music and applied arts classes, courses that feature field trips, or other experience-based learning.
- Create three-dimensional models.
- Use your index finger to write difficult-to-spell words and important terms in the air or on a tabletop. You can also trace the letters with your finger. Review the word and look up and to the left.
- When you study, take breaks every half hour or so. Stand up, stretch, or run in place for a few minutes.
- Gesture as you are rereading or saying material you are trying to learn.
- Walk back and forth while you are trying to learn information. Review information by repeating it aloud as you jog, walk to class, clean house, or work out.
- Chew gum if it helps you deal with nervous energy.
- Review material using a question-and-answer format; change your body position as you switch from question to answer and back again.
- When you study, change subjects rather than trying to study the same subject for a long period of time. For example, read only part of a long reading assignment, shift to some math homework, and then return to the reading assignment.
- Create a game or act out concepts you need to remember.
- Relate material to a football game or some other activity.
- Sit in the front of the room to help you stay focused and involved.

ANALYTICAL/ SEQUENTIAL LEARNERS

- Seek out instructors who are organized and present material in a clear, organized, step-by-step fashion and who give out an assignment calendar. (Ask other students who have taken a course you are planning to take.)
- Create outlines of material you need to learn. (See Ch. 14, Organize Information for Study.)
- Ask for clear written or verbal directions, whichever works better for you.
- Write or repeat aloud down the steps in any important procedure or process.
- Break a process down into separate steps. Break information down into smaller pieces and put them in an order that makes sense to you.
- Trial-and-error learning may work well for you.
- You are probably well organized and aware of time. If you have not already done so, create a study routine, make a schedule, use a calendar, To Do List, and other organizing aids.

- Repetition is usually an effective way to reinforce your learning.
- You may do better reading and studying in a place where the light is bright.
- You may find it more productive to study in the morning or early evening; staying up late probably does not work well for you.
- Eating a good breakfast and having regular meals are likely to work better for you than skipping breaking or snacking while you study.
- You may be able to concentrate better when there is silence.

GLOBAL/INTUITIVE LEARNERS

Global learners like to get the "big picture" first. *Intuitive learners* are often spontaneous in their decision making, and often go with what "feels right."

- Before you read an assignment, preview it to see what it will be about. If there is an introduction or a summary, read it first. Turn through the chapter to see what it contains and how the topics are organized.
- Ask for or find several examples so that you can see what they have in common.
- Find out what the goal or end product is before you begin.
- Start with the end product and work backward to see how the parts fit together.
- Read your course syllabus (description) to see what the overall goals of the course are.
- Read the introduction in your textbooks to get an overview and to find out what the overall goals are.
- You may do better reading and studying in a place where the light level is very low.
- Some background sound may be helpful to you when you study. If you play music, play it at a low level. Use instrumental music rather than songs with lyrics.
- Snacking while you study may help you. Choose high-protein snacks rather than sugary or high-fat ones.
- You may like to study on the bed or the floor.
- Similes and metaphors may help you learn because you like to see similarities and connections.
- Wear a watch because you may tend to run late.
- For school, use a planner or organizer and an assignment notebook because your normal tendency may be to "go with the flow" rather than to plan.
- You will benefit from working with others. Find a study-buddy or study group.
- If possible, sign up for courses in which there are opportunities to discover the answers rather than being told them.
- Study a picture of the way something will look when it is complete before you begin assembling it.
- You may find it more comfortable to study in the afternoon and at night, or even very late at night.

6 Four Common Figures of Speech

Figurative language, or figures of speech, are nonliteral ways of saying things; that is, the words have to be interpreted in order to understand the intended meaning. Authors use figures of speech to paint vivid pictures in the reader's mind or to achieve some other specific effect (such as emphasis or humor). You, too, use and encounter them every day. For example, you tell a friend that your *new boss is a prince* (a wonderful person), or you hear a classmate say he *worked his fingers to the bone* to finish his science project in time (worked long and hard).

Four common figures of speech are simile, metaphor, hyperbole, and personification. (See the Online Learning Center for a complete module on interpreting figurative language. It also includes additional figures of speech beyond the four described below.) Here are descriptions and examples of them:

1. **Simile** (sĭm′ə-lē) Comparison between two things that, in most respects, are totally unlike, but which actually are alike in some significant way. Similes generally use the term *like* or *as* in the comparison. Example: Joannie's eyes *twinkle like stars*. (The comparison is between her eyes and stars that twinkle. The meaning is that her eyes are bright.)

2. **Metaphor** (mĕt′ə-fôr′, -fər) Implied comparison between two seemingly dissimilar things by saying that one of them *is* the other. (As the word *seemingly* suggests, the two things are, in fact, similar in some significant way.) Example: In the weeks after the tornado destroyed their home, she was *a pillar of strength* to her family. (She is compared with a column of stone. The meaning is that she was emotionally strong, able to cope well under difficult circumstances.)

3. **Hyperbole** (hī-pûr′bə-lē) Obvious exaggeration made for emphasis or to create some other specific effect. Example: I have *ten thousand things to do* before everyone arrives for the party tonight. (The exaggeration is "ten thousand things to do." The meaning is that the person has many things left to do to prepare for the party that night.)

4. **Personification** (pər-sŏn′ə-fĭ-kā′shən) Speaking about nonhuman or nonliving things as if they were human. Example: These shoes are *determined to torture me!* (Shoes are spoken about as if they can deliberately choose to cause pain to the wearer.)

As you read, watch for figurative language. Here are the questions and strategies you can use for each of these four figures of speech.

Simile and metaphor: Is the author making a comparison between two seemingly dissimilar things? If so, in what significant way are they actually alike?

■ Watch for the clue words *like* and *as* in similes.

■ For both similes and metaphors, determine the two things that are being compared, and then decide in what important way they might be alike.

Hyperbole: Is the author using an obvious exaggeration?

■ Determine what the exaggeration is.

■ Decide what point the author is trying to make or what effect the author is trying to achieve with the exaggeration.

Personification: Is the author attributing human characteristics to nonliving things?

■ Determine the nonliving thing that is being given human characteristics.

■ Determine which human characteristics are being attributed to it.

■ Decide the point the author is making.

For practice, identify and interpret the figure of speech in each of these sentences.

1. "Resentment is like drinking poison and waiting for it to kill your enemy." —*Nelson Mandela*

   Figure of speech: _____

   Meaning: _____

2. "Opportunity makes thieves." —*European saying*

   Figure of speech: _____

   Meaning: _____

   _____

3. My brother can eat a mountain of pancakes!

   Figure of speech: _____

   Meaning: _____

4. "Life is a foreign language; all men mispronounce it." —*Christopher Morley, writer (1890–1957)*

   Figure of speech: _____

   Meaning: _____

   _____

   _____

5. "Job offers are a little like romance. You wait by the phone for months and no one calls—then suddenly everyone wants you." —*H. J. Cummins*

   Figure of speech: _____

   Meaning: _____

   _____

6. The coach was so angry he had steam coming out of his ears.

   Figure of speech: _____

   Meaning: _____

7. "Education is our passport to the future, and tomorrow belongs to those who prepare for it today." —*Malcolm X*

   Figure of speech: _____

   Meaning: _____

   _____

8. "A good example is the best sermon." —*Ben Franklin*

   Figure of speech: _____

   Meaning: _____

   _____

9. "Earth is here so kind, that just tickle her with a hoe and she laughs with a harvest." —*Douglas Jerrald, playwright and humourist (1803–1857)*

   Figure of speech: _____

   Meaning: _____

   _____

10. "Ideas are like rabbits. You get a couple and learn how to handle them, and pretty soon you have a dozen." —*John Steinbeck, novelist, Nobel laureate (1902–1968)*

    Figure of speech: _____

    Meaning: _____

    _____

Photo Credits

Introduction: *Benjamin Carson,* M.D. Director of Pediatric Neurosurgery at Johns Hopkins Hospital in Baltimore, Maryland. Overcame an early life of hardship and extreme poverty; internationally known for his success in hemispherectomies (removal of half of the brain) and separating conjoined twins who are joined at the head. (© Keith Weller/Johns Hopkins)

"Secrets" of Success: Page S-1, © Royalty-Free/CORBIS

Chapter 1: Page 3, © Royalty-Free/CORBIS

Chapter 2: Page 23, © Lawrence Lawry/Getty Images

Chapter 3: Page 41, © Lawrence M. Sawyer/Getty Images

Chapter 4: Page 63, © Photolink/Getty Images

Chapter 5: Page 95, © Karl Weatherly/Getty Images

Chapter 6: Page 125, © Royalty-Free/CORBIS

Chapter 7: Page 165, © Didrik Jonck/CORBIS SYGMA

Chapter 8: Page 201, © Royalty-Free/CORBIS

Chapter 9: Page 219, © Rim Light/Photolink/Getty Images

Chapter 10: Page 247, © Photolink/Photodisc/Getty Images

Chapter 11: Page 273, © Photolink/Photodisc/Getty Images

Chapter 12: Page 301, © Roualty-Free/CORBIS

Chapter 13: Page 321, © Photolink/Photodisc/Getty Images

Chapter 14: Page 355, © Ryan McVay/Getty Images

Chapter 15: Page 393, © Lawrence M. Sawyer/Getty Images; Page 394, Courtesy of Roger That Productions

Appendix 4: Page A-25, © Photodisc/Getty Images; Page A-31, © The McGraw-Hill Companies, Inc./Christopher Kerrigan, photographer

Index of Key Terms and Skills

Index of Excerpt Topics